CRIMINAL
Justice in the
United States

Nelson-Hall Series in Law, Crime, and Justice

Howard Abadinsky, Series Consulting Editor
Saint Xavier University

CRIMINAL
Justice in the
United States

SECOND EDITION

Dean J. Champion

Minot State University

NELSON-HALL/Chicago

Project Editor: Dorothy Anderson
Copy Editor: Susan McCloskey
Production: Jane R. Brown
Illustrations/Photo Research: Nicholas Communications
Compositor: E.T. Lowe
Manufacturer: Quebecor Printing
Cover Painting: *I.A.C.* by Peter Volay

Library of Congress Cataloging-in-Publication Data

Champion, Dean J.
    Criminal justice in the United States / Dean J. Champion.
-- 2nd
  ed.
      p.   cm.
     Includes bibliographical references.
     ISBN 0-8304-1485-1
      1. Criminal justice, Administration of--United States.
I. Title.
  HV9950.C45 1997
  384.973--dc2l
97–21722
                                CIP

Manufactured in the United States of America

10 9 8 7 6 5 4 3 2 1

The paper used in this book meets the minimum requirements of American National Standard for Information Sciences—Permanence of Paper for Printed Library Materials, ANSI Z39.48-1984.

Contents in Brief

Contents

CHAPTER 2
An Overview of the American Criminal Justice System   37

CHAPTER 3
Constitutional Criminal Law and Procedure   53

CHAPTER 4
Law Enforcement: Forms, Functions, and History

77

CHAPTER 5
The Police: Operations and Procedures

117

CHAPTER 6
Court Organization: Structure and Process 149

CHAPTER 7
Processing Defendants: Pretrial Procedures I 179

CHAPTER 8
Processing Defendants: Pretrial Procedures II 203

CHAPTER 9
Juries and Trial Procedures 227

CHAPTER 10

The Sentencing Process

CHAPTER 11

Correctional Institutions: Forms and Functions

CHAPTER 12

Corrections Operations and Issues   329

CHAPTER 13

Probation, Parole, and Intermediate Punishments   359

CHAPTER 14

The Juvenile Justice System   *391*

Preface

This book is about the criminal justice system, a vast network of agencies and persons who react to and deal with crime. Each component of the criminal justice system is described in the following chapters, including the police, the courts, and correctional institutions. Students of criminal justice can see the entire criminal justice process from beginning to end and thus acquire a better understanding about how criminals are processed.

The criminal justice system for adults is paralleled by a justice system for juvenile offenders. In the 1960s and 1970s, juveniles were vested with various legal rights through U.S. Supreme Court decisions. While there remain several important distinctions between the adult and juvenile systems, many important rights once exclusively reserved for adults have been extended to juvenile offenders.

The criminal justice system takes the leading role in dealing with crime. It attempts to minimize crime by preventing and controlling it. Thus, *crime prevention and control* are two important objectives of the criminal justice system.

The objectives of this text are:

1. to acquaint students with all components of the criminal justice system,
2. to help students understand those components, and
3. to prepare students for subsequent courses in criminal justice programs.

Some of these programs are included in the curricula of departments such as sociology, psychology, public administration, and political science. Of course, many schools also offer specific criminal justice programs. These programs are of interest to law enforcement officers, prelaw students, persons preparing for careers in corrections, and those engaged in private security work. Of course, many students enroll in these programs to learn more about how the U.S. criminal justice system works.

The following pedagogical features will help the reader understand material presented. Questions at the end of each chapter help the reader review important information. Suggested readings for each chapter encourage additional study of highlighted concepts. A comprehensive glossary of key terms provides students with definitions of difficult terminology. An up-to-date bibliography of sources helps those interested in further study of particular issues and subjects. Important concepts are highlighted in each chapter and concise definitions are furnished. The glossary is a summary compilation of these concepts. Finally, each chapter is supplemented with material on specialized topics, interesting anecdotes, and observations that accompany the discussion of particular subjects. These materials are intended to supplement the text and to show how particular concepts are applied.

My appreciation is also extended to those who provided some of the photos for this book. These include Corky Stromme, Chief of Security, North Dakota State Penitentiary; Lt. Darrell Theurer, North Dakota State Penitentiary; Darin Egge, Steve Whitesell, Rodney L. Tryhus, Bryan M. Durham, DeVawn Beckman, Kari Sage, William A. Brown, and Jay Laudenschlager, Minot (N.D.) Police Department; Scott Kast, Minot State University; Thom Mellum, Penny Erickson, Deryl Martin, Deb Armstrong, Deanna Flagstad, Corie A. Delzer, Laura Forbes, Jeremy Mattison, Glennis Knudsvig, Donald Williams, Ward County (N.D.) Jail; and Jarrett Wold, Jennia Green, Eric Pinnick, Jordan Hendershot, and Zach Schultz of Minot, North Dakota.

CHAPTER 1

Law and Crime

- Smile! It's *against the law* in Pocatello, Idaho, to frown or look gloomy!
- It's *against the law* in Raton, New Mexico, for any woman to ride horseback down the street while wearing a kimono!
- Do you have an unbeatable football team? Don't ever play against the Arizona Wildcats in Tucson, Arizona, because it's *against the law* to beat them in Tucson.
- Planning on dancing in the dark in Des Moines, Iowa? Better cancel. It's *against the law* to dance in the dark in Des Moines, according to a 1950 ordinance prohibiting dancing after 2:00 A.M.

Believe it or not, these laws are on the books. From one city to the next, there may even be seemingly *contradictory* laws. For instance,

- It's *against the law* in Morton Grove, Illinois, for private citizens to possess a firearm.
- It's *against the law* in Kennesaw, Georgia, for private citizens *not* to possess a firearm.

The U.S. Constitution, Second Amendment, says that "the right of the people to keep and bear arms shall not be abridged."

The Constitution was prepared in part to define certain basic rights that must not be abridged by the federal government. It was also designed to protect people and their property, their right to privacy, and their right to worship, to voice their opinions, and to lawfully dissent from those in political control.

One important feature of the U.S. Constitution is that it gives states considerable control over their own territories. While no state can pass laws that infringe on the rights of U.S. citizens, handgun legislation is state-regulated. Hence, each state, including Illinois and Georgia, is entitled to regulate the ownership of firearms. Each locality is free to establish laws that express the will of the people. However, Amendment II of the U.S. Constitution, though saying citizens may "bear arms," was never intended to suppress or replace state powers. Gun control is a persistent issue in the courts, and groups such as the National Rifle Association seek to interpret this Amendment in ways that favor their own interests. Other interest groups opposing gun control interpret Amendment II differently. The U.S. Supreme Court is the ultimate arbiter when disputes such as these occur.

During the 1960s and 1970s, citizens protested the Viet Nam war and rising crime rates. Civil disobedience increased as prospective draftees burned their draft cards and held sit-ins in public buildings to protest government policies. Supreme Court decisions then seemed directed toward shielding criminals from the law, and crime's victims were virtually ignored. The criminal justice system itself was put on trial, and no component of it escaped criticism.

The Study of Criminal Justice

What Is the Field of Criminal Justice?

Criminal justice is an interdisciplinary science, including but not limited to law, sociology, psychology, political science, public administration, history, and economics. In fact, many of these departments at universities and colleges offer courses in criminal justice as a part of their regular curriculum. August Vollmer, a former chief of police in Berkeley, California, established the first School of Criminology at the University of California—Berkeley in 1916. His primary interest was improving police officer training and professionalism. Other schools were eventually established with similar curricula and aims, and the formal study of criminal justice was created. Currently, over two thousand criminal justice programs have been established, serving over 1 million students annually.

What Does Criminal Justice Study?

Criminal justice is an interdisciplinary field that studies the nature and operations of organizations providing justice services to society. The criminal justice system consists of lawmaking bodies such as state legislatures and Congress, as well as local, state, and federal agencies that try to enforce the laws and punish law violators. These agencies and organizations include the police, the courts, and corrections. The police detect crime and attempt to control and prevent it. The courts deal with the issue of a defendant's guilt and sentence those found guilty of crimes. Corrections supervises offenders in jails or prisons as well as in probation and parole programs. Students of criminal justice learn about the criminal justice system, its components, and how it deals with crime and processes criminals.

Besides examining criminal justice, students study various aspects of this process, such as the police and their activities. Prosecutors and judges are also examined. Decisions about who should be prosecuted and how trials ought to be conducted are a part of this examination. Correctional institutions including jails and prisons are also studied. Students learn about programs for offenders who either are not incarcerated or who are released after serving a period of time. Thus, corrections includes prison/jail culture, management and administration, prisoners' rights, and probation and parole services.

An important dimension of the criminal justice system is a parallel system for juveniles. While not the same as the justice process for adult offenders, the juvenile justice system focuses upon apprehending, classifying, and rehabilitating juvenile offenders. In juvenile justice the terms *offense* and *crime* are often used interchangeably because juveniles do not commit crimes that carry adult penalties. Juveniles commit "offenses," and depending upon the evidence presented, these juveniles are determined by the judge to be delinquent or nondelinquent. Appropriate juvenile punishments are prescribed, such as warnings, foster home placement, fines, compensation to victims, or detention in secure facilities.

For some experts, criminal justice is applied criminology (Wilson and Petersilia, 1996). **Criminology** *means the study of crime. It is a discipline that scientifically examines crime and criminal behavior, the forms of criminal behavior, the causes of crime, the definition of criminality, and the societal reaction to crime* (Wilson and Petersilia, 1996). Because criminology involves the extensive use of theory in the explanation of crime and the etiology of criminals, and because criminal justice focuses largely upon the processing of criminals, some writers use the *applied criminology* label in their references to criminal justice. *Applied* has the connotation of action or utility. Thus, those in criminal justice do something about crime and criminals, whereas criminologists are primarily concerned with speculating about crime and its causes through their theories. This is an exaggeration, of course, although it highlights the topical extremes of both disciplines.

Thus, criminal justice is not synonymous with criminology, although there is considerable overlap between the two disciplines. Numerous members of professional organizations in criminal justice also belong to criminology organizations, and both do research on the same types of subjects. One convenient way of distinguishing between criminology and criminal justice is to say that *criminology studies the etiology of crime, its causes, forms, and patterns, while criminal justice studies how offenders are processed by the criminal justice system.* Thus, the focus of criminologists is upon *explanation* while the focus of criminal justicians is upon *process.*

The Purpose of This Chapter

This chapter examines the origin of our present laws and how those laws affect us. Different kinds of crime are described as well as crime patterns. Some crime victims are featured, especially the very old or very young. The criminal justice system has become increasingly formalized and bureaucratic in order to cope more effectively with growing amounts of crime and changing crime trends.

The Sources of Law

The legal system of the United States is derived from the English system of **common law**. This system was based on decisions by judges who settled complaints according to custom or precedent. Thus, judges rather than legislative lawmakers were re-

sponsible for defining crimes such as murder and theft. Over the years, most state legislatures have gradually incorporated common laws into their own legal codes and statutes that reflect social changes involving threats to society (Boostrom, 1995). A distinction has been made between common law and **statutory law**.

Common and Statutory Law

Common-law authority is based upon court decrees and judgments that recognize, affirm, or enforce certain usages and customs of the people. Statutory-law authority is based upon enactments of legislatures. The Indiana Legislature, for instance, enacts, eliminates, or changes statutory laws in every session.

There are two types of common law. One type pertains to *acts of violence*, such as murder and assault. Another type applies to *violations of property rights*. These offenses were typical law violations that occurred in early English communities. Property was an important possession, and citizens were identified with and derived social status from their land holdings. Property trespass was considered a very serious offense. Deceit and misrepresentations about property sales or exchanges were equally offensive.

Some statutory laws have been derived from these common laws. Other statutory laws have been passed because of technological changes in society. For instance, early English communities did not have automobiles or computers. Thus, in recent times legislatures have passed laws regulating vehicular traffic and the misuse of computers. Where statutory law fails to include a particular offense, however, the courts will often rely on common law as a way of reaching a "holding" or decision for a specific case. Two instances of common law applied to settling disputes and determining possible law violations are shown in Highlight 1.1.

Every U.S. Supreme Court decision has the potential for setting a legal policy or precedent. In 1972, for example, the Supreme Court held in *Furman v. Georgia* that the death penalty, *as it was then applied*, was "cruel and unusual punishment" for convicted offenders, primarily because it was

---

Highlight 1.1. Two Examples of Common Law

The Case of Ghen, the Whale Hunter

In Massachusetts Bay, a whale hunter, Ghen, shot a whale with a bomb lance. The whale swam away and died about twenty-five miles from where it had been shot. Rich, a wandering beachcomber, came upon the dead whale lying on the beach. He stripped the blubber from the beached whale and converted the fat to oil, which he later sold at a nearby market. Subsequently, he bragged about his luck, and eventually word reached Ghen about where his whale had gone. Ghen tracked down Rich and accused him of converting the whale remains for profit, thus denying Ghen any revenue from the whale he had shot. Rich refused to turn over the money he had received from the whale remains, arguing that he had found the whale, didn't know it was someone else's property, and did a lot of work converting the remains to fat. Ghen sued Rich, seeking to recover damages.

An interesting case was presented to the presiding judge. In the Cape Cod area, there were no laws governing whale rights. However, it was customary for those finding whales to alert the whale hunters where the whale had washed ashore. The bomb lances used by different whalers were thus marked distinctively, so that anyone familiar with whaling knew whose lance it was and thus who "owned" the whale. In Massachusetts, the custom was that the whale hunter who shot a whale "possessed" it through a type of ownership, regardless of where the whale eventually swam or washed ashore. When Rich found the beached whale, he either knew or should have known the proper procedure to follow in turning the whale remains over to the rightful owner. In his case, he ignored custom and precedent and converted the whale remains for his own benefit. Thus, the judge ruled against Rich and in favor of Ghen, who was subsequently reimbursed for his loss by Rich.

The Case of Bradbury's Dead Sister

Bradbury lived in a large two-story building with his sister, Harriet, in a Maine community. During a particularly severe winter, his sister became ill and died in the apartment. Bradbury had little money and could not afford to pay for a funeral for his sister. Therefore, he concluded, he could dispose of his sister in the large furnace in the basement. He dragged her body to the basement, where he cremated it. Neighbors detected a foul odor and called police, who investigated. They determined what Bradbury had done and arrested him. At the time, there was no law or written statute prohibiting anyone from disposing of a dead body in an apartment furnace. However, the court determined that Bradbury had violated the *common law*, which spoke against indecent burials. The fact that Bradbury had *indecently disposed of his sister's body and had not given her a decent Christian burial* was sufficient to find him in violation of the prevailing common law.

In both the *Ghen* and *Bradbury* cases, no statutes existed that prohibited the specific conduct described. In both cases, judges decided these matters strictly on the basis of prevailing precedent established by common agreement through common law. Today in the United States, many states continue to have common law, although statutory law has replaced much of it. At the federal level, common law has been replaced entirely by statutory law.

Sources: Ghen v. Rich, 8 F. 159 (1881), and *State v. Bradbury*, 136 Me. 347 (1939).

---

racially discriminatory. Disproportionately large numbers of blacks were on death row compared with whites, who might instead be serving life terms for committing identical offenses. Some death sentences were imposed on blacks for noncapital crimes, such as rape, armed robbery, or nighttime burglaries of occupied dwellings, whereas whites convicted of identical crimes might be sentenced to ten- or fifteen-year prison terms instead. Another reason the Court gave was that death penalties were imposed without a full consideration of circumstances that might lessen or intensify one's punishment. For instance, if someone was convicted of killing a police officer during the commission of a felony, a death sentence was automatically imposed, without a consideration of extenuating circumstances, either good or bad, that led to the killing. Juries were not asked to consider or weigh any factors that might reduce one's punishment to life imprisonment. Persons who opposed the death penalty claimed a "victory" and interpreted the *Furman* decision as a definitive ban against capital punishment per se. However, this interpretation was both premature and false.

For several years following the *Furman v. Georgia* decision, the death penalty was suspended in all states. Many state legislatures were concerned about whether their procedures for imposing the death penalty complied with Supreme Court guidelines. Understandably, these legislatures were hesitant to move forward with their scheduled executions because they didn't want to have their own death penalty statutes and procedures declared unconstitutional.

In 1976, the Supreme Court said in *Gregg v. Georgia* that the death penalty is *not* a form of punishment that may never be imposed, regardless of the circumstances of the offense. Further, the Court condoned Georgia's revised version of death penalty procedures and accepted the new procedures as constitutional. The fixed and arbitrary nature of the death penalty was abandoned and replaced with a more rational, objective system. Despite this setback, death penalty opponents continued to lodge appeals with the Supreme Court on behalf of their clients. For example, in 1987, the Supreme Court heard the case of Warren McCleskey, a forty-one-year-old black who had been sentenced to death for the 1978 murder of a white police officer in Georgia. McCleskey alleged that because he was black, the death penalty in his case was discriminatory. In a narrow 5–4 decision, the Supreme Court rejected his argument and upheld his original death sentence (*McCleskey v. Kemp*, 1987). Speaking for the majority, Justice Lewis Powell, a black, said "there is . . . some risk of racial prejudice influencing a jury's decision . . . but apparent disparities in sentencing are an inevitable part of our criminal justice system."

The Civil Rights Acts of 1957, 1960, and 1964 established several federal statutes using the federal government's power to force state and local governments to grant citizens civil rights under the Constitution. Discrimination because of race, religion, color, or age was prohibited by some of these statutes. As a result, judges at local, state, and federal levels were obligated to decide cases of defendants charged with certain violations of the Civil Rights Acts, regardless of their race, color, or creed. In subsequent years, a number of cases have reached the Supreme Court. The rights of several types of minorities including women have been the subject of recent rulings under Title 42, Section 1983 of the U.S. Code (U.S. Code Annotated, 1996). While these cases are primarily civil, many criminal cases have also been heard by the Supreme Court. *Our laws are made by our legislatures, the executive branch, and the judiciary, and the criminal justice system is the process of administering the enforcement of these laws.* However, we often rely on the Supreme Court to interpret these laws and their application in criminal cases.

Presidents of the United States are authorized to use their executive privilege to change laws or to pass new laws on certain occasions or under certain emergency conditions. Presidents may also approve or veto laws submitted by Congress. Congress is the primary lawmaking body of the United States. During each session, new laws are recommended, some old laws are abolished, and other laws are changed significantly. The Supreme Court also establishes new laws through its interpretation of Constitutional amendments.

Substantive and Procedural Law

Laws are either substantive or procedural. *Statutes that prohibit people from doing certain things or require them to act in particular ways are* **substantive laws**. Substantive laws are the statutes that comprise statutory law. All of our criminal statutes for both the state and federal governments are not only statutory laws but substantive laws as well.

Procedural laws *specify how the criminal statutes should be applied against law violators.* Trials are held according to certain established procedural laws and rules of criminal (or civil) procedure. Persons accused of crimes are tried in a court of law, and the government must follow rules of criminal procedure and rules of evidence when introducing evidence against the alleged offenders. All rules of law are numbered and codified. These compilations of rules are found in published state or federal regulations and dictate whether certain kinds of evidence are legally admissible.

The Meaning of Law

Law is more than the expression of the will of the people or government. *Law is a body of rules of specific conduct, prescribed by existing, legitimate authority, in a particular jurisdiction and at a particular point in time.*

Rules of Specific Conduct

Criminal laws apply to specific prohibited behaviors or acts and not to mere thoughts. Whether a statute pertains to concealing faulty construction or assaulting another person, it defines the behaviors of criminal conduct. The mere act of "thinking" about committing a crime is not a crime; it must be followed by one or more overt acts that set in motion the conditions for crimes to be committed.

Legitimate Authority and Jurisdiction

In the United States, the Congress, the president, and the Supreme Court constitute the *legitimate authority*. These positions and bodies represent the interests of the people of the United States and maintain the existing social organization. In different ways, they administer the rules created by statute or common law. Each level of authority in local, state, or federal government oversees a particular jurisdiction. Lower or municipal courts, for instance, make decisions about lesser offenses such as traffic violations or minor infractions. Thus, defendants accused of murder would not be within the jurisdiction or power of the municipal court. By the same token, federal district court judges would never conduct jury trials involving trivial city traffic tickets. These minor matters are not within the range of serious offenses handled by U.S. district court judges. One exception is that U.S. magistrates frequently hear cases involving traffic citations issued in national parks and recreational areas. Each of these courts has a specific jurisdiction or "sphere of authority" governing the kinds of cases heard.

Particular Point in Time

The phrase *particular point in time* means that current laws apply in specific criminal cases, whereas former laws are not applicable. For example, *prohibition* was the law during the 1920s. But most laws are subject to change and dependent upon the will of the people. Prohibition was subsequently repealed. States also differ regarding the application of identical laws. In one state, the age for consuming alcoholic beverages legally may be twenty-one. In an adjacent state, legal alcohol consumption may be permitted for eighteen-year-olds. Those age eighteen in a state that prohibits them from drinking may drink in an adjacent state where such behavior is lawful.

If a state wishes to *decriminalize* a particular act, such as smoking marijuana, drawing graffiti, or gambling, then it may become lawful in that state to smoke marijuana, write graffiti on public walls, or gamble after a law prohibiting it is abolished (Gomez, 1993; Kindt, 1994). However, while the law is operative, it is enforceable. By the same token, it may be that a state wishes to *criminalize* a particular conduct. Until a law is passed prohibiting that conduct, however, it is legal to engage in it. Various chemicals are discovered from time to time that may be harmful to one's health. Until their hazardous effects become known, using such chemicals is not specifically prohibited. However, the previously lawful behavior becomes unlawful when certain laws or ordinances are passed by the legislature or other governmental bodies.

The Functions of Law

The functions of law are to:

1. legitimize the existing social structure and its continuation;
2. regulate social conduct;
3. regulate freedom; and
4. resolve disputes.

Legitimizing the Existing Social Structure and Its Continuation

A body of laws exists requiring citizens to follow particular *standards of conduct*. By conforming to these standards, existing social arrangements are endorsed and perpetuated. Laws also provide a degree of predictability. For instance, we expect other drivers to yield when we have the right of way. We also expect drivers to obey traffic lights. These standards are not limited to traffic ordinances. They also include criminal and civil laws contained in our local, state, and federal statutes. Regulatory agencies such as the Federal Communications Commission (FCC) also issue rules and regulations for citizens to follow.

Regulation of Social Conduct

Local police forces, state militia (particularly under conditions of mass rioting or natural disasters), state police, the FBI, and many other agencies maintain order through the regulation of social conduct. People who violate these laws or prescribed rules are often apprehended by these law enforcement agencies and processed through the criminal justice system. Laws cause many people to refrain from unacceptable conduct.

O. J. Simpson in 1995 (left) after hearing the jury's verdict that he was not guilty of the murders of his ex-wife Nicole Brown Simpson and Ronald Goldman. Fred and Patti Goldman with their daughter Kim (right) in 1997 at a press conference following the guilty verdict in the wrongful death litigation against Simpson. Although Simpson was on trial both times for the same alleged wrongdoings, the first proceedings involved criminal charges and the second, civil allegations.

Highlight 1.2. Losing Your Assets:
The Case of John and Tina Bennis and the Confiscated Car

Tina Bennis jointly owned an automobile with her husband, John Bennis. John Bennis was observed by Detroit police officers engaging in a sexual act with a prostitute in his car on a Detroit city street in public view. John Bennis was arrested and convicted of gross indecency. The automobile was seized by the government as a *public nuisance* under a Michigan statute. Tina Bennis sued for recovery of her jointly owned vehicle, claiming that she was an innocent owner of the car and didn't know that it would be used for illegal purposes. The Supreme Court upheld Michigan's seizure of the vehicle as a public nuisance, defined as any object or place kept for the use of prostitutes. The Court referred to a *"long and unbroken* *line of cases [as precedent] [that hold] that an owner's interest in property may be forfeited by reason of the use to which the property is put, even though the owner did not know that it was to be put to such use."*

Should the government be allowed to seize assets under the circumstances of this particular case? What is the difference between this case and one in which a car is seized as the instrument of a driving violation committed by someone convicted of driving while under the influence of drugs or alcohol? Where is the line to be drawn regarding forfeiture of assets?

Source: Bennis v. Michigan, ___U.S.___, 116 S.Ct. 994 (1996).

Regulation of Freedom

The U.S. Constitution, the nation's highest law, provides us with several individual freedoms or rights, including the right to free speech, a speedy trial, assembly, and worship of any religion. The laws of the United States insure that these individual freedoms should not be infringed by any state. Laws ensure all citizens the right to "due process," or the guarantee of fair procedures if they are ever charged with crimes. Due process also protects citizens against unwarranted government seizures of property or interference with other freedoms provided in the Constitution. All citizens accused of crimes have the right to have their cases aired in court, regardless of the seriousness of the offenses.

Resolution of Disputes

If citizens cannot resolve disputes about property or other matters, they can seek assistance from the courts. Our courts interpret the law based on precedent or statute. If you loan your car to a friend and the friend uses your car to commit a crime, it is possible that the government may move to seize your car as a "fruit" or instrument of the crime. You may lose your car through asset forfeiture (Miller and Selva, 1994). How can you recover your car? What laws govern whether your car can be seized by the government? (See Highlight 1.2.)

The Definition of Crime

The criminal justice system includes the entire process of administering the enforcement of laws (Black, 1990). Before we examine these basic components of the criminal justice system, we must distinguish between *civil* and *criminal* actions.

Civil and Criminal Actions

The criminal justice system focuses exclusively on criminal laws and those who violate these laws. However, courts generally deal with both criminal and civil matters. With the exception of special criminal courts in various jurisdictions, much "action at law" in courts is civil. In federal district courts, for instance, about 85 percent of all cases are civil, while only about 15 percent involve alleged criminal acts (Langan and Graziadei, 1995; U.S. Department of Justice, 1995). Civil court actions may include resolving child custody disputes, settling conflicting land claims, fulfilling the terms of wills, and deciding whether someone's civil rights have been violated. Other civil actions involve claims for damages arising from negligence or intentional misconduct. These civil actions involve *tort claims.*

Torts and Crimes

A **tort** *is a civil wrong involving one's duty to someone else, a breach of that duty, and injuries arising from that breach* (Black, 1990). Civil wrongs include injuries arising from an automobile accident and printing allegedly false statements in public documents such as newspapers. Many of these civil wrongs involve *tort law.* If retail store owners are negligent and permit slippery substances to accumulate on their store floors, for instance, customers may suffer injuries. Tort actions may follow such incidents. But store owners will not be charged with committing a criminal act. Criminal laws do not apply in cases such as these.

Crimes *are violations of criminal laws by people held accountable by those laws.* A useful distinction between criminal and tort actions is that tort actions seek damages, usually monetary compensation, for injuries sustained, while criminal actions are conducted to punish alleged offenders of criminal laws by imprisonment, fines, or both. In all actions at law, one party opposes another party for a wrong allegedly committed, for the protection of a right, or for the prevention of a wrong. Normally, criminal actions are prosecutions of alleged wrongdoers. In civil actions, the proceedings are called litigations.

Crime is defined by seven specific criteria or elements (Cole, 1975:79–81; Hall, 1947:18). These elements are:

1. *Legality*, where a specific behavior must be described by statute or constitutional provision.
2. *Actus reus,* or an overt "act" by a person that is prohibited by statute or other provision.
3. *Mens rea,* or the intent to do harm. Known as

"evil intent," this element is crucial in determining whether someone "premeditated" a crime or thought about committing it.
4. *Consensus*, or the combination of *mens rea* and *actus reus.* A prohibited act must be accompanied by the thought or evil intent to commit it.
5. *Harm*, where damage to people or property results from the act, although "victimless" crimes, where no one is actually harmed or injured directly, may also be perpetrated.
6. *Causation*, where there is a cause-effect relation between the perpetrator of the act and the harm inflicted. If a truck driver negligently fails to set the brakes on a steep hill and the truck goes out of control and kills or injures a pedestrian, the truck driver's negligence would be the cause of the death, although the *mens rea* or intent to commit a criminal act could not be proved.
7. *Punishment*, where a specific punishment accompanies criminal conduct. Punishments may include fines, imprisonment, or both.

Laws and Jurisdictions

The criminal justice system refers to (1) *a set of agencies and organizations*, and (2) *a series of interrelated stages by which alleged criminal offenders are processed.* Clearly, this process is prefaced by established criminal laws. These criminal laws have been created by the legislatures or executives and interpreted by the courts, and they are usually made explicit through local, state, and federal statutes and ordinances.

While the criminal justice system is procedurally uniform, it may be analyzed according to several different *levels*. Thus, violations of *federal laws* locate alleged offenders within the jurisdiction of the federal criminal justice system. Violations of *state laws* will place alleged criminals within the jurisdiction of the state criminal justice system. **Jurisdiction** *is the power of a court to hear and decide particular kinds of cases.*

If the laws of one state conflict with the laws of other states, for instance, the Supreme Court has the jurisdiction or power to resolve such a dispute. No state may dictate to another state which laws and policies it must follow. If a burglary is committed at a branch of the U.S. Post Office, the law violation occurs within the jurisdiction of one of several U.S. district courts. At the same time, the post office branch is located in a given state and community, and the burglary violates the law in each of these jurisdictions as well. Therefore, concurrent jurisdiction may exist, where alleged burglars may be prosecuted in federal court and/or in one of the state courts in a city or township. Thus, there may be several separate prosecutions for the same offense.

For example, a U.S. Post Office branch is a federally protected government unit, as is a bank insured by the Federal Deposit Insurance Corporation. The Federal Bureau of Investigation would have jurisdiction to pursue those responsible for robbing these organizations. Further, the city, county, and state in which such a robbery occurred would each have some claim against the crime's perpetrators. Conceivably, charges could be brought against the robbers by the city, county, and state contemporaneously with the charges filed against them by the federal government.

Rodney King and Simi Valley

A memorable real-life example is the matter of Rodney King, a motorist who was stopped and beaten by police in Southern California in 1991 (*Time*, 1993:21). Several Los Angeles Police Department officers, including Laurence Powell and Stacy Koon, were charged under California law with causing serious bodily injury to King under color of their police authority. They were tried in a Simi Valley, California, state court and acquitted of these state charges. Subsequently, the U.S. attorney in Los Angeles filed federal charges against these same officers, alleging that Rodney King's civil rights had been violated in the same incident. In a later federal trial, the officers were convicted and sentenced to a period of years in federal prison.

Criminal laws vary among states. Some states have more (or fewer) criminal laws than other states. Also, states vary in their procedures for punishing persons who commit the same types of crimes. As we saw at the beginning of this chapter, in Morton Grove, Illinois, it is against the law to possess a gun. In Kennesaw, Georgia, however, it is against the law *NOT* to have a gun on one's

premises. This is just one of numerous instances where cities and states are divided on particular issues, such as gun ownership and use.

The Model Penal Code

In 1962, the American Law Institute developed a Model Penal Code that unified diverse state and federal laws. The Institute's efforts led to a uniform set of laws with consistent punishments as guidelines for both the states and the federal government. While neither is obligated to follow or adopt any part of the Model Penal Code, it nevertheless provides a consistent definition of criminal conduct. Several jurisdictions have adopted portions of the Model Penal Code in their own codifications of statutes and penalties. Terms such as *knowingly, purposefully, recklessly, entrapment,* and *deadly force* are given precise definitions. One objective of the Model Penal Code is to establish consistency among the states regarding the fair application of the law to everyone as well as uniformity of punishment for similar offenses.

Crime Distinguished from Deviance

Throughout the United States, certain social customs are followed, ranging from regular bathing to respecting the rights and property of others. These accepted codes of behavior are followed by most persons. Those who do not follow these accepted codes of conduct are labeled "deviant." **Deviance** *is any departure from the accepted code of conduct.*

There are many degrees and types of deviance. When "streaking" was a fad in the 1970s, for instance, many college students ran nude across their campuses. These acts were violations of public decency laws and exhibitionism, but authorities were lenient in dealing with streakers. Even though some of these students were apprehended, most were given a stern warning and released without any further punishment. Punk hairstyles and strange clothing might be regarded as deviant, but such deviance is not criminal.

Of course, there are more serious kinds of deviant conduct. Persons may rob others or steal their property. Or they may physically assault persons or commit homicide or murder. It does not follow, however, that *all* deviance per se is the same as criminal conduct. *Criminal behavior is the violation of codified criminal laws by persons who are held responsible by those laws.* Responsibility is determined by one's capacity to understand the laws and the consequences for violating the law. Those defined as "insane" or mentally retarded or who are senile, for example, are often treated as incapable of understanding the law. Ordinarily, they are not held accountable for the consequences of their actions. These people are not necessarily "above the law" or immune from punishment, but allowances are usually made for their limited abilities or diminished mental capacity. Primarily because they are incapable of formulating the requisite criminal intent, medical or psychological treatment and/or hospitalization is prescribed for them rather than punishment by confinement in a jail or prison.

When John Hinckley attempted to assassinate then-President Ronald Reagan, he was arrested and brought to trial. His attorney used the "insanity" defense and sought to show that Hinckley was not responsible for his actions. The defense was successful, and Hinckley was acquitted in 1982 (Steadman, McGreevy, and Morrissey, 1993; Wahl and Kaye, 1991). Nevertheless, he was hospitalized under strict supervision.

Public outrage over Hinckley's use of the insanity defense caused many lawmakers to revise their insanity statutes and the frequency with which such a defense can be used. Many states either eliminated or redefined their concept of insanity, and several jurisdictions created a "guilty but mentally ill" plea to replace the "not guilty by reason of insanity" standard (Perlin, 1994). Chapter 3 discusses several defenses used by criminal defendants besides insanity, including mistake, duress, and intoxication.

Some deviance is classified as "residual rule breaking," because it does not fit easily into any identifiable crime category (Kaplan, 1995). Some political and religious leaders have had their private lives exposed to the national media. Former senator Robert Packwood, Senator Edward Kennedy of Massachusetts, and President Bill Clinton have been labeled by some media sources as "womaniz-ers" or accused of sexual harassment (Associated Press, 1996:A2; Elson, 1992:46; Kaplan and Cohn, 1991:30–31; Painton, 1991:47). In some instances, lawsuits have been filed against these public figures and assorted allegations have been made. While not all forms of sexual misconduct are illegal, some sexual misconduct, if brought to the public's attention, may result in moral condemnation by those who think these behaviors are sinful or plainly wrong (Denno, 1994; Roberts, 1994).

Criminal Responsibility and Legal Definitions

Victimless Crimes

Certain law violations are labeled **victimless crimes** *because the "victims" are willing participants in the illegal activity* (Buchanan and Hartley, 1992; Stitt, 1988). Thus, no one is actually victimized or harmed (Stitt, 1988). Prostitution and gambling are considered by some observers to be victimless crimes. Those seeking sexual gratification solicit it from others for a fee. This is a violation of the law, although the prostitute and client mutually consent to the conditions of the illegal activity. In localities where gambling is outlawed, covert gambling operations are often conducted. Those who want to gamble seek out these gambling establishments. Thus, there is mutual consent between gamblers and gambling house operators about participating in these illegal activities. Some criminologists have labeled automobile theft as a victimless crime (Thomas, 1990). As certain experts see it, no one is harmed by these activities. (See Highlight 1.3.)

It is helpful to contrast such crimes with certain violent crimes where persons are injured, or with property crimes where things of value are taken. In these instances, "victims" of crimes can easily be identified, compared with a prostitute's customers, occasional poker players, or persons whose automobiles have been stolen.

In recent years, however, the public has been confronted with the spread of AIDS, Acquired Im-

---

Highlight 1.3. Nonviolent and Nonharmful Deviance: The Case of Pee-Wee Herman

---

In some instances, highly visible personalities are cast into the limelight as law violators, although their crimes are relatively minor. For example, in 1991 Paul Reubens, a thirty-eight-year-old actor better known as Pee-Wee Herman, was arrested at a hothouse known as the XXX South Trail Cinema in Sarasota, Florida, on charges of indecent exposure. It seems that Herman allegedly exposed his genitals to various persons in the theater, including three detectives. "The suspect was observed with his exposed penis in his left hand," said one of the arresting detectives (Leerhsen, 1991:55).

According to a Florida obscenity statute, his behavior was "a natural and nonharmful behavior for individuals of all ages and both sexes." The problem was that he *went public* with that behavior. Many would argue that Reubens's conduct was victimless. However, Soupy Sales indicated little sympathy for Reubens when he said, "He [Reuben] can masturbate his brains out, but you don't do that in a porno theater when you're a role model." Also, would role models for children be in a porno theater at all? (Leerhsen, 1991:55).

How should sexual deviance of this sort be punished? Should rapists be punished to a greater degree than those committing nonviolent, nonharmful sexual deviance? Should places where such behaviors are portrayed through film or other visual media, such as pornographic shops or stores, be exempted from laws prohibiting nonharmful deviance among patrons? Should nonharmful sexual deviance be decriminalized?

Source: Adapted from Charles Leerhsen, "'His Career Is Over,'" *Newsweek*, August 12, 1991: pp. 54–55.

---

mune Deficiency Syndrome, which is a deadly virus often spread through sexual contact. Prostitution is one means of spreading this virus, and therefore experts question whether this offense is really a "victimless crime." As evidence of the seriousness with which AIDS is treated by the courts, a man was convicted in Westminster, Maryland, in February, 1996, for sexually molesting his eight-year-old step-grandson. The forty-seven-year-old man, who had the AIDS virus, was sentenced to ninety years in prison for *intent to murder*, precisely because he had a deadly virus that could be transmitted sexually. The judge remarked when the sentence was imposed, "What you have done is horrific beyond description . . . you have robbed this young man of his childhood" (Associated Press, 1996:A2).

In addition, some authorities say that gambling, another "victimless crime," causes the financial ruin of families or those dependent upon gamblers. Organized crime also realizes substantial profits from gambling and prostitution, and these profits support other illegal activities. Therefore, it is sometimes claimed that there is no such thing as a "victimless crime." Someone is inevitably hurt as a direct or indirect result of engaging in unlawful conduct of any kind (Bastian, 1995).

Classifying Crimes

Felonies and Misdemeanors

Law enforcement officials have designated major or more serious crimes as **felonies** and minor or less serious crimes as **misdemeanors**. These categories of crimes are ordinarily distinguishable according to the severity of punishment prescribed. *Felonies are crimes punishable by imprisonment in a state or federal prison for one year or longer. Misdemeanors are crimes punishable by fines or imprisonment in a city or county jail for less than one year.* There are exceptions to these definitions among jurisdictions, however. For instance, some persons who are supposed to be housed in state or federal penitentiaries for committing serious felonies may actually be confined in local jails because of prison overcrowding. Thus, the location of one's confinement is no longer a reliable indicator of whether the offender has been convicted of a felony or a misdemeanor.

Felonies include murder, rape, robbery, aggravated assault, arson, vehicular theft, larceny, and selling or distributing controlled substances such as marijuana and cocaine. Misdemeanors include simple possession of marijuana (not for resale), reckless driving or driving while intoxicated, and simple trespass. In the former felony cases, the penalties are usually severe, while in the case of misdemeanors, misdemeanants, those who commit misdemeanors, are usually fined or receive suspended sentences.

Mala in Se *and* Mala Prohibita

Crimes can also be classified according to whether they are *mala in se* or *mala prohibita*. **Mala in se** *refers to crimes that are intrinsically wrong, such as murder, rape, and arson.* In contrast, **mala prohibita** *offenses are defined by legislatures that pass criminal laws.* Such offenses might include selling liquor on Sunday and vagrancy. Most *mala in se* offenses are statutorily prohibited anyway. For instance, in the 1880s, a man came home one evening from a tavern after drinking heavily. His wife awaited him but did not have his dinner prepared. The intoxicated man picked up a lit kerosene lantern and threw it at his wife, breaking the lantern and splashing kerosene over her clothing. The kerosene caught fire and the woman suffered serious burns over 90 percent of her body. While there was no specific statute preventing husbands from throwing lit kerosene lanterns at their wives for not having dinner ready, his behavior was inherently wrong and definitely *mala in se.*

The Measurement of Crime

The Uniform Crime Reports (UCR)

The **Uniform Crime Reports (UCR)** are published monthly by the Federal Bureau of Investiga-

tion. These publications *include statistics about the number and kinds of crimes reported in the United States annually by over fifteen thousand law enforcement agencies.* The *UCR* is the major source of crime statistics in the United States (Maguire and Pastore, 1995).

The *UCR* is compiled by gathering information on twenty-nine types of crime from participating law enforcement agencies. Crime information is requested from all rural and urban law enforcement agencies. However, not all agencies report their crime information to the FBI on a regular basis. Others don't report at all, while still others report their information inconsistently (e.g., the same offense may be reported differently by New Mexico and California authorities).

Many jurisdictions use the *UCR* as a way of evaluating the effectiveness of their law enforcement agencies. Higher numbers of reported crimes may mean less efficient police work, while lower numbers of crime reports might signify better police work. Of course, higher numbers of reported crimes may also mean better police-community relations, or there may be several other explanations unrelated to crime per se. During mayoral campaigns in various cities, *UCR* statistics are widely quoted by incumbent candidates to show the effectiveness of their administrations. Opposition candidates use the same information to draw different conclusions. Depending upon the particular crime and the time period covered, many contradictory interpretations can be made about crime trends in any city.

The FBI has established a crime classification index. **Index offenses** *include eight serious types of crime by which the FBI measures crime trends.* Information is also compiled on twenty-one less serious offenses, ranging from forgery and counterfeiting to curfew violations and runaways. Index offense information is presented in the *UCR* for each state, city, county, and township that has submitted crime information during the most recent year.

The eight index offenses and their definitions according to the Uniform Crime Reporting Program are shown below:

1. *Murder and Nonnegligent Manslaughter:* the willful (nonnegligent) killing of one human being by another.

2. *Forcible Rape:* the carnal knowledge of a female forcibly and against her will; assaults or attempts to commit rape by force or threat of force are also included.

3. *Robbery:* the taking or the attempt to take anything of value from the care, custody, or control of a person or persons by force or threat of force or violence and/or by putting the victim in fear.

4. *Aggravated Assault:* an unlawful attack by one person upon another for the purpose of inflicting severe or aggravated bodily injury.

5. *Burglary:* the unlawful entry of a structure to commit a felony or theft.

6. *Larceny-Theft:* the unlawful taking, carrying, leading, or riding away of property from the possession or constructive possession of another; includes shoplifting, pocket picking, purse snatching, thefts from motor vehicles, and thefts of motor vehicle parts or accessories.

7. *Motor Vehicle Theft:* theft or attempted theft of a motor vehicle, including automobiles, trucks, buses, motorcycles, motor scooters, and snowmobiles.

8. *Arson:* any willful or malicious burning or attempt to burn, with or without intent to defraud, a dwelling house, public building, motor vehicle or aircraft, or the personal property of another.

Table 1.1 shows a distribution of arrests for these index offenses and others for the year 1994. Table 1.2 shows arrest rates for crimes against property for the years 1971–1994.

Violent and Property Crimes

Index crimes reported by the *UCR* are divided also into crimes against the person (violent crimes) or crimes against property. **Crimes against the person,** or **violent crimes,** are those committed directly against persons in their presence. Aggravated assault (possibly involving a personal attack with a dangerous weapon), rape, homicide, and robbery (the felonious taking of something of value from others in their immediate presence, against their will, and by using force or fear) are crimes against persons or violent crimes. **Crimes against property,** or **property crimes,** are considered nonviolent or passive. No physical harm is inflicted upon crime victims, because victims are ordinarily absent when these crimes are committed. Examples of property crimes are vehicular theft, burglary (breaking and entering unoccupied premises), and larceny (theft).

Crime clocks are used to provide information about how often violent and property crimes are committed. Figure 1.1 shows a crime clock for these index offenses. For instance, a violent crime is committed every twenty-four seconds somewhere in the United States, while a property crime occurs every three seconds. And one forcible rape occurs every six minutes somewhere in the United States.

The frequency of these offenses does not mean that there is a rape every six minutes in Philadelphia or New York City or Los Angeles. Nor does it mean that because a larceny-theft occurs every five seconds, there is a larceny-theft occurring every five seconds in Detroit or Miami. These are aggregate statistics that reflect nationwide figures for the entire year. The total annual number of specific crimes reported is divided by some unit of measurement such as seconds or minutes. For example, if 240 rapes occur in a twenty-four-hour period, 240/24 = 10 rapes per hour. But many rapes occur during evening hours. Thus, these crime clock figures are somewhat misleading.

Crimes fluctuate from one month to the next and vary in frequency among cities and towns. Crime clocks provide us with general information about the frequency of certain crimes. But they fail to take into account population increases, and thus they do not provide a per capita measure of crime frequency. The mode of display in the crime clock should not be taken to imply a regularity in the commission of these offenses, however. Rather, it represents the "annual ratio" of these crimes according to fixed intervals (*Uniform Crime Reports,* 1996).

Criticisms of the *UCR*

Even though the *UCR* publishes the most current crime figures from reporting law enforcement agencies, many experts believe crime clocks are inaccurate in several respects (McDowall and Loftin, 1992; U.S. Bureau of Justice Statistics, 1994).

Table 1.1

Arrests by Offense Charged and Age, United States, 1994 (10,654 agencies; 1994 estimated population 207,624,000)

Offense charged	Total all ages	Ages under 15	Ages under 18	Ages 18 and older	Under 10	10 to 12	13 to 14	15	16	17	18	19
Total	11,877,188	780,979	2,209,675	9,667,513	37,130	176,289	567,560	428,697	489,089	510,640	520,831	505,122
Percent[a]	100.0%	6.6	18.6	81.4	0.3	1.5	4.8	3.6	4.1	4.3	4.4	4.3
Murder and nonnegligent manslaughter	18,497	379	3,102	15,395	3	31	345	535	912	1,276	1,418	1,418
Forcible rape	29,791	1,863	4,859	24,932	103	442	1,318	892	993	1,111	1,217	1,158
Robbery	146,979	13,543	47,094	99,885	245	2,478	10,820	10,008	11,753	11,790	10,653	8,701
Aggravated assault	449,716	23,190	70,030	379,686	1,043	5,261	16,886	13,219	15,993	17,628	17,857	17,030
Burglary	319,926	47,481	115,681	204,245	3,135	11,833	32,513	22,232	23,413	22,555	20,223	15,889
Larceny-theft	1,236,311	185,811	412,349	823,962	9,145	51,765	124,901	76,459	77,418	72,661	62,806	49,702
Motor vehicle theft	166,260	21,867	73,265	92,995	206	2,592	19,069	17,986	18,087	15,325	11,698	8,718
Arson	16,764	6,289	9,268	7,496	1,153	2,041	3,095	1,224	964	791	531	488
Violent crime[b]	644,983	38,975	125,085	519,898	1,394	8,212	29,369	24,654	29,651	31,805	31,145	28,307
Percent[a]	100.0%	6.0	19.4	80.6	0.2	1.3	4.6	3.8	4.6	4.9	4.8	4.4
Property crime[c]	1,739,261	261,448	610,563	1,128,698	13,639	68,231	179,578	117,901	119,882	111,332	95,258	74,797
Percent[a]	100.0%	15.0	35.1	64.9	0.8	3.9	10.3	6.8	6.9	6.4	5.5	4.3
Total Crime Index[d]	2,384,244	300,423	735,648	1,648,596	15,033	76,443	208,947	142,555	149,533	143,137	126,403	103,104
Percent[a]	100.0%	12.6	30.9	69.1	0.6	3.2	8.8	6.0	6.3	6.0	5.3	4.3
Other assaults	991,881	72,514	171,642	820,239	3,731	18,961	49,822	32,005	33,602	33,521	31,173	31,652
Forgery and counterfeiting	93,003	927	7,013	85,990	33	184	710	981	2,057	3,048	4,199	4,512
Fraud	330,752	4,409	18,594	312,158	127	657	3,625	4,082	4,120	5,983	8,969	11,896
Embezzlement	11,614	92	803	10,811	8	22	62	60	211	440	574	631
Stolen property; buying, receiving, possessing	134,930	10,751	36,218	98,712	240	1,890	86,621	7,376	8,714	9,377	9,690	8,078
Vandalism	259,579	60,250	122,085	137,494	6,074	17,782	36,394	21,415	21,381	19,039	13,965	11,017
Weapons: carrying, possessing, etc.	213,494	16,661	52,200	161,294	611	3,424	12,626	9,963	12,199	13,337	14,213	12,554
Prostitution and commercialized vice	86,818	120	1,013	85,805	10	18	92	129	289	475	1,317	1,900
Sex offenses (except forcible rape and prostitution)	81,887	7,506	14,418	67,469	658	2,081	4,767	2,442	2,230	2,240	2,205	2,183

20	21	22	23	24	25 to 29	30 to 34	35 to 39	40 to 44	45 to 49	50 to 54	55 to 59	60 to 64	65 and older
459,948	433,449	419,027	420,909	406,399	1,761,357	1,713,145	1,298,615	796,890	433,908	227,419	120,448	70,677	79,369
3.9	3.6	3.5	3.5	3.4	14.8	14.4	10.9	6.7	3.7	1.9	1.0	0.6	0.7
1,215	1,097	938	803	706	2,538	1,847	1,342	856	533	271	164	113	136
1,156	1,065	990	1,107	1,001	4,674	4,617	3,382	2,023	1,120	621	334	216	251
6,808	5,946	5,398	5,130	4,740	19,712	15,823	9,621	4,432	1,745	658	255	118	145
16,115	16,485	16,315	16,741	16,195	72,265	70,262	52,262	31,176	17,003	8,763	4,920	2,862	3,435
11,818	10,234	9,497	9,258	8,385	38,079	35,507	24,140	12,426	5,180	2,017	805	355	432
39,440	34,473	31,926	31,928	30,636	140,027	141,593	109,829	68,611	36,125	18,320	10,259	6,854	11,433
6,516	5,510	4,989	4,642	4,217	17,153	13,812	8,348	4,133	1,848	761	305	132	213
341	283	263	264	245	1,178	1,268	1,069	665	407	238	99	80	77
25,294	24,593	23,641	23,781	22,642	99,189	92,549	66,607	38,487	20,401	10,313	5,673	3,309	3,967
3.9	3.8	3.7	3.7	3.5	15.4	14.3	10.3	6.0	3.2	1.6	0.9	0.5	0.6
58,115	50,500	46,675	46,092	43,483	196,437	192,180	143,386	85,835	43,560	21,336	11,468	7,421	12,155
3.3	2.9	2.7	2.7	2.5	11.3	11.0	8.2	4.9	2.5	1.2	0.7	0.4	0.7
83,409	75,093	70,316	69,873	66,125	295,626	284,729	209,993	124,322	63,961	31,649	17,141	10,730	16,122
3.5	3.1	2.9	2.9	2.8	12.4	11.9	8.8	5.2	2.7	1.3	0.7	0.5	0.7
30,938	33,605	35,257	36,524	36,465	163,495	160,971	117,939	67,879	35,759	17,997	9,173	5,401	6,011
4,308	4,174	4,115	4,088	4,086	17,829	16,234	11,234	6,046	2,856	1,226	540	258	285
13,192	13,559	14,146	14,739	14,606	63,001	57,461	43,331	27,414	15,181	7,271	3,425	1,900	2,067
599	556	553	499	519	2,042	1,716	1,295	799	513	260	123	62	70
6,440	5,754	5,158	4,833	4,503	18,057	14,875	10,417	5,761	2,708	1,237	616	282	303
8,347	7,804	6,898	6,664	6,200	24,811	21,565	14,552	7,794	3,853	1,872	917	481	754
10,361	10,462	9,449	8,650	7,827	28,035	21,742	15,325	9,676	5,663	3,282	1,735	1,047	1,273
2,275	2,727	2,953	3,501	3,876	20,017	20,712	13,527	6,851	2,962	1,429	786	460	512
2,058	2,127	2,244	2,227	2,167	11,056	12,191	9,903	6,695	4,483	2,853	1,849	1,333	1,895

(continued next page)

Table 1.1. *(continued)*

Arrests by Offense Charged and Age, United States, 1994 (10,654 agencies; 1994 estimated population 207,624,000)

Offense charged	Total all ages	Ages under 15	Ages under 18	Ages 18 and older	Under 10	10 to 12	13 to 14	15	16	17	18	19
Drug abuse violations	1,118,346	21,830	131,220	987,126	266	2,281	19,283	24,103	36,747	48,540	60,142	57,786
Gambling	15,845	242	1,493	14,352	2	24	216	299	423	529	531	537
Offenses against family and children	92,133	1,475	4,234	87,899	98	293	1,084	815	978	966	2,009	2,207
Driving under the influence	1,079,533	329	10,573	1,068,960	117	24	188	534	2,708	7,002	15,769	22,312
Liquor laws	424,452	10,083	94,030	330,422	153	832	9,098	14,001	27,520	42,426	60,029	59,868
Drunkenness	571,420	2,065	14,778	556,642	120	197	1,748	2,298	3,606	6,809	12,831	14,090
Disorderly conduct	601,002	48,868	137,328	463,674	1,741	10,752	36,375	27,057	30,178	31,225	30,639	27,148
Vagrancy	21,413	925	3,657	17,756	19	154	752	773	946	1,013	1,072	860
All other offenses (except traffic)	3,046,100	99,318	343,669	2,702,431	5,396	20,348	73,574	61,382	81,918	101,051	124,694	132,388
Suspicion	11,395	551	1,712	9,683	39	128	384	396	385	380	407	399
Curfew and loitering law violations	105,888	31,609	105,888	X	537	4,552	26,520	24,667	28,098	21,514	X	X
Runaways	201,459	90,031	201,459	X	2,117	15,242	72,672	51,634	41,246	18,548	X	X

Source: U.S. Department of Justice, Federal Bureau of Investigation, *Crime in the United States, 1994* (Washington, DC: U.S. Government Printing Office, 1995), pp. 227, 228.

Note: This table presents data from all law enforcement agencies submitting complete reports for 12 months in 1994. Population figures represent U.S. Bureau of the Census July 1, 1994, estimates.

a. Because of rounding, percents may not add to total.

b. Violent crimes are offenses of murder and nonnegligent manslaughter, forcible rape, robbery, and aggravated assault.

c. Property crimes are offenses of burglary, larceny-theft, motor vehicle theft, and arson.

d. Includes arson.

First, when criminals have been questioned about other crimes they have committed, the results show discrepancies between *UCR* figures and "self-report" information. In short, criminals escape detection or capture for many crimes they commit. Thus, *it is generally accepted that there is more crime committed each year than official estimates such as the UCR disclose.*

Second, *not all law enforcement agencies report crimes in a uniform manner. Many jurisdictions define the same crimes differently* (Coyle, Schaaf, and Coldren, 1991). Errors also occur in tabulating arrest statistics by clerks in local police departments (e.g., a clerk may classify a robbery as a burglary). Some critics say that the *UCR* is more a reflection of police arrest practices than a true measure of the amount of crime that really occurs (Blumstein, Cohen, and Rosenfeld, 1991).

Third, *in some jurisdictions, police "crackdowns" will lead to numerous arrests, but there will be few convictions.* The implication is that arrest statistics are more a measure of police activity rather than criminal activity (Blumstein, Cohen, and Rosenfeld, 1991; Winsberg, 1993). In these instances, there is often an underlying political motive, such as a mayor's election. A police department making numerous arrests gives voters the impression that the incumbent mayor is really doing something about crime. However, arrests of suspects on weak provocation means that many of these cases are dismissed outright. A continuing hazard of police work is that citizens may file lawsuits alleging false arrest. The weaker the provoca-

20	21	22	23	24	25 to 29	30 to 34	35 to 39	40 to 44	45 to 49	50 to 54	55 to 59	60 to 64	65 and older
51,330	48,063	45,564	45,455	43,839	190,382	183,565	133,141	73,403	32,406	12,773	5,170	2,270	1,837
533	466	389	433	389	1,770	1,880	1,775	1,563	1,191	970	726	601	598
2,383	2,731	2,916	3,256	3,465	16,778	19,310	15,461	8,913	4,419	1,980	989	534	548
27,223	38,711	40,866	44,180	43,818	195,657	201,508	161,847	111,111	70,710	41,984	23,910	14,628	14,726
47,987	14,628	11,150	9,477	8,012	29,069	27,355	22,918	16,126	9,964	6,035	3,657	2,112	2,035
14,841	19,260	18,959	18,928	18,599	87,057	101,426	90,333	65,154	40,160	24,643	13,776	8,502	8,083
24,627	26,244	23,791	23,202	20,985	81,732	76,119	56,300	33,277	18,142	9,664	5,078	3,083	3,643
677	580	591	647	602	2,930	3,265	2,747	1,739	1,009	541	227	141	128
128,076	126,545	123,337	123,304	119,931	510,184	484,602	365,026	221,462	117,530	59,593	30,525	16,798	18,436
344	360	375	429	385	1,829	1,919	1,551	905	438	160	85	54	43
X	X	X	X	X	X	X	X	X	X	X	X	X	X
X	X	X	X	X	X	X	X	X	X	X	X	X	X

tion for an arrest, the greater the likelihood that a suit will be filed.

Nevertheless, high arrest rates have apparent political advantages. For instance, an investigation found that arrest rates and crime levels fluctuated significantly during sheriff campaigns in different counties in Florida. Using 1976 Florida County Sheriff election data, it was shown that winners and losers of sheriffs' elections could be predicted fairly accurately by arrest figures (Surrette, 1979, 1985). This reinforces the notion that "arrest statistics" may be a better measure of police activity than actual criminal activity. This observation has historical precedent, because immigrants in the early 1900s were arrested more frequently because of prevailing political agendas (Brown and Warner, 1992), and because arrests in the 1980s and 1990s have been a part of racially motivated political strategies in various cities (Tonry, 1994). This is especially true regarding the promotion of strong drug and sanctioning polices that do not significantly reduce crime rates or drug use (Tonry, 1994) but satisfy certain political policy objectives instead.

"Better" police work (i.e., more aggressive arrest strategies) actually may cause the "crime rate" to increase significantly, even though there is no real increase in crime committed in the community. But in the view of the public, "better" police work means more arrests because they demonstrate that law enforcement agencies are doing something to "combat" crime. In reality, this is not the case. Police action or inaction may have little or nothing to do with crime fluctuations and in fact represent ar-

Figure 1.1 Crime Clock

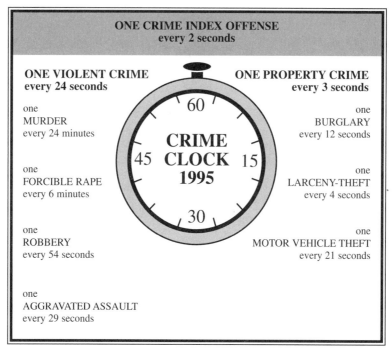

Source: National Victim Center.

tificially created crime waves or crises (Caringella-MacDonald, 1990).

A fourth criticism is that *not all law enforcement agencies report their crime figures on a consistent basis.* Sloppy record keeping and lax record keeping policies contribute to faulty reporting. Also, *many crimes are never reported to the police.* For instance, someone soliciting a woman for prostitution may be beaten and robbed by the woman's associates. Under these circumstances, he may be reluctant to report the incident to the police because of possible ridicule and embarrassment. Furthermore, soliciting prostitutes is unlawful. And if a person engages another for purposes of prostitution and the act is completed, no one may find out about it. In both instances, crimes have been committed but not reported. Also, women may be afraid to report a rape because of personal embarrassment or potential reprisal from the rapist (Eigenberg, 1990).

Fifth, *when a crime is reported and a report is submitted to the* UCR, *only the most serious offense is often reported.* For example, a burglary suspect is arrested at a crime scene in possession of burglary tools (a law violation), stolen goods (another law violation), and a concealed weapon (another law violation). However, law enforcement officials may report a single crime, burglary. This practice (i.e., reporting the most serious offense where two or more offenses have been committed by a single suspect), together with the fact that many crimes remain undetected or are not reported, causes some experts to charge that the *UCR* underestimates the actual amount of crime committed in the United States.

In the matter of juveniles, the presence or absence of curfew laws can increase or decrease the number of juvenile arrests. If a city were to change a curfew law from 9:00 P.M. to 10:00 P.M., fewer juveniles would be stopped by police, detained,

Table 1.2

Arrest Rates for Property Crimes by Offense Charged and Region, 1971-94 (Rate per 100,000 inhabitants)

	Offense charged and region															
	Burglary				Larceny-theft				Motor vehicle theft				Arson			
	Northeast	Midwest	South	West	Northeast	Midwest	South	West	Northeast	Midwest	South	West	Northeast	Midwest	South	West
1971	173.7	170.7	204.8	295.2	302.1	455.8	445.2	572.1	72.1	69.5	67.5	151.2	X	X	X	X
1972	164.0	157.9	200.3	306.7	281.8	447.2	431.0	593.5	66.6	61.2	62.3	137.4	X	X	X	X
1973	189.6	154.3	193.9	314.2	280.8	424.6	425.7	572.6	77.1	58.9	60.6	126.0	X	X	X	X
1974	207.9	213.5	269.5	361.5	398.0	586.0	542.5	680.9	67.3	62.3	66.7	139.9	X	X	X	X
1975	222.0	186.5	271.0	344.3	393.7	528.8	571.7	658.1	63.1	49.9	56.8	112.2	X	X	X	X
1976	232.9	170.2	241.5	307.2	423.8	491.9	550.4	692.3	65.9	46.4	51.1	115.0	X	X	X	X
1977	243.6	178.8	233.8	320.8	452.0	507.9	521.3	658.1	66.4	57.7	53.6	125.4	X	X	X	X
1978	259.6	166.7	231.5	304.5	475.7	485.9	515.9	646.2	77.9	55.4	57.5	124.0	X	X	X	X
1979	221.0	163.2	237.9	315.8	447.4	499.5	537.9	697.5	60.6	52.2	58.1	129.2	9.9	8.1	7.9	11.2
1980	226.1	167.2	239.0	303.5	463.5	535.1	516.3	674.8	60.1	46.0	50.2	107.4	9.8	8.3	8.1	9.8
1981	213.4	172.5	235.0	305.9	474.2	558.2	541.7	685.9	55.2	42.8	47.8	93.9	9.2	8.6	8.5	10.5
1982	199.5	188.8	234.5	304.9	492.4	661.6	590.4	735.4	57.8	49.4	47.6	83.7	9.0	11.5	7.5	9.9
1983	177.9	166.2	209.7	275.9	475.8	593.9	566.4	703.1	49.5	41.7	46.0	78.1	8.5	9.1	7.8	9.3
1984	159.6	139.3	194.3	247.9	466.2	545.8	549.9	692.6	50.0	38.3	49.5	71.2	8.0	8.0	7.1	10.2
1985	156.7	133.0	197.6	258.7	477.9	549.5	572.2	723.5	47.7	38.4	53.0	90.9	8.8	7.9	7.2	9.9
1986	151.1	129.6	206.7	253.9	478.5	563.4	590.7	738.4	54.8	43.4	60.0	101.7	8.0	7.7	7.1	8.8
1987	151.7	136.5	204.9	235.8	514.9	622.7	602.1	739.2	67.3	50.3	66.3	109.2	7.8	7.7	6.4	8.6
1988	145.2	131.3	182.7	234.9	511.6	625.8	579.3	730.6	77.1	60.6	64.7	124.4	7.6	8.2	6.9	8.2
1989	153.6	135.5	181.9	239.8	527.1	650.2	599.4	729.0	90.7	73.1	73.1	134.2	7.2	7.6	6.7	7.9
1990	145.1	121.4	192.9	229.0	533.3	626.9	647.0	729.0	79.7	56.3	81.0	128.5	7.2	8.0	7.4	8.4
1991	142.0	127.8	182.7	223.9	536.0	660.4	650.0	693.8	78.6	56.0	78.2	122.4	7.1	7.7	8.0	8.3
1992	137.0	122.4	174.8	222.2	499.8	610.1	607.5	686.6	69.6	52.7	72.7	122.5	7.1	8.6	6.8	8.7
1993	126.2	110.4	168.7	206.4	466.4	577.7	598.2	666.1	65.7	57.0	71.7	118.1	6.8	8.0	7.1	8.5
1994	120.0	113.9	165.5	194.0	468.7	593.9	635.0	643.4	61.3	64.4	74.8	114.6	6.9	9.5	7.1	9.5

Source: Maguire and Pastore (1996), p. 424.

Note: Arson was designated an Index property crime in October 1978. Data collection began in 1979. The number of agencies reporting and the populations represented vary from year to year.

and/or arrested. If the curfew were changed from 9:00 P.M. to 8:00 P.M., however, more juveniles would be stopped by police, detained, and/or arrested. Of course, juveniles are often arrested for offenses besides curfew violations.

Some investigators feel that the *UCR* is a valid indicator of the incidence of serious crimes (Biderman and Lynch, 1991). This belief is supported by the fact that crimes involving death, serious bodily injury, and thefts of valuable property have a greater likelihood of being reported to police and to insurance companies. In contrast, lesser offenses or petty crimes leaving the victim uninjured may not be reported. The paperwork required of crime victims may not be worth their time in relation to the money or property stolen (U.S. Bureau of Justice Statistics, 1993).

Other experts believe that the *UCR* should improve the quality of information reported and ensure greater comparability with other crime databases. Massive crime legislation in various states, such as Michigan, has been described as "piecemeal" by various agencies and experts. The Michigan Council on Crime and Delinquency has suggested a moratorium on further crime legislation until more systematic information mechanisms can be implemented to give crime policy greater focus and direction (*Corrections Compendium*, 1993).

How well do law enforcement agencies respond to various crimes? The *UCR* maintains records indicating the proportion of crimes cleared by arrest each year. *Cleared by arrest means that a law enforcement agency has identified possible offenders, has sufficient evidence to charge them, and actually takes them into custody.* Crimes may also be cleared by exceptional means, such as when the offender dies, offers a deathbed confession, or commits suicide. Also, crime victims may decide not to prosecute simply because the time consumed is not worth the loss sustained from the crime committed. In these instances, law enforcement officers know the identity of offenders, have sufficient evidence to support their arrest, and/or know the offenders' whereabouts. Thus, "crimes cleared by arrest" do not reflect these exceptional cases.

It should be noted that the phrase "crimes cleared by arrest" does not mean that those crimes have been solved. It means simply that someone has been arrested and charged with a particular crime. Overzealous law enforcement in selected jurisdictions may lead to many arrests, but how many persons are actually convicted of the crimes charged or alleged? More than half of all arrests do not result in convictions. Therefore, the information in figure 1.1 is somewhat misleading because it causes us to believe that the criminals who committed the crimes have been apprehended, prosecuted, and convicted. Despite the poor relation between the number of "crimes cleared by arrest" and the resulting convictions, these figures are indicative of some degree of crime control, although we don't know how much.

The National Crime Victimization Survey (NCVS)

The limitations of the *UCR* and other official documents measuring the amount of crime have led some experts to draw comparisons between the *UCR* and the **National Crime Victimization Survey (NCVS),** which until 1991 was called the *National Crime Survey* (Rand, 1991). The *NCVS* has been conducted annually in cooperation with the U.S. Bureau of the Census. The *NCVS* is an annual random survey of approximately fifty thousand households, involving interviews with one hundred thousand persons age twelve and over, and approximately fifty thousand businesses (Eigenberg, 1990). Smaller samples of persons from these original figures form the database from which crime figures are compiled. Carefully worded questions lead people to report incidents that can be classified as crimes. This material is statistically manipulated in such a way as to make it comparable with *UCR* statistics. This material is usually referred to as *victimization data.*

The *NCVS* distinguishes between victimizations and incidents. *A victimization is the basic measure of the occurrence of a crime and is a specific criminal act that affects a single victim. An incident is a specific criminal act involving one or more victims.*

Comparing *NCVS* (victimization) information with *UCR* (officially reported) data shows that *the amount of crime reported by the NCVS is from two to three times greater than the amount of crime re-*

ported by the UCR. Despite this clearly different indication about the actual *volume* of crime in the United States annually, some experts say that both the *UCR* and *NCVS* behave similarly over time according to actual *crime trends* (Blumstein, Cohen, and Rosenfeld, 1991). Other experts disagree and challenge the validity of correlations between these two reporting outlets (Menard et al., 1992). However, some researchers caution that comparing *UCR* data with *NCVS* data is both difficult and unreliable. Comparing burglary and robbery rates in both the *NCVS* and *UCR* for a given time, such as between 1973–1989, shows very low correlations (McDowall and Loftin, 1992). Still other experts suggest that we utilize *calls-for-service* data as a more reliable indicator of crime activity than either the *UCR* or *NCVS* (Bursik and Grasmick, 1993). *Calls-for-service data are tabulated from police agencies where calls are received requesting police assistance, whether the assistance is for crimes in progress or non-crime-related emergencies.* Data are retrieved from agency records and used as an indication of crime trends in cities and regions.

Despite its safeguards, however, the *NCVS* has certain persistent problems. Some crime victims cannot remember when or where the offense occurred. Other victims are reluctant to report a rape, particularly if the rapist is a family member or a close friend. Nonreporting is also related to victim fear, feelings of helplessness or apathy, the perceived powerlessness of police, and fear of the authorities themselves. Neither the *UCR* nor the *NCVS* report victimless crimes (Boggess and Bound, 1993). The poor are especially reluctant to report crime because they fear reprisals from the criminals, who are often known to them. Also, police may detect evidence of other crimes or statutory violations such as health code infractions, illegal aliens, and overcrowded apartment dwellings (Marshall and Webb, 1994).

Additionally, both the *UCR* and *NCVS* overemphasize street crimes and deemphasize corporate crimes. It is often difficult to know, for instance, who has been a direct victim of corporate crime such as the theft of a company's secrets by a current or former trusted employee. Sometimes embezzlement of a corporation's funds is handled internally without police intervention. Some indication of the amount of crime in the United States as reflected by victimization data from the *NCVS* is shown in table 1.3.

In 1993, for instance, the *NCVS* showed that there were 43.6 million victimizations (Bastian, 1995:1). Violent crimes accounted for about 10.6 million or 24.9 percent of these. Reported offenses included rape, robbery, burglary, and assault. For comparative purposes, there were 34.7 million victimizations in 1991. The 43.6 million victimizations in 1993 represent a 25.6 percent increase between these two years (Maguire, Pastore, and Flanagan, 1993).

Crime Patterns and Offender Characteristics

About two-thirds of all single-offender violent crimes are committed by whites. Although handguns are frequently blamed for much violent crime, deadly weapons are not used in 80 percent of all violent crime cases. About 71 percent of all violent crimes (primarily rapes and assaults) are committed by offenders acting alone, while over half of the robberies are committed by two or more offenders. Currently, the experts say that the relationship between gun availability, gun laws, and gun usage in crimes is "inconclusive" (Annest, Mercy, and Gibson, 1995; Burstein, Kopel, and Ram, 1995; Edel, 1995; Sheley and Wright; 1995; Zawitz, 1995).

Most violent crimes occur between 6:00 P.M. and midnight. Streets are common sites for personal crimes of violence, and most of these crimes involve strangers. Nonstranger, violent crimes, including rape and assault, often occur in the victim's home or somewhere on the victim's property.

In 1994, over 50 percent of all crimes were committed by persons under age twenty-five. Involvement in criminal activity declines with age, although recent data suggest that crime committed by the elderly is on the increase (Maguire and Pastore, 1995:384–85). Also, attempts to account for variations in crime based on age ignore important variables such as personality and socioeconomic characteristics (Whitaker, 1989). Considering the

Table 1.3

Criminal Victimizations and Victimization Rates, 1992–93: Estimates from the Redesigned National Crime Victimization Survey

Type of Crime	Number of Victimizations (1,000's)		Victimization Rates (per 1,000 persons age 12 or older)	
	1992a	1993	1992a	1993
All Crimes	42,912	43,622	...	...
Personal Crimesb	10,692	11,409	51.1	53.9
Crimes of violence	10,317	10,896	49.3	51.5
Completed violence	3,311	3,226	15.8	15.3
Attempted/threatened violence	7,006	7,670	33.5	36.3
Rape/Sexual assault	607	485	2.9	2.3
Rape/attempted rape	374	313	1.8	1.5
Rape	175	160	.8	.8
Attempted rape	200	152	1.0	.7
Sexual assault	233	173	1.1	.8
Robbery	1,293	1,307	6.2	6.2
Completed/property taken	862	826	4.1	3.9
With injury	310	276	1.5	1.3
Without injury	552	549	2.6	2.6
Attempted to take property	431	481	2.1	2.3
With injury	81	100	.4	.5
Without injury	350	381	1.7	1.8
Assault	8,416	9,104	40.2	43.0
Aggravated	2,317	2,578	11.1	12.2
With injury	671	713	3.2	3.4
Threatened with weapon	1,646	1,865	7.9	8.8
Simple	6,099	6,525	29.1	30.8
With minor injury	1,445	1,358	6.9	6.4
Without injury	4,655	5,167	22.2	24.4
Property Crimes	32,220	32,213	325.3	322.4
Household burglary	5,815	5,995	58.7	60.0
Completed	4,756	4,835	48.0	48.4
Forcible entry	1,845	1,858	18.6	18.6
Unlawful entry without force	2,911	2,977	29.4	29.8
Attempted forcible entry	1,059	1,160	10.7	11.6
Motor Vehicle theft	1,838	1,967	18.6	19.7
Completed	1,203	1,297	12.1	13.0
Attempted	635	670	6.4	6.7
Theft	24,568	24,250	248.0	242.7
Completedc	23,474	23,033	237.0	230.5
Less than $50	10,313	9,642	104.1	96.5
$50-$249	7,976	7,688	80.5	76.9
$250 or more	4,144	4,264	41.8	42.7
Attempted	1,094	1,217	11.0	12.2

Source: Bastian (1995), p. 2.

Note: These data are preliminary and may vary slightly from the final estimates. Completed violent crimes include completed rape, sexual assault, completed robbery with and without injury, aggravated assault with injury, and simple assault with minor injury. The total population age 12 or older was 209,352,860 in 1992; in 1993 it was 211,524,770. The total number of households in 1992 was 99,046,200; in 1993 it was 99,926,400.

a. These 1992 estimates are based on a half sample of data from the redesigned National Crime Victimization Survey and are not directly comparable with figures previously published for 1992, which were estimated under the previous, and now superseded, survey design.

b. The victimization survey cannot measure murder because of the inability to question the victim. Personal crimes include purse snatching and pocket picking, not shown separately.

c. Includes thefts in which the amount taken was not ascertained.

unreliability of the *UCR* and *NCVS* in accounting for the true amount of crime in the United States, it is unlikely that we will ever know the real relationship between age and crime.

Emerging Issues in Criminal Justice

Elderly Victims

In 1992, persons aged sixty-five and older experienced approximately 2.1 million criminal victimizations (U.S. Bureau of Justice Statistics, 1994). This group was the least likely of all age groups to experience crime. The elderly appeared to be particularly susceptible to crimes motivated by economic gain, and injured elderly victims were more likely than their younger counterparts to suffer a serious injury. Further, elderly victims were more likely to face assailants who were strangers, with 38 percent facing armed offenders. The elderly victims tended not to protect themselves during a crime, but they reported these offenses to police more frequently. Despite these elderly victimizations, victimization rates generally decline with age. For instance, the rate of assaults in 1993 was 98.1 per 1,000 for persons age sixteen to nineteen, while persons sixty-five or over had an assault rate of 4.1 per 1,000 (Bachman, 1994a:1; Bastian, 1995:4).

A growing area of concern is the victimization and abuse of elderly persons by their own children. The elderly may be physically assaulted, verbally insulted or degraded, starved, or deprived of needed health services. Because much elderly abuse is unreported, accurate and reliable estimates of its occurrence cannot be made. However, human services and other interested agencies report annual increases in the number of cases involving elderly abuse (Macolini, 1995).

Why would adult children abuse their elderly parents? One hypothesis is that the abuse is an outlet for financial frustration (Reulbach and Tewksbury, 1994). The cost of caring for aging parents is increasing annually, but many families cannot afford to place their parents in homes or hospitals for the elderly. Instead, the children must bear this burden. Like child abuse, elderly abuse will continue to be an important social and criminal issue well beyond the 1990s.

The elderly often suffer abuse from people besides family members. Because they are often unable to defend themselves and live alone, they are targeted by muggers and other criminals for various crimes (U.S. Bureau of Justice Statistics, 1994). The number of elderly victims is small in proportion to the number of victims in other age categories, but that number is growing proportionately each year.

With the exceptions of purse snatching and pocket picking, the 1995 *NCVS* data shown in table 1.3 disclose that the elderly are victimized less often than any other age category (Bastian, 1995). But elderly victims are different in several respects from their younger counterparts. First, elderly victims pose little or no physical threat to criminal offenders who prey upon them (U.S. Bureau of Justice Statistics, 1994). Second, elderly females are increasingly the targets of rapists because of their greater physical vulnerability (Davis, Taylor, and Bench, 1995). Third, elderly victims are unable or unwilling to appear in court to testify against their assailants for fear of retaliation. Fourth, elderly victims heal less quickly when physically attacked. This means that their victimization is frequently more serious and of longer duration compared with younger victims. Perhaps the greatest problem confronting the elderly is the fear of being victimized (Davis, Taylor, and Bench, 1995). Threats of mugging, purse snatching, robbery, and assault make many elderly persons avoid routine trips to the store or to places of entertainment ordinarily available to others.

Elderly Criminals

As the proportion of elderly increases in our population, there is also a corresponding increase in the frequency of crimes committed by the elderly (Champion, 1988b). Some researchers refute the idea of a growing "crime wave" among the elderly. For instance, Lydia Long has noted that between 1970 and 1987, there was a 27 percent increase in the overall elderly population, although during that same period, no commensurate increase in crime among these persons was detected (Long, 1992). While these figures may be true of the general elderly population, they may mask actual crime escalation among elderly offenders in selected geographical areas with high elderly concentrations (Aday, 1994; Midwinter, 1991; Zimbardo, 1994). Variations in arrest policies and sentencing provisions may account for substantial fluctuations in these figures.

Estimates of the number of elderly who commit crimes range from 300,000 to 500,000. This is less than 1 percent of all crimes in the United States. While the elderly currently have little if any significant impact on the amount of crime in the United States, their numbers are growing (Maguire and Pastore, 1995). This situation is problematic for judges when sentencing elderly offenders. Ordinarily, a convicted robber or drug dealer might receive a five- or ten-year sentence. For a ninety-year-old thief or drug dealer, a ten-year term would be the equivalent of a death sentence. The convicted elderly offender would probably die in prison.

Currently, the criminal justice system makes no distinction between adults of different ages who commit similar offenses. However, judges are often more lenient in sentencing elderly offenders (McCarthy and Langworthy, 1988; Champion, 1988b). For example, an eighty-year-old woman was arrested in Kentucky for growing one hundred marijuana plants. She claimed the marijuana helped her glaucoma and that she was growing the illegal plants for her health (one hundred plants?). The judge gave her a small fine, a lecture, and a suspended sentence. In a similar case, a twenty-six-year-old person was convicted of growing thirty marijuana plants and received a three-year sentence in the Kentucky state penitentiary from the same judge who sentenced the eighty-year-old woman.

Presently, judges attempt to dispense justice impartially for all offenders, regardless of age (with noted exceptions). Police officers are reluctant to arrest elderly citizens for offenses, even serious ones. But by the year 2000, the sheer numbers of elderly offenders will be such that police and judicial discretion will have to be modified. There are no easy answers to the question of how elderly offenders ought to be punished. A more pressing question is how to manage the expense of maintaining elderly offenders in jail and prison facilities. Aging inmates pose increasingly serious medical problems for these facilities, so that elderly prisoner care and treatment are now more of a problem than their actual rate of offending (Aday, 1994; Kratcoski and Babb, 1990; Zimbardo, 1994).

Child Abuse and Missing Children

Child Abuse

Child abuse *is any form of cruelty to the physical, moral or mental well-being, the sexual abuse or exploitation, negligent treatment, or maltreatment of a child under the age of eighteen by a person who is responsible for the child's welfare.* (42 U.S.C., Sec. 5101–5105, 1996). In many states, child abuse is a felony; in a few states, it is a misdemeanor (Greenfeld, 1996). In 1991, about 16.8 percent of all state prison inmates were serving time for violent crimes against persons under age eighteen (Greenfeld, 1996:1). More than half of these offenders victimized children under twelve years of age.

Child abuse is a problem of interest to many agencies and organizations. Health departments and child welfare services try to identify and prevent child abuse whenever it is detected. The *UCR* and *NCVS* do not collect data about child abuse. Child abuse may also involve child pornography or sexual abuse, including prostitution.

At present, little is known about how much child abuse occurs nationally. Media reports and human services agency data suggest that child abuse is an increasingly pervasive phenomenon. It is not clear whether there is really more child abuse today or whether public awareness of child abuse is increasing because of greater media coverage of child abuse incidents. Statistically, estimates of child abuse range from 1 million to 5 million abused children each year (Steidel, 1994; Wynkoop, Capps, and Priest, 1995). Some researchers estimate that 95 percent of all parents have physically abused their children at least once, although this figure may be exaggerated (Girdner and Hoff, 1994).

In 1978, the Child Abuse Prevention and Treatment Act was passed. This act provides for a national center to collect and disseminate information regarding child abuse and neglect and a national adoption information exchange system to facilitate the adoptive placement of children (42 U.S.C., Sec. 5107, 1996). While no reliable statistics exist to show how much child abuse actually occurs in the United States annually, in 1994 the federal government appropriated $30 million to deal with this growing problem (Asdigan, Finkelhor, and Hotaling, 1995; Elliott, 1995).

An attempt to profile child abusers has been made. Abusive persons have been described as "low in self-esteem, emotionally immature and self-centered, and feeling incompetent as parents" (Allen, 1991). But child abuse cuts across all socioeconomic levels and genders and occurs in all types of families (Milner, 1992). Many child sexual abusers were abused themselves as children (Allen and Lee, 1992; Milner and Robertson, 1990). Increasing numbers of female child sexual abusers are being reported, and there is some indication that they have suffered childhoods similar to those of their male abuser counterparts (Wakefield and Underwager, 1991).

Missing Children

Missing children comprise a different category than abused children or sexually abused youths (National Center for Missing and Exploited Children, 1992, 1994). Unless the child is quite young (i.e., under five or six years of age), the missing child is assumed to be a runaway (Collins et al., 1993). While missing infants are sometimes victims of kidnapping, the most common form of abduction occurs when divorced noncustodial parents take their children from the custodial parents without their knowledge or permission (Forst and Blomquist, 1991; Pollet, 1993).

A missing child is "any person under eighteen years of age whose whereabouts are unknown to such individual's legal custodian and the circumstances of the individual's disappearance are such as to indicate his/her removal without consent of the legal custodian and/or there are strong indications of abuse or sexual exploitation" (42 U.S.C., Sec. 5772, 1996). When runaways are involved, sexual exploitation may include prostitution as a means of surviving and paying for necessities (National Center for Missing and Exploited Children, 1992). Or the exploitation may be child pornography (Best, 1990).

Some experts believe that too much has been made of the "missing children" phenomenon and that the media has sensationalized reports about it (Best, 1990; Forst and Blomquist, 1991). This does not mean that these experts have trivialized the problem of missing children but rather that they have given the problem a more realistic focus by directing our attention toward parentally abducted youths rather than those who have disappeared into some invisible underground of sexual slavery and exploitation (Girdner and Hoff, 1994). Forst and Blomquist (1991) suggest that the most pressing issue is parental abduction and what to do about it. They contend that more children are parentally abducted than are kidnapped by strangers. Best (1990) agrees with Forst and Blomquist and suggests that crusades about missing children result from socially constructed problems created and perpetuated by the media and child advocates with hidden political agendas. Nevertheless, a substantial proportion of missing children *do* become child prostitutes and vagrants (National Center for Missing and Exploited Children, 1992).

Under the provisions of the Missing Children's Assistance Act of 1984, the Advisory Board on Missing Children was established to provide information about and coordinate the efforts of child welfare agencies to locate missing children (42 U.S.C., 1996). In 1985, $10 million was appropriated by Congress for this Advisory Board. In 1992, the U.S. Department of Justice reported that there were over 500,000 missing children. The Department of Justice maintains computerized files of missing children and assists agencies in locating them (Collins et al., 1993).

Domestic Violence

During the 1980s and well into the 1990s, greater concern has been shown for domestic violence. Known also as *intimate-violence, spousal abuse, and wife battering, domestic violence is assault upon one spouse by another, usually involving physical harm or injury to one or both partners.* One difficulty in providing an adequate definition of domestic violence is the fact that domestic living has taken on many new meanings in recent years. Persons may live together and not be married. Persons may be living together and married, but not to each other. Persons may be in same-sex relationships. Domestic violence may occur between one or both parents and siblings or other close relatives. The term *wife battering* is inaccurate because often *males* are the battered victims, despite conventional and gender-biased police interpretations and definitions (Lanza-Kaduce, Greenleaf, and Donahue, 1995:526–29). Nevertheless, wives are about six times more likely to be victimized or abused by their husbands than men are by their wives (Bachman and Saltzman, 1995:1).

Domestic violence often includes murder of one spouse by another. Over 60 percent of all murders in large urban counties are committed by family members or close acquaintances of victims (Dawson and Langan, 1994:1; Gwinn, 1995:11–14). The problem has become so severe that Congress has created the Violence Against Women Act (VAWA) as

a part of the Violent Crime Control and Law Enforcement Act of 1994 (Travis, 1995:1). Among other things, the Act provides for a national domestic violence hotline; severe penalties for sex crimes; education and prevention grants to reduce sexual assaults against women; grants to prevent crime on public transportation and in parks; and increased efforts on the part of law enforcement to enforce laws against domestic violence, prosecute offenders, and provide victim services.

In many jurisdictions, police departments have mandatory arrest policies that provide for the arrest of whichever spouse is deemed by police officers to have caused the incident and/or inflicted physical injury on the other (Zorza and Woods, 1994; Virginia Department of Criminal Justice Services, 1993). However, there is strong evidence that domestic violence is not deterred by such arrests. In fact, the violence may intensify when the arrested spouse is released, sometimes resulting in the death of the other spouse (Corsilles, 1994). Another problem complicating the situation is that even under mandatory-arrest policies, testimony from the injured spouse is often vital to a successful prosecution. But after typical cooling-off periods, spouses are reluctant or unwilling to testify against their

A crowd protests a court decision that released a man who was charged with wife abuse and who subsequently murdered her. Awareness and concern for domestic violence have been growing in America since the 1980s.

Highlight 1.4. Six Years for an Abuser: The Case of Dennis Conklin, Jr.

Some domestic situations can turn extremely violent. In New Town, North Dakota, Dennis Conklin, Jr., twenty-three, had been living with a woman, Tanya Haddeland, forty-six. One evening he returned home to find her with another man. His anger resulted in his arrest for stabbing Ms. Haddeland in the face and throat and hitting her on the head and face with a hammer.

Conklin was charged with attempted murder. Had it not been for the other person in the home with Haddeland, she may very well have been murdered. Conklin was permitted to plead guilty to a lesser charge of assault resulting in bodily injury. He was sentenced to fifty-seven months in a federal prison by U.S. District Court Judge Patrick Conmy. This sentence was to be followed by two years of probation, during which time Conklin would be ex-

pected to perform seventy-five hours of community service and pay $1,000 restitution to the victim of his assault. He was also ordered to pay fifty dollars to a crime victim's defense fund that was set up to assist victims of domestic violence in cases against their spouses. The woman, Ms. Haddeland, was hospitalized for several days following her attack by Conklin.

Should stiffer penalties be imposed on those committing assault against their spouses or partners? What else should Conklin have been expected to do in this case? Is there any protection for Haddeland once Conklin is released from prison?

Source: Adapted from Associated Press, "New Town Man Given 57 Months for Attack on Woman," *Minot (ND) Daily News*, November 30, 1995, p. B1.

---

partners. Thus, in many cases, the prosecutions are terminated (Virginia Department of Criminal Justice Services, 1993; Zorza and Woods, 1994).

Organized Crime

At the heart of much of the street crime in the United States is **organized crime**. *Organized crime is a social network created for the purpose of perpetrating illegal acts such as illegal gambling, prostitution, and drug trafficking.* During the 1920s, Prohibition banned alcoholic beverages. Al Capone and other notorious crime figures organized syndicates to distribute alcohol in various cities, such as Chicago. Capone's organization was also known for its gambling and prostitution activities (Schoenberg, 1992).

Perhaps the best-known crime organization is the Mafia, a powerful international network of families that continues to provide illegal goods and services to consumers (Brewton, 1992; Jamieson, 1992; Shawcross, 1994). The organizational appa-

ratus of the Mafia is much like that of IBM or any other large-scale corporation, with a chain of command or authority hierarchy, a division of labor, spheres of competence, and appointment or promotion on the basis of merit (Wallek, 1991). The origin of the Mafia is traceable to Italy and Sicily (Catanzaro, 1994; Salzano, 1994). In recent decades, organized crime has involved itself in political corruption, transnational crimes, and drug trafficking (Flood, 1991; Godson, Olson, and Shelley, 1995). Even bingo is not immune to the Mafia and other organized criminal organizations (Pennsylvania Crime Commission, 1992).

Frustrating efforts of law enforcement agencies is that much of organized crime's operations are funneled through legal fronts or conduits, such as banks, department stores, discount houses, liquor wholesalers, investment companies, and major retail outlets (Dick, 1995; Moore, 1992). Furthermore, these organizations use state-of-the-art technology in their business dealings and other illicit transactions (Findlay, 1992; Moore, 1992).

The government's efforts against the Mafia and organized crime generally were strengthened greatly by the Organized Crime Control Act of 1970 and its subsequent amendment, known as RICO or Racketeer Influenced and Corrupt Organizations Act (18 U.S.C. Sec. 1951–1968, 1996). Federal racketeering statutes, which were enacted originally in 1934 and periodically amended, target a number of offenses, such as conspiracy to obstruct, or obstruction of, interstate commerce by robbery or extortion; travel in interstate or foreign commerce, or use of the mails to facilitate any unlawful activity; and any offer, acceptance, or solicitation of bribes to influence an employee benefit plan (*Corrections Compendium*, 1994:4–5).

Specific RICO prohibitions include the following four activities:

a. investing the proceeds of a pattern of racketeering activity in an enterprise that engages in interstate or foreign commerce;
b. acquiring or maintaining an interest in such an enterprise by means of a pattern of racketeering activity;
c. using a pattern of racketeering activity in conducting the affairs of such an enterprise; or
d. conspiracy to do (a), (b), or (c). (*Corrections Compendium*, 1994:4–5).

Some of the more notorious activities linked with organized crime and the Mafia include the Mafia's "cooperation" with a CIA plot to murder Fidel Castro in Cuba; the events of the day Jimmy Hoffa was killed; and the origins of the confrontation between Hoffa and U.S. Attorney General Robert Kennedy (Flood, 1991; Ragano and Raab, 1994). Evidence suggests that the federal government has been able to utilize RICO and its various provisions to cripple organized crime in various parts of the country through asset forfeiture and other crime prevention and control measures (U.S. Bureau of Justice Assistance, 1992). Illicit drug trafficking by the Mafia has also been minimized through RICO and other anticrime provisions (Jamieson, 1992; Shawcross, 1994).

White-Collar Criminality

Sometimes confused with organized crime is **white-collar crime**. *White-collar crime is generally understood to refer to illegal activities of businesspersons that occur during the legitimate day-to-day activities of their business or profession.* Probably the best-known type of white-collar crime is embezzlement, although the term may encompass both violence and theft in the workplace (Bachman, 1994b:1; Shockman, 1995:B1). Actually, Edwin H. Sutherland coined the phrase in his work "White-Collar Criminality" in 1940. Professionals generally are dissatisfied with the term "white-collar" crime because it means many things in many contexts. Reiss and Tonry (1993) call it a "plastic phrase" with many meanings, and thus it is considered undesirable usage when referring to a variety of similar phenomena. They suggest that one reason for the confusion in terminology is that acts of individuals in organizations often are treated as organizational acts. Thus, the focus of law enforcement agencies is upon organizations involved in crime rather than on specific individuals in those organizations.

In recent decades, stock market insider trading and savings and loan company scandals have also received considerable media attention, with personalities such as Charles Keating headlining the news. As head of California's Lincoln Savings and Loan, Keating sold investors over $250 million in worthless junk bonds (Greenwald, 1990:34).

Not all white-collar scams are big-city based. In 1995, in Minot, North Dakota, with a population of thirty-five thousand, sixteen cases of embezzlement resulted in a revenue loss of over $520,000 to local businesses (Shockman, 1995). Each of the thefts involved an employee who stole either money or property.

Attempts to prevent white-collar crime have been hit-and-miss, according to some experts. Criminal penalties, such as the threat of imprisonment, are believed to be a deterrent by some, but other experts say that white-collar offenders believe, often rightly so, that even if they are apprehended, their punishment will be minimal (Weisburd, Waring, and Chayet, 1995).

Highlight 1.5. Telemarketing Scams:
The Case of the Telemarketing Arrest Blitz

Mail or wire fraud is punishable by up to five years in prison. If ten or more elderly persons are victimized, sentences can be increased by up to ten years.

Telemarketing is big business. Telemarketing involves calling persons by telephone and selling them something. Presumably, what is offered for sale is legitimate and as represented. Presumably, it is a good value and worthwhile to potential consumers. But it doesn't always work this way. In Las Vegas, for example, a telemarketing enterprise called thousands of potential consumers with offers of valuable prizes, vacations, and lucrative investment schemes. The only problem was that none of these benefits were legitimate or as advertised.

A woman from Ohio lost $240,000 to telemarketers in Las Vegas. She was promised that her money would go to a worthwhile charity. In another case, a ninety-two-year-old California woman lost $180,000 on a similar charity pitch. She lost an additional $5,000 when a man from the same telemarketing firm called and told her he could get her money back if she paid him that sum.

The Department of Justice estimates that over $40 billion is lost by the elderly and other unwary victims of telemarketing schemes. While many telemarketing firms are reputable, many others take advantage of persons who are gullible enough not to see through the promotions and schemes. Promotional items of great value are offered to consumers, but they turn out to be cheap imitations of the real thing. Attorney General Janet Reno says that many persons are victimized by phony charities and investment schemes. An FBI raid in Las Vegas in December 1995 netted 422 persons. One way the FBI lured criminal telemarketers was to use elderly volunteers, members of the American Association of Retired Persons, who posed as unwary consumers.

What should the penalties be for illegal telemarketing schemers? Are present punishments sufficient? What types of regulations should be implemented to protect citizens from future exploitation?

Source: Adapted from Kevin Johnson and Gary Fields, "FBI Nabs 422 in Telemarketing Scams," *USA Today,* December 8, 1995, p. A1.

Hate Crimes

Hate crimes have always been prevalent in the United States. *A hate crime is any offense committed against another person because of that person's nationality, race, religion, or sexual orientation* (Rush, 1994:159). President George Bush signed the Hate Crimes Statistics Act in April 1990. Subsequently, hate crime laws have been enacted in most states. These laws permit judges to impose harsher and longer sentences on those convicted of hate crimes.

Traditional hate crime perpetrators might be members of the Ku Klux Klan (KKK), centered largely in the South, although the KKK has members in virtually every state (Alexander, 1995; Bensinger, 1992). Most often, activities of KKK members have been directed toward harassing or intimidating blacks and Jews (Martin, 1995). In recent years, persons known as neo-Nazis or skinheads have emerged to perpetuate hatred toward blacks, Jews, gays, and others (Bensinger, 1992). In many instances, various hate groups have joined forces to fight "common enemies."

Hate crimes have been directed increasingly at gays and lesbians (Jenness, 1995). Specific instances of harassment toward these persons have led to the establishment of crisis intervention programs, victim assistance programs, education programs, and street patrols. Increasingly, women seem to be the victims of gender-based hate crimes (Hood and Rollins, 1995). Hate crime is not unique to the United States. It also exists in countries·such as England and in areas such as Southeast Asia (Virdee, 1995). Hate crime laws have done much to subdue various hate groups and organizations, although hate crimes continue to flourish (Czajkoski, 1992).

Drug Trafficking and Money Laundering

Often closely linked with organized crime are **drug trafficking** and **money laundering** (Potter, 1994). *Drug trafficking is any scheme established to fa-*

Highlight 1.6. Hate Crimes in Denver: The Case of William and Dorothy Quigley

William and Dorothy Quigley are next-door neighbors to Mitchell and Candice Aronson, a Jewish couple. The Aronsons began receiving threatening telephone calls, seemingly from the Quigleys. Allegations were that the caller(s) wanted the Aronsons "out of the neighborhood," an upscale area of Evergreen, Colorado, a suburb of Denver. According to the Aronsons, they recorded over 250 telephone calls with a scanning device designed to intercept cordless telephone conversations. The conversations included specific threats of burning down the Aronsons' home, burning crosses in their yard, and other violent acts. Additionally, on one occasion, William Quigley drove his BMW *near* Mrs. Aronson's Jeep as she drove down a street. No accident or injuries resulted. Subsequently, the Aronsons made transcripts of the telephone conversations and turned them over to the Anti-Defamation League office in Denver.

Spurred to action by a recently enacted hate crimes law, Denver prosecutor Dave Thomas filed thirteen hate crime charges against the Quigleys. The Jefferson County Sheriff's Department arrested the Quigleys on the basis of the charges filed. Considerable activity occurred between the DA's office, the Aronsons, and heads of the Anti-Defamation League as they moved to prosecute the Quigleys.

But wait a minute! Who said the Quigleys had violated the law or actually said the things alleged? An attorney for the Quigleys moved to inspect the supposedly incriminating evidence. There wasn't any!

When the dust finally settled, the Denver DA's office issued a public apology to the Quigleys, dropped all charges against them, and awarded them $75,000 for their trouble! Local news agencies re-

ported that most, if not all, of the Aronsons' allegations were self-inflicted. The Anti-Defamation League became involved on the basis of the word of the Aronsons. The DA's office became involved on the word of the Aronsons. No one bothered to check the factual details contained in the allegations. The prosecutor's office admitted that they had not listened to the tapes recorded by the Aronsons— they had only read transcriptions of the tapes. When the tapes were actually heard, the case was dropped for lack of evidence.

Colorado's ethnic-intimidation statute specifies that persons commit ethnic intimidation if, because of another person's race, color, religion, ancestry, or national origin, they knowingly cause bodily injury to another person, or by words or conduct, knowingly place other persons in fear, or if they knowingly cause damage to or destruction of the property of another. In the case of the Quigleys, even the "near-miss" car incident was referred to by police as a nonincident.

What criteria should district attorneys use before deciding to prosecute a case? How much evidence should be needed to go forward with a prosecution? In this case, was the Anti-Defamation League at fault for believing the Aronsons without further investigation? What other recourse for justice is available to the Quigleys? Can anything undo the damage caused to their reputation by the notoriety of the case?

Source: Adapted from Al Knight, "Hate Crimes Law Is Bad—Its Application Was Worse," *Denver Post*, December 10, 1995, p. 5D.

Organized crime, drug trafficking, and money laundering are intimately connected and international in scope. Here, Colombia's chief police officer inspects some of the $5.5 million seized at a drug cartel's house in Cali, Colombia, in 1997.

cilitate the sale and distribution of illegal substances, such as heroin, cocaine or crack, marijuana, and prescription drugs. Money laundering is the act of converting money or securities from illegal enterprises so that it appears as revenue from legitimate enterprises. In some instances, money laundering is referred to as shadow banking (New Jersey Commission of Investigation, 1994). Drug trafficking and money laundering are worldwide enterprises (Beare, 1995; Reuvid, 1995; U.S. General Accounting Office, 1995).

Drug Trafficking

In 1994 in the United States, approximately 18,573,000 persons reported using marijuana; 4,530,000 persons used cocaine, including crack (Timrots and Byrne, 1995:1–2). These do not re-

flect the *unreported* or *undetected* cases. Thus, illicit drug use in the United States is a major problem (Eck, 1995).

Organized crime figures prominently in drug trafficking, and it is widely known that U.S. gangs in virtually every city are conduits through which illegal drugs are distributed (Johnson, Webster, and Connors, 1995; Spergel, 1995). One way of attacking illicit drug trafficking is by meting out tougher sentences to drug traffickers. The U.S. Sentencing Commission has implemented more severe penalties for drug offenses in recent years, including a *mandatory* five-year penalty for simple possession of crack cocaine and a statutory *minimum penalty* of one year for simple possession of any other kind of drug (U.S. Sentencing Commission, 1995).

Drive-by shootings between rival gangs, often drug-related, contribute to rising numbers of deaths of innocent bystanders (Johnson, Webster, and Connors, 1995). In some jurisdictions, actions at the community level have been instrumental in reducing or eliminating drug trafficking and in reducing neighborhood violence. In 1988, for instance, the Chicago Housing Authority implemented the Public Housing Drug Elimination Program. This program was designed to "sweep out" drug dealers and others from buildings; remove weapons and unauthorized tenants; improve residential services; and implement large-scale drug intervention/ prevention programs (Popkin, Olson, and Lurigio, 1995). Evidence in a six-year follow-up suggests that the program has been modestly successful at reducing street crime in affected neighborhoods by decreasing drug trafficking.

On an international scale, there has been greater global cooperation in decreasing the flow of narcotics (Burns and Pomainville, 1995; Thoumi, 1995). *Interpol* and other international crime-fighting organizations have also joined together in an effort to combat drug trafficking. Greater emphasis upon local enforcement practices and street-level self-regulation are viewed as key elements in this form of crime prevention as well (Eck, 1995; Green, 1995).

Money Laundering

It is estimated that over $500 billion per year in illegal organized crime profits is laundered through various outlets (Raine and Cilluffo, 1994). One of the largest money-laundering schemes uncovered by the Drug Enforcement Administration involved several jewelry districts in New York City and Los Angeles and the Colombian drug cartel (Woolner, 1994). Drug trafficking generates so much hard cash that it is physically impossible to disguise it as legitimate business revenue. Sometimes substantial sums of money are plowed into failing businesses where large losses are anticipated. The losses are only on paper, however, because the drug money shows up as revenue from wholesale or retail sales, which are subsequently written off as losses. Entire store inventories are sold off at a fraction of their original cost, although there is no real loss incurred by the illegal investors.

Because banks and other types of financial institutions are money launderers, international efforts have been made to improve substantially record-keeping and auditing practices of various types of financial institutions (Reuvid, 1995). International cooperation is evidenced by information exchange systems implemented by Japan and Great Britain (Katoh, 1994; Robinson, 1994).

Technology and the Criminal Justice System

Widespread technological developments in electronics and computer innovations have contributed to significant improvements in our ability to monitor crime and criminal activity. Initiated by the FBI in 1967, the National Crime Information Center (NCIC) is a central source of information about stolen vehicles, car accidents, stolen property of every description, arrested persons, fingerprint identification, criminal offenses, and criminal offenders and their whereabouts.

For example, if a driver is stopped for a minor traffic violation, information may be quickly relayed to the NCIC and back to the officer as to whether the driver is wanted for a criminal offense in another jurisdiction or whether the automobile is stolen. All information exchange between police departments occurs in seconds. The computerization of record keeping applies to all jurisdictions in

the United States, regardless of their remoteness or size (U.S. Department of Justice, 1995).

The United States Bureau of Prisons, under the direction of the attorney general of the United States, supervises the management and regulation of all federal penal and correctional institutions. Information about the locations of prisoners, projected parole dates, and other relevant subjects is available at the touch of a button.

Thus, the criminal justice system is becoming increasingly streamlined (U.S. Department of Justice, 1995:1–4). Although the gradual switch to computerized record-keeping has been helpful in some respects, it has created some new problems. For instance, the proliferation of rules and regulations for processing alleged offenders has created courtroom backlogs. Judges are increasingly overworked, and legal paperwork is ever-expanding.

Summary

The criminal justice system of the United States is rooted in the common law of Great Britain. Common law has evolved through judicial decrees and decisions, whereas statutory laws are established through legislative action. The laws are always being changed to reflect the customs and preferences of society. Law regulates social conduct in a particular jurisdiction at a given point in time. It facilitates dispute resolution and assures that individual freedoms will be preserved.

Crime is a violation of criminal laws by persons held accountable by those laws. It is also a form of deviant behavior. Crimes are greater or lesser offenses known as felonies and misdemeanors. Measures of crime include the *Uniform Crime Reports (UCR)* and the *National Crime Victimization Survey (NCVS)*. These measures are only approximations of the actual amount of crime that exists in the United States. Most authorities consider them underestimates of the actual amount of crime committed.

Victims of crimes include persons of all ages. Most crime victims are young, single people, although crimes against the elderly are increasing. The elderly criminal is increasingly problematic, as judges, police officers, and others must decide their appropriate punishments. Victims of crime also include children, who are frequently abused, physically or mentally, by their parents or legal guardians. Missing children and child abuse account for an annual expenditure by the federal government of $40 million. Streamlining the efforts of the criminal justice system to monitor and control crime has resulted in increasing bureaucracy.

Key Terms

Actus reus
Child abuse
Common law
Crimes
Crimes against the person
Crimes against property
Criminology
Deviance
Drug trafficking
Felonies
Hate crimes
Index offenses
Jurisdiction
Mala in se
Mala prohibita
Mens rea
Misdemeanors
Money laundering
National Crime Victimization Survey (NCVS)
Organized crime
Procedural laws
Property crimes
Statutory law
Substantive laws
Tort
Uniform Crime Reports (UCR)
Victimless crimes
Violent crimes
White-collar crime

Questions for Review

1. What is meant by "common law"? Who makes the laws and decides how they should be applied?

2. Differentiate between *mala in se* and *mala prohibita*.

3. What are three functions of law? What are the significance of time and jurisdiction in defining the law for a given community or state?

4. Are crime and deviance the same thing? Give an example of deviant behavior that is not criminal.

5. What are some potential sources of error in crime measurement in the *UCR* and *NCVS*?

6. Which measure of crime do you prefer: the *Uniform Crime Reports* or the *National Crime Victimization Survey*? Why?

7. Differentiate between crimes against persons, or "violent crimes," and crimes against property, or "property crimes." If a person commits robbery and larceny, which type of crime has the person committed?

8. What are some of the characteristics of crime victims in the United States? Is a victimization the same as an incident?

9. Does the fact that "crimes are cleared by arrest" mean that we are cutting down the actual amount of crime in the United States? Explain. When a crime is "cleared by arrest," does that necessarily mean the crime has been solved? Explain.

10. What kinds of crimes are committed by elderly criminals? Is there any reason to believe that crimes committed against the elderly are more serious than crimes committed against younger victims?

Suggested Readings

Briggs, Freda (ed.). *From Victim to Offender: How Child Sexual Abuse Victims Become Offenders.* St. Leonards, Australia: Allen and Unwin, 1995.

Close, Daryl and Nicholas Meier. *Morality in Criminal Justice: An Introduction to Ethics.* Belmont, CA: Wadsworth, 1995.

Cordess, Christopher and Murray Cox (eds.). *Forensic Psychotherapy: Crime, Psychodynamics, and the Offender Patient.* Bristol, PA: Taylor and Francis, 1995.

Green, Gary S. *Occupational Crime*. 2d ed. Chicago: Nelson-Hall, 1996.

Harr, J. Scott and Karen M. Hess. *Criminal Justice System: Seeking Employment in Criminal Justice and Related Fields*. 2d ed. St. Paul, MN: West, 1996.

Jenness, Valerie. *Making It Work: The Prostitutes' Rights Movement in Perspective*. Hawthorne, NY: Aldine de Gruyter, 1993.

Kappeler, Victor E., Mark Blumberg, and Gary W. Potter. *The Mythology of Crime and Criminal Justice*. Prospect Heights, IL: Waveland, 1996.

Kenney, Dennis Jay and James O. Finckenauer. *Organized Crime in America*. Belmont, CA: Wadsworth, 1995.

Klofas, John and Stan Stojkovic. *Crime and Justice in the Year 2010*. Belmont, CA: Wadsworth, 1995.

Linsky, Arnold S., Ronet Bachman, and Murray A. Straus. *Stress, Culture and Aggression*. New Haven, CT: Yale University Press, 1995.

Messner, Steven and Richard Rosenfeld. *Crime and the American Dream*. Belmont, CA: Wadsworth, 1994.

Pollock, Jocelyn M. *Ethics in Crime and Justice: Dilemmas and Decisions*. 2d ed. Belmont, CA: Wadsworth, 1994.

Tower, Cynthia Crosson. *Understanding Child Abuse and Neglect*. 3d ed. Needham Heights, MA: Allyn and Bacon, 1996.

Walker, Samuel. *Sense and Nonsense about Crime and Drugs: A Policy Guide*. 3d ed. Belmont, CA: Wadsworth, 1994.

Wallace, Harvey. *Family Violence: Legal, Medical and Social Perspectives*. Needham Heights, MA: Allyn and Bacon, 1996.

Weed, Frank J. *Certainty of Justice: Reform in the Crime Victim Movement*. Hawthorne, NY: Aldine de Gruyter, 1995.

Winfree, Jr., L. Thomas and Howard Abadinsky. *Crime Theory: An Introduction*. Chicago: Nelson-Hall, 1996.

Wright, James D. and Peter H. Rossi. *Armed and Considered Dangerous: A Survey of Felons and Their Firearms*. Hawthorne, NY: Aldine de Gruyter, 1994.

CHAPTER 2

An Overview of the American Criminal Justice System

In 1994, there were 43.6 million victimizations in the United States (Bastian, 1995). There were over 14 million arrests during the same period (Maguire and Pastore, 1995:374). The task of investigating these crimes, dealing with and processing alleged offenders, and ultimately housing and/or rehabilitating criminals is performed by the **criminal justice system**. *The criminal justice system is an interrelated set of agencies and organizations whose aims are to control criminal behavior, to detect crime, and to apprehend, process, prosecute, punish, and/or rehabilitate criminal offenders.*

Consider the following comments of E. Z. Thief, arrested for vehicular theft in New Jersey in November 1995:

> I stole a '93 Ford from a supermarket parking lot in late September of 1995. In early October, I got pulled over by the cops, who said I was speeding. I didn't have a driver's license, and when they checked the registration of the car, they found it was reported stolen. They arrested me and took me to jail. They booked me and charged me with vehicular theft. They set my bail at $5,000. I called my brother and he came down and bailed me out. They set my preliminary hearing for December 5th. They let me have a public defender because I couldn't afford a regular attorney.
>
> I met with my public defender before the preliminary hearing and he asked if I wanted to cop a plea. I didn't want to do that, and so they had my hearing and set my trial date for January 20, 1996. We went to trial, and they had a jury there. The trial went on for about two days, and there were all kinds of people who testified. Anyway, the jury found me guilty of vehicular theft, and the judge sentenced me to four years in prison. When I went to prison, I was there for about a year. But they let me out early because of my good behavior, and they put me on parole. I had to report to a parole officer every month for the rest of the four-year sentence. Now it's all over.

While this story is hypothetical and omits significant stages of criminal processing, E. Z. Thief's narrative does indicate contact with most agencies or components of the criminal justice system. A crime was committed when the automobile was stolen. A report was filed, and the crime was investigated by police. Subsequently, a suspect, E. Z.

Thief, was arrested. At this point Mr. Thief entered the criminal justice system. Mr. Thief was booked at the police station, where he was fingerprinted and photographed. Other personal information about him was collected by police. An initial appearance before a magistrate led to bail being set at $5,000. His brother bailed him out, pending a subsequent trial. After determining that sufficient evidence and probable cause existed to proceed with a prosecution of Mr. Thief in a preliminary hearing, a trial date was established and a trial was held. The issue of Mr. Thief's guilt or innocence was ultimately decided by an impartial jury, who considered evidence and arguments from both prosecutors and defense attorneys. The sentence was pronounced by the judge, and E. Z. Thief was incarcerated for a period of time in a prison facility. Finally, Mr. Thief was paroled and assigned to a parole officer. Upon completion of the term of parole, Mr. Thief exited the criminal justice system.

This chapter is about the different components of the adult criminal justice system in the United States. It is not intended to be an in-depth description of all agencies and organizations associated with the system. Later chapters will provide detailed coverage of the functions and operations of all aspects of the criminal justice system.

The Organization of the Criminal Justice System

The basic components of the criminal justice system include (1) the legislatures; (2) law enforcement agencies; (3) the prosecution and defense; (4) the courts; and (5) corrections.

Legislatures

There is a sound basis for including legislatures in the criminal justice process. **Legislatures** *create, enact, or pass the criminal laws for the states and the federal government.* Accordingly, legislatures modify existing laws or repeal them. Law enforcement agencies enforce these laws, while the prosecution, courts, and corrections subject al-

leged offenders or violators of these criminal laws to further processing.

Criminal laws come from several different sources. State and federal constitutional provisions give legislatures the authority to enact any civil or criminal law. The United States Code (U.S.C.) contains all civil and criminal laws of the United States. The U.S.C. contains over two hundred twenty volumes setting forth all U.S. statutes governing almost every aspect of citizens' lives (United States Code, 1996). Title 18 of the U.S.C. contains all federal crimes and criminal procedures. It consists of seventeen volumes.

The states have similar codes containing state statutes enacted by legislatures. These are identified as statutory compilations. They include the Oregon Revised Statutes, the Oklahoma Statutes Annotated, the Code of Alabama, the Annotated California Code, the Hawaii Revised Statutes, the Idaho Code, and the Laws of Nebraska.

These laws are continually changing. When a state legislature convenes, legislators often enact new laws or modify or eliminate old ones. In 1996, it was a violation of one of Oregon's criminal statutes to possess marijuana for resale and/or personal consumption. The Oregon legislature has considered legalizing marijuana possession in recent years. Should the legislature decide to decriminalize marijuana possession, the old Oregon statute prohibiting this substance would be eliminated. Such action is sometimes termed **decriminalization**. *Decriminalization is legislative action by which an act or omission formerly criminal is made noncriminal and without punitive sanctions* (MacCoun, Kahan, and Gillespie, 1993).

As an example, while prostitution is illegal in almost every jurisdiction, it has been decriminalized in certain Nevada counties, where considerable revenues accrue from this activity. Nevada authorities contend that state-regulated prostitution decreases the spread of infectious diseases such as AIDS. Since prostitution exists everywhere in the United States anyway, some Nevada officials believe that state control of this activity is a safe alternative to prohibiting it outright.

Sometimes acts that were formerly non-criminal are defined as criminal through legislative action. Marijuana possession and distribution were lawful until legislation prohibited them in the 1930s (Inciardi, 1991; MacCoun, Kahan, and Gillespie, 1993). Thus, while new drugs and/or modifications of existing ones (e.g., various herbal substances) may not at the present time be officially classified as harmful and/or illegal by the Food and Drug Administration, legislative action may eventually address such substances and either sanction or prohibit them. Currently, proposed drug legislation is more acceptable if it is oriented toward regulating controlled substances rather than decriminalizing them outright (Krause and Lazear, 1991). However, there is every indication that law enforcement agencies will continue to disapprove of the use of such drugs as marijuana even if they are legalized (Evanson, 1991).

Supreme Court decisions also influence state legislative actions. Until 1985, for example, it was permissible for police officers to use deadly force to apprehend those committing serious crimes. Thus, if a burglar ran from police officers to avoid apprehension, officers were authorized by state statutes to use deadly force to catch the burglar. This was known as the fleeing felon rule (Fyfe, 1988). But in 1985, the Supreme Court declared the fleeing felon rule unconstitutional (*Tennessee v. Garner*, 1985). Since then, deadly force may be used only in defense of a police officer's life or the life of a bystander. The fleeing felon rule remains in many state codes simply because the state legislatures have not repealed it. Laws that are no longer valid continue to exist in the codes of many states. Again, this is largely the result of legislative inattention or the triviality of the law.

Even before the *Garner* decision, however, various jurisdictions such as Pennsylvania applied the "defense-of-life" standard in all situations that involved the use of deadly force (Waegel, 1984a). Once the Supreme Court decided the *Garner* case, however, the use of deadly force was governed for *all* jurisdictions by clear criteria (Fyfe, 1988).

Once laws are in place, certain mechanisms ensure that they will be upheld or enforced. At the threshold of the criminal justice system are several law enforcement agencies whose jobs are to detect crime and apprehend offenders.

Law Enforcement Agencies

The combination of all law enforcement agencies in the United States makes this the largest component of the criminal justice system. The most visible law enforcement officers are the uniformed police who enforce the laws of cities and townships. Less conspicuous law enforcement officers include the FBI, IRS agents, city and county detectives, agents of the Bureau of Alcohol, Tobacco, and Firearms, and agents of the Drug Enforcement Administration.

All law enforcement officers have powers of arrest. Police officers, for example, have the authority to make arrests whenever law violations occur within their jurisdictions. Offenses justifying arrests may range from traffic violations such as driving recklessly to suspicion of first-degree murder, forcible rape, or kidnapping.

Primarily an investigative body, the FBI has arrest powers covering violations of over two hun-

Local uniformed police are the most visible law enforcement officers. This highly visible team is part of a unit employed in the Miami, Florida, area as a crime-prevention measure.

dred federal laws and statutes. FBI agents observe all appropriate jurisdictional boundaries associated with their position. Thus, these agents do not issue traffic citations or monitor speeders on interstate highways. Similarly, state troopers do not ordinarily investigate and arrest counterfeiters or conspirators in interstate gambling. A more thorough examination of law enforcement agencies and their functions will be presented in chapters 4 and 5.

Arrest involves taking suspected law violators into custody. These suspects are ordinarily taken to a jail, where they are "booked." **Booking** *is the process of making a written report of the arrest, including the name and address of the suspect, a description of the crime(s) alleged, the name of arresting officer(s), the time and place of the arrest, a physical description of the suspect, and photographs (so-called "mug shots") and fingerprints.* At the time of the booking, arresting officers often run a computer check of suspects to determine if they have any "priors," or prior arrests or convictions.

Depending upon the seriousness of the offense and the circumstances of the arrest, a bail bond is usually established. This is a monetary amount that must be paid for a pretrial release. The bail bond functions as a "surety" to guarantee the defendant's subsequent appearance in court. If suspects want to remain free until their trials, they must post a bail bond as a surety against flight. Bonding companies post bail bonds. A suspect's community standing, prior record, and other relevant factors are considered in bond setting and posting. Most defendants are released on their own recognizance, without having to post bail. Usually these defendants have jobs and ties with the community and for these reasons are considered unlikely to flee from the jurisdiction before trial occurs.

If the charges are extremely serious, such as murder, robbery, or some other aggravated offense, bail may be quite high. In some cases, authorities may hold the suspect without bail if it is likely that their pretrial release will result in further harm to others or that they may flee the jurisdiction to avoid prosecution. This is known as preventive detention. After suspects have been arrested and booked, they may contact an attorney and reply to the charges.

The Prosecution and Defense

Suspects' having been arrested and booked does not automatically mean that they will remain in custody or that they will eventually be prosecuted for the alleged offenses. Sometimes there is insufficient evidence to pursue the case. In the case of minor offenses, a monetary punishment such as a bail bond or a cash bail may be imposed. Most traffic violations require paying a fine.

Prosecutors

Most persons suspected of serious crimes come to the attention of prosecutors. City and county attorneys (frequently called district attorneys, or DAs) and their assistants determine which cases should be prosecuted. Not all arrests for serious crimes result in prosecutions. Furthermore, not all prosecutions result in convictions.

Figure 2.1 compares the process of arrest and subsequent punishment to a "leaky funnel." Of five hundred serious crimes in an average community, four hundred will remain unsolved. Felony arrests will be made in the remaining one hundred cases. Of the suspects in these cases, thirty-five will be juveniles and sixty-five will be adults who will be brought to the prosecutor's attention. The prosecutor will actively pursue cases against forty of these suspects. Of these, eight will be tried and convicted, two will be acquitted, and the remaining thirty will plead guilty and will be convicted. Only twenty of these thirty-eight convicted offenders will be incarcerated. In short, a ratio of 1 in 25 will be incarcerated from an initial sample of five hundred felonies reported.

A **prosecution** *is the carrying forth of criminal proceedings against a person, culminating in a trial or other final disposition such as a plea of guilty in lieu of trial.* Many factors influence a prosecutor's decision to prosecute suspects. Factors such as the sufficiency of evidence against the accused, the seriousness of the crime, the availability of witnesses, and the general circumstances associated with the arrest are taken into consideration.

Some experts believe that some gender disparity exists in prosecutions throughout the United States, where prosecutors exercise differential dis-

Figure 2.1 Funneling Effect of 500 Serious Crimes from Arrest to Imprisonment

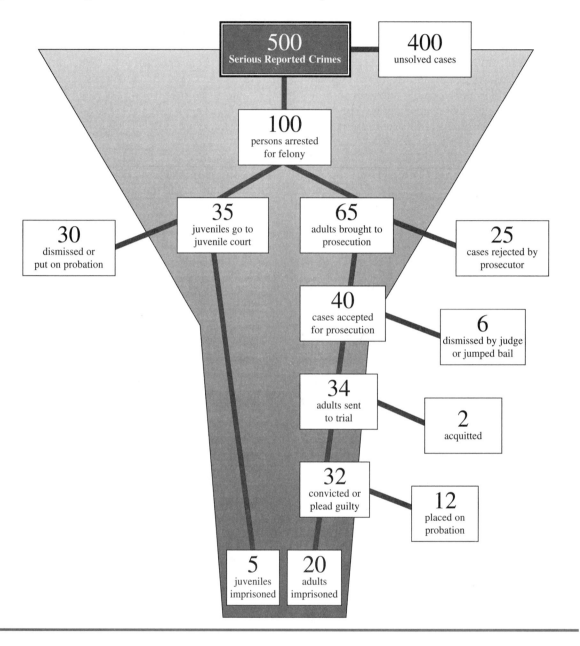

Highlight 2.1. Crimes Without Victims?
Three Cases of Conspiracy

Bourjaily v. United States, 483 U.S. 171, 107 S.Ct. 2775 (1987). William Bourjaily was convicted in U.S. District Court of possessing and conspiring to distribute cocaine. Earlier, several tape-recorded conversations had been made between Bourjaily and undercover FBI agents. Various friends of Bourjaily had been implicated initially, and Bourjaily became a suspect through evidence obtained in the recorded telephone conversations. An FBI informant, Lonardo, also implicated Bourjaily. During his subsequent trial, Bourjaily protested that the government had permitted Lonardo's statements as proof of a conspiracy to distribute cocaine. Further, Bourjaily argued that as evidence, Lonardo's statements supported the conspiracy only according to a "preponderance of the evidence" standard. Finally, Lonardo himself did not testify; his statements against Bourjaily were read into the record. Bourjaily appealed his conviction, alleging that his Sixth Amendment rights were violated because he was unable to cross-examine Lonardo. He also alleged that Lonardo's statements amounted to hearsay and were thus excludable as evidence against him. The U.S. Supreme Court decided otherwise and upheld his conviction. *The U.S. Supreme Court declared that evidence of a co-conspirator is not hearsay if such evidence is obtained during the course and in the furtherance of a conspiracy. Thus, Lonardo's out-of-court statements were ruled admissible against Bourjaily. Further, out-of-court statements may only be proven by the offering party (the prosecution) on the basis of the preponderance of the evidence.*

Rutledge v. United States, ___U.S.___, 116 S.Ct. 1241 (1996). Tommy L. Rutledge was convicted in federal court of charges relating to conspiracy to distribute controlled substances and of one count of conducting a continuing criminal enterprise in concert with others. Both convictions stemmed from the conspiracy to distribute cocaine. The court sentenced Rutledge to two concurrent terms of life without parole and imposed special assessments of fifty dollars for each count. Rutledge appealed on the grounds of double jeopardy. The Supreme Court held that *because Congress intended to authorize only one punishment, one of [Rutledge's] convictions as well as its concurrent sentence was unauthorized punishment for a separate offense and must be vacated.* Thus, because Rutledge was convicted based upon the same underlying conduct of both the offense of conducting a continuing criminal enterprise and of conspiracy to distribute controlled substances, which was a *lesser included offense* of the "continuing criminal enterprise" offense, one of his convictions and concurrent sentences had to be vacated. Courts cannot impose multiple punishments for the same criminal activity, as this would violate one's right against double jeopardy.

United States v. Karo, 468 U.S. 705, 104 S.Ct. 3296 (1984). Karo was suspected as a co-conspirator in an enterprise to distribute cocaine. DEA agents obtained a court order to install a beeper in a clothing container used by Karo and others to smuggle cocaine. By tracking the can through monitoring the beeper, agents discovered various homes and businesses that appeared to be involved in the cocaine distribution conspiracy. The monitoring was done without a specific search warrant. DEA agents eventually obtained a search warrant based upon probable cause and entered several of the homes and businesses. Karo and others were eventually convicted of conspiracy and appealed. The Supreme Court overturned Karo's conviction on other grounds but declared that in order for beepers to be installed and monitored, especially in private dwellings, a valid search warrant based upon probable cause must be obtained first.

In each of these three cases there were no immediate victims. Persons were alleged to have conspired to distribute cocaine or controlled substances. No persons were directly injured or killed as a result of the alleged conspiratorial actions. Yet prosecutors moved forward with conspiracy charges based upon their own discretionary authority.

The Supreme Court justices are (top row, left to right) Ruth Bader Ginsburg, David H. Souter, Clarence Thomas, and Anthony M. Kennedy; (bottom row, left to right) Antonin Scalia, John Paul Stevens, Chief Justice William H. Renquist, Sandra Day O'Connor, and Stephen Breyer.

cretion and prosecute either fewer females than males or reduce charges against more female defendants than male defendants (Farnworth and Teske, 1995). Other methods leading to a prosecution may be invoked that are independent of prosecutorial discretion. These will be described in chapters 7 and 8.

The prosecution represents the state in any criminal proceeding. It is not always necessary that a specific victim be available to press charges against the accused. As a representative of the state, the prosecution may move against any suspect, regardless of the victim's unwillingness to press charges or even if there is no apparent victim. The prosecuting attorney screens cases and determines which ones have the highest probability for conviction. The prosecutor also prioritizes cases according to the severity of the crimes. The defense attorney opposes the prosecuting attorney at every stage. If defendants are brought to trial, defense attorneys will act to protect their clients' interests, while prosecuting attorneys will protect the government's interests.

Defense Attorneys

Defense attorneys *are licensed lawyers retained by defendants or appointed by the court to defend suspects unable to afford an attorney.* The defense attorney has access to much of the evidence against the accused and can usually determine the prosecution's probable course of action. If the evidence against the accused is weak or exclusively circumstantial, defense attorneys may attempt to persuade prosecutors to drop formal proceedings against their clients. On the other hand, if the evidence against the accused is strong and likely to result in a guilty verdict, *defense attorneys try to negotiate with prosecutors for a reduction in charges and/or punishment in exchange for a guilty plea. This is known as* **plea bargaining** (McConville and Mirsky, 1995). Plea bargaining accounts for 90 percent of all criminal convictions in cases that have not been formally tried, although it is prohibited in a few states, such as Alaska (Marenin, 1995). Plea bargaining is allowed in many countries besides the United States, includ-

By the policy of stare decisis, *the superior court at Olympia, Washington, and all other courts of descending order in the United States, must stand by the precedents of the Supreme Court, the highest court in the land.*

ing Germany (Ludemann, 1994) and England (Mulcahy, 1994).

The Courts

Judges, especially those in courts of appeals, including the Supreme Court, contribute to law making in certain ways. Both state and federal courts are based on a hierarchy. The highest court in the land is the U.S. Supreme Court. In each state, a similar court decides various issues.

Normally, a lower court in the judicial hierarchy must rely on rulings from higher courts under the doctrine of **stare decisis**. *Stare decisis is the policy of courts to stand by a particular precedent and not to disturb a settled point of law* (Black, 1990:1406). For instance, there are thirteen judicial circuits at the federal level. These are the "courts of appeals" for decisions rendered in federal district courts. Judges in cases brought before the Ninth Circuit, which includes Alaska, Arizona,

California, Idaho, Montana, Nevada, Oregon, Washington, and Hawaii, are obliged to follow any ruling of the Supreme Court that pertains directly to issues involved in the present case.

As a general rule, lower court judges have the prerogative of interpreting a decision by a higher court as it applies to a case pending before their courts. Is the case "on point"? Does it contain most of the same characteristics of the case decided by the higher court? If, in the opinion of the lower court judge, the case does not conform to the one decided earlier by the higher court, the judge is not bound to abide by it. Later, however, that particular interpretation may be appealed by the defendant.

If the issue is unique and has not been addressed by the Supreme Court, a Ninth Circuit ruling will be made. This ruling will either affirm or overturn a decision from one of several lower federal district courts. As a result, *all* district courts within the Ninth Circuit will be obligated under the policy of *stare decisis* to adhere to and be consistent with the decision of the Ninth Circuit whenever a case is heard involving the same issue of law. No district court in the Ninth Circuit is obliged to follow precedents established by other circuits, however, but it may be influenced by the decisions made by another court at the same level. Thus, the Ninth Circuit may choose to rely upon another circuit court's decision in a particular case as a way of justifying its own decisions.

Only the U.S. Supreme Court can overturn decisions made by lower circuit courts. The Supreme Court can also act to create uniformity among circuits on certain issues. If one circuit court decision is to permit a certain type of evidence to be introduced in a criminal trial and another circuit decision is to prohibit that same type of evidence, the Supreme Court will act to create uniformity as it pertains to the admissibility of evidence (Pohlman, 1995).

It is apparent that the judiciary functions differently from the legislature at both the federal and state levels. Judges do not propose legislation. But their rulings and interpretations often have the same impact on existing criminal laws. As a part of their law-making authority, for instance, legislators deal principally with substantive criminal laws. *Substantive criminal laws embody all activities defined by statute as criminal as well as punishments accompanying such activities* (Kadish, 1987). The judiciary is often, though not always, concerned with procedural laws. *Procedural laws pertain to the implementation of substantive laws.*

The courtroom is where the defendant's guilt is ultimately determined. It functions as a public forum for the airing of all relevant information in the case. The government presents its evidence against the accused, and the defense presents its side. Witnesses are called to testify both for and against the accused, and defendants have the right to cross-examine their accusers. The courtroom is also where the sufficiency of evidence against the accused is tested.

The state and federal court systems operate in a similar fashion. Violations of federal laws are usually prosecuted in federal district courts. Violations of state and local criminal laws are prosecuted in either courts of general jurisdiction or criminal courts. Each state has a different court organization with a particular nomenclature applying to the courts' different functions. For example, California

has "Superior Courts" while Tennessee has "Circuit Courts" and "Criminal Courts." Minor offenses in each state jurisdiction are tried before magistrates, justices of the peace, sessions judges, or municipal judges. These are considered lower criminal courts and are frequently associated with misdemeanor offenses.

If prosecutors persist in a prosecution against a particular suspect, the suspect becomes a **defendant** in the subsequent criminal proceeding. Again, depending upon the jurisdiction within which a crime has been committed, a defendant will eventually appear in a courtroom to face formal criminal charges.

All defendants are entitled to a jury trial in any criminal proceeding, *if the charges are serious and could result in incarceration for more than six months.* This applies to either misdemeanors or felonies. *A* **jury** *is an objective, impartial body of persons who convene to hear the case against the accused and make a determination of guilt or innocence on the basis of the factual evidence presented.* Jury members are ordinarily selected from the community and are unrelated to the accused. They are sworn to be objective and impartial in their assessment of the facts presented to them by the defense and prosecution (Roberts, 1994).

Defendants may waive their right to a trial by jury and elect instead to permit the judge to decide guilt or innocence on the basis of the facts presented. Sometimes the accused is charged with a crime that is so emotionally charged that there is ample reason to believe that no jury could be objective and return an impartial verdict. In these cases, the judge might evaluate the facts more impartially than the jury.

When defendants are found guilty, an appeals process at both the state and federal levels enables them to appeal the verdict and request a new trial. At the federal level, thirteen circuit courts of appeal exist to evaluate decisions rendered in all of the federal district courts. Beyond these appellate bodies is the U.S. Supreme Court. The U.S. Supreme Court is the highest appellate body. Most states have supreme courts where decisions made by criminal courts of appeal may be challenged (Williams, J., 1995a, 1995b). State and federal court organizations are described in chapter 6.

If defendants in a criminal proceeding are found not guilty and acquitted, they are freed by that court action. While the government may appeal verdicts to higher courts in those cases where judges have decided in favor of the defendant, such appeals are relatively rare. If defendants are convicted of the crime alleged, they are sentenced by the court in a manner prescribed by law. A judge has several options in sentencing criminal defendants. For example, first-offenders may receive light sentences and not be incarcerated. Those who have committed previous offenses may receive harsher sentences. If the judge decides not to incarcerate the defendant, the defendant may be placed on probation for a prescribed period. *Probation is a sentence involving a conditional release from incarceration, usually with a number of behavioral provisions or conditions.* These conditions include not associating with other known criminals, refraining from further criminal acts, obtaining employment, or participating in medical or counseling programs.

Corrections

The last component of the criminal justice system is **corrections**. *Corrections includes all of the agencies and personnel who deal with a convicted offender after a court proceeding.* Even in cases of plea bargaining, one correctional agency or another will become involved in the further processing of the convicted person. Convicted offenders may be assigned to the supervision of probation officers or to community agencies for treatment.

Typically, corrections is associated with **jails** and **prisons**. *Jails are confinement areas associated with local city and county police departments. They usually house persons sentenced to short-term confinement for misdemeanor offenses or persons charged with more serious offenses who are awaiting trial. Prisons are much larger facilities that are owned and operated by the state or federal government. These facilities house criminals sentenced to terms of one or more years.* While these facilities are an important feature of the corrections process, they are not the dominant component.

The number of jail inmates per 100,000 U.S. residents increased from 96 in 1983 to 188 in 1994. In 1993, eight states had over 200 jail inmates per 100,000 residents. Between 1983 and 1993, the number of jail inmates increased by 106 percent; the total jail staff by 156 percent; and correctional officers by 165 percent. By mid-1994, the capacity of the nation's local jails was 504,324. The jail population was at 97 percent of the rated capacity. Jail space increased 93 percent between 1983 and 1994. Factors accounting for the growth of the jail population included increases in adult arrests, felons sentenced to local jails, inmates charged with or convicted of drug offenses, and inmates held in jails because of crowded state or federal prisons (Perkins, Stephan, and Beck, 1995).

Convicted offenders sentenced to either jail or prison may be released early. This early release is known as parole, and parolees are routinely assigned to particular parole officers. In many instances, there is no difference between a parole officer and a probation officer. The same officer may supervise both parolees and probationers. Probation or parole workers make up a large portion of correctional personnel beyond those who staff jails and prisons. They are responsible for monitoring the behaviors and progress of probationers and parolees for a fixed period of time. This is usually the remainder of the original sentence imposed by the judge in court.

Prisons and jails are the most visible corrections facilities. Most are staffed by government employees, although there have been some efforts within the private sector to take over selected prison operations (Hanson and Daley, 1995; Reynolds, 1994). Jails and prisons have their own rules and regulations, which are rigidly enforced. The custodial function of jails and prisons is apparent, although some citizens would prefer to see these facilities accomplish more rehabilitative objectives (Sexton, 1995; Walla, 1995).

Some Goals of the Criminal Justice System

Each of the major components of the criminal justice system performs specific functions. Apart from individual organizational goals and agency objectives, the criminal justice system itself has a set of identifiable goals that shape its policies and practices. While not everyone agrees about what these goals are or to what degree they are being achieved, there are several common concerns. These include (1) crime prevention and deterrence; (2) crime detection and control; (3) criminal punishment and societal retribution; (4) criminal rehabilitation; and (5) the assurance of due process.

Crime Prevention and Deterrence

Criminal laws are derived from several sources. The purposes of criminal laws are to regulate social conduct and protect citizen's rights. Crime infringes these rights to varying degrees. Establishing criminal laws with accompanying prescribed punishments deters most people from committing crimes (Veneziano and Veneziano, 1995). Obviously, not everyone is equally deterred from committing crimes through the threat of punishment. Some information shows that increasing the severity of punishment does not affect crime rates (Clarke and Weisburd, 1994; Homel, 1994; Niskanen, 1994).

Crime prevention is improved through the efforts of criminal justice agencies. Counselors and therapists work with first offenders who are either on probation or on parole to help them develop constructive strategies to cope with their problems rather than resort to crime.

Crime prevention strategies also include making homes more secure against burglars (Tunnell, 1992). This is known as "target hardening." Several new home and building designs have been developed for this purpose (Bannister, 1991). Police officers have helped communities develop their own crime prevention programs and community patrols (Titus, 1984). Preventive strategies include "Operational Identification," in which citizens imprint their personal possessions with an electronic identification label such as a social security number. This strategy minimizes the chances that thieves will be able to resell stolen property easily (Cromwell, Olson, and Avary, 1991; Meredith and Paquette, 1992).

Crime Detection and Control

Another goal of the criminal justice system is to detect and control crime. The *National Crime Victimization Survey* indicates that only about a third of all crimes are reported to the police annually (Bastian, 1995).

One of the more well-known crime detection organizations in the United States is the FBI. The FBI's extensive files on convicted felons includes their prior arrests, fingerprints, and other pertinent information. The FBI's laboratory facilities assist interested law enforcement agencies in several ways through materials identification, analyses of numerous substances, missing persons identification, and investigative techniques.

Criminal Punishment and Societal Retribution

The criminal justice system seeks to punish offenders for the crimes they have committed. The courts dispense justice and impose sentences on those convicted of crimes. The fines and sentences imposed are punishments for these crimes. The more serious the offense, the more severe the sentence. Or at least this is how it is supposed to work.

All criminal offenses have prescribed punishments established by statute. The United States Code or any compilation of state criminal laws shows maximum penalties for all criminal acts. For instance, Title 18, Section 1953 of the U.S. Code (1996) indicates the following punishment for "interstate transportation of wagering paraphernalia": "[The offender] . . . shall be fined not more than $10,000 or imprisoned for not more than five years or both." For an offense against personal property belonging to the United States, 18 U.S.C. Sec. 2112 (1996) provides that "whoever robs another of any kind or description of personal property belonging to the United States, shall be imprisoned not more than fifteen years."

Even illegal weather forecasting is prohibited by federal statute. Under 18 U.S.C. Sec. 2074 (1996), "Whoever knowingly issues or publishes any counterfeit weather forecast or warning of

Highlight 2.2. On the Death Penalty: Death Penalty Opponents Running Out of Money?

In Columbia, South Carolina, defense attorney David Bruck leaned forward and spoke to the man strapped to the prison gurney. He said, "I'll see you. Take care, man." He was speaking to condemned killer Sylvester Adams. A few minutes later, Adams was administered a lethal injection.

Adams was convicted of capital murder following a bungled 1979 robbery-turned-kidnapping. He had wrapped a tablecloth around the neck of sixteen-year-old Bryan Chambers and twisted it until Chambers died. Defense attorneys argued that Adams was mentally incompetent to stand trial, that he didn't realize what he was doing. Nevertheless, the judge barred defense attorneys from introducing such evidence at Adams's trial, and he was convicted of first-degree murder.

An avid opponent of the death penalty, David Bruck was appointed to handle Adams's unsuccessful appeal to the U.S. Supreme Court. Bruck expresses extreme bitterness over the Adams case. One major reason for his bitterness is that over fifty death row inmates have been found innocent following the discovery of exculpatory or exonerating evidence. Much of this evidence was discovered by public defender organizations hired by states to assist death row inmates in their appeals. Now there is imminent danger that the federal funds supporting such appeals will be withdrawn.

In 1996, the U.S. House of Representatives voted to cut the $20 million used to support public defender appeals work and groups that counsel and assist death row inmates. No doubt the pace of executions will increase as funds for appeals become unavailable.

Bruck says that the average wait between conviction and execution is about eight years. He says that most inmates on death row die of natural causes. He notes that in 1996, there were three thousand inmates on death row and that about two hundred fifty are joining their ranks each year, while we are executing only about thirty of them. He expects that this situation will change now that appeals are being increasingly restricted and that the funding for such appeals is being withdrawn.

Prosecutors, however, allege that the lengthy appeals are nothing more than the attempts of "philosophical think-tanks" to stall executions. Surveys of private citizens conducted by many independent agencies and media organizations, such as *USA Today*, report that upwards of 75 percent of the citizenry support capital punishment.

Should appeal money be retained by Congress for death row inmates? Should the death penalty be abolished? Should the cost of execution be a consideration in whether it is applied?

Source: Adapted from Associated Press, "Death Row Defenders: Funds for Nation's Death Row Defender System Endangered," *Minot (N.D.) Daily News*, May 6, 1996, A6.

weather conditions falsely representing such forecast or warning to have been issued or published by the Weather Bureau, United States Signal Service, or other branch of the Government service, shall be fined not more than $500 or imprisoned not more than ninety days, or both." All states and territories of the United States have similar statutory provisions addressing various crimes and accompanying punishments. No punishment has aroused as much controversy as the death penalty. The Supreme Court has debated the capital punishment issue for years, and it is no closer in the 1990s to resolving this issue than it was in the 1970s.

The death penalty has been investigated extensively as a possible deterrent to capital crimes (Dieter, 1994; Howells, Flanagan, and Hagan, 1995). Opponents of the death penalty argue that it fails as a crime deterrent and is cruel and unusual punishment (Carter, 1995). Those favoring the death penalty say there is retributive value derived from executing those criminals who deprive others of life. Yet others emphasize the *costs* of executing those convicted of capital crimes. These experts question whether the cost of an execution should be a major consideration in whether or not the death penalty should be administered (Carter, 1995). While the U.S. Supreme Court has not resolved all controversies about the death penalty, it has specified the manner in which the death penalty may be invoked by any state. It is unlikely that the death penalty issue will ever be resolved to everyone's satisfaction, despite all legal efforts thus far. Chapter 10 discusses the capital punishment issue in greater detail.

Criminal Rehabilitation

Rehabilitation of criminals, *correcting criminal behavior,* has been a dominant correctional goal. But corrections critics say that prisons and jails do not rehabilitate but rather that they are institutions of higher criminal learning and basically dehumanizing (Holton, 1995).

Alternative sentencing, or sentencing offenders to some type of nonincarcerative program such as home confinement, electronic monitoring, community service, or restitution, has become popular in recent years, not only as a method of easing prison and jail overcrowding but also as a more effective means of establishing more humane, noncustodial environments where true rehabilitation may occur (Sharbaro and Keller, 1995; Wright, 1995). Alternatives such as the private financing and operation of jails and prisons have also been considered in recent years (Logan, 1992; Sechrest and Shichor, 1993). Some authorities believe that private enterprise can do a better job in treating criminals and furnishing them with needed educational, vocational, and counseling services than bureaucratic governmental agencies (Casarez, 1995; Logan, 1992; Shichor, 1995).

Rehabilitation is concerned in part with providing incarcerated offenders with useful vocational and educational skills that can help them find good jobs when they are released from prison. Many prisons have counseling programs in which offenders can discuss their problems with trained therapists and psychological counselors. Many prisons have special counseling programs for child sexual abusers, drug and alcohol abusers, and those with various psychological disorders. However, incarceration fails to achieve the rehabilitative ideal for most offenders. For this reason, many critics have concluded that existing offender programs are coercive rather than rehabilitative. Inmates may enroll in educational courses or engage in extensive counseling, but these activities are cosmetic and designed primarily to impress those who make decisions about their early release from prison—parole boards. Other experts argue that rehabilitation has not succeeded on a large scale primarily because treatment programs have lacked the financial resources and personnel necessary to change inmate lives (DiPiano, 1995).

Before any rehabilitation program is rejected outright, it should be examined closely to see whether its objectives are being implemented and whether the program description is being followed by program personnel. High rates of recidivism among offenders who have been enrolled in rehabilitation programs have created some skepticism among correctional critics and the public. But there is ample evidence to show that some properly managed rehabilitative programs do assist some offenders (Casarez, 1995; Shichor, 1995).

The Assurance of Due Process

Due process *is the basic constitutional right to a fair trial, a presumption of innocence until guilt is proven beyond a reasonable doubt, the opportunity to be heard, to be aware of a matter that is pending, to make an informed choice before a judicial official.* The accused is entitled to the full protection of the law in any criminal proceeding. Several constitutional safeguards ensure that a suspect's rights will be respected at every stage of the criminal justice process.

Law enforcement officers must have probable cause whenever they make an arrest. Prosecutors must observe all criminal defendants' rights to due process. They must undertake no action that will violate these rights. By the same token, the judge must ensure in subsequent court action that all courtroom procedures are carefully observed. The judge must make appropriate rulings as to the admissibility of evidence against the defendant. If a judge rules inappropriately, the defendant's rights may be violated, and the subsequent conviction may be reversed or overturned. All of the officials with whom convicts interact must continue to ensure that their rights are not violated. At any stage in this process, defendants may challenge any procedure or decision affecting them.

Summary

The criminal justice system is a vast network of agencies, organizations, and individuals who attempt to control crime through detection and apprehension of alleged criminals. It processes them through a sequence of legal events culminating in a determination of their guilt or innocence. Eventually, it oversees and enforces their punishment or rehabilitation.

Most criminal laws originate in legislative action and in statutes. All federal laws are listed in the U.S. Code and other compilations. These laws are continually subject to revision. Some laws are dropped or revised, and new laws are developed as society requires. The courts interpret these laws and establish precedents through the principle of *stare decisis.* The Supreme Court is the final arbiter of actions pertaining to constitutional law and reviews decisions made by all lower courts.

The largest component of the criminal justice system is law enforcement. Law enforcement officers are empowered to arrest suspects for alleged crimes, to investigate crimes, and to enforce all laws within their jurisdictional boundaries. Depending upon the severity of the alleged offense and other information such as probable cause and the quality of evidence obtained, certain suspects are prosecuted. Defendants are tried, and a determination of guilt or innocence is made, often by a jury. Defendants may waive their right to a jury trial and permit the judge to decide the case. Or defendants may plea bargain with prosecutors at an earlier stage in these proceedings. If defendants are found innocent or if the charges against them are dropped, they are released from the criminal justice system. If defendants plead guilty or are found guilty by the court or jury, the final disposition of the case is determined by the judge through a sentence prescribed by law.

Corrections is concerned with supervising convicted offenders. Corrections may include probation or parole, or it may include incarceration in jail or prison, depending upon the nature and seriousness of the offense. The goals of the criminal justice system are to prevent and deter crime, to detect and control it, to punish and monitor criminal offenders, to rehabilitate them and accelerate their return to society, and to assure that all of those who enter the criminal justice process receive due process under the U.S. Constitution.

Key Terms

Arrest
Booking
Corrections
Criminal justice system
Decriminalization
Defendant
Defense attorneys
Due process
Jails
Jury
Legislatures
Plea bargaining
Prisons
Prosecution
Rehabilitation
Stare decisis

Questions for Review

1. Identify the major components of the criminal justice system. Are they independent of one another or related? Explain.
2. Do judges hand down statutes? Why or why not? Where do statutes come from? Do judges make laws? Do judges modify existing laws?
3. What is the difference between a jail and a prison? Do persons usually serve different terms in each facility?

4. What is meant by decriminalization? What kinds of criminal acts are most likely to be decriminalized?

5. When a lower court makes a decision, what principle applies that governs that decision, to the extent that a precedent exists or a similar ruling has been made that might affect the original decision? Are two federal district courts bound to observe decisions made in either court?

6. Differentiate between substantive and procedural law.

7. What is the largest component of the criminal justice system? What federal law enforcement agencies represent the government's interests?

8. Why is due process important in the criminal justice process?

9. What is plea bargaining? How much is plea bargaining used in the United States? Is plea bargaining increasing or decreasing? In what ways does plea bargaining benefit the criminal justice process?

10. Distinguish between probation and parole. In what sense are parolees and probationers supervised by the same persons?

Suggested Readings

del Carmen, Rolando V. *Criminal Procedure: Law and Practice*. 3d ed. Belmont, CA: Wadsworth, 1995.

Eck, John E. and David Weisburd. *Crime and Place*. Monsey, NY: Criminal Justice Press, 1995.

Eskridge, Chris. *Criminal Justice: Concepts and Issues*. Los Angeles, CA: Roxbury, 1996.

Rutledge, Devallis. *Courtroom Survival: The Officer's Guide to Better Testimony*. Placerville, CA: Copperhouse, 1992.

Steury, Ellen Hochstedler and Nancy Frank. *Courts: Criminal Court Process*. St. Paul, MN: West, 1996.

CHAPTER 3

Constitutional Criminal Law and Procedure

Scenario 1. You are a motorist traveling through Ohio. A state trooper pulls you over, suspecting that you are driving while intoxicated. You tell the officer that you have consumed two beers and smoked some marijuana. The officer arrests you, takes you to jail, and administers a test to determine the amount of alcohol in your blood. The test shows *no alcohol.* At no time are you advised of your *Miranda* rights to counsel and to refuse to be questioned, or that anything you say can and will be used against you in a court of law. You continue to make incriminating statements. Subsequently, you enter a plea of "no contest" or *nolo contendere* to a charge of DUI (driving under the influence) and are convicted. Later, you hire an attorney, who presents your case to the Supreme Court, alleging that your conviction should be overturned because the officers who interrogated you never gave you a *Miranda* warning. (*Berkemer v. McCarty,* 468 U.S. 104, 104 S.Ct. 3138 [1987])

Scenario 2. You are a woman working in a heavy-equipment company. Your male boss refers to you frequently as a "dumb-ass woman," says to you, "What do you know?"; "We need a man as the rental manager"; and "Why don't we go to the Holiday Inn and negotiate your raise?" At other times, the boss puts coins in his pockets and asks you to retrieve them. You politely ask the boss to stop this abusive behavior, but he persists. You sue your boss and the company, alleging that your psychological well-being has been affected and that an abusive work environment exists that is very upsetting to you. Lower courts dismiss your suit, saying that the offensive conduct by your boss has not seriously affected your psychological well-being. Your attorney takes the case to the Supreme Court. (*Harris v. Forklift Systems, Inc.,* 114 S.Ct. 367 [1993])

Scenario 3. You are an anti-abortion protester demonstrating in front of a clinic where abortions are performed. You confront pregnant women entering the clinic, giving them pamphlets and saying things intended to deter them from having abortions. You show them pictures of fetuses and tell them about the lives their unborn children may lead. You sing, chant, shout, yell, and use amplification equipment to get across your message. The sheriff arrests you. You are advised by the sheriff that you cannot demonstrate within thirty-six feet of the clinic's property line and that you cannot approach anyone seeking the services of the clinic. Further, you are prohibited from singing, chanting, whistling, shouting, or using sound equipment to protest what is going on inside the clinic, if such noise is within earshot of clinic patients. Also, you are forbidden to show any pictures, such as of unborn fetuses, to make patients think about what they are doing by having an abortion. When released from jail, you go back to the clinic and continue to do what you were doing earlier. You are arrested again. You complain that you have a right of *free speech* and *free assembly* and that the sheriff has no business arresting you for exercising these rights. You and your attorney present your case to the Supreme Court. (*Madsen v. Women's Health Center, Inc.*, 114 S.Ct. 2516 [1994])

In these three scenarios, several important constitutional issues are raised. In the first scenario, the Fifth Amendment guarantee against self-incrimination is highlighted. In the second, the Fourteenth Amendment guarantee of equal protection under the law as well as protection offered by the Civil Rights Act are called into question. In scenario 3, First Amendment issues of freedom of assembly and speech are raised. How did the Supreme Court decide in these cases?

In scenario 1, the conviction of the suspected drunk driver was overturned by the U.S. Supreme Court. The Court said that, although the driver had made incriminating statements *before* he was arrested, the driver had *not* been given the *Miranda* warning *following his arrest*. Thus, any incriminating statements he made following his arrest were inadmissible as evidence. The Court said, however, that any routine traffic stop by police is *not* considered a custodial interrogation for purposes of Mirandizing DUI suspects.

In scenario 2, the court held that the company environment was indeed hostile and abusive toward women. The Court said, however, that while mere utterances of epithets that cause bad feelings

are not severe enough to create an abusive work environment, conduct that *does* interfere with one's work performance and is sufficiently unreasonable *would* be considered abusive and thus illegal. The Court ruled in favor of the woman suing the large-equipment company and declared that she had, indeed, been sexually harassed.

In scenario 3, the Court ruled against the anti-abortion protester, holding that protesters are barred from blocking entrances and exits within thirty-six feet of clinics where abortions are performed, although so-called buffer zones for protesters do not apply to private property on the sides of clinics. Nevertheless, protesters are barred from singing, chanting, or otherwise creating noises that can be heard by those inside clinics. The Court said, however, that displays of pictures are not in violation of the First Amendment. Essentially, the Court said that it is much easier for clinics to close their curtains than to plug their ears (McCormack, 1994:27–32).

This chapter is about the constitutional foundation of U.S. criminal laws. All criminal laws are contained in local ordinances and state and federal statutes. They specify acts defined as criminal as well as punishments for those acts. The criminal justice system deals exclusively with those accused and convicted of violating these laws. The Supreme Court is responsible for interpreting the U.S. Constitution and its amendments and for deciding important cases, such as the above, where infringements of rights are alleged.

Several important constitutional amendments ensure the basic rights of U.S. citizens to fair treatment by the police and courts. Some of these amendments have been prominent in Supreme Court decisions in recent years. Several of the important landmark cases that have changed or modified laws are described in this chapter.

Some of the functions of criminal law are also described, as well as the legal basis for defining certain behaviors as criminal. Also, several defenses used by alleged law violators are presented. Some of these defenses have prompted legislators and others to support legal reforms such as the decriminalization of certain offenses and the abolishment of the insanity plea.

The Bill of Rights and State/Federal Law

The violation of criminal laws threatens not only the safety and security of citizens but also the perpetuation of an orderly social, political, and economic arrangement. The criminal justice system exists, in part, to punish the guilty and protect the innocent. Numerous safeguards exist to ensure an accused person's right to due process. Ideally, everyone has his or her "day in court." However, the system is far from perfect. Occasionally, guilty defendants are acquitted and freed, and innocent defendants are found guilty and punished.

At the foundation of the criminal justice system is the U.S. Constitution. This document has established several guarantees or rights for all citizens. The first ten amendments to the Constitution, known collectively as the Bill of Rights, makes some of these guarantees explicit. Figure 3.1 shows each of these amendments.

The Articles of Confederation, a document developed in 1781 by the Continental Congress, contained statements about personal liberties and freedoms, but they failed to make explicit the respective powers of the states in relation to the federal government. The Congress convened later and devised the Constitution as a way of making these powers more explicit.

It is important to understand the historical context in which the Constitution was created. Colonists were being exploited by Great Britain in different ways. They were denied trials by jury. Taxes were levied upon them without their consent. And in a bill of particulars the colonists accused the King of England of cutting off their trade with other countries, ravaging their coasts, plundering their seas, burning their towns, and destroying their lives.

The provisions of the Constitution, including the Bill of Rights and other amendments, were originally developed in the context of the prevailing common law, the **law of tradition and precedent.** These constitutional provisions were intended to secure existing guarantees and not necessarily to create new ones (U.S. Code Annotated, *Constitution of the United States*, 1996:62–63). Only in the

last few decades has the Bill of Rights been extended to the states. Some of these rights continue to be the subject of Supreme Court action.

Supreme Court Interpretation of Selected Rights

The U.S. Supreme Court is petitioned annually to hear cases requiring an interpretation of one or more constitutional amendments. Ordinarily, the petitioners have been convicted of violating local or state ordinances or statutes. The cases are first appealed to higher courts within the state. If petitioners receive an unfavorable judgment from the supreme court of the state in which they reside, they may then appeal to the U.S. Supreme Court, especially if the appeal involves constitutional issues.

The Supreme Court's interpretations of constitutional amendments depend on its composition. Justices are appointed by the president of the United States, subject to Senate confirmation.

While the Supreme Court receives at least five thousand cases a year, it hears oral arguments and writes opinions in only about two hundred fifty of them. Six of the first ten amendments to the Constitution have been frequently cited in criminal appeals to the Supreme Court. These include the First, Second, Fourth, Fifth, Sixth, and Eighth Amendments. This section examines each of these Amendments and provides sample cases associated with each.

The First Amendment: Freedom of Speech, the Press, and Religion

When does speech become defamatory and injure others? When does a group's assembly become unlawful and harmful? When does religious expression become criminally harmful?

The notion of *free speech* has been liberally interpreted. Some groups seek to prohibit speech and depictions of sex that demean women or are obscene, while others seek to promote such rights (Assister and Avedon, 1993; Martin and Sussman, 1993). Some interesting examples suggest the types of issues addressed by the First Amendment.

Figure 3.1 The Bill of Rights of the U.S. Constitution

Amendment	*Provision*
Article I	Congress shall make no law respecting an establishment of religion, or prohibiting the free exercise thereof; or abridging the freedom of speech, or of the press; or the right of the people peaceably to assemble, and to petition the Government for a redress of grievances.
Article II	A well-regulated militia, being necessary to the security of a free State, the right of the people to keep and bear arms, shall not be infringed.
Article III	No soldier shall, in time of peace, be quartered in any house, without the consent of the owner, nor in time of war, but in a manner to be prescribed by law.
Article IV	The right of the people to be secure in their persons, houses, papers, and effects, against unreasonable searches and seizures, shall not be violated, and no warrants shall issue, but upon probable cause, supported by oath or affirmation, and particularly describing the place to be searched, and the persons or things to be seized.
Article V	No person shall be held to answer for a capital, or otherwise infamous, crime unless on a presentment or indictment of a Grand Jury, except in cases arising in the land or naval forces, or in the militia, when in actual service in time of war or public danger; nor shall any person be subject for the same offense to be twice put in jeopardy of life or limb; nor shall be compelled in any criminal case to be a witness against himself, nor to be deprived of life, liberty, or property, without due process of law, nor shall private property be taken for public use without just compensation.
Article VI	In all criminal prosecutions, the accused shall enjoy the right to a speedy and public trial, by an impartial jury of the State and district wherein the crime shall have been committed, which district shall have been previously ascertained by law, and to be informed of the nature and cause of the accusation, to be confronted with the witnesses against him; to have compulsory process for obtaining witnesses in his favor, and to have the assistance of counsel for his defense.
Article VII	In suits at common law, where the value in controversy shall exceed twenty dollars, the right of trial by jury shall be preserved, and no fact tried by a jury, shall be otherwise reexamined in any court of the United States, than according to the rules of the common law.
Article VIII	Excessive bail shall not be required, nor excessive fines imposed, nor cruel and unusual punishments inflicted.
Article IX	The enumeration in the Constitution, of certain rights, shall not be construed to deny or disparage others retained by the people.
Article X	The powers not delegated to the United States by the Constitution, nor prohibited by it to the States, are reserved to the States respectively, or to the people.

It has been determined that verbally soliciting for purposes of prostitution is not within the right of free speech guaranteed by the First Amendment (*Eissa v. United States*, 1984). In a 1969 free speech case, Mr. Brandenburg was arrested, tried, and convicted of "advocating . . . the duty, necessity, or propriety of crime and . . . voluntarily assembl[ing] with [a] society, group, or assemblage of persons formed to teach or advocate the doctrines of criminal syndicalism" (*Bradenburg v. Ohio*, 1969). Brandenburg was believed to be a member of the Ku Klux Klan, and he publicly advocated a "march on Congress" on the Fourth of July to protest a racial issue. He was prosecuted under a controversial 1919 Ohio Criminal Syndicalism Statute. The Supreme Court reversed his Ohio conviction, noting that "we are here confronted with a statute which . . . purports to punish mere advocacy, and to forbid, on pain of criminal punishment, assembly with others merely to advocate the described type of action. Such a statute falls within the condemnation of the First and Fourteenth Amendments."

In another case, several black police officers in Columbus, Georgia, removed the American flags from their uniforms to protest racially discriminatory hiring practices by the city's police force (*Leonard v. City of Columbus*, 1983). They were dismissed from their jobs by city officials and appealed their dismissal on the grounds that their "symbolic" speech rights had been violated by the city under the First Amendment provision. The U.S. Supreme Court ruled the city's action unconstitutional and ordered the reinstatement of the officers.

In Vermont, a defendant convicted of using marijuana claimed the marijuana use was religious in nature and part of the doctrine of Tantric Buddhism (*State v. Rocheleau*, 1982). He claimed that his freedom of religion was violated by the marijuana conviction. The U.S. Supreme Court disagreed. It said, "Assuming that the defendant fully subscribed to the doctrines of Tantric Buddhism and that such is a genuine religion which includes the use of marijuana for spiritual purposes, compelling state interest in regulating marijuana use was of sufficient magnitude to override defendant's interest claiming protection under this clause, particularly where defendant did not assert that he would be unable to practice his religion without the use of marijuana and it was doubtful that he was actually practicing his religion while in the restroom of a nightclub" (*State v. Rocheleau*, 1982).

In another case, a man named Meyers drove around Louisiana streets with a bumper sticker

Freedom of speech, a basic right set forth in the First Amendment, is subject to many interpretations.

reading "Fuck [criminal sheriff or parish]." Meyers was arrested and convicted for possessing an obscene bumper sticker. Meyers's conviction was later overturned in a ruling that declared the bumper sticker to be *constitutionally protected free speech* (*State v. Meyers*, La.App.4 Cir. 1984, 462 So.2d 227). A similar ruling was made in the case of Cohen, who walked through a California courthouse corridor wearing a jacket with the words "Fuck the Draft" emblazoned upon it. Despite the fact that women and children were present when Cohen wore his jacket, the Supreme Court held that his "breach of the peace" conviction could not be upheld because it could not be plausibly maintained that the vulgar allusion to the selective service system would conjure up such psychic stimulation in anyone likely to be confronted with Cohen's crudely defaced jacket (*Cohen v. California*, 403 U.S. 15 [1971]).

Finally, city officials in Oklahoma City, Oklahoma, sought to prohibit the use of a convention center for the Miss Gay America Pageant in which male contestants would compete in female attire. Officials believed that the pageant would include obscene depictions of sexual conduct in violation of state law. Thus, the pageant was declared "immoral" and illegal. Pageant organizers sought relief from the court. The court declared that city officials failed to present any tangible evidence that such a pageant would be immoral or contain distasteful expressions, and thus the pageant was permitted. The ordinance invoked to prohibit it was declared unconstitutional (*Norma Kristie, Inc. v. City of Oklahoma City*, D.C.Okla., 572 F.Supp. 88, 1983).

The Second Amendment: Right to Keep and Bear Arms

The Second Amendment is frequently misinterpreted (Kates, 1994; LaPierre, 1994). Each state has the power to regulate the possession and registration of firearms. The original intent of this amendment was to preserve the right of states to maintain armed militia (Malcolm, 1994). Hence, it refers to a "collective right" rather than to an individual one (*United States v. Warin*, 1976). In 1981, the Supreme Court held that it was not a violation of the Second Amendment for the city of Morton Grove, Illinois, to ban the possession of handguns (*Quilici v. Village of Morton Grove*, 1981).

The Supreme Court also held in a 1983 case that it was not unconstitutional for Texas to bar the defendant from carrying two "sword-like weapons" in his belt "in case he might need them" for self-protection (*Masters v. State*, 1983). All states have the right to regulate the possession and/or distribution of firearms and to license and oversee their ownership. The Second Amendment places no limitation on the power of states to enact their own gun control legislation (*People v. Morrill*, 1984), and it does not prohibit state statutes from defining the crime of unlawfully carrying a weapon (*State v. Young*, 1985).

The Supreme Court has held that the Second Amendment is applicable only to federal laws (*Presser v. Illinois*, 1886) and that the right to bear arms is closely linked with the preservation of *state militias* (*United States v. Miller*, 1939) (Vernick and Teret, 1993). However, other experts challenge abolitionist arguments and suggest that the constitutional right to bear arms for purposes of self-defense ought to be preserved (LaPierre, 1994).

The Fourth Amendment: Right of Search and Seizure Regulated

The key elements of the Fourth Amendment are *unreasonable* **search and seizure** of persons, houses, papers, and effects, and the issuance of search and seizure warrants *upon probable cause*. This amendment has frequently been interpreted to restrict law enforcement officers rather than to protect the rights of private citizens (*Greene v. United States*, 1981; Bradley, 1993; Davey, 1994; McWhirter, 1994). It has also been applied to searches of homes, automobiles, bodies, lunch boxes, dormitory rooms, and blood and urine specimens.

The Supreme Court has broadly construed the Fourth Amendment and has created several exceptions to it. Not all warrantless searches are illegal. Not all seizures of personal possessions violate this amendment. For instance, under the "plain view" doctrine, illegal contraband may be seized if it is in plain view and is in a place where the police officer

Highlight 3.1. Fourth Amendment Searches

Arizona v. Hicks, 480 U.S. 321, 107 S.Ct. 1149 (1987). One evening, people in an apartment reported that someone in the apartment above had fired a bullet through their ceiling, injuring one of the lower apartment's occupants. Police investigated the upstairs apartment, rented by Hicks, and discovered some weapons and a stocking cap mask. They also found that while the apartment was run-down, new stereo equipment was *in plain view*. The police wrote down serial numbers from the stereo equipment. In order to see the stereo's serial numbers, however, they had to move the equipment. Later, these stereo items were found to have been stolen, and a search warrant was obtained for Hicks's apartment. Hicks was arrested, charged with robbery, and convicted. Hicks sought to suppress the evidence against him, alleging that his Fourth Amendment rights had been violated. The U.S. Supreme Court overturned Hicks's conviction, saying that in order for police officers to invoke the *plain view rule* regarding the stereo equipment, they required probable cause to believe the stereo equipment was stolen. However, the police used *reasonable suspicion* when moving the stereo equipment, which caused their act to be a *search* requiring a proper warrant based upon probable cause. *Reasonable suspicion does not rise to the level of probable cause, however.*

Brinegar v. United States, 338 U.S. 160, 69 S.Ct. 1302 (1949). Probable cause exists whenever the apparent facts and circumstances available to officers, combined with reasonably trustworthy information, cause the officers to believe that a crime has been or is being committed. Brinegar was known by police to be a bootlegger and to transport illegal liquor across state lines. Federal revenue agents observed Brinegar driving his car in Oklahoma, five miles west of the Missouri line. They noticed that his speeding car was weighed down in the back. After a short chase they forced Brinegar off of the road and observed in plain view a case of liquor in Brinegar's car. Twelve more cases of untaxed liquor were found under the car seats. Brinegar was convicted of transporting illegal liquor across state lines. He appealed, arguing that the officers lacked probable cause to stop him and search his vehicle. The Supreme Court disagreed and adopted a totality-of-circumstances test for this type of situation.

From past observation and experience, the officers who surveilled Brinegar's car knew who he was and what he did. They knew various contact points where illegal liquor was obtained. Given all of the events the officers observed, the Supreme Court believed that they had probable cause to intercept Brinegar and search his vehicle. His conviction was thus upheld.

California v. Ciraolo, 476 U.S. 207, 106 S.Ct. 1809 (1986). Ciraolo was growing marijuana in his backyard, according to an anonymous tip received by police. Ciraolo's backyard could not be seen from the street, and so police flew over Ciraolo's home and photographed the backyard. Officers detected marijuana plants in the photographs. On this basis they obtained a search warrant for Ciraolo's premises, where they found growing marijuana plants. Ciraolo was convicted of cultivating marijuana. He appealed, contending that he had a reasonable expectation of privacy that included his backyard and that viewing his yard from an airplane constituted unreasonable search. The Supreme Court upheld the aerial use of photography in identifying illegal contraband, such as growing marijuana. The Court declared that one's property, such as a backyard, cannot be barred from public view from the air; thus, anything seen from the air is subject to being seized.

Dow Chemical Co. v. United States, 476 U.S. 227, 106 S.Ct. 1819 (1986). Dow Chemical brought suit against the U.S. government when the Environmental Protection Agency conducted an aerial surveillance of their property as part of the Clean Air Act. Dow Chemical, which had been fined for various violations of the act, claimed that their Fourth Amendment right had been violated by the "unreasonable" aerial surveillance of their property. The Supreme Court disagreed, holding that inspections by means of aerial photography are reasonable and do not constitute a "search" in the context of the Fourth Amendment.

Illinois v. Rodriguez, 497 U.S. 177, 110 S.Ct. 2793 (1990). A woman named Fischer called police and reported that she had been beaten by her boyfriend, Rodriguez. The police went with Fischer to Rodriguez's apartment. She allowed them entry into the

---

Highlight 3.1. Fourth Amendment Searches *(continued)*

apartment, because she lived there with Rodriguez and had a key. Indeed, her clothes, furniture, and other personal effects were in Rodriguez's apartment as proof of her statements. When police entered the apartment, they saw *in plain view* containers of cocaine and drug paraphernalia and arrested Rodriguez. The seized evidence was used against him, and he was convicted. He appealed, contending that Fischer had moved out weeks earlier and that she did not have the

right to permit police entry. It turned out that Fischer had indeed moved out. Nevertheless, the police had acted *in good faith* that she had the authority to admit them. Thus, the Court upheld Rodriguez's conviction, saying that a warrantless entry and search based on the consent of someone the police believed to possess *common authority over the premises* but who did not have such common authority was a valid entry and search.

---

has a right to be. For instance, a man was taken to an emergency room of a local hospital. While awaiting treatment, he placed the contents of his pockets on a table in a public hallway. A passing police officer observed and inspected a bag that appeared to contain marijuana. Finding that it was marijuana, he arrested the patient for possession of a controlled substance. The court upheld the warrantless search and seizure of the marijuana because the emergency room was a public place and the officer had a right to be there (*People v. Torres*, 1986).

In another case, a police officer patrolling in his cruiser observed a pedestrian with a gun butt protruding from his belt. He stopped the pedestrian and confiscated the pistol, which was in plain view. This search and seizure was upheld by the courts as valid because the gun was in plain view when the officer observed it (*United States v. Jenkins*, 1967).

In order to legally seize contraband, the police must have a right to be where they are and must also have reasonable certainty that the item observed is illegal. It is insufficient for police to confiscate a "brown paper bag" that they believe might contain an illegal substance unless there is substantial supporting evidence associated with their seizure. Furthermore, even if the search and seizure is later held to be unlawful, illegal drugs or other contraband seized, such as counterfeit money, are illegal *per se* and will not be returned to the defendant (*United States v. Low*, 1966).

The Fifth Amendment: Right Against Double Jeopardy and Self-Incrimination

This amendment guarantees at least two important rights: (1) *the right against self-incrimination*, and (2) *the right against double jeopardy*. In any criminal case, defendants cannot be compelled to testify against themselves (Rosenberg and Rosenberg, 1991). And if those charged with crimes are subsequently acquitted, they cannot be tried again for those same crimes. In federal courts, the Fifth Amendment also protects citizens from being charged with capital offenses without first having those charges presented to a grand jury. The grand jury is convened to determine probable cause that a crime was committed and that the defendant probably committed it. Individual states do not have to abide by this provision. About half the states do not use the grand jury system, but employ other means for filing serious charges against suspects.

When police officers have reason to believe that a felony has been committed and that a particular person committed it, they may make an arrest. At the time of the criminal arrest police must advise suspects of their constitutional "rights." These rights include (1) the right to remain silent, (2) the right to an attorney, (3) the right to have the attorney present during all questioning, and (4) the right to give up the right to remain silent. Anything sus-

---

Highlight 3.2. What Is Self-Incrimination? The Case of Massiah

Interrogations are not always conducted in the immediate presence of the police, and police officers do not have to be physically present. An interesting case of an illegal interrogation is *Massiah v. United States* (1964). Massiah and a co-defendant were formally charged with violating federal narcotics laws. Massiah pleaded not guilty and was released on bail. While Massiah was out on bail, his co-defendant, Mr. Colson, decided to cooperate with the police and agreed to spy on Massiah.

On November 19, 1959, Colson had a lengthy conversation with Massiah while sitting in Massiah's automobile. By an earlier arrangement, an FBI agent sat in a car parked near Massiah's. Massiah's car had been secretly outfitted with a small radio transmitter, and the FBI agent was able to record the entire conversation between Colson and Massiah. Massiah made several incriminating statements in that conversation. These statements led to his conviction on the narcotics charges. The Supreme Court reversed his conviction, however, saying that Massiah was actually "under interrogation" by the FBI agent, even though the FBI agent was not physically present in Massiah's vehicle. While under interrogation, Massiah had the right to have his attorney present. The Court also said that if the rule against self-incrimination "is to have any efficacy, it must apply to indirect and surreptitious interrogations as well as those conducted in the jailhouse."

Source: Massiah v. United States, 377 U.S. 201, 84 S.Ct. 119 (1964).

---

pects say after being placed under arrest can and will be used against them in a court of law.

The police are not required to advise suspects of their rights as long as the criminal case they are investigating is in the "investigatory phase." However, once the investigation progresses to accusation and enters the accusatory or "critical" phase, suspects' rights "attach" and must be invoked. Placing suspects under arrest and restricting their movements (e.g., placing them in a patrol car or in jail) are part of the accusatory phase. Any interrogation of suspects under such conditions must be preceded by advising these suspects of their rights under the law.

Some confessions or admissions are obtained without police prompting or interrogation. In 1984, a man named Connelly approached a uniformed Denver police officer and commenced to confess to a 1982 murder. The officer advised him of his Miranda rights. Connelly stated that he understood and continued his confession. A detective who arrived later again advised Connelly of his Miranda rights. Connelly continued to confess. In fact, he led officers to the site of the murder and

furnished them with incriminating details of the crime. During his confession, he said that he was "following the advice of God" by confessing. Psychiatrists examined Connelly and found him incompetent to assist in his own defense but *competent* to stand trial. Connelly was convicted. He appealed, contending that his mental state rendered him incompetent to be properly advised of his Miranda rights. The Supreme Court disagreed and upheld his conviction. The Court said that Connelly's belief that he was confessing because of God's advice did not automatically exclude his confession as admissible evidence against him (*Colorado v. Connelly*, 479 U.S. 157, 107 S.Ct. 515, 1986).

Another source of self-incrimination might be one's spouse. Spousal testimony is no longer privileged as long as the testimony is voluntary and does not compromise a confidential marital communication. For instance, the U.S. District Court of Colorado convicted Otis Trammel of importing and conspiring to import heroin. Before the trial, government prosecutors indicated their intention to call Trammel's wife to testify against him. Tram-

---

Highlight 3.3. Double Jeopardy: The Case of Alvin Dixon

Alvin Dixon was indicted for possession of cocaine with intent to distribute. Earlier, Dixon had been arrested for second-degree murder and released on bond. While out on bond, Dixon was "forbidden from committing any criminal offense." It was during this period that Dixon was arrested and charged with cocaine possession. Shortly thereafter he was convicted of contempt (because of the cocaine possession) and was sentenced to 180 days in jail. Later, he moved to have the cocaine indictment dismissed, because his "contempt" conviction involved the identical drug charges. The trial court granted his motion and dismissed the indictment. The government appealed to the Supreme Court. The Court upheld the dismissal, holding that *because a criminal contempt sanction was imposed upon Dixon for violating an order of conditional release by violating a drug offense that was incorporated into his release conditions, the later attempt to prosecute him for the drug offense itself is barred by double jeopardy.*

Source: United States v. Dixon, 507 U.S.___, 113, S.Ct. 2849 (1993).

---

mel objected on the grounds that spouses cannot be compelled to make incriminating statements about their spouses. Trammel's wife was granted immunity and testified against Trammel voluntarily. He was convicted. On appeal, Trammel moved to suppress her testimony. The Supreme Court upheld Trammel's conviction, holding that spouses may act as witnesses against their spouses as long as they do so voluntarily. Trammel's wife had been granted immunity from prosecution and thus testified freely. The fact that she was the defendant's wife was immaterial to whether she testified voluntarily. Trammel's wife could have refused to testify. Thus, Trammel's claim of spousal privilege was rejected (*Trammel v. United States*, 1980).

The Sixth Amendment: Right to a Speedy Trial and Assistance of Counsel

The Sixth Amendment guarantees the right to a speedy trial by an impartial jury, to the assistance of counsel, and to confront one's accusers in open court. The phrase **speedy trial** is vague. In order to make this concept more explicit, the Speedy Trial Act of 1974 was passed (U.S. Code Annotated,

1996). Amended several times since 1974, this act provides for a hundred-day period between an arrest and the trial for the alleged offense. While there are exceptions to this fixed time period, ordinarily a defendant being arrested for a crime on August 1, 1996, for example, will be tried no later than November 10, 1996. Only exceptional circumstances, such as a crowded court docket, may be grounds to delay a trial beyond the hundred-day period (*United States v. Nance*, 666 F.2d 353 [1982]).

This act overcomes certain delays and limits the period within which a defendant's guilt is in question. However, sometimes defendants may be granted additional time in order to file appeals and make motions in other proceedings. For instance, a man named Cook was charged with income tax evasion. He sought to have the charges reduced and/or thrown out on various grounds. He also was filing appeals in a tax case in another state. He asked the court for delays, which were granted. Eventually, he entered a guilty plea. Thirty-two months had passed since his indictment. Cook challenged the delay as a violation of his right to a speedy trial. The court rejected his assertion and upheld his criminal conviction (*United States v. Cook*, 1972).

The Sixth Amendment guarantees the assistance of counsel. The leading case on defining at-

Highlight 3.4. On the Trail of the Speedy Trial

Barker v. Wingo (1972). In September 1958, Barker and another person were indicted for shooting an elderly couple in July 1958. Kentucky prosecutors sought sixteen continuances to prolong Barker's trial. Barker's companion, Manning, was tried five times. Four of the trials resulted in hung juries; the fifth resulted in his conviction. During these five trials, Barker made no attempt to protest or to encourage a trial on his own behalf. Barker's trial was postponed several times but was finally held in October 1963. He was convicted. He appealed, alleging a violation of his right to a speedy trial. The Supreme Court declared that since Barker had apparently not wanted a speedy trial, he was not entitled to one. The case illustrates that defendants must state their desire to have a speedy trial in order for the Sixth Amendment guarantees to be enforceable (*Barker v. Wingo*, 407 U.S. 514, 92 S.Ct. 2181 [1972]).

Klopfer v. North Carolina (1967). Klopfer was tried for criminal trespass. A mistrial was declared. Klopfer asked whether the government intended to continue its prosecution and was advised that the state was filing a *nolle prosequi* with leave, meaning that it might retry Klopfer at a later date. Klopfer sought relief from the Supreme Court, declaring that he be-

lieved that *nolle prosequi* with leave left him in a vulnerable position and that he was entitled to a speedy trial under the law according to the Sixth and Fourteenth Amendments. The Supreme Court agreed with Klopfer and endorsed a speedy trial provision. Justifications for a speedy trial include: (1) witnesses are more credible; (2) a defendant's ability to defend himself and trial fairness are not jeopardized; and (3) a defendant's pretrial anxiety is minimized (*Klopfer v. North Carolina*, 386 U.S. 213, 87 S.Ct. 988 [1967]).

Strunk v. United States (1973). Strunk was arrested and eventually tried ten months later. He was convicted and appealed, arguing that the ten-month delay was a violation of his right to a speedy trial. The Supreme Court heard the case and noted several considerations in determining whether speedy trial rights of suspects have been violated. These considerations are: (1) whether there are overcrowded court dockets and understaffed prosecutors' offices; (2) whether there is substantial emotional distress caused to defendants because of long delays; and (3) whether an accused is released pending a trial and whether there is little or no immediate interest in having a trial (*Strunk v. United States*, 412 U.S. 434, 93 S.Ct. 2260 [1973]).

torney competence is *Strickland v. Washington* (1984). More than a few defendants have raised the issue of the *effective assistance of counsel* as grounds for reversing their convictions. In most of these cases, higher courts have held that the level of effectiveness provided by one's counsel is usually *not* unconstitutional (U.S. Code Annotated, Amendment VI, Supplementary Pamphlet, Notes 2292–2308, 1996) because whatever the omission or error, it was *not of sufficient seriousness to alter the case outcome*. Thus, if one's attorney fails to introduce certain evidence or call particular witnesses, these omissions are insufficient to cause juries to change their minds about the defendant's guilt. There are exceptions, however.

For instance, counsel for a Cuban citizen living

in Illinois charged with delivery of cocaine failed to advise his client that entering a guilty plea might result in deportation. The Cuban citizen entered a guilty plea and was ordered deported. He appealed, claiming ineffective assistance of counsel, and that he did not know that a guilty plea would result in his deportation. His conviction was overturned *on the basis of ineffective assistance of counsel, because his counsel failed to inform him of the possibility of deportation following his entering a guilty plea* (*Moreno v. State*, 1992).

In North Dakota, a state court arrived at a different conclusion when a woman was not advised of the possibility that she might be deported if she pled guilty to a crime (*State v. Dalman*, 1994). In the North Dakota case, the woman *failed to establish*

Highlight 3.5. On the Effective Assistance of Counsel

Strickland v. Washington (1984). Strickland's case was evaluated according to the following standards: Did counsel's conduct undermine the adversarial process to such an extent that the trial could not render a just result? Did counsel's behavior fall below the objective standard of reasonableness? There must be a reasonable probability that, but for counsel's unprofessional errors, the result of the proceedings would have been different (*Strickland v. Washington*, 466 U.S. 668, 104 S.Ct. 2052 [1984]).

Lozada v. Deeds (1991). José Lozada was convicted of four crimes relating to narcotics. He had been convicted earlier in Nevada on four counts of possession and sale of controlled substances. Following the trial proceedings, Lozada alleged that his attorney failed to notify him of his right to appeal, of the procedures and time limitations of an appeal, and of his right to court-appointed counsel. Further, Lozada alleged, his attorney failed to file a notice of appeal or to ensure that Lozada received court-appointed counsel on appeal. Finally, Lozada alleged that the attorney misled Lozada's sister, and hence Lozada, when he mistakenly told her that the case had been forwarded to the public defender's office. Lower appellate courts dismissed Lozada's subsequent *habeas corpus* petition on the grounds that he had ineffective assistance of counsel. The Supreme Court found otherwise, however, and reversed his convictions, holding that Lozada had made a substantial showing that he was denied the right to effective assistance of counsel (*Lozada v. Deeds*, 498 U.S. 430, 111 S.Ct. 860 [1991]).

that her counsel was ineffective after he failed to advise her of the possibility that she might face deportation following a guilty plea to an alleged criminal offense. She entered a guilty plea and was ordered deported. She appealed on the grounds of ineffective assistance of counsel, but her appeal was rejected. This shows that different state courts might interpret the standard of ineffective assistance of counsel differently. In many cases today, clients *cannot* successfully argue ineffective assistance of counsel *merely* based on the fact that their counsel failed to advise them of *every* consequence associated with entering a guilty plea (*People v. Huarte*, 1991).

The Sixth Amendment also guarantees defendants the right to cross-examine witnesses. If this right is denied, it may be the basis for the reversal of a conviction. Cross-examination also gives the judge and jury an opportunity to observe witnesses' demeanor and thus evaluate their veracity (*Breeden v. State*, 1993).

However, the right to confront everyone who testifies against the defendant is not absolute. In many cases, the government employs informants, or persons who acquire incriminating information about the defendant surreptitiously. Informants may infiltrate organized crime syndicates and gather incriminating information. When many of these informants testify in open court, their identities are disguised or protected so that their lives can also be protected from those they testify against. But not all informants are entitled to have their identities protected. For example, in the case of *United States v. Bateman* (1992), Bateman was being prosecuted for producing child pornography. An informant against Bateman was called as a witness, but the court refused to identify the informant. Bateman was subsequently convicted, but the conviction was overturned because Bateman was denied the opportunity to directly confront the witness. The government had argued earlier that the witness's identity should be protected because he was a child when Bateman involved him in the illegal creation of pornographic materials. The Court rejected the government's argument and entitled Bateman full opportunity to confront his accuser, now an adult. There was no reason to protect the witness's identity that outweighed Bateman's right to confrontation.

The Eighth Amendment: Right Against Excessive Bail and Cruel and Unusual Punishment

The Eighth Amendment pertains to **excessive bail** and **cruel and unusual punishment**. It is a common misconception that all citizens have an absolute right to bail, regardless of the offenses alleged (Alexander, 1992). In some cases, it might be harmful to society to release suspects on bail. Where there is sufficient evidence (e.g., several witnesses to a brutal murder) permitting the suspect to go free while awaiting trial may result in additional crimes. In cases involving nonviolent crimes, those who are likely to flee the country are sometimes denied bail (e.g., a banker who has a home in Portugal and has been accused of stealing $20 million in negotiable securities from a California bank).

Thus, the right to bail is not an absolute one, and Congress may restrict the categories of cases where bail is allowed (*Augustus v. Roemer*, 1991; *People v. Burton*, 1990; *State v. Boppre*, 1990; *United States v. Salerno*, 1987). Bail is also discretionary in every jurisdiction. For the same offense of burglary committed by two different persons, for instance, bail for an habitual or an especially dangerous offender might be higher than bail for a first offender. In the case of *Wischmeier v. State* (1991), for instance, a $50,000 bond was not considered excessive by a Nevada court. In another drug case, bail for a defendant facing possible imprisonment of from fourteen to twenty-nine years was set at $25,000 (*Ballard v. Walker*, 772 F.Supp. 1335, 1991). In yet another case, a defendant had his bail reduced from $250,000 to $60,000 after the first bail was declared excessive. The defendant, Nguyen, was charged with aggravated assault, robbery, and burglary, but he did not have a prior record and had extensive community ties (*Nguyen v. State*, 1994).

Issues of *cruel and unusual punishment* include police brutality, prison overcrowding, indifference of prison officials, and capital punishment for either adults or juveniles (Acker and Lanier, 1994; Crosby, Britner, and Jodl, 1995). For example, in-mates do not lose all of their rights. The Eighth Amendment guarantees that prisoners have the right to be treated in a reasonable manner. However, courts are consulted about kinds of treatment that may be "unreasonable" or "cruel and unusual." These are highly subjective concepts that the Supreme Court has never explicitly clarified. Each case is decided on its "individual merits." The general standard is that conditions of confinement must not involve wanton or unnecessary infliction of pain, must not be grossly disproportionate to the severity of the crime, and must not involve conduct that demonstrates more than ordinary lack of due care for the prisoner's safety or interest (*Wright v. Caspari*, 1992).

For instance, a California prison superintendent had the capacity to change prison conditions and improve prisoner safety, but he failed to do so. The superintendent apparently condoned improper and inadequate staff training methods, failed to control illegal activities within the prison, provided inadequate supervision of inmates and insufficient controls in dormitories, failed to investigate thoroughly allegations of inmate rapes, and failed to provide safe controls for prisoners' movements within and without the facility. In this instance, the courts declared that inmate rights were violated and that the conditions constituted "cruel and unusual punishment" (*LaMarca v. Turner*, 1993).

Allegations of cruel and unusual punishment might also be related to the severity of a sentence in relation to the crime committed. For example, Jonas sold one marijuana cigarette to a fourteen-year-old and was also caught trafficking in stolen property. He was convicted for both offenses. His sentence was twenty-five years in prison for the marijuana cigarette sale, plus twenty-one years without parole for the stolen property charge, both sentences to run *consecutively*. These sentences were *not* considered "cruel and unusual punishment" within the Eighth Amendment context (*State v. Jonas*, 1990). In another case, Jenkins was convicted of possessing 0.33 grams of cocaine and sentenced to fifty years. While this sentence was considered excessive by the court, it was *not* considered "cruel and unusual" (*Jenkins v. State*, 1994).

The Fourteenth Amendment: The Equal Protection Clause

Shortly after the Civil War in 1868, Congress ratified the Fourteenth Amendment, which made explicit a citizen's right to due process. It also made a clear distinction between state and federal law. Section I of the Fourteenth Amendment:

All persons born or naturalized in the United States, and subject to the jurisdiction thereof, are citizens of the United States and of the State wherein they reside. No State shall make or enforce any law which shall abridge the privileges or immunities of citizens of the United States; nor shall any State deprive any person or life, liberty, or property, without due process of law; nor deny to any person within its jurisdiction the equal protection of the laws.

The significance of Section I is twofold. First, *it assures all citizens of their right to due process.* In any criminal matter where charges are brought against any citizen, the Fourteenth Amendment gives that citizen an absolute right to a trial. There are some limitations to the right to a trial by jury, however. These are discussed in chapters 8 and 9. Second, it guarantees that *no state shall make or enforce any law which abridges or deprives citizens of their rights as provided by the Constitution.*

The original intent of the Fourteenth Amendment was to extend the rights to due process to all citizens, particularly former slaves, and to equal protection under the law. Shortly after the Civil War, the Fourteenth Amendment was established, technically giving full rights of citizenship and the full protection of the law to former slaves. In reality, however, racial discrimination was not abolished. Despite changes in the law designed to repair previous injustices against blacks and other minorities, injustices continue. Disproportionate administration of the death penalty to black prisoners is of concern to more than a few experts, and the Fourteenth Amendment is a means of redressing allegations of racial discrimination in capital cases (Hanson, 1988). Chapter 10 examines disparities in sentencing that are attributable in part to racial and ethnic factors, gender differences, and socioeconomic variables.

Evidence also suggests that discrimination based on race, ethnicity, gender, and socioeconomic differences continues to be prevalent in law enforcement, police discretion, officer recruitment practices, prosecutorial decisions, and corrections. Hate crimes against members of various ethnic and racial groups are relevant to the Fourteenth Amendment provision of equal protection under the law (Alexander, 1991; Winer, 1994). Female inmates raise Fourteenth Amendment issues when they perceive injustices or inequities in how they are treated compared with their male counterparts (Knight, 1992). Each of these areas will be addressed in later chapters.

One purpose of the Fourteenth Amendment is to create uniformity in state and federal civil and criminal statutes. The main effect of this amendment is to bar any state from passing a law inconsistent with federal law. Furthermore, no state may pass a law that infringes any federal law applying to U.S. citizens. The Fourteenth Amendment does not deny a state the right to enact laws that conflict with those of other states. Thus, while in one state the legal age for drinking might be twenty-one, in another state it might be eighteen. Citizens of the United States must adhere to all federal laws as well as those of states where they reside, including those states they enter temporarily.

Rules of Criminal Procedure

At the heart of the criminal justice system is a set of **rules of criminal procedure**. Just as debates and public forums are conducted according to established rules of procedure, such as *Robert's Rules of Order*, the processing of criminal defendants is governed by established rules. These rules apply from the time a crime comes to the attention of police to the time when an arrest is made. The rules continue to apply throughout a defendant's subsequent processing, trial, conviction, appeal, sentencing, and eventual parole or release from the criminal justice system. While these rules have evolved in a fairly systematic fashion, some experts believe that they have been formulated on a piecemeal, case-by-case basis. Thus, at times their application is cumbersome and complex (Bradley, 1993; Heller, 1990).

At the federal level, the U.S. Code has established Federal Rules of Criminal Procedure under Title 18, U.S. Code (1996). As the code specifies under Federal Rules of Criminal Procedure 1 and 2, "these rules govern the procedure in all criminal proceedings in the courts of the United States. . . . These rules are intended to provide for the just determination of every criminal proceeding. They shall be construed to secure simplicity in procedure, fairness in administration and the elimination of unjustifiable expense and delay" (U.S. Code Annotated, 1996:11).

Each state and all U.S. possessions have rules of criminal procedure. In many states, the Federal Rules of Criminal Procedure have been reproduced verbatim, with minor variations and exceptions to reflect local customs or crimes unique to particular jurisdictions (e.g., shooting alligators in Florida or rustling cattle in Wyoming). Each state has statutory compilations of laws. For instance, Maine has "Maine Revised Statutes Annotated," Alabama has the "Code of Alabama," and Oregon has "Oregon Revised Statutes." Included in these statutory compilations are state rules of criminal procedure that govern the processing of defendants.

Presently, there are sixty federal rules of criminal procedure. These apply to various stages of the process of dealing with alleged criminal offenders. Table 3.1 shows selected rules that apply from pre-

Table 3.1

Selected Federal Rules of Criminal Procedure and Stages of the Criminal Justice Process

Federal Rules	Subject	Stage
3	Complaint	Preliminary proceedings
4	Arrest warrant	Preliminary proceedings
5	Appearance	Preliminary proceedings
5.1	Preliminary examination	Preliminary proceedings
6	Grand jury	Indictment/information
7	Indictment	Indictment/information
8	Joinder/offenses	Indictment/information
9	Warrant/summons	Indictment/information
10	Arraignment	Arraignment/trial preparation
11	Pleas	Arraignment/trial preparation
12	Pleadings/motions	Arraignment/trial preparation
15	Depositions	Arraignment/trial preparation
16	Discovery	Arraignment/trial preparation
17	Subpoena	Arraignment/trial preparation
23	Trial by jury	Trial proceedings
24	Trial jurors	Trial proceedings
26	Taking testimony	Trial proceedings
30	Instructions	Trial proceedings
31	Verdict	Trial proceedings
32	Sentences/judgments	Judgments
33	New trial	Judgments
34	Arrest judgment	Judgments
35	Corrections/sentences	Judgments

Source: 18 United States Code, 1996.

Note: Several rules have been omitted because of their incidental nature to this process or because of their special application to particular motions or technicalities.

liminary proceedings through judgment. It is beyond the scope of this book to examine all of these rules in detail. Rather, several have been selected for discussion largely on the basis of their immediate relevance for criminal defendants.

Table 3.1 shows that a federal criminal action is commenced by filing a **complaint** under Rule 3. *The complaint is a written statement of the essential facts constituting the offense charged.* Rule 4 applies to issuing arrest warrants or summonses. Arrest warrants or summonses contain statements of probable cause. Once an arrest warrant or summons has been issued by the court, an arrest is made and defendants are brought before a U.S. magistrate. All procedures to be followed at this initial appearance are outlined in Rule 5.

State courts follow similar procedures for processing criminal defendants. The rules and procedures may vary among jurisdictions, but all state jurisdictions follow a general procedural pattern such as the one described in table 3.1. Chapters 7 through 10 describe arrests of alleged offenders and the procedures followed in their processing.

Functions of Criminal Law

Criminal law performs two important functions: (1) defining criminal conduct and (2) prescribing the punishment for such conduct.

Defining Criminal Conduct

All criminal conduct is specified in federal, state, and local statutes. Criminal conduct violates criminal laws in each jurisdiction. Sometimes local laws and state statutes conflict with certain constitutional guarantees extended to citizens.

Criminal laws are subject to modification, change, elimination, or amplification. Every year in every jurisdiction, some laws change. For example, in 1987, Los Angeles prosecutors filed attempted murder charges against Joseph Markowski for selling his blood and engaging in male prostitution, even though he knew he had AIDS. At that time, no statute prohibited "knowingly transmitting

AIDS" (Lacayo, 1987:63). But the lethal nature of AIDS and Markowski's knowledge of this fact brought his conduct within the context of an attempted murder statute. But by 1996 there were statutes on the books of most states prohibiting the knowing transmission of HIV. In that year a man in Westminister, Maryland, was convicted of sexually molesting his eight-year-old step-grandson and sentenced to ninety years for assault with intent to murder (Associated Press, 1996d: A2). One reason for the lengthy sentence was that the man *knew* that he had the AIDS virus and thus that his actions were potentially lethal for his eight-year-old victim.

Prescribing Appropriate Punishment for Criminal Conduct

Criminal law prescribes punishments for violations of the law. From time to time, there are revisions of punishments prescribed for various criminal offenses. States differ about the definitions of crimes as well as about how those crimes should be punished. One state may recognize the offense of third-degree burglary, whereas another state may not. The punishment for simple breaking and entering varies among states from ten years to probation. The seriousness of the offense and the suspect's previous record are considered in determining punishment.

In an Illinois case, a murderer and his accomplice received widely different sentences. Together they had abducted and murdered a victim. At trial, one of the accomplices testified for the government and received a sentence of forty years. The other defendant was sentenced to death. The Supreme Court held that this disparity did not violate either accomplices' rights under the Eighth Amendment (*People v. Flores*, 1992). It is a well-documented fact that when judges sentence offenders, they consider factors such as the gravity of the offense, the harshness of the penalty, and sentences imposed on offenders in the same and other jurisdictions.

Sentences are considered "excessive" if they are grossly disproportionate to the severity of the crime. But individual states are not required to review intercase proportionality to determine whether particular sentences are more or less excessive among cases with similar factual circumstances (*People v. Danielson*, 1992; *People v. Fierro*, 1991; *People v. Mincey*, 1992). But decisions about the excessiveness of punishment are subjective and depend on court discretion (*State v. Davis*, 1994).

The American Bar Association, the American Law Institute, and several states have created uniformity in their penal sanctions for all major criminal offenses. However, these efforts have not been adopted on a national scale. One attempt to introduce uniformity and systematization is the American Law Institute's Model Penal Code and its subsequent revisions (American Law Institute, 1962). The penal code outlines types of offenses and prescribes uniform punishments for each. Fines are suggested for first, second, and third degree felonies of $10,000 and $5,000, respectively. A $1,000 fine is prescribed for a petty misdemeanor violation.

Elements of a Crime: *Mens Rea* and *Actus Reus*

A **crime** *is a violation of the criminal law by anyone held accountable by that law.* Simply committing an act defined as criminal is insufficient—there must also be the intent to commit that act. Criminal intent is known as *mens rea*. The criminal act is the *actus reus*. Combining these two elements, the *actus reus* and the *mens rea*, may result in criminal penalty (Shute, Gardner, and Horder, 1993). Some experts have observed that it is difficult to apply the principle of *mens rea* and *actus reus* to environmental crime and corporate deviance, although often criminal penalties are exacted against specific *persons* in organizations found guilty of such crimes (Ridley and Dunsford, 1994; Thornburgh, 1991).

In a California case, Lawrence Robinson was arrested and charged with the willful and unlawful use of narcotics (*Robinson v. California*, 1962). A California statute said that it was a criminal offense for a person to be "addicted to the use of narcotics." Under this statute, Robinson was convicted and sentenced to jail. Robinson's attorney argued that Robinson had not committed a crime but rather was being punished for a disease. The Supreme Court agreed and reversed his conviction.

The Court said that "it is unlikely that any State at this moment in history would attempt to make it a criminal offense for a person to be mentally ill, or a leper, or to be afflicted with a venereal disease. . . . Even one day in prison would be a cruel and unusual punishment for the 'crime' of having a common cold." In this case, narcotic addiction was a status or condition, not an "act" in the traditional sense. Without an *actus reus* or a criminal and overt act, there is no crime. Obviously, merely *thinking* about committing a crime is not a crime.

It is difficult for prosecutors to convict defendants who lack the requisite criminal intent (Acker and Lanier, 1993), such as when the defendant's sanity or ability to differentiate between right and wrong is at issue. Mental illness and diminished capacity are sometimes defenses for negating the *mens rea* or "guilty mind."

In an unfortunate 1969 Idaho case, a woman was charged with voluntary manslaughter after she picked up her three-month-old infant and threw her on the floor (*State v. White*, 1969). The defendant, Janet White, claimed that "my mind snapped, and I threw her [the baby] to the floor." Mrs. White then put her baby in the crib. The baby died a few hours later from massive head injuries. Subsequently, Mrs. White was tried on charges of voluntary manslaughter. She relied on the defense of insanity and was acquitted. The State of Idaho appealed the case, but the Supreme Court upheld the acquittal. In that instance, a jury had determined that Mrs. White lacked the *mens rea* that would justify a guilty verdict.

In recent years, several plea options have been proposed that relieve the state of the burden of proving defendants' sanity in criminal cases (Bumby, 1993; Steadman, McGreevy, and Morrissey, 1993). The American Psychiatric Association has proposed a "guilty but mentally ill" alternative to the "not guilty by reason of insanity" verdict (Slovenko, 1995). Some states, such as Georgia, accept this verdict (Callahan, McGreevy, and Cirincione, 1992).

Defenses for Criminal Conduct

What are some defenses for a person's alleged criminal conduct? Besides insanity, a partial list of other defenses includes (1) self-defense, (2) protection of property, (3) duress, (4) ignorance or mistake, and (5) intoxication.

Self-Defense

The successful claim of **self-defense** in criminal proceedings must show that *defendants had the reasonable belief that they were in grave danger of death or great bodily injury and that the action taken to repel the aggressor was absolutely necessary* (Cascardi and Vivian, 1995). Historians have examined self-defense in the context of a "duty to retreat." That is, when one is confronted or threatened, one should attempt to get away before resorting to violent defense. However, in 1921 the Supreme Court sanctioned a "*no* duty to retreat" concept, thereby condoning a violent defense in many cases. Some of the violence in American society has been attributed to this concept (Brown, 1994).

In a 1975 Massachusetts case, a woman was convicted of homicide in the shooting death of her estranged husband (*Commonwealth v. Shaffer*, 1975). On the morning of the homicide, her husband came to her home and threatened her. The defendant ran downstairs to her basement and picked up a .22 caliber rifle. She began to telephone the police but hesitated. Five minutes later, her husband came down the stairs. She fired the rifle, mortally wounding him. The Massachusetts Supreme Court upheld her conviction, saying that she had the means to escape—a basement door— but did not do so. Because of the *totality of circumstances*, the court decided that she was *not* in grave peril. Therefore, they concluded that the killing was not justified by self-defense.

In a Missouri case, a man pleaded self-defense in a stabbing death but was convicted of second-degree murder (*State v. Mayberry*, 1950). In this case, Mr. Mayberry was chased around his own home by Charles Talley, the ex-husband of his present wife. Mayberry ran from one room to another, seeking an exit. Finally, he was cornered and pulled a knife to defend himself. In the final confrontation, he stabbed Talley. The trial court convicted him of murder, but the Missouri Supreme Court reversed the conviction on the grounds of self-

defense. While they did not absolve him from all blame, they said that the "defendant in good faith sought to withdraw from the encounter" and that the original charge should be reduced.

In noncapital cases, self-defense might excuse someone from criminal liability if that person fights to avoid personal bodily injury. A court would probably not convict defendants of assault if it could be shown they were acting only to protect themselves from bodily harm.

Gayle Boone pleaded self-defense in shooting and killing the man she claimed had terrorized her for more than a year and then invaded her house and threatened her with a knife. Nevertheless, she was convicted of first-degree murder. Shown here at Renz Correctional Facility in Jefferson City, Missouri, six years after the incident in early 1997, Boone, age thirty-three, tells a reporter she has asked the governor for clemency. Seven hundred people—half the adults in her hometown—signed a petition on her behalf.

CRIMINAL JUSTICE IN THE UNITED STATES

Defense of Property

Sometimes the claim of *defense of property* is sufficient to free a defendant of criminal liability. If someone damages another's automobile or home, it is proper for the automobile or home owners to defend their property by any force necessary, short of taking the life of the aggressor. Killing someone else to prevent property damage is *never* justified (*Tennessee v. Garner*, 1985).

A Washington case (*State v. Marfaudille*, 1907) illustrates the improper use of lethal force in the protection of personal property. Marfaudille rigged a gun to discharge inside a trunk that stored his personal possessions. The landlady entered his apartment and opened the trunk. The gun inside the trunk discharged and killed the landlady. Marfaudille was convicted of second-degree murder. The Washington Supreme Court upheld his conviction on the grounds that "[Marfaudille] had no greater right to take the life of the deceased by indirect means than he would have had to take it by direct means under the same circumstances if personally present."

Duress

Duress *is a defense for criminal conduct under circumstances of coercion.* If people are overpowered and coerced or constrained to perform a particular criminal act against their will, duress is a defense for the criminal conduct (Corrado, 1994). As the Model Penal Code states, duress excuses criminal conduct when a person "was coerced to do [a criminal act] by the use of, or a threat to use, unlawful force against his person or the person of another, which a person of reasonable firmness in his situation would have been unable to resist."

In a 1974 California case, two women escaped from the California Rehabilitation Center (*California v. Lovercamp*, 1974). They were later captured and convicted of felonious escape. They appealed the conviction, arguing that they were placed in a hazardous situation involving fifteen lesbian inmates who had threatened them with great bodily harm unless they submitted to sexual advances. They fought with some of the women

and were further threatened that the group would "see them again." Therefore, believing their lives were in danger, they fled the prison. The California Court of Appeals accepted the duress defense in that situation. While this action did not necessarily excuse all acts of escape from California penal facilities by inmates who believed their lives were in danger, the court said that "the prisoners were faced with a specific threat of forcible sexual attack in the immediate future." The court also noted a legal principle applied in seventeenth-century England that held that "some conditions excuseth the felony." Subsequently, courts have increasingly allowed juries to consider whether, in light of all the circumstances, the crime of escape was justified because no reasonable alternative was available at the time (Jeffries, 1979).

Ignorance or Mistake

The old adage "ignorance is no excuse" is frequently flung at defendants who claim ignorance of the law. Sometimes **ignorance of the law** *does* excuse criminal conduct. The defense of *deliberate ignorance* is sometimes offered to negate the *mens rea* requirement for criminal conduct. Thus, some defendants may escape conviction by deliberately maintaining ignorance despite indications of their involvement in criminal activity (Robbins, 1990; *United States v. Jewell*, 1976).

In *Morrissette v. United States* (1952), Morrissette was hunting deer one afternoon on a government practice bombing range in Michigan, although there were signs stating "Danger—Keep Out—Bombing Range." While hunting, he came across a number of spent copper shell casings that appeared to be discarded. Morrisette took some of the casings to sell them. He was arrested and charged with stealing government property. He was convicted, given a sentence of two months, and fined $200. The Supreme Court reversed Morrissette's conviction, holding that Morrissette had no intention of committing a crime, that he did not know that what he was doing was unlawful, and that through his good character and openness in the taking of the casings he demonstrated that his action was not deliberately criminal.

Sometimes persons may *think* they are permitted to engage in particular kinds of conduct when in fact the conduct is criminal. Cases like this involving **mistake of fact** sometimes involve people of other cultures. For example, in some cultures, genital mutilation is a common practice, especially on females undergoing puberty. U.S. laws ordinarily prohibit such mutilation. When people belonging to cultures that condone such behavior are arrested for engaging in genital mutilation, they may claim either ignorance of the law or mistake of fact (Sams, 1986). Mistake of fact is often used as a defense against charges of income tax evasion. The Internal Revenue Service may charge certain taxpayers with deliberately failing to declare particular types of income, while the taxpayers may believe that the unreported income is exempt from taxation. Many of these tax cases have civil solutions rather than criminal ones, because taxpayers can legitimately claim ignorance of the law or mistake of fact when completing their increasingly complex tax returns.

Intoxication

The position of the American Law Institute and the Model Penal Code concerning **intoxication** as an excuse for criminal behavior is that it should not be used *unless it negates an element of that offense* (Melroy, 1992). For instance, in order for defendants to be convicted of first-degree murder, they must murder with *premeditation*. Often, intoxication might be used effectively as a mitigating factor to lessen the severity of one's punishment (Felker, 1990; Mitchell, 1990).

In a 1983 Tennessee case, Wayne Adkins was convicted of first-degree murder in the shooting death of Junior Adams (*State v. Adkins*, 1983). Evidence submitted by the defendant showed that on the day of the shooting, he had drunk large quantities of beer. In fact, witnesses testified that Adkins had consumed at least twenty-four cans of beer before the shooting incident. The victim of the shooting, Adams, had been a witness to an earlier shooting incident in which Adkins shot a girlfriend in the stomach. It was common knowledge that Adams planned to testify against Adkins in a future

trial. Coupled with Adkins's intoxicated state, these facts led to an argument between Adkins and Adams that resulted in Adams's murder. The Supreme Court affirmed Adkins's conviction for murder, but it reversed the death penalty, holding that "[Adkins's] drunkenness may be considered in determining whether he specifically intended [premeditated] the particular act for which he is on trial."

Other Defenses

Necessity

There are several other defenses that defendants may use when charged with crimes. Defendants might act out of **necessity** to save someone else (Lippman, 1990). If a home is on fire and the owners are out of town, a neighbor may "break and enter" in order to put out the blaze and save the home from certain destruction. A charge of burglary would not be upheld because the neighbor acted "out of necessity" (Corrado, 1994).

Entrapment

Sometimes people are entrapped into committing a crime (Camp, 1993). *Entrapment is the act of law enforcement officers inducing a people to commit crimes not contemplated by them* (del Carmen, 1995). In a California case, John DeLorean was acquitted of cocaine charges in federal court when it was shown that he was induced to participate in a cocaine sale by undercover FBI agents who offered him a large sum of money. This was considered entrapment. DeLorean had no history of cocaine dealing and was not known for any involvement in the "drug community." Therefore, he had been induced to do something that he was not ordinarily disposed to do and that he had not contemplated doing. A landmark case involving the entrapment defense is *Jacobson v. United States* (1992).

Alibi

If a suspect can prove that he or she was not in the vicinity of a crime when it occurred, the suspect has an **alibi**. Usually the police interview friends and acquaintances of suspects or others familiar with their whereabouts at the time of the crime. If

---

Highlight 3.6. Entrapment: The Case of *Jacobson v. United States* (1992)

In early 1984, Jacobson ordered several books from an adult bookstore. The books contained pictures of nude young boys. Ordering such books was not illegal at the time, because the Child Protection Act of 1984 had not been passed. After the passage of this act, U.S. Postal Inspectors found Jacobson's name on the mailing list of an adult bookstore and commenced to send him fictitious catalogues and other materials. Jacobson responded to many of these solicitations over the next *three years*. All of this activity was generated by U.S. Postal Inspectors as well as the U.S. Customs Office, because some of the materials were sent from other countries. Finally, in May 1987, U.S. Postal Inspectors sent Jacobson a catalogue offering photos of young boys in sexually explicit poses. Jacobson ordered a magazine from the catalogue. When it was delivered by the U.S. Postal Inspector, Jacobson was arrested for receiving child pornography through the mail. He was convicted and appealed, arguing entrapment. The Supreme Court overturned his conviction, saying that the government may not originate a criminal design, implant in an innocent person's mind the disposition to commit the criminal act, and then induce commission of the crime so that the government can prosecute.

Source: Jacobson v. United States, 503 U.S. 540, 112 S.Ct. 1535 (1992).

---

it is reasonably determined that suspects were not in the vicinity and could not possibly have committed the crime, the alibi will be a strong defense against prosecution (Connelly, 1983).

These are some of the common defenses used in criminal actions to explain and justify otherwise criminal conduct. These defenses are not always successful, but they are considered by juries or the court for their mitigating value. Judges and juries may not punish offenders as harshly if they believe plausible circumstances contributed to the crime.

Criminal Law Reforms and Decriminalization

An examination of federal and state criminal laws and statutes reveals the legal equivalent of culture lag: criminal laws do not keep pace with an ever-changing society. Some states still have statutes prohibiting cattle rustling. Of course, in some farming areas, cattle rustling still occurs and is considered a serious crime. But such laws are irrelevant in large urban areas. Federal criminal laws continue to prohibit selling alcoholic beverages to Indians on their reservations and committing piracy on the high seas.

Further, the punishment for certain law violations is sometimes disproportionate to the offense. For instance, 18 U.S. Code, Section 1154 (1996) provides that anyone who sells beer or wine to any Indian on any government land shall be fined $500 and sentenced to one year in prison. Subsequent offenses are punishable by a fine of $2,000 and imprisonment for up to five years. The most recent case cited by the U.S. Code concerning a criminal violation on Indian land involving intoxicating beverages took place in 1943! There is also little uniformity in criminal laws and prescribed punishments among states. In thirty-four state jurisdictions, public drunkenness is not a criminal act, whereas other states include it in one or more of their criminal statutes (Mitchell, 1990; Tiffany and Tiffany, 1990).

That criminal laws and their accompanying statutory punishments need to be revised and standardized is evident from judicial sentencing practices. There is considerable variation among judges in sentencing criminal offenders and setting bail

(Myers and Reid, 1995). In most jurisdictions, about 90 percent of the criminal offenders avoid jail or prison sentences and are placed on probation. These arrangements are usually negotiated through *plea bargaining, an arrangement where defendants plead guilty to one or more charges and have their sentences reduced.*

With more offenders avoiding prison or jail and a growing number of probationers, questions arise about the reality of punishments for criminal offenses. One trend in sentencing practices is **creative sentencing** (Czajkoski and Wollan, 1986). *Creative sentencing applies to a broad class of punishments that are alternatives to incarceration and that are designed to fit the particular crime.* Sometimes, a creative sentence means compensating victims for their losses and injuries or doing "good works." Florida uses activities such as "aiding the handicapped" and using rehabilitation or counseling services as alternatives to incarceration (Gitchoff and Rush, 1989).

Some people say that creative sentencing encourages judicial abuse of their sentencing discretion (Czajkoski and Wollan, 1986:228). In one situation, a judge had before him a woman convicted of a marijuana offense. The judge noted that the woman was receiving considerable public assistance and had several children out of wedlock. He placed her on probation for the marijuana offense, but as a part of her probationary requirements, she was forced to undergo sterilization. Analysts observed that "the sterilization could not be justified, however, as relating to her marijuana offense or to her personal rehabilitation, and so the judge must have had in mind some benefit to the community by reducing the number of illegitimate children and welfare recipients" (Czajkoski and Wollan, 1986:228).

Decriminalization has also played a part in criminal law reform. *Decriminalization is the elimination of certain acts from the body of criminal laws or the removal or lessening of sanctions applied to particular criminal conduct.* One example is the decriminalization of public drunkenness in various states (Weisheit and Johnson, 1992). Punishments for some offenses such as prostitution and minor drug violations have also been considered for removal or modification (McCaghy and Cernkovich, 1991).

Decriminalization is quite controversial (Mac-Coun, Kahan, and Gillespie, 1993). Critics are skeptical about the effectiveness of decriminalizing such acts as the use and possession of marijuana, believing that it will lead to substantial increases in the consumption of potentially harmful substances. However, an historical investigation into the decriminalization of marijuana use and possession in eleven states during the early 1990s revealed only small increases in marijuana use when the threat of incarceration was removed (DiCharia and Galliher, 1994).

Summary

Criminal laws have been developed as a means of protecting society from the harmful acts of others. Criminal laws define criminal conduct and prescribe appropriate punishments. Criminal laws change as society changes. Criminal laws and sanctions are applied in the context of certain Constitutional guarantees. The Bill of Rights makes several guarantees that must be observed by the criminal justice system. These guarantees are designed to ensure due process. Defendants are guaranteed the right to a trial by jury in any major criminal action and the right to privacy. They have the right to a speedy trial, to the benefit of counsel, and to confront their accusers in court. They are protected against self-incrimination as well as against unreasonable searches and seizures of person and property.

The basic elements of a crime include the *mens rea*, or the guilty mind or guilty intent, and the *actus reus*, the criminal act itself. All citizens are presumed innocent until their conduct is judged impartially in court. Certain defenses may explain and excuse criminal conduct at particular times and under particular circumstances. A person may be intoxicated or mentally ill. A person may engage in criminal conduct while under duress or while acting in self-defense or to protect others.

As society changes, certain laws become outmoded and less useful. These are eventually eliminated or revised. At the same time, new laws are created to fit newly acquired societal needs and interests. Among the problems confronting the criminal justice system are sentencing disparities among jurisdictions and decriminalization issues. Legal reforms attempt to resolve these disparities and issues.

Key Terms

Alibi
Complaint
Creative sentencing
Crime
Cruel and unusual punishment
Decriminalization
Duress
Excessive bail
Ignorance of the law
Intoxication
Law of tradition and precedent
Mistake of fact
Necessity
Rules of criminal procedure
Search and seizure
Self-defense
Speedy trial

Questions for Review

1. Which of the amendments to the Constitution covered in this chapter pertain to due process? What is due process, and what importance does it have for alleged offenders entering the criminal justice system?
2. Who is entitled to bail under the Bill of Rights? Under what circumstances might a person not be considered for bail?
3. What are the primary functions of criminal law? What is decriminalization, and how is it related to criminal laws specifically?

4. Does a person have to testify against himself or herself in court? Why or why not? What constitutional provisions are relevant here?
5. Under the Fourteenth Amendment, is it lawful for a state to enact a law that is different from and contrary to a federal law? Why or why not?
6. What is meant by an "unreasonable" search and seizure? Is evidence obtained by an unreasonable search and seizure necessarily excluded from court? Why or why not?
7. Some people think that the Second Amendment gives them the right to carry a lethal weapon such as a firearm anytime they want. What does the Second Amendment provide in this regard?
8. What is meant by "probable cause"? Which of the amendments discussed in this chapter include probable cause as an integral feature?
9. Identify and discuss two important cases having to do with ineffective assistance of counsel.
10. What is the difference between the "investigatory phase" and the "critical or accusatory phase" of crime investigation?

Suggested Readings

James A. Holstein. *Court-Ordered Insanity: Interpretive Practice and Involuntary Commitment.* Hawthorne, NY: Aldine de Gruyter, 1993.

Kappeler, Victor E., Mark Blumberg and Gary W. Potter. *The Mythology of Crime and Criminal Justice.* 2d ed. Prospect Heights, IL: Waveland, 1996.

Mays, G. Larry and Peter R. Gregware. *Courts and Justice: A Reader.* Prospect Heights, IL: Waveland, 1996.

Rutledge, Devallis. *Search and Seizure Handbook.* 5th ed. Placerville, CA: Copperhouse, 1995.

CHAPTER 4

Law Enforcement: Forms, Functions, and History

In 1990 a speeding motorist named Rodney King led police officers on a lengthy chase through Los Angeles streets. After stopping King, more than twenty officers surrounded him, beating him with nightsticks and shooting him several times with a stun gun before "subduing" him. An attentive apartment dweller who lived across from the scene recorded several minutes of the incident on videotape, particularly the portion where officers beat King with their sticks. Subsequently, two trials were held that alleged assorted violations of King's rights as a citizen and certain criminal claims. A California state jury acquitted three out of four officers charged with criminally assaulting King. A federal court tried the officers on a different set of criminal charges stemming from the same incident. Two of the officers, Stacy Koon and Laurence Powell, were found guilty. In the meantime, King sued the City of Los Angeles for injuries he sustained when arrested.

The Rodney King case is an example of *overlapping jurisdictions*. In that case, the overlapping jurisdictions were the State of California and the U.S. government. King was assaulted by officers of the Los Angeles Police Department. Citizens of California are protected not only by California law but also by federal law. Therefore, the incident of police officers, under cover of their authority, inflicting great bodily harm upon a U.S. citizen made the case a federal one also and exposed the police officers accused of King's beating to the weight of federal criminal laws.

Many people still don't understand why these police officers were tried twice, seemingly for the same offense. They regard the treatment of these officers as *double jeopardy* and believe that what happened to them in federal court is unconstitutional. We know, of course, that this is not the case and that the officers were actually prosecuted under different sets of criminal laws in two separate jurisdictions. Trying the officers again in a California court on the same charges of which they were acquitted earlier would indeed have been a case of double jeopardy. But federal violations were alleged following the state proceedings, and a federal jury found the officers guilty.

This chapter seeks to distinguish between federal, state, and local law enforcement jurisdictions and to identify and examine several general classes of law enforcement agencies at these different levels, including their major functions and operations. One troublesome feature of these agencies is that their overlapping jurisdiction in many criminal matters fosters competitiveness, which sometimes lessens agency effectiveness.

As law enforcement agencies expand their services and functions, questions may arise about their goals and purposes and how these are fulfilled. This chapter gives an overview of some of the major issues and problems confronting law enforcement agencies. These issues will be examined in greater detail in later chapters.

This chapter also examines the history and role of police in society, including how police departments are organized and administered, how police officers are selected and trained, and how police professionalism is measured. Various sources of stress are highlighted, and means of coping with stress are investigated. Because attempts have been made to profile the personalities of police officers, a brief discussion of police personality and police subculture will be presented.

State and Federal Law Enforcement Agencies and Organizations

By 1993, there were 17,358 police and sheriff's departments in the United States, including 12,502 general-purpose local police departments, 3,086 sheriffs' departments, and 1,721 special police agencies (Reaves, 1993:1). These agencies employed over 604,000 full-time sworn officers with general arrest powers and 237,000 nonsworn civilian personnel (Reaves, 1993:1). Combined local, state, and federal public law enforcement expenditures were estimated at between $65 billion and $75 billion annually, with a total of approximately 1.6 million sworn and nonsworn law enforcement personnel (El Nasser, 1993:9A; Lindgren, 1992). According to Hallcrest Systems, Inc., in the private sector in 1993, over 4,000 private police and security agencies employed an additional 1.6 million officers and other personnel with a budget of $64

billion (El Nasser, 1993:9A). Thus, about $140 billion is spent annually on both public and private law enforcement and security.

Considering the number of law enforcement personnel in the public sector, it is ironic that 70 to 90 percent of their time is spent performing activities only incidentally related to law enforcement per se (Bohm, 1986). The bulk of their activities includes traffic control, public service, social services, crowd control, supervision of licensed establishments, settling of citizens' disputes, emergency health care, and ceremonial functions. It is a myth that these persons are primarily crime fighters (Bohm, 1986).

At the federal level, several government departments and bureaus oversee a number of law enforcement agencies. By January 1994, federal law enforcement agencies employed about sixty-nine thousand full-time personnel authorized to make arrests and carry firearms (Reaves, 1994:1). Three major federal organizations are discussed here. Each includes several agencies with specific powers and law enforcement responsibilities. They are the Department of Justice, the Department of the Treasury, and the Central Intelligence Agency. Table 4.1 lists specific agencies within each of these organizations, together with their personnel and major states of employment.

The Department of Justice

The **Department of Justice** is headed by the attorney general, who is appointed by the president with Senate approval. The president also appoints the attorney generals' assistants as well as U.S. attorneys for each of the judicial districts. These may appoint committees to investigate other governmental agencies or offices where questions of wrongdoing are raised or where possible violations of the laws of the United States are suspected or detected. Figure 4.1 shows the organization of the Department of Justice. Of particular interest are the Federal Bureau of Investigation, the Drug Enforcement Administration, the Immigration and Naturalization Service, and the U.S. Marshals Service. These organizations are most directly involved in enforcing criminal laws.

Table 4.1

Federal Agencies Employing 500 or More Full-Time Officers with Authority to Carry Firearms and Make Arrests, by Function and Major States of Employment, December 1993

Agency	Total	Police response and patrol	Criminal investigation and enforcement	Other	Major States of employment
U.S. Customs Service	10,120	43	10,077	0	Texas (1,764), California (1,581), New York (1,249), Florida (1,174), Arizona (434), New Jersey (421)
Federal Bureau of Investigation	10,075	0	10,000	75	District of Columbia (1,356), New York (1,206), California (1,191), Texas (743), Florida (549), Illinois (448), Pennsylvania (393), Virginia (368)
Federal Bureau of Prisons	9,984	0	0	9,984	Pennsylvania (1,161), California (949), Texas (919), New York (626), Florida (608), Georgia (538), Colorado (472), Kentucky (467)
Immigration and Naturalization Service	9,466	3,920*	4,457	1,089	Texas (2,547), California (2,352), New York (846), Arizona (651), Florida (514)
Administrative Office of the U.S. Courts	3,763	0	0	3,763	Texas (366), California (360), Florida (295), New York (270), Georgia (212), Illinois (144)
Internal Revenue Service	3,621	0	3,621	0	California (407), New York (371), Texas (307), Florida (215), Illinois (214), Pennsylvania (176), District of Columbia (149), Ohio (144)
U.S. Postal Inspection Service	3,587	0	2,129	1,458	New York (580), California (492), Illinois (285), District of Columbia, (254), Pennsylvania (253), New Jersey (196), Texas (163), Florida (150)
Drug Enforcement Administration	2,813	0	2,813	0	California (458), Florida (375), New York (362), Texas (340), Illinois (114)
U.S. Secret Service	2,186	0	1,594	592	District of Columbia (1,063), New York (166), California (155), Texas (123), Florida (105)
National Park Service	2,160	439	1,563	158	
Ranger Activities Division	1,500	0	1,500	0	Not available
U.S. Park Police	660	439	63	158	District of Columbia (423), New York (64), Maryland (63), California (55), Virginia (32)
U.S. Marshals Service	2,153	0	0	2,153	California (194), District of Columbia (165), New York (154), Florida (145), Texas (128)
Bureau of Alcohol, Tobacco and Firearms	1,959	0	1,832	127	California (182), District of Columbia (151), Texas (151), Illinois (129), New York (128), Florida (126), Michigan (97), Georgia (84)
U.S. Capitol Police	1,080	122	41	917	District of Columbia (1,080)
Tennessee Valley Authority	740	357	0	383	Tennessee (456), Alabama (250)
U.S. Forest Service	732	527	205	0	California (191), Oregon (73), Arizona (39), Idaho (34), Montana (34), Colorado (32)
General Services Administration— Federal Protective Services	732	505	66	161	District of Columbia (200), California (79), Texas (55), New York (52), Missouri (51), Massachusetts (37), Illinois (30)
U.S. Fish and Wildlife Service	620	397	223	0	Alaska (45), Texas (44), North Dakota (35), Arizona (25), Oklahoma (25), Montana (24)

Source: Reeves (1994), p. 2.

Note: State of employment was unavailable for 70 U.S. Marshals providing federal court security.

*Border Patrol agents

Figure 4.1 The Department of Justice

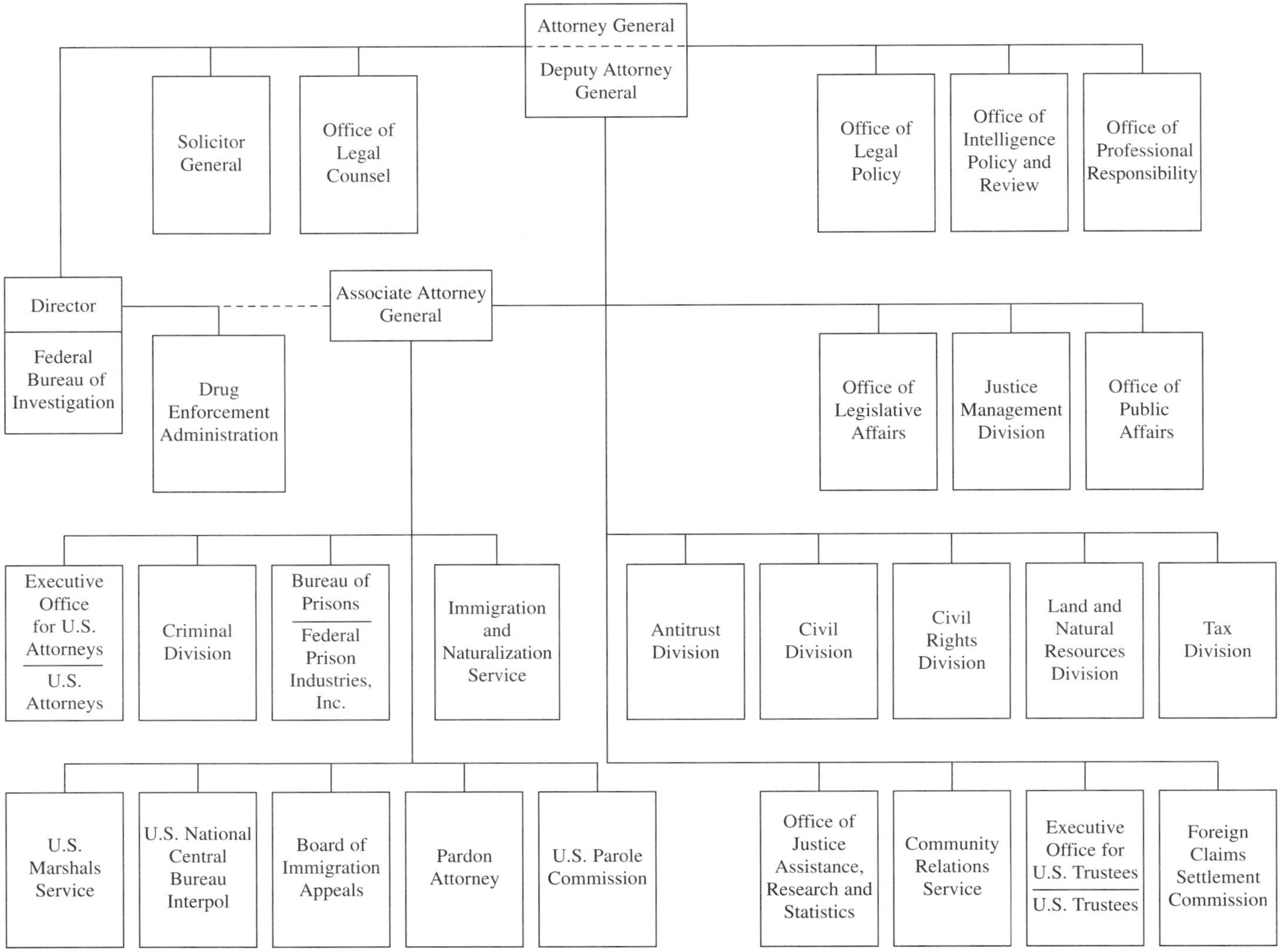

Source: Adapted from the United States Code (1989).

The Federal Bureau of Investigation (FBI)

The **Federal Bureau of Investigation (FBI)** was created and funded through the Department of Justice Appropriation Act of May 22, 1908 (U.S. Code Annotated, 1996). It was originally known as the Bureau of Investigation. It had no specific duties or responsibilities other than the broad charge of the Appropriation Act, which made funds available to the Department of Justice "for the prosecution of crimes." Since the Department of Justice was established to enforce the laws of the United States, the Bureau of Investigation assumed the general responsibility of enforcing these laws, especially the criminal statutes.

In 1933, all of the Bureau's functions, including those of the old Bureau of Prohibition, were consolidated and transferred to the Division of Investigation, which was headed by a director of investigation. Finally, the Division of Investigation became the Federal Bureau of Investigation by the act of March 22, 1935, Chapter 39, Title II, U.S. Code (1996).

The FBI investigates cases involving at least two hundred federal criminal statutes covering civil matters and intelligence cases of national security. It also cooperates with other federal, state, county, and local authorities in cases of mutual interest, assisting them with information or laboratory services. The FBI also provides extensive professional training to all interested law enforcement officers (Torres, 1985:135–136). In 1993, there were 10,075 FBI agents with various law enforcement duties (Reaves, 1994:2).

The FBI is one of the more colorful law enforcement organizations and has captured the attention of the media in past years. During Prohibition, the FBI was instrumental in bringing to justice several infamous criminals, such as George "Machine Gun" Kelly in 1933, John Dillinger in 1934, and Charles "Pretty Boy" Floyd that same year. More recently the FBI has investigated the murder of Congressman Leo J. Ryan at Bob Jones's People's Temple in Jonestown, Guyana, in November 1978, the murder of U.S. District Court Judge John H. Wood of San Antonio, Texas, in May 1979, and public corruption in

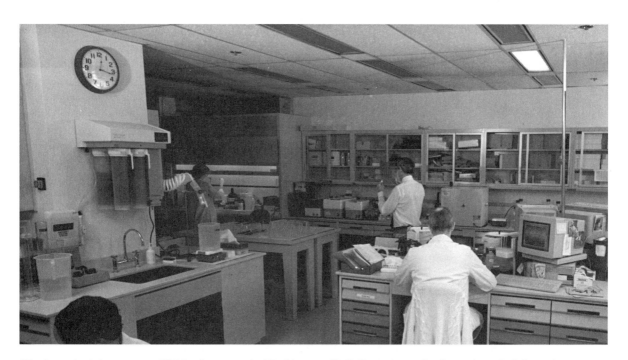

The forensics laboratory at FBI headquarters in Washington, D.C. Preeminent in the nation, the lab conducts examinations not only for its own investigations but also for other law enforcement agencies.

the ABSCAM operation in the early 1980s, which led to the conviction of several congressmen and state government leaders (Torres, 1985:136).

The FBI does not have an untarnished reputation, however. In 1986, the federal racketeering trial of John DeLorean, a former car maker, disclosed evidence of FBI misdeeds, including perjured testimony and the concoction of incriminating evidence intended to make De-Lorean appear guilty. DeLorean was acquitted of all criminal charges, and numerous instances of FBI misconduct were disclosed in posttrial interviews.

Furthermore, in August 1992, numerous FBI agents, together with a contingent of U.S. marshals, used deadly force against Randy Weaver, a white supremacist, and his wife and family. Weaver was wanted on a minor firearms charge and in various public speeches had also advocated the overthrow of the U.S. government. The incident occurred at Ruby Ridge in the Idaho mountains. Following an eighteen-month surveillance of Weaver's movements, FBI agents and others decided to arrest Weaver at his mountain home. They knew Weaver was armed and likely to resist. Nevertheless, they stormed the home, firing their weapons into the dwelling. When Weaver was finally subdued, FBI agents discovered that they had shot and killed Weaver's wife and son. The media seized this incident to illustrate that some federal agencies, such as the FBI and U.S. Marshals Service, were capable of entrapment, cover-ups, and the killing of innocent people (Bock, 1995).

More favorably, FBI assistance to other law enforcement agencies is unsurpassed. In 1996, the FBI had over 200 million fingerprints on file, of which about 85 million belonged to criminals. The Identification Division of the FBI has helped many state and local police departments identify not only criminal suspects but also missing persons and accident victims. The FBI also maintains the Instrumental Analysis Unit, where samples of various substances are stored. This unit can examine and identify almost any type of material evidence. In 1996, it conducted over 1 million scientific examinations of physical evidence for various agencies.

The Criminal Investigation Division of the FBI is most directly involved in combating criminal activity. In 1993, for instance, special agents of the FBI spent about 25 percent of their time on organized crime investigations, leading to the conviction of over one thousand individuals. The FBI also convicted about five thousand white-collar criminals during that time (Reaves, 1994).

The Drug Enforcement Administration (DEA)

The **Drug Enforcement Administration (DEA)** is an outgrowth of the former Bureau of Narcotics, established in 1930 under the direct control of the Treasury Department. In 1968, the Bureau of Narcotics was placed under the authority of the Department of Justice and renamed the Bureau of Narcotics and Dangerous Drugs. This transfer occurred partly because of a scandal involving Bureau of Narcotics special agents who were accused of selling confiscated drugs (Torres, 1987: 126–127).

In 1973, the DEA was established under a general reorganization plan that combined the functions of several agencies. In January 1982, the DEA was given primary responsibility for enforcing drug and narcotics laws. It presently shares concurrent jurisdiction with the FBI in this regard (Torres, 1985:126). The major responsibilities of the DEA include (1) developing overall federal drug-law enforcement strategy, programs, planning, and evaluation; (2) investigating and preparing for prosecution those suspected of violating federal drug-trafficking laws; (3) investigating and preparing for prosecution suspects connected with illicit drugs seized at U.S. ports of entry and international borders; (4) conducting all negotiations with drug-law enforcement officials of foreign governments; (5) cooperating with state and local law enforcement officials on joint drug-law enforcement efforts; and (6) regulating the legal manufacture of drugs and other controlled substances (29 U.S.C., Sec. 509, 1996).

In 1993, the DEA employed over twenty-eight hundred persons, most of them special agents authorized to carry firearms, make arrests, and seize property when violations of federal drug laws occur. Drug busts and arrests by the DEA are numerous—twenty-two thousand in 1990 alone. These investigations and arrests usually involve *interstate* and *international* trafficking in narcotics and other controlled substances. However, the DEA observes that *most* drug enforcement activity is the responsibility of state and local jurisdictions, where 1.1 million drug-related arrests were made in 1990 (Bureau of Justice Assistance, 1992:76–77). Most of these arrests involved drug possession, sales, and trafficking intrastate.

The Immigration and Naturalization Service (INS)

Congress was originally authorized to establish a naturalization service under Article I, Section 8 of the Constitution (Torres, 1985:178). In 1798, the Alien and Sedition Act was passed, which gave the president the power to expel aliens who were considered threats to the security of the United States. The Office of Commissioner of Immigration under the Department of State was created in 1864, and in 1898 the Bureau of Immigration was established.

In 1903, this bureau was placed under the control of the Department of Commerce. By 1913, it was divided into the Department of Labor and the Bureau of Naturalization and placed under the control of the Department of Labor. These two bureaus were combined into the **Immigration and Naturalization Service (INS)**. In 1940, the INS was transferred to the Department of Justice.

Perhaps the best-known agency of the INS is the *Border Patrol* (*BP*), which in 1924, the year it was established, consisted of 450 officers (Torres, 1985:178). The original purpose of the BP was to police U.S. borders between Canada and Mexico. Under the McCarran-Walter Act of 1952, the INS was charged with three goals: (1) to reunite families; (2) to encourage the immigration of persons with needed labor skills; and (3) to protect the domestic labor force. The BP is most visible today in its fight against illegal entry into the United States (Clarke, 1993; U.S. General Accounting Office, 1995; U.S. Senate Committee on Governmental Affairs, 1995). In 1993, there were 9,466 officers with the INS; of these 3,920 were BP officers (Reaves, 1994:2).

The BP patrols over eight thousand miles of international boundaries. Under Title 8 U.S.C. (1996) INS agents have the power of arrest and of search and seizure. In 1982, the BP apprehended 819,919 aliens, many of whom were involved in illegal activities, including drug smuggling and theft. In 1982, 3,112 aliens were convicted of smuggling-related charges. Also in 1982, the INS apprehended 3,564 aliens on criminal, morals, and narcotics charges (Torres, 1985:182). The budget for the INS is over $500 million. Between 1991 and 1995, 1,200 sector agents monitored the 2,000-mile border between Mexico and the United States. During that period, the BP apprehended 1.9 million persons from ninety-four different countries and seized over 203,000 pounds of marijuana, 11,200 pounds of cocaine, and 15,500 vehicles that were forfeited through drug and illegal-immigrant smuggling operations (Nicely, 1995:8–9; U.S. General Accounting Office, 1995).

The United States Marshals Service (USMS)

The **United States Marshals Service (USMS)** is one of the oldest federal law enforcement agencies in existence (Torres, 1985: 360). The office of U.S. marshal was established under the Judiciary Act of 1789. George Washington appointed thirteen marshals, one for each of the original thirteen colonies. Wyatt Earp was one of the more famous U.S. marshals.

In 1969, the USMS was established; it formally became a bureau in 1974. In 1985, there were ninety-four judicial districts and ninety-three U.S. marshals, with at least one marshal per state. The budget for the USMS in 1984 was $117.7 million. In 1984, in addition to the U.S. marshals there were ninety-three chief deputy marshals, sixteen hundred deputy marshals, and over four hundred staff employees (Torres, 1985:363). By 1993, there were 2,153 U.S. marshals (Reaves, 1994:2).

Duties of U.S. marshals include executing warrants and orders issued by federal courts; conducting investigations of fugitives; arresting dangerous fugitives; providing security for federal courts and the judiciary; managing the Federal Witness Protection Program; managing the asset seizure and forfeiture program of the Department of Justice; suppressing riots on federal lands or in federal prisons; and escorting missile convoys (Reaves, 1994:3). An arm of the U.S. Marshals Service is the Fugitive Investigative Strike Team (FIST), which cooperates with local fugitive enforcement agencies to apprehend federal fugitives (Morris, 1985). Less glamorous work associated with U.S. marshals is the supervision of pretrial detainees. Between 1985 and 1993, for instance, the number of federal pretrial detainees under the supervision of U.S. marshals grew by 262 percent (Caudell-Feagan, 1993).

In an effort to enforce U.S. laws, the U.S. Marshals Service is sometimes drawn into situations that generate bad publicity. For instance, as we saw earlier, some U.S. marshals were involved in killing the wife and child of Randy Weaver, a white supremacist, in the "Ruby Ridge" incident (Bock, 1995). This incident received even more public scrutiny as the subject of a 1996 made-for-television movie.

An important function of the U.S. Marshals Service is the operation of the *Witness Protection Program*, in which federal witnesses are offered protection against reprisal that, depending upon the case (e.g., a conspiracy trial against a member of the Mafia or other organized crime figure), might extend to establishing complete changes of identity, including new names, Social Security numbers, residences, and employment for witnesses and their families. The Witness Protection Program was established in 1984 and within a year had afforded protection to nearly fifteen thousand individuals, including the successful relocation of 4,250 witnesses. By 1996, over twenty-five thousand persons were under the protection of this program.

Other Department of Justice Activities

The Department of Justice also has a Civil Rights Division, which is authorized to investigate allegations of civil rights violations. In 1982, the Civil Rights Division prosecuted fifty-six criminal actions against ninety-eight defendants accused of various discriminatory acts and other violations (Torres, 1985:31).

The attorney general is also empowered to conduct investigations of organized crime and racketeering under the amended Racketeer Influenced and Corrupt Organizations Act (RICO) of 1984 (Rebovich, 1995: *United States v. DiCaro*, 1985). In recent years, the American Bar Association has attempted to coordinate state and federal anti-racketeering efforts by developing some common goals and objectives for interested law enforcement agencies (Albanese, 1995; American Bar Association, 1985).

The Department of the Treasury

The **Department of the Treasury** controls many agencies that have law enforcement functions, including the Bureau of Alcohol, Tobacco, and Firearms, the United States Customs Service, the Internal Revenue Service, and the Secret Service.

The Bureau of Alcohol, Tobacco, and Firearms (BATF)

The **Bureau of Alcohol, Tobacco, and Firearms** was organized as a subunit within the Internal Revenue Service in 1862, when certain alcohol and tobacco tax statutes were created (Torres, 1985:63). It was originally called the Alcohol, Tobacco, Tax Unit and was later named the Alcohol, Tobacco, and Firearms Division. In 1972 it acquired its current name and was put under the direct control of the Department of the Treasury. The BATF's general mission in combating crime is to reduce the illegal use of firearms and explosives. In its further mission to curtail arson-for-profit schemes, its agents investigate scenes of fires of mysterious origins (Torres, 1985)

Like the FBI, the BATF has a fairly colorful history, which began in 1919, when Congress ratified the Sixteenth Amendment prohibiting the manufacture, sale, and/or importation of intoxicating liquors. For a twelve-year period, the underworld thrived on sales of bootlegged liquor and the operation of speakeasies or secret bars where the public could purchase illegal liquor. This era bolstered the fame of persons such as Elliot Ness, a BATF agent who chased bootleggers and organized gangsters who were profiting from illegal liquor sales. *The Untouchables*, a television program of the 1960s, was based upon Ness's exploits during the 1920s and 1930s.

The BATF has a budget of $300 million and employs 1,959 special agents (Reaves, 1994:2). Its law enforcement functions extend to areas such as arson investigation, high explosives including

One of the criminal enforcement activities of the BATF is suppressing illegal trafficking and possession of firearms.

bombs, and automatic weapons. It is illegal for a private citizen to possess an automatic weapon such as a submachine gun without official authorization from the Department of the Treasury and the purchase of an expensive tax stamp. Before granting authorization the BATF thoroughly investigates the character and background of the applicant. Unauthorized possession of an automatic weapon in any state is a felony.

The BATF also authorizes licenses for firearms dealers, importers and exporters, and ammunition manufacturers. Estimates are that over 223 million guns were available to the general public in 1994 (Zawitz, 1995:1). At least 80 percent of all guns in the United States are manufactured within the country (Zawitz, 1995:3). The BATF presently operates the *National Tracing Center*, which enables the BATF to trace firearms from their original point of sale (Zawitz, 1995:4). In 1994, there were 2 million reports of stolen guns, about 60 percent of which (1.26 million) were hand guns (Zawitz, 1995:3). The FBI's National Crime In-

formation Center (NCIC) also maintains a computerized file of stolen guns, including make, caliber, and serial number. Entries are maintained until the gun's recovery is reported.

The United States Customs Service (USCS)

The **United States Customs Service** was created under the Tariff Act of 1789 to collect duties on goods, wares, and merchandise (Torres, 1985:353). Under Title 19 of the U.S. Code (1996), the Customs Service is authorized to conduct searches and inspections of all ships, aircraft, and vehicles entering the United States. USCS agents may seize illegal merchandise or wares and arrest suspects engaging in illegal activities.

The USCS employs over ten thousand law enforcement personnel (Reaves, 1994:2). In 1995, USCS officers and agents seized large amounts of narcotics and made many arrests in the process. In 1991, the USCS spent $674 million, mainly in seizing illegal drugs as well as vessels, aircraft, vehicles, and money used in the drug trade (Bureau of

Highlight 4.1. Tracing an Illegal Gun: The Case of Rashid Baz

A van filled with Jewish Talmudic students was crossing the Brooklyn Bridge on the way to a religious event. Suddenly, the van was riddled by gunfire from a passing car. One student, Aaron Halberstam, sixteen, was killed in the attack, while a friend, eighteen-year-old Nochum Sasonkin, was critically wounded.

Subsequently arrested for these crimes were a twenty-eight-year-old Lebanese immigrant, Rashid Baz, a Jordanian named Bassam Mousa Reyati, and Hlal Mohammad. A 9mm Glock Model 17 pistol was one of two weapons used in the attack; the other was manufactured by the Mac Gun Company of Copperhill, Tennessee. The Mac gun was available for $189 in a kit, with some assembly required.

Police and the BATF traced the Glock 17 to Albert Jeanniton, twenty-eight, who bought the gun legally from Homestead Arms of Miami, Florida. The gun had been shipped to Homestead Arms from Glock, Inc., in Smyrna, Georgia, where it had previously been shipped from Austria as a Glock import.

Jeanniton purchased the weapon for $579.95 on October 30, 1991. Jeanniton owned a Miami car window-tinting firm, but police say that he trafficked in illegal firearms on the side. Police say that the gun was illegally shipped to New York City, where firearms are prohibited. "That's how 90 percent of them come into New York," said BATF agent John O'Brien. Jeanniton allegedly purchased at least 130 guns between September and December of 1992. He was subsequently convicted on federal drug charges by a Miami federal district court.

The pistol used to kill Aaron Halberstam "was one of those," said O'Brien, referring to one of the guns that Jeanniton had purchased and that eventually came into the possession of the killers.

Source: Adapted from Bruce Frankel, "New York Shooting Investigation Zeroes in on Gun," *USA Today,* March 9, 1994, p. 10A.

Justice Assistance, 1992:128). It seized almost 68,000 pounds of cocaine, 2.4 million pounds of marijuana (Bureau of Justice Assistance, 1992), and nearly ten thousand vehicles and two hundred aircraft that were used in illegal drug trafficking (Bureau of Justice Assistance, 1992).

The USCS works closely with other law enforcement agencies, particularly responsible for combating international drug trafficking and smuggling. The USCS interfaces with the National Crime Information Center, operated by the FBI, as well as with the DEA (Torres, 1985:356). Customs patrol officers enforce federal laws at airports and in cargo areas, piers, and terminals. They perform their duties on foot, and on horseback and in helicopters, boats, and by airplanes. They use drug-sniffing dogs to locate contraband. The USCS also investigates firearm smuggling and, in close cooperation with the Immigration and Naturalization

Service under the Department of Justice, trafficking in illegal aliens.

The Internal Revenue Service Criminal Investigation Division (CID)

Another agency within the Department of the Treasury is the Internal Revenue Service (IRS). The main role of the IRS is to monitor and collect federal income taxes from individuals and businesses. The **Internal Revenue Service Criminal Investigation Division** (CID) investigates possible criminal violations of income tax laws and recommends appropriate criminal prosecution (Torres, 1985:97). The first chief of the Special Intelligence Unit, Inspector Elmer I. Irey, gained notoriety by investigating income tax evasion charges against Al Capone and the kidnapping of Charles Lindbergh's baby (Kennedy, 1985:104–5).

The CID cooperates with the U.S. Attorney's

Office of the Department of Justice in investigating possible criminal violations of federal income tax laws and recommending appropriate criminal prosecutions and civil penalties. CID agents carry weapons and are authorized under 18 U.S.C., 26 U.S.C., and 31 U.S.C. (1996) to execute and serve search warrants, to make arrests without warrant for any offense relating to internal revenue laws, and to make appropriate seizures of property in relation to these criminal offenses. In 1993, there were 3,621 agents authorized to carry firearms and enforce federal tax laws (Reaves, 1994:2).

The United States Secret Service (USSS)

The United States Secret Service originated in 1865 as the Secret Service Division (SSD). Its primary responsibility was to capture counterfeiters. In 1908, the SSD was transferred to the Department of Justice. From 1912 to 1918, the SSD made numerous arrests and secured over one thousand counterfeiting convictions involving about $250,000 in fake coins and currency (Johnson, 1995).

Presidential security became another SSD function in 1917. In 1965, shortly after President Kennedy was assassinated, the SSD was placed under the Department of the Treasury and renamed the United States Secret Service (Torres, 1985:370). In 1975, USSS agents prevented the assassination of President Gerald R. Ford by Lynette "Squeaky" Fromme in Sacramento, California. USSS agents also overpowered John Hinckley when he attempted to assassinate President Ronald Reagan in Washington, DC, in 1981.

USSS personnel are authorized to carry firearms and make arrests for violations of any federal laws. They are empowered to investigate credit and debit card frauds and anything related to electronic fund-transfer frauds (18 U.S.C., Sec 3056, 1996). In a Texas case, the USSS arrested and prosecuted persons who had stolen Treasury checks and were attempting to cash them in various stores (*United States v. Collins*, 1982).

Another major function of the USSS is the investigation of fraudulent documents (Riley, Stader, and Lancaster, 1995). The USSS also cooperates with other federal and local agencies in cases involving computer fraud and money laundering (Powis, 1992).

The Central Intelligence Agency (CIA)

The National Security Council was established under the National Security Act of 1947. The purpose of the act was to provide a comprehensive program for the future security of the United States and to provide for the establishment of integrated policies and procedures for the departments, agencies, and functions of the government responsible for national security. Under the CIA Act of 1949, the National Security Council established a subordinate organization called the Central Intelligence Agency.

The CIA participates in undercover and covert operations on an international scale. It has been linked to the ill-fated invasion of the Bay of Pigs in Cuba and to the supply of arms to Nicaraguan rebel forces. CIA links to the plot to murder Fidel Castro, to various savings and loan scandals, to anti-Mafia activities, and to the infiltration of various South American drug cartels have also been alleged or established (Brewton, 1992; Long, 1993; McCoy and Block, 1992; Ragano and Raab, 1994).

The functions of the CIA include (1) collecting, producing, and disseminating foreign intelligence and counterintelligence and (2) collecting, producing, and disseminating intelligence on the foreign aspects of narcotics production and trafficking. *This function is of particular interest to criminal justice.* The CIA transmits information it obtains to other interested agencies, including the FBI and the USCS, as a part of a nationwide program to curtail the distribution of illegal narcotics. In 1991, the CIA was directly responsible for seizing over one thousand pounds of cocaine and other narcotics having a value of $6 million (Bureau of Justice Assistance, 1992). However, the CIA's intelligence-gathering functions greatly overshadow its participation in the investigation of international drug trafficking.

Other Federal Agencies

The federal law-enforcement agencies and organizations described here are just a few of the many that exist. *Although each agency has specific functions and goals, some overlap occurs in critical areas* such as drug trafficking and contraband smuggling. These **overlapping jurisdictions** sometimes create internal conflicts, where one organization attempts to "steal the show" from another. If the FBI becomes involved in investigating an illegal international drug transaction, it probably will proceed independently, without involving the USCS or BATF. By the same token, the BATF sometimes acts independently without notifying other interested agencies. Although it is inefficient for these agencies not to share valuable information, it is unlikely that such interorganizational jealousies will soon end.

State Police Agencies

In 1993, about 9 percent (78,570) of all local and state law enforcement officers (841,099) were members of the **state police** (Reaves, 1993:2). One of the most well-known state police organizations is the Texas Rangers. Established in 1835, it was the first state police department. However, some historians argue that the Pennsylvania State Police, established in 1905, was the first "true" or modern state police agency.

The Pennsylvania State Police organization became one of several different models of state law enforcement. The Pennsylvania State Police model required that all officers function as a uniformed force. Besides enforcing state laws, Pennsylvania troopers have arrest powers similar to those of local police, perform investigatory functions when major crimes are committed, and have units or teams of specialists who engage in forensic and laboratory work. Other states, such as Delaware and New York, have emulated the Pennsylvania model. Other models have been developed that focus almost exclusively on the enforcement of state highway laws. Thus, highway patrols in states such as Utah, Kansas, Georgia, and Kentucky spend most of their time enforcing state traffic laws, although they may perform additional functions.

Most people are acquainted with state police in the form of **state highway patrols**. With the exception of Hawaii, most states have a highway patrol or its equivalent. *The responsibilities of highway patrol officers, often known as state troopers, include enforcing state motor vehicle laws on major state roads and federal interstate highways.*

In some states, state police conduct training centers for local city and county officers. These centers offer courses on crime detection, personal safety, and weapons training. In New Mexico, for instance, traffic enforcement is only one of several functions of the state police, who are also trained in techniques of criminal investigation. These officers cooperate with other authorities in cases that cross jurisdictional boundaries.

As a part of their official duties, in some states troopers and other state police are obligated to assist in collecting state taxes and other revenue. In Tennessee, state troopers establish roadblocks to determine whether motorists have appropriate driver's licenses and they use drug-sniffing dogs in searches of automobiles. They carry weapons and make arrests for various law violations.

Some states have "bureaus of identification" similar to the FBI's. Agents of these state bureaus perform routine criminal investigation functions. When state police become involved in such operations, they usually perform supporting functions, such as by making arrests, interviewing witnesses, and gathering evidence from crime scenes.

County and Metropolitan Police

Ninety-one percent of law enforcement personnel are officers of city and county governments. In 1993, there were 762,529 city, county, and special police officers in the United States (Reaves, 1993:2–3). Sheriff's department personnel numbered 225,342, while local police agencies had 476,261 employees. About 30 percent of all personnel in these city and county agencies were nonsworn, with no arrest powers, while 562,583 were sworn officers. Special types of police officers (60,926) include airport and park police, transit police, public school police, college and university police, and housing police (Reaves, 1993:2), as well as investigative units attached to city and county law enforcement agencies and investigators with prosecutor's offices.

While the *notion* of police work is much older, the roots of the modern police department can be traced to eighteenth-century England. During this period, a magistrate, Patrick Colquhoun (1745–1820) made several innovative proposals, several of which were influenced by an earlier writer, Henry Fielding (1707–1754).

Colquhoun proposed the establishment of a bureaucratic law enforcement organization with full-time, paid personnel, each specializing in a particular function, such as detection and prevention (Becker and Whitehouse, 1980). Colquhoun outlined his proposals in his *Treatise on the Police in the Metropolis* in 1806: "Police in this country may be considered as a new science; the properties of which consist not in the judicial powers which lead to punishment, and which belong to magistrates alone; but in the prevention and detection of crimes; and in those other functions which relate to the internal regulations for the well ordering and comfort of civil society" (Colquhoun, 1806: preface).

In 1829, England's home secretary and political reformer, Sir Robert Peel, established the Metropolitan Police of London through the Act for Improving the Police in and Near the Metropolis (Lee, 1901). This act created two positions of justice of the peace to conduct the business of the Police Office and framed a number of regulations for managing the force (Manning, 1977:77–78). Two police commissioners who gave considerable substance and direction to early English police work were an army officer, Charles Rowan (1783–1852), and a lawyer, Richard Mayne (1796–1868), appointed by Peel to head his new force (Becker and Whitehouse, 1980:6–8; Miller, 1985:49).

Modern police organization in the United States has been patterned on the Metropolitan Police of London of 1829 (Becker and Whitehouse, 1980:34). The first U.S. police force was established in Boston in 1838, and the next in New York City in 1845 (Miller, 1985:49–50).

In 1992, there were 17,358 local police and sheriff's agencies and departments in the United States (Reaves, 1993:2). Table 4.2 shows a breakdown of the numbers of police and sheriff's departments by state and type of agency for 1992. Tables 4.3 and 4.4 show the numbers of full-time employees in police and sheriff's departments by state and type of agency for 1992 as well as the number of full-time sworn officers employed by police and sheriff's departments per 10,000 residents, by state and type of agency, for the same year.

On average, cities in the United States have 21 officers per 10,000 residents. The highest rate of officers to population occurs in the Northeast, where there are 28 officers per 10,000 residents. The lowest rate occurs in the West, where there are 16 officers per 10,000 inhabitants (Reaves, 1993:7, 1996:1).

There is considerable variation in police organization among jurisdictions in the United States. Some police departments in rural areas are staffed by one police officer or sheriff, whereas in New York City there are nearly twenty-nine thousand police officers. There is also great variation in the functions performed by the police. In some jurisdictions, police perform only civil functions such as regulating traffic and serving warrants for magistrates; in others police may conduct criminal investigations.

Private Police

In 1993, 4,000 agencies spent more than $64 billion in the employment of over 1.6 million persons as **private police** or security personnel (El Nasser, 1993:9A). One reason for the rapid increase in the hiring of private security police is that the cost of crime has risen to over $40 billion per year (National Institute of Justice, 1991). Among other reasons cited for the growth of private security forces are (1) increasing public awareness and fear of crime; (2) the trend toward specialization of all services; (3) more sophisticated electronic surveillance devices and monitoring systems; (4) lowering of insurance rates when private police are on the premises of businesses; and (5) a lack of confidence in the ability of regular police officers to protect business interests (Maguire and Pastore, 1995; Rand, 1991).

Table 4.2

Police and sheriff's departments, by State and type of agency, 1992

		Number of agencies			
		General purpose police			Special
State	Total	Local	State	Sheriff	police
All States	17,358	12,502	49	3,086	1,721
Alabama	377	285	1	67	24
Alaska	48	43	1	0	4
Arizona	102	75	1	15	11
Arkansas	277	185	1	75	16
California	493	341	1	58	93
Colorado	218	140	1	63	14
Connecticut	133	108	1	8	16
Delaware	42	33	1	3	5
District of Columbia	3	1	0	0	2
Florida	371	285	1	65	20
Georgia	540	343	1	159	37
Hawaii	6	4	0	0	2
Idaho	112	66	1	44	1
Illinois	894	748	1	102	43
Indiana	448	336	1	91	20
Iowa	427	321	1	99	6
Kansas	345	221	1	105	18
Kentucky	377	240	1	120	16
Louisiana	348	256	1	64	27
Maine	142	119	1	16	6
Maryland	124	78	1	24	21
Massachusetts	388	341	1	14	32
Michigan	578	474	1	83	20
Minnesota	456	359	1	87	9
Mississippi	297	189	1	82	25
Missouri	594	463	1	114	16
Montana	119	59	1	55	4
Nebraska	247	149	1	93	4
Nevada	35	14	1	16	4
New Hampshire	228	214	1	10	3
New Jersey	534	488	1	21	24
New Mexico	115	72	1	33	9
New York	578	463	1	57	57
North Carolina	458	332	1	100	25
North Dakota	134	76	1	53	4
Ohio	908	776	1	88	43
Oklahoma	410	312	1	77	20
Oregon	183	137	1	36	9
Pennsylvania	1,167	1,049	1	66	51
Rhode Island	48	39	1	4	4
South Carolina	255	188	1	46	20
South Dakota	171	102	1	66	2
Tennessee	326	211	1	95	19
Texas	1,712	632	1	255	824
Utah	127	84	1	29	13
Vermont	73	57	1	14	1
Virginia	327	167	1	125	34
Washington	252	202	1	39	10
West Virginia	228	158	1	55	14
Wisconsin	506	417	1	72	16
Wyoming	77	50	1	23	3

Source: Reaves (1993).

Note: Special police total for Texas includes 751 constable offices. Local police category includes consolidated police-sheriff departments.

Table 4.3

Full-time employees in police and sheriff's departments, by State and type of agency, 1992

State	Total	General purpose police		Sheriff	Special police
		Local	State		
All States	841,000	476,261	78,570	225,342	60,926
Alabama	12,517	7,295	1,281	3,172	769
Alaska	1,645	1,071	439	0	135
Arizona	13,243	7,178	1,611	4,196	258
Arkansas	6,823	3,262	679	1,849	1,033
California	100,582	46,947	8,894	36,243	8,498
Colorado	12,559	6,445	688	4,513	913
Connecticut	9,276	7,236	1,321	425	294
Delaware	2,006	1,047	687	40	232
District of Columbia	6,174	5,750	0	0	424
Florida	54,011	25,598	2,106	24,426	1,881
Georgia	24,516	12,524	1,900	8,381	1,711
Hawaii	3,478	3,384	0	0	94
Idaho	2,922	1,151	254	1,502	15
Illinois	46,189	30,971	3,300	10,817	1,101
Indiana	14,935	7,864	1,745	4,601	725
Iowa	6,257	3,476	459	2,058	264
Kansas	7,832	4,215	821	2,397	399
Kentucky	7,949	4,721	1,654	1,141	433
Louisiana	17,370	6,760	1,042	8,889	679
Maine	3,313	1,766	460	896	191
Maryland	16,871	10,156	2,400	2,546	1,769
Massachusetts	21,181	14,217	2,579	3,615	770
Michigan	26,375	15,636	2,913	6,861	965
Minnesota	10,171	5,506	723	3,466	476
Mississippi	6,689	3,633	838	1,768	450
Missouri	15,370	10,395	1,833	2,619	523
Montana	2,121	733	262	1,034	92
Nebraska	4,194	2,147	643	1,303	101
Nevada	4,993	3,175	459	1,142	217
New Hampshire	2,894	2,191	340	158	205
New Jersey	32,785	22,793	3,550	4,706	1,736
New Mexico	4,957	3,003	552	1,241	161
New York	85,177	56,406	4,684	9,284	14,803
North Carolina	19,633	9,805	1,602	7,109	1,117
North Dakota	1,449	674	199	503	73
Ohio	29,718	17,936	2,348	7,522	1,912
Oklahoma	9,554	6,028	1,406	1,736	384
Oregon	8,310	3,883	1,145	3,107	175
Pennsylvania	28,326	19,907	5,232	1,453	1,734
Rhode Island	2,891	2,456	203	125	107
South Carolina	10,099	4,323	1,193	3,423	1,160
South Dakota	1,592	804	169	603	16
Tennessee	16,349	8,204	1,543	5,927	675
Texas	64,247	33,059	5,605	19,077	6,506
Utah	4,833	1,882	395	1,709	847
Vermont	1,329	752	426	119	32
Virginia	21,454	10,529	2,206	6,550	2,169
Washington	12,733	6,246	2,074	4,090	323
West Virginia	3,912	1,527	734	1,373	278
Wisconsin	15,279	8,795	665	4,752	1,067
Wyoming	2,016	799	308	875	34

Source: Reaves (1993).

Note: Special police category includes both State and local agencies.

Special police total for Texas includes 2,006 employees working for constable offices.

Figures are for pay period that included June 30, 1992.

Table 4.4

Number of full-time sworn officers employed by police and sheriffs' departments per 10,000 residents, by State and type of agency, 1992

State	Population in 1992	Number of full-time sworn officers per 10,000 residents				
		Total	General purpose police		Sheriff	Special police
			Local	State		
All States	255,082,000	24	15	2	5	2
Alabama	4,136,000	21	14	2	5	1
Alaska	587,000	18	12	4	0	2
Arizona	3,832,000	21	14	3	4	–
Arkansas	2,399,000	19	10	2	4	2
California	30,867,000	21	11	2	7	1
Colorado	3,470,000	25	14	1	9	1
Connecticut	3,281,000	23	18	3	1	1
Delaware	689,000	23	13	7	–	2
District of Columbia	589,000	89	83	0	0	6
Florida	13,488,000	24	13	1	9	1
Georgia	6,751,000	25	14	1	9	1
Hawaii	1,160,000	24	23	0	0	1
Idaho	1,067,000	20	9	2	10	–
Illinois	11,631,000	31	21	2	7	1
Indiana	5,662,000	18	11	2	4	1
Iowa	2,812,000	17	10	1	4	1
Kansas	2,523,000	22	13	2	6	1
Kentucky	3,755,000	16	10	3	3	1
Louisiana	4,287,000	35	13	2	19	1
Maine	1,235,000	18	11	3	3	1
Maryland	4,908,000	26	17	3	3	3
Massachusetts	5,998,000	27	20	3	2	1
Michigan	9,437,000	21	14	2	4	1
Minnesota	4,480,000	16	10	1	4	1
Mississippi	2,614,000	18	11	2	4	1
Missouri	5,193,000	22	15	2	4	1
Montana	824,000	17	7	2	7	1
Nebraska	1,606,000	19	11	3	5	1
Nevada	1,327,000	23	14	2	6	1
New Hampshire	1,111,000	19	15	2	1	1
New Jersey	7,789,000	34	25	3	5	1
New Mexico	1,581,000	22	13	3	5	1
New York	18,119,000	38	25	2	3	7
North Carolina	6,843,000	21	12	2	7	1
North Dakota	636,000	17	8	2	5	1
Ohio	11,016,000	19	13	1	4	1
Oklahoma	3,212,000	20	14	2	3	1
Oregon	2,977,000	18	9	3	6	–
Pennsylvania	12,009,000	20	14	3	1	1
Rhode Island	1,005,000	24	20	2	1	1
South Carolina	3,603,000	22	10	3	7	2
South Dakota	711,000	16	9	2	5	–
Tennessee	5,024,000	21	12	2	6	1
Texas	17,656,000	23	14	2	6	2
Utah	1,813,000	16	9	2	5	1
Vermont	570,000	17	10	5	1	–
Virginia	6,377,000	26	13	3	9	2
Washington	5,136,000	16	9	2	4	–
West Virginia	1,812,000	14	7	3	4	1
Wisconsin	5,007,000	23	14	1	7	1
Wyoming	466,000	26	13	3	10	–

Source: Reaves (1993).

Note: Special police category includes both State and local agencies.

Population figures are Census Bureau estimates as of April 1, 1992.

Personnel figures are for pay period that included June 30, 1992.

Detail may not add to total because of rounding.

–Less than 0.5.

In fairness to police departments, however, it should be noted that private security forces are proprietary or operated on a contractual basis. As such, they can devote unlimited time to certain types of crime problems associated with the industries and businesses they serve. One result is that their effectiveness in crime control is greater than that of many public police departments, which must perform diverse police tasks (Maxwell, 1993).

While some private police are private detectives and investigators, over 90 percent of the private security force consists of guards, watchmen, doorkeepers, crossing guards, and bridge tenders. The oldest security firm in the United States is Pinkerton's, established in 1850 by Allan Pinkerton. Pinkerton's continues to provide contract guard and investigative services. It currently has more than thirty thousand personnel and revenues of over $150 million. Other private companies marketing crime-protection services include Brink's, American District Telegraph Company (ADT), Baker Industries, Burns, Wackenhut, and Globe Security Systems (Albanese, 1989).

Training for most private guards and police is less organized than that for municipal police. Its quality varies but in most cases is considered inadequate by critics (Johnston, 1992; Maxwell, 1993). North Carolina and several other states have developed fairly stringent licensing and regulation codes for companies furnishing private security. Most other jurisdictions do not have licensing mechanisms and regulations to ensure consistency and quality in training recruits for private guard positions. Nevertheless, some experts believe that the notion that private police are somehow inferior to public law enforcement officers is a myth. Given the great emphasis upon more extensive training and experience, private police officers increasingly exhibit as much competence as public law enforcement officers (Walsh, 1989). In fact, some jurisdictions, such as Sussex Borough in New Jersey, have privatized their police forces, with apparently successful results (O'Leary, 1994).

Some types of security personnel belong to unions. For example, the Union of Plant Guard Workers of America has a membership of over twenty-five thousand, who represent about 10 percent of all private sector guards in the United States. Union members are encouraged to upgrade their skills in various kinds of guard duty. In almost all of the programs, there is little, if any, in-class instruction and almost no on-the-job training provided. Bank guards and in-house guards in research organizations tend to receive the most on-the-job training, usually from their immediate supervisors. The average company offering guard-training programs allocates twelve hours to seventeen topical areas at the discretion of the local trainer (Maxwell, 1993; Nemeth, 1992).

All states have regulations governing handgun ownership, registration, and possession. California follows a model statute specified by the Uniform Firearms Act, which does not require a license to purchase a handgun. However, handgun sellers are required to provide local police with descriptions and other information about all purchasers of handguns and to prohibit sales to minors, drug addicts, and criminals. California also requires a permit to carry a concealed weapon. Private investigators and off-premises security guards must comply with these provisions, making it possible for the state to check backgrounds and prior arrest records before issuing permits.

Security regulations lack uniformity among the states. In 1976, the National Advisory Committee on Criminal Justice Standards and Goals released a report encouraging improvements in licensing requirements and regulations for three major types of private police, including (1) guard services, (2) private investigators, and (3) alarm system contractors. In 1981, the licensing requirements in all states were investigated (Buikema, Horvath, and Dodson, 1983). Of the forty-seven states that responded, thirty-seven states said their jurisdictions regulate at least one of the three types of security services mentioned above. The most common requirement for licensing is the absence of a felony conviction. Grounds for revoking licenses include previous felony convictions, false statements made on job application forms, and dishonesty or fraud associated with the clients served. Most respondents indicated that their jurisdictions are reviewing current licensing requirements and considering proposals for upgrading licensing criteria (O'Leary, 1994; Walsh, 1989).

Private guards and other law enforcement personnel in the private sector have the same powers of arrest as citizens, who may make citizen's arrests when they observe suspects committing crimes. Of course, it is dangerous for untrained citizens to attempt to subdue and detain criminal suspects. In many communities, groups of citizens band together for self-protection, particularly where there is distrust of or lack of confidence in the police (Marx and Archer, 1971).

Business establishments have certain rights pertaining to the arrest and detention of suspects. For example, a department store may detain someone suspected of shoplifting for a reasonable period without fear of liability. There is nothing to prevent citizens from suing businesses for false arrest or imprisonment, however, even when the arrest and detention appeared justified. In some jurisdictions, private security forces must be deputized by the county executive (e.g., the county sheriff) before they can carry a concealed firearm or simply "go armed," even on private premises such as large industrial plants or businesses.

Private policing will probably continue to grow at a rate similar to that of past years, and the training and employment requirements for those performing guard services will improve substantially (Cunningham, Strauchs, and VanMeter, 1990). This is true particularly for those services that require firearms and that perform tasks similar to those of the regular police (Johnston, 1992). Regular police still perceive their private police counterparts to be deficient in professional training, however (Morley and Fong, 1995). Indeed, sometimes regular police officers must intervene to rescue private police from dangerous criminals. These negative impressions will change gradually as the recruitment, education, and training of private police become more regulated (Morley and Fong, 1995; O'Leary, 1994).

Overlapping Jurisdiction and a Lack of Interagency Cooperation

When Charles Lindbergh's baby was kidnapped in 1932, several law enforcement agencies became involved, including the New Jersey State Police, local

officials, and the FBI. In November 1933, when the FBI asked the New Jersey Police what progress it had made in its investigation, they were told, "None" (Kennedy, 1985:203). On the contrary, they had made extensive progress in their investigation, and they certainly could have used FBI laboratory assistance in identifying various objects associated with the kidnapping.

There has always been rivalry among the various branches of law enforcement. There are several theories that explain such rivalry. One of the more convincing explanations is interagency jealousy. In the Lindbergh kidnapping, the New Jersey State Police wanted to "solve the crime" and not rely on the FBI or any other agency. Similarly, the FBI refused help from other agencies in its final attempt to capture John Dillinger. The FBI wanted Dillinger's capture to be "their show."

As has already been noted, there is considerable jurisdictional overlap in law enforcement. Narcotics trafficking is within the jurisdiction of almost every law enforcement agency, including the FBI, the BATF, the USCS, and even the CIA! Even though these agencies are supposed to coordinate their activities with other agencies, such cooperation does not often happen. While head of the FBI, J. Edgar Hoover deliberately advocated a pattern of noncooperation with local police agencies. Some experts say that law enforcement agencies must overcome their "turf jealousies" and develop more effective anticrime alliances (Shanahan, 1985:449–52).

The History and Role of Police in Society

The word *police* stems from the Greek word *polis*, meaning "city." It has been applied historically to the exercise of civil or collective authority (Manning, 1977:39). In 1800, the French viewed police unfavorably because they spied on and tyrannized citizens (Manning, 1977:39; Reith, 1938).

In England, however, the police force was originally created to maintain state security and protect citizens. In 1829, **Sir Robert Peel** (1788–1850) passed a bill through the British Parliament establishing the first formal police department, the **Metro-**

politan Police of London (Manning, 1977:39–40; Becker and Whitehouse, 1980:6). Historians say that the development of the police force in England can best be understood by examining certain societal changes, including various reforms of the political-legal system (Manning, 1977:52–71).

Between 1750 and 1820, the population of London doubled from 676,000 to 1.3 million. In fact, between 1801 and 1831 alone, England's population grew from 8.9 million to 13.9 million. These population changes resulted in part from a growing birth rate, a sharp reduction in the death rate, and extensive migration from rural areas to densely populated cities (Manning, 1977:53–54). Simultaneously, several significant occupational changes occurred. Many people switched from agricultural to nonagricultural employment, there were growing numbers of skilled workers and artisans, and the middle class began to form (Manning, 1977:54). There was similar growth in the professions, such as medicine, law, and the ministry.

The Napoleonic Wars of the early nineteenth century eroded England's economy to a critical level (Manning, 1977:57–59). Prices of goods and wares skyrocketed while postwar unemployment levels surged because of the large numbers of soldiers and sailors looking for work. These people often committed fraud and petty crimes to support themselves and their families.

The years between 1770 and 1828 saw at least six major political and legal reforms involving struggles for power and competition for political domination among various classes. London in the late 1700s "was a hell of a place at night. There was almost no street lighting and no police worth the name. Burglary and robbery with violence were widespread, and the roads on the outskirts of London were infested with highwaymen" (Pringle, 1955:29–30).

It was in the context of these great social, economic, and political changes that Peel made his idea for an organized and professional metropolitan police force a reality. His thinking about such an organization was influenced by other reformers, such as Patrick Colquhoun (1745–1820) and Henry Fielding (1707–1754).

Peel's original plan provided for detectives and for "bobbies" or "peelers" (after Sir Robert "Bobby" Peel) to walk the streets twenty-four hours a day (Becker and Whitehouse, 1980:34). Bobbies wore special uniforms, and detectives wore street clothing. Detectives' duties included collecting evidence and presenting it in court, while police officers tried to minimize crime by their visibility and arrested suspects (Becker and Whitehouse, 1980:34–35).

Recruitment for the Metropolitan Police of London emphasized criteria such as sex, height, weight, character, and ability to read and write. Training was mandatory, although it consisted mainly of close-order drill (Gorer, 1955). The size and strength of police officers was considered important because police were often required to quell public disorders and make arrests by sheer physical force. Their military-type training instilled discipline among them and made it easier to function as a unit when confronting large numbers of law-breakers or rioters.

The aim of the Metropolitan Police of London was simple: to protect citizens and their property (Manning, 1977:82–83). Sir Robert Peel outlined several principles to guide the Metropolitan Police of London. He stated that:

> The police were initially designed to prevent crime without resort to repressive legal sanctioning and to avoid military intervention in domestic disturbances; to manage public order nonviolently, with the application of violence viewed as an ultimate means of coercing compliance; to minimize and indeed reduce, if at all possible, the schism between police and public; and to demonstrate efficiency by the absence of crime and disorder, not visible evidence of police action in dealing with them. (Manning, 1977:98–99)

During these same years, some of the larger cities in the United States, such as Boston and New York, were also experiencing rapid population growth and increasing urban density from migration and industrialization. Formal police departments were created first in Boston in 1838; next in New York in 1845; and then in Chicago, 1851; Cincinnati and New Orleans, 1852; Philadelphia, 1854; and Newark and Baltimore, 1857 (Manning, 1977:123). In Boston especially there were widespread thievery, drunkenness, vagabondage, lewd and lascivious behavior, assault and battery, and many other forms of unruly conduct (Lane, 1967:6). New York City faced similar problems.

That city's streets were called "pathways of danger" (Richardson, 1970:25).

Policing in the United States was not unknown before 1838, however. In 1643, every settlement in New Amsterdam (later New York) appointed or elected constables, marshals, and watches (i.e., guards or lookouts on duty) (Bayley, 1985:32). The emerging government of the United States created specialized federal marshals in 1789.

Early police departments in the United States were patterned largely on England's 1829 model of the Metropolitan Police of London. The objectives of these police departments were similar to those of their British counterparts (Johnson, 1981). Boston and New York City police officers were responsible for "keeping the peace" (hence, "peace officers") and for deterring crime by patrolling the streets. Their effectiveness was measured by the absence of crime in their jurisdictions. Police departments have undergone many reforms since their origins in Boston and New York, partly because the original police role was somewhat diffuse and influenced by conflicting moral codes and political interest groups.

The Prohibition Era of the 1920s and 1930s marked a turning point in police organization (Manning, 1977:96–98). Three major changes occurred in the 1930s that profoundly affected the role of the police: (1) the development of a systematic method of collecting and publishing crime statistics in the form of the *Uniform Crime Reports*, distributed by the FBI; (2) the linking of criminal statistics published in such reports to the notion of police professionalism; and (3) the police use of radios and automobiles, which permitted more mechanized and immediate response to reports of crime.

The motto "To serve and to protect" is emblazoned on police cars in many cities. However, while it is true that police officers serve and protect the citizenry, it is also true that most of their time is consumed by non-crime-related activities such as public service and traffic control (Bohm, 1986). This results in two conflicting images of police work. One image is embodied in the public's conception of the "ideal" police officer, the Hollywood image that portrays police officers who spend much of their time catching, prosecuting, and convicting criminals, and thus "clearing" most

crimes. Police officers not engaged in fighting crime are usually shown either on foot or in patrol cars "preventing crime" by their high visibility.

The second image of the police role is based on a practical assessment of the *actual* work of police officers. Some studies show that police officers spend less than 10 percent of their time on crime-related business (Bohm, 1986). The rest of police officers' work involves traffic control, leading funeral processions, lecturing high school students about police methods, getting cats down from trees, counseling husbands and wives in family disputes, and filling out daily service reports.

Despite efforts to dispel certain "myths" about law enforcement (Crank, 1994; Marsh, 1988; Stewart, Lieberman, and Celester, 1994), there is a prevailing public misconception about police work. Why? According to some critics, "Myths about crime, criminals, and crime control policy are perpetuated because they serve a variety of interests. Among the interests served are those of the general public, the media, the politicians, academic criminologists, criminal justice officials, and social elites" (Bohm, 1986:199–209).

The public itself perpetuates myths about crime and crime control because they help forge common bonds and create and reinforce a sense of community. The community distinguishes between the "good guys" and the "bad guys" and takes pride in the "fact" that the police, through "law and order" campaigns, are doing something about crime. This gives citizens a sense of public order (Bohm, 1986:204).

The media and politicians benefit from myths about crime control. The media sells more papers, gets higher television ratings, and markets more of a sponsor's product, while politicians get more votes by reassuring their constituencies that they are "doing something about the crime problem" (Bohm, 1986:205–6).

Even academicians and those conducting police research benefit from perpetuating certain myths about crime control. For instance, considerable grant money is allocated annually by the National Institute of Justice and the Bureau of Justice Statistics to support projects for improving crime detection and preventing crime. Many criminologists in colleges and universities derive several profes-

Here, police officers check motorists' driver's licenses at a roadblock. Most police work is not directly related to serious crime.

sional benefits from receiving these grants. Police department budgets, salary increments, and other allocations are made often on the basis of the effectiveness of a department's crime-fighting efforts (Bohm, 1986:206–7). Thus, dispelling myths about the police and crime control would only undermine the rationale for a larger crime-control budget.

Does spending more money on crime control actually decrease crime? This question is difficult to answer. One widely held view is that changing a police department's budget has little or no impact on the level of crime (Bayley, 1985; Decker and Kohfeld, 1985). However, considerable improvements have been made in the recruitment and training of police officers in all major U.S. police departments (Strawbridge and Strawbridge, 1990), largely in response to a more critical public demanding greater professionalism among those who enforce the law.

The Administration of Police Organization

The structural features of police organization and administration in the United States and other

countries have been remarkably consistent over time (Barker, Hunter, and Rush, 1994). Indeed, many U.S. police departments are similar to their 1829 British counterpart in several respects (Becker and Whitehouse, 1980:34–36). But public demand for greater police effectiveness in reducing crime together with administrative concerns for organizational efficiency and the elimination of corruption have resulted in significant reforms in recent years.

Figure 4.2 shows an organizational chart of the offices and divisions of the Washington, D.C., Metropolitan Police Department. This department is headed by a chief of police, who oversees four bureaus. In turn, these bureaus supervise "divisions," including patrol, traffic, and criminal investigations. This type of organization is "traditional." It reflects a highly centralized operating unit in which four bureau heads report directly to the chief of police, who is responsible to a commissioner or some other public official.

Police organization is divided into line, staff, and auxiliary functions (Souryal, 1995). Line functions are patrol, traffic, juvenile, and detective work. Staff functions are performed by both civilians and police officers, who may work as clerks or in public relations jobs. They are responsible for improving police-community relations. They coordinate internal organizational activities and law enforcement assignments among different police divisions. Auxiliary personnel include maintenance employees, jail guards, and other supporting workers (Becker and Whitehouse, 1980:38–40).

Police departments in most cities are municipal agencies under the direct control of the chief executive, such as the mayor or the city manager (Coleman, 1995). In Chicago, the police superintendent is appointed by the mayor, while in Los Angeles, the commissioner of police is appointed by the Board of Police Commissioners (Ruchelman, 1973:6). In Indianapolis, the mayor appoints a public safety director, who in turn appoints a police chief, who must be approved by the mayor (Hudnut, 1985:21).

Historically, police departments in the United States have been political bodies, extensions of municipal political authority (Crank and Rehm, 1994: Souryal, 1995). Because of the close relationship between police departments and the political leadership of the community, mayoral abuse of political power has occurred (Sheehan and Cordner, 1995). Some people say that *police* and *politics* are the same word pronounced differently. Because political systems developed at about the same time as police agencies, there has always been a close relation between the two bodies. Also, some mutual exploitation has occurred to further the interests of both political groups and police organizations.

According to Richard J. Brzeczek, a former superintendent of police in Chicago:

Figure 4.2 Traditional Department Organization: An Outline of the Washington, D.C., Metropolitan Police Department

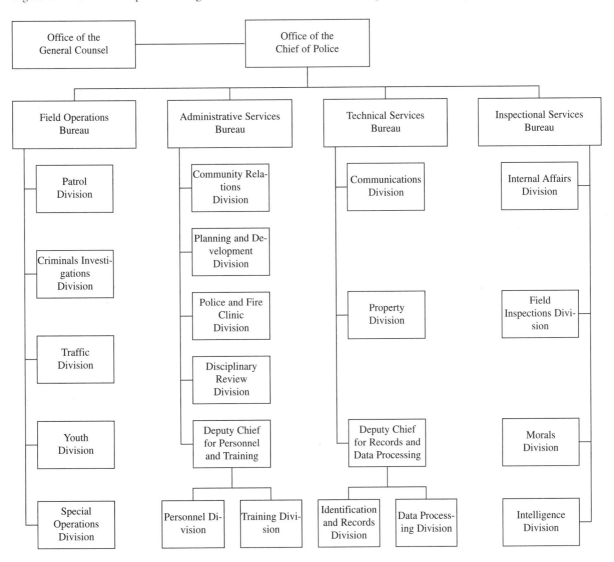

Source: "The Shadow of the Past—The Light of the Future: 1974 Annual Report" (Washington, D.C.: Metropolitan Police Department, Planning and Development Division), p. 4.

Historically, mayors abused their power over the police department, placing inept cronies on its payroll and using its members as footsoldiers in political skirmishes. Remnants of such inappropriate mayoral meddling can be found in modern times in a number of cities. For example, Minneapolis, during the 1970s, suffered from mayoral abuse of the police personnel structure, and Chicago only within the past decade (1975–1985) ceased the unconstitutional use of police for surveillance of the mayor's political enemies. (Brzeczek, 1985:51)

In 1982–1983, a nationwide study examined the training and background of 493 police chiefs of state, county, or municipal agencies employing seventy-five or more persons (Witham, 1985). The typical respondent was about forty-nine years old, had been a police chief for about five years, and had had an average of twenty-four years' experience as a law enforcement officer. Fifty percent had bachelor's degrees, and most had experience with at least one other law enforcement agency.

Police chiefs' credentials were *not* impressive compared with those of administrators of similar sized corporations (Witham, 1985), nearly 80 percent of whom had bachelor's degrees. Chiefs often defined their roles too narrowly and were not involved directly in formulating policies affecting their department's officers. Recommendations for improvements included establishing and enforcing minimum educational standards as well as trying to recruit chiefs from outside law enforcement. Some critics have said that police chiefs are nothing more than fifty-year-old police officers, although this conception is gradually changing.

Other criticisms of police management and administration suggest that police chiefs should have exposure to practices and principles of business management (Cox and Moore, 1992). Such exposure may enhance police administrators' job performance by familiarizing them with a variety of managerial strategies that would help them meet their departmental needs (Bennett, 1992; Cox and Moore, 1992).

Because of the limited training and effectiveness of many police chiefs and administrators, police department administration has been the subject of reform for several decades (Bennett, 1992). Several suggestions for administrative reform were contained in the 1967 report of the President's Crime Commission. This report reflected a "traditional approach" to police reform: (1) greater administrative efficiency; (2) more expert leadership; and (3) higher qualifications for police officers. In more recent years, studies have suggested that in order to be more successful in their work, police chiefs are going to have to alter their approaches to leadership and redesign their organizations to fit the more diverse needs of contemporary society (Bennett, 1992:257–58).

Other reforms being implemented in most major police departments have been described in the 1981 Civil Rights Commission report, "Who Is Guarding the Guardians?" (Hanewicz, 1985:50–51). The report recommends that police departments develop clear and restrictive rules governing the use of force, better regulation of weaponry and training, and stricter procedures for reporting firearms discharges. However, some experts say that policy statements about the use of firearms and other issues often have little effect on how police officers act on the job when confronted with a dangerous situation (Mays and Taggert, 1985).

Police reforms have not eliminated mayoral interference in police departments. Mayors continue to influence police actions, including how police should respond to a disturbance, when deadly force should be used, and how certain laws should be enforced (Brzeczek, 1985:51; Tunnell and Gaines, 1992).

A current trend in police reform is greater police-community interaction (Dantzker, Lurigio, and Hartnett, 1995a, 1995b). Many communities are moving away from the traditional view of police and toward a definition of police skills that is more consistent with the service nature of the police role (Weisheit, Wells, and Falcone, 1994). Specifically, reforms are directed at (1) improving police-public communication, (2) emphasizing the service function of the police and rewarding officers for doing well in that area, and (3) democratizing police departments by increasing the involvement of rank-and-file police officers in policy making (Walker, 1979:168). One effort to increase police-community interaction is through "team policing," in which several officers work intensively in a small geographical area. Reactions to this concept have been mixed (Walker, 1993b).

The Selection of Police Officers

As has already been stated, early selection criteria for police officers included size, gender, age, and the ability to read and write. While more sophisticated criteria have been developed in recent years, some of the original criteria, such as physique, continue to attract interest of researchers. A 1985 Florida study examined the relation between an officer's height and potential for aggression. It was found that "shorter" officers had greater "aggression potential" and issued more "warnings" compared with their taller counterparts (Willoughby and Blount, 1985).

Little progress occurred in developing better police selection criteria until the establishment of the first police training school in the United States in 1908 by Berkeley, California, Chief of Police **August Vollmer**. Vollmer, considered the father of scientific police investigation, pioneered such innovations as a fully mechanized patrol system and two-way radios.

In 1916, Vollmer and Professor Alexander M. Kidd developed the first criminology curriculum in the United States at the University of California at Berkeley. This program became a division of the Department of Political Science in 1939, and in 1963, a Doctor of Criminology degree program was established (Becker and Whitehouse, 1980:49–51). Other institutions such as the University of Southern California, the University of Chicago, and Michigan State University developed similar programs during the late 1920s and the 1930s. These programs were developed largely because of the recommendations of the National Commission on Law Observance and Enforcement, chaired by George W. Wickersham. Wickersham, who was appointed by President Herbert Hoover, published several reports in 1931 on the state of police training in the United States. These documents were known as the **Wickersham Reports**.

In 1979, there were over seven hundred academic degree programs in law enforcement offered in community colleges and universities throughout the United States (Becker and Whitehouse, 1980:51). It is difficult to know for sure how many degree programs in criminal justice exist today, because so many of these programs are intertwined with the programs of departments of political science, public administration, sociology, and other behavioral sciences. Estimates of the number of programs range from eight hundred to twelve hundred.

Vital to the growth and development of law enforcement programs in colleges and universities in the United States were the educational recommendations of the Commission on Law Enforcement and the Administration of Justice and the Omnibus Crime Control and Safe Streets Act of 1968. During the 1970s, the Law Enforcement Assistance Administration (LEAA) was established by the federal government in 1969, and allocated billions of dollars toward the development of law enforcement education and criminal justice programs (Becker and Whitehouse, 1980:51–52). The functions of the LEAA are described in chapter 5.

In 1973, the National Advisory Commission on Criminal Justice Standards and Goals strongly recommended that by 1982, all police agencies require a bachelor's degree from an accredited college or university (Becker and Whitehouse, 1980:51). Interestingly, in 1940, over 50 percent of the police officers in the New York City Police Department (NYPD) had college degrees. However, the general level of education among law enforcement officers nationwide was not of equivalent quality during that period (Geary, 1975:87). One explanation for the higher educational level of NYPD officers was that the NYPD paid its officers well. Thus, the NYPD attracted numerous applicants and was also able to be highly selective about whom it hired. Another reason for the higher NYPD educational level is that during the Depression years of the early 1930s, many college graduates were unable to find work in their chosen professions. Thus, some of them turned to law enforcement. This phenomenon occurred in jurisdictions besides New York, although it was not particularly widespread.

There is considerable variation in recruitment

programs among police departments (Ash, Slora, and Britton, 1990). In rural areas with small police departments, there may be no formal selection criteria. Applicants "off the street" might be hired as police officers with only a cursory check of their background, or nepotism may result in the appointment of close friends or relatives to law enforcement positions. But usually in such remote areas, there is not a great deal of competition for these jobs.

In most of the larger municipal police departments where there are numerous applicants, however, the selection process is more formal (Burbeck and Furnham, 1985). It may include completing numerous personal data forms, submitting college transcripts or records of university work completed, taking several personality and abilities tests, taking a polygraph or "lie detector" test, and responding to situational "screening" devices (Kornfeld, 1995: Scogin, Schumacher, and Gardner, 1995).

The primary objective of such screening procedures is to select people who will make the best police officers. The purpose of some of the psychological tests is to identify "well-adjusted" officers or those who can handle stressful situations.

The Minnesota Multiphasic Personality Inventory (MMPI) and the California Personality Inventory (CPI) are administered to prospective police recruits in California and other states and in some foreign countries, including Canada (Scogin, Schumacher, and Gardner, 1995: Winters, 1992). These instruments purportedly measure personality dimensions such as anxiety, sociability, personal adjustment, and social adjustment. Precisely how such personality dimensions relate to choosing good police officer candidates is unknown at present.

One problem with any paper-and-pencil personality test is that answers can be faked. However, the MMPI, CPI, and other personality assessment devices contain "lie factors" consisting of questions or statements that detect whether applicants are "faking it." Usually, these statements have obvious answers or describe most people. Some examples might be, "I never question my ability to accomplish difficult tasks" and "I never worry about my work quality or social relations with others." Since many persons occasionally worry about their ability to carry out difficult job assignments and have oc-

casional interpersonal problems, disagreement with these items may be indicative of the applicant's attempt to fabricate an image of the "ideal" police recruit. In short, applicants sometimes want to project an image of perfection and will deliberately give untrue statements about themselves. Police officers should be strong, confident, and secure in their mental and social well-being. Anything that would lead recruiters to believe that prospective applicants do not possess these qualities might result in rejection.

Of course, there are several other methodological problems associated with personality tests (Talley and Hinz, 1990). Sometimes they are used as "negative predictors." Thus, a police department may use them to determine whom it does *not* want to hire, such as persons with "problem" or "maladjusted" personalities (Winters, 1992).

In spite of these methodological drawbacks, such tests are used increasingly to select police recruits. Law enforcement agencies stress the need for persons who can cope with "personal stress" (Nietzel, 1993). Psychological clinicians interpret test results, designating applicants as "acceptable," "unacceptable," and "marginal" (Winters, 1992). When the MMPI and CPI have been used as screening tools, drop-out rates among recruits have been lower than when alternative selection procedures, including personal interviews and review board decisions, have been used (Hargrave, 1985; Hargrave and Berner, 1986). The effectiveness of these instruments is questionable. In some jurisdictions, these instruments may be used by highly trained professionals skilled in selecting applicants for different types of jobs, while in other jurisdictions they may be administered haphazardly, with little or no professional interpretation of test results. In any case, test results on any personality assessment device should be cautiously interpreted and supplemented with interviews and other situational criteria.

In some jurisdictions, prospective police recruits are asked how they would handle certain problem situations such as disputes between neighbors, violations of community statutes, and lost drivers. Responses to such questions were quite successful as predictors of job performance in a study of sixty-one police recruits in Alberta, Canada

(Pugh, 1985). "Situation" tests also permitted recruiters to identify prospective candidates who had high verbal expression skills, which are of value to police officers in their early years of service.

If psychological tests are a key part of an agency's personnel selection process, the agency should be prepared to experiment with various tests and to continuously evaluate and revise their standard measures (Gettys and Elam, 1985). The goals of such tests are to establish legitimate selection criteria that can be reasonably quantified, to identify the tests that most accurately predict job performance, and to refine selection procedures so that they meet the staffing needs of the agency (Gettys and Elam, 1985).

While the results of polygraph tests are inadmissible in court, their use in the screening process of police recruits is widespread. In 1983, for instance, the Vermont State Police administered polygraph tests to 181 applicants. One hundred and nine of them were rejected, primarily because of former drug offenses and undetected larcenies (Prior, 1985). The polygraph test is used to identify persons who are attempting to deceive recruiters about their backgrounds and police records (Garwood, 1985). These persons are excluded as candidates for police positions. In recent years, the use of polygraph tests has either declined or been discontinued in various jurisdictions. A national survey of 626 police agencies serving 50,000 or more citizens and of sheriffs' agencies employing one hundred or more sworn personnel has revealed that although most agencies valued polygraph tests, their use among agencies was not uniform. How such screening was conducted tended to determine whether it was viewed positively or negatively. Thus, polygraph screening was discontinued not because of dissatisfaction with it but rather because various states passed legislation barring its use (Horvath, 1993). Another reason cited, especially by some of the smaller police agencies, was a general lack of confidence in pre-employment polygraph screening (Meesig and Horvath, 1995).

In 1979, the U.S. Equal Employment Opportunity Commission (EEOC) raised several important ethical and legal issues about police selection criteria and proposed the Uniform Guidelines on Employment Selection Procedures (Inwald, 1985). These guidelines include (1) using psychological screening only as one component of the overall selection process; (2) devising a reliable validation scheme that can determine the usefulness of test results; (3) selecting a variety of tests and procedures for verification purposes; (4) avoiding arbitrary "cutoff" scores on psychological tests or scales; (5) documenting all selection procedures with written progress reports available for public inspection; (6) educating appropriate staff members on testing procedures and interpretive guidelines; (7) interviewing all candidates who have taken written psychological tests; (8) using well-defined and reliable psychological tests and scales; (9) being flexible in the use of various evaluative procedures; and (10) sharing information with state and local agencies through networking (Inwald, 1985).

At this time paper-and-pencil personality measurement devices cannot distinguish between a police officer and a member of the general public on the basis of answers given (Corey, 1988). This means that psychological testing for police recruitment has only limited use. In short, tests should be interpreted cautiously by both large and small police departments (Alpert, 1991). However, there is some agreement among police departments about desirable qualities for police officers: honesty, reliability, emotional stability, patience, and good character (Hogue, Black, and Sigler, 1994).

All states require that police officers be certified by Peace Officer Standards and Training (POST) Commissions or their equivalent (Shigley, 1987). Florida requires prospective police recruits to acquire certificates that essentially guarantee that they have never committed a felony or misdemeanor involving "moral turpitude" and that they have high school diplomas and meet other standards (Levinson, 1983). In order to maintain certification, police officers must continue to demonstrate that they have not been guilty of insubordinate conduct, gross immorality, habitual drunkenness, or gross misconduct (Levinson, 1983). The principal objectives of POST licensing procedures are (1) to keep bad officers (e.g., those with felony convictions or disciplinary problems or who have filed false statements) out of law enforcement and (2) to contribute to higher quality law enforcement by requiring officers to have a certain level of basic training (Shigley, 1987:10).

Minority Hiring Practices

In 1968, the National Advisory Commission issued its Report on Civil Disorders. Among the causes of civil disorders was discrimination directed against minorities by police. The Commission noted that although blacks made up at least 12 percent of the population, they represented less than 5 percent of police officers.

The underrepresentation of minorities in police departments has resulted in many racial conflicts in the United States. Before 1948, blacks could not join the Atlanta, Georgia, police department (Kuykendall and Burns, 1983:64). When some blacks were finally hired in 1948, they were initially not permitted to wear uniforms like those worn by white officers. By 1981, black officers in the Atlanta police department made up 46 percent of the force, although blacks make up 67 percent of the total population (Kuykendall and Burns, 1983; Stroup, 1985).

Such underrepresentation has not been limited to southern cities. Every major municipal jurisdiction in the United States has had the same problem for decades. In 1981, 9 percent of the Los Angeles Police Department were black, even though 17 percent of the city consisted of blacks. And even in Washington, D.C., where blacks make up 70 percent of the population, the police department in 1982 had only 50 percent black membership. Among the fifty largest cities in the United States in 1982, only Toledo, Ohio, had a proportion of black police officers (18 percent) commensurate with the proportion of blacks in the city as a whole (17 percent). In the other forty-nine cities, the discrepancy was sizeable (Walker, 1983:5).

In 1988, a five-year follow-up study was conducted to determine whether affirmative action policies were improving the proportionate representation of blacks and others in law enforcement (Walker, 1989). Data were collected on the numbers of sworn officers in forty-seven police departments in the fifty largest U.S. cities. Nearly half (45 percent) of all departments surveyed reported significant progress in the employment of black officers, while only 17 percent of the departments reported progress on the recruitment of Hispanics. Of all departments surveyed, about 10 percent reported a decline in minority recruitment, while another 17 percent reported no change. It was determined that in twenty-three departments, affirmative action policies leading to substantial increases in the number of black and Hispanic hires were court-ordered (Walker, 1989).

In 1973, the National Advisory Commission on Criminal Justice Standards and Goals adopted the following standard:

> Every police agency should engage in positive efforts to employ ethnic minority group members. When a substantial ethnic minority population resides within the jurisdiction, the police agency should take affirmative action to achieve a ratio of minority group employees in approximate proportion to the make-up of the population. (National Advisory Commission on Criminal Justice Standards and Goals, 1973:329)

Blacks in Law Enforcement

Between 1973 and 1983, the affirmative action proposal from the National Advisory Commission on Criminal Justice Standards and Goals resulted in a racially representative police force in only one of the fifty largest cities in the United States. The results of a 1992 survey were compared with those of 1983 (Maguire and Pastore, 1995:49). Table 4.5 shows the number, percentage, and percentage increase/decrease of black police officers in the fifty largest U.S. cities for the period 1983–1992. The table shows that only five cities (Milwaukee, Wisconsin; El Paso, Texas; Tucson, Arizona; Albuquerque, New Mexico; and Toledo, Ohio) had decreases in the proportionate employment of blacks, while the remaining forty-four cities had increases in the proportionate representation of black officers in law enforcement. Only New York City registered no change. The highest increase (217 percent) was in Jacksonville, Florida (Maguire and Pastore, 1995:49). Police departments with the largest percentages of black officers in 1992 were Washington, D.C. (68 percent), Detroit, Michigan (53 percent), New Or-

Table 4.5

Number of Police Officers and Number of Black Police Officers in the Fifty Largest Cities

City	Total Number of Officers 1983	Total Number of Officers 1992	Black Officers 1983 Number	Black Officers 1983 Percent	Black Officers 1992 Number	Black Officers 1992 Percent	Index of Black Representation 1983	Index of Black Representation 1992	Percent change
New York, NY	23,408	27,154	2,395	10.2	3,121	11.4	0.40	0.40	0.0
Los Angeles, CA	6,928	8,020	657	9.4	1,127	14.1	0.55	1.00	81.8
Chicago, IL	12,472	12,291	2,508	20.1	3,063	24.9	0.51	0.64	25.4
Houston, TX	3,629	4,056	355	9.7	595	14.7	0.35	0.52	48.5
Philadelphia, PA	7,265	6,280	1,201	16.5	1,615	25.7	0.44	0.64	45.4
San Diego, CA	1,363	1.937	76	5.5	146	7.5	0.62	0.80	29.0
Detroit, MI	4,032	4,787	1,238	30.7	2,556	53.3	0.49	0.70	42.8
Dallas, TX	2,053	2,878	169	8.2	546	19.0	0.28	0.64	128.5
Phoenix, AZ	1,660	1,644	48	2.8	66	4.0	0.58	0.77	32.7
San Antonio, TX[a]	1,164	1,606	54	4.6	90	5.6	NA	0.80	NA
San Jose, CA	915	1,223	20	2.1	50	4.1	0.46	0.85	84.7
Baltimore, MD	3,056	2,822	537	17.5	851	30.2	0.32	0.51	59.3
Indianapolis, IN	936	979	123	13.1	174	17.8	0.60	0.78	30.0
San Francisco, CA	1,957	1,818	159	8.1	170	9.4	0.64	0.85	32.8
Jacksonville, FL[a]	1,263	1,205	78	6.1	232	19.2	0.24	0.76	216.6
Columbus, OH	1,197	1,444	133	11.1	256	17.7	0.50	0.78	56.0
Milwaukee, WI	1,438	1,971	168	11.6	283	14.4	0.50	0.47	-6.0
Memphis, TN	1,216	1,403	268	22.0	481	34.3	0.46	0.62	34.7
Washington, DC	3,851	4,396	1,931	50.1	2,980	67.8	0.71	1.03	45.0
Boston, MA	1,871	1,972	248	13.2	404	20.5	0.59	0.80	35.5
Seattle, WA	1,011	1,231	42	4.1	105	8.5	0.43	0.84	95.3
El Paso, TX	650	787	13	2.0	17	2.2	0.63	0.62	-1.5
Cleveland, OH	2,091	1,668	238	11.3	439	26.3	0.26	0.56	115.3
New Orleans, LA	1,317	1,551	276	20.9	608	39.2	0.38	0.63	65.7
Nashville, TN	969	1,058	114	11.7	139	13.1	0.50	0.54	8.0
Denver, CO	1,379	1,348	82	5.9	130	9.2	0.49	0.72	46.9
Austin, TX	607	830	43	7.0	81	9.8	0.57	0.78	36.8
Fort Worth, TX	766	967	43	5.6	112	11.6	0.25	0.52	108.0
Oklahoma City, OK	662	932	27	4.0	69	7.4	0.27	0.47	74.0
Portland, OR	688	877	19	2.7	32	3.6	0.36	0.46	27.7
Kansas City, MO	1,140	1,166	123	10.7	156	13.4	0.39	0.45	15.3
Long Beach, CA	637	696	20	3.1	39	5.6	0.27	0.41	51.8
Tucson, AZ	549	771	17	3.0	25	3.2	0.81	0.74	-8.6
St. Louis, MO	1,763	1,552	346	19.6	437	28.2	0.43	0.59	37.2
Charlotte, NC	644	872	144	22.3	167	19.2	0.72	0.60	-16.6
Atlanta, GA	1,313	1,223	602	45.8	668	54.6	0.69	0.81	17.3
Virginia Beach, VA	NA	599	NA	NA	50	8.3	NA	0.60	NA
Albuquerque, NM	561	765	14	2.4	16	2.0	0.96	0.67	-30.2
Oakland, CA	636	549	147	23.1	144	26.2	0.49	0.60	22.4
Pittsburgh, PA	1,222	1,128	175	14.3	289	25.6	0.60	0.99	65.0
Sacramento, CA	NA	607	NA	NA	38	6.3	NA	0.41	NA
Minneapolis, MN	672	840	20	2.9	46	5.5	0.38	0.42	10.5
Tulsa, OK	695	718	30	4.3	68	9.5	0.36	0.69	91.6
Honolulu, HI	1,557	1,870	11	0.7	28	1.4	0.58	1.07	84.4
Cincinnati, OH	971	927	89	9.1	176	19.0	0.27	0.50	85.1
Miami, FL	1,051	1,032	181	17.2	231	22.4	0.69	0.81	17.3
Fresno, CA	NA	412	NA	NA	33	8.0	NA	0.96	NA
Omaha, NE	551	610	46	8.3	70	11.5	0.69	0.87	26.0
Toledo, OH	757	639	139	18.3	119	18.8	1.05	0.94	-10.4
Buffalo, NY	1,018	963	86	8.4	195	20.2	0.37	0.66	78.3

Source: Maguire and Pastore (1995), p. 49.

Note: Data were obtained through a questionnaire mailed to the office of the chief of police and the office of the municipal director of personnel (or equivalent position) in the 50 largest cities in the United States. Forty-seven cities returned completed questionnaires in 1983; all 50 cities returned completed questionnaires in 1992. Cities are listed in rank order of size based on the 1990 census of the population.

The index of black representation is calculated by dividing the percent of black police officers in a department by the percent of blacks in the local population. An index approaching 1.0 indicates that a city is closer to achieving a representation of black police officers equal to their proportion in the local population. The black population of a city is derived from the 1990 census of the population.

a. Data for 1983 are based on 1980–81 information from the Police Executive Research Forum, *Survey of Police Operational and Administrative Practices 1981* (Washington, DC: Police Executive Research Forum, 1981).

leans, Louisiana (39 percent), Memphis, Tennessee (34 percent), and Baltimore, Maryland (30 percent). In 1993, black police officers accounted for 11.3 percent of all local police officers; this figure was up from 10.5 percent in 1990 and 9.3 percent in 1987 (Reaves, 1996:1).

Women in Law Enforcement

A significant trend is the growing number of women in law enforcement. In 1993, women comprised 8.8 percent of all full-time local police officers, up from 8.1 percent in 1990 and 7.6 percent in 1987 (Reaves, 1996:1).

Prior to 1967, there were only a few female patrol officers in most jurisdictions. Many female police officers were "meter maids" largely restricted to issuing parking tickets; other female officers performed routine clerical tasks (Segrave, 1995). During the 1950s the numbers and roles of female officers increased substantially (Schultz, 1993). By 1981, *affirmative action* had increased the number of women to 6 percent of all law enforcement officers nationally. While this percentage was well below the proportionate representation of women

in the total population, few critics propose a 50–50 balance of males and females in law enforcement.

Many police departments find it difficult to attract, hire, and retain women (as well as certain racial and ethnic groups). A major influence on the number of women in police work is the "self-selection process." An investigation into women's reasons for entering police work reveals that little is known about them (Thomann, Pilant, and Kay, 1994). What little information that does exist shows that women are attracted to police work because of salary and because it offers an opportunity to help others (Austin and Hummer, 1994; Morash and Haarr, 1995). In short, women do not appear to be motivated by the desire to enter a male-dominated occupation as a protest prompted by the ERA or the Women's Movement.

Many women who enter police work are initially self-confident and idealistic about their roles and interactions with male co-workers. But after eight weeks of training, many become disillusioned and experience sex-role conflict, self-doubt, repressed anger, and confusion. There have also been reports of sexual harassment by male officers

This officer of the Metro-Dade Police Department appears totally at ease as a firearms instructor, a position that a decade ago most likely would have been filled by a man.

(Felkenes and Schroedel, 1993). However, in some jurisdictions, such as Miami, veteran women police officers form support networks and function as role models for less experienced female recruits who otherwise might be inclined to quit. Furthermore, female officers seem to be less dissatisfied with police work over time compared with their male counterparts (Buzawa, Austin, and Bannon, 1994; Culliver, 1993).

Some critics say that female trainees generally will not be as successful as their male counterparts. Other experts suggest that while women may not perform their general police tasks as well as men, they might perform better at such tasks as preventing crime and handling female and juvenile cases (Appier, 1993). This view has been labeled as the *crime prevention model* of police work (Appier, 1993). Research investigating the training experiences of women and minorities has found some confirmation of this model, with higher attrition rates and lower training satisfaction levels among women recruits compared with men (Felkenes and Schroedel, 1993). It appears that even undergraduate criminal justice majors who intend to work in law enforcement feel negatively about women as police officers, with over 50 percent of the 809 male students harboring such unfavorable attitudes (Austin and Hummer, 1994). Despite the existence of hostile, gender-biased environments, women and minorities generally have fought to overcome racism and sexism in law enforcement recruitment and training (Martin, 1994; Thomann, Pilant, and Kay, 1994).

Female officers in police departments where the proportion of women is lower seem to be more aware of their gender in performing police work compared with women in police departments where the proportion of female officers is higher (Belknap and Shelley, 1993). Female officers are also more conscious of their gender in smaller police departments compared with women in larger police departments (Belknap and Shelley, 1993).

The mandatory hiring of female officers in many police departments has made them a target of on-the-job hostility from more than a few male officers (Felkenes, Peretz, and Schroedel, 1993). In Washington, for instance, a study of sixty-seven male police officers following the recruitment of

female officers suggested that although male attitudes toward female officers have improved, about 20 percent of the officers continued to exhibit hostility toward women in law enforcement (Grown and Carlson, 1993). Observers might think that under such circumstances stress levels among women officers might be higher than for male officers. However, this has not been the case, at least in those jurisdictions where this issue has been studied (Morash and Haarr, 1995).

Reactions to Affirmative Action and Minority Recruitment

Affirmative action policies increase the proportion of minorities and women in police departments throughout the nation (Felkenes and Unsinger, 1992). The use of quotas in establishing appropriate racial/ethnic/gender balances is legally justified, particularly if there is a compelling state interest in rectifying past discrimination in any particular municipal department, and most police executives are complying with the general principles of affirmative action (Carter and Sapp, 1991). One problem noted by Carter and Sapp (1991) is that although the educational backgrounds of many minority recruits are similar to those of their white counterparts, the requirement of a college education continues to be perceived as discriminatory and thus as disadvantageous to blacks desiring law enforcement careers. Thus, affirmative action has been labeled as shortsighted and has led to organizational conflict and allegations that law enforcement agencies have somehow recruited less qualified minority personnel. While women and minorities in law enforcement may never achieve their proportional representation in the population, affirmative action efforts will continue (Felkenes and Unsinger, 1992).

Professionalism: Education and Training

Early police reformers such as August Vollmer sought to: (1) eliminate political influence from police administration; (2) secure expert leadership in police management; (3) modernize the organizational structure of police departments; and (4) raise the quality of rank-and-file police officers (Walker, 1979:164). It is doubtful whether political influence has been eliminated from police administration. It is also doubtful that profound changes have occurred in the organizational structure of police departments. Furthermore, it is doubtful whether police reform efforts have resulted in expert leadership. However, the quality of rank-and-file police officers has substantially improved.

Police professionalism has drawn increasing interest from criminal justicians. The term *professional* has been elusive, however, as few attempts have ever been made to define it or give it a precise and consistent interpretation (Skolnick, 1994; Virginia State Crime Commission, 1994a). However, it has often been used to explain such variables as victim satisfaction with police services, police discipline, conduct and corruption, and general effectiveness of police (Brandl and Horvath, 1991; Hickman, 1990; Woods, 1993). The average number of training hours required of new police recruits in 1993 ranged from over 1,100 hours in departments serving populations of at least 100,000 to less than 500 hours in those serving populations of fewer than 2,500 (Reaves, 1996:1).

Professionalism ordinarily is marked by the attainment of at least five general objectives. These include (1) a clearly defined body of knowledge, (2) a code of ethics, (3) ongoing education, (4) uniform standards of excellence for selection, education, and performance, and (5) an unequivocal service orientation (Shigley, 1988). If these standards are stringently applied to law enforcement, it is questionable whether professionalism among police officers has been fully realized. Increasingly, law enforcement officers are expected to attain minimal educational levels and receive fixed amounts of in-service training. In many jurisdictions, relevant educational courses are recommended but not required. While greater amounts of training are equated with greater professionalism, the type and amount of training are often vaguely defined or unspecified.

Improving the "quality" or professionalism of the rank-and-file police officer means several things. Most large police departments use psychological tests to screen their police recruits (Korn-

feld, 1995). Many of these departments also use professional psychologists as members of their oral screening boards (Faulkner, 1994; Lumb, 1995; Pollock and Becker, 1995). Many municipal police departments have established minimum educational requirements as prerequisites for employment. Also, prospective candidates must meet stringent physical standards and withstand a thorough background check. In most states, the prospective recruit must be certified by a regulatory board before being hired. All of these criteria are associated with improving the quality of the rank-and-file police officer (Lumb, 1995).

Nevada police officers are exposed to a wide variety of practical and theoretical experiences aimed at enhancing job performance. They receive training in language skills and learn how to testify in court, how to perform field sobriety tests, and how to deal with gangs, cults, and hate crimes (Brand and Peak, 1995). Officers in Chicago receive various forms of training to help them become more proficient at police work. In 1995, there was a strong emphasis on community-oriented policing, and under the Chicago Alternative Policing Strategy (CAPS), officers were evaluated on a variety of "hands-on" experiences and innovative problem-solving techniques (Dantzker, Lurigio, and Hartnett, 1995a). Some police training programs, such as the one in Rochester, New York, focus on an anger-management training module to increase rapport between police officers and citizens (Abernethy and Cox, 1994). The training has shown favorable results, as is indicated by the significant reduction in use-of-force arrests.

Some critics question whether these requirements and restrictions necessarily produce the right kind of police officer (Shigley, 1987). How do we know that any psychological screening device accurately measures one's ability to handle stressful situations? And how does being able to run a mile in under seven minutes make a police officer better at promoting good police-community relations? Will a police officer who has a college degree act more decisively when being fired upon by a bank robber than a police officer who has only a high school diploma?

Currently, a majority of police officers in large municipal police departments either have completed college or have some post-secondary educational training (Carter and Sapp, 1991). In 1993, for instance, 12 percent of all local police departments required new officer recruits to have some college education (Reaves, 1996:1). Another 8 percent required some type of degree (either an associate of arts degree or a bachelor's degree), and about 1 percent required a degree from a four-year college (Reaves, 1996:1).

An argument can be made that college-educated police officers communicate more effectively with the public because of their greater verbal skills. Those with college degrees may also have better chances at promotion. But a study of Illinois police departments showed that being promoted depended more on politics than on merit or education (Fischer, Golden, and Heininger, 1985). Data were obtained from 537 police officers above the rank of patrol officer who had more than eight years' experience. The majority of the veteran police officers who sought promotion and who had college educations were unable to get promoted. Most officers believed that education or merit had little or nothing to do with who gets promoted (Fischer, Golden, and Heininger, 1985).

Apart from a college education, what accounts most for success on the job is on-the-job training (Pugh, 1985). In some jurisdictions, such as White Plains, New York, all personnel below the rank of captain must complete a forty-hour in-service training program that is designed to increase job proficiency and enhance self-image and motivation (Bradley, 1986). In most departments, training in human relations skills is increasingly a part of a recruit's instruction as well (Das, 1985). This relatively new emphasis on human relations dovetails nicely with the trend toward greater police-community interaction, and it illustrates the concern given to the real kinds of tasks and problems confronting police officers in over 75 percent of their daily routine (Bohm, 1986). Some training programs are faulted for being too structured and for not cultivating the flexibility a police officer must have in making split-second, on-the-spot decisions in dealing with an increasingly diverse public (Faulkner, 1994; Pollock and Becker, 1995). Cultural sensitivity training is increasingly encouraged in police training programs (Barlow and Barlow, 1994).

Police officers' ideas about professionalism reflect their desire to increase their knowledge about police operations and their ability to cope with a wide range of problems requiring the exercise of discretion as well as their pride in uniform and appearance that is not unlike that of the military (Brown and Vogel, 1983). In some jurisdictions where computer-assisted instruction is used in police training, police officers pride themselves in acquiring useful and essential information concerning criminal justice procedures, such as using the exclusionary rule (Wilkenson and Chattin-McNichols, 1985). Most police officers are genuinely concerned with their image as professionals and support programs designed to enhance that image (Fisher, Golden, and Heininger, 1985).

One way of making police officer training official and certifying that the curriculum teaches universally accepted behaviors is to accredit the training program. *Accreditation is the certification by an officially recognized body or agency that any particular training program complies with national standards and requirements* (Bizzack, 1993; Williams, 1989).

Accreditation of police training programs has been conducted on a large scale since 1979 (Williams, 1989). Law enforcement training programs are required to meet certain minimum expectations. Thus, after the acceptance of accreditation by most police departments, substantial changes in police training took place. Further, in most jurisdictions, police departments modified their policies to bring them into compliance with nationally mandated accreditation standards. Subsequent surveys of a cross section of police departments suggest that accreditation has been effective in bringing about improvements in officer training and effectiveness (Bizzack, 1993; Vaughn, 1992). Accreditation has also helped improve officer accountability by making officers more aware of their responsibilities in serving citizens (Bizzack, 1993).

Measuring Police Performance

How can we determine whether police officers are doing their jobs responsibly and in accordance with department policies? Early attempts to assess police effectiveness and evaluate their performance were plagued by methodological and theoretical problems. In order to understand what police officers are supposed to do, we should know the general mission of the police departments where they work. Early surveys of mission statements suggested that few existed (Cordner and Kenney, 1996) and that these were often too general to determine whether they were being fulfilled. For example, one early study of the performance of Arkansas state police revealed that in most instances, officers could not agree on specific performance criteria. Further, even when such criteria was identified, there was little or no agreement about how it should be used to evaluate performance (Neufeldt, 1983). Even subsequent research into factors most likely to accurately measure police performance has been sketchy (Oettmeier and Wycoff, 1994).

One way of evaluating an officer's or an agency's performance is to consider the number of complaints filed by citizens. Officers who receive more complaints than others might be considered "less effective," while officers receiving fewer or no complaints might be considered "more effective." We don't know this for sure, however. By the same token, agencies receiving large numbers of citizen complaints might be considered less effective than agencies that receive fewer complaints. In fact, this type of assessment has been used by police departments such as the New York City police department to predict an officer's career performance (Mealia, 1990).

Another way of evaluating performance is to determine the association between an officer's educational level and his or her ability to handle stressful situations. It has been found in at least some departments that a college degree increases patrol effectiveness (Dantzker, 1989) in that better-educated officers handle stressful situations better than less-educated officers. Thus, requiring officers to have college degrees might be one way of ensuring that more competent officers are hired and that their performance levels will generally be higher. However, this thinking has had only limited testing. Research from the RAND Corporation in Santa Monica, California, for instance, suggests that it is difficult to find strong correlations between police performance and conventional indicators of it, such as arrest rates, complaints, departmental policies, and victim response to police action (Petersilia, Abrahamse, and Wilson, 1990).

The Police Personality and Subculture

Apart from the military-like uniformity that typifies police officers and the regimentation they observe in their routine activities, is there a **"police personality"** that is unique and different from other personalities (Franz and Jones, 1987)? And is there a police subculture with its own norms and belief systems apart and distinct from, yet within, the larger culture of the American public? Social psychologists have portrayed police officers as having a distinct set of personality characteristics, including cynicism, aggressiveness, conventionalism, and authoritarianism (Krug, 1961; Watson and Sterling, 1969; Wilson, 1974).

The term **working personality** *has been used to describe police officers' similar and distinctive cognitive tendencies and behavioral responses and particular "life style"* (Skolnick, 1994). This working personality emerges through a combination of two principal variables—danger and authority. Police officers are trained to be "suspicious persons," and the element of danger inherent in the police role sets them apart from those not exposed to it. Furthermore, arrest powers and authority set police officers apart from others, because officers are required to enforce laws that regulate the flow of public activity and morality (Baker and Meyer, 1980:102–103).

There is a pervasive *esprit de corps* that binds police officers to one another (Bittner, 1970:63). "Police officers often remark that one of the most cherished aspects of their occupation is the spirit of 'one for all, and all for one'. To the extent that the fraternal spirit binds members of the police, it also segregates them from the rest of society" (Bittner, 1970:63–64). Police develop a code of secrecy and exhibit a high degree of fraternal loyalty.

Most close friends of police officers are other police officers, although this is not atypical of other professions or occupational categories (Skolnick, 1994). This "pattern" of social interaction continues over time to give outsiders the impression that police do, indeed, have their own subculture. This view is reminiscent of Homans's notion of interactions, activities, and sentiments (Homans, 1950). Although somewhat oversimplified, this view holds that persons who engage in similar activities and interact with one another frequently will develop similar sentiments. Applied to police officers and the associations they develop with one another, it suggests the development of a rather unique police subculture or police "family" (Drummond, 1976).

Several factors may account for this subculture and its perpetuation over time. For one thing, police officers are selectively recruited and screened through interviews and psychological tests and measures. Most officers are conservative and conventional. Unconventional types of persons would probably be excluded by the selection process. It may be that certain types of persons are attracted to police work, such as persons who want to exert authority over others, who want to control the actions of people, or who want absolute power (Bonifacio, 1991).

Police officers are obligated to enforce the law and are often regarded as "the enemy" by many citizens who exceed the speed limit or commit other minor violations. They are alienated from many people because they are sworn to uphold a code of conduct that is supposedly higher than the conduct expected of others. In addition, they work shifts that cause them to keep unusual hours; thus, they are not able to socialize frequently with people who hold down routine, nine-to-five jobs.

Subsequent large-scale studies of police officer candidates have suggested that they have as personality characteristics self-discipline or self-control, tough poise, and low anxiety (Lorr and Strack, 1995). However, other studies indicate that officers' personality characteristics may change over time as they acquire more experience. Some investigations suggest that officers with more than twelve years' experience tend to be cynical, aloof, tough-minded, independent, aggressive, hostile, and more authoritarian than officers with less work

experience (Evans, Coman, and Stanley, 1992). Thus, time on the job might be an overriding factor leading to less flexibility in dealing with occupational stress.

But there probably is the same degree of dissimilarity among police officers that there is among the general public. However, serious efforts to identify a particular type of police personality have not been successful (Broderick, 1987). Further, police officers in every jurisdiction socialize with persons from every walk of life. It is probably most accurate to say that police officers manifest their "working personality" primarily when they are on the job. And while instances of social aggregation among police officers may give the impression of a police subculture, it is more likely that they maintain loose social ties with many persons so that there is no police subculture as such.

Police Officer Deaths in the Line of Duty

Between 1978 and 1995, 1,346 police officers were killed in the line of duty (Maguire and Pastore, 1995:357). Between 1983 and 1995, officer deaths per year ranged from 63 to 80, with an average of about 72 per year (Maguire and Pastore, 1995:357). Over half of these deaths occurred during arrests or investigations of suspicious persons and circumstances. An average of 55 officers per year are killed accidentally in the line of duty (Maguire and Pastore, 1995:360).

In response to these deaths, police departments have equipped their officers with weaponry at least as sophisticated as that of criminals on city streets. In 1993, for instance, 84 percent of all local police departments authorized their officers to carry semi-automatic sidearms, up from 73 percent in 1990. Furthermore, in 1993 a third of all local police departments required all regular field officers to wear protective body armor while on duty (Reaves, 1996:2). The late 1980s and early 1990s saw an increase in the use of nonlethal weaponry as well. By 1993, nearly every police department authorized the use of the sophisticated and powerful PR-24 baton. Chemical agents, such as pepper

---

Highlight 4.2. Police Officer Killed in Line of Duty: The Case of the Police Officer and the Farmer

Not much happens in Watford City, North Dakota. But one night police received a call that a local farmer was drunk and disorderly in one of the bars. In fact, some eyewitnesses said that the farmer was holding some people hostage.

Officer Keith Braddock, thirty-nine years old, a husband and a father, went to the bar to investigate. As he walked through the door, the farmer blew him away with a high-caliber rifle. The farmer was Robert Meade, forty-one years old. He had been in trouble with the law before, but he had never been violent.

Braddock was everyone's friend. He had no enemies, not even Meade, whom he knew from previous incidents. He had volunteered for military service and served some time in the Gulf War in 1990, guarding enemy prisoners as a military policeman. Braddock's commanding officer, Col. Scott Brand of the North Dakota National Guard's 191st Military Police Unit, said of Braddock, "He did a very good job for us . . . very well respected and relied upon." Braddock was honorably discharged from military service in 1991, and returned to his police job in Watford City.

Townspeople were shocked at the shooting. Nothing like it had ever happened in Watford City. People just don't go around shooting other people here, said many of the residents. Meade immediately surrendered to authorities when they stormed the bar and pled not guilty by reason of insanity at his subsequent arraignment.

The North Dakota Peace Officer's Association (NDPOA) swung into high gear. A critical response team went to Watford City to comfort Braddock's grieving family. Captain Dan Draovitch, a Minot, North Dakota, detective and president of the NDPOA, summed it up by saying, "Emotionally, this occupation is pretty tough. I've known him [Braddock] through the years as a very personable, well-trained officer." The critical response team exists for just such occasions. Its purpose is to lend support to the family suffering the loss as well as to other officers and their families.

Source: Adapted from Associated Press, "Peace Officers Association Supports Families," *Minot (ND) Daily News*, May 6, 1996, p. B3.

---

spray, also became a part of officers' growing arsenal of nonlethal weaponry (Reaves, 1996:2).

The mortality rate of police officers is of increasing interest to researchers. While some experts suggest that a major cause of police deaths is psychological stress, the National Center of Health Statistics found that the leading cause of mortality among police officers is heart disease (Reviere and Young, 1994). An international study of suicide during the period 1980–1989 showed that the suicide rate for police officers was somewhat higher than that for other workers (Lester, 1992). Firearms were most often used in police suicides. Data from the National Mortality Detail File show findings consistent with those of Lester—police officers in public agencies tend to have slightly higher suicide rates compared with age-matched counterparts in other occupations and professions (Stack and Kelley, 1994).

Studies of specific police departments yielded insights into the problem of suicide among police officers. For instance, in a study of police suicides from 1977 to 1988 at the Los Angeles Police Department (Josephson and Reiser, 1990) it was found that the suicides increased from 8.1 per 1,000 officers in 1977 to 12 per 1,000 officers in 1988. The variables cited as most responsible for officer suicides were marital discord, job-related stress, and alcohol abuse. Research into other police departments (Bonifacio, 1991) has also found that alcohol abuse, marital difficulties, trauma, and line-of-duty injuries were highly correlated with officer suicides. Some observers indicate that police suicides may in fact be underreported and that the

---

Box 4.3. Cop Bulldozed by Thief: The Case of the Speeding Ten-Ton Tractor

Policing is risky business. Consider the case of Officer Mike Hanke of York, Nebraska. Officer Hanke was on patrol in York when he received a report from Champion Home Builders, Inc., that one of their tractors had just been stolen. In fact, they said, the thief had earlier rammed two pickup trucks into a wall, smashed a car into a telephone pole nearby, and pushed a twenty-foot flatbed trailer through another wall. The thief was definitely on a rampage.

When Officer Hanke spotted the tractor coming down the middle of the road, he flashed his patrol car lights and blocked the tractor's path. Bad idea. The thief didn't stop. In fact, he drove the tractor right over Officer Hanke's cruiser, pinning him inside. Officer Hanke managed to squeeze off twelve rounds from his 9mm pistol, but he suspects that none of the bullets hit the thief. The thief escaped in the tractor, which was later found abandoned several miles from the scene of Officer Hanke's ordeal.

Source: Adapted from Associated Press, "Cop OK after Cruiser Crushed," *Minot (N.D.) Daily News,* June 5, 1996, p. A2.

---

actual number of police suicides might be much higher (Stack and Kelley, 1994). This is particularly true among officers assigned "high-risk" street duties, who are subjected to more stress.

Police Stress and Burnout

In recent years, two psychological phenomena appear to have affected police officers to a critical degree. These are **stress** and **burnout**. *Stress is defined as the body's nonspecific response to any demand placed on it.* While stress may be either positive (e.g., the body's response to a sports event or to an examination) or negative, *police stress specifically refers to negative stress that is accompanied by an alarm reaction, resistance, and exhaustion.* Stress is often measured by the twenty-two-item Langer Stress Index (Violante, Marshall, and How, 1985).

Stress is not unique to police work. All jobs have some stress. Most studies of police stress have been theoretical, speculative, and full of conjecture. Comparatively little empirical research has rigorously investigated police stress and the sorts of problems such stress creates (Violante and Aron, 1995).

Several "police stressors" have been identified

that cause an increase in the incidence of coronary heart disease, ulcers, high blood pressure, headaches, and gastric disorders. Some of these are the constant threat to an officer's health and safety; boredom alternating with the need for sudden alertness and mobilizing energy; responsibility for protecting others' lives; continual exposure to people in pain or distress; post-shooting trauma; the need to control emotions, even when provoked to anger; the presence of a gun, sometimes even during off-duty hours; and the fragmented nature of police work, with only rare opportunities to follow a case to conclusion or obtain feedback or follow-up information (Anderson, Swenson, and Clay, 1995; Violante and Aron, 1995).

Stressors also come from the police department itself, from the criminal justice system, and from society at large. Poor administrative supervision, few rewards for a good job performance, insufficient training and experience, excessive paperwork, and inadequate job opportunities often are cited as major causes of stress for police officers (Morash and Haarr, 1995). Court decisions such as the exclusionary rule and other legal restrictions on the freedoms of police officers when doing their jobs also contribute to stress (Turco, 1986). The conspicuous lack of public support for police work is yet another source of stress (Anderson, Swenson, and Clay, 1995).

Police officers sometimes experience personal and internal stress when they worry excessively about their ability to cope with certain assignments or fear dangerous assignments. For instance, over 950 police officers were killed in the line of duty between 1976 and 1983 (Schmidt, 1985). Of course, officers are much more likely to die in a traffic accident than in the line of duty. The unusual working hours and the degree of risk also affect police officers' families, which is another source of stress. While previous research showed that female police officers have especially high stress levels as they strive to compete physically with male officers in difficult police roles (O'Brien, 1986), more recent evidence suggests that female police officers exhibit no more stress than their male counterparts (Morash and Haarr, 1995).

Closely associated with stress is burnout. *Burnout is the psychological equivalent of physical stress. It is a disorder characterized by the loss of motivation and commitment related to task performance.* Police burnout is the loss of commitment to the job and of motivation to be successful at police work (Hendricks and McKean, 1995). Burnout is frequently measured by the Maslach Burnout Inventory, a psychological device consisting of a number of subscales, each designed to tap selected psychological dimensions (Maslach and Jackson, 1979).

Stress and burnout are important because they influence the quality of a police officer's job performance. Such phenomena as high absenteeism, low or poor morale, inefficiency, and poor judgment are direct results of stress and burnout. Other phenomena related to burnout and stress include high suicide and divorce rates and alcoholism (Anderson, Swenson, and Clay, 1995).

Investigations of how police officers deal with stress have led researchers to conclude that alcohol is the most convenient and socially acceptable "coping" method (Violante and Aron, 1995). In fact, there is evidence that the police "subculture" accepts and reinforces the use of alcohol. Coping methods such as cynicism and deviance have also been identified, although these types of responses have often triggered even greater stress levels (Violante and Aron, 1995).

Several strategies have been used to combat stress and burnout among officers. These strategies are stress-management focused and include employee assistance, home visits, and peer counseling programs (Anderson, Swenson, and Clay, 1995; Morash and Haarr, 1995). Employee assistance programs are designed to offer diagnostic, referral, and treatment services (Beehr, Johnson, and Nieva, 1995). In Florida, employee assistance programs offer prevention, intervention, and after-care counseling. They help police officers with such problems as substance abuse disorders; family, child, or interpersonal difficulties; legal concerns; and emotional problems (Violante and Aron, 1995).

The Indiana State Police Employee Assistance Program (EAP), created in 1978, is designed to assist officers or their families with problems such as alcoholism, drugs, or emotional difficulties. It was the first of its kind in the country and has enjoyed a fairly high success rate (Lambuth, 1984). In fact, in 1984 the program began training all new state police recruits to recognize stress, to handle co-worker's problems, and to become acquainted with the hazards and pressures of their jobs (Lambuth, 1984).

The Los Angeles Police Department has experimented with a limited home-visit program that includes an outreach approach in which in-house mental health specialists work with distressed officers to reduce sick time, medical costs, and civil liability (Petrone and Reiser, 1985). During a four-month evaluation period, eighty-eight officers were questioned about the program. Over 50 percent supported it, and many indicated a willingness to accept home visits (Petrone and Reiser, 1985).

Using peer counselors to help officers suffering from work stress means that one police officer functions as a "counselor" for other officers (Goolkasian, Geddes, and DeJong, 1985:64–66). Police departments in Rochester, New York; New Haven, Connecticut; and Tucson, Arizona, have experimented with peer counselors and report favorable results. In Tucson, only one officer acts as a peer counselor. This officer is a sergeant, but the patrol officers he counsels look up to and feel comfortable with him. In order to be effective, peer counselors must have the trust and respect of their fellow officers. The cost of these programs ranges from $10,000 to $200,000 annually, depending on their sophistication and operations and the services provided.

Summary

Federal law enforcement agencies for the most part belong to two major departments: (1) the Department of Justice and (2) the Department of the Treasury. The Department of Justice heads up the Federal Bureau of Investigation and the Drug Enforcement Administration. The FBI investigates violations of over two hundred federal statutes involving both criminal and civil offenses, and the DEA investigates a variety of narcotics violations. The Department of the Treasury encompasses several law enforcement agencies, including the Bureau of Alcohol, Tobacco, and Firearms; the United States Customs Service; the Internal Revenue Service Criminal Investigation Division; and the Secret Service.

The CID within the Internal Revenue Service investigates and recommends for prosecution anyone who violates federal income tax laws or engages in tax fraud. The Secret Service, originally assigned to investigate counterfeiting, is also responsible for protecting the president and other dignitaries. It also investigates any fraud involving electronic funds transfers in banking institutions.

State police agencies operate primarily to enforce state traffic laws, although their duties vary considerably from one state to the next. County and metropolitan police are charged primarily with enforcing local laws and conducting local criminal investigations.

Law enforcement in the United States suffers from several problems. There is little coordination between major agencies at the federal, state, and local levels. Criticisms have been made of the quality of police training and professionalism, the use of deadly force in making arrests, police corruption, and the use of deception and entrapment. Critics stress the need for greater cooperation between the community and the various law enforcement agencies and encourage greater citizen participation in police affairs.

Modern-day policing is patterned after the military model. The Metropolitan Police of London, established in 1929, still influences police organization and administration. Police officer selection and training underwent considerable transformation as the result of the work of August Vollmer, a police chief in Berkeley, California, in 1916. The Wickersham Commission's 1931 criticisms of police operations and effectiveness focused more attention on police training methods.

Currently, there is considerable variation in police recruitment programs, although accreditation procedures have resulted in greater uniformity and professionalism. The use of psychological screening mechanisms and thorough background investigations has done much to improve the quality of police recruits. Affirmative action programs and other pressures have caused police departments to be more aggressive in hiring women and minorities. The performance levels of women and minorities are at least equal to those of male and non-minority officers. In recent years, the trend has been to require new recruits to have higher levels of education and even college diplomas in some jurisdictions. Higher levels of education are equated with greater professionalism, although professionalism may be measured in several other ways.

Some people believe that there is a distinctive police personality, although evidence of such a personality is not strong. Although experts say that compared with other occupations and professions, police work is not particularly stressful, it can lead to burnout and other personal and social problems. Suicide rates among police officers tend to be higher than for other occupations. Many larger police departments have programs to assist officers suffering from work-related stress or who have chemical or alcohol dependencies. These employee-assistance programs enable officers to cope more effectively with their jobs.

Key Terms

Bureau of Alcohol, Tobacco, and Firearms (BATF)
Burnout
Department of Justice
Department of the Treasury

Drug Enforcement Administration (DEA)
Federal Bureau of Investigation (FBI)
Immigration and Naturalization Service (INS)
Internal Revenue Service Criminal Investigation Division (CID)
Metropolitan Police of London
Overlapping jurisdictions
Police professionalism
Police personality
Private police
Sir Robert Peel
State highway patrols
State police
Stress
United States Customs Service (USCS)
United States Marshals Service (USMS)
August Vollmer
Wickersham Reports
Working personality

6. What are the various duties and responsibilities of the Secret Service? Which bureau oversees the Secret Service?

7. Differentiate between the state and local police in terms of their respective functions. Are all state police assigned identical functions? What are some of the duties of state police besides traffic control?

8. Discuss briefly the history of the modern-day police department. Are modern police departments based on any particular historical model?

9. What were some of Colquhoun's proposals for a proper police agency? Discuss the importance of these proposals for modern police work.

10. Who was Sir Robert Peel, and what was his contribution to the development of police departments?

Questions for Review

1. What program was initiated in 1968 to coordinate police activities in local and state jurisdictions? Briefly explain the functions of the program.

2. What are the responsibilities of the Criminal Investigation Division of the Internal Revenue Service? What bureau or agency oversees the CID?

3. Identify the major law enforcement agencies supervised by the Department of Justice. Briefly discuss the functions of each.

4. What law enforcement agencies have some jurisdiction over illegal drug trafficking? Briefly discuss some of the problems associated with overlapping jurisdictions.

5. What agency investigates arson-for-profit and illegal possession of automatic weapons? What other duties and responsibilities are associated with this agency?

Suggested Readings

Brandl, Steven G. and David E. Barlow. *Classics in Policing.* Cincinnati, OH: Anderson, 1996.

Chevigny, Paul. *Edge of the Knife: Police Violence in the Americas.* New York: New Press, 1995.

Gaines, Larry K., Victor E. Kappeler, and Joseph B. Vaughn. *Policing in America.* 2d ed. Cincinnati, OH: Anderson, 1996.

LaGrange, Randy L. *Policing American Society.* 2d ed. Chicago: Nelson-Hall, 1997.

Peak, Kenneth J. and Ronald W. Glensor. *Community Policing and Problem Solving: Strategies and Practices.* Upper Saddle River, NJ: Prentice-Hall, 1996.

Poveda, Tony G. *Lawlessness and Reform: The FBI in Transition.* Belmont, CA: Wadsworth, 1990.

Violence Policy Center. *Cop Killers: Assault Weapon Attacks on America's Police.* Washington, DC: Violence Policy Center, 1995.

CHAPTER 5

The Police: Operations and Procedures

You are a female officer assigned to vice. Dressed in a miniskirt, you are ordered to arrest anyone soliciting for prostitution. You see a man driving down the road. He does not seem interested in you. You stand provocatively by the roadside and wave at him, motioning him to pull over. He stops and rolls down his window. You smile and ask him if he is looking for a good time. He smiles back and asks you what you mean. You respond that you might go with him to a motel, where "one thing might lead to another." He asks you to "hop in," and as you do, you flash your badge and arrest him for soliciting for prostitution.

You are a police officer walking a neighborhood beat downtown. Passing a delicatessen known for its good food, you notice a delivery van that is double-parked. You go in the delicatessen and ask whose van it is. The manager says, "Oh, that's my brother-in-law Tony delivering some fresh meats. Want a pastrami sandwich on the house?" "Sure," you say. You eat the sandwich and leave, ignoring the double-parked van. Soon you pass a battered pick-up truck parked in a space with an expired parking meter. You write a parking ticket and place it on the front windshield.

You are a white police officer riding with a white partner who pulls over a black motorist for "weaving." You didn't see the black motorist weaving or doing anything unusual. Your partner writes a ticket, citing the motorist for speeding and reckless driving. The angry motorist mutters something about "racism" and that you will see him in court later. Your partner, obviously angry, acts as if he is going to arrest the motorist but changes his mind and tells the motorist to be on his way. A month later, you and your partner are called to testify in municipal court, where the motorist is contesting the ticket your partner gave him. Your partner gives his testimony, saying that the motorist was "all over the road." You corroborate what your partner has said. You say to the judge, "Yes, the guy was driving all over the road. I thought he might be drunk or something."

These scenarios and others like them are played out every day in cities throughout the United States.

We know, or at least we *think* we know, how each scenario ought to be resolved. In the case of the undercover female police officer, you might think that she deliberately encouraged the motorist to stop and talk with her. She presented a powerful temptation to the motorist and made an arrest before probable cause could be established. The motorist never should have been arrested without more incriminating information. Right? Not necessarily.

The second scenario involving the officer who accepted the pastrami sandwich and decided not to ticket the double-parked van is fairly easy to resolve as well. Since the officer ticketed the truck because of the expired parking meter, he certainly should have ticketed the double-parked van. Right? Not necessarily.

The third scenario involving the white police officer who stopped and ticketed the black motorist for speeding and reckless driving when, in fact, he had apparently done nothing wrong is also clear-cut. The partner should have told the truth in court to exonerate the motorist. This would have been a simple case of doing the right thing and not committing perjury. Right? Not necessarily. In policing, deciding what to do is not always clear-cut and simple.

In each of these cases, **police discretion** was at work. The officers were making on-the-spot judgments about someone's conduct. Both legal and extralegal factors were operating to influence officer decision making in each case. In each case, abuses of discretion occurred. Citizens were jeopardized, to one degree or another, by officer misconduct. But little or nothing could be done about it.

This chapter is about the work police officers do. Police officers are in daily contact with citizens. They are hired to enforce the law and protect the community. Departmental policies address how these officers will perform their diverse tasks.

A key topic of study about police departments and the administration of police services is the nature of patrol activities. What styles of patrol best fit the communities? Various patrol styles are described in this chapter. An important development in the early investigation of patrol styles was the establishment of the Law Enforcement Assistance Administration (LEAA). The LEAA, which lasted through the 1970s, prompted numerous studies of policing and police department effectiveness. Much was learned through the experiments that were funded, either in whole or in part, by the LEAA. The information these experiments yielded was inconsistent with what experts anticipated. Some of this research, especially in Kansas City, Missouri, will be described.

The nature of police discretion is also examined here. Under what circumstances do police exercise their discretion? This discussion of police discretion involves arrests and detentions; searches and seizures of persons, their personal effects, and their automobiles and homes; the use of deadly force; and perjury as a form of police misconduct.

An important area of interest to criminal justicians is community-oriented policing. More and more attention is given to programs that bring police officers closer to the public they serve. Neighborhood programs are enhanced by officers who organize watch groups and other crime prevention efforts.

Several key issues of importance to police agencies and researchers are discussed. These include police training, police discretion, police deception and entrapment, police-community relations, police violence and the use of excessive force, police administration and corruption, police misconduct and internal affairs, and accountability and civilian complaint review boards. The significance of these issues for criminal justice is discussed.

What Is "Real Police Work"?

James Q. Wilson says that for police officers, real police work is catching real criminals or felons, preferably while the crime is in progress (Wilson, 1968:68). But on average, police spend only 10 or 20 percent of their time doing real police work (Bohm, 1986:198). Police officers spend most of their time on patrol. They perform many necessary community services, including first aid and various types of citizen assistance. In the 1980s and 1990s, homeless persons have become increasingly visible on city streets. While police agencies have been moderately responsive to the needs of the homeless, many police officers view their interactions with the homeless as a burden, and not a part of "real" police work (Plotkin and Narr, 1993).

Real police work has been portrayed on television programs such as *Top Cop* and *Real Stories of the Highway Patrol*. But police work has also been sensationalized on programs such as *N.Y.P.D. Blue, The Commish,* and *Silk Stalkings.* The public has mixed sentiments about what police actually do. About 40 percent of a sample of 796 New York City residents believed that TV depictions of police work are accurate, while 84 percent of a sample of 502 New York City police officers considered the depictions inaccurate and resented the stereotypical depictions of their roles (Penn and Schoen Associates, Inc., 1987).

Citizen complaints were most often focused on police officers' irresponsible use of their weapons, violations of suspects' constitutional rights, and police officers' reckless driving during high-speed chases. Called **hot pursuit**, such high-speed chases once took place relatively frequently (Crew, Kessler, and Fridell, 1994). However, most police departments now have policies governing hot pursuit and the conditions under which it is warranted (Crew, 1993). Public safety and citizen reactions to hot pursuit have influenced police department policy.

One important issue is police discretion to use deadly force in making arrests. Many states once observed the **fleeing felon rule**. *This rule authorized police officers to use deadly force, if necessary, to prevent felons from escaping* (Fyfe, 1988; Sarre, 1993). However, the fleeing felon rule has been replaced by the defense-of-life standard, which says that deadly force may be used to apprehend fleeing felons only if an officer's life is in immediate danger or the lives of others are seriously jeopardized (Fyfe, 1988). The Supreme Court has applied this restriction to officers in *all* jurisdictions (Fyfe and Blumberg, 1985: *Tennessee v. Garner*, 1985).

Depending upon the jurisdiction, police officers spend from 50 to 90 percent of their time on patrol (Crank and Langworthy, 1992; Cordner and Hale, 1992). Day and night, alone or in pairs, on foot, on a motorcycle, or in a cruiser, police officers patrol. Most routine work (e.g., giving first aid, counseling, mediating, citing, investigating auto accidents, and locating lost children) is unrelated

to crime fighting. However, it is that small fraction of time police officers spend on patrol, doing "real police work" that has relevance here (Bohm, 1986:198–199). This is the type of work that brings suspects into the criminal justice system for processing.

Police patrol activity is designed to prevent crime. It is also designed to provide more direct services to neighborhoods whenever crimes occur. Some experts refer to this type of patrolling activity as **preventive patrol** (Crank and Langworthy, 1992; Lund, 1988). Several types of police patrol will be described in a later section of this chapter.

Real police work begins when one of two things happens. First and most often, police officers are notified by a dispatcher that a crime has been committed or is in progress. Silent alarms in banks are triggered, and police departments are notified by burglar alarm companies, such as ADT. Or citizens call the police and report victimizations or crimes being committed. Or a report may be made about someone's suspicious behavior, which may or may not be criminal. Police officers investigate these reports.

Second, police officers sometimes observe crimes being committed, although this is relatively rare—obviously, criminals usually try to commit crimes when and where police are unlikely to appear. In any case, patrolling officers may drive by a liquor store and see someone in a ski mask pointing a pistol at a store clerk. Or they may see a woman being attacked by a street gang. Or they may hear a burglar alarm in a nearby building. When any of these events occur, the police officers' "real police work" begins.

Police officers have broad discretionary powers when making arrests. However, the courts have restricted the types of things they can do while patrolling their community. The rights of suspects and the responsibilities of police officers sometimes conflict. Under certain circumstances, police officers may be accused of misconduct, dishonesty, or corruption. Most officers attempt to walk a fine line, balancing their job expectations with those of community residents.

Finally, other types of officers—private police—supplement the routine tasks performed by regular police officers on patrol. As we have seen, private police make up a growing proportion of law enforcement personnel, contributing to community welfare in various ways.

The Law Enforcement Assistance Administration (LEAA)

In 1968, Congress established the **Law Enforcement Assistance Administration** (LEAA) (U.S. Code Annotated, 1996). Under 42 U.S. Code Section 3701, Congress declared that

> the high incidence of crime in the United States threatens the peace, security, and general welfare of the nation and its citizens. To reduce and prevent crime and juvenile delinquency, and to insure the greater safety of the people, law enforcement and criminal justice efforts must be better coordinated, intensified, and made more effective at all levels of government.

The purposes of the LEAA were to provide necessary resources, leadership, and coordination to various state and local law enforcement agencies to prevent and/or reduce adult crime and juvenile delinquency. The LEAA recognized crime as a local problem and stressed the financial and technical resources of the federal government in helping local jurisdictions combat it. Therefore, the LEAA attempted to more effectively coordinate the anti-crime activities of law enforcement agencies at local, state, and federal levels as one means of reducing interagency rivalries and turf jealousies.

Congress authorized grants as well as other financial and technical assistance to state and local agencies. The objectives of such assistance were to devise new ways to prevent and reduce crime and to improve methods of detecting crime, apprehending suspects, and rehabilitating criminals. It was generally understood that under the provisions of the LEAA, local law enforcement agencies were to improve their operations and streamline their police-services delivery systems (Nelson, Cushman, and Harlow, 1980).

Unfortunately, the goals of the LEAA were not realized within the period originally projected, and funding for the program was gradually withdrawn in the early 1980s. In 1979, the National Institute of Justice (NIJ) was established to provide for and encourage research for the purpose of (1) improving federal, state, and local criminal justice systems; (2) preventing and reducing crimes; (3) ensuring citizens' access to appropriate dispute-resolution forums; and (4) identifying programs of proven effectiveness or programs that offer a high probability of improving the criminal justice system (Feeley and Sarat, 1980; U.S. Code Annotated, 1996).

Also established in 1979 was the **Bureau of Justice Statistics** (BJS) to provide for and encourage the collection and analysis of statistical information concerning crime, juvenile delinquency, and the operation of the criminal justice system. Currently, much information concerning local and federal criminal justice systems is distributed by the BJS and NIJ. In addition, these bureaus give grants to persons and interested organizations for studying criminal victimization, crimes against the elderly, and gathering statistical information.

Since October 1984, the LEAA has been referred to as the Bureau of Justice Assistance, a grant-making body within the Department of Justice. Also established in 1984 was the Office of Justice Programs, headed by the assistant attorney general of the United States. These new agencies assumed some of the functions of the earlier LEAA, such as research and grant activities relating to criminal justice investigations.

In 1983, a project was undertaken to evaluate the effectiveness of the LEAA in improving criminal justice (Hudzik, 1984). Data were obtained from thirty-three state planning agency directors through questionnaires and in-depth interviews. One disappointing finding was that LEAA-assisted programs continued to thrive in only about a third of the states, and in those states where LEAA did not succeed, independent funding was not made available when LEAA funds were discontinued (Hudzik, 1984).

On Preventive Patrol and Golf Carts

The Houston, Texas, police department believes that crime prevention is its most important goal and that it should "vigorously pursue those who commit serious crimes" (L. Brown, 1984). Among other aims of the Houston police department are: (1) to involve the community in all policing activities that directly affect the quality of community life; (2) to manage its resources carefully and effectively; (3) to structure service delivery so as to reinforce the strengths of the city's neighborhoods; and (4) to use policing strategies in such a way that democratic values are preserved and advanced (Houston Police Department, 1991). Thus, it implemented **neighborhood-oriented policing**, *an integrative program that decentralizes police patrol by establishing neighborhood command stations and promoting better police-community relations* (Oettmeier and Bieck, 1989).

The goals of the Houston police department are not that different from those of other large municipal police departments. All police departments attempt to prevent crime and apprehend criminals. And all police departments share a common problem: they must operate within limited budgets based upon community resources and needs. Some police departments are better off financially than others, and some are able to hire larger numbers of highly qualified police officers than police departments with limited financial resources.

Some police departments must patrol large areas, while others oversee small areas. Even in jurisdictions of the same size, population density varies greatly. These are several of the factors that influence the officer/citizen ratio in any community.

Preventive patrol reflects the belief that high visibility of police officers will deter crime. But evidence shows that the size of a police department and officer visibility have little effect on crime rate (Crank and Langworthy, 1992; Cordner and Hale, 1992). In a study of crime rates in 252 suburbs and 269 cities in 1960 and 1970, the amount of crime and police visibility was correlated. It was originally believed that increasing the number of police officers in selected community areas would lessen crime, but investigators found no evidence that either violent or property crimes were reduced as a result of these areas increasing the size of their police forces (Greenberg, Kessler, and Loftin, 1983).

The Kansas City Preventive Patrol Experiment

One controversial study that tested the effectiveness of preventive patrols and their influence on the crime rate took place in 1972 in Kansas City, Missouri. Called the **Kansas City Preventive Patrol Experiment** (Kelling, Pate, Dieckman, and Brown, 1974), the study was controversial because it disproved the notion that spending more money on police services and increasing police visibility through more patrolling decreases crime. In fact, it showed that increasing or decreasing the number of police patrols in Kansas City suburbs had no effect on the amount of crime in those suburbs.

In this study, funded by a grant from the Police Foundation, the Kansas City Police Department conducted a comprehensive experiment to determine the effectiveness of routine preventive patrol (Kelling, Pate, Dieckman and Brown, 1974). The experiment varied the number of routine preventive patrols in fifteen police beats, police officers' habitual patrols. The fifteen beats were divided into three groups of five each. In the **control beats**, routine preventive patrol was maintained by the usual one-car patrol. In the **reactive beats**, routine patrols were eliminated. Instead, police officers responded only to calls for assistance from citizens. In the **proactive beats**, routine preventive patrol was increased to three cars per patrol. The Kansas City Police Department randomly dispersed 1,300 police officers throughout the southern district of the city of 500,000 according to these different beat groupings.

The experiment lasted from July 1972 to September 1973. During that period data were collected about crime rates, citizens' perceptions of police service and visibility, police response time to citizens calls, and citizens' satisfaction with police services. The results showed that the presence or absence of police patrols had no effect on the number of residential and nonresidential burglaries, auto thefts, larcenies, robberies, and vandalism. These findings were important because it is usually assumed that preventive patrol deters these crimes. Furthermore, citizens' fear about crime was unaffected. The attitudes of businesspersons toward crime and police services were unaffected also, as was the level of citizens' satisfaction with police services and response time.

These findings do not necessarily mean that preventive patrol doesn't prevent crime. Nor do they mean that preventive patrols in large cities should be discontinued. However, citizens' satisfaction with police officers' responses suggests that preventive patrols did enhance police-community relations.

It has been suggested that one reason for the apparent lack of effect of police visibility on crime in Kansas City is the *phantom effect*. Thieves, robbers, and burglars may have "thought" patrols were present because of the previous police patrols in those areas. However, this is only speculation.

The experiment has been faulted in other respects. To what extent is Kansas City representative of other cities? Would the same results be observed in small communities or larger cities? No investigations were conducted that examined the effectiveness of one- or two-officer patrol cars. Team policing was untested, as were a number of other experimental patrolling styles used during that period. Nor did the findings suggest that police forces be reduced or that police be withdrawn from certain areas. Nevertheless, questions were raised that challenged traditional beliefs about police visibility as a crime deterrent. Because the findings were neither conclusive nor absolute, further experimentation with police patrols was strongly encouraged.

Patrol Alternatives

The years after the Kansas City study saw much research into management and the effectiveness of police patrols. Subsequent experiments with varying styles of police patrol styles were largely unsuccessful at preventing crime (Wagner, 1978). However, almost no one disputes the value of these experiments in improving social relations between police officers and community residents. One topic investigated was the **scale of police patrol** (Whitaker, 1984), which is the geographical scope of a police officer's routine patrol responsibilities (Mastrofski, 1981b; Whitaker, 1984).

It is not clear whether the scale of police pa-

trols should be extensive or limited. One view holds that large-scale police patrols are better because they keep police officers from becoming too attached to any given community (T. Johnson, 1993). As a result, the likelihood that police officers will become corrupt by engaging in clandestine gambling or other illicit activities in those areas might be reduced, and so might officers' potential of becoming complacent or stale (Mastrofski, 1981a). The view favoring small-scale police patrols is that police officers' continuous contact with citizens in the beat area would enhance their understanding of citizens' problems and customs. Officers with greater familiarity with citizens on the beat would be less likely to stereotype them or misinterpret their actions, and thus there would be fewer occasions for using unnecessary force to make arrests and uphold the law (Tonry and Morris, 1992).

Reducing the scale of patrol is aimed at linking police officers with a small population (Whitaker, 1984:25). Among the proposals for reducing the scale of patrolling are neighborhood, territorial, and team policing. The Tampa, Florida, police department experimented with a community-based patrol called the Neighborhood Sector Patrol System (Smith and Taylor, 1985). Under this **sector patrol** system, police officers were assigned to sector commanders in those areas where "police-citizen relationships were most vital because of conditions including economics, population, crime problems, and crowd behavior." Sector offices were manned eighteen hours a day. Police officers were permanently assigned specific areas to "become familiar with the characteristics of individual neighborhoods, and to become acquainted with the inhabitants and the problems peculiar to the area." Reported crime in those sectors decreased significantly during the first six months of the experiment and police-citizen cooperation improved (Smith and Taylor, 1985).

In another Tampa experiment, a permanent patrol assignment system called the back-to-the-people program was supplemented with **golf cart patrols** (Morrill, 1984). The golf cart patrols responded more rapidly to citizen calls, and dispatchers' efficiency at dealing with citizens' complaints was increased.

In Flint, Michigan, a **foot patrol program** was

started in 1979 (Payne, and Trojanowicz, 1985). The Flint Police Department assigned twenty-two officers to foot patrol in selected neighborhoods as a supplement to officers in patrol cars. By 1984, the number of foot patrol officers had been increased to sixty-four, and other cities such as Newark, New Jersey, began experimenting with similar foot patrols (Trojanowicz and Banas, 1985a). Administrative concerns about the foot patrols were related to program costs, attitudes of officers toward their work, and potential communication problems resulting from patrolling on foot rather than in cruisers. First, the Flint community supported the foot patrol program. The taxpayers agreed to increased property tax assessments in exchange for the expansion of the foot patrol. Between 1981 and 1985, Flint residents appeared increasingly satisfied with the deterrent value of foot patrols in neighborhoods with formerly high crime rates (Trojanowicz, Steele, and Trojanowicz, 1986).

Second, a comparison between officers in cruisers and those on foot patrol showed that foot patrol officers believed they were doing a more important job in their patrol areas, that they were dealing with crime and other local problems more effectively, that they were improving police-community relations, and that they were doing work that their department considered important (Trojanowicz and Banas, 1985a). Third, both foot and motorized patrol officers said that although foot patrol officers found it more difficult to communicate with their dispatchers and with other patrolling units, cruiser officers had greater difficulty maintaining high morale and work satisfaction (Trojanowicz and Banas, 1985b). Interviews with sixty-four foot patrol officers and fifty cruiser officers showed that foot patrol officers believed they were safer in the neighborhoods they patrolled. They also sensed greater closeness to community residents and believed these residents would come to their aid if necessary (Trojanowicz and Banas, 1985a).

One interesting implication of this foot patrol research involved attitudes of blacks and whites toward the foot patrol program and their respective satisfaction with officer performance (Trojanowicz and Banas, 1985b). Interviews were conducted with 1,220 blacks and whites in Flint in 1979,

1981, 1982, and 1983. While the 1979 interviews showed that blacks perceived police officers less favorably than whites, by 1983, blacks not only viewed the foot patrol program and police officers favorably, but they also viewed police more favorably than whites did (Trojanowicz and Banas, 1985b).

There is disagreement about whether small-scale police patrolling is the most effective means of combating community crime (Green, 1993; Lurigio and Rosenbaum, 1994). Some experts believe that emphasizing neighborhood sector patrols creates a "localism" that isolates communities rather than uniting citizens in working on common problems, including crime (Einstadter, 1984). Despite this disagreement, more active citizen involvement in policing has occurred where foot patrol programs have been implemented (Walker and Caudell, 1993). In Boston, for example, citizens actively participate with police officers in neighborhood crime and street patrol committees (Graves, et al., 1985). In Atlanta, the Bureau of Police Services Partnership Against Crime Program has actively involved citizens in devising ways of attacking crime through more aggressive prevention and control (Napper, 1986).

One innovative type of police patrol is **team policing**. *Team policing is the assignment of a small area to a team of police officers commanded by a team leader* (Greenwood, Chaiken, and Petersilia, 1977). Terry (1985:346) says that "the basic concept of team policing involves assigning complete responsibility for police service in a small geographical area to a team of police officers, commanded by a team leader. Using this pattern a city of several hundred thousand may be divided into six to ten team areas, with each area covered by a team of twenty to forty police officers."

In team policing, decentralization of police authority is maximized because it is distributed among numerous teams. Team policing has been implemented in cities such as Albany, Albuquerque, Charlotte, Cincinnati, Dayton, Hartford, Rochester, Los Angeles, and St. Louis. It transforms a department's specialized, segregated pockets of expertise into all-encompassing, flexible units of generalists; these units are self-supporting, with specialists providing cross-training to the team as a whole (Davis, 1973). The Los Angeles

Police Department Team Policing Project, known as Team 28, is a forty-one-officer unit consisting of detectives, patrol officers, traffic specialists, supervisors, and civilians charged with twenty-four-hour protective responsibility for a specified area and instructed to develop means and methods to decrease crime and traffic accidents, mobilize community residents, and foster positive attitudes among them (Davis, 1973). Public education, awareness and security techniques, and improved investigation are stressed.

Team policing and foot patrolling have at least one goal in common: *to bring police officers closer to citizens and to be more effective in providing police services.* It is unclear whether team policing has achieved this objective, however (Walker, 1993a). In Los Angeles, police officers have been found to be more aggressive in law enforcement under team-policing arrangements compared with non-team-policing arrangements (Brown, 1981). The Directed Area Responsibility Team (DART) was implemented by the Houston, Texas, police department in the early 1980s (Bales and Oettmeier, 1985). Results suggest that the program was successful, largely through a redistribution and redeployment of personnel, team interaction, job diversification, knowledge gaining/sharing, and increased community interaction.

James Q. Wilson and other criminologists have said that police patrol practices should return to the "watchman" style of policing that was typical of pre-1930 police patrols. According to Wilson, during the 1930s, patrol practices were changed toward more crime-control-oriented policing. One type of crime-control-oriented policing took the form of police officers in cruisers patrolling specific geographical beats. Some cities say that this type of policing tended to depersonalize police officers and isolate them from their communities. Wilson and a colleague, Kelling, have recommended strengthening police officer ties with the community through closer contacts with citizens in small business and residential sectors (Kelling and Wilson, 1982). Known as the *broken-windows approach,* this form of police patrol emphasizes better communication between police and citizens. "Little problems" such as managing juveniles and preventing them from pestering store owners and customers, inves-

tigating suspicious persons, and paying occasional visits to store proprietors and others to check on their personal safety are part of the broken-windows approach. Foot patrols, team policing, and other "back to the people" programs are consistent with the broken-windows approach espoused by Kelling and Wilson (Matthews and Young, 1992).

Walker (1984) disagrees with Wilson, saying that such talk about the depersonalization caused by crime-control-policing is greatly exaggerated. Innovations such as the telephone have promoted rather than lessened police-citizen contact. Furthermore, it is difficult to discount the value of any type of police patrol, in which officers interact directly with the public.

The trend is toward more experimentation with alternative forms of patrolling. Police administrators are pragmatic, and eventually they will adopt the patrol alternative that best suits their community's needs. In the meantime, no single patrol style is considered "best" for *all* communities.

Discretionary Powers of Police

"Police roles are best understood as *mechanisms for the distribution of non-negotiably coercive force employed in accordance with the dictates of an intuitive grasp of situational exigencies*" (Bittner, 1970:46; emphasis added). This means that police officers have the authority to use force, and that force may be used to enforce the law if, in the officer's opinion, the situation demands it (Bittner, 1985).

A key objective of police professionalization is producing well-trained officers who can make informed choices in everyday encounters and properly exercise their discretionary powers. A critical part of such professionalization is learning about and understanding their responsibilities as well as the reasonable limits of their discretion.

Confronting police officers in both "real police work" and service activities is the public mandate to enforce the laws of the community. However, the overwhelming number of technical violations being committed, together with limited police resources, require that police officers *exercise discretion* (Ohlin and Remington; 1993; Walker,

1993a). This means that police officers enforce some laws but not others. However, this situation is not necessarily what police officers desire. The nature of their position demands it. Therefore, police officers create mental lists of enforcement priorities, where more serious offenses head the list. Thus, officers will more likely chase a speeding, weaving driver rather than a plodding motorist with a broken taillight, unless there is nothing better to do at the time.

According to some authorities, *how police exercise their discretion* is the most pressing and complex problem confronting modern law enforcement (Ma-Omar, 1990; Walker, 1993b). There are at least three ways of examining police discretion: (1) the legal approach, (2) the organizational approach, and (3) the behavioral approach.

The **legal approach** *is to codify discretion according to specific legal proscriptions and to adjust discretionary behavior to the amount of deviation from these rules. In the* **organizational approach**, *police administrators create lists of organizational priorities for officers and clarify explicitly how to handle a wide array of police-citizen encounters. The* **behavioral approach**, *a blend of management, sociology, psychology, and political science, is a development scheme whereby police officers negotiate their way through each encounter with alternative behavioral choices that seem to fit the situation* (Hanewicz, 1985:43–47).

The behavioral approach is based on the highly subjective word *depends*. Whether to arrest a drunk in a bar *depends* on the drunk's attitude. Whether to cite a speeding driver *depends* on how the driver reacts to the officer's lectures about speeding and traffic safety. Whether to arrest juveniles who are having a loud party and disturbing their neighbors *depends* on their cooperation with officers and whether they are willing to "hold things down."

Police Discretion: Arrest and Detention

The **Model Penal Code (MPC)** outlines law enforcement officers' authority to make arrests without warrants (Singer, 1988). Under Section 120.1 of the MPC, (1) officers may arrest suspects without a warrant *whenever they have reasonable cause to believe that the suspects have committed a felony*. The MPC further provides that (2) suspects may be arrested without warrant *for committing misdemeanors, if officers have reasonable cause to believe that they will not be apprehended unless immediately arrested, or if the suspects may cause injury to themselves or others, or if they may cause damage to property*. Also, (3) arrests without warrant may be made *for misdemeanors committed in the officer's presence*. Most jurisdictions follow these guidelines in making arrests without warrant.

To illustrate the first instance, suppose police officers patrolling First Avenue in a large city are notified that a Mini-Mart has just been robbed by two suspects, one white and one black, who escaped in a blue 1994 Ford station wagon with broken tail lights. They were last seen headed west on First Avenue. At that moment, suppose that a blue, 1994 Ford station wagon with broken tail lights, driven by a black with a white passenger, speeds west past the officers. While there is no absolute proof that these men committed the robbery, the circumstances give the officers reasonable suspicion and probable cause to make an arrest. Thus, the officers do not have to see the crime being committed in order to make an arrest. They only need to have probable cause to believe that a felony was committed and certain suspects committed it.

To illustrate the second instance, suppose someone is traveling to Denver and has just gotten off a bus stopped at a Trailways terminal in St. Louis. The person is drunk and disorderly and steals a magazine from the terminal gift shop. Police officers are called to the terminal, talk with the gift shop owner, who points out the disorderly passenger. In this situation, the officers are empowered to make an arrest because there is a good chance that if they don't, the disorderly drunk will board the bus to Denver and never return to the St. Louis jurisdiction. Also, there is a good chance that the drunk bus passenger will injure himself or others. These conditions permit arrests without warrant, even though the crime is a misdemeanor and has been committed outside the officers' presence.

To illustrate the third instance, if police officers are standing in the bus terminal and see the drunk passenger steal a magazine from the gift shop, they may make an arrest immediately and without warrant because the crime was committed in their presence.

Stop and Frisk

In warrantless arrests and stops and frisks, police discretionary power is influenced by *probable cause*. Is there probable cause to believe that a crime has been committed and that a specific suspect has committed the crime? Police officers learn that each case has its own merits, and there are often fine lines between cases, regardless of their factual similarities (Albanese, 1988). A **stop and frisk** *is a search in which the police* **pat down** *a person's outer clothing to determine whether there are any dangerous weapons that may pose a danger to officer safety.* A stop and frisk is thus a defensive action. It is *not* intended to be a thorough search of one's person, including his or her pockets. The two leading cases dealing with stop-and-frisk are *Terry v. Ohio* (1968) and *Sibron v. New York* (1968) (del Carmen, 1995; Mertens, 1984). A more recent case, *Minnesota v. Dickerson* (1993), upholds the spirit of the *Terry* and *Sibron* cases (see Highlight 5.1 for a synopsis of the three cases).

Limitation of Stop and Frisk

In *Terry v. Ohio* (1968), an off-duty police officer arrested Terry after discovering a weapon in his jacket during a pat-down of Terry's outer clothing. Terry was convicted of carrying a concealed weapon and appealed. The U.S. Supreme Court upheld the conviction, saying that the officer was entitled to ensure his safety when questioning Terry. In *Sibron v. New York* (1968), Sibron was convicted of unlawful possession of heroin after Martin, an officer, thrust his hands into Sibron's pockets and found small envelopes of heroin. Sibron moved to suppress the heroin seized because the officer's search of his person went well beyond patting down his outer clothing for dangerous weapons. The U.S. Supreme Court overturned his conviction.

The court distinguished between Sibron's case and *Terry v. Ohio* (1968) by noting that the search for Terry's weapon consisted solely of "patting down" the suspect's outer clothing and not thrust-

Police detectives stop and frisk a suspected car burglar at a mall. "Stop and frisk" is a discretionary procedure prompted by officers' sense of probable cause that a crime has been committed.

ing hands into his pockets. The court concluded that Martin's search of Sibron violated the Fourth Amendment and was not an act of self-protection by disarming a potentially dangerous man. Had officer Martin merely patted down Sibron, it is unlikely that he would have found the heroin envelopes. Certainly, these envelopes of heroin would not feel like a .38 caliber revolver. Therefore, no cause would exist for officer Martin to search Sibron further for a dangerous weapon.

Police Discretion: Search and Seizure

Ordinarily, police officers may make arrests without warrant under the conditions outlined earlier: (1) the officer has probable cause, or the reasonable belief that a felony has been committed and that the suspects have committed it, (2) the officer knows that a misdemeanor has been committed and reasonably believes that the suspects may injure themselves or others if they are not immediately arrested, and (3) the officer has seen a crime being committed. In the cases discussed above, suspects were stopped, questioned, frisked, or searched, depending upon the particular circumstances. Evidence seized and used in court to convict suspects was either suppressed or not suppressed by the Supreme Court. The Court's decision depended on whether the officers had probable cause to detain the suspects initially and whether the officers had reason to believe that the suspects possessed a dangerous weapon.

These cases involved personal encounters with suspects on the street, searches and seizures of items on their person, and arrest and detention without a warrant. Ordinarily, when police officers stop a suspect in an automobile or go to their res-

---

Highlight 5.1. Stop and Frisk: Three Leading Cases

Terry v. Ohio, 392 U.S. 1, 88 S.Ct. 1868 (1968). In Cleveland, a thirty-five-year veteran police officer observed Terry and two companions walking up and down the street looking in store windows and returning frequently to the street corner to talk. Suspicious of this behavior, the officer confronted them. He patted down Terry and discovered a revolver. Terry was later convicted of carrying a concealed weapon. Terry appealed. The Supreme Court upheld Terry's conviction, holding that police officers may pat down suspects as a means of protecting themselves and determining whether suspicious persons may be armed and dangerous. See *Sibron v. New York* (1968) as a limitation to the "pat down and frisk" ruling in *Terry*.

Sibron v. New York, 392 U.S. 40, 88 S.Ct. 1889 (1968). A police officer watched as Sibron, a convicted drug user and ex-con, sat in a New York diner. Over a period of a few hours, as many as six or eight persons, also known to be involved with drugs, approached Sibron and spoke with him. The officer did not see Sibron and the men exchange anything. When Sibron left the diner, the officer approached and said, "Sibron, you know what I want." Sibron began to place his hand in his pocket, but the officer quickly thrust his hand in instead. The search yielded several glassine envelopes containing heroin. Sibron was subsequently convicted of heroin possession. However, the Supreme Court overturned his conviction, saying that the officer had a right to "pat down" Sibron but not to thrust his hands into Sibron's pockets. The purpose of *Terry* was to enable officers to protect them-

selves against possible armed suspects. Thus, a patdown and frisk are warranted under certain conditions. However, Sibron had not been observed doing anything illegal, and thus his pocket search by the observing officer was *unreasonable* according to the Fourth Amendment. In short, the officer was entitled to pat down Sibron to detect a possible weapon; the officer would not have detected small glassine envelopes of heroin in such a pat-down, however. This is a landmark case limiting the scope of a police officer's search of suspicious persons to pat-downs and frisks, unless other special circumstances apply. Sibron's case did *not* involve special circumstances.

Minnesota v. Dickerson, 507 U.S. __, 113 S.Ct. 2130 (1993). Police officers saw Dickerson walking down an alley after emerging from a known crack house. When he saw the officers walking toward him, Dickerson turned around and walked away from them. They stopped him for a pat-down. They discovered no weapons, but one of the officers thrust his hand into Dickerson's pockets and found a small quantity of crack cocaine in a glassine envelope. He later claimed that he had "felt a small lump that felt like crack cocaine" through Dickerson's clothing during the pat-down and frisk. Dickerson was convicted of cocaine possession. He appealed, and the Supreme Court overturned his conviction on the ground that the police officers' search of Dickerson *went well beyond the scope specified in Terry v. Ohio*, which held that pat-downs and frisks of suspects must be exclusively for the purpose of determining whether they possess a dangerous weapon.

Highlight 5.2. Searches of Refuse: The Case of the Incriminating Garbage

California v. Greenwood, 486 U.S. 35, 108 S.Ct. 1625 (1988). Greenwood, a suspected drug dealer, was under surveillance by police. They inspected some trash Greenwood had placed out for trash collectors and discovered sufficient incriminating evidence to obtain a search warrant of Greenwood's premises based upon probable cause. A search yielded large quantities of cocaine and hashish. Greenwood was subsequently convicted of various drug violations. He appealed, contending that police should have obtained a search warrant before inspecting his trash and thus that the evidence used against him in court should be excluded. The Supreme Court disagreed, saying that warrantless searches of trash or garbage are permissible, because persons give up their right to privacy of refuse whenever they place it in public places in trash containers readily accessible to others.

---

idences, they are prevented from searching the automobile or home and from seizing contraband found in the course of their search unless they have a warrant authorizing the search and seizure. Several important exceptions exist to this requirement.

Warrantless Searches of Private Dwellings

The first landmark case involving a warrantless search of a dwelling is *Payton v. New York* (1980). On January 14, 1970, New York detectives pieced together sufficient evidence to show probable cause that Theodore Payton had murdered the manager of a gas station two days earlier. On January 15, six police officers and detectives went to Payton's apartment in the Bronx, where they intended to arrest him. They did not have a warrant. They knocked on Payton's door. Receiving no reply, they used crowbars to forcibly enter his apartment. At that point, they observed *in plain view* a 30-caliber shell casing, which was subsequently introduced as evidence against Payton in a murder trial. The **plain view rule** says that *if police officers are in a place they have a right to be and observe illegal contraband or activity, they may seize the contraband and conduct a search without warrant* (R. Allen, 1991; George, 1990).

The Supreme Court reversed Payton's murder conviction because the police failed to obtain search or arrest warrants, although they had time to do so. Thus, the evidence against Payton was suppressed because it had been unlawfully seized. Without the incriminating evidence, Payton's conviction was overturned.

The plain-view rule has been extended to warrantless searches of garbage. Persons who leave their garbage cans on city streets relinquish their privacy relative to the contents of the garbage. Police officers do not need a warrant to search a person's garbage. Sometimes garbage can be incriminating. Officers may even develop sufficient probable cause to conduct searches of a person's premises with a lawful warrant, depending upon what they find in that person's garbage (Watson, 1989). (See Highlight 5.2.)

Exigent Circumstances

In an earlier landmark case, *Ker v. California* (1963), Ker and his wife were convicted of unlawful possession of marijuana. Like Payton, they claimed that a warrantless search of their home revealed illegally seized evidence. Some of the facts in their case are these: several narcotics agents from the Los Angeles County Sheriff's Office purchased some marijuana from a man named Murphy. Undercover officers observed Murphy contact Ker on several occasions, and they eventually learned that Ker was selling marijuana from his apartment. Without either an arrest or a search warrant, Los Angeles police officers went to Ker's apartment building, obtained a key from the building manager, and, without warning, entered Ker's apartment, where they discovered a large quantity of marijuana. The marijuana was eventually used as evidence at Ker's trial.

The U.S. Supreme Court upheld Ker's conviction, reasoning that the police officers were justified in not giving Ker notice of their intent to search his premises because narcotics dealers are known to quickly dispose of their drugs by flushing them down the toilet or throwing them out the window. The officers had to act quickly because **exigent circumstances** required fast action to prevent destruction of the incriminating evidence.

In the search of Payton's premises, however, no exigent circumstances justified the warrantless search. Also, no arrest warrant had been issued. Police officers learn to discern situations where exigent circumstances exist. As the two cases illustrate, the decision to search without a warrant often involves police officer discretion. Warrantless searches of premises depend on the personal judgment of police officers (Mascolo, 1983). If police lack the requisite grounds to conduct these searches, the case against a suspect may be thrown out.

Searches Incident to an Arrest

Another discretionary situation arises when police officers possess an arrest warrant. When they arrest the suspect, they are permitted to conduct a limited search of the immediate vicinity to determine the presence of dangerous weapons (Bradley, 1993). This is similar to the warrantless "patdown-and-frisk" procedure articulated in *Terry*, discussed earlier. This limited search is called a **search incident to an arrest**. The purpose of a search incident to an arrest is to enable police to determine if suspects possess any weapons or *fruits of the crime*, either on their person or in the immediate vicinity. No police officer has the authority to conduct a warrantless search of the suspect's entire premises, however.

In a landmark case involving a search incident to an arrest, an officer's search of an entire dwelling "incident to the arrest" of a suspect was challenged. In the case of *Chimel v. California* (1969), Chimel was suspected by police of burglarizing a coin shop. On September 13, 1965, three officers armed with an arrest warrant went to Chimel's apartment in Santa Ana, California, and were ad-

mitted to the apartment by Chimel's wife. When Chimel returned from work, they handed him the arrest warrant and asked if they could "look around." Chimel objected, but the police said that "on the basis of the lawful arrest, they had the right to conduct a search anyway." No search warrant had been issued. The officers searched the entire three-bedroom house, including the attic, the garage, and a small workshop, and found some coins that may have come from the coin shop. Chimel was convicted of burglary largely on the basis of evidence seized by these officers.

The Supreme Court reversed his conviction because the arrest warrant did not entitle the officers to search the entire premises. The arrest warrant limited them to a search only of the suspect and the area in the immediate control of that suspect. The high court indicated that while a gun on a table or in a drawer in front of the suspect is just as dangerous as a gun concealed on his person, there is no justification for routinely searching any room other than that in which the arrest occurs. The court maintained that Chimel could have been arrested at his place of work or outside his apartment. Letting Chimel's conviction stand would give officers license to conveniently wait for suspects to return home in order to conduct a search of their entire premises. This would eliminate completely the need to obtain a proper search warrant.

Warrantless Searches of Automobiles

The police officer's discretion to conduct a warrantless search of automobiles must be based upon probable cause (*Carroll v. United States*, 1925; *Chambers v. Maroney*, 1970). By the same token, if police officers stop a vehicle for a traffic violation and observe a pistol or illegal narcotics *in plain view* on the seat inside the vehicle, they have probable cause to conduct a more extensive search of the car without a warrant (*Cooper v. California*, 1967; *Harris v. United States*, 1968).

Warrantless Searches as the Result of Hot Pursuit

Sometimes police officers find themselves in *hot pursuit* of a fleeing suspect. Hot pursuit may be ample justification for officers to search a suspect's premises and seize evidence related to a crime. In

Highlight 5.3. Searches Incident to Arrest, Exigent Circumstances, and Consent

Vale v. Louisiana, 399 U.S. 30, 90 S.Ct. 1969 (1970). A search may be incident to an arrest only if it is contemporaneous with the arrest and is confined to the immediate area of the arrest. Vale, a suspected drug user, was under police surveillance. One evening while police were observing his home, a known drug addict spoke with Vale on Vale's front porch and exchanged some object with him. The police intercepted the drug addict as he left and arrested Vale outside his front door. Police proceeded to enter Vale's home and search it in the context of a *search incident to an arrest*. Police discovered heroin and other narcotics in Vale's bedroom. Vale was convicted. He appealed, contending that police needed a valid search warrant to search his premises and that a "search [of his home] incident to an arrest of Vale [outside of his home] violated his Fourth Amendment right against an unreasonable search and seizure." The Supreme Court agreed with Vale and overturned his conviction. Police cannot drag an arrestee into his or her home for the purpose of searching it. If they wish to search the home, they must obtain a valid search warrant.

Steagald v. United States, 451 U.S. 204, 101 S.Ct. 1642 (1981). Gary Steagald and another man, Gaultney, were mistaken for a wanted fugitive in Atlanta, Georgia. Agents had earlier been advised by a confidential informant that the wanted fugitive would be at a particular house. Authorities obtained an arrest warrant and went to the house, which was Gaultney's. Police saw Gaultney and Steagald talking in front of the house. They drew their weapons, approached Steagald and Gaultney, and frisked them. Determining that neither was the fugitive they sought, they went to the house, where Mrs. Gaultney met them. They ordered her to place her hands against the wall and then proceeded to search the premises thoroughly for their wanted fugitive, who was not there. However, the police discovered a small quantity of cocaine. They obtained a warrant for a search that uncovered forty-three pounds of cocaine. Steagald was convicted of possession of cocaine. He appealed, contending that the officers should have

obtained a search warrant before entering the house and that their subsequent search of the premises was unreasonable and unlawful. The police contended that their arrest warrant "entitled" them to search the premises to hunt for their fugitive, and that as the result of their search, the illegal contraband was discovered lawfully. The Supreme Court strongly disagreed, saying that neither exigent circumstances nor consent existed to entitle the officers to search the premises. Steagald's conviction was overturned, because a valid search warrant was required, based upon probable cause, and the officers conducting the search possessed no such warrant. Thus, all evidence subsequently seized was inadmissible. The U.S. Supreme Court specifically noted that *arrest warrants do not authorize searches of premises in any absolute sense. Search warrants are necessary for the types of searches conducted of Gaultney's residence.* Otherwise, such searches are unlawful and violate the Fourth Amendment guarantee against unreasonable searches and seizures.

Illinois v. Condon, 507 U.S. 948, 113 S.Ct. 1359 (1993). Condon was suspected of dealing in cocaine. An informant provided police in DuPage County, Illinois, with sufficient information to obtain a warrant to search Condon's home. One evening, a team of police officers stormed Condon's home without knocking or announcing their presence and found a large quantity of cocaine, marijuana, and several weapons. Condon was convicted. He appealed, alleging that police did not knock and announce their intentions before conducting the search. Police countered that their search and unannounced entry into Condon's home were based on *exigent circumstances*. Condon's conviction was overturned. This reversal was upheld by the Illinois Supreme Court, which held that the unannounced entry was not prompted by exigent circumstances and that it conflicted with the protocol to be followed in Illinois in searches and seizures of residences. The U.S. Supreme Court declined to hear Illinois's appeal of this ruling.

the case of *Warden v. Hayden* (1967), for instance, a cab company in Baltimore was robbed on the evening of March 17, 1962. Police and cab company employees chased a suspect to his residence. Mrs. Hayden, the suspect's wife, let police officers in, and they conducted a search of the premises. Hayden was found pretending to be asleep in an upstairs bedroom. Police found a shotgun and pistol in the bathroom and trousers and a jacket in a washing machine in another part of the house. These items matched those worn by the robber. The Supreme Court upheld Hayden's conviction, holding that the police officers' warrantless search in the course of a hot pursuit was justified. In some respects, hot pursuit is similar to exigent circumstances, where it is imperative that officers act quickly to prevent a suspect from secreting or destroying evidence (Crew, Kessler, and Fridell, 1994).

Warrantless Searches by Consent

Finally, sometimes suspects will voluntarily permit officers to search their homes or automobiles. Warrantless searches and seizures are permissible when suspects voluntarily give their consent to the search. Of course, the circumstances must be scrutinized carefully to determine if, in fact, the suspects voluntarily consented. If police officers threaten to arrest suspects "unless they allow a search," the discretionary action by police officers may be successfully challenged.

In the case of *Schenckloth v. Bustamonte* (1973), for instance, a police officer stopped a car at 3:00 A.M. because one of the car's headlights and the license plate light were burnt out. The driver could not produce a driver's license, and the officer asked permission to search the car. One of the occupants, a brother of the car owner, said, "Sure, go ahead." With this consent, the officer opened the trunk and discovered three checks that had been stolen from a car wash. This evidence was used in obtaining a conviction against Robert Bustamonte, one of the passengers and the person who had hidden the checks in the trunk.

The Court of Appeals for the Ninth Circuit in California reversed Bustamonte's conviction, saying that the government had failed to established that Bustamonte "knew that he had a right not to consent to the search." But the United States

Supreme Court reversed this decision, stating that when a subject is not in custody and when consent is given in the absence of duress or coercion, voluntariness is presumed. Bustamonte's conviction was upheld.

Warrantless Searches in "Good Faith" and on the Basis of "Totality of Circumstances"

Sometimes police officers may have invalid search warrants to search one's automobile or premises. Having a defective search warrant is very much like not having one at all. When police officers search property on the basis of an invalid warrant, it is often argued that any illegal contraband seized should be excluded as evidence against the defendant (Moneymaker and Janikowski, 1990). However, the Supreme Court has ruled that illegal contraband *is* admissible against criminal suspects if police are acting in "good faith" when they search one's person, automobile, or premises (*United States v. Leon,* 1984).

Also, suspicious circumstances may lead police to believe that a crime is being committed. They may believe that the *totality of circumstances* is such that criminal activity is definitely occurring. If events, considered in their totality, lead officers to conclude that a crime is occurring or if illegal contraband is observed, police may conduct warrantless searches and make arrests (*Illinois v. Gates,* 1983). Each situation poses slightly different issues for police officers to resolve. The courts consider these differences between cases when deciding the validity of searches and seizures.

Summary of Search and Seizure Without Warrant Options

Police discretion to search a suspect's premises and seize evidence without a warrant is influenced in part by probable cause. Officers may be in *hot pursuit* of suspects, or they may observe evidence *in plain view*. Officers may determine that *exigent circumstances* justify a warrantless search as well. And suspects may *voluntarily consent* to a search (Peak and Stitt, 1993). If officers believe that they are acting in *good faith* when searching someone's premises, their search will be upheld, regardless of whether they have a valid search warrant. Also, the *totality of circumstances* might justify warrantless

Highlight 5.4. Good Faith and the Totality of Circumstances

A Case of "Good Faith"

Arizona v. Evans, __ U.S. __, 115 S.Ct. 1185 (1995). Evans was arrested by Phoenix police during a routine traffic stop when it was discovered that there was an outstanding warrant against him. In a search incident to his arrest, marijuana was found in his trunk. Evans was convicted of marijuana possession. It was determined later that the computer that indicated an outstanding arrest warrant was in error—the warrant was associated with a person with a similar name. Thus, police officers had arrested the wrong man and searched the *wrong man's automobile trunk*. Evans sought to have his conviction overturned, because, he said, his Fourth Amendment guarantee against unreasonable search and seizure had been violated. After various state appeals, the Ninth Circuit Court of Appeals overturned Evans's conviction. The government appealed to the Supreme Court. The Court reinstated Evans's original conviction, saying that the "good faith" exception to the exclusionary rule was in effect because the arresting officers acted appropriately and did not engage in misconduct while searching Evans's automobile trunk incident to a lawful arrest. The police had no knowledge of computer errors in this case. This case is significant because it establishes that, *if police, acting in "good faith," discover contraband or controlled substances incident to the arrest of the wrong person, the evidence they discover may be admissible in court*. The primary function of the exclusionary rule is to guard against police misconduct. In Evans's case, there was no police misconduct, only clerical error unattributable to police. Thus, illegal contraband seized by police in good faith does not become inadmissible as evidence simply because of clerical error.

United States v. Leon, 468 U.S. 897, 104 S.Ct. 3405 (1984). Evidence seized on the basis of a warrant later found defective is valid if officers were acting in "good faith." Leon, a suspected drug trafficker, was placed under surveillance by police in Burbank, California. Police later obtained search warrants for three residences and several automobiles under Leon's con-

trol. Acting on the search warrants, police seized large quantities of drug evidence that was used against Leon during his trial. Leon was convicted. The Supreme Court upheld Leon's conviction, even though it declared the search warrants *invalid*. The Court noted in a rambling and expansive opinion that the officers *acted in good faith*, presuming that the issued warrants were valid. The significance of this case is that it creates a "good faith" exception to the exclusionary rule. In its opinion, the Supreme Court also noted that its decision was not to be interpreted as a blanket authorization for officers to conduct searches despite defective warrants. The Court simply weighed the benefits of suppressing the evidence obtained in Leon's case against the costs of exclusion. The Court's message is that evidence may be admissible if the fault for defective warrants rests with judges, not police officers. The target of the exclusionary rule is police misconduct, not judicial misconduct.

A Case of the "Totality of Circumstances"

Alabama v. White, 496 U.S. 325, 110 S.Ct. 2412 (1990). An anonymous tipster told police that a woman named White would be leaving her apartment at a particular time carrying a brown briefcase containing cocaine and that she would get in a particular type of car and drive to a particular motel. Police watched as White emerged from her apartment and entered the described vehicle. They followed her to the motel and stopped her car. They approached and advised her that she was suspected of carrying cocaine. At their request, she permitted them to search her vehicle, where they discovered the described briefcase. They asked her to open it; inside they found some marijuana. A search of her purse incident to her arrest for marijuana possession disclosed a quantity of cocaine. She was charged and convicted of possessing illegal substances. She appealed to the Supreme Court, arguing that the police lacked *reasonable suspicion* to stop her initially and that therefore the dis-

(continued next page)

Highlight 5.4. Good Faith and the Totality of Circumstances *(continued)*

covered drugs were inadmissible as evidence. The Supreme Court disagreed, holding that the anonymous tip and the totality of circumstances observed during subsequent police surveillance more than satisfied the less-demanding standard of *reasonable suspicion* contrasted with the more-demanding standard of *probable cause.* (See especially *Illinois v. Gates* (1983) for a more extensive discussion of anonymous informants and the totality of circumstances justifying police stops and searches of suspicious persons and their effects.)

Illinois v. Gates, 462 U.S. 213, 103 S.Ct. 2317 (1983). Based upon an anonymous letter sent to the police, Lance and Sue Gates, of Bloomingdale, Illinois, were accused of selling drugs. A fairly detailed description of the couple's activities was contained in the anonymous letter. Police placed the two under surveillance and ob-

served the activities described in the letter. The Gates were moving large quantities of drugs between Florida and Illinois by automobile and airplane. The police obtained a search warrant and searched the Gates's home, where they discovered large quantities of drugs. The two were convicted. In an appeal to the Supreme Court they argued that because the reliability of the informant could not be determined, there was no basis for the search warrant leading to the discovery of the drugs. The Gates moved to suppress evidence of all drugs found as the result of this allegedly faulty search. In a landmark decision, the Court held that the "totality of circumstances," not informant reliability, justified the search warrant. Thus, it is now easier for police to obtain search warrants by stating that a "totality of circumstances" suggests that a crime is being or has been committed and that specific, named persons are responsible.

searches of persons, automobiles, and homes. These are several of the options available to officers when they exercise their discretion in making arrests and conducting searches and seizures.

Police Discretion: The Use of Deadly Force

The use of deadly force to make an arrest is perhaps the most sensitive issue in police work (Tennenbaum, 1994). Whether police can use force is *not* the issue, however. Rather, the matter is, how much force should they use? Public reaction to the use of force by police is mixed (DeSantis, 1994; Doerner and Ho, 1994).

In 1980, the National Opinion Research Center in Chicago surveyed 1,468 respondents. Would they approve of a policeman striking an adult male under any of the following circumstances: (1) if the suspect was being questioned as a suspect in a murder case; (2) if the suspect had said something vul-

gar or obscene; (3) if the suspect was attempting to escape from custody; and (4) if the suspect was attacking an officer with his fists. Those interviewed condoned the use of physical force by police if suspects were attempting to escape from custody or if they were attacking the officer. Although most of those surveyed did not approve of the use of physical force by police against suspects who made obscene remarks or against suspects in a murder case, some respondents did condone force in these situations (Williams et al., 1983).

A Force Continuum

Experts have devised a *force continuum.* Among the weapons or techniques available to officers, which may range from "no force" to "extraordinary force," are (1) controlled confrontation, (2) body language, (3) verbal persuasion, (4) contact controls, (5) joint restraints, (6) nerve center controls, (7) weapon-assisted pain compliance techniques, (8) chemical irritants such as mace, (9) electrical devices, (10) intimate impact weapons, (11) extended impact weapons, (12) weaponless techniques with debilitating potential, (13) weapon techniques with debilitating potential, (14) service firearms, and (15) supplemental firearms and shotguns (Conner, 1986). Some experts also recommend "indexing" and reporting the use of *all* force, not just *bad* force, as a means of keeping track of the type of force being used by police officers in any given department and perhaps protecting the department and the officer from potential lawsuits (Patti, 1984).

Deadly Force

Of interest to criminal justice researchers and citizens alike is the discretionary power of police officers to use **deadly force** in making arrests. This topic has stimulated much controversy and has been the subject of important court decisions (DeSantis, 1994; Sorensen, Marquart, and Brock, 1993). *Deadly force is any force likely or intended to cause death or great bodily harm, and it may be reasonable or unreasonable, depending upon the circumstances* (Black, 1990:398). For many years, law enforcement officers followed the *fleeing-felon rule.* This rule permitted them to exercise deadly force to apprehend anyone attempting to elude police who was believed to have committed a felony. (*Cunningham v. Ellington,* 1971; *Beech v. Melancon,* 1972; *Smith v. Jones,* 1973).

During the 1970s, several studies examined police shootings and the implications of the fleeing-felon rule. The Police Project of the Philadelphia Public Interest Law Center compiled information on all police shootings in the city in the years 1970–1978 (Waegel, 1984a). Many of the lethal-force incidents were not split-second reactions to life-threatening situations. About 20 percent of them were violations of legal standards for the use of deadly force that Philadelphia had statutorily changed in 1973. Burglary suspects or purse-snatchers were shot and killed while running away after police officers had ordered them to halt. Suspicious persons who committed minor speeding violations were occasionally shot and killed after attempting to elude police.

Despite more restrictions on officers' use of firearms, many continued to use deadly force in "legally impermissible circumstances," and several officers faced serious penalties for doing so. The

decision to use deadly force has been largely situational, consisting of a series of interactional stages (Scharf and Binder, 1983). The outcome of the potential deadly force situation is influenced by the type of suspect (e.g., a criminal or an insane person), the mode of contact (e.g., off-duty or regular patrol or planned apprehension), and the number of police officers present. Using the phase model of police decision making, Scharf and Binder (1983) have proposed that there are four stages in a confrontation between police and suspect: (1) an anticipation phase, (2) an initial confrontation, (3) a dialogue and information exchange, (4) a final decision to shoot or not to shoot, and (5) the aftermath. Some officers have been dissuaded from shooting at suspects by back-up officers. Psychological training of officers teaches them several options to deadly force.

Deadly force is not limited to shooting at suspects or fleeing felons. High-speed police chases such as those seen on television programs are examples of deadly force as well (Alpert and Anderson, 1986) because cruisers can injure or kill innocent bystanders.

Prior to 1985, twenty-five states permitted police to use deadly force to arrest fleeing felons. Seven other states had restrictions on the use of deadly force, and seven other states adopted the Model Penal Code provision (Griswold, 1985). The Model Penal Code provision states that "the use of deadly force is not justifiable . . . unless the . . . officer . . . believes that such force is necessary to protect himself against death, serious bodily harm, kidnapping, or sexual intercourse compelled by force or threat" (Griswold, 1985).

A significant change in the use of deadly force occurred in the 1985 case of *Tennessee v. Garner* (1985); (Coddon, 1985). Garner was a fifteen-year-old who was allegedly burglarizing an unoccupied house in Memphis, Tennessee. Police arrived on the scene, and Garner fled on foot. After ordering him to halt, police fired several shots at Garner. One of the bullets struck Garner in the back of the head, killing him instantly.

The decision in a suit against the Memphis police department filed on behalf of Garner upheld an 1858 Tennessee statute, TCA 40-7-108, that states, "If, after notice of the intention to arrest the defendant, he either flee or forcibly resist, the officer may use all the necessary means to effect the arrest" (*Garner v. Memphis Police Department,* 1979). Tennessee courts interpreted the statute as the codification of the common-law rule allowing officers to kill fleeing felons suspected of property crimes, even those that did not endanger human life, as well as felons who may be dangerous to others if left at large (*Garner v. Memphis Police Department,* 1979).

In an appeal the Sixth Circuit Court of Appeals ruled the Tennessee statute unconstitutional because it violated the Fourth Amendment guarantee against *unreasonable seizure of the person (Garner v. Memphis Police Department,* 1983). The State of Tennessee appealed the case to the Supreme Court, which eventually restricted the use of deadly force by all law enforcement officers and others to *situations involving the defense of one's life (Tennessee v. Garner,* 1985).

Until the *Garner* decision, police officers' right to use deadly force in apprehending suspects had been taken for granted by most police departments. However, this "right" raises an important ethical question. Justice may indeed be undermined when police officers are licensed to kill people before a trial, especially people who probably would not be executed even if convicted (Elliston, 1985). The application of the death penalty, even in capital cases, is extremely limited. Authorizing police officers to make death penalty decisions when attempting to arrest low-risk property offenders or even violent felons raises the question of the suspect's right to due process under the Constitution. But the issue cannot be settled here. Because of the *Tennessee, v. Garner* (1985) decision, many police departments have revised their deadly force provisions. The "defense of life" standard set forth in *Garner* currently takes precedence over existing state statutes that authorize deadly force under the fleeing-felon rule.

Police Discretion: Dropsy Testimony

Following various Supreme Court decisions on the admissibility of evidence, particularly *Mapp v. Ohio* (1961) (see chapter 8), prosecutors found it increasingly difficult to obtain convictions when their evidence was weak. Police officers who testified in court were sometimes obliged to admit that their actions in conducting searches of a suspect's person, automobile, and/or residence were not in accord with Fourth Amendment requirements governing searches and seizures. If a law enforcement officer failed to follow constitutional guidelines for seizing incriminating evidence, the evidence would be ruled inadmissible, which often caused the case to deteriorate and the defendant to escape conviction.

Requiring police to adhere to a higher standard when conducting searches and seizures created a subtle backlash. Some officers resented that criminals were getting off on "legal technicalities." The movie *Dirty Harry,* featuring Clint Eastwood as Detective Harry Callahan, demonstrated police attitudes in the early 1970s. In the movie, Callahan is investigating killings by a San Francisco sniper. Eventually, the identity of the sniper becomes known, and Callahan moves to seize incriminating evidence and make an arrest. Without a warrant, he breaks into the alleged sniper's residence and seizes a rifle and other items that prove that the man is the sniper. However, a judge later rules that the incriminating evidence cannot be used because Callahan *seized them without first obtaining a lawful warrant.* We have already seen how exigent circumstances or the totality of circumstances legitimates some warrantless searches. But in Callahan's case, a warrant could have been obtained but wasn't. The sniper was freed on a technicality.

The same type of real-life scenario happens almost daily. When their search methods are challenged in court, some officers may deliberately perjure themselves on the witness stand. For instance, they may testify that they observed *in plain view* a plastic bag full of drugs *protruding from underneath the defendant's car seat,* when in fact they conducted a warrantless search of the defendant's vehicle and reached under the seat to find the incriminating drugs. Or they may testify that when the defendant got out of his automobile, some drugs or marijuana cigarettes were seen *dropping to the ground.* The fact that these officers *saw* the drugs authorized them to seize the drugs and arrest the suspect. This type of perjured testimony has been called *dropsy testimony.*

Perjury committed by police officers to solidify a case is not new, nor is it limited to uniformed police officers. Agents of the DEA, the FBI, the IRS, and the CID, as well as officers of state highway patrols and state bureaus of investigation, have occasionally succumbed to the temptation to give dropsy testimony. Thus, many officers, especially those involved in narcotics investigations, have thwarted the intent of the Fourth Amendment by committing perjury (*Georgetown Law Journal*, 1971).

Occasionally police officers also deliberately plant evidence to incriminate suspects. In the O. J. Simpson trial in Los Angeles in 1995–1996, Simpson was acquitted of double-murder charges. Without proof or even evidence, Simpson's defense alleged that an investigating detective, Mark Fuhrman, planted at Simpson's residence a glove used in the murders. Thus, defense attorneys wanted Simpson's jury to believe that Fuhrman perjured himself when he testified about finding the glove. If Fuhrman *had* perjured himself when testifying about the glove, it would have been the symbolic equivalent of dropsy testimony. In fact, Simpson's prosecutors suggested that Simpson himself *dropped* the incriminating glove while returning home after the murders. Thus, a fairly wide gap exists between formal police department policy about *how* officers should conduct their business and what actually happens in drug and victimless crime cases (Cohen, 1985). Fortunately, incidents of dropsy testimony are somewhat infrequent.

Some Contemporary Law Enforcement Issues

Law enforcement officers at the federal, state, and local levels experience moral/ethical dilemmas, conflicting expectations, and organizational problems that affect how they do their job. Over the last decade, several problem areas have emerged as law enforcement issues. This does not mean that these problems did not exist earlier but rather that they are currently attracting much attention from criminal justice professionals, law enforcement personnel, and the public. These issues include (1) police training and professionalism; (2) police discretion in law enforcement; (3) police deception and entrapment; (4) police-community relations; (5) police violence and excessive force; (6) police administration and corruption; and (6) overlapping jurisdiction and lack of interagency cooperation.

Police Training and Professionalism

The present level of police training and professionalism has been criticized not only by the media but also by criminal justicians, politicians, and others. Police officers committing violent acts against others and acting out of control are indicators of the ineffectiveness of their training (Faulkner, 1994; Shigley, 1988). When police officers act unprofessionally or show deficiency in training, the solution seems to be that they should cultivate more professionalism and acquire more training. This is not a new issue.

In 1967, the President's Commission on Law Enforcement and Administration of Justice recommended that all police officers be required to possess at least a college degree. This conclusion was reached because the average police officer received less than two hundred hours of formal training while teachers, for example, received more than seven thousand hours and barbers more than four thousand hours (McLeod, 1979:201). Despite recent improvements in police training and efforts to raise education requirements for law enforcement officers generally, most agencies are far from achieving their minimum educational objectives for new recruits (Bureau of Justice Statistics, 1992).

Police training enhances officer productivity concerning specific types of law violations. Various Pennsylvania police agencies, for example, have always enforced drunk-driving laws but individual police officers have believed that this policy has not gotten the strong support of either their departments or the public (Mastrofski and Ritti, 1996:291). In fact, some police officers in various Pennsylvania jurisdictions have sensed public hostility to DWI arrests, especially after several important public figures were charged with this offense. In recent years, however, police training programs in Pennsylvania have emphasized the importance of

DWI arrests and how to effect them most professionally. After receiving training, 443 police officers were interviewed. They expressed the opinion that because of new departmental support for DWI arrests, their efforts were legitimized. Thus, their attitudes toward their work became more professional, and their job performance improved (Mastrofski and Ritti, 1996:315–16). Therefore, it is clear that training in particular law enforcement activities, such as DWI arrests, coupled with institutional and public support create an organizational climate that encourages police officers to do their best work.

In 1976, the Police Foundation established the National Advisory Commission on Higher Education for Police Officers, which identified six critical problem areas: (1) What should be the objectives of education for police officers? (2) What should be the curriculum for pre-employment and in-service police education as opposed to vocational and liberal arts subjects? (3) What experience should police instructors have (e.g., academic and/or police experience)? (4) What kind of student should receive federal funding? (5) Should an associate or bachelor's degree be required for entry and/or promotion? and (6) How can curriculum be changed, if necessary, within the many instructional institutions? (Becker and Whitehouse, 1980:50).

As we saw in chapter 4, one of the early advocates of education for police was August Vollmer, an early chief of police in Berkeley, California. The criminology curriculum developed by Vollmer and law professor Alexander M. Kidd at the University of California-Berkeley in 1916 was the first in the country. Since then, over a thousand college and university programs have been established. In 1990, only about 6 to 10 percent of local police departments, state police departments, and sheriff's departments required their new recruits to have some college education (Bureau of Justice Statistics, 1992). Most officers in these organizations were encouraged to seek additional college training in order to advance their careers and improve their academic skills. Presumably, over time these greater academic achievements will improve overall officer quality. However, whenever some police officers engage in misconduct, particularly against citizens, renewed cries for "something to

be done" to professionalize an already professionalized police force are heard from police chiefs and city officials. It sometimes seems that no matter how much professional skill police officers acquire, that skill is insufficient (Lumb, 1995; Pollock and Becker, 1995).

Becoming skilled at police work has been compared with becoming skilled at a craft. Some experts say that the transition from apprentice police officer to "master craftsperson" is more assured if formal training programs stress the problem-solving nature of policing, if master police officers act as field instructors for rookie police recruits, and if such training involves developing skills related to experience (Bayley, 1984).

Experts disagree about the effectiveness of greater police professionalization. The prevailing view is that better-educated police officers are more likely to observe their responsibilities and to violate fewer rules (Heffernan, 1985). Most police reform movements stress improvement through professionalization and more rational policy making. But recent evidence indicates such reforms have given the *appearance* of change without actually increasing police professionalization (Sykes, 1985).

Police Discretion in Law Enforcement

The police are authorized to enforce all laws. However, officers often enter situations in which formal law enforcement conflicts with community attitudes and expectations. The President's Commission on Law Enforcement and Administration of Justice has identified several factors that influence a police officer's discretion. These include (1) the sheer volume of technical violations; (2) limited police resources; (3) overgeneralized legislative enactments; and (4) various pressures that reflect community values and attitudes (Johnson, Misner, and Brown, 1981:28).

For police officers, using discretion is a necessary and unavoidable part of their job (Ohlin and Remington, 1993). But the area of discretion is very gray and calls for wisdom and judgment (Hanewicz, 1985:52–53; Cohen, 1985:29). Seasoned and skilled police officers frequently say that discretionary situations call for common sense because they often do not present clear choices or strategies for police officers to follow (Cohen, 1985:28). For example, in the case of an unruly crowd in a bar, it is difficult to distinguish between the "good guys" and the "bad guys." Sometimes it is wiser for police officers to separate the trouble-makers and ask certain people to leave the bar rather than to make arrests (Cohen, 1985:29).

Legislatures have been reluctant to limit the discretionary powers of police officers. This reluctance stems from the prevailing myth that the police officer has no choice in determining how and against whom to enforce the law (R. J. Allen, 1991). Prosecutors also prefer to avoid criticizing police discretion in arrest situations because of their own broad discretionary powers in prosecution decisions (Sherman, 1984).

Highlight 5.5. Illegal Immigrants Beaten by Police: The Case of Funez and Gonzales

In late March of 1996, a pickup truck carrying illegal aliens crossed the border from Mexico into the United States. Police officers and sheriff's deputies followed the truck, which suddenly increased its speed to 100 mph. A lengthy pursuit followed. The truck's flimsy exterior blew away piece by piece as its driver attempted to elude capture. During the chase, passengers threw rocks, bottles, tire irons and other items from the fleeing truck, striking some of the pursuing cruisers. Some civilian vehicles were also hit by some of the debris. The truck was finally halted near El Monte, California, about 120 miles from the Mexico-U.S. border. A dozen or so illegal aliens scattered, but sheriff's deputies caught two persons as they tried to get out of the truck.

What happened next was recorded on videotape by an overhead helicopter from the local television station. It was Rodney King revisited. Several sheriff's deputies dragged the two Mexicans from the truck. They stomped on the Mexicans, slammed them against the hood of the truck, and beat them repeatedly with their batons. One officer held his baton like a baseball bat as he clubbed a woman named Leticia Gonzales, who had been shoved to the ground. Another alien, Enrique Funez, was beaten repeatedly with batons as he attempted to comply with shouted police orders.

Almost immediately after the videotape of these events was broadcast, the officers involved were suspended pending an investigation. In the meantime, the U.S. Attorney's Office in Los Angeles announced

that the FBI was beginning an investigation to determine whether police had violated the Mexicans' civil rights.

Sergeant Mark Lohman, a sheriff's deputy, said that "people inside [the fleeing truck] were throwing things at officers in the chase and at other cars, hitting some of them." The videotape showed that when Leticia Gonzales got out of the cab, a deputy beat her on the back with his baton and then grabbed her by the hair and threw her to the ground, for no apparent reason. At least one other deputy also hit Gonzalez with his baton. Neither Funez nor Gonzalez appeared to resist arrest or to attempt to flee from the officers, all of whom were white.

In the weeks following these beatings, Funez and Gonzalez filed multimillion dollar lawsuits against the officers and the jurisdictions that employed them. The Mexican government condemned the beatings as a flagrant violation of the rights of its citizens.

Under what conditions should officers use force in subduing suspects, including illegal aliens? What factors potentially triggered the sheriff's deputies' behavior? What policies should determine how illegal aliens should be processed when apprehended? What sanctions should be imposed against these officers? What sanctions should be imposed against these illegal aliens for violating U.S. laws?

Source: Associated Press, "FBI Opens Probe into Taped Beating," *Minot (N.D.) Daily News,* April 3, 1996, p. A1.

Police Deception and Entrapment

Closely related to police discretion is police deception and **entrapment**. To what extent is it proper for law enforcement officers to employ trickery and deceit in their law enforcement practices? (Elliston and Feldberg, 1985:73). Is perjury by police officers to increase their chances of obtaining a criminal conviction ever acceptable? Is it sometimes all right for a police officer to actively participate in illegal activities in order to obtain incriminating evidence against a suspect?

Entrapment by law enforcement officers or agents of the government is inducing persons to commit crimes not otherwise contemplated by them for the purpose of instituting a criminal prosecution against them. One of the scenarios at the beginning of this chapter involved the use of entrapment. Consider these additional scenarios:

A businessman has just checked into a hotel. He is unpacking when an attractive young woman dressed in a very short skirt and halter knocks on his door. She asks him to invite her in for a drink. A little later, when he offers her money to engage in sexual intercourse, she pulls out a badge, identifies herself as a policewoman, and arrests him for soliciting for prostitution.

A customer in a bar asks the bar owner if he would like to buy a color television set very cheaply and adds, "Don't ask me how I got it." The owner purchases the television set and is then arrested for receiving stolen property. (Stitt and James, 1985:129)

These are obvious entrapment situations. Or are they? The decision of whether the situation is entrapment is made by determining whether the police planned, suggested, encouraged, or aided an individual in committing a specific crime that would not have occurred otherwise in order to make an arrest (Stitt and James, 1985:130).

The earliest criminal case that applied the entrapment defense was *Sorrells v. United States* (1932). In this case, a federal prohibition agent posing as a tourist approached Sorrells and engaged him in conversation about their common war experiences. After gaining Sorrells's confi-

dence, the agent asked him for some liquor (liquor was prohibited in Sorrells's community). Sorrells refused several times but eventually agreed to supply the agent with illegal liquor and was promptly arrested. The Supreme Court overturned his conviction on the grounds of entrapment. In a later case, a government investigator was found to be "so enmeshed in the criminal activity" himself that the Supreme Court declared his behavior "repugnant to the American criminal justice system" (*Greene v. United States*, 1970).

Two tests are used to evaluate whether law enforcement activity is entrapment: the **subjective test** and the **objective test.** *In the subjective test, if suspects have criminal records and/or are possibly disposed toward a particular kind of criminal activity, then whatever means the police use to elicit their criminal behavior are permissible.* Defendant are responsible for their own actions (Krakovec, 1986; Marcus, 1986). *In the objective test, regardless of a person's record, certain police conduct is reprehensible per se and should not be tolerated* (Leidheiser, 1983; Stitt and James, 1985:132).

Police misrepresentation and deception in entrapment situations cause mistrust of the police and put the victims of entrapment in the unfortunate position of having to admit an unlawful act if they elect to use the entrapment defense (Stitt and James, 1985:133).

Deception usually occurs at one or more of three stages of the police detection process: investigation, interrogation, and testimony in court (Skolnick, 1985:76). Particularly objectionable to citizens is a police officer's lying under oath. However, much evidence suggests that there are "tolerable" levels of perjury among police officers when testifying in court (Vaughn, 1992). During interrogation of criminal suspects, sometimes police deceive to entice suspects to plead guilty to a crime. Many confessions have been given under conditions that violate the Constitution. In short, police officers *know* the confessions they obtain will probably be rejected if tested, but there is always the chance that the suspect or the suspect's attorney will not question the methods or circumstances used to obtain the confession (McMahon, 1995).

Police-Community Relations

Police-community relations is an operational concept that originated in 1957 in the St. Louis, Missouri, Police Department (Geary, 1975:211). Since then, community relations has been emphasized by many police departments throughout the nation. *Police-community relations is the philosophy of involving members of the community and the police in determining (1) what police services will be provided; (2) how they will be provided; and (3) how the police and members of the community will resolve common problems* (Attorney General's Advisory Commission, 1973).

Is Police-Community Relations a Key Police Department Priority?

Promoting community relations is a major priority of many police departments. Many large municipal police departments have special public relations divisions and bureaus staffed by persons whose sole function is to harmonize the interests of the police and the community. In 1972, for instance, the Omaha police department implemented

Officers discuss home security and residential safety measures with concerned families and public housing managers. Such meetings help to harmonize the interests of the police and the community they serve.

the Omaha Police-Community Relations Camp run by six police officers, six YMCA personnel, and one special consultant (Tooley, 1972). Fifty-three youths from the Omaha suburbs attended the camps, where both police officers and campers lived together for a short period. The objective was to allow the youths to observe lifestyles different from their own and develop more positive perspectives. Most camp participants reported the camp to be a success, especially at generating experiences that reduced tension between the youths and police.

Community-Oriented Policing and Police-Community Relations

It should be noted that police-community relations is not the same thing as community-oriented policing. Police-community relations seeks to foster better relations between the public and police department. Whenever incidents involving police misconduct and violence against citizens make the news, the police department involved must attempt some sort of damage control. Usually, the public information officers in the department will attempt to offset the negative image created by these incidents by highlighting the department's accomplishments (Trojanowicz, 1990; U.S. Community Relations Service, 1993).

Do Different Groups View Police Differently?

It is a commonly held view in criminal justice that nonwhites and minorities tend to hold less favorable views than whites toward police officers. However, many of the studies about citizen perceptions of police were conducted during the 1960s, 1970s, and early 1980s when civil disobedience was pervasive in virtually every large city. When police officers moved to quell civil disobedience and enforce laws, many citizens believed that police were being abusive toward them. Additionally, more than a few police officers appeared to single out minorities for their special attention. Consequently, many minorities, especially African Americans, reasonably believed that they were being discriminated against.

However, interest in community-oriented policing and in other police-community relations programs has drastically changed many police department policies. While charges of racism and unfair treatment of minorities continue to emerge, some experts believe that minority attitudes toward police have improved. For instance, during a 1996 study of 526 residents of Detroit, Michigan, Frank et al. interviewed about three-fourths of these individuals. The sample consisted of 339 blacks and 187 whites, primarily from poor neighborhoods. All participants were asked about their attitudes toward police and whether they believed police were doing a good job of maintaining order on the streets and controlling drugs.

Frank et al. found that black citizens' attitudes toward police were significantly more favorable than in previous years. Furthermore and quite surprisingly, blacks' attitudes toward police were more favorable than whites'. As Frank et al. correctly observed, this finding contradicts much of the earlier research, which found clear differences between black and white attitudes toward police. In previous research, whites overwhelmingly felt more favorable toward police than nonwhites. Given that this study took place in Detroit, which has a history of abusiveness toward minorities, it is somewhat surprising to find such a change in attitudes. One key element explaining this finding was that the Detroit Police Department has implemented several important reforms. For example, it appointed its first black police chief, Coleman Young, in 1976 and changed its policy on the use of force by police. As these and other new policies became standard practices, complaints about police officers declined. While this is only one study, it suggests a subtle shift in public attitudes toward police in the wake of reforms that are being implemented nationally.

It is also significant that Detroit was also the site of an experimental program offering police services directly to residents. This experiment, called the Detroit Police Ministation Program (Detroit Police Department, 1983; Holland, 1985), places police officers in neighborhood *ministations,* or smaller police precincts. These ministations, which provide all the services of a regular precinct except detention facilities, are staffed by officers twenty-four hours a day. In order to build better police-community relations, the police department has encouraged citizen involvement in staffing these ministations, of which there are nearly forty. Be-

cause community residents perceive police interest in these ministations as genuine, citizen participation has increased, and citizen volunteers have become valuable assets to the program (Holland, 1985). In some jurisdictions, however, police-community relations programs have been nothing more than public relations gimmicks. In these instances, police departments have promoted the appearance of working with the community while maintaining the status quo.

Few dispute that the goal of police-community relations is to improve relations between police departments and various ethnic and racial minorities. In West Virginia, for instance, officers assigned community relations tasks worked with black members of the community to address community grievances and allegations of racism and poor treatment (U.S. Commission on Civil Rights, 1993). In many instances, new departmental policies and operations incorporate civil rights training to make officers more aware of their relations with everyone, especially minority citizens. Principles of good policing promoted by the programs include using violence only as a last resort (U.S. Community Relations Service, 1993). Trojanowicz (1990) has suggested that officers should get such training much earlier, even while they are new recruits. Additionally, surveys of community needs and interests should be conducted fairly regularly to determine citizens' needs and the types of problems police officers will confront in the streets (Marenin, 1989).

Police Violence and Excessive Force

One sensitive subject of interest to the community and police officers alike is the use of violence in apprehending criminal suspects. Violence most often occurs when officers must use extraordinary force to subdue arrestees. Experts have described such violence as a three-stage process: arousal, reaction, and outcome (Ross, 1995). Because most police violence occurs in public, there are reactions from different actors: the victims, police officers, the public, and the government (Ross, 1995). *The use of more force than is necessary to make arrests has been called* **excessive force** (Smith, 1994).

Whenever citizens see police officers arresting a suspect, they judge the amount of force exerted as being either appropriate or excessive. Most citizens understand that force is often warranted when police arrest resisting suspects. The more the community knows about police policies regarding the use of force, the more residents understand why police act as they do. Most experts concede that any force police use to subdue a suspect must be legitimate and justified and that people consent to the use of such force whenever necessary. This consent and understanding are important to good police-community relations (Smith, 1994). However, if citizens perceive that ethnic or racial factors influence an officer's treatment of a suspect, they regard *any* force as excessive (Geller and Toch, 1995; Rome, Son, and Davis, 1995). The most extreme form of force is deadly force. Deadly force is any force likely or intended to cause death or great bodily harm (Black, 1990:398). Consider these hypothetical examples.

> A fifteen-year-old boy has just stolen a jacket from a department store. He runs from the store and flees in a car that he stole a few hours earlier. The police are notified about the car theft and shoplifting incident and observe the fleeing boy. They follow in their cruiser at speeds in excess of 90 miles per hour through congested city streets, firing at the suspect with .357 magnum revolvers. Eventually, they succeed in wounding the boy, stopping the vehicle, and retrieving the stolen goods. In the process, they damage fifteen automobiles, cause considerable damage to their own cruiser, and endanger the lives of many innocent pedestrians.

> A suspect has shot and killed two bank employees during a hold up and is being pursued by police, again at high speed. The suspect fires at the police with a shotgun, and they return the suspect's fire. Eventually, they wound the suspect and capture him.

Are either of these incidents justified? Are the lives of the officers in jeopardy in the incident involving the fifteen-year-old shoplifter? Is there any difference in either of the two hypothetical cases? Civil rights groups and concerned citizens have expressed disapproval over police use of deadly force

in situations that are not life-threatening. In 1984, twenty-four states permitted police officers to use deadly force to apprehend fleeing felons (Griswold, 1985). But the decision in *Tennessee v. Garner* (1985) renders the fleeing-felon rule invalid. All states must modify their deadly force policies and statutes that apply when police officers attempt to apprehend fleeing felons. The "defense of life" standard has replaced the fleeing felon rule. It specifies that deadly force may be used only when the police officer's life or the life of a bystander is in jeopardy.

Police officers in Washington, D.C., are required to use only soft-lead bullets rather than copper-jacketed rounds, and they must use no larger than a .38-caliber cartridge. Such lead bullets are less powerful in that they travel at slower speeds. They are thus less likely to pass through more than one body than jacketed higher-caliber ammunition, which may pass through as many as five or six persons. Thus, if police must fire their guns near a crowd, fewer innocent people will be wounded. When these police officers face suspects using a .357 or .44 magnum revolver, they justifiably feel that they are at a distinct disadvantage.

Studies of public attitudes about the use of force by police are mixed. For instance, a 1991 study tallied responses to the statement "A policeman striking an adult male citizen under some circumstances is warranted." About 70 percent of white respondents and 43 percent of black respondents agreed with this statement (Arthur and Case, 1994). Researchers found that members of groups with greater power, status, and advantage (whites, males, the more educated, and the more wealthy) were more likely to favor police use of force than less privileged groups.

The years since *Garner* (1985) have seen a noticeable decline in killings of suspects by police officers. Following the *Garner* case, there was a 16 percent decrease in work-related homicides committed by police officers according to an official Supplementary Homicide Reports data base (Tennenbaum, 1994). Virtually every police department now has more restrictive shooting policies. The number of shots fired by police has also declined dramatically. The racial imbalance of persons shot and killed by police has been significantly reduced, an achievement that has not been accompanied by a noticeable increase in crime or life-threatening risk to police officers (Walker and Fridell, 1992).

Police Administration and Corruption

Corruption exists when a public official accepts money or the equivalent of money for doing something he has a duty to do anyway or a duty not to do or for exercising a legitimate discretion for improper reasons (Elliston and Feldberg, 1985:251). Police officers engage in corruption when they permit pimps and prostitutes to operate in exchange for a share of the profits, when they accept bribes to permit illegal gambling and bookmaking, or in any way permit violations of the law in exchange for rewards (Barker and Carter, 1986).

Police corruption received national attention when the Knapp Commission investigated corruption among New York City police (Barker and Carter, 1986). One NYC police officer, Frank Serpico, testified extensively about payoffs to police by business owners and organized crime figures. His story was popularized in the 1970 movie *Serpico*. Despite the Knapp Commission investigation and the eradication of corruption in certain police precincts in the early 1970s, corruption continued to flourish at many administrative levels.

In 1992, then-mayor David Dinkins appointed an official commission chaired by Milton Mollen to investigate police corruption in New York City (New York Commission to Investigate Allegations of Police Corruption, 1994). The New York Commission found that corruption flourishes because of a police culture that exalts loyalty above integrity; because of the silence of honest officers who fear the consequences of scandal more than corruption itself; because of hostility and alienation between the police and the community in certain precincts; and because for years the police department abandoned its responsibility to ensure the integrity of its members. During the Commission's investigation, its members' attempts to acquire information about officers and department activities were thwarted by higher-ups who refused to disclose records. The Commission recommended to

Mayor Dinkins that a permanent, independent body be charged with the task of uncovering corruption and that the department enact measures to more effectively screen recruits and improve their training and integrity.

Corruption in police departments and in government is neither uncommon nor recent. It undermines public faith in law officers whenever it is made known (McAlary, 1994). During the 1920s, Al Capone bragged that he "owned" a number of police officers in Chicago and that much of his criminal activity was permitted to flourish in exchange for police payoffs. Police corruption still exists in many cities, such as Chicago, Boston, and Miami (Lindberg, 1991; Sechrest and Burns, 1992). One of the more infamous examples involves New York City Police Department officer Michael Dowd, who was convicted of bribery and extortion in connection with his sheltering of a gang of drug traffickers (McAlary, 1994). And in Miami, the great influx of Cuban refugees caused several racially sensitive incidents that resulted in numerous disciplinary actions (Sechrest and Burns, 1992).

Several stages of the "moral career" of police officers in becoming "grafters" have been identified: (1) officers engage in minor "perks" (e.g., free meals from restaurants); (2) officers do not enforce bars' closing hours; (3) officers accept gratuities from motorists and other persons guilty of minor law violations; (4) officers permit more serious crimes, such as gambling, in exchange for larger financial payoffs; (5) officers permit prostitution and other more serious offenses; and (6) officers permit narcotics trafficking and other more serious crimes in exchange for bribes (Sherman, 1985:258–60). The existence of these "stages" is not accepted by all, nor do all police officers follow this pattern. Even police officers who are familiar with their fellow officers' misdeeds may not "blow the whistle" on them (Wren, 1985). There appears to be some gradualism in the accepting of graft. "Offense escalation" has been described in studies of drug abuse and juvenile delinquency. Should it be assumed that police officers will rapidly progress from accepting free cups of coffee to shaking down drug dealers?

It is difficult to distinguish between genuine gifts (e.g., Christmas gifts) and gratuities, bribes, and corruption (Feldberg, 1985:267). Sometimes accepting any kind of gift may be the beginning of the *slippery slope*, which paves the way for accepting other, larger gratuities and eventually bribes (Feldberg, 1985:267–68). Greater citizen involvement in police administration is one community response to police corruption. Thus, citizen review boards may have merit, despite some police chiefs' negative feelings toward them (Reiss, 1985; Fyfe, 1985).

Police Misconduct and Internal Affairs

While police misconduct and dishonesty are often linked to individual police officers, misconduct can also originate within the police organization itself (Lundman, 1979:218). Three conditions characterize organizationally condoned police misconduct:

1. The misconduct is supported and encouraged by peer norms at some level in the organization.
2. Mechanisms exist whereby new officers are taught the norms that are supportive of misconduct.
3. The misconduct is supported by police administrators (Lundman, 1979:218–19).

Thus, police abuse of their discretionary powers when making arrests is easily explained, because these abuses are supported either overtly or covertly by the entire department (Bratton, 1995; New York Civil Liberties Union, 1990). This does not mean that all police officers in all police departments abuse their arrest powers, but for those who do engage in such abuses, there are no organizational penalties in certain jurisdictions.

During the 1970s, the Philadelphia Police Department was involved in several federal civil suits that alleged police brutality against minorities (Anechiarico, 1984). The outcomes of these suits (*COPPAR v. Rizzo*, 1973; *Rizzo v. Goode*, 1976; *United States v. Philadelphia*, 1979) did not favor the plaintiffs. The plaintiff-citizens' having to prove intentional discrimination and injury seriously weakened their cases. Sometimes lawyer apa-

thy or unwillingness to sue police officers may cause delays in civil actions alleging police misconduct. If the legal delays are excessive, the statute of limitations may expire, and the cases will be dismissed outright (Harrison, 1985).

Mechanisms exist for investigating police corruption and misconduct. Most large urban police departments have internal affairs divisions whose job is to investigate allegations of police misconduct or corruption. Internal affairs divisions are unpopular with many police officers, who believe that these agencies are "out to get them" (St. Clair et al., 1992).

Victims of police misconduct can seek damages against the police officers themselves. Also, the Supreme Court has made it possible for citizens to pursue legal action against the municipal agency itself under the **municipal liability theory** embodied in 18 U.S.C., Sec. 1983 (Alpert and Smith, 1991; Friedman, 1988; U.S. Community Relations Service, 1993). Awards to victims of police brutality and other forms of officer misconduct have reached $1 million, and such suits have done much to improve and modernize police operations and procedures. But victims of police brutality and misconduct still find it difficult to win their cases in court.

Accountability and Civilian Complaint Review Boards

Many municipalities have created *citizen complaint review boards*, also called simply complaint review boards. These boards, which are independent of the police department, have as members civilians from the community who are often appointed by the mayor or other officials (Kerstetter, and Rasinski, 1994). One reason for establishing independent review boards is that many citizens distrust department mechanisms for "policing" the police. Citizens suspect collusion between officers who are members of internal affairs divisions and regular line officers who have been charged with misconduct. It is not unusual, therefore, to find citizen review boards that are comprised of *both* officers and citizens (St. Clair et al., 1992). The success of both internal and external review mechanisms continues to be debated (West, 1988).

Police officers often feel that they are accountable only to the chief of police. They see civilian review boards as an infringement on police authority because they involve "lay people with little knowledge" of police work (Fyfe, 1985). Because these citizen review boards have little or no independent investigative capability, they ordinarily rely on what police tell them anyway.

If police organizations covertly support police misconduct, more effective departmental monitoring is needed. As we have seen, civilian complaint review boards have been used as independent monitoring mechanisms for regulating police conduct. These boards also aim at increasing police accountability. Theoretically, they independently and objectively judge the grounds underlying citizen complaints against the police (Kerstetter and Rasinski, 1994). However, the boards of many municipalities, such as Boston, Philadelphia, and Detroit, are sometimes considered ineffective because of (1) police resistance, especially from chiefs who regard the boards as infringements on their authority; (2) officers' feelings of being singled out for close scrutiny by citizens who have little or no knowledge of police work; and (3) unrealistic expectations about what these boards can accomplish (Fyfe, 1985; St. Clair et al., 1992).

An alternative to citizen review boards is to improve the mechanisms for receiving, investigating, and reviewing complaints against police officers. What is needed is a thorough review of complaints that involves several officers at different administrative levels. Most important, citizens must be provided meaningful feedback on what has been done about their complaints (Fyfe, 1985), because many people feel that no action is taken regarding allegations of police misconduct. Establishing a feedback system would increase police credibility and ensure greater fairness for both citizens and officers.

At least two important factors have shaped people's attitudes toward police officers: (1) the actual contact they have with police, and (2) the impressions they have of fairness, bias, or prejudice on the part of police. Citizen participation in sanctioning police for alleged misconduct is a sensitive issue. Community residents believe that more citizens should be involved in reviewing allegations of police misconduct. More effective means of registering and even encouraging complaints should be adopted. Better feedback about the status of investigations of complaints would greatly improve police credibility and ensure that the system is more fair.

Summary

The organization and operation of modern police departments in the United States are based largely on the 1829 model of the Metropolitan Police of London established by Sir Robert Peel. The police were originally conceived as protectors whose functions included the general security of the state and individuals. The first police departments in the United States were created in Boston in 1838 and New York City in 1845, although policing activities were not unknown in earlier periods under different names.

The Law Enforcement Assistance Administration was established in 1968 to coordinate many of the anticrime activities of local, state, and federal agencies, but it failed to achieve its goals over the next fifteen-year period. It has gradually been replaced by the Office of Justice Programs and National Institute of Justice, which fund criminal justice research and compile statistics relating to crime trends and criminal characteristics.

Police officers are expected to exercise their discretion when investigating criminal activity, and they are also expected to use reasonable judgment when making arrests. Thus, discretion is important at every stage of the investigatory process, from arrests and detentions; to searches of persons, their automobiles, and their homes; to seizures of contraband. Sometimes police use deception in order to detect criminal activity and to ferret out lawbreakers. Questions arise about the use of deception in order to create the conditions of probable cause necessary before an arrest can be made. Some citizens allege entrapment and believe they should not be held accountable for criminal activity generated by these means.

Most police departments have made serious efforts to improve their relationships with community residents, often through community-oriented policing programs and other activities aimed at enhancing or improving police-community relations.

Presently, most police officers are aware of their high visibility and of the importance of presenting themselves in the best possible light.

Police misconduct and corruption are unwarranted and are given intense publicity. Many police departments have established internal affairs divisions to conduct investigations into allegations of police misconduct. Many jurisdictions have established independent citizen complaint review boards to supplement the work of internal affairs divisions. Efforts are being made to hold officers more accountable while enforcing criminal laws.

Key Terms

Behavioral approach
Bureau of Justice Statistics
Control beats
Deadly force
Entrapment
Excessive force
Exigent circumstances
Fleeing felon rule
Foot patrol program
Golf cart patrol
Hot pursuit
Kansas City Preventive Patrol Experiment
Law Enforcement Assistance Administration
Legal approach
Model Penal Code (MPC)
Municipal liability theory
Neighborhood-oriented policing
Objective test
Organizational approach
Pat down
Plain view rule
Police-community relations
Police discretion
Preventive patrol
Proactive beats
Reactive beats
Scale of police patrol
Search incident to an arrest
Sector patrol
Stop and frisk
Subjective test

Team policing
Tennessee v. Garner

Questions for Review

1. Briefly discuss the Kansas City Preventive Patrol Experiment. Why was this experiment controversial?
2. What do regular police officers mean by "real police work"? What kinds of functions do police perform most of the time?
3. Did the Kansas City Preventive Patrol Experiment reduce crime in Kansas City? Why or why not?
4. What is a foot patrol? Briefly compare patrol car officers and foot patrol officers concerning their effectiveness and ability to communicate with headquarters.
5. What is meant by team policing? Does team policing foster better police-community relations? Why or why not?
6. James Q. Wilson favors a return to the "watchman" style of patrolling. Other researchers disagree. Briefly discuss Wilson's rationale and the opinions of his critics about patrol styles.
7. A police officer saw a person he didn't like driving down the road. The officer pulled him over for no reason and searched his car. Finding some marijuana in a small bag in the person's trunk, he arrested the person for possession of marijuana. Criticize the officer's action in view of the Supreme Court cases discussed in the chapter. Should the marijuana found in the car be used as evidence against the person? Why or why not?
8. A police officer saw a person sitting in a bus station at 3:00 A.M. He made the person stand against the wall. The officer thrust his hands into the person's pockets and found a pocketknife. He arrested the person for "going armed." Criticize his actions in view of the cases discussed in this chapter.
9. What are exigent circumstances? Give some examples of exigent circumstances that would justify a police officer breaking into a person's home to seize evidence.

10. What is the significance of *Garner v. Memphis Police Department*? Briefly discuss the case and its results.

Suggested Readings

Alpert, Geoffrey P. and Roger G. Dunham. *Policing Urban America*. 3d ed. Prospect Heights, IL: Waveland, 1996.

Bennett, Wayne W. and Karen M. Hess. *Policing: Management and Supervision in Law Enforcement*. 2d ed. St. Paul, MN: West, 1996.

Cordner, Gary and Donna Hale. *What Works in Policing? Operations and Administration Examined*. Cincinnati, OH: Anderson, 1992.

Cordner, Gary W. and Dennis J. Kenney. *Managing Police Organizations*. Cincinnati, OH: Anderson, 1996.

Cox, Steven M. *Police: Practices, Perspectives and Problems*. Needham Heights, MA: Allyn and Bacon, 1996.

Ebbe, Obi N.I. *Comparative and International Criminal Justice Systems: Policing, Judiciary, and Corrections*. Newton, MA: Butterworth/Heinemann, 1996.

Klotter, John C. *Legal Guide for Police*. 4th ed. Cincinnati, OH: Anderson, 1996.

Kraus, Melvyn B. and Edward P. Lazear (eds.). *Searching for Alternatives: Drug-Control Policy in the United States*. Stanford, CA: Hoover Institution Press, 1991.

Leonard, V.A. and Harry M. More (eds.). *Police Organization and Management*. 8th ed. Mineola, NY: Foundation Press, 1993.

More, Harry W. and Fred Wegener. *Effective Police Supervision*. 2d ed. Cincinnati, OH: Anderson, 1996.

Murrell, Dan S. and William O. Dwyer. *Constitutional Law and Liability for Agents, Deputies and Police Officers*. Durham, NC: Carolina Academic Press, 1992.

Rabon, Don. *Investigative Discourse Analysis: Statements, Letters and Transcripts*. Durham, NC: Carolina Academic Press, 1994.

Roberg, Roy R. and Jack Kuykendall. *Police & Society*. Belmont, CA: Wadsworth, 1993.

Souryal, Sam S. *Police Organization and Administration*. 2d ed. Cincinnati, OH: Anderson, 1996.

Tonry, Michael and Norval Morris (eds.). *Modern Policing*. Chicago, IL: University of Chicago Press, 1992.

Weisheit, Ralph A., L. Edward Wells, and David N. Falcone. *Crime and Policing in Rural and Small-Town America*. Prospect Heights, IL: Waveland, 1996.

CHAPTER 6

Court Organization: Structure and Process

Where should suspected terrorists be tried? On April 19, 1995, the federal building in Oklahoma City was bombed. The culprits had loaded a Ryder rental truck with numerous barrels of fertilizer and other chemicals to produce a bomb capable of leveling a multi-story building. They parked the truck in front of the federal building at 9:00 A.M., setting a timer to detonate the mixture. The explosion blew away half of the federal building, killing 169 persons and seriously injuring another 500, and damaged property over several blocks.

A short time later, Timothy McVeigh and Terry Nichols were arrested and charged with murder and conspiracy. According to the government, McVeigh and Nichols blew up the federal building to protest and avenge the assault on the Branch Davidian compound in Waco, Texas, a few years earlier.

Actually, state, city, and county officials could also act to bring charges against these men for violating state, city, and county statutes and ordinances. However, since the building was a federal facility, the federal government acted first to bring charges. McVeigh and Nichols were scheduled to be tried in federal court in late 1996. Because of the heavy publicity surrounding the bombing, attorneys for McVeigh and Nichols requested a change of venue, whereby their cases would be transferred to another jurisdiction. Changes of venue, or jurisdiction, are made whenever it is believed that the defendants might not receive a fair trial in the jurisdiction where the crime occurred. The federal trial for McVeigh and Nichols was transferred to Denver, Colorado (Associated Press, 1996:A4). McVeigh was convicted in June 1997.

This chapter is about court organization. In order to understand why the federal government acts as it does when trying cases, we need to understand how the *federal court system* is organized. We also need to know how the *state court system* operates when pursuing cases against defendants accused of state crimes. This chapter examines and describes both systems.

The first part of the chapter describes the federal judiciary, beginning with the U.S. Supreme Court. Circuit courts of appeal are also discussed, including U.S. district courts and the U.S. magistrate. State court organization is then described and various functions of state and local courts are identified.

Court personnel are also discussed, including the court reporter, court clerk, bailiff, and prosecutor. The role of defense attorney is discussed, and judges and various judicial selection methods are presented. Various plans, including the Missouri and Kales plans, are described. The chapter concludes with an examination of various court reforms and efforts to unify various court systems.

Levels of Court Systems

The federal government and fifty state governments make and enforce criminal laws. Therefore, fifty-one systems co-exist (Abraham, 1968: 138–39; Neubauer, 1979). Abraham (1968:139) says: "The character, jurisdiction, quality, and complexity of these [state] courts vary considerably from state to state in accordance with the myriad considerations of public policy, need, size, and constitutional practice that characterize the heterogeneous component parts of the nation."

Despite the diversity among state court organizations and operations, these systems share several common features. The Fourteenth Amendment forbids any state to create laws that conflict with the Constitution or that would "abridge the privileges and immunities of citizens of the United States." Frequently, local and state laws are challenged regarding their constitutionality. On these occasions higher courts consider possible conflicts between federal and state statutes.

Both the federal and state court systems have higher and lower courts. Each court has a *jurisdiction*, or *the power and authority to hear and resolve certain matters or controversies*. A chart of the federal and state court system is shown in figure 6.1.

Figure 6.1 shows that the highest of all state and federal courts is the U.S. Supreme Court. Beneath the U.S. Supreme Court are federal and state courts. These comprise two parallel court systems, each with a particular jurisdiction (Lieberman, 1984). The federal court has jurisdiction over all federal laws, while the state court has jurisdiction over state and local statutes and ordinances (National Center for State Courts, 1995). There is some interplay between federal and state courts. State court cases may enter the federal ap-

pellate process at some point. This interface of state and federal courts will be described later in this chapter.

Federal Court Organization

Many state courts copy federal court structure and process (Flango, 1994a). In fact, some states have adopted almost verbatim the Federal Rules of Criminal Procedure contained in the U.S. Code, changing them only slightly to fit their own needs.

Most courts trace their roots to the Constitutional Convention in the 1780s. Prior to the final vote on the Bill of Rights, convention delegates passed the Judiciary Act of 1789, which was influenced by the **Virginia Plan** (sometimes called the **Randolph Plan**) (Carp and Stidham, 1993).

The Virginia Plan presented the concept of superior and inferior courts, with the former having considerable appellate authority over the latter (Goebel, 1971). Interestingly, the Virginia Plan stemmed from England's royal court system. Royal judges in England had served "at the King's pleasure during good behavior," which was the equivalent of a lifetime appointment. This practice is still followed in all federal courts and in some state courts, where judges are appointed to serve for life or until they retire.

The Judiciary Act of 1789 created three "tiers" of courts: (1) thirteen *federal district courts,* each presided over by a district judge; (2) three higher-level *circuit courts,* each made up of two justices of the Supreme Court and one district judge; and (3) a *Supreme Court,* consisting of a chief justice and five associate justices (Carp and Stidham, 1993).

The federal district courts have jurisdiction over all civil and criminal cases. The circuit courts review decisions of federal district courts, although they also have some limited original jurisdiction (Flango, 1994b). And finally, the Supreme Court was given jurisdiction that included the interpretation of federal legislation and balancing the interests of the state and the nation (Hughes, 1966:1). Figure 6.2 shows the structure of the federal judicial system.

Figure 6.1 The Federal and State Court System

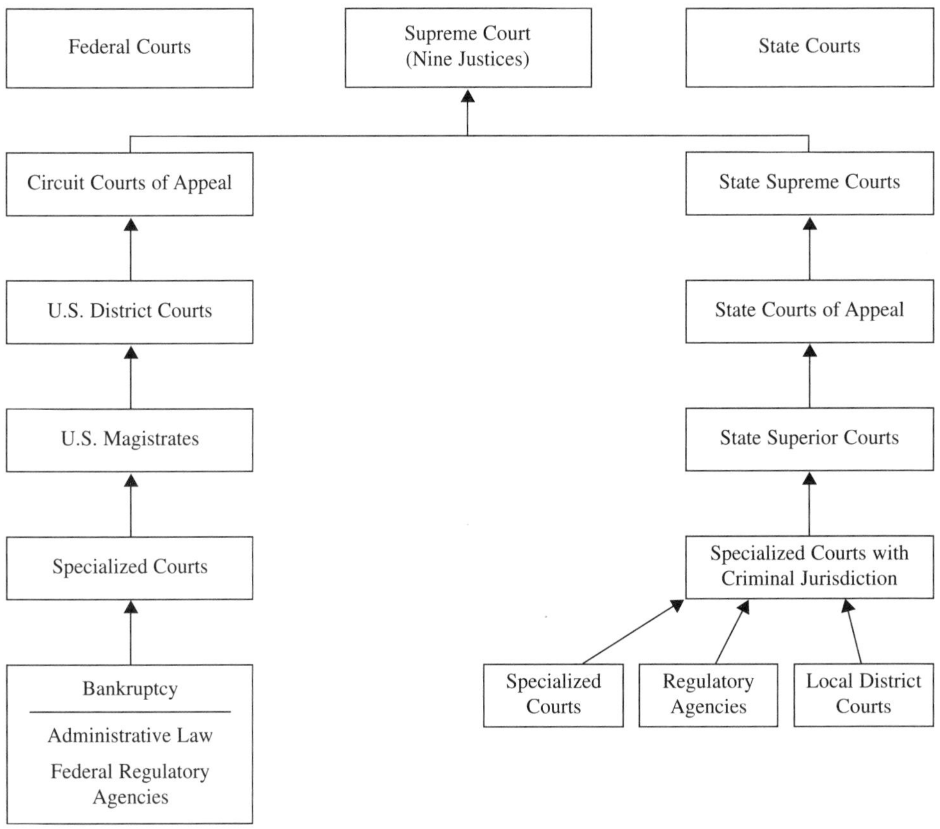

The U.S. Supreme Court

Original and Exclusive Jurisdiction

The **U.S. Supreme Court** has both original and exclusive jurisdiction over (1) all actions or proceedings against ambassadors or public ministers of foreign states; and (2) all controversies between two or more states. *Original jurisdiction means the court may recognize a case at its inception, hear that case, and try it without consulting other courts or authorities. Exclusive jurisdiction means that no other court may decide certain kinds of cases.* For example, a juvenile court has exclusive jurisdiction over juvenile matters.

The Case of *Marbury v. Madison* (1803)

One of the most important cases in establishing the review powers of the Supreme Court was *Marbury v. Madison* (1803). This case resulted from a political conflict between the Federalists and anti-Federalists. Outgoing president John Adams signed commissions for several new circuit court appointments on his last day in office. However, Secretary of State James Madison withheld the processing of these commissions, anticipating that the new president would want to make his own appointments to the circuit court. One of the thwarted appointments was that of William Marbury, who petitioned the Supreme Court to force Secretary of State Madison to issue his appointment. Chief Justice John Marshall ruled in Marbury's favor and issued a *writ of mandamus* to compel the Secretary of State to issue the commissions authorized by ex-president John Adams. Thus, the right of **judicial review** was established—the *power of the Supreme Court to review and determine the constitutionality of acts of Congress and the executive branch.* In 1810 this judicial review power was also extended to state governments in *Fletcher v. Peck.*

Supreme Court Jurisdiction and Salaries

The Supreme Court also has original, but not exclusive, jurisdiction over (1) all actions or proceedings brought by ambassadors or other public ministers; (2) all controversies between the United States and states; and (3) all actions or proceedings by a state against citizens of another state or aliens (U.S. Code, 1996).

The Supreme Court is the most powerful court in the land. It is directly instrumental in shaping diverse policies, including those governing abortion rights and the death penalty. Abortion reforms have been attempted on numerous occasions, although reformists have been unsuccessful thus far in changing policies established by *Roe v. Wade* (1973; Farr, 1993). The Supreme Court has also influenced how death penalty cases are decided and how death sentences are imposed (*Gregg v. Georgia*, 1976), how to bring about greater racial equity in the jury selection process (*Batson v. Kentucky*, 1986), and how due process can be preserved in prison disciplinary hear-

Figure 6.2 The Federal Judicial System

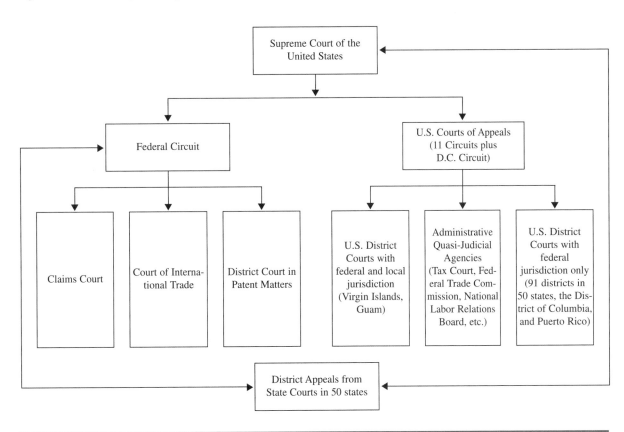

Americans differ openly about the death penalty. People demonstrating outside the gates of San Quentin State Prison in California show support for the execution of a convicted killer, soon to take place. A few hours after his death, a small group (facing page) organized by the ACLU protested the execution at the State Building in San Francisco.

ings (Epstein and Kobylka, 1992; Golash, 1992; Jacobson, 1977; Trugman, 1986).

The Supreme Court is the ultimate reviewer of decisions made by lower appellate courts or state supreme courts. The Supreme Court is primarily an appellate court, because it devotes most of its time to reviewing decisions of lower courts (Carp and Stidham, 1993). It is the final arbiter of lower court decisions unless Congress declares otherwise. Congress may change Constitutional Amendments or other acts. The Supreme Court meets thirty-six weeks a year, from the first Monday in October until the end of June. In 1994, annual salaries of the chief justice and associate justices were, respectively, $171,500 and $164,100 (U.S. Code, Title 28, Sec. 5, 1996). Salaries of all federal judges are fixed by the Federal Salary Act of 1967 (Title 2, Secs. 351–61, 1996).

The Nature of U.S. Supreme Court Appointments

The president of the United States appoints judges to the Supreme Court, subject to the ap-

proval of Congress. These lifetime appointments often reflect a president's vested interests. Therefore, judges with judicial philosophies consistent with those of the president are sometimes appointed instead of more qualified judges who hold contrary philosophies (Goldman, 1985; Solomon, 1984). Former President George Bush's nomination of Clarence Thomas to the Supreme Court was hotly debated by the U.S. Senate Judiciary Committee, which spent considerable time examining accusations of sexual harassment brought against Judge Thomas by Anita Hill, a University of Oklahoma professor who at one time worked for him. Conflicting testimony before the Judiciary Committee left many persons doubting Hill's accusations, and Judge Thomas's appointment was approved.

The Composition of the U.S. Supreme Court

The composition of the Supreme Court strongly influences the court's interpretations of the Constitution. Since the president of the United

exceptions to the Fourth Amendment were introduced that liberalized search and seizure regulations and policies. These exceptions broadened police powers and eased restrictions that the Warren Court had imposed earlier. In 1986, William H. Rehnquist became chief justice, replacing Warren Burger. No doubt his philosophies and opinions will also influence Supreme Court decisions.

One issue of importance to most citizens is the death penalty. The Supreme Court has never banned the death penalty, although it has narrowed the circumstances under which it may be applied. Abortion is another burning issue. The Warren Court issued a dramatic ruling (*Roe v. Wade*, 1973) that declared unconstitutional those state statutes that prohibited it.

The composition of the Supreme Court is vital to whether capital punishment will eventually be abolished. In the 1980s and early 1990s, two former justices, William J. Brennan and Thurgood Marshall, consistently opposed the majority of justices by declaring their belief that the death penalty was cruel and unusual punishment and violated the Eighth and Fourteenth Amendments "under all circumstances" (Brennan et al., 1994; *Monroe v. Butler*, 1988). These justices were appointed in 1956 and 1967 respectively. In fact Justice John Paul Stevens (appointed in 1975) is the only one of the justices on the Court in 1996 to be appointed prior to 1980. As the composition of the Supreme Court changes, it becomes more liberal or conservative. While later Supreme Courts have not been inclined to reverse previous Court decisions, they have decided narrow issues that have the effect of law. Capital punishment and abortion are two such issues that may be affected by subsequent Supreme Court decisions.

A president's political philosophies and interests figure prominently in selecting replacement justices for those who die or retire. Selecting justices who favor capital punishment or abortion or who favor their abolishment will sway future U.S. Supreme Court decisions toward or away from vested interest groups advocating opposing views. During his first presidential term, President Clinton appointed Justices Stephen Breyer and Ruth Bader Ginsburg to replace retiring Justices Byron R. White and Harry A. Blackmun.

States appoints justices subject to congressional approval, these appointments influence Supreme Court decision making in favor of liberal or conservative interests. When Earl Warren was chief justice, the Court's decisions were directed at minimizing the abuse of police discretion in matters of arrest and search and seizure. The Court introduced stringent requirements that emphasized the rights of criminal suspects and minimized police misconduct. The exclusionary rule and "pat-down" doctrines are part of the legacy of the Warren Court, which also instituted the *Miranda* doctrine guaranteeing suspects' rights to counsel and against self-incrimination. In the perception of some law enforcement officers, these Supreme Court decisions are restrictive and favor the interests of criminals. However, the American Civil Liberties Union and other rights groups were pleased with these decisions because they demonstrated concern for the rights of individuals, regardless of their guilt or lack of guilt.

In 1969, Warren Burger became chief justice of the Supreme Court. During his tenure several

---

Highlight 6.1. Chief Justice Says Congress Threatens Justice: The Case of Chief Justice William H. Rehnquist

In late 1995, Congress planned a study aimed at evaluating how well federal judges perform their jobs. In the study, sponsored by the chairman of the Senate Judiciary Committee, Senator Charles Grassley (R-Iowa), all federal court judges will complete a self-administered questionnaire that solicits detailed information about the amount of time judges actually devote to official tasks.

Chief Justice William H. Rehnquist most vigorously opposes such a study. "There can be no doubt that answers to some form of such questions could aid Congress in making decisions about judicial salaries, permitting outside income from teaching, creating new judgeships, and filling existing vacancies. There can also be no doubt that the subject matter of the questions and the detail required for answering them could amount to an unwarranted and ill-considered effort to micromanage the work of the federal judiciary." Rehnquist hopes that the committee's inquiries are aimed at obtaining information that is of legitimate interest to Congress without encroaching on judicial independence. These words of Justice Rehnquist amuse various congresspersons, who regard Rehnquist's own year-end reports about the Supreme Court as "dryly worded volumes devoted to judicial administration."

Senator Grassley defended his study by saying that "the purpose of my inquiry is simply to initiate dialogue between Congress and members of the judiciary. It is my hope that these questions will help activate the participatory process between members of the federal judiciary and Congress."

Are such "accountability" questionnaires within the scope of congressional authority? Who should monitor the tasks, job performance, and effectiveness of the federal judiciary? Some people think that federal judges have too much power. Will a study such as this highlight potential abuses of power? What can be done if some judges clearly abuse the powers they have been given? Should the Supreme Court intervene in this congressional action?

Source: Associated Press, "Rehnquist: Congress Threatens Justice," *Minot (N.D.) Daily News,* January 1, 1996, p. A1.

Justices have a duty to be objective in their resolution of any constitutional issue, but frequently individual justices register their personal views in the form of dissenting opinions. The rationales underlying such dissenting opinions are often as persuasive as the rationales accompanying majority opinions. Thus, the composition of the Supreme Court cannot be taken lightly. Table 6.1 shows the composition of the Supreme Court in 1997, the years the justices were appointed, and the presidents who appointed them.

Supreme Court Caseloads

The caseload of the Supreme Court has grown considerably since the early 1960s. In 1963, the Supreme Court was presented with 2,294 case filings. In 1973, 5,079 cases were filed, for an increase of 121 percent. In 1994, 5,450 cases were filed. These figures are somewhat misleading, however. Congress has given the Court considerable power to determine which cases it will hear. The fact that a case appears on the Supreme Court docket is not a guarantee that it will be heard. Each year the Court hears only a few hundred cases in which full-text opinions are prepared. This means that each year at least 90 percent of appeals to the Court either are denied or not heard at all (Carp and Stidham, 1993). Table 6.2 shows the number of cases reviewed by the Supreme Court and the numbers of full opinions written from 1976 through 1994.

Gaining Access to the Supreme Court

How does a case get to the Supreme Court? Most cases reach the Court either directly from state supreme courts or from the various federal

Table 6.1
U.S. Supreme Court Composition, Year of Appointment, and U.S. President Who Nominated Justices, 1997

Supreme Court Justice	Year of Appointment	U.S. President Appointing Justice
Chief Justice William H. Rehnquist	1986	Ronald Reagan
Justice David H. Souter	1990	George Bush
Justice Clarence Thomas	1991	George Bush
Justice Atonin Scalia	1986	Ronald Reagan
Justice John Paul Stevens	1975	Gerald Ford
Justice Ruth Bader Ginsburg	1993	Bill Clinton
Justice Sandra Day O'Connor	1981	Ronald Reagan
Justice Stephen G. Breyer	1994	Bill Clinton
Justice Anthony M. Kennedy	1988	Ronald Reagan

circuit courts of appeal. **Writs of *certiorari*** are filed by *petitioners*. *Writs of certiorari are requests for the Supreme Court to hear particular cases. These writs are certifications of lower court records that present the lower court's decision, together with a statement of the legal issues or questions involved, as well as a brief rationale for why the Supreme Court should hear and decide the case.*

Some types of sentences are automatically appealed, including all death sentences. In the decision to hear a case, the *rule of fours* is invoked, meaning that *four or more justices must agree that the case deserves to be heard* (Kadish, 1994). Once the case is scheduled for a hearing, there is no guarantee that it will eventually be heard. As we have seen, only a small proportion of the cases before the court are actually heard and decided, with full opinions written in less than 4 percent of all cases.

Many cases presented to the Supreme Court are settled in a short paragraph. For instance, *disbarment proceedings* against attorneys in various states are often appealed to the Supreme Court. A disbarment is a court action suspending an attorney's license to practice law. Some of the reasons for disbarment might include incompetence, illegal acts, conduct unbecoming attorneys, acting in bad faith on behalf of one's client, and fraud and deceit. The reasons for disbarments are not usually specified. If someone wanted to know why a particular attorney was being disbarred, the original case would have to be consulted. Each case is designated by a *date* and a *docket number.* For instance, a typical statement in the *Supreme Court Reporter* about a disbarment proceeding and the Supreme Court's opinion is as follows:

In the Matter of DISBARMENT
OF Richard L. Karch
No. D–1450
Sept. 14, 1994

It is ordered that Richard L. Karch of Los Angeles, California, be suspended from the practice of law in this Court and that a rule issue, returnable within forty days, requiring him to show cause why he should not be disbarred from the practice of law in this Court.

The date is shown as is the docket number: September 14, 1994, and D–1450.

Whenever the Supreme Court denies *certiorari* to a petitioner, again only a short sentence appears in the *Supreme Court Reporter.*

Donald Ray BOLTON, petitioner
v. Edward HARGETT, Superintendent,
Mississippi State Penitentiary
No. 94–5257
October 3, 1994

Petition for writ of certiorari to the United States Court of Appeals for the Fifth Circuit denied.

If *certiorari* is granted, a similar short phrase will appear, and later, the case may be decided with a full text opinion written for it.

Table 6.2

Cases Filed with the Supreme Court and Numbers of Cases with Full Opinions Written, 1976–1994.

Year	Number of Cases Filed	Number of Full-Text Opinions	Percentage
1976	4,730	176	3.7%
1977	4,704	172	3.6
1978	4,731	168	3.5
1979	4,781	156	3.2
1980	5,144	154	3.0
1981	5,311	184	3.4
1982	5,079	163	3.2
1983	5,100	184	3.6
1984	5,006	175	3.5
1985	5,158	172	3.3
1986	5,134	175	3.4
1987	5,268	167	3.2
1988	5,657	170	3.0
1989	5,746	146	2.5
1990	6,316	125	2.0
1991	6,770	127	1.9
1992	7,245	116	1.6
1993	7,786	99	1.3
1994	8,100	91	2.4

Source: Administrative Office of the United States Courts, *Annual Report of the Director*, 1994 (Washington, DC: U.S. Government Printing Office, 1994), p. 161, Table A–1; Maguire and Pastore (1996), pp. 520–21.

Death Penalty Appeals to the Supreme Court

One of the court's most important tasks is to review death penalty appeals. Each of the nine justices has primary responsibility for emergency pleas in death-penalty cases in certain areas of the nation and in U.S. territories. About three hundred death-penalty cases go before the Supreme Court annually. Some death row inmates file emergency pleas whenever their executions are imminent. The appeal process for handling *emergency applications* for stays of execution involves six stages. These are:

1. Applications are addressed to the justice assigned to cases from a specific region.
2. The justice can halt the execution or refer the case to the full court; justices are supposed to weigh the merits of the issues raised in the appeal and the potential harm to the defendant and to society if execution is stayed or allowed.
3. Applications are handled "on paper," meaning that no oral hearings are held. Justices are often contacted at home or while traveling. Some justices are known to turn down appeals without reading the late-night proceedings, based upon their previous knowledge of the case.
4. If the region's justice turns down the appeal, the inmate can apply to any other justice.
5. A stay granted by a justice or the Court usually lasts until the Court decides the case through its normal nonemergency process, which can take a year or more.
6. If the stay is rejected, the execution proceeds, unless new avenues or issues for appeal are found. (Mauro, 1994)

Each of the nine justices is assigned to hear death-penalty appeals of various states and territories.

Justice Ruth Bader Ginsburg: Colorado, Kansas, Oklahoma, New Mexico, Utah, and Wyoming

Justice Antonin Scalia: Canal Zone, Louisiana, Mississippi, and Texas

Justice John Paul Stevens: Illinois, Indiana, Kentucky, Michigan, Ohio, Tennessee, and Wisconsin

Justice Anthony Kennedy: Alabama, Florida, and Georgia

Justice William Rehnquist: Washington, DC, Maryland, North Carolina, South Carolina, Virginia, and West Virginia

Justice Sandra Day O'Connor: Alaska, Arizona, California, Guam, Hawaii, Idaho, Montana, Nevada, Oregon, and Washington

Justice David Souter: Delaware, Massachusetts, Maine, New Hampshire, New Jersey, Pennsylvania, Puerto Rico, Rhode Island, and Virgin Islands

Justice Clarence Thomas: Connecticut, New York, and Vermont

Justice Stephen G. Breyer: Arkansas, Iowa, Minnesota, Missouri, Nebraska, North Dakota, and South Dakota

A death-row inmate's chances of having the death penalty overturned are greatly influenced by the composition of the Supreme Court and how many justices favor its use. For instance, before Justice Harry Blackmun retired in 1994, he oversaw the states currently assigned to Justice Breyer. Blackmun said that he always "cringed" whenever a death penalty appeal came before him. "It occasions a little bit of sleeplessness in me," he told a National Public Radio interviewer in December 1993. In fact, Blackmun announced a reversal of his position favoring the death penalty when he told National Public Radio that he was now against it in *all* cases. Thus, he became the only justice since the late Justice Thurgood Marshall and retired Justice William Brennan, Jr., to oppose the death penalty. With his retirement, however, virtually every justice in 1996 supported the death penalty whenever it was imposed.

Circuit Courts of Appeal

In the early years of the United States, there were only three circuit courts of appeal without any

permanent personnel (Goebel, 1971). Two Supreme Court justices and a federal district judge comprised the transient judiciary of the circuit courts. These judges, called *circuit riders,* were obligated to hold twenty-eight courts per year. This created considerable hardship because transportation was poor. Furthermore, because federal district judges were a part of the original circuit judiciary, this placed them in the prejudicial position of reviewing their own decisions (Goebel, 1971).

Circuit courts' activity in their early years may be gleaned by examining the number of criminal prosecutions they handled. From 1790 to 1797, circuit courts handled a grand total of 143 criminal prosecutions, with half of these originating in Pennsylvania. A majority of the Pennsylvania cases were connected with the Whiskey Rebellion (Henderson, 1971:70–71). With the exception of insurrection cases in Pennsylvania during that same period, most of the criminal prosecutions could have been conducted in state courts where the crimes were allegedly committed (Henderson, 1971:71). By comparison, over 2,800 civil or common law cases were handled by these circuit courts during the period from 1790 to 1797. But the activity of circuit courts soon increased. From 1797 to 1801, they handled 3,316 civil cases. The courts handled 283 criminal cases during the same five-year period, twice as many as they handled during the previous eight years.

Over the next century, the structure of the circuit court underwent numerous changes. Several reforms, such as the Judiciary Act of 1891, or Evarts Act, were introduced to create the current scheme for federal appellate review. In 1996, there were thirteen judicial circuits at the federal level (these include the District of Columbia and Federal Circuits), with 179 circuit court judges (U.S. Code, Title 28, Section 41, 1996). These are shown in table 6.3. The district and appellate court boundaries are also shown in figure 6.3.

Circuit Court Jurisdiction

Each of the circuit courts of appeal has appellate jurisdiction for all federal district courts in the states under its jurisdiction. These states are divided into several areas, each containing one or more federal district courts. Thus, an appeal of a

Table 6.3

The Thirteen Judicial Circuits, Composition, and Number of Circuit Judges, 1996

Circuits	Composition	Number of Circuit Judges
District of Columbia	District of Columbia	12
First	Maine, Massachusetts, New Hampshire, Puerto Rico, Rhode Island	6
Second	Connecticut, New York, Vermont	13
Third	Delaware, New Jersey, Pennsylvania, Virgin Islands	14
Fourth	Maryland, North Carolina, South Carolina, Virginia, West Virginia	15
Fifth	Canal Zone, Louisiana, Mississippi, Texas	17
Sixth	Kentucky, Michigan, Ohio, Tennessee	16
Seventh	Illinois, Indiana, Wisconsin	11
Eighth	Arkansas, Iowa, Minnesota, Missouri, Nebraska, North Dakota, South Dakota	11
Ninth	Alaska, Arizona, California, Idaho, Montana, Nevada, Guam, Oregon, Washington, Hawaii	28
Tenth	Colorado, Kansas, New Mexico, Oklahoma, Utah, Wyoming	12
Eleventh	Alabama, Florida, Georgia	12
Federal	All Federal Judicial Districts	12
Total		179

Source: Title 28, U.S.C. Sec. 44, 1996.

decision of any federal district court in Alabama, Florida, or Georgia is directed to the Eleventh Circuit Court of Appeals. Panels of three circuit judges convene at regular intervals to hear appeals from federal district courts. If a defendant disagrees with the decision of a circuit court, he or she can appeal to the Supreme Court.

The caseload for circuit courts of appeal increased substantially between the early 1960s and the 1990s. Table 6.4 shows the number of cases heard in courts of appeals from 1982 to 1994.

In 1963, for instance, 5,437 cases were filed. Of these 965 or 17.7 percent were criminal cases. In 1973, there were 15,629 total cases. About a fourth of these were criminal cases. In 1983, the total number of cases had virtually doubled to 29,630, but only 16 percent, or 4,790 of these were criminal. By 1994, 48,322 cases were filed in federal courts of appeal. Civil case filings accounted for most of the increase in caseload between 1983 and 1994 (Administrative Office of the United States Courts, 1994:57).

The litigation explosion of the 1980s has increased the use of the appeals process. Some analysts believe that if the appellate judiciary is not increased substantially over the next few years, a "watering-down" effect will probably occur in circuit courts, where judges will increasingly rely on professional staff for case processing (Daniels, 1984; Sarat, 1985). One proposed solution to the problem of growing caseloads is *subject matter specialization, where certain circuit judges will have exclusive control over particular areas of the law.* Currently, three-judge panels preside over all appeals, regardless of subject matter. Organizing appeals by subject matter may maximize the efficiency of the appeals process (Meador, 1983).

In 1982, the U.S. Ninth Circuit Court of Appeals incorporated several innovations suggested by the Federal Judicial Center to improve the processing of cases awaiting argument (Cecil, 1985). The **Innovations Project** was a submission-without-argument program, where cases were presented without oral argument. A prebriefing conference program was also implemented, in which attorneys filing appeals met with court-designated staff members to discuss the length and structure of appeals briefs. The median time between the filing of an appeal to its final disposition was reduced from 17.4 months in 1980 to 10.5

Figure 6.3 District and Appellate Court Boundaries

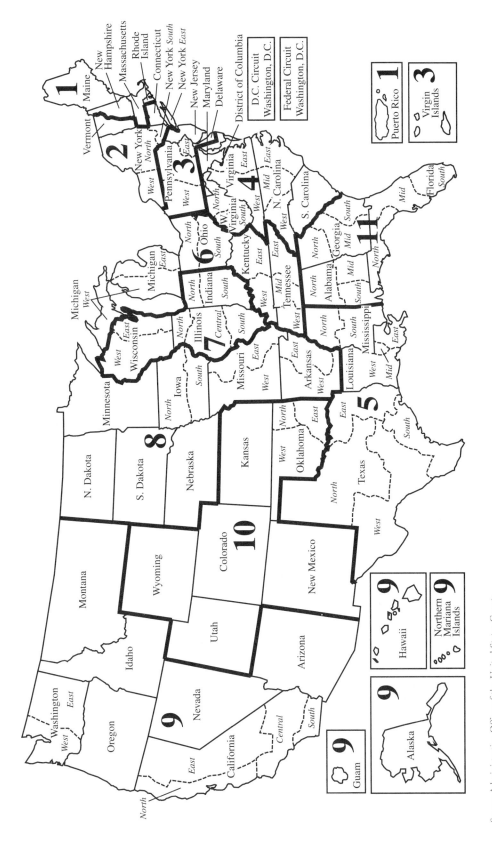

Source: Administrative Office of the United States Courts.

Note: The large numerals indicate the Court of Appeals, and the broken lines represent jurisdiction boundaries of district courts.

Table 6.4

Appeals Commenced in U.S. Circuit Courts of Appeal, 1982–1994.

Year	Number of Appeals
1982	27,946
1983	29,630
1984	31,490
1985	33,360
1986	34,292
1987	35,176
1988	38,239
1989	39,900
1990	40,858
1991	43,027
1992	47,013
1993	50,224
1994	48,322

Source: Administrative Office of the United States Courts, *Annual Report of the Director* (Washington, DC: U.S. Government Printing Office, 1994), p. 57, Table 1.

months in 1983. The average number of case participations by active circuit judges increased by 27 percent, from 229 cases in 1981 to 291 cases in 1982 (Cecil, 1985). This process continues to alleviate case backlogs and greatly enhances the effectiveness of case processing.

Circuit Court Judgeships and Presidential Nominations

The president of the United States nominates circuit judges. Their nomination must be approved by Congress. The Senate Judiciary Committee hears arguments both for and against these nominations and either approves or rejects them. One such rejection occurred in the case of Miami District Court Judge Kenneth L. Ryskamp, who had been appointed as a federal district judge by then-president Ronald Reagan in 1986. At that time, the Senate Judiciary Committee approved his nomination, and his appointment was confirmed. However, during his next five years on the federal bench, Judge Ryskamp made numerous disparaging remarks about racial and ethnic minorities.

During the Senate Judiciary Committee's April 1991 hearings on Ryskamp's qualifications for the circuit court of appeals judgeship, committee members called to Ryskamp's attention remarks that he had made once to four blacks who filed suit after being mauled by police dogs. Ryskamp told the four blacks that "it might not be inappropriate to carry around a few scars to remind you of your wrongdoing," even though two of the men were never actually charged with a crime. He also complained from the federal bench that some people were "thin-skinned" if they took offense at a black neighborhood being called "colored town."

Judge Ryskamp also belonged to a Miami country club that excluded blacks and Jews. Also, while in Washington, Ryskamp failed to "play ball" with politicians and to adhere to advice from his aides. When then-president George Bush nominated Ryskamp to the influential Eleventh Circuit Court of Appeals, his approval would have tipped the appeals court in favor of conservatives. Although George Bush had had seventy-six confirmation victories in a row and the Senate Judiciary Committee hadn't rejected a nomination from any Republican president since 1988, they decided to derail Ryskamp. Ryskamp reinforced the committee's response for rejecting him by confiding to an aide to Senator Paul Simon that "Miami is like a foreign country, where the store clerks speak Spanish and stock only ethnic food. Cubans always show up two hours late to weddings." Despite this setback for President George Bush, by 1992 approximately 70 percent of all federal judiciary would be Reagan or Bush appointees (Cohn, 1991:31).

Circuit Judges' Salaries

All circuit court judges serve for life or until he or she retires. In 1996, the annual salary of a circuit court judge was $141,700.

Federal District Courts

In 1996, there were 603 active federal district judges in the various circuits (Title 28, U.S.C. Sec. 133, 1996). Like circuit court judges, federal district judges are appointed by the president and approved by Congress. They also serve life terms. In 1996, the annual salary of a federal district court judge was $133,600. Federal district judges who serve ten or more years with *good behavior* are entitled to retire anytime thereafter and keep their annual salary. Although judicial appointments are ideally made without regard to race, color, sex, religion, or national origin, they are primarily political and reflect the interests and views of the president.

The Jurisdiction of U.S. District Courts

The federal district court is the major trial court for the United States. All violations of federal criminal laws are tried in district courts. Besides hearing criminal cases, federal district courts have the following authority:

1. To hear all civil actions in which the matter exceeds $10,000 and arises under the laws, the Constitution, or treaties of the United States;
2. To try a diversity of citizenship matters and to determine amounts in controversy and costs;
3. To hear bankruptcy matters and proceedings;
4. To hear interpleaders or third-party complaints;
5. To enforce ICC orders;
6. To hear commerce and antitrust suits;
7. To hear cases involving patents, copyrights, trademarks, and charges of unfair commercial competition;
8. To hear internal revenue cases and customs duty matters;
9. To judge tax matters by states;
10. To hear civil rights cases; and
11. To hear matters in which the United States is a plaintiff or defendant.

Criminal cases heard in these district courts are initiated in the same way as cases in local and state courts. Federal law enforcement officers arrest suspects directly, or federal grand juries or federal prosecutors issue indictments, presentments, or criminal informations against defendants. These defendants appear before magistrates who establish their bonds or release them on their own recognizance.

Arraignment proceedings at the federal level are conducted in district courts by federal judges. Since arraignments include the entry of a plea by criminal defendants and the determination of a trial date, federal judges and their staffs can best determine an appropriate trial date because of the schedule of events on the federal court docket or calendar.

U.S. District Court Caseloads

Table 6.5 shows the number of criminal cases filed in district courts for 1964, 1974, and 1984 through 1994. Fluctuations in criminal cases during the 1984–1994 period do not reflect increases or decreases in federal crimes. Rather, a complex constellation of factors determines which cases will be prosecuted. Some cases take many months to conclude, while other cases can be concluded in a few days. U.S. attorneys and their assistants in each judicial district determine which cases will be prosecuted. Cases are prioritized. Because federal district judges hear *both* civil and criminal cases, their trial dockets vary annually in volume. Again, many factors influence the number of cases filed.

In 1963, 95,376 civil and criminal cases were filed in district courts. Of these, 31,746 (48.5 percent) were criminal cases. In 1973, 140,994 cases

Table 6.5

Criminal Cases Filed in U.S. District Courts for 1964, 1974, 1984–1994.

Year	Number of Criminal Cases Filed
1964	9,282
1974	24,416
1984	18,587
1985	19,938
1986	22,299
1987	24,453
1988	25,263
1989	27,722
1990	30,910
1991	35,021
1992	39,562
1993	34,078
1994	28,701

Source: Administrative Office of the United States Courts, *Annual Report of the Director,* 1994 (Washington, DC: U.S. Government Printing Office, 1994) pp. A111–A112, Table D–1.

were filed; 42,434 (30 percent) of these were criminal cases. In 1983, the caseload had nearly doubled to 277,714 cases. Of these, only 35,872 (12.9 percent) were criminal cases. In 1994, the number of criminal cases filed in U.S. district courts was 28,701. This represented about 15 percent of all cases, both civil and criminal, filed in U.S. district courts (Bork, 1994).

One explanation for the decline in the percentage of criminal cases filed might be that more of these cases are being plea-bargained, and trial proceedings are increasingly avoided at the time of arraignment (McDonald, 1985). (Plea bargaining will be discussed in chapter 8.) Another explanation for this decrease is that many cases are returned, or *remanded*, to state courts for processing. Certain Supreme Court decisions have directed state courts to handle particular criminal cases involving previously resolved constitutional issues (*Stone v. Powell*, 1976). Federal and state prisoners strain the courts by filing petitions, containing various allegations against prison and jail officials. Petitions filed by federal prisoners, for example, escalated from 19,537 in 1977 to 57,940 in 1994. State prisoners can also file petitions in U.S. district courts. State prisoners filed 14,846 petitions in U.S. district courts in 1977 and 50,240 in 1994 (Administrative Office of the United States Courts, 1994: Table C–2).

Presently, U.S. district courts direct petitioners from state prisons back to state courts unless these prisoners have exhausted *all* legal state court remedies. While this policy has lessened the number of petitions filed in federal district courts, these petitions continue to overburden federal district court judges (Ostrom and Gallas, 1990). Although state and federal courts process annually about the same volume of criminal and civil cases, there are fewer state court judges to process these cases. Thus, by comparison, federal district court judges have somewhat lower caseloads (Ostrom and Gallas, 1990).

Other Federal Courts

Other federal courts include the U.S. Magistrate, Bankruptcy Court, the Court of International Trade, and the Court of Federal Claims. U.S. mag-

istrates are judicial officers appointed to each of the U.S. district courts. Authorized by the 1968 Federal Magistrate's Act, these judges have fewer powers than U.S. district court judges. U.S. magistrates set bail bond for federal defendants and hear numerous minor cases that often involve federal misdemeanors, such as driving recklessly in a national park or building a campfire in a federally protected area. U.S. magistrates hear both civil and criminal cases. Criminal cases heard by U.S. magistrates do not involve juries—the judge decides the case. Appeals of U.S. magistrates' decisions are made to the U.S. district court. U.S. magistrates hear about 100,000 cases annually.

State Courts

State court systems are diverse, and no single generalization applies to all of them. One reason for this diversity is the number of reforms that have been directed at state court systems (Flango, 1994a, b, c); court reform will be examined later in this chapter. The purpose of this section is to generally describe the organization and operation of state courts.

A debtor talks with an attorney in a Nashville, Tennessee, Federal Bankruptcy Court.

Figure 6.4 shows a general sketch of state court organization. It shows a state supreme court, to which all appeals from lower courts are directed. There are also intermediate courts of appeal, a su-

perior court, and lesser courts including probate, county, municipal, magistrate, and domestic relations courts. Not all states follow this model. Some states do not have justices of the peace, and even

Figure 6.4 The State Judicial System

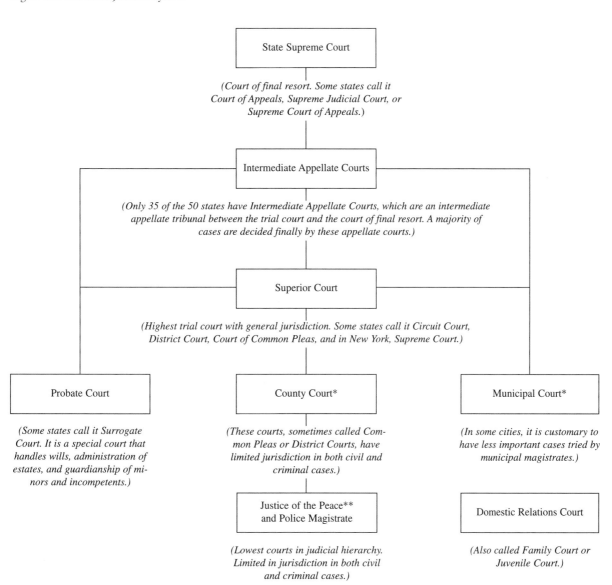

*Courts of special jurisdiction, such as probate, family, or juvenile courts, and the so-called inferior courts, such as common pleas or municipal courts, may be separate courts or part of the trial court of general jurisdiction.
**Justices of the peace do not exist in all states. Where they do exist, their jurisdictions vary greatly from state to state.

the same kinds of courts may have different names. Some states have chancery courts where civil matters and child custody cases are litigated. Other states refer to these courts as courts of common pleas, or circuit courts.

The highest state courts are called supreme courts in most states, but there are exceptions. In Massachusetts, the highest court is called the Supreme Judicial Court; in New York, this court is called the Court of Appeals; and in West Virginia, it is called the Supreme Court of Appeals (Harvard Law Review Association, 1994).

Beneath the state supreme court are intermediate appellate courts. Over two-thirds of the states have these courts, which hear appeals directly from local trial courts. For example, Tennessee has a Court of Appeals and a Court of Criminal Appeals, which function as conduits through which civil and criminal cases must pass on their way to the Tennessee Supreme Court.

Figure 6.4 depicts a **superior court**, *the court of record or trial court*. At the lower levels of court organization are probate courts, county courts, municipal courts, and domestic relations courts. Sometimes these are known as courts of **limited jurisdiction.** *Limited or special jurisdiction means that the court is restricted to handling certain kinds of cases, such as probate matters or juvenile offenses. Criminal courts deal only with violations of criminal laws.* Often, the amount of money in controversy limits the court's jurisdiction. Therefore, courts of domestic relations do not conduct murder trials, and a lawsuit for negligence demanding $1 million in compensatory damages is not within the jurisdiction of a justice of the peace. In 1996, there were over fourteen thousand courts of limited jurisdiction in the United States.

Another common classification is a *court of general jurisdiction*. In many states trial courts are courts of general jurisdiction because they are not restricted to certain kinds of cases (Black, 1990:684). Some states have both civil and criminal trial courts, or even more elaborate court systems that carry out a wide variety of jurisdictional functions. When applied to jurisdiction, the terms *general* and *limited* differentiate between a legal authority that has authority over an entire subject and one limited to a part of it.

Limited jurisdiction is also called *special jurisdiction* (Black, 1990:927–28). In 1996, there were five thousand courts of general jurisdiction in the United States.

Many county jurisdictions have no criminal trial courts. In those counties, the circuit court functions the way it did in federal circuits in the 1790s. Circuit courts convene at regular intervals in certain areas of a state to hear a wide variety of both civil and criminal matters, including domestic relations and juvenile adjudication proceedings.

The most popular model of state court organization is the **traditional model,** or **Texas Model,** shown in figure 6.5 The Texas Model includes two courts of last resort: (1) the supreme court, which hears civil cases and juvenile matters; and (2) the court of criminal appeals, which has final appellate jurisdiction in criminal cases. Both of these courts have nine judges.

Between the major trial courts and the supreme court is a **court of civil appeals.** This court hears all civil appeals from lower trial courts. These trial courts are called district courts, and each is assigned a jurisdiction. Thus, the family district court oversees matters having to do with child custody questions, juvenile delinquency, and child abuse cases, while the criminal district court has exclusive jurisdiction over criminal cases. Finally, there is a general district court, which hears both civil and criminal cases.

At the lower levels of the Texas court system are various county and municipal courts. Texas also has a justice of the peace court staffed with twelve hundred judges. These are courts of limited jurisdiction. Some experts have proposed more simplified versions of state court systems. For example, Pound (1940) proposed a three-tiered system of state court organization, called the **Pound Model.** He outlined four principles that influenced his model: (1) unification, (2) flexibility, (3) conservation of judicial power, and (4) responsibility. According to Pound:

> Basic to the achievement of these principles is the establishment of a single three-tiered state court system. At the top sits the ultimate court of appeal (the supreme court). A trial court of general jurisdiction for all major civil and criminal proceedings consti-

Figure 6.5 The Traditional Court Model (Texas Model)

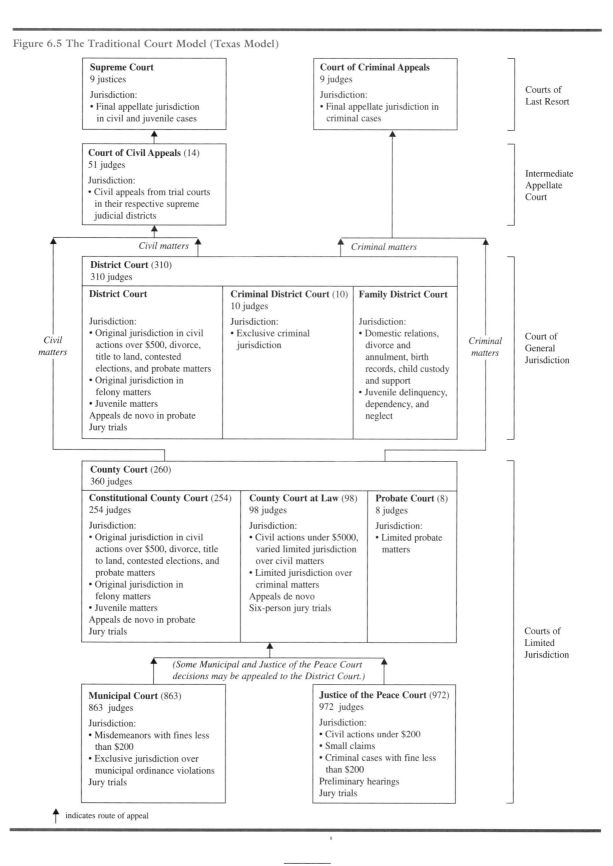

Figure 6.6 Pound's Model, the ABA Model of 1962, and the ABA Model of 1974

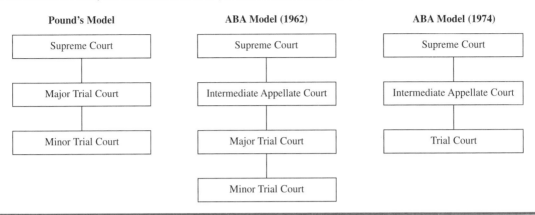

tutes the second level. Depending upon the volume of litigation or on the traditions of the state, this tier might be organized into divisions specializing in certain types of litigation. Finally, the lowest tier of the court, a minor trial court, hears cases of lesser magnitude. (Pound, 1940:230).

During the last several decades, the American Bar Association has submitted many proposals for state court organization. In 1962, it proposed a model with a four-tiered system, including a supreme court at the top, an intermediate appellate court, a major trial court, and a minor trial court. In 1974, it modified this model somewhat by combining the major and minor trial courts into a "trial court" at the lowest level of a three-tiered system. Pound's model and the two **ABA models** are shown in figure 6.6.

Functions of State and Local Courts

While rules of procedure in administering the law are reasonably clear in their prescriptions for judges to follow while on the bench, judges have considerable authority over the conduct of their courts and the behaviors of litigants. Each case brought before judges has unique aspects, and it is difficult for judges to promote fairness, regardless of the precision of procedural rules and court administra-

tive polices (American Bar Association, 1975:1). Decisions judges make about the admissibility of evidence are often subjective, because there are so many exceptions to the rules of evidence. Sometimes a judge's ruling about the admissibility of evidence is appealed to a higher court, because it often helps decide a defendant's guilt or innocence.

The diverse functions of state and local courts are closely linked with their respective jurisdictions. For instance, the American Bar Association has described standards relating to trial courts and their administration (American Bar Association, 1975). While these standards do not bind individual trial courts, judges have been persuaded to abide by them because of their objectivity and clarity. According to these standards, the trial court performs three primary functions:

1. Decides conflicting contentions of law and disputed issues of fact;
2. Formulates sanctions and remedial orders; and
3. Supervises the activity of persons subject to the authority of the court.

Figure 6.5, the Traditional or Texas Model, shows the diverse functions of various courts of limited jurisdiction. The county court, which has jurisdiction over civil actions involving amounts between $200 and $1,000, consists of 254 judges. It hears probate matters in which wills are read and estates settled. It also has jurisdiction over misdemeanors that involve fines greater than $200 or that can result in jail sentences. It conducts six-person jury trials and can also grant appeals for new trials.

The county court at law has one hundred judges and jurisdiction over civil actions involving amounts less than $5,000. It may conduct six-person jury trials and grant appeals for new trials. It also has jurisdiction over certain types of criminal matters. The probate court has fewer than ten judges and deals exclusively with probate matters such as wills and estates.

Most of the Texas courts are municipal and justice of the peace courts. They have jurisdiction over misdemeanors involving fines of less than $200, traffic offenses, and violations of municipal ordinances. They can settle small claims in civil actions and also conduct preliminary hearings to determine probable cause.

Court Personnel

Court personnel and their respective functions are similar in most jurisdictions. Besides the judge, there are several other personnel, including (1) the court reporter, (2) the court clerk, (3) the bailiff, and (4) the prosecutor.

The Court Reporter

All **courts of record** maintain written or taped records of all court proceedings. The trial court in most states is a court of record. At the federal level, U.S. district courts are courts of record. Typically, **court reporters** are appointed who *make verbatim or "word-for-word" transcriptions of court proceedings.*

In criminal trials, transcriptions of court proceedings are often quite important, particularly if defendants appeal their convictions. A defendant's guilt or innocence may rest upon evidence that was presented or excluded. If the admissibility of evidence is at issue, or if questions arise about the integrity of judges' rulings on motions or objections, a "guilty" verdict may be overturned by a higher court. Thus, judges must follow certain rules of procedure in their courts, and their failure to do so may result in reversals of their decisions.

In the Palm Beach, Florida, courtroom of the William Kennedy Smith rape trial can be seen the standard personnel of a criminal trial: judge, court reporter, court clerk, bailiff, prosecutor, defense attorney, and another increasingly familiar player in criminal proceedings involving celebrities, the television camera.

In criminal cases before U.S. district courts, federal judges must follow the Federal Rules of Criminal Procedure and the Federal Rules of Evidence. While judges are not infallible, most of their errors of judgment are harmless. On some occasions, however, these errors may be serious. Serious errors committed by judges are termed **harmful errors** and **reversible errors** (National Center for State Courts, 1989). *Harmful errors are often prejudicial to a defendant's case, and juries might render guilty verdicts because of such judicial errors. The same is true about reversible error. Reversible error is considered by appellate courts when reviewing transcripts of lower court proceedings.* If judges have committed reversible errors, their judgments are ordered reversed by higher courts. A record of court proceedings made by the court reporter is essential for determining whether harmful or reversible errors have been made. Defendants' appeals often allege that guilty verdicts result from errors such as these.

For instance, in a 1981 Tennessee case, Larry Hamm and some friends stole a truck belonging to Don Bailey and drove it around for about an hour (*State v. Hamm*, 1981). When the truck was recovered by police, evidence linked Larry Hamm to the theft. At his trial, Hamm contended that he was only "joyriding," although he was charged with grand larceny, a more serious offense. When the judge instructed the jury, he failed to charge the jury concerning the state's joyriding statute, which carried less severe penalties. Hamm was convicted of grand larceny and sentenced to six years in prison. Hamm's lawyers appealed on the grounds that the judge had erred by failing to instruct the jury about the joyriding statute. The court reporter's transcript of the proceedings proved the judge's omission, and the Tennessee Court of Criminal Appeals reversed Hamm's conviction.

The Court Clerk

In most local jurisdictions, court clerks are elected officials. In federal district courts, the court clerk is often the district judge's secretary or personal aide. *The* **court clerk** *is a court officer who may file pleadings, motions, or judgments, issue process, and keep general records of court proceedings.*

Each district court may appoint a clerk, who may, in turn, appoint (with the approval of the court) necessary deputies, clerical assistants, and other employees. These court clerks keep records of judges' court dockets and may advise them concerning the scheduling of cases.

The Bailiff

Bailiffs *are court officers who have charge of maintaining order while the court is in session. The bailiff is often placed in custody of the jury in a trial proceeding, and sometimes the bailiff has custody of prisoners while they are in the courtroom.*

Bailiffs, known also as *criers* and *messengers* in district courts, may be given additional duties by federal judges, including the duties of law clerks, if they are qualified. These criers call the court to order, attend to the needs of jury members while deliberations are taking place, and generally serve the various interests of the federal judge (Title 28, U.S. Code, Sec. 751–755, 1996).

The Prosecutor

A key figure in any court proceeding is the **prosecutor**. At the state and local levels, the prosecutor may be called the district attorney, city attorney, county attorney, or simply the prosecuting attorney. At the federal level, each district has a United States attorney appointed by the president, with the advice and consent of the Senate. These attorneys are appointed for four-year terms and are subject to removal by the president. The attorney general of the United States appoints one or more assistant United States attorneys (AUSAs) as they might be required depending on the caseload of any particular district. These AUSAs are subject to removal by the attorney general. Except as otherwise provided by law, each United States attorney, within his or her district, shall:

1. prosecute all offenses against the United States;
2. prosecute or defend for the government all actions, suits, or proceedings in which the United States is concerned;

3. appear on behalf of the defendants in civil actions and suits or proceedings pending in his or her district against collectors, or other officers of the revenue or customs departments for any act done by them or for the recovery of any money exacted by or paid to these officers;

4. institute and prosecute proceedings for the collection of fines, penalties, and forfeitures incurred for violation of any revenue law; and

5. make such reports as the attorney general may direct.

At the state and local levels, the **district attorney**, or DA, decides which cases to prosecute and represents local government in all civil and criminal matters. Like their federal counterparts, DAs initiate prosecutions and seek grand jury indictments, or they may issue criminal informations.

Prosecutors exercise considerable discretion in determining which cases to prosecute. They appoint assistant district attorneys according to their respective caseloads and city or county budgets. They are also pretrial intermediaries between judges and criminal defendants and may negotiate plea agreements. In the courtroom, prosecutors present evidence against defendants and seek convictions for crimes alleged.

Judges and Judicial Selection

The key figure in any courtroom is the **judge.** In their own courtrooms judges are all-powerful, and their decisions affect defendants and influence decisions made by lower courts. A judge decides whether certain evidence should be allowed or excluded. The judge decides what is relevant testimony. The judge controls the conduct of all trials. Sometimes judges' decisions are reversed by higher courts.

As we have seen, harmful or reversible error may result in judicial decisions being overturned by higher appellate courts. But (1) not all errors are detected in a trial; (2) not all *guilty* verdicts are appealed; and (3) not all appeals are heard on their merits by higher courts. The Supreme Court hears only about 4 percent of the appeals it schedules annually.

It is assumed by all appellate courts that the judgment or verdict rendered by a lower trial court was correct. Therefore, a defendant must present clear and convincing evidence that a verdict should be reversed. It is insufficient simply to prove that errors were committed. Under certain conditions, even harmful errors will not result in the reversal of a judge's decision.

In a murder case, a judge admitted into evidence photographs of the victim's mutilated corpse. The photographs had absolutely no bearing on the guilt or innocence of the accused. There were eyewitnesses to the murder, and the defendant's guilt had been proven beyond a reasonable doubt without the photographs. But the photographs obviously inflamed the jury and influenced their decision to impose the death penalty. The murder conviction was appealed, but the verdict was affirmed by the higher court, which held that there was so much evidence against the accused that the admission of these inflammatory materials into evidence resulted in **harmless error**. Under other circumstances, however, the admission of inflammatory photographs might be the "finishing touch" and persuade the jury to render a "guilty" verdict in a weak case against the defendant. Again, the trial judge controls the courtroom and influences the general course of the trial as well as the defendant's chances for conviction or acquittal.

One misconception among citizens is that all judges are lawyers and know the fine points of the law (Provine, 1986; Gordon, 1985). Many judges have no legal training.

Judges are either appointed or elected (Dubois, 1990). Alfini (1981:253) has identified five methods of judicial selection: (1) popular election by partisan ballot; (2) gubernatorial (or presidential) appointment; (3) popular election by nonpartisan ballot; (4) legislative election; and (5) selection through the merit plan.

At the federal level, the president recommends candidates for district, circuit, and Supreme Court judgeships, with congressional advice and consent (Solomon, 1984). Supreme Court appointments do not necessarily have previous judicial experience, however. From 1930 to 1967, twenty-three Supreme Court justices were appointed. Of these, only seven had been federal judges, with all but one serving five or fewer years on the federal bench.

Highlight 6.2. State Supreme Court Justices Are Not Particularly Popular: The Case of the Pennsylvania Supreme Court and a New Definition of Rape

Nobody believed the case was going to be particularly easy. A woman claimed that she was raped. The victim, a student at East Stroudsburg University in Monroe County, Pennsylvania, alleged that Robert Berkowitz, another student, raped her. It seemed that she entered Berkowitz's room looking for a friend. Berkowitz closed and locked the door, placed her on the bed, and raped her. Both Berkowitz and the victim testified that during the sexual encounter, the woman continuously said "no," although she offered no physical resistance, did not scream, and was neither threatened nor restrained by Berkowitz.

Berkowitz was later convicted of assault and rape. The Pennsylvania Supreme Court reviewed the case and noted that the victim was not "raped" because rape implies force, and the woman made no mention during her testimony of even the threat of force. Thus, the Pennsylvania Supreme Court, an all-male body, declared that in order for a rape conviction to stand, a woman must be physically threatened into having sex. Thus, the Court established a *forced-compulsion requirement* necessary to sustain rape charges against criminal suspects. Berkowitz's conviction for assault was upheld, however. He faced from six months to one year in jail for the misdemeanor conviction.

By comparison, the California Supreme Court declared that a man could be convicted of rape even if he was unarmed and the victim didn't struggle. Feminist leaders were appalled by the Pennsylvania high court ruling. "I was shocked by this decision, because this state has strong domestic violence legislation," said Eleanor Smeal. State NOW president Barbara DiTullio said that "it sends a clear message to the women in Pennsylvania that they have to fight for their very lives."

What do the Pennsylvania and California Supreme Court decisions about rape cases say about the diversity of decision making regarding our criminal laws? Throughout the states, should every criminal act have the same definition and punishment? What are the advantages of states' choosing their own definitions and punishments?

Source: Adapted from Steve Marshall, "Ruling that Rape Must Be Forced Is Criticized," *USA Today,* June 3, 1994, p. 3A.

And only four of these twenty-three appointments had been state judges. Only Justice Cardozo, appointed in 1932, had more than eight years' experience, having served eighteen years in state courts.

In most states, the governor appoints judges to high court posts. In many other jurisdictions, candidates campaign for judgeships much as candidates run for political office. In fact, politics is the primary reason for the large numbers of nonlawyers serving as municipal judges, justices of the peace, and county court judges. There has been considerable debate about whether judges should be appointed or elected, although no judicial selection method has been found to be superior to others (Dubois, 1990; Feeley, 1983).

Politically appointed or elected judges raise several important issues, however. Are the most qualified persons selected for the judgeship? An investigation of elected and appointed judges for the California Superior Court from 1959 to 1977 compared their demographic characteristics, educational backgrounds, and previous careers (Dubois, 1990). Of the 739 judges investigated, 662 had been appointed. Most of these had been attorneys or had some previous legal experience. When their decisions were examined for technical accuracy and legal justification, however, no significant differences between elected or appointed judges were found (Dubois, 1990). No conclusions could be reached about which selection method was best when the quality of their judicial decision making was compared.

Another issue is *whether making political appointments contributes to corruption in the judiciary* (Blankenship, Spargar, and Janikowski, 1994; Scheb, 1988). Because of their powerful positions, judges may influence trial outcomes, dismiss cases, or find innocent defendants guilty. They can also regulate the harshness of penalties when a guilty verdict is rendered. All states have judicial sanctioning boards, which are usually operated through state bar associations, and there are provisions for officially questioning judicial behavior. Studies comparing the quality of elected judges and appointed judges tend to show little difference between them (Blankenship, Spargar, and Janikowski, 1994). Thus, judicial independence does not seem to significantly improve the quality of judges generally.

State appellate judges, for example, overwhelmingly favor merit selection (Scheb, 1988). However, no one has ever said *which* qualities judicial applicants should possess and how those qualities should be considered in choosing judges. A report of the Committee on Qualification Guidelines for Judicial Candidates indicated nine criteria for judicial selection: (1) age; (2) communication skills; (3) health; (4) industry; (5) integrity; (6) judicial temperament; (7) justice (impartiality, fairness, objectivity); (8) professional skills; and (9) social consciousness (American Judicature Society, 1983). This general list is used only in the initial screening of judicial nominations.

The Missouri Plan

A popular method of judicial selection that has been adopted by several states is the **Missouri Plan**. Originally proposed in 1940 *the Missouri Plan is a method of judicial selection using the merit system for appointments to judgeships* (President's Commission on Law Enforcement, 1967:66–67). The essential features of the Missouri Plan are:

1. A nominating committee is formed consisting of lawyers and nonlawyers appointed by the governor and chaired by a judge.

2. The committee nominates qualified candidates for each judicial vacancy.

3. The governor files each judicial vacancy from the list of candidates nominated by the committee.

4. An appointed judge seeking re-election runs only on the basis of merit.

The Missouri Plan is a variation of the much earlier **Kales Plan** (Kales, 1914). The Kales Plan has survived in various forms in several states. Its influence on the Missouri Plan is obvious. For instance, the Kales Plan requires a nonpartisan aggregate of lawyers, judges, and nonjudicial personnel to list the most qualified candidates on the basis of their records and expertise. This list is then submitted to the governor. The governor fills vacancies from the list, without reference to political affiliation or association. Ideally, any choice a governor makes from the list would, by definition, be a good choice. The important point is that the element of politics is minimized in the selection process.

But some critics question whether *any* merit plan can eliminate politics from judicial selection (Blankenship, Spargar and Janikowski, 1994; Champagne, 1988). However, other analysts find that the merit plan promotes greater accountability and fairness among judges (Scheb, 1988).

Court Reforms

The courts of the United States have been criticized for their *assembly-line justice* (*Northern Kentucky Law Review*, 1982). The courts have been depicted as overworked, inadequately staffed, glutted with case overloads, unsympathetic and unfair, and extremely lethargic in resolving legal disputes. There are indications that at least some of these accusations are true. During the past few decades Congress has introduced bail reforms, speedy trial rules, sentencing reforms, and pretrial diversionary measures for low-risk defendants.

Within the courtroom, trial delay is a frequent subject of investigation (Rottman, Flango, and Lockley, 1995). Perhaps trial delays strengthen the court's image as an assembly-line process. Courts have extensive caseloads primarily because the United States has become an extremely litigious society. But the courts are dispatching cases today with greater frequency than in previous years (Maguire and Pastore, 1996). A major problem is the great increase in the number of case **filings** that consume valuable court time.

An investigation of misconceptions about state trial courts found that traffic cases make up the bulk of court activity (Rottman, Flango and Lock-

---

Highlight 6.3. Judicial Misconduct Off the Bench: Judges Are Not Above the Law

Judge Albert Garcia

Are judges above the law? Hardly. In Compton, California, a municipal court judge, Albert Garcia, was sentenced to a year in jail and three years of probation for crashing his car while drunk and leaving his girlfriend dead at the scene.

Garcia had a wife of twenty-two years and a son living in Berkeley. While on the bench he had sentenced many drunk drivers. He grew up in an East Los Angeles barrio and graduated from law school. He was appointed Municipal Court judge in 1986 by then-governor George Deukmejian. Many Compton attorneys praised his skills as a judge.

Eventually, Garcia's marriage soured and he began dating Josie Smith, a thirty-five-year-old co-manager of a Highland Park restaurant. After a while he broke off the relationship and attempted to reconcile with his wife. Smith was upset because of Garcia's decision not to continue seeing her, and a fight ensued. Smith says that Garcia threatened her with physical force, although she never filed charges.

One evening after Smith and Garcia had made up over a friendly dinner, Garcia drove her toward her home on the Ventura Freeway. His Mercedes-Benz suddenly went out of control on an off-ramp on Colorado Boulevard in Eagle Rock, striking a post. Smith was thrown from the car and died instantly. Garcia left the scene immediately but surrendered to police about four hours later. He had been drinking and wanted to protect his family from the impending scandal.

Garcia resigned his judgeship the day he pled guilty to vehicular manslaughter, driving under the influence, and leaving the scene of an accident. He told his attorney that he no longer wished to practice law. As punishment he was ordered to pay $7,000 restitu-

tion to Smith's children and enlist in an alcohol treatment program. He listed eleven mitigating factors, including his crime-free record, his early admission of guilt, his remorse, and his exemplary life as a role model to disadvantaged youths. Smith's sister was disappointed with Garcia's punishment. "The sentence wasn't harsh enough. I am heartbroken. I just miss her [Josie] very much," said Virginia Gallegos.

Should judges who violate the law be punished more severely than nonjudges? Why or why not? Was Garcia's punishment too lenient? What sentence would you have imposed?

Judge Sol Wachtler

Chief Judge of the New York Court of Appeals Sol Wachtler, sixty-two, resigned in late 1992 following a seven-week FBI investigation. Judge Wachtler had been arrested in November on charges of blackmail and attempted extortion against his ex-mistress, Joy Silverman, forty-five, a wealthy Republican fundraiser. He was placed under house arrest after formally being charged. Accusations against him included bombarding Silverman with many anonymous letters and phone calls that included a demand for $20,000 and a threat to kidnap her fourteen-year-old daughter. Wachtler remained confined to his Long Island home under house arrest. He was subsequently convicted. After serving some prison time, Wachtler was paroled. He was permanently barred from practicing law.

Sources: Adapted from Sabrina Hockaday, "Judge Sentenced for Manslaughter," *Long Beach Press-Telegram,* August 10, 1994, p. A1, A7; "There Goes the Judge: The Distinguished Career of New York State's Chief Jurist Ends in Disgrace," *Time,* November 23, 1992, p. 20.

ley, 1995). Civil cases make up most of the activity in courts of general jurisdiction. In criminal cases, most defendants plead guilty. In cases where not guilty pleas are entered, about half the cases are heard by judges, and about half are decided by juries. Between 1972 and 1977, filings of civil cases increased more than three times faster than the general population (Rottman, Flango and Lockley, 1995).

Between 1977 and 1983, civil case filings increased by 20 percent, while criminal filings increased by 23 percent. Between 1977 and 1981, however, the number of trial judges increased by only 7 percent, while the number of appellate judges increased by only 15 percent (Mahoney, 1987; National Institute of Justice, 1986:2).

Several states have implemented alternative strategies for preventing trial court delays. Hudson County, New Jersey, has a Central Judicial Processing (CJP) Court (Conti et al., 1985). This program handles all initial appearances of defendants charged with indictable offenses. The main goal of CJP is to eliminate municipal court delays and free judges to deal with more serious cases. Since the program was implemented in 1980, court backlogs of over thirty-eight hundred cases have been eliminated. Furthermore, the program has (1) assured greater consistency in the treatment of defendants, (2) decreased paperwork, (3) improved the efficiency of the grand jury operation, and (4) greatly enhanced prosecutor and defense services (Conti et al., 1985).

Court reform programs emphasize better coordination and management of court resources (Feeley, 1983). District judges in the District Court for the Western District of Missouri have developed a **joint trial calendar system** for processing various cases (Stienstra, 1985). For example, all judges share a common trial calendar for cases that are ready for trial. A criminal calendar is used for all but the most complicated cases, and a civil calendar is used for jury cases that can be tried in four days or less. During a particular two- to three-week period, judges suspend all their activities and try all the cases on the calendar. This procedure guarantees a trial and at the same time stimulates pre-trial settlements by defense attorneys who are unsure about the particular judge who will preside over their case.

Some attorneys wish to avoid judges who have a history of dealing harshly with particular kinds of offenses (Stienstra, 1985; Champion, 1987).

One of the more successful programs is the use of **volunteer lawyer-judges** as a means of bolstering court resources (Aikman, 1986:2). A project undertaken by the National Center of State Courts has examined the influence of **judicial adjuncts** on reducing caseloads and backlogs of regular judges. *Judicial adjuncts are lawyers who assist courts on a temporary basis while maintaining an active law practice.* They are considered attorneys rather than full-time judicial officers.

The study found judicial adjuncts of significant benefit in (1) assisting in alternative dispute resolution, (2) handling settlement conferences, (3) holding quasi-judge positions, (4) holding commissioner/magistrate positions, and (5) acting as temporary trial/appellate judges. In civil cases where a certain amount of arbitration is necessary, a judicial adjunct can save valuable court time by getting the litigants to agree on a settlement. These judicial adjuncts also conduct preliminary hearings and arraignment and set bail. They are empowered to sign warrants and subpoenas, preside over nonjury misdemeanor cases, and decide small claims issues (Aikman, 1986:2–3).

For several years various jurisdictions have used **community dispute resolution programs** to resolve legal matters that would otherwise have to be heard in courts (National Center for State Courts Information Service, 1992). Currently, there are thirty-five dispute resolution centers that serve thirty-seven different counties in states such as New York. In that state in 1982–1983, for example, these centers handled 54,254 cases resulting in 15,280 conciliations, mediations, or arbitrations. Most (81 percent) of the referrals to the centers were from the courts. The average cost per conciliation was only $67, including state administrative costs. Ninety percent of the cases reaching the mediation stage were successfully resolved, thus avoiding the expense and time of a trial (New York State, 1984). Mediation programs are particularly desirable in dealing with juvenile issues, such as dependency court proceedings (Libow, 1993).

One of the more useful mechanisms for eliminating trial court delays occurs before a defendant enters the courtroom. This is a *pretrial settlement* or *plea bargain agreement* reached between the prosecution and defense attorneys. Plea bargaining is described in chapter 8.

Court Unification

Early observations about court reform and reorganization emphasized three basic themes: (1) improved quality of justice; (2) better court management; and (3) an enhanced political position for the courts (Henderson and Kerwin, 1982). The present diversification of courts is replete with overlapping jurisdictions, duplication, and disputes concerning where a case should be heard. One proposal receiving increased attention is **court unification**. *Court unification is the consolidation and simplification of court services into one system.* Centralized rule making is emphasized, with centralized budgeting, case planning, and scheduling, and state financing (Berkson, 1977).

Court unification is a hierarchical plan for state court organization administration designed to streamline the court system and make it more efficient. State constitutional restraints are one of the largest obstacles to court unification. Critics of court unification say that decision making will become increasingly rigid and uniform throughout the entire system. Proponents counter by saying that unification will be "mandatory consultive," meaning that previously autonomous professional personnel will be required to interact with all members of the judiciary and set collective priorities and goals (Berkson and Carbon, 1978). Vested interests might be expected to lobby for continued court decentralization and fragmentation, because some judges find it difficult to consider consolidating with other courts. To many judges, unification means a loss of power, because they would become more dependent upon a more centralized rule structure and be held more accountable. Presently, there is little evidence to suggest that court unification is more economical and efficient than existing court systems (Miner et al., 1987; Flango, 1994a).

Summary

Courts are the cornerstone of the criminal justice system. There are two major court systems at the federal and state levels. These are parallel systems, each having particular jurisdictions and responsibilities. On the federal side, the court organization is headed by the U.S. Supreme Court, which consists of nine justices. This court is the highest appellate body in the United States. Beneath the Supreme Court are thirteen circuit courts of appeal. These are intermediate courts with appellate jurisdiction over U.S. district courts. The U.S. district court is the federal trial court. It has exclusive jurisdiction over many subjects, including all violations of federal criminal laws. All major federal court appointments are made by the President of the United States, with the advice and consent of the Senate.

State court organization is similar to that of federal court organization. However, states vary considerably in the number of different courts and their operations. Most state courts have a supreme court, a court of appeals (either criminal, civil, or both), several trial courts, and local municipal courts and justices of the peace. While groups such as the American Bar Association have advanced a number of models over the years, no single model of court organization typifies our state court systems.

Court officers include the court reporter, who makes and maintains verbatim records of court proceedings in courts of record. The bailiff is responsible for maintaining order in the courtroom. The court clerk has diverse functions, including maintaining the judicial calendar and serving the needs of particular judges. The prosecutor initiates cases against defendants and represents the state's interests in prosecutions.

Judges at both the federal and state levels are either appointed or elected. Critics of judicial appointments cite political favoritism and corruption as reasons for rationalizing the judicial selection process. Among the many court reforms suggested over the years are appointing judges with legal expertise and law backgrounds, centralizing trial court decision-making procedures and unifying court rules on a statewide basis, and using judicial adjuncts to speed up the processing of cases and reduce trial backlogs.

Key Terms

ABA models
Bailiffs
Circuit courts of appeal
Community dispute resolution programs
Court clerk
Court of civil appeals
Court reforms
Court reporters
Court unification
Courts of record
District attorney
Federal district courts
Filings
Harmful errors
Harmless errors
Innovations Project
Joint trial calendar system
Judge
Judicial adjuncts
Judicial review
Kales Plan
Limited jurisdiction
Missouri Plan
Pound Model
Prosecutor
Randolph Plan
Reversible errors
Superior court
Texas Model
Traditional model
U.S. Supreme Court
Virginia Plan
Volunteer lawyer-judges
Writs of *certiorari*

Questions for Review

1. What is the jurisdiction of the U.S. Supreme Court? Who appoints judges to the Supreme Court? Can these appointments be challenged, and if so, by whom?
2. Among the different kinds of federal judgeships discussed in this chapter, which ones are life appointments? How long does a district judge have to serve before he or she can retire with full salary benefits?
3. How did the Virginia Plan affect court organization?
4. Approximately how many cases does the U.S. Supreme Court actually hear each year? What proportion of cases is this in relation to the total number of cases submitted to the Court annually?
5. Why were early circuit judges known as circuit riders? Do any states have circuit judges?
6. Describe the functions of the following court personnel: (a) court reporters; (b) criers; (c) bailiffs; (d) prosecutors.
7. What is the community dispute resolution program run by New York State officials, and what are some of its objectives?
8. What are some personal characteristics of judges cited by the American Judicature Society that are used in judicial selection procedures by at least thirty-three states?
9. What is a judicial adjunct? What sorts of functions does a judicial adjunct perform?
10. What is court unification? What are the advantages of unifying state court systems? What are some of the disadvantages?

Suggested Readings

Epstein, Lee. *Contemplating Courts.* Washington, DC: CQ Press, 1995.

Finn, Peter and Maria O'Brien Hylton. *Using Civil Remedies for Criminal Behavior: Rationale, Case Studies, and Constitutional Issues.* Washington, DC: U.S. National Institute of Justice, 1994.

Hewitt, William E. *Court Interpretation: Model Guides for Policy and Practice in State Courts.* Williamsburg, VA: National Center for State Courts, 1995.

Mays, G. Larry and Peter R. Gregware (eds.). *Courts and Justice: A Reader.* Prospect Heights, IL: Waveland, n.d.

Rothwax, Harold J. *Guilty: The Collapse of Criminal Justice.* New York: Random House, 1996.

Walker, Samuel. *Taming the System: The Control of*

Discretion in Criminal Justice. New York: Oxford University Press, 1993.

Welsh, Wayne N. *Counties in Court: Jail Overcrowding and Court-Ordered Reform.* Philadelphia: Temple University Press, 1995.

Wice, Paul B. *Court Reform and Judicial Leadership: Judge George Nicola and the New Jersey Justice System.* Westport, CT: Praeger, 1995.

CHAPTER 7

Processing Defendants: Pretrial Procedures I

You are in a bus depot and see someone point a pistol at a clerk who issues bus tickets and take money from the clerk by force. *You* can arrest the robber. Or you observe a woman chasing a young man with a purse down the street. The woman is shouting, "Stop that man. He stole my purse!" Again, *you* can arrest the mugger. These are examples of a **citizen's arrest**. *A citizen's arrest occurs whenever a private citizen makes an arrest of another citizen (1) who committed or attempted to commit a misdemeanor offense in the citizen's presence; (2) whom the citizen suspects has committed a felony, although not necessarily in his or her presence; and (3) whom a citizen has reasonable cause to believe has committed a felony* (Black, 1990:244). Police also have these arrest powers. As we have seen, police powers also include stop and frisk or pat downs, searches of dwellings and automobiles without warrant under certain circumstances, searches incident to an arrest, and other arrest and search and seizure privileges not extended to citizens in general. *Arrests of criminal suspects by either citizens or police set in motion a sequence of pretrial events.* (*Most* police officers *do not recommend* citizen's arrests, mainly because ordinary citizens are not usually trained to make arrests and may jeopardize their own lives or the lives of others.)

This chapter is about the pretrial processing of defendants. Besides being arrested, there are several other ways defendants may be brought into the criminal justice system for processing. In the case of known suspects, complaints are filed, bench warrants are issued, grand juries may be convened, indictments or presentments are forthcoming, or a criminal information may be filed by the prosecutor. These actions include the arrest and "booking" of a defendant, a preliminary examination or hearing, an arraignment involving a specification of charges against the accused, a plea by the defendant to the charges, and setting bail for the suspect's pre-trial release.

Whenever police officers arrest suspects with or without a warrant, they must bring the suspects before a magistrate or other judicial officer **without undue delay** (*United States v. Duvall*, 1976). Most jurisdictions have provisions for bringing suspects before magistrates or local judicial officers without unnecessary delay. The primary purposes

---

Highlight 7.1. Citizen Attacks Mugger: The Case of Citizen Ybarra

Augustine Reyes, twenty-one years old, approached a twelve-year-old girl on a sidewalk in downtown Dallas. When she spurned his advances, he shouted vulgar insults at her. Then he threw her to the ground and began to fondle her. The girl screamed for help. Dozens of passers-by ignored the incident and continued on their way.

About that time, a thirty-eight-year-old electrician, Stephen Ybarra, saw the incident as he was driving down the street. He was outraged that no one was helping the girl. "I got out of my truck and tackled him," said Ybarra. According to witnesses, when Ybarra approached Reyes, Reyes began to run away. Ybarra and his ex-wife helped the girl into his truck. Then Ybarra sped after Reyes, who continued running down the sidewalk.

Ybarra pulled about even with Reyes, who had just accosted another young girl, this time a seventeen-year-old. Reyes had begun to molest her in the same way. "That's when I jumped out of my truck and tackled him," said Ybarra. Ybarra pulled Reyes to the sidewalk. "I was just thinking that I have two daughters that age. I hit him in the ribs and hit him in the jaw and held him down until police got there," Ybarra said.

Was Ybarra wrong to come to the aid of the twelve-year-old? Should there be laws compelling persons to come to the aid of people being attacked by molesters like Reyes? Do you think Reyes can sue Ybarra for his injuries? How do *you* feel about citizens such as Ybarra getting involved in other people's troubles?

Source: Adapted from Associated Press, "Passer-By Tackles Molester after Dozens of People Ignore Attacks," *Minot (N.D.) Daily News*, March 7, 1996, p. A2.

---

of this rule are (1) to prevent the unlawful detention of suspects; (2) to protect suspects' rights; and (3) to satisfy courts, juries, and the public that coercion has not been used and that defendants know their rights (*United States v. Carnigan,* 1951; *Naples v. United States,* 1962; *United States v. Smith,* 1962).

The provision *without unnecessary delay* upholds the suspect's constitutional right to due process. This does not mean instantly or immediately, but rather *as quickly as possible or as soon as is reasonable (Muldrow v. United States,* 1960; *Mallory v. United States,* 1957). The test of the unreasonableness of delay from the time suspects are arrested to the time they are brought before a magistrate is not measured in hours or days (*United States v. Gorman,* 1965). In fact, there is much variation in how unnecessary delay is interpreted by the courts. Much attention is given to the circumstances leading to delays of suspect appearances before magistrates. Currently, a forty-eight hour rule exists that functions as a standard against which delays are judged. This forty-eight-hour rule was established in *County of Riverside v. McLaughlin* (1991). (See Highlight 7.2 for a discussion of this case).

In a California case, a defendant was not taken before a magistrate for seventeen hours following his arrest, despite the fact that a magistrate was available. In that case, the police subjected the suspect to a grueling interrogation. They eventually obtained a confession from him, but the confession was ruled inadmissible by the trial judge (*United States v. Mayes,* 1969).

In contrast, there was a thirty-seven-hour delay before a Kansas defendant was taken to a magistrate. In that instance, the arrest occurred on a weekend, and the magistrate was not available until the following Monday morning (*Davis v. United States,* 1969). Arrests made on holidays, weekends, or on other special occasions; arrests of intoxicated suspects; and arrests that take place at a considerable distance from the nearest magistrate are exceptional circumstances. Most courts will

Highlight 7.2. "Without Undue Delay" Cases: The Cases of *Mallory, McLaughlin,* and *Powell*

Mallory v. United States, 354 U.S. 449, 77 S.Ct. 1356 (1957). Mallory's confession was held inadmissible in court because, while police were required to take the arrestee before a magistrate without unnecessary delay, they had questioned him for seven hours first. A woman had been raped in the early morning hours of April 7, 1954. While the victim was doing laundry in the basement of her apartment building she had trouble with the washing machine. She called the janitor, Mallory, who lived in the building with his wife and two sons. The janitor fixed the washing machine, left the laundry room, and later reappeared masked with his two sons. The men raped the woman and left the basement shortly thereafter. The victim gave police an account of the rape and named Mallory as a key suspect. Later that afternoon, Mallory and his sons were arrested and taken to police headquarters. Mallory was questioned intensively and given a lie detector test. At about 10 P.M. he confessed. Because a magistrate could not be found, Mallory was arraigned before a commissioner the following morning. For various reasons, Mallory's trial was delayed for a year. Mallory was convicted. He appealed, arguing that he was not brought before a magistrate *without undue delay and that his extensive interrogation by police was without probable cause and of unreasonable duration.* The Supreme Court overturned his conviction, holding that police only had reasonable suspicion for arresting Mallory and that his subsequent detention and interrogation yielded probable cause for rape charges. The Supreme Court also noted that during the afternoon that Mallory was arrested, numerous magistrates were available to police. Thus, Mallory was not brought before them without undue delay. Thus, his due process rights were violated. The Supreme Court said that *it is not the function of police to arrest at random, as it were, and to use an interrogating process at police headquarters to determine whom they should charge before a committing magistrate on "probable cause."*

County of Riverside v. McLaughlin, 500 U.S. 44, 111 S.Ct. 1661 (1991). Donald McLaughlin was arrested without a warrant and detained for several days over a weekend in the Riverside County Jail in California.

The policy of arrest and detention in Riverside County provided for arraignments, without unnecessary or undue delay, within forty-eight hours, excluding weekends and holidays. He appealed his conviction to the Supreme Court, which determined that a forty-eight-hour period is *presumptively reasonable,* provided that an arraignment immediately follows. If not, then the government bears the burden of showing why a period *beyond* forty-eight hours is reasonable detention of an accused person. If the period is *less than* forty-eight hours, the burden shifts to the accused to show unreasonable delay.

Powell v. Nevada, 507 U.S. __, 114 S.Ct. 1280 (1994). Powell was convicted of the murder of his girlfriend's four-year-old daughter. He was arrested on November 3, 1989, for felony child abuse. However, it was not until November 7, 1989, that a magistrate found probable cause to hold him for a preliminary hearing. Subsequently, the child died, and Powell was accused of murder and convicted. He appealed, alleging that the four-day delay between his warrantless arrest and the finding of probable cause to conduct a preliminary hearing violated the forty-eight-hour rule set forth in a subsequent case, *County of Riverside v. McLaughlin* (1991). The Nevada Supreme Court upheld his conviction, saying that because the *McLaughlin* forty-eight-hour rule came about *after Powell's conviction, it cannot be retroactively applied to his case.* Powell appealed to the U.S. Supreme Court. The Supreme Court overturned Powell's conviction, saying that the *McLaughlin* rule had indeed been violated by the excessive delay between his arrest and a finding of probable cause. This case is significant because it establishes that certain rules, such as the *McLaughlin* forty-eight-hour rule, *may be retroactively applied in capital cases.* Thus, the Nevada court erred by allowing the presumptively unreasonable delay of four days between a warrantless arrest, detention, and finding of probable cause. The U.S. Supreme Court did not say, however, that Powell was automatically entitled to be set free. Rather, Nevada courts were encouraged to explore other remedies for their error in violating the forty-eight-hour rule under *McLaughlin.*

hold that suspects arrested under these circumstances were not subject to any unnecessary delay. (*Wakaksan v. United States*, 1966; *United States v. Blocker*, 1973; *United States v. Sterling*, 1971; *United States v. Burke*, 1963).

Exceptions to the forty-eight-hour rule are allowed when: (1) circumstances beyond the government's control render them unable to bring a suspect before a magistrate within forty-eight hours. For example, if a suspect is arrested Friday evening and the magistrate has gone fishing for the weekend, the delay until Monday is excusable and does not violate a suspect's rights, even though the suspect's period of confinement greatly exceeds forty-eight hours; (2) the suspect or suspect's attorney requests a delay. For example, the suspect or suspect's attorney may wish to study arrest records and speak with witnesses to learn about the circumstances of the crime(s) alleged; or the suspect may be ill or recovering from adverse reactions to drugs or alcohol. Thus, exceptions to the forty-eight-hour rule occur because of circumstances beyond the government's control or because of delays requested by the suspect or suspect's lawyer. Neither of these situations violates a suspect's right to appear before a magistrate without undue or unnecessary delay, and appellate courts would consider both delays reasonable if they were to be challenged.

Alternative Procedures Leading to Arrests

Besides being arrested by police or private citizens, suspects may be taken into custody in other ways, including (1) being issued a warrant or summons based upon the filing of a criminal complaint; (2) being issued an indictment or a presentment; and (3) being issued a criminal information.

Issuance of Warrants and Summonses

When suspects have been identified, a complaint is filed. *A complaint is a written statement of the essential facts constituting the offense alleged. It is made under oath before a magistrate or other qualified judicial officer.* On the basis of the facts stated in the complaint, the oath of the citizen making the complaint, and the presiding judge's general consideration of all relevant circumstances, a warrant or a summons will be issued (Bell and Bell, 1991). One question that arises at this point is whether the citizen filing the complaint or supplying the information supporting it is *trustworthy*.

The test for determining the trustworthiness of a citizen or of information supplied is whether the facts as stated would persuade a reasonably prudent person that there is probable cause to believe that an offense has been committed and that suspects named in the complaint committed the offense (United States v. Cooperstein, 1963). If a reliable informant tips off the police that suspects are exchanging cocaine and heroin in an airport lobby, these officers feel confident in asserting this information under oath before a judicial officer, who is persuaded by the officers' presentation of facts from reliable informants. Thus, probable cause exists to support the issuance of a warrant (*United States v. Salliey*, 1966; *United States v. Casanova*, 1963). However, if an irate citizen storms into the courthouse demanding that his neighbor be arrested for vehicle theft and it is determined that (1) no one saw the vehicle stolen, and (2) both neighbors have been feuding for several weeks, the magistrate will be unable to support an arrest warrant solely on the word of the hostile neighbor.

If the magistrate determines that there is probable cause to support the complaint and the information contained in it, a **warrant** will be issued for the arrest of the suspect named in the complaint. *A warrant is a written order issued by an official with appropriate authority directing a suspect's arrest.* An example of an arrest warrant is shown in figure 7.1. A warrant commands a defendant to be arrested and brought before the nearest available magistrate, who is not necessarily the same magistrate who issued the warrant. Sometimes the magistrate will issue a **summons**. *A summons is in the same form as a warrant, except it commands a defendant to appear before the magistrate at a particular time and place.* An example of a summons on a complaint is shown in figure 7.2.

Figure 7.1 An Arrest Warrant Based on a Filed Complaint

FORM 4.
WARRANT OF ARREST ON COMPLAINT

(RCr 2.04, 2.06)
(Caption)

TO ALL PEACE OFFICERS IN THE
COMMONWEALTH OF KENTUCKY:

You are hereby commanded to arrest _____
(Name of defendant)
and bring him forthwith before a judge of the District
Court in Franklin County, Kentucky (or, if he be absent
or unable to act, before the nearest available magistrate),
to answer a complaint made by _____
charging him with the offense of reckless driving.
  Issued at Frankfort, Franklin County, Kentucky, this
_____ day of _____, 19__.

_____
                        Judge, District Court of Kentucky
                        Franklin County

(Indorsement as to bail)
  The defendant may give bail in the amount of $_____.

_____
                        Judge, District Court of Kentucky
                        Franklin County

(Amended October 14, 19 , effective January 1, 19 .)

A warrant permits officers to arrest defendants named in the warrant. A summons is merely served, however, often for traffic violations. If suspects fail to appear at the particular time and place indicated by the summons, judicial officers may issue a **bench warrant** ordering the immediate arrest of the suspect. *Bench warrants are used to compel suspects to appear before legal authorities.*

John Doe Warrants

Police officers serve arrest warrants on suspects accused of criminal offenses. These suspects are taken into custody and brought before the local magistrate or judicial official. If the name of the person to be arrested is unknown or if the person is known by some other name such as an alias, a *particularized description* of the defendant is sufficient. In some cases, the magistrate issues a *John*

Doe warrant, which contains an adequate description of the defendant (*United States v. Jarvis,* 1977; *United States ex rel. Savage v. Arnold,* 1975; *Clark v. Heard,* 1982).

Sometimes an arrest warrant will be held invalid if it lists an *alias* by which the defendant is *not*

Figure 7.2 A Summons on Complaint

FORM 2.
SUMMONS ON COMPLAINT
(RCr 2.04, 2.06)

DISTRICT COURT OF KENTUCKY

Franklin County

COMMONWEALTH OF KENTUCKY
    V.   SUMMONS
_____
          Defendant.

TO THE ABOVE NAMED DEFENDANT:

You are hereby summoned to appear before the District
Court, in the Franklin County Court House at Frankfort,
Kentucky, at 9:00 A.M. (Eastern Standard Time) on
Wednesday, October 31, 19 , to answer a complaint made
by _____ charging you with the offense of
reckless driving.
  Issued at Frankfort, Franklin County, Kentucky, this
_____ day of _____, 19__.

_____
                        Judge, District Court of Kentucky
                        Franklin County
(Amended October 14, 19 , effective January 1, 19 .)
                        _____

FORM 3. SUMMONS IN INDICTMENT
          (RCr 6.52, 6.54)
(Caption)

TO THE ABOVE NAMED DEFENDANT:
  You are hereby summoned to appear before the
Franklin Circuit Court in the Franklin County Court
House at Frankfort, Kentucky, at 9:00 A.M. (Eastern
Standard Time) on Wednesday, October 31, 19 , to
answer an indictment charging you with the offenses of
(1) malicious shooting and wounding with intent to kill
and (2) carrying concealed a deadly weapon.
  Issued at Frankfort, Franklin County, Kentucky, this
_____ day of _____, 19__.

_____
                        Clerk, Franklin Circuit Court
                        By _____
                        Deputy Clerk

A warrant commands a defendant to be arrested and brought before the nearest available magistrate. This man, a staff member of a Florida prison, was served a warrant at the facility itself.

and Jim Jenkins will be called as a witness against him. Jim Jenkins does not personally prosecute Fred Smith, however. The offense committed was a violation of a Philadelphia criminal law. Through its prosecutors, Philadelphia, not Jim Jenkins, prosecutes Fred Smith.

This principle is frequently misunderstood. For example, suppose a woman alleges that she has been raped, and she files a complaint against the alleged rapist. Later the woman decides to *drop the charges* against the rapist because he is a close friend of her brother's. The state may decide to prosecute anyway. Thus, the jurisdiction where a law was violated is the final arbiter of whether to prosecute. A similar situation exists in child sexual abuse cases. If a father sexually abuses his daughter, it is a public offense and the public is entitled to appropriate action by authorities. In this type of situation, however, it is often difficult to get close friends or family members to testify against one another. And if no one testifies, pursuing the case is pointless. However, in some situations, there may be incriminating physical evidence that allows the prosecutor to develop and support a convincing case without relying on the testimony of witnesses.

An Indictment and a Presentment

Because different states process defendants differently, the federal system will be discussed here as an example. Many state and local jurisdictions emulate the federal system in processing criminal defendants. However, other jurisdictions have quite different criminal processing systems. Throughout this discussion, some of these exceptions will be noted.

In federal proceedings and in many state jurisdictions, a **grand jury** is convened. *Grand juries are investigative bodies whose numbers vary from state to state and whose duties include determining whether probable cause exists that a crime has been committed and whether formal charges should be returned against a suspect.* Federal grand juries consist of no fewer than sixteen and no more than twenty-three citizens who are selected from the jurisdiction of each federal district court. These jury members represent average socioeconomic levels

known. In a Tennessee case, an arrest warrant was prepared against a person described as "John Doe alias Bud Ferguson." While other aspects of the description on the arrest warrant were accurate, the defendant had never been known as "Bud Ferguson." The warrant was declared invalid because "the defendant had never been known or called by the alias of 'Bud Ferguson' and was not himself a party to the officer obtaining such a misnomer" (*United States v. Swanner,* 1964).

When a criminal complaint is filed either by police officers or by private citizens, the government can either pursue the case or not pursue it. If Jim Jenkins has filed a complaint in Philadelphia saying that Fred Smith has stolen his car, and if there are reasonable grounds to support the complaint, the magistrate will issue an arrest warrant against Fred Smith, and police officers will attempt to arrest him. When Fred Smith is brought to trial for vehicle theft, the state (through the district attorney in Philadelphia) will prosecute Fred Smith,

because their names and addresses are selected from voter registration lists or property tax records.

Grand juries convene at different times and meet for various periods, such as ninety days, or one hundred and twenty days. They hear complaints and consider the government evidence against defendants (Neubauer, 1979). After deliberating, they return either a **no bill** or a **true bill**. *A no bill means that in the jury's opinion, the government did not produce sufficient evidence to determine that probable cause exists that a crime has been committed.* If the grand jury returns a true bill, *the grand jury was convinced that probable cause exists that a crime was committed and that the defendants should be charged with that crime.* The true bill is an **indictment.** *An indictment is a charge or a written accusation found and presented by a grand jury that a particular defendant has committed a crime.* It is the means whereby defendants are brought to trial to answer the charges against them.

Normally, government prosecutors present complaints to the grand jury alleging that certain crimes have been committed by particular suspects. These presentations are accompanied by government evidence that a crime has actually been committed. Such evidence links the defendant with the crime, and the prosecutor tries to convince the grand jury that sufficient probable cause exists to issue an indictment against the accused. Once a true bill or indictment has been issued by the grand jury, either an arrest warrant or a summons is prepared. Police then apprehend the defendants and bring them before a magistrate without unnecessary delay, or the officers serve the summons, which directs defendants to appear before a magistrate at a particular time and place.

Grand juries are not "juries" in the sense that they convene to determine guilt or innocence of suspects. They determine whether probable cause exists to support charges against defendants. Some grand juries perform investigative functions to determine if crimes have been committed. Many people mistakenly believe that if a grand jury decides to indict someone, the indicted individual must be guilty of the crimes alleged. An indictment is simply a charge, and one's guilt remains to be proved in a court of law. A presumption of innocence underlies all charges of crimes against defendants. If a

defendant is indicted by a grand jury and eventually tried in court, another jury will hear the case and decide the defendant's guilt or innocence. This latter jury is the one with which we are most familiar. It is called a *petit jury* to distinguish it from the grand jury (Black, 1990).

Procedurally, the government representative or prosecutor prepares an indictment or bill of particular charges against a defendant, including any supporting evidence. Suspects do not appear before the grand jury and do not have the opportunity to present exculpatory evidence. Grand juries are most definitely one-sided affairs. Depending upon the enthusiasm of the prosecutor, indictments are fairly easily obtained. Only the most incriminating evidence is presented, and any evidence favorable to the defendant is conveniently kept from the grand jury. Thus, the prosecutor leads the grand jury in the desired direction (Champion, 1988a).

Grand juries may make recommendations independently of the prosecutor, however. When considering evidence against defendants, they may determine that others have committed crimes as well. In some jurisdictions, grand juries issue their own indictments against defendants. These indictments are called presentments. *A* **presentment** *is an accusation, initiated by the grand jury on its own authority from their own knowledge or observation. It functions as an instruction for the preparation of an indictment* (Black, 1990:1184). The government prosecutor does not seek presentments. In effect, presentments bypass prosecutors.

Presentments have the same effect as indictments. Once they are issued, arrest warrants or summonses are prepared ordering that defendants be brought before magistrates without unnecessary delay either directly or at a particular time in the future.

An Information

A **criminal information** (or simply an information) is to the prosecutor what a presentment is to the grand jury. In the case of presentments, a grand jury can, on its own authority, prepare an indictment against a defendant. In the case of an information, a prosecutor can bypass the grand jury and obtain the equivalent of an indictment against an accused. *A criminal information is a written accusation made by a public prosecutor against a person for some criminal offense, without an indictment.* Informations are formulated against defendants by prosecutors when minor offenses are involved and when the punishment by imprisonment is less than one year (Title 18 U.S.C., Rule 6, 1996). If the crime is punishable by imprisonment of one year or more, prosecutors may use informations if indictments are waived by criminal suspects. Otherwise, informations cannot be used to prosecute criminal defendants.

In most states, informations may be used in place of grand juries to bring defendants to trial, provided that the punishment by imprisonment is less than one year (Black, 1990:779). When an information is obtained, an arrest warrant or a summons is prepared, and officers bring the defendant before a magistrate without undue delay (or command the accused to appear before the magistrate at a particular time in the future). Again, criminal informations are most often issued for minor offenses such as misdemeanors.

In many jurisdictions, indictments, presentments, and criminal informations result in the issuance of a **capias.** *A capias refers to several different kinds of writs issued for the purpose of making arrests.* These writs have the same effect as arrest warrants because they require law enforcement officers to take suspects into custody and bring them before a magistrate without undue delay. *A capias describes the offense charged and commands an officer to bring the defendant before the court where the charge is pending.*

Summarizing, a suspect may be arrested and brought before a magistrate in the following ways: (1) a citizen's arrest without an arrest warrant; (2) a direct arrest by a police officer, with or without an arrest warrant; (3) the issuance of an arrest warrant by a judicial official following a complaint; or (4) the issuance of a criminal summons or a capias or an arrest warrant by the court as the result of grand jury action leading to indictments, presentments, or informations.

Normally, before an arrest warrant is issued, a *determination of probable cause* is made by the official according to the information accompanying a criminal complaint. In the case of grand jury action, the grand jury itself or the prosecutor determines whether probable cause exists to proceed with an indictment, a presentment, or an information. If these documents are issued, arrest warrants, summonses, or capiases are prepared, and suspects may be taken into custody.

Statutes of Limitations

Can the government maintain an active case against a defendant indefinitely? It depends. Most offenses have a **statute of limitations.** *Statutes of limitations are maximum time periods set by states and the federal government during which certain actions can be brought against defendants or rights can be enforced* (Black, 1990:926–27). Once the statute of limitations has expired, no legal action can be brought regardless of whether any cause of action ever existed. This means that if someone has committed a burglary, is charged with the burglary, but somehow escapes the jurisdiction where the burglary was committed, after a substantial period of time, the burglary charge expires because of the run of the statute of limitations for the burglary offense. Suppose the statute of limitations is six years for burglary in Nevada. Once six years have passed, the person who committed the burglary can no longer be prosecuted for it. Some crimes, such as murder, have *no* statute of limitations. (See Highlight 7.3.)

Some offenses, such as child sexual abuse, often are not reported until those who were abused as children reach adulthood. By then, many years have passed, and the statute of limitations governing prosecutions of child abuse offenses has long expired (Bulkley and Horwitz, 1994). Some jurisdictions have passed laws that delay the time when the statute of limitations begins to run for the offense. Thus, the statute of limitations for some offenses can be *tolled,* or delayed, as a legal remedy so that charges can be brought against alleged child sexual abusers years after the offense occurred (Bharam, 1989; Bulkley and Horwitz, 1994).

Booking

Once defendants have been taken into custody, with or without a warrant or capias, or present

Highlight 7.3. On the Statute of Limitations: The Case of William Henry Redmond

Her name was Jane Marie Althoff. She was an eight-year-old who was strangled to death near a carnival outside Trainer, Pennsylvania, in April 1951. Suspected of the crime was William Henry Redmond, the Ferris wheel operator at the carnival.

Shortly after the murder, Redmond was questioned by police. His answers made police suspicious, and an arrest warrant was issued in 1952 directing police to take him into custody for the murder of Althoff. Before police could arrest Redmond, he disappeared.

For the next thirty-three years, no action was taken by any police agency to determine Redmond's whereabouts. However, in 1985, Trainer Borough Police Chief Hubert Morris revived Althoff's murder investigation. Morris, fifty-seven, said that he had heard about Jane Althoff's murder since he was a little boy. It had always bothered him that no one had been prosecuted for her murder.

When he investigated the files, he decided to try to track down Redmond. Using court records and the expertise of State Police trooper Malcolm Murphy, he examined many driver's license registrations. Trooper Murphy discovered that Redmond was living quietly as a retired trucker in Grand Island, Nebraska. Morris and Murphy went to Nebraska and confronted Redmond. Redmond broke down and confessed.

When he was brought back to Paoli, Pennsylvania, he leaned on the arms of his captors and clasped a towel to his face to protect his emphysema-weakened lungs from the cold. The frail prisoner looked nothing like a man who had committed murder. At age sixty-six, William Henry Redmond would face a trial by jury for the 1951 murder of Jane Marie Althoff. No statute of limitations would protect him. Justice for the family of Jane Marie would prevail.

Should there continue to be no statute of limitations on heinous crimes such as murder? Should *all* crimes have no statute of limitations?

———————

Source: Adapted from *Time*, February 8, 1988, p. 20.

themselves to law enforcement officers after being served with a criminal summons, they are usually booked. **Booking** *is an administrative procedure designed to furnish personal information about the defendant to the police. Booking includes the compilation of a file for a defendant, including his or her name, address, telephone number, age, place of work, relatives, and other personal data.* The extensiveness of the booking procedure varies among jurisdictions. In some jurisdictions, the suspect may be photographed and fingerprinted, while in others, the defendant may merely be asked a few personal questions.

At the federal level, booking is performed by federal marshals, who photograph defendants in a variety of poses. Front and side pictures are often taken, fingerprints obtained, and an extensive questionnaire administered that includes questions about close associates and social habits. "Just in case we have to track you down," answered one federal marshal when asked by this author why such extensive information was required.

The Initial Appearance

The **initial appearance** of a defendant before a magistrate *is a formal proceeding during which the judge advises the defendant of the charges. This proceeding usually follows the booking process. The presiding judicial official determines from a reading of the charges whether or not they constitute petty offenses.*

Different states have different opinions of what constitutes petty or minor offenses. The maximum fine imposed or the length of sentence associated with the criminal offense usually indicates whether the state considers it major or minor. In *Duncan v.*

Louisiana (1968), the Supreme Court discussed this issue in the matter of a nineteen-year-old man who was sentenced to serve sixty days in jail and pay a $150 fine for simple battery. Duncan had requested a jury trial but was denied one. The state of Louisiana claimed that Duncan's crime was a *petty offense* and that therefore he was not entitled to a jury trial.

The Supreme Court disagreed. It noted that Louisiana's law pertaining to battery carried a two-year maximum sentence and a $300 fine. The Supreme Court observed that most states define petty offenses as those punishable with terms of less than one year; in some jurisdictions, the maximum punishment is a sentence of no more than six months and a $50 fine. Without defining precisely the meaning of a petty offense, the Supreme Court nevertheless concluded: "We need not . . . settle in this case the exact location of the line between petty offenses and serious crimes. It is sufficient for our purposes to hold that a crime punishable by two years in prison is . . . a serious crime and not a petty offense." Duncan's conviction was overturned.

More recently, Title 18 U.S.C., Sec. 3401 (1996) has specified that at their first appearance magistrates must inform those accused of petty crimes that they have a right to a trial by jury:

Any person charged with a misdemeanor may elect . . . to be tried before a judge of the district court for the district in which the offense was committed. The magistrate shall carefully explain to the defendant that he has a right to trial, judgment, and sentencing by a judge of the district court and that he may have a right to a trial by jury before a district judge or magistrate. (Title 18, U.S.C., Section 3401(b), 1996:14)

The Sixth Amendment guarantees the right to a speedy and public trial by an impartial jury. But different jurisdictions interpret the amendment differently. Some prosecutors resent it when an accused person requests a jury trial for a petty offense. In a New Jersey case, a defendant was indicted by a federal grand jury on federal misdemeanor charges, and the prosecutor for the government strongly opined that the accused ought to waive his right to a trial by jury. The man refused, so in retaliation the prosecutor brought new felony charges against the man. This created such an atmosphere of coercion that as the fairest remedy the court dismissed all indictments against the man and criticized the prosecutor for his improper conduct (*United States v. Lippi,* 1977). Because the penalties for felony are substantially more severe, it is especially important that defendants be

The initial appearance of a defendant in a civil case conducted in Orange County, California

advised of the specific charges against them as well as of their rights under the circumstances.

In the case of those arrested by police on either misdemeanor or felony charges, their initial appearance before a magistrate is the formal proceeding at which they are advised of the charges against them. At that time, the magistrate or presiding official advises the defendants of their rights and considers bail. On this occasion magistrates also determine the date for a **preliminary examination** or a **preliminary hearing** to establish whether probable cause exists to move forward toward a trial. The time interval between the defendant's initial appearance and the date of the preliminary hearing or examination allows defendants to secure legal counsel.

A defendant's initial appearance may also be ordered by an indictment, presentment, or criminal information (in those cases where indictments have been waived by defendants or the crime is punishable by possible imprisonment for less than one year). Defendants' initial appearance is for the purpose of advising them of the indictment, presentment, information, or specification of the charges and allegations and furnishing them with a copy of same. It is also when the conditions for bail are determined and bail, if any, is established. Finally, a time is set for the defendant to appear for a preliminary hearing (which the defendant may waive). Before we examine the procedures associated with preliminary examinations or hearings and arraignments, however, bail will be described.

Bail

Release on One's Own Recognizance (ROR)

When a defendant has been arrested, a determination is made concerning whether he or she will be brought to trial. If a trial is likely, most defendants can obtain temporary release from detention. They may be released on their own recognizance. If their reputation in the community is such that it is unlikely that they will flee the jurisdiction, a **release on own recognizance,** or ROR, will be ordered by the presiding magistrate or judicial officer (Na-

tional Center for State Courts, 1990). One reason for granting pretrial release is to alleviate jail overcrowding (Mauer and Young, 1992).

Motorists charged with minor traffic offenses may be required to post a **cash bond,** which guarantees their appearance in court later to face charges. If the motorist fails to appear, the cash bond is forfeited. The bond set is often the exact amount of the fine for violating the traffic law.

The Use of Bail Bonds

In those situations when the character of the defendant is unknown or the offenses alleged are quite serious, the magistrate will often establish **bail** or a **bail bond.** *Bail is a surety to procure the release of those under arrest, to assure that they will appear to face charges in court at a later date. A bail bond is a written guarantee, often accompanied by money or other securities, that the person charged with an offense will remain in the court's jurisdiction to face trial in the future* (Hawaii Office of the Auditor, 1992). An example of a bail bond form is shown in figure 7.3.

Defendants who have real property may give written pledges of this to the court as a bail bond. The court may also accept other assets as a bail bond, such as bank deposits, securities, or valuable personal property (Black, 1990).

Bail bond companies are found near most jails. Company representatives appear at the jail and "post bond" for defendants. Defendants pay the bonding company a fee for this service, often 10 percent of the bail bond established by the magistrate. For instance, if the bond set by the magistrate is $5,000, the bonding company may post this bond if the defendant is considered a "good risk" and if the defendant or an associate of the defendant pays the bonding company a nonrefundable fee of $500. If a defendant is unable to pay the fee and no one else will pay it, he or she must remain in jail until trial is held.

Jumping Bail and Bounty Hunters

Some defendants released on bail jump bail and attempt to escape prosecution by leaving the vicinity. Many bonding companies employ bounty

Figure 7.3 A Bail Bond Form

```
BAIL BOND
(Caption)
_____being in custody charged with
(Name of defendant)
the offense of _____ and being admitted to bail in
the sum of $_____, we undertake that he will appear and
be amenable to the orders and process of this and any
other court in which this proceeding may be pending
hereafter for any and all purposes and at all stages of the
proceeding (including, in event of indictment, proceed-
ings thereafter) in accordance with
(Name of defendant)
   Executed this ____ day of _____, 19__.
_____    _____
(Name of defendant)             (Address)
_____    _____
(Name of surety)                (Address)
   Taken and subscribed before me this
_____day of _____, 19__.
                          _____
                                (Signature)
                          _____
                                (Title)
   I, _____, by entering into the (above) bond
obligation, do hereby submit to the jurisdiction of the
courts of          in which any forfeiture proceeding
arising out of my bail obligation may be pending, and do
further irrevocably appoint the clerk of such court as my
agent upon whom any process affecting my liability on
such bond may be served, such clerk to forthwith mail
copies to me at _____ City
                (Street address)

of _____, County of _____, State
of _____, or at my last known address.
   Date this ____ day of _____, 19__.
                          _____
                                (Name)
```

hunters to track down such persons and bring them to court (Burton, 1984). If the defendant is not found, the bonding company forfeits the bond it has posted.

Excessive Bail

The Eighth Amendment guarantees that *excessive bail shall not be required, nor excessive fines imposed.* Some people believe that regardless of the offense alleged, bail will be set and defendants posting bail will be permitted to remain free until the date of trial. This is not true. Depending on circumstances, some defendants may have a very high bail while others may not be granted bail at all. They will be required to remain in jail until trial.

The constitutional prohibition against excessive bail means that bail shall not be excessive in those cases where it is proper to grant bail (*United States, v. Giangrosso,* 1985). The right to bail is not an absolute one under the Eighth Amendment (*United States v. Bilanzich,* 1985; *United States v. Provenzano,* 1985; *United States v. Fernandez-Toledo,* 1984). In some cases, suspects are detained for trial without bail (*United States v. Acevedo-Ramos,* 1984), while in others, defendants must be confined if they are unable to pay high bail ranging from $25,000 to $1 million (*United States v. Szott,* 1985; *United States v. Jessup,* 1985). A murder suspect caught in the act, an habitual offender, or other such defendant will likely be denied bail, because it is highly likely that they will attempt to escape prosecution. Do suspects pose a danger to the community? Not all states permit judges to make this determination. But in thirty-one states and the District of Columbia, this is a judicial consideration that often results in preventive pretrial detention (Gottlieb, 1984).

Violent criminals aren't the only defendants denied bail. The magistrate considers the totality of circumstances in setting bail for anyone. A former bank president was denied bail in a case alleging fraudulent manipulation and theft of depositors' funds. While the former bank president had substantial community ties and property interests to protect, he also had a recently acquired passport and travel visas to several foreign countries where he also maintained property and business interests. In addition, a federal audit had revealed that several million dollars in bank funds were unaccounted for. For these reasons, he was considered a poor risk for bail.

The American Civil Liberties Union and a number of other groups have challenged the bail provisions of the Constitution. Their efforts as well as those of a variety of special interest groups have prompted a number of bail reforms over the years. Some of the reasons given for such bail reforms have included: (1) bail is inherently discriminatory against the poor or indigent defendant (Goldkamp,

1984); (2) those who are unable to post a bail bond and must remain in jail cannot prepare an adequate defense or correspond effectively with their attorneys; (3) bail for similar offenses often varies considerably from one jurisdiction to the next and even from one case to the next within the same jurisdiction; (4) withholding bail or prescribing prohibitively high bail offends our sense that one is presumed innocent until proven guilty; and (5) those who pose no risk to the community may lose their jobs or other benefits as a result of being detained because of failure to post bail (Gibbs, 1975).

Do racial or gender differences make a difference to judges when making pretrial release and/or bail decisions about particular defendants? Milton Heumann and Colin Loftin collected data on 8,414 defendants charged with one or more of eleven felonies in the years 1976, 1977, and 1978 (Heumann and Loftin, 1979). Their original interest was to explore the impact of the then-new Michigan Felony Firearm Law on the processing of defendants in the Detroit Recorder's Court. In 1995, this information was re-analyzed by Charles Katz and Cassia Spohn, who were interested in controlling for the effects of race and gender in examining decisions on bail.

Katz and Spohn (1995:161–63) wanted to know whether these data showed any pattern of discrimination in bail decision making according to race and/or gender. The original sample of 8,414 defendants was divided according to both race and gender. Some of the records did not contain race information. The resulting sample consisted of records for 6,625 black defendants and 1,005 white defendants. A small proportion of the sample consisted of female defendants. Katz and Spohn asked whether it made any difference in the bail decision, as well as the amount of bail, whether defendants were black or white or male or female. They found that when taking offense and prior record of defendants into account, *race made no difference* on the bail decision. However, *gender did make a difference*. For certain types of offenses, female defendants were set significantly *lower* bails than their male counterparts. However, white defendants were more likely than black defendants to be released before trial. Further, females were more likely than males to be granted pretrial release.

While these findings are not conclusive, they do suggest that while race and gender may help explain bail and pretrial release decisions, they may not influence these decisions as strongly as previously thought. In any case, a significant change in bail decision-making policies occurred a few years later in 1984.

The Bail Reform Act

At the basis of the bail reform movement is the argument that bail is inherently discriminatory. In 1966, the Bail Reform Act was passed, which stated, "the purpose of this Act . . . is to revise the practices relating to bail to assure that all persons, regardless of their financial status, shall not needlessly be detained pending their appearance to answer charges." The most recent federal action relating to bail has been the passage of the **Bail Reform Act of 1984**, which gives magistrates and judicial officers considerably more leeway in setting bail and releasing persons on their own recognizance. Presently, bail is available only to those entitled to bail (Hirsch and Sheely, 1993; Reed, 1983). These are usually persons who do not pose a threat to themselves or others and/or are not likely to flee. There is nothing inherently unconstitutional about keeping persons jailed prior to their trials, however, under various forms of pretrial detention (*United States v. Salerno*, 1987) (See Highlight 7.4). Some experts believe that sometimes pretrial detention of suspects is abused and that lawmakers should keep its use within reasonable limits (Miller and Guggenheim, 1990). One reason for this belief is that it is often difficult to forecast accurately who will or will not be dangerous or good candidates for bail.

Some states have enacted *sexual predator laws* targeted at violent sex offenders. In 1990, the state of Washington, for instance, passed a Sexual Predator Act aimed at those likely to commit acts of sexual violence. However, the act was roundly criticized because of its failure to propose realistic criteria that would predict *which* sex offenders would commit dangerous sexual acts after therapy or treatment (Brody and Green, 1994). Similar laws contemplated by other states have also been criticized

---

Highlight 7.4. Pretrial Detention: The Case of *United States v. Salerno*

United States v. Salerno, 481 U.S. 739, 107 S.Ct. 2095 (1987). Salerno and others were arrested for several serious crimes and held without bail under the Bail Reform Act of 1984 because they were considered *dangerous.* Salerno was among the first to challenge the constitutionality of the new Bail Reform Act and its *dangerousness* provision, which specifies that persons may be held until their case is decided. Salerno was subsequently convicted and sentenced to one hundred years in prison. He appealed on the grounds that the act violated the Eighth Amendment's guarantee against cruel and unusual punishment. The Supreme Court upheld the constitutionality of pretrial detention and declared that it did not violate specific criminal defendants' rights under the Eighth Amendment following a finding of *dangerousness.*

(Cleary and Powell, 1994). According to some experts, between 51 and 95 percent of the predictions made by various agencies and states about the future dangerousness of offenders have been wrong (Ewing, 1991; Miller and Guggenheim, 1990).

ROR and Bail Experiments

One of the more innovative aspects of the 1984 act was a provision for judicial officers to release suspects who agreed to certain conditions, such as (1) complying with a curfew, (2) reporting regularly to a designated law enforcement agency, (3) abiding by specific restrictions on their personal associations, places of abode, and travel, (4) participating in an educational program, and (5) maintaining or seeking employment.

Preceding the Bail Reform Act of 1984 and possibly contributing to its subsequent passage were various experiments that studied the effectiveness of ROR. Between 1962 and 1971, the National Bail Study was conducted in twenty jurisdictions (Thomas, 1976, 1977). During those years there was a significant drop in the number of people jailed for felonies and misdemeanors and an accompanying increase in the number of defendants released on their own recognizance (ROR). The study concluded that judges were relying more on ROR and that this caused a sizeable reduction in the use of cash bail, a favorite target of bail critics.

In the mid-1970s, the use of ROR in lieu of cash bail was investigated in Duluth, Minnesota, San Mateo, California, and Salt Lake City, Utah (Bynum, 1977). ROR was most frequently used for defendants who had good incomes and strong employment records. The economically disadvantaged did not benefit at all from the greater use of ROR by participating judges.

Between January 1981 and March 1982, the Philadelphia Experiment (Goldkamp and Gottfredson, 1984) examined bail guidelines in the Philadelphia Municipal Court. Twenty-two judges were selected for the study, one objective of which was to create concrete guidelines for judges to follow in using ROR in lieu of bail. The median bail amount set by judges not following prescribed guidelines was $2,000, whereas the median bail figure was $1,500 for those judges adhering to the guidelines provided.

While the findings regarding the use of ROR were mixed (e.g., more guidelines judges used ROR for misdemeanor cases, and more nonguidelines judges used ROR for felony cases), the researchers said that in general the experiment significantly improved the equity of bail decisions. The study also encouraged greater use of supervised or conditional release programs as outlined by the Bail Reform Act of 1984. As the Philadelphia Experiment suggested, at the very least this alternative would somewhat relieve jail overcrowding.

For instance, the New York City Department

---

of Correction discharged 611 jail inmates in November 1983 (Gerwitz, 1987). Of these, 75 percent were released on bail, while 25 percent were released on their own recognizance. Only four ROR defendants were charged with felonies, while about 75 percent of those on bail were similarly charged. Forty percent of the bail-released defendants failed to appear for at least one pretrial hearing, while ROR defendants were far less likely to appear in court later. Over a third of the ROR defendants were rearrested before trial. Other investigators also conclude that obligating defendants to post bail does not necessarily guarantee that they will appear in court later, but it does result in fewer *failures to appear* than the use of ROR (Goodman, 1992; Pretrial Resources Service Center, 1994; Reaves and Perez, 1994).

Preliminary Hearings

Preliminary hearings are held after defendants have been arrested and have had their initial appearance before a magistrate (Emerson and Ames, 1984). *Preliminary hearings are conducted by the magistrate or judicial official to determine whether defendants charged with a crime should be held for trial.* It is an opportunity for magistrates to determine if probable cause exists that a crime has been committed and the person charged committed it. The preliminary hearing is the first "screening" of charges against defendants (Black, 1990:1180).

The purpose of preliminary hearing is not to establish the defendant's guilt or innocence but only that (1) a crime has been committed, and (2) it is likely that the defendant committed it. If the government fails to present a convincing case to the magistrate, the charges against the defendant will be dismissed.

Even if the magistrate dismisses charges against the defendant, the prosecutor may take the case to a grand jury. However, if the magistrate believes that the prosecutor has presented a weak case, a grand jury probably will not issue an indictment either. But there is an important difference between preliminary hearings and grand juries. In preliminary hearings, defendants have the right to present

facts and evidence supporting their innocence. Defendants may even cross examine witnesses and bring in witnesses supportive of their own position. Grand juries, however, hear only the government's side of the matter. Thus, even if magistrates determine that the accused should be released for lack of probable cause, subsequent grand juries may issue indictments or presentments against defendants. Preliminary hearings are also used for the purpose of establishing probable cause.

When the defendant first appears before a magistrate, the magistrate will determine whether the defendant wishes to waive the preliminary hearing. With the exception of certain petty offenses, which may be tried by the magistrate directly, the defendant may either (1) waive the right to a preliminary hearing or (2) not waive that right.

The Defendant Waives the Right to a Preliminary Hearing

If the defendant *waives* the right to a preliminary hearing, the magistrate or judicial official will *bind over* the defendant to the grand jury. The grand jury will hear evidence from the prosecutor against the defendant and issue either a true bill or a no bill. If a no bill is issued, the defendant is discharged and the criminal charges are dismissed. If a true bill is issued, the defendant faces arraignment.

The Defendant Does Not Waive the Right to a Preliminary Hearing

If the defendant does not waive the right to a preliminary hearing, the hearing is held. The magistrate will determine either that probable cause exists or does not exist. If probable cause does not exist, in the opinion of the magistrate, the defendant is discharged. However, the defendant is subject to a subsequent indictment or presentment by the grand jury. On the other hand, if probable cause exists, again in the opinion of the magistrate, the defendant will face arraignment on the criminal charges.

Lawyers approach the bench during an arraignment.

Grand Jury Action

A charge from the grand jury alleging certain criminal offenses brings a defendant to the arraignment stage of the justice process. Thus, the arraignment stage is reached through (1) a finding of probable cause in a preliminary hearing (possibly resulting from a criminal information filed by the prosecutor), or (2) an indictment or presentment from a grand jury. Figure 7.4 shows a summary of events leading to an arraignment stemming from preliminary hearings, informations, or grand jury action.

Arraignments

At the federal level and in many state and local jurisdictions, the **arraignment** *is the official proceeding at which defendants are informed of the formal criminal charges against them and enter a plea of (1) guilty, (2) not guilty, or (3) nolo contendere.* An alternative set of pleas in the State of Kentucky includes (1) not guilty, (2) guilty, and (3) guilty, but mentally ill. Pleas of *nolo contendere* in Kentucky are prohibited (*Commonwealth v. Hillhaven Corp.*, 1984).

If the arraignment stems from grand jury action rather than a preliminary hearing, a copy of the indictment or presentment is given to the defendant. In many arraignments, indictments or presentments are read to the defendant by either the magistrate or the clerk of the court. At this stage, the defendant is usually, although not always, represented by counsel. An example of a federal arraignment order is shown in figure 7.5.

Guilty Plea
A guilty plea is the equivalent of a confession of guilt in open court (Black, 1990:708). While the

---

Figure 7.4 Alternative Procedures Leading to Arraignment

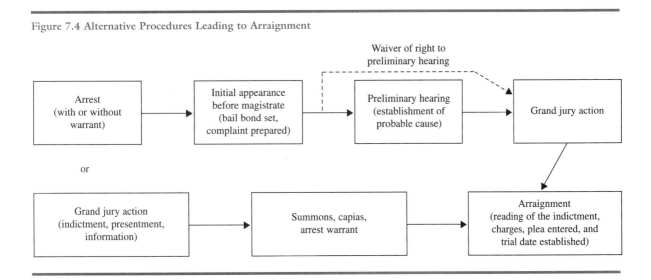

Figure 7.5 A Federal Arraignment Order

DC 15
(Rev. 1/62)

NOTICE OF SETTING OF CASE FOR _____ ARRAIGNMENT _____

United States District Court
FOR THE

_____

THE UNITED STATES OF AMERICA
vs.

Criminal No.

To

☐ [1]   TAKE NOTICE that the above entitled case has been set for **arraignment** in said Court at Federal Courtroom ,
on , 19 , at

☐ [1]   As surety for the said defendant
you are required to produce [2] in said Court at said time, otherwise the bail may be forfeited.

_____, 19____   _____

[1] Sentences following boxes which have been checked are applicable.

[2] Insert "him," "her," as appropriate.

procedures vary among jurisdictions, judges usually are expected to inquire of defendants if their plea is voluntary and if they understand the nature of the charge or charges, the mandatory minimum penalty under the law, the maximum penalty under the law, and that they are still entitled to an attorney if they have not obtained one. Furthermore, the judge will likely ask defendants if the guilty plea has been obtained through threats or coercion and inform them that the plea can be withdrawn and a plea of *not guilty* entered, even at that late hour, that they are entitled to a trial, that they have the right to confront and cross-examine witnesses against them, that they have the right not to incriminate themselves, and that there is a factual basis for that plea. In short, the judge usually extends every opportunity to defendants to exercise all possible constitutional rights to which they are entitled.

Not Guilty Plea

A plea of not guilty obligates the judge to fix a date for trial. The judge also determines whether bail will be continued, if the defendant is currently out of jail on bail. Or the judge may permit defendants to continue ROR if that is their current pretrial release status. Any number of options are available to the judge at this stage. The primary decision reached in an arraignment proceeding after a plea of not guilty is the establishment of a trial date, however.

Nolo Contendere Plea

A plea of ***nolo contendere*** *is the legal equivalent of a guilty plea.* Technically, it is not a plea of guilty, but rather a plea of *no contest*. The defendant is not contesting the facts as presented by the prosecution. However, the defendant may take issue with the legality or constitutionality of the law allegedly violated. For instance, the defendant may say, "Yes, your honor, I do not question the facts presented by the prosecution that I possessed two ounces of marijuana, but I also do not believe that the law prohibiting marijuana possession is constitutionally valid."

Businesspersons sometimes enter pleas of *nolo contendere*. Even though these pleas are treated as the equivalent of guilty pleas in criminal proceedings, they are not considered admissions of guilt in possible future civil proceedings. If a businessperson is charged with the criminal offense of fraud in the construction of a large building, a plea of nolo contendere or "no contest" will result in criminal penalties being invoked. The plea will be treated as though the businessperson had actually pled guilty. However, if the building collapses and people are injured or killed as a result, they may sue the businessperson for damages, but they may not use the *nolo contendere* plea as evidence of an admission of guilt to fraud charges. If the businessperson had pled guilty to the same fraud charges, the guilty plea could have been used against him or her in the subsequent civil action as evidence not only of guilt in the fraud scheme but also of negligence. Therefore, a *nolo contendere* plea is sometimes a strategic option for a person wishing to avoid civil liability connected with criminal activities, traffic accidents, or some other law infraction where civil liability may be incurred.

The Speedy Trial

There are many options available to defendants from the time they are arrested to the time they are arraigned and a trial date is set. In fact, there are many contingencies available to defendants even during the trial and after its conclusion. A general view of trial procedures and an examination of the contingencies available to defendants during the arrest-trial period is presented in chapters 8 and 9.

This last section focuses *only* upon the trial op-

tion. A plea of not guilty by a defendant will obligate the presiding judge to set a trial date and eventually conduct a trial. Normally, this is the case unless some alternative plea is entered, if the prosecution elects to drop charges against the defendant, or if an agreement can be reached between the defendant and prosecutor whereby a formal trial can be avoided. This last contingency is usually referred to as a plea-bargain agreement. *Plea-bargain agreements are preconviction agreements in which a guilty plea from a defendant is exchanged for some type of leniency from the prosecutor* (McDonald, 1985). A more extensive discussion of plea bargaining is presented in chapter 8. But to illustrate some important pretrial requirements and procedures, assume that the defendant does not wish to enter a guilty plea and *persists* in a plea of not guilty to all offenses alleged.

Federal courts are bound by law to observe the **Speedy Trial Act** of 1974 and its subsequent 1979 and 1984 amendments (Steinberg, 1975; Yanich, 1990). The purposes of the Speedy Trial Act are (1) to clarify the rights of defendants, (2) to ensure that (alleged) criminals are brought to justice promptly, and (3) to give effect to a citizen's Sixth Amendment right to a speedy trial (*Klopfer v. Carolina*, 1967; *United States v. Pollock*, 1984; *United States v. Horton*, 1983; *United States v. Nance*, 1982; *United States v. Tunnessen*, 1985; *United States v. May*, 1985).

According to the provisions of this act, suspects must be charged with a criminal offense within thirty days following their arrest or receipt of a summons. Then the trial should commence not less than thirty days nor more than seventy days after the suspect's initial appearance. A hundred-day federal provision is spread out as follows, thirty days from arrest to initial appearance, ten days from initial appearance to arraignment, and sixty days from arraignment to trial.

The leading case relating to a speedy trial is *Klopfer v. North Carolina* (1967) (See Highlight 7.5 for additional "speedy trial" cases). Klopfer was charged with criminal trespass. He eventually went to court, and his case resulted in a mistrial. Klopfer then tried to find out if the government intended to prosecute him again for the same crime, but government officials declined to say. Instead, they

Highlight 7.5. On Speedy Trials

Dickey v. Florida, 398 U.S. 30, 90 S.Ct. 1564 (1970). Dickey was charged in 1968 with various crimes he allegedly committed in 1960. He made motions to have an immediate trial in several different court appearances, but for various reasons his trial was delayed until 1968. Between 1960 and 1968, some witnesses died while others became unavailable for various reasons. Also, some relevant police records were destroyed or misplaced. Following his conviction, he appealed, arguing that his right to a speedy trial had been violated. The Supreme Court overturned his conviction, saying that *prompt inquiry is a fundamental right and that the charging authority has a duty to provide a prompt trial to ensure the availability of records, recollection of witnesses, and availability of testimony.*

Barker v. Wingo, 407 U.S. 514, 92 S.Ct. 2182 (1972). Barker and Manning were alleged to have shot an elderly couple in July 1958. A grand jury indicted them in September 1958. Kentucky prosecutors sought sixteen continuances to delay Barker's trial. Manning, in the meantime, was tried five times. The first four resulted in hung juries; the fifth resulted in his conviction. During Manning's five trials, Barker made no attempt to protest or to encourage a trial on his own behalf. Barker's trial was scheduled and postponed for various reasons but was finally held in October 1963. He was convicted. He appealed, alleging a violation of his right to a speedy trial. The Supreme Court declared that because apparently Barker had not wanted a speedy trial, he was not entitled to one. The case is significant because it establishes that defendants must assert their desire to have a speedy trial in order for the speedy-trial provision of the Constitution to be enforceable.

Strunk v. United States, 412 U.S. 434, 93 S.Ct. 2260 (1973). Strunk was arrested for a crime and tried ten months later. He appealed his conviction, arguing that the ten-month delay was a violation of his right to a speedy trial. On hearing the case the Supreme Court noted several considerations in determining whether speedy-trial rights of suspects have been violated. These considerations are: (1) whether court dockets are overcrowded and prosecutors' offices understaffed; (2) whether defendants have been caused substantial emotional stress because of long delays; and (3) whether the accused is released pending a trial and whether he or she has little or no interest in a speedy trial.

Dillingham v. United States, 423 U.S. 64, 96 S.Ct. 303 (1975). Dillingham was arrested for a crime. After twenty-two months an indictment was issued against Dillingham, and twelve months later he was brought to trial. Dillingham was convicted. He appealed, arguing that the twenty-two-month interval between his arrest and indictment violated his right to a speedy trial. The Supreme Court overturned his conviction, declaring that invocation of the speedy trial provision did not require him to await indictment, information, or other formal charge. Thus, the delay between Dillingham's arrest, indictment, and trial was unreasonable and violated his Sixth Amendment right to a speedy trial.

Doggett v. United States, 505 U.S. 647, 112 S.Ct. 2686 (1992). Doggett was convicted in a U.S. district court of conspiracy to distribute cocaine. Because of various delays, mostly caused by the government, Doggett's trial was not held for eight and one-half years. He appealed his conviction, contending that the eight-and-a-half-year delay violated his right to a speedy trial under the Sixth Amendment. The Supreme Court overturned Doggett's conviction, concluding that the eight-and-a-half-year delay, largely because of government causes, did indeed violate the Sixth Amendment rights of the accused.

Fex v. Michigan, 507 U.S. 403, 113 S.Ct. 1085 (1993). Fex, a prisoner in Indiana, was brought to trial in Michigan 196 days following his trial request to Michigan officials and 177 days after the request was received by Michigan prosecutors. Fex was convicted and appealed, alleging that the 180-day speedy trial time period was violated, inasmuch as his trial commenced 196 days after his own request to have a trial was submitted to Michigan. The Supreme Court heard Fex's appeal and upheld his conviction, noting the detainer warrant phraseology that the statutory 180-day period *did not begin until the Michigan prosecutor received his request.* The U.S. Supreme Court said that if the warden in Indiana delayed the forwarding of a prisoner's request for a speedy trial, this *merely postponed the starting of the 180-day clock.* Thus, the receipt of such a notice from a prisoner under a detainer warrant in another state by the state prosecutors triggers the 180-day clock to determine whether the prisoner's speedy trial rights are being observed.

formally entered in the court record a "*nolle prose-qui* with leave," which meant that while they were permitting the defendant to be discharged, they were allowing themselves an opportunity to retry him at a future unspecified date. The Supreme Court declared that the government violated Klopfer's Sixth and Fourteenth Amendment rights and that it was unconstitutional to indefinitely postpone his trial without providing an adequate reason. Some of the reasons the Supreme Court cited for the decision to endorse a speedy trial provision were: (1) witness testimony would be more credible through an early trial; (2) the defendant's pretrial anxiety would be minimized; and (3) the defendant's ability to defend himself or herself and the fairness of the trial would not be jeopardized through extensive, adverse pretrial publicity.

Notwithstanding certain delays for a variety of reasons attributable to the defense, the prosecution, or both, the Speedy Trial Act of 1974 provides:

1. In a case where a plea of "not guilty" is entered, the trial shall commence within seventy days from the date when an information or indictment has been made public or from the date of the defendant's arraignment, whichever date last occurs.
2. Unless the defendant consents in writing to the contrary, the trial shall not commence less than thirty days from the date on which the defendant first appears through counsel or expressly waives counsel and elects to proceed *pro se* (on his own).

These provisions not only make it possible for a criminal defendant to enjoy the right to a speedy trial but also eliminate delays caused by crowded court dockets (*United States v. Nance*, 1982). Some courts have been notorious for their slowness in conducting trial proceedings. A judge may allow into evidence lengthy tape recordings of conversations between an FBI agent and a defendant, which may consume many hours. In another district court, however, the judge may insist that such materials be presented through more direct and brief testimony from witnesses. With the provisions of the Speedy Trial Act in force, all federal judges

are obligated to comply with these provisions in spite of the "general congestion of the court's calendar" (Title 18, U.S.C., Sec. 3161 (h)(8)(C), 1996). Certainly, one consequence of this provisions is a more rapid trial proceeding.

The "not less than thirty nor more than seventy days" provision of the Speedy Trial Act applies to the period between a defendant's initial appearance and his or her arraignment, which is usually ten days. A federal trial date should be set within sixty days of a defendant's arraignment. The purpose of the time interval is to allow a defendant and his or her lawyer adequate time to prepare a defense and to spare the defendant any undue delay in coming to trial. Under the act, however, the defendant has a right to an earlier trial.

There are many factors that affect the seventy-day requirement. Defendants may discharge one attorney and appoint another. New attorneys will need sufficient time to examine the case and prepare a defense (*United States v. Darby*, 1984). The defendant may be ill (*United States v. Savoca*, 1984), or an important witness may require additional time to arrive (*United States v. Strong*, 1985). The judge may even request a psychiatric examination of a defendant if, in the judge's opinion, there is reason to believe that the defendant is not competent to stand trial (*United States v. Howell*, 1983; *United States v. Crosby*, 1983).

Many local and state jurisdictions follow the federal provisions set forth in the Speedy Trial Act, although they are not bound to do so. For example, North Carolina has a 90-day limit from the time of arrest or arraignment to trial, while New Mexico has a 180-day limit. The "speedy trial" provision of the Sixth Amendment is construed differently from one jurisdiction to the next. However, federal courts are bound by the Speedy Trial Act provisions.

Summary

Defendants are brought into the criminal justice system through an arrest by a police officer or a private citizen. Complaints alleging law violations are filed. Grand juries and prosecutors can also bring defendants into the system through indictments, presentments, and criminal informations.

When suspects are arrested, they are booked, and records of personal data are compiled. Usually, a magistrate or other judicial officer will establish a bail bond for a defendant in order for the defendant to gain pretrial release. A date for a preliminary hearing is usually established, unless the defendant wishes to waive that right. If that right is waived, the magistrate binds over the defendant to the grand jury where the particular case is heard. Grand jury action leads to either a no true bill or a true bill. A true bill means that the grand jury has determined that probable cause exists to charge a defendant with a crime.

When persons are brought into the justice system through grand jury or prosecutor action, they are arraigned before a magistrate. When a defendant is subjected to a preliminary hearing, a judicial official determines if there is probable cause to support the criminal charges against the defendant. If probable cause is determined to exist, the defendant is subsequently arraigned.

During arraignment a defendant is confronted with formal criminal charges, enters a plea, and has a trial date established by the court. The plea may be guilty, not guilty, guilty but mentally ill, nolo contendere, or some other plea consistent with the rules of criminal procedure followed in particular jurisdictions. A plea of not guilty obligates presiding judges to set a trial date for the defendant.

Under the Speedy Trial Act of 1974 and its 1979 and 1984 amendments, trial dates set in federal court proceedings must be not less than thirty days nor more than seventy days from the date of the arraignment. There are many exceptions to these requirements, however. Federal judges are bound by the provisions of the Speedy Trial Act, whereas local and state judges follow particular rules peculiar to their own jurisdictions.

Key Terms

Arraignment
Bail
Bail bond

Bail Reform Act of 1984
Bench warrant
Booking
Capias
Cash bond
Citizen's arrest
Criminal information
Grand jury
Indictment
Initial appearance
Nolo contendere
No bill
Preliminary examination
Preliminary hearings
Presentment
Release on own recognizance (ROR)
Speedy Trial Act
Statute of limitations
Summons
True bill
Warrant
Without undue delay

Questions for Review

1. What are the arrest powers of citizens? Do police officers have the same arrest powers as citizens, or do they have more arrest powers? Explain.
2. What does "without undue delay" mean in reference to bringing arrested persons before magistrates?
3. Differentiate between a summons and a complaint. How does a magistrate evaluate the trustworthiness of a person filing a complaint?
4. Differentiate between an indictment and a presentment. If a prosecutor wants to avoid the grand jury altogether and file charges against a particular defendant, what does the prosecutor file?
5. Distinguish between a "true bill" and a "no bill." In grand jury actions, do defendants usually get a chance to present their side of the story regarding pending criminal charges?
6. Which amendment to the Constitution pertains to speedy trials? What legislation pertain-

ing to speedy trials has the federal government enacted?

7. What is bail? What is the primary purpose of bail? Does bail always have to be in the form of money? Why or why not?

8. Are only violent criminals likely to be denied bail in certain situations? What are some other kinds of offenses and conditions that might result in the denial of bail?

9. What generally happens to a defendant at an arraignment?

10. Do all states have pleas of guilty, not guilty, and *nolo contendere*? What other plea is used in some states, such as Kentucky?

Suggested Readings

Hirsch, Alan and Diane Sheely. *The Bail Reform Act of 1984.* 2d ed. Washington, DC: Federal Judicial Center, 1993.

Inciardi, James A. *Examining the Justice Process: A Reader.* Ft. Worth, TX: Harcourt Brace, 1996.

Mauer, Marc and Malcolm C. Young. *Feasibility of the Expansion of Alternatives to Incarceration for Essex County, New Jersey.* Washington, DC: The Sentencing Project, 1992.

Stenning, Phillip C. (ed.). *Accountability for Criminal Justice: Selected Essays.* Cheektowaga, NY: University of Toronto Press, 1996.

CHAPTER 8

Processing Defendants: Pretrial Procedures II

This chapter describes the interval between arraignment and trial. For those suspects charged with one or more criminal offenses, several pretrial options may be considered. The defense attorney represents the client's interests, while the prosecution represents the state's interests. While some criminal defendants never use an attorney to represent them, the Sixth Amendment guarantees *all* criminal defendants access to a lawyer at every stage of the criminal proceeding. If defendants cannot afford an attorney, one will be appointed for them at the state's expense.

When a suspect is formally charged with a crime, a *Miranda* hearing is often conducted to determine if the police observed the suspect's rights during interrogation. This is especially crucial in cases where serious crimes are alleged and where suspects have made statements to police.

The importance of pretrial proceedings is measured by the number of convictions obtained by prosecutors without a formal trial. Ninety percent of all criminal convictions are obtained without trial (Miller, Cramer, and McDonald; 1978; McDonald, 1985; Meeker, 1984; Stitt and Siegel, 1986; Alschuler, 1979; Mather, 1979). In many of these cases, a defendant will simply plead guilty after discussing his or her situation with a prosecutor. In other instances, the defendant's attorney and the prosecution have worked out an agreement satisfactory to both sides. One reason for the lengthy time between an arrest and a final disposition of a case is to enable the prosecutor to evaluate the strength of the evidence and the probability of obtaining a conviction *if the case were to go to trial*. Also, this includes time spent conferring with defense attorneys about the disposition of the case and the defendants' feelings and intentions in the matter.

The Prosecution and Its Functions

Local, state, and federal prosecutors represent the government's interests whenever criminal laws are violated. The U.S. Attorney's Office makes decisions concerning which cases to prosecute and which ones lack prosecutive merit when federal laws are broken. At the state and local levels, city and county attorneys make similar decisions about filing criminal charges against defendants.

In some states, the state supreme court appoints a state attorney general for a specified term. The Tennessee Supreme Court appoints an attorney general for a term of eight years. In New Mexico, the state attorney general is elected through a partisan election and serves one four-year term. In other states, the attorney general may be appointed by the governor. In city and county government, the position of district attorney is often an elected position.

The functions of the prosecutors at the local, state, and federal levels include, but are not limited to, the following: (1) deciding, or **screening**, cases slotted for prosecution; (2) representing the government in presenting cases against suspects before the grand jury; (3) conferring with police participating in the initial arrest and ensuring the suspect's right to due process; (4) evaluating the sufficiency of evidence against the accused; (5) conferring with defense attorneys in pretrial conferences in an effort to avoid a trial proceeding; and (6) presenting the case against the defendant in court.

Screening Cases

A prosecutor must look at each potential case in terms of how it would appear to a judge and jury if it were to come to trial. This view of the case often differs from the view of arresting officers who are familiar with the crime scene and the circumstances leading to a suspect's arrest. For instance, police may arrest a suspect and charge him with attempted rape. The following dialogue between an El Paso, Texas, prosecutor and an interviewer serves as an example of this process:

Q: What types of things do you look for on deciding if a case should be screened out?
A: We look for elements that constitute that particular penal offense.
Q: What if you have an eighteen-year-old kid who is with his date and pulls off her underwear,

and then she jumps out of the car screaming? What do you do with that?
A: Well, it's attempted rape. But how are you going to prove it? What were his intentions? Well, you can't prove he intended to rape her. Maybe he wanted to look at her. Attempted rape is an impossibility to make. We'd probably have an assault by contact case. When it boils down to it, that's all we've got. That's assuming she'll press charges. (McDonald, 1985:41)

In this situation, the officers making the arrest at the crime scene observed the woman's torn and dishevelled clothing and listened to the suspect as he made admissions to them. But the prosecutor reviewing the arrest report considers how a jury would react to the evidence presented several months after the incident. In the meantime, the woman may change her mind about prosecuting, and she may even marry the accused. The El Paso, Texas, Screening Bureau, consisting of two attorneys with some trial experience and two investigators from the police department, uses as the standard of case strength whether the case can be won at trial. In that jurisdiction, the screening bureau rejects 60 percent of all cases forwarded to it (McDonald, 1985:42).

Presenting Cases Before the Grand Jury

A prosecutor presents cases to grand juries. If defendants waive their right to a preliminary hearing, the prosecutor must present the evidence to the grand jury and try to obtain a true bill or an indictment. Of course, the prosecutor can act independently and secure a criminal information against the accused without resorting to a grand jury. This is sufficient to start proceedings that may eventually lead to trial.

Conferring with Police Concerning a Defendant's Right to Due Process

Part of the screening process of a criminal case involves consulting with arresting officers and determining the circumstances surrounding the arrest. Were the accused informed of their constitutional rights? Did the police give suspects the Miranda warning? While a hearing on this matter may be held at a later date, the prosecutor usually conducts an independent investigation before recommending prosecution of a case.

Evaluating the Sufficiency of Evidence Against the Accused

The evidence linking the suspect with the crime is crucial to a successful prosecution. Sometimes evidence is purely circumstantial. Suppose a person wearing blue jeans and a red shirt robbed the Convenient Food Store. He used a "silver-looking" pistol, according to eyewitnesses. Later, police stop and question a suspect wearing jeans and a red shirt. They frisk the suspect and find a nickel-finished ("silver-looking") pistol tucked inside his belt. Although eyewitnesses can't positively identify the suspect, there is some circumstantial evidence connecting that suspect with the robbery.

Some suspects are homeowners who have acted to protect their property. Some states have passed "make my day" laws authorizing people to defend their homes against intruders. These are difficult cases to screen and unpopular to prosecute. The jury almost always sides with the homeowner.

The prosecutor must examine all witnesses who may have relevant information about the case. Will they be willing to testify in court later? Sometimes a conviction hinges on the availability of a witness. Depending upon the sufficiency of evidence against the accused, the prosecutor will either drop the case or prosecute.

Conferring with Defense Attorneys

A suspect is entitled to certain information from the prosecution. This is known as **discovery** (*Brady v. Maryland,* 1963). For instance, a defendant is entitled to see the results of any tests conducted, including blood tests or psychiatric examinations. Defendants also have the right to review any statements they made to police at the time

of arrest or during any custodial interrogation. The defense attorney will seek to obtain these discoverable materials (sometimes referred to as "Brady" materials). This information gives defense attorneys a more accurate picture of the state's case against their clients.

Another purpose of a pretrial conference with the defense attorney is to attempt to work out an arrangement whereby a trial can be avoided. Based on the sufficiency of the evidence, the prosecutor may feel that the suspect is guilty of the crime alleged. If the evidence is strong and incriminating, the prosecutor may ask the defendant (perhaps through the defendant's attorney) to plead guilty to the offenses alleged. A guilty plea saves the state considerable time and expense. In exchange for a guilty plea, the prosecutor may offer leniency or a reduction in the seriousness of charges. This process, known as *plea bargaining,* is discussed in more detail later in this chapter.

The prosecutor's meeting with the defense attorney is one way of "testing the waters." In many criminal cases, the defendant has information that is unknown to the prosecutor. The information and evidence may be **exculpatory evidence,** or *evidence favorable to defendants that supports their innocence.* Unknown to the prosecution, there may be witnesses who can testify as to the true whereabouts of a defendant at the time the offense was committed. *Incriminating evidence or evidence that tends to show one's guilt is called* **inculpatory evidence**. Both the prosecution and the defense exchange limited information in an effort to work out the most equitable arrangement for everyone concerned.

A further inducement for defendants to plead guilty, especially when the evidence against them is strong, is that sentences imposed after a jury trial are from two to three times as severe as sentences imposed by the judge after a plea of guilty and a waiver of a trial (Greenstein, 1994; McConville and Mirsky, 1995; Nelson, 1994). The message from the prosecution: "If you force us to take you to trial by pleading not guilty, prepare yourself for a stiffer sentence if you're convicted." Sometimes this tactic works, and a stubborn defendant pleads guilty in exchange for lenient treatment by the court.

Presenting the Case Against the Defendant in Court

The prosecutor presents the government's case against the accused in court. This responsibility includes calling witnesses who can give testimony supporting the accused's guilt. It also involves coordinating the presentation of other relevant evidence with detectives, police officers, and laboratory experts. If it is a jury trial, the prosecutor must persuade the jury that the accused is guilty beyond a reasonable doubt. In fact, the standard of *guilt beyond a reasonable doubt* makes the prosecutor's role especially difficult to perform. *The finder of fact* is the jury, which must weigh all the evidence and decide if it is sufficient to prove the defendant's guilt beyond a reasonable doubt. In a weak case, a prosecutor must give serious thought to what the jury's opinion of the evidence will be. In a borderline case, the prosecutor may eventually decline to prosecute simply because the probability of a conviction is not very strong (Roberts, 1994).

Prosecutorial Misconduct

Prosecutors do not always adhere to the high standards they are expected to observe. Occasionally they engage in various forms of *prosecutorial misconduct* or *immoral, unethical, or illegal acts associated with their prosecutorial duties*. It is unethical for a prosecutor to pursue a case against a defendant when the prosecutor knows that the defendant is innocent. In some cases, prosecutors may dislike particular defendants and desire to make their life miserable by subjecting them to criminal prosecution. **Malicious prosecution** *is any prosecution begun in malice without probable cause to believe that the criminal charges will ever be sustained* (Black, 1990:958). It is also unethical for prosecutors to threaten defendants with prosecutions for very serious offenses (for which there is little evidence, if any) unless these defendants plead guilty to lesser charges. In some cases, defendants have pleaded guilty to offenses where there is no evidence against them. Their motive is a simple one: they wish to avoid a prosecution on more serious, yet groundless, charges, because there is a chance that a jury might find them guilty. The public seldom hears about such prosecutions or guilty pleas entered by innocent defendants.

An assistant U.S. attorney in Chattanooga, Tennessee, once threatened a poor defendant with a felony charge if the defendant did not enter a guilty plea to a federal misdemeanor. The prosecutor advised the defendant that if he didn't plead guilty, then a long trial was promised. Such a trial would exhaust the defendant's savings. Grudgingly, the defendant entered a guilty plea. An alert federal judge oversaw the plea agreement hearing. When the judge asked the prosecutor for evidence he would have presented to support a conviction against the defendant, the prosecutor fumbled with some papers and said that there was no evidence. The federal judge threw out the guilty plea, dismissed the defendant from the courtroom, and verbally reprimanded the federal prosecutor for his conduct and for wasting valuable court time. This type of prosecutorial misconduct is sometimes called *prosecutorial bluffing*. Circumstantial evidence may exist to suggest that a particular person may have knowledge about the crime, but there may be insufficient evidence for a criminal information to be filed or for an indictment to be issued by a grand jury. More than a few defendants will admit to crimes they have not committed if it means getting probation, serving no time, paying no fine, and not getting prosecuted for more serious offenses. The mere thought of going through a humiliating public trial causes some defendants to "confess" to things they have never done.

Another type of prosecutorial misconduct is to encourage witnesses to slant their versions of events when testifying during trials. FBI agents, DEA agents, local and state police officers, and a host of other witnesses are sometimes rehearsed in particular versions of cases to fit a certain prosecutorial scenario. The testimony given by these persons may or may not be factually accurate, but the prosecutors succeed in getting their witnesses to tell the story *the prosecutors' way*. A particular spin on a witness's version of events may prejudice juries against defendants. In the trial of O. J. Simpson in 1995–1996, for instance, prosecutors led various witnesses to tell more incriminating versions of what they had seen or heard. However, de-

Highlight 8.1. Talk about Getting Rid of the Competition! The Case of Lovesick Prosecutor William Jones, Jr.

In 1987, Allegheny County (Pennsylvania) judge David Cashman was presiding over a case against Thomas Balenger, thirty-four. Balenger was convicted of robbing a delicatessen and sentenced to a five- to ten-year term. He was also convicted of robbing a jeweler at gunpoint in 1988. He has been serving a thirteen- to twenty-six-year sentence for that conviction.

In March 1996, Judge Cashman ordered that Balenger be given a new trial on the delicatessen robbery charge. It seems that the prosecutor in *both* cases, William Jones, Jr., was in love with Balenger's girlfriend at the time he was prosecuting Balenger. Jones wanted to put Balenger away for a *long time*, the longer the better. A long prison term would keep Jones's competition away. The new information about Jones's love affair with Balenger's girlfriend came to light when Balenger lodged a protest and appealed his first conviction.

In 1990, Jones left the district attorney's office and went to work in the state attorney general's office, where he was still employed in 1996. When Judge Cashman learned of Jones's love affair with Balenger's girlfriend, he was furious. He ordered a new trial for Balenger, largely because of the prosecutorial misconduct and conflict of interest. The judge declared that because there was *still* evidence to suggest that Balenger had committed the crime, he couldn't drop all of the charges. But he ordered a new trial nevertheless.

Balenger was delighted. "Justice was served. I didn't do the crime. I'll get a new trial," he declared after learning of Cashman's decision. Referring to his *former* girlfriend, Balenger said, "She's an evil temptress, and he's a dog" (referring to Jones).

How would you punish the prosecutor, Jones, for what he did to Balenger? While we don't know all the facts about Balenger and whether he actually committed the crimes of which he was convicted, should any special leniency be extended to him because of such prosecutorial misconduct? Does he have any legal recourse for civil damages?

Source: Adapted from Associated Press, "Man Gets New Trial Because Prosecutor Fell in Love with His Girlfriend," *Minot (N.D.) Daily News,* March 7, 1996, p. A2.

---

fense attorneys for Simpson were able to catch some of these witnesses in factual inconsistencies or to get them to admit that their testimony had been rehearsed with prosecutors in pretrial sessions. The most important ally and advocate of a defendant facing *any* criminal charge is the defense attorney.

Defense Attorneys and Their Functions

Defense attorneys appear on behalf of clients who are charged with crimes. They file appearances on behalf of their clients and represent their interests in court (Black, 1990:420). A defense attorney's job is not an easy one. For one thing, the attorney comes into contact with every sort of defendant imagin-

able. Alleged burglars, child sexual abusers, murderers, rapists, robbers, drug dealers, arsonists, prostitutes, thieves, and organized crime figures appear at the defense attorney's doorstep looking for legal aid.

The major function of criminal defense attorneys is to secure the best possible disposition of a case for their clients. This means either (1) to convince a judge or jury of the accused's innocence if the case goes to trial, or (2) to get the client the best possible bargain in terms of dismissal of all charges, or a light sentence, or probation, or a general mitigation of punishment.

To accomplish either of these feats, the attorney must resort to investigative tactics practiced by detectives and police. Defense attorneys should contact all prospective witnesses for the government as well as those supporting their client's case. In short, a defense attorney must attempt to formulate a picture of the case from the prosecutor's standpoint. Only then will certain crucial flaws in the case emerge. Interviewing witnesses for either the prosecution or the defense will lead to disclosures that were unknown earlier to either side. Inconsistencies in recollections will be detected, and the defense attorney will get a better grasp of the entire affair.

Criminal lawyers are often criticized by other attorneys. In particularly brutal murder or rape cases, for instance, or in cases where severe bodily injury has resulted from the criminal offenses alleged, defense attorneys who agree to handle the case for the defendant often are asked, "How can you defend those people?" (Kunen, 1983). Some attorneys reject requests from alleged drug dealers to represent them in court. Many attorneys avoid criminal work altogether.

In spite of the crimes alleged, however, all defendants facing felony or misdemeanor charges that could result in imprisonment are entitled to counsel whether they can afford it or not (*Gideon v. Wainwright*, 1963; *Argersinger v. Hamlin*, 1972; *Baldasar v. Illinois*, 1980). While federal courts have always complied with the Sixth Amendment and provided defendants with an attorney if they could not afford one, state courts have not always done the same.

Public Defenders

When defendants are indigent and cannot afford an attorney, a defense lawyer is appointed by the court to represent them. These lawyers are **public defenders.** Each jurisdiction has different arrangements for providing counsel to indigent defendants. In some communities, for instance, courts require attorneys to allocate a certain amount of time each year to represent indigent clients. These attorneys sometimes perform defense services without remuneration from the government or other sources. More frequently, however, the attorneys are paid nominal sums. Other communities have public defender offices that employ attorneys on a full-time basis. These attorneys' exclusive role is to provide legal counsel to all indigent defendants. In yet other jurisdictions, attorneys volunteer as counsels for indigents, rotating with other attorney-volunteers as

A public defender checks her notes in court as the defendant stands in a holding cell.

their caseloads vary. An early survey of funding available to public defender systems in most state criminal courts suggested that most of these systems were chronically *underfunded* (Lefstein, 1982). This continued to be the case well into the 1990s (Flango, 1994b; Worden, 1993).

Sometimes indigent defendants turn to legal aid clinics for assistance. These agencies and organizations are usually operated by persons less trained in legal fundamentals than bonafide attorneys. They are frequently staffed by law students in their last years of legal training, who are under the direction or supervision of a court-approved attorney. Often, public defenders are new attorneys looking for legal experience. They are not usually paid well, and as a result, their motivation to assist criminal defendants may not be as strong as it should be.

How Do Public Defenders Compare with Private Counsel?

Some evidence suggests that a privately obtained defense attorney will do a better job than a

Highlight 8.2. Defense Attorneys for Indigent Clients: Some Leading Cases

Gideon v. Wainwright, 372 U.S. 335, 83 S.Ct. 792 (1963). Indigent defendants have a right to counsel in felony cases; the *Gideon* decision required that all states provide counsel to all indigent defendants in all felony trials. Clarence Gideon broke into a poolroom, allegedly with the intent to commit larceny, a felony in Florida. Gideon, an indigent, asked for a lawyer to represent him. He was advised by the judge that counsel could only be appointed to persons if the offense was a capital one (involving the death penalty). Thus, Gideon represented himself. He was convicted and appealed. The U.S. Supreme Court overturned his conviction, saying that all indigent defendants are entitled to court-appointed counsel in *felony cases.*

Argersinger v. Hamlin, 407 U.S. 25, 92 S.Ct. 2006 (1972). The *Gideon* decision was extended by the Supreme Court to include misdemeanor offenses; no sentence involving the loss of liberty (incarceration) can be imposed where there has been a denial of counsel. Thus, defendants have a right to counsel when imprisonment might result. Argersinger, an indigent, was charged with carrying a concealed weapon. In Florida, this crime is a misdemeanor punishable by imprisonment of up to six months and a $1,000 fine. Argersinger was not allowed to have court-appointed counsel, since his crime was not a *felony* (see *Gideon v. Wainwright,* 1963), and thus Florida was not obligated to provide him with court-appointed counsel. Argersinger was convicted of the

misdemeanor and sentenced to ninety days in jail. He appealed, and the Supreme Court overturned his misdemeanor conviction. The Court said that any indigent defendant is entitled to counsel for *any* offense involving *imprisonment, regardless of the shortness of the length of incarceration.* Essentially, the Court said that anyone facing possible imprisonment is entitled to court-appointed counsel if they are indigent and cannot afford their own private counsel.

Baldasar v. Illinois, 446 U.S. 222, 100 S.Ct. 1585 (1980). Thomas Baldasar was convicted in a theft of property not exceeding $150 in value. Although this offense was a misdemeanor, it was Baldasar's second offense, and therefore it became a felony. He was convicted of the felony and sentenced to one to three years in prison. He appealed, claiming that he was not represented by counsel at the time of his first conviction. Therefore, the enhanced penalty from the second conviction was not constitutional. The Supreme Court agreed with Baldasar and overturned his conviction, holding that no indigent criminal defendant shall be sentenced to prison unless the state has afforded him counsel. Baldasar requested but was denied counsel in his original misdemeanor conviction, which became a crucial step in enhancing the penalty resulting from his second conviction. *Uncounseled misdemeanor convictions may not be used to enhance or convert subsequent misdemeanor convictions into felony convictions with prison terms.*

court-appointed lawyer, although the defendant's prior record and the seriousness of the offense seem to have more effect on the severity of a sentence than the quality of the attorney (Willison, 1984; Champion, 1988a). However, other experts have concluded that it makes little difference whether one is represented by private counsel or a public defender (Hanson, Ostrom, and Hewitt, 1992; Lehtinen and Smith, 1974). Williams (1995b) found, for instance, that the effectiveness of court-appointed attorneys did not differ significantly from that of

privately acquired counsel in filing criminal appeals on behalf of convicted offenders.

Other research suggests that the quality of public defenders varies among jurisdictions. For example, in a study of public defenders in Fulton County, Georgia, it was found that attorneys who defended indigent clients in the public defender's office got no training and no supervision by more experienced counsel. Low salaries and low morale also added up to unfavorable results for indigent clients (Spangbenberg Group, 1990).

Highlight 8.3. Taking the Defense Attorney to Jail: The Case F. Lee Bailey Didn't Win

F. Lee Bailey, one of the most successful defense attorneys in the United States, has defended the worst of clients. He defended Albert DeSalvo, the "Boston Strangler." He won an acquittal for Dr. Sam Sheppard. He defended Patty Hearst. He was part of the defense team that successfully defended O. J. Simpson on double-murder charges.

In March 1996, it was F. Lee Bailey's turn to be the defendant. His attorney was Roger E. Zuckerman of Tallahassee, Florida. Bailey was led away by U.S. marshals after defying a federal court order to produce $25 million in stock and other securities that he had obtained from a drug dealer he once represented.

Bailey claimed the stock was owed him as his fee. The government said that the stock and securities were a part of the drug dealer's cash and assets to be seized under asset forfeiture.

Bailey was fingerprinted, photographed, and searched before being taken to a federal jail in Tallahassee. He served approximately two months in jail before his release. The claim against the stocks continues to be disputed.

Source: Adapted from Associated Press, "Bailey Reports to Jail in Stock Controversy," *Minot (N.D.) Daily News,* March 7, 1996, p. A5.

Despite the apparent contradictions in the research literature about the quality of public defenders, the prevailing opinion is that privately acquired counsel are in a position to do *more* for their clients than public defenders. For his double-murder trial of 1995–1996, for instance, O.J. Simpson employed a multimillion dollar defense team consisting of internationally known defense attorneys, forensics experts, and investigators. His formidable defense easily matched the prosecution appointed to convict him. In Simpson's case, the jury rendered a "not guilty" verdict because reasonable doubt had been created. It is likely that the same high-quality, expensive, and successful defense could not have been mounted by a public defender.

It should be noted that a good defense attorney does not always have to win a not guilty verdict for the client. If a defense attorney is successful is dissuading a jury from imposing the death penalty in a capital case in favor of life without parole or from imposing the severest possible prison sentence, his or her work is judged successful.

Sometimes criminal defense attorneys encourage their clients to persist in pleading not guilty if the case against them is weak. This form of bluffing is practiced by both sides. Prosecutors frequently drop charges against a criminal defendant at the last minute before trial. Some prosecutors have gone so far as to impanel a jury before dropping a case. This tactic is meant to frighten defendants into pleading guilty (McDonald, 1985).

Ineffective Assistance of Counsel

Sometimes defendants will argue on appeal that they had ineffective assistance of counsel. Ineffective assistance of counsel occurs when (1) the counsel's conduct fell below the objective standard of reasonableness, and (2) the counsel's functioning undermined the adversarial process to the point that a fair and just trial could not be conducted. The leading case in determining whether counsel is ineffective is *Strickland v. Washington* (1984). (See Highlight 8.4 for a brief account of *Strickland* and three other cases describing U.S. Supreme Court appeals where ineffective assistance of counsel was raised as an issue.) If one's defense counsel was indeed ineffective, it might be argued that a new trial is warranted. The convicted offender reasons that if the defense attorney was ineffective, his or her right to a fair trial was violated. Hence, a new trial ought to be granted. However, appellate courts require considerable persuasion that a defense counsel is ineffective, even when the attorney commits seemingly outrageous behaviors or acts of omission are committed. As *Strickland* illustrates, an attorney may have been *deficient* or *incompetent*, but the case itself may have been sufficiently strong against the defendant that the deficiencies and incompetencies of the defense attorney would have made no difference to the final outcome (Flango, 1994b; Guggenheim, 1986; Hengstler, 1987; Sevilla, 1986).

Highlight 8.4. Determining Counsel Ineffectiveness: Four "Ineffective Assistance of Counsel" Cases

Strickland v. Washington, 466 U.S. 668, 104 S.Ct. 2052 (1984). In this case, the attorney's conduct was measured according to the following standards: Did it undermine the adversarial process to such an extent that the trial could not be relied upon to render a just result? Did it fall below the objective standard of reasonableness? To find an attorney guilty of rendering ineffective assistance there must be a reasonable probability that, but for counsel's unprofessional errors, the result of the proceedings would have been different.

Jones v. Barnes, 463 U.S. 745, 103 S.Ct. 3308 (1983). A New York jury convicted David Barnes of robbery and assault. Barnes attempted to launch several appeals through a court-appointed attorney. The attorney advised Barnes that most of his suggested claims were groundless. Defense counsel advised Barnes of at least seven claims of error which he considered including in his brief, but when the case was eventually appealed, the counsel focused on primarily three of the claims. Barnes filed a *habeas corpus* petition, alleging ineffective assistance of counsel. The Supreme Court heard Barnes' appeal and rejected his argument that his counsel had been ineffective. Rather, the Court declared, defense counsel assigned to prosecute an appeal of a criminal conviction does not have a constitutional duty to raise every nonfrivolous issue requested by a defendant. In the Court's opinion, the counsel was effective and supported Barnes' claims to the best of his ability, which was reasonable.

Murray v. Carrier 477 U.S. 478, 106 S.Ct. 2639 (1986). Clifford Murray was convicted in a Virginia court of rape. Prior to his trial, Murray demanded to see statements made by the rape victim, but the trial judge refused to disclose them. Murray's counsel appealed his conviction but did not include the matter of the victim's testimony or the denial of the discovery motion pertaining to it. The appeal was denied. On his own, Murray filed a *habeas corpus* petition alleging ineffective assistance of counsel and a failure of the prosecution to disclose the victim's statement. The Supreme Court upheld Murray's conviction, holding that the mere fact that counsel failed to recognize the factual or legal basis for a claim or failed to raise it despite recognizing it does not constitute cause for procedural default. Further, defense counsel inadvertently neglected to include the discovery matter in his later motion filed with the court. Thus, the U.S. Supreme Court dismissed Murray's defaulted discovery claim and rejected his appeal.

Lozada v. Deeds, 498 U.S. 320, 111 S.Ct. 860 (1991). José Lozada was convicted of four crimes relating to narcotics. He had been convicted earlier in Nevada of four counts of possessing and selling controlled substances. Following the trial proceedings, Lozada's attorney failed to notify him of his right to appeal, of the procedures and time limitations of an appeal, and of his right to court-appointed counsel. Further, Lozada alleged that his attorney failed to file a notice of appeal or to ensure that Lozada received court-appointed counsel on appeal. Finally, it was alleged that the attorney misled Lozada's sister, and hence Lozada, when he told her that the case had been forwarded to the public defender's office. Lower appellate courts dismissed Lozada's subsequent *habeas corpus* petition, which stated that he had ineffective assistance of counsel as the result of these alleged events. The Supreme Court found otherwise, however, and reversed his convictions, holding that Lozada had made a substantial showing that he was denied the right to effective assistance of counsel.

Alternatives to Criminal Court

Between the time a person is arrested and the day her or his trial begins, a number of things usually happen "behind the scenes" involving exchanges of information between the prosecutor, the prosecutor's staff, and the defendant's attorney. Assuming that the prosecutor intends to prosecute the defendant (i.e., believes the evidence sufficient to convict the defendant), the defendant's attorney attempts to convince the prosecutor to either drop the charges or at least reduce their severity (Adams, 1983).

Some of the alternatives to a formal criminal trial include (1) police cautioning; (2) diversion to a civil court; (3) pretrial diversion; and (4) plea bargaining.

Police Cautioning

Police cautioning *is verbally warning an alleged offender of further police action and of the certainty of prosecution if the offender persists in committing additional offenses* (Lee, 1994; Marshall et al., 1985). Such a tactic is often useful in dealing with those caught committing petty crimes such as voyeurism or soliciting a prostitute.

In jurisdictions where court dockets are overcrowded, police cautioning might be in order. Of course, this alternative almost always applies to minor misdemeanor offenses, with some exceptions. For instance, suppose a woman was arrested for using cocaine at a small party. Others were also arrested, including the cocaine supplier. Police might permit the cocaine user to go free with the stern warning that if she is caught using or possessing cocaine again, she will be arrested and prosecuted.

Diversion to a Civil Court

In some cases there is a fine line between a civil and a criminal violation. For instance, assault and battery is considered a tort in every jurisdiction. It is "any unlawful touching of another which is without justification or excuse" (Black, 1990). Assault may be a verbal threat of harm, whereas battery is actual harmful contact with another. Assault and battery is also a crime, although its description varies among states. Usually, *aggravated assault* is used for the criminal classification.

If two or more persons get in a fight, either person may charge the other with *assault and battery*. If the charge is filed with the police department and a warrant alleging assault and battery is issued, the person named in the warrant will be arrested and charged with the crime of aggravated assault and battery. A prosecutor may recommend that the charge be changed to *simple assault and battery* and transferred from criminal to civil court, where it can be dealt with as a tort action. In that situation, plaintiffs will not be seeking the defendant's imprisonment, but rather *they will seek damages, usually a sum of money for injuries sustained.* Transferring the case from criminal to civil status keeps the defendant from acquiring a criminal record and alleviates an already crowded criminal court docket.

Pretrial Diversion

Pretrial diversion *is a procedure that diverts criminal defendants to either a community-based agency for treatment or to a counselor for social and/or psychiatric assistance* (President's Commission on Law Enforcement and the Administration of Justice, 1967). Pretrial diversion may involve education, job training, counseling, or some type of psychological or physical therapy (Broderick et al., 1993; Hepburn et al., 1992).

A pretrial diversion temporarily removes a case from the criminal justice system. For instance, those who have been arrested for driving under the influence or have committed child sexual abuse involving family members may be granted pretrial diversion by the prosecutor rather than forced to go through a trial and admit their guilt publicly. Usually, a pretrial diversion involves complying with a number of conditions.

In Indianapolis, Indiana, for example, a study investigated the handling of spousal abuse complaints (Ford and Regoli, 1993). Victim-initiated complaints caused police to go to scenes of domestic violence and arrest batterers, who were mostly spouses but sometimes boyfriends. The experiment involved warrantless arrests, pretrial diversion, counseling as a condition of probation, fines, and probation or jail. Counseling and pretrial diversion seemed effective in decreasing the incidence of repeat assaults.

In many cases involving misdemeanor arrests, defendants have been found to be mentally disturbed. Courts have diverted the most serious cases to mental hospitals, where these defendants can be treated rather than punished. In a great proportion of the cases, the long-range outcomes included reductions of charges and outright case dismissals. Thus, diverting persons from the system who may be mentally disturbed seems to be effective (Ford and Regoli, 1993).

Unless the crime alleged is particularly serious, prosecutors usually try to keep first offenders out of prison. Not all first offenders are considered eligible for pretrial diversion programs, however. Usually, the prosecutor evaluates and determines the suitability of a particular alleged offender for pretrial diversion. Does the person have a prior criminal record? Is the person employed? Does the person have a good reputation in the community? Is the offense inconsistent with the person's character? Were there extraneous variables that contributed to the offender's conduct, such as financial hardship, divorce, loss of a family member, or some other traumatic event?

If a defendant is recommended for pretrial diversion, the court must approve the diversion and assign the offender to the supervision of an appropriate agency or service for a specified period. If offenders fail to comply with the terms of the diversionary program, their status reverts to whatever it was at the time pretrial diversion was granted, and the prosecution of the case will proceed. The importance of pretrial diversion cannot be underestimated, however. It helps the defendant avoid the criminal label and further involvement in the justice system.

Pretrial diversion is not without its critics. Implicit in any pretrial diversionary program is the defendant's admission of guilt to the crime(s) alleged. Technically, a courtroom appearance is avoided, and the defendant must comply with certain terms and conditions for a fixed period. At the end of the diversion period, defendants may have their records erased through **expungement orders,** provided that they complied with the provisions of the diversion. *Expungement orders are court-ordered suppressions of criminal or juvenile cases.* Thus, the defendant will have no police record (Blunt, 1976).

Plea Bargaining

The most popular pretrial alternative is **plea bargaining.** *Plea bargaining or plea negotiating is a preconviction agreement between the state and the accused whereby the defendant exchanges a plea of guilty or nolo contendere for a reduction in charges, a promise of sentencing leniency, or some other concession from full, maximum implementation of the conviction and sentencing authority of the court* (McDonald, 1985:5). The defendant enters a guilty plea with the reasonable expectation of receiving some consideration from the state (McDonald, 1985:6).

Plea bargaining is not new. Evidence of its use can be traced to the twelfth century (Alschuler, 1979). Plea bargaining is so pervasive in the United States today that many persons regard it as a standard feature of our criminal justice system (Alschuler, 1979). At the local, state, and federal levels, 80 to 90 percent of all criminal convictions annually are obtained through plea bargaining (Sanborn, 1993).

Plea bargaining is controversial. It is regarded as a time-saving device by its supporters. It is viewed as a denial of due process by its opponents. Some states, including Alaska, have prohibited it altogether in criminal cases, although most other states and the federal government condone it (Marenin, 1995).

If a defendant pleads guilty to certain criminal charges, the state is spared the time and expense of a trial. In fact, there is evidence that if the defendant refuses to plea bargain and is eventually convicted at trial, the sentence is often more severe than that proposed during the attempt to plea bargain (McConville and Mirsky, 1995; Myers and Reid, 1995).

Plea bargaining was officially condoned by the Supreme Court in the landmark case of *Brady v. United States* (1970). Brady and a codefendant were charged with kidnapping in violation of 18 U.S.C. Sec. 1201(a) (1996). Because the indictment charged that the victim of the kidnapping was not liberated unharmed, Brady faced the maximum penalty of death if the jury so recommended. The trial judge was reluctant to try the case without a jury, and in the meantime, a codefendant pleaded guilty and was available to testify against Brady. Brady entered a guilty plea and was subsequently sentenced to thirty years in prison.

In 1967, Brady petitioned the Supreme Court, contending that his plea was not voluntary because government prosecutors pressured him to plead guilty. The Supreme Court upheld the original verdict, holding that "although Brady's plea of guilty may well have been motivated in part by his desire to avoid a possible death penalty, we are convinced that his plea was voluntary and intelligently made and we have no reason to doubt that his solemn admission of guilt was truthful."

In that same case, the Court declared, "We cannot hold that it is unconstitutional for the State to extend a benefit to a defendant who in turn extends a substantial benefit to the State and who demonstrates by his plea that he is ready and willing to admit his crime and to enter the correctional system in a frame of mind that affords hope for success in rehabilitation over a shorter period of time than might otherwise be necessary."

In *North Carolina v. Alford* (1970), Alford was charged with first-degree murder, a capital crime in North Carolina at that time. There was considerable evidence against him. Although Alford protested his innocence, his attorney advised him to enter a plea of guilty to second-degree murder, which carried a maximum prison term of twenty years. Although he continued to maintain his innocence, Alford entered a guilty plea to second-degree murder and was sentenced to twenty years. Subsequently, Alford sought relief from a court of appeals, arguing that his plea was not voluntary but that he had entered the plea in order to escape the possible death penalty that may have been imposed had he been found guilty on the first-degree murder charge. The court of appeals overturned Alford's conviction for second-degree murder on the grounds that he was coerced into a guilty plea because of the possible imposition of the death penalty. The State of North Carolina appealed to the U.S. Supreme Court.

The Supreme Court reversed the court of appeals, reasoning that Alford was not unconstitutionally coerced into the plea of guilty to second-degree murder. Despite his protestations of innocence, the overwhelming evidence against him suggested that a trial on the first-degree murder charge would have resulted in a verdict of guilty. Thus, Alford had nothing to gain through a trial on first-degree murder, but he had much to gain by pleading guilty to a reduced murder charge.

In later years, the Supreme Court extended to the government wide discretion in the kinds of pressures it may exert on defendants if they do not agree to plea bargain with the government (*Bordenkircher v. Hayes,* 1978; *Santobello v. New York,* 1971) (see Highlight 8.5 for a brief discussion of the *Santobello* case). In the case of *Bordenkircher v. Hayes* (1978), the Supreme Court said, "The disposition of criminal charges by agreement between the prosecutor and the accused, sometimes loosely called 'plea bargaining,' is *an essential component* of the administration of justice. Properly administered, it is to be encouraged" (emphasis added).

About four times as many cases are plea-bargained as are brought to trial (McConville and Mirsky, 1995; McDonald, 1985). This proportion varies from one jurisdiction to the next, and it also varies when misdemeanor cases are compared with felony cases. A study of the misdemeanor disposition process in Philadelphia, Pennsylvania, municipal courts showed that one-fifth of all misdemeanor dispositions and one-half of all guilty verdicts resulted from genuine adversarial trials (Schulhofer, 1985). An examination of six hundred misdemeanor cases showed that even routine misdemeanor cases benefit from guarantees of fairness and accuracy afforded by trial. In many other jurisdictions, however, felony as well as misdemeanor convictions from trials are proportionately few compared with convictions obtained through plea bargaining (Fletcher, 1995; Pohlman, 1995).

There are four different systems of plea bargaining in the United States. One system is **implicit plea bargaining,** *where the defendant pleads guilty in the expectation of receiving a more lenient sentence.* The second is **charge-reduction bargaining,** *where the prosecutor downgrades the charges in return for the defendant's guilty plea.* A third is **judicial plea bargaining,** *where the judge offers a specific sentence in exchange for a guilty plea.* And the fourth is **sentence recommendation plea bar-**

Highlight 8.5. Plea Bargaining:
The Case of *Santobello v. New York*

Santobello v. New York, 404 U.S. 257, 92 S.Ct. 495 (1971). Santobello was charged with two felonies and pleaded guilty to a lesser-included offense following a promise by the prosecutor *not to make a sentence recommendation* at the plea bargain hearing. Several months lapsed, and in the meantime, a new prosecutor was appointed. At Santobello's plea hearing, the new prosecutor recommended *the maximum sentence under the law*, and Santobello moved to withdraw his guilty plea. The judge refused to allow the withdrawal of the guilty plea, and Santobello was sentenced to the maximum sentence. The Supreme Court heard San-

tobello's appeal. Santobello alleged that the prosecutor was honor-bound to stand by his promise not to make a sentence recommendation, despite the fact that the judge said that he was "uninfluenced" by the prosecutor's recommendation. The Court overturned Santabello's conviction and allowed him to withdraw his guilty plea, saying that when a guilty plea rests to a significant degree on a promise or agreement by the prosecutor, such a promise *must be fulfilled*. This case is significant because it establishes that prosecutors must fulfill promises they make to defendants to elicit guilty pleas.

gaining, *where the prosecutor proposes a sentence in exchange for a guilty plea* (Padgett, 1985). A plea bargain agreement may contain one or more promises or provisions, including a reduction in charges, leniency in sentencing or a recommendation for a specific type of sentence, and proposals *not* to prosecute the defendant for other crimes alleged or seek enhancement of punishment.

Historically, some form of plea bargaining has always been observed in the United States and even in the colonies. After the founding of the United States, various state courts gradually incorporated plea bargaining into their justice systems. In New York State in 1839, for instance, only 22 percent of all criminal convictions for the entire state were obtained through plea bargaining. By 1869, this figure had risen to 70 percent, and by 1920, it had reached 88 percent (McDonald, 1985:3).

But federal court rules are not binding on state courts. For instance, the rules governing plea bargaining in federal district courts are not constitutionally mandated for state courts. The Supreme Court has held that the federal procedural rule relating to the acceptance of guilty pleas must be observed scrupulously by the federal courts, but the precise terms of this rule are not constitutionally applicable to state courts (*Roddy v. Black,* 1975; *Osborne v. Thompson,* 1979; *Neeley v. Duckworth,*

1979; *Winegar v. Corrections Department,* 1975). Most states use plea bargaining, however, and some states have copied the rules followed by federal district courts in their own plea agreement procedures.

The most prevalent plea bargaining systems involve charge reduction and leniency. But in every jurisdiction the final arbiter in a plea bargaining agreement is the judge. Judges are not bound to observe the conditions of any plea agreement. They usually approve the plea agreement between the prosecution and defense, but they reserve the right to reject the plea agreement. Also, they may decide to impose maximum sentences and fines upon a defendant who pleads guilty even when a prosecutor favors milder sanctions or even probation (Pohlman, 1995).

Federal prosecutors may make only four concessions in a plea bargain agreement. First, the charge may be reduced to a lesser or related offense. Second, the prosecutor may promise to move for dismissal of other charges. Third, the prosecutor may agree to recommend or at least to not oppose a particular sentence. And fourth, the prosecutor and the defense may agree on a given sentence.

An example of an actual plea bargain agreement between the U.S. Attorney's Office and a defendant in the Eastern District of Tennessee is shown in figure 8.1. In this plea agreement, the

Figure 8.1 Federal Plea Bargain Agreement

United States Department of Justice

UNITED STATES ATTORNEY
EASTERN DISTRICT OF TENNESSEE
P.O. BOX 872
KNOXVILLE, TENNESSEE 37901
July 15,

IN REPLY, PLEASE
REFER TO FILE NO.

Dear

RE:

On May 2,   , Ed Wilson and I met with   regarding a proposed plea bargain for the captioned individual. Due to your absence from the office the original deadline for acceptance was informally extended "until you had time to discuss the situation with   ". To date, I have not heard anything relative to acceptance or rejection.

As we are now prepared to begin Grand Jury proceedings in the immediate future on this matter which will involve calling a number of witnesses from various parts of the country at significant expense to the Government, I want to clarify our offer and set a firm deadline for action.

We believe that Mr.   violated 18 U.S.C.   and   as the result of his purchasing, transporting and subsequently selling certain stolen   beginning in the summer of   . This Office has proposed the following plea bargain which if accepted would be followed by the filing of an information and subsequent presentation of the plea bargain to Judge Taylor for approval. This offer is also contingent upon a proffer by you or your client's testimony regarding this matter and which, if acceptable to us, would be followed by the following plea bargain presentation to the Court:

1) $10,000 fine
2) Three year probation (payment of fine condition thereto)
3) Furnish detailed account of his dealings with the stolen   to FBI
4) No   prosecution
5) Immunity for any further violations arising from transactions from June,   , to date of information. (Please note as I have advised you earlier this is not as broad as the "transactional immunity" previously discussed with Mr.   on May 2nd.)

If in fact the case is going to be plea bargained, it must be done so before the Government incurs additional significant expense. Therefore, I am placing a deadline of July 31,   , on the offer. If the bargain is not accepted by the end of that date, it will be withdrawn and terminated. Please discuss this matter with Mr.   and advise us of your decision.

Very truly yours,

JOHN H. CARY
United States Attorney

J. Michael Haynes

BY: J. MICHAEL HAYNES
Assistant United States Attorney

JMH:sjv

U.S. attorney at that time, John H. Cary, and assistant U.S. attorneys J. Michael Haynes and Edward Wilson offered a defendant in a criminal prosecution involving several counts of interstate transportation of stolen property and conspiracy a number of concessions in exchange for a guilty plea. The total fines and maximum statutory imprisonment for the original charges totalled $285,000 and forty-five years.

In exchange for a plea of guilty to one count of interstate transportation of stolen property having a value in excess of $5,000, the government offered the following plea bargain: (1) the defendant must pay a $10,000 fine; (2) the defendant must accept a three-year probation term; (3) the defendant must testify against a codefendant in a later trial and disclose all transactional details of the stolen property matter; (4) there would be no further prosecution of the defendant for any of the other charges; and (5) the defendant would receive immunity from prosecution for any further violations arising from the original transactions (e.g., receiving and concealing stolen property, selling stolen property, and so on).

In this case, the defendant rejected the plea agreement, went to trial twice in the federal district court (the first trial resulted in an undecided jury and a mistrial was declared), and was subsequently acquitted of all charges. The codefendant was offered a similar plea bargain agreement, accepted it, and served one year in a medium-security federal prison.

Because a defendant waives a number of important constitutional rights when he or she enters a guilty plea, both federal and state trial courts make especially sure that the defendant's due process rights are fully observed. When one or more of these rights are violated or infringed by the courts and prosecutors, the defendant has grounds to appeal the case to a higher court (Dixon, 1995).

While state and local trial courts are not bound to comply strictly with the same plea bargaining rules governing federal trial judges, and while these same courts are not bound to accept plea bargaining in any form as an alternative to trial, these courts *are bound* to observe defendants' constitutional rights. These rights override and take precedence over local and state procedures and are guaranteed to every citizen under the Fifth, Sixth, and Fourteenth Amendments of the U.S. Constitution (*United States v. French*, 1983; *United States v. Carter*, 1981; *Clemmons v. United States*, 1983).

Because the rules followed by federal district judges in plea bargain agreements and the general plea agreement procedure encompass all of a citizens' rights in this regard, it is helpful to examine the substance of these rules. Under the provisions of Title 18 U.S.C., Rule 11 (1996), whenever defendants enter a plea of guilty or *nolo contendere*, a judge MUST address these defendants personally in open court to determine if they understand the following:

1. The nature of the charge(s) to which the plea is offered;
2. The maximum possible penalty provided by law;
3. The mandatory minimum penalty as provided by law;
4. The effect of any special parole term, and any special provisions for compensating victims;
5. If defendants do not have an attorney, they have a right to one; if one cannot be afforded, one will be appointed at state expense;
6. Defendants have a right to plead not guilty and withdraw the guilty plea at any time;
7. Defendants have the right to a trial by jury, and they have the right to assistance of counsel at the trial;
8. Defendants have the right to confront and cross-examine witnesses against them;
9. Defendants have a right not to incriminate themselves;
10. If the plea of guilty or *nolo contendere* is accepted, there will be no further trial of any kind; therefore the plea is a waiver of a right to a trial;
11. There is a factual basis for the plea;
12. That the plea is voluntarily given and that it is not the result of force or threats or coercion apart from a plea agreement;
13. That the judge may accept or reject the plea agreement;
14. That the plea is accurate; and
15. If the plea is the result of prior discussions between prosecutors and defendants or their attorney.

Title 18 U.S.C., Rule 11 (1996) also prohibits the district judge from participating in the plea agreement negotiations between the prosecution and defense. This prohibition protects defendants from a conflict of interest that might arise from the fact that federal judges would be faced with approving or disapproving a plea agreement that they helped to formulate.

Highlight 8.6. Plea Bargaining Gone Awry

Can Judges Ignore Sentences Contemplated in Plea Agreements and Impose Harsher Sentences? Yes!

Alabama v. Smith, 490 U.S. 794, 109 S.Ct. 2201 (1989). A grand jury indicted James Smith for burglary, rape, sodomy, and assault. Smith entered a guilty plea and was convicted of first-degree burglary and rape. In exchange he received a thirty-year sentence, and the sodomy charge was dropped. The judge sentenced Smith to concurrent terms of thirty years on each of the other charges. Later, Smith succeeded in having his guilty plea vacated. A trial was held on the three original charges. The jury found him guilty on all counts, and this time the judge sentenced Smith to life imprisonment for the burglary and sodomy convictions and one hundred fifty years on the rape conviction. The judge justified the different sentences on the grounds that he had not been fully aware of the circumstances under which these terrible crimes had occurred. Smith appealed, alleging that the sentence was *vindictive. The U.S. Supreme Court rejected Smith's claim that the new sentence was vindictive, because it could not be demonstrated that the judge deliberately enhanced these sentences on account of the previous vacating of Smith's earlier guilty plea. The Court also stressed that in cases that go to trial, greater and more detailed information is available to sentencing judges compared with the information received as a part of a plea bargain agreement.*

Can Judges Flout Mandatory Sentencing and Get Away with It? No!

People v. Hipp, 861 S.W.2d 377 (1993). The court determined that Hipp was addicted to gambling.

Mandatory sentencing laws compel the court to prescribe a jail term as well as therapy for the addiction. In this instance, the judge simply accepted a plea agreement, accepting the defendant's guilty plea in exchange for a term of probation. The New York Court of Appeals overruled the judge, indicating that New York statutes do not authorize a trial court to ignore clearly expressed and unequivocal mandatory sentencing provisions of the New York Penal Law.

Can Defendants Not Uphold Their End of a Plea Bargain and Get Away with It? No!

Ricketts v. Adamson, 463 U.S. 1, 107 S.Ct. 2860 (1987). Defendants must uphold their end of the plea agreement or suffer the consequences. Adamson was convicted of murder. Prior to his conviction, he entered into a plea bargain whereby he would plead guilty to second-degree murder and testify against his co-defendants. The prosecutor indicated that if Adamson *refused to cooperate,* the terms of his plea agreement would be *null and void.* Adamson was convicted of second-degree murder, but during the later trial of his co-defendants, he refused to testify. The Arizona Supreme Court reversed his conviction on the grounds outlined by the prosecutor, and Adamson was tried again for *first-degree murder.* Adamson appealed his conviction, contending that this retrial constituted double jeopardy. The Supreme Court upheld his first-degree murder conviction, saying that his prosecution for first-degree murder did not violate the principle of double jeopardy, because his breach of the plea agreement removed the double jeopardy bar that otherwise would prevail, assuming that under state law second-degree murder is a lesser-included offense of first-degree murder.

All plea agreement hearings and proceedings are recorded. This is a requirement in the event that a defendant wishes to appeal the decision of the trial judge or any portion of the plea agreement. For example, some defendants have appealed to higher courts on the grounds that the federal judge did not advise them of all their rights as stated in 18 U.S.C., Rule 11 (1996) (*United States v. Thompson*, 1982; *United States v. Cooper*, 1984).

In the Illinois case of *United States. v. Thompson* (1982), Thompson claimed in his appeal that the district judge failed to read verbatim the admonitions for federal judges to follow as set forth in 18 U.S.C., Rule 11 (1996). The Supreme Court affirmed Thompson's conviction and held that "[t]his rule should not be read as requiring litany, or any other ritual which can be carried out by word-for-word adherence as to set script, but rather, it is sufficient if colloquy between the court and the defendant would lead a reasonable person to believe that the defendant understood the nature of the charge."

However, in the 1981 Arkansas case of *United States v. Riegelsperger,* the district judge asked Riegelsperger general questions about whether threats or promises had been made but failed to advise him that the court was not obligated to follow the plea agreement. The judge also failed to ask if the guilty plea was the result of prior discussions between the prosecution and defense. The Supreme Court reversed Riegelsperger's conviction on these grounds and sent the case back to the lower court for further processing. At least for the federal judiciary, these rules are extremely important; and everything in these rules pertaining to a defendant's constitutional rights is critical in all state trial courts where plea agreements are arranged.

In state and local trial courts where plea bargaining is permitted, there is considerable variation in plea agreement hearings as well as in the procedures prosecutors follow in constructing plea bargains.

In some jurisdictions, prosecutors engage in **overcharging** criminal defendants (McDonald, 1985:20; Utz, 1979:105). *Overcharging is filing charges against a defendant more serious than the ones the prosecutor believes are justified by the evidence and charging more, or more serious, counts than those on which the prosecutor wants a conviction*

(Bond, 1981:231). Overcharging is a crude form of blackmail (Alschuler, 1975). A defendant facing many charges will often feel relieved when the prosecution offers to drop all but one in exchange for a guilty plea. The prosecutor's original intention may have been to secure a guilty plea to the single charge anyway (Holten and Jones, 1982).

The American Bar Association (1971) and the American Law Institute (1975) have outlined some of prosecutors' ethical obligations relating to overcharging. Some of these obligations are that (1) it is unprofessional to institute criminal charges without probable cause; (2) the prosecutor is not obligated to present all of the charges that the evidence might support; (3) the prosecutor should not bring or seek more, or more serious, charges than the evidence can support; (4) the prosecutor shall not seek to obtain a plea of guilty or *nolo contendere* by charging or threatening to charge a defendant with a crime not supported by the facts believed by the prosecutor to be provable; and (5) the prosecutor shall not charge or threaten to charge a defendant with a crime not ordinarily charged in the jurisdiction for the conduct allegedly engaged in by him or her.

While overcharging probably occurs in all jurisdictions, some critics have cautioned that more often than not, overcharging is a misnomer. This is because the defendant has, in fact, committed all of the crimes alleged (McDonald, 1985). But overcharging does pressure defendants to seriously consider pleading guilty to at least one of the offenses alleged.

The plea bargaining process proceeds differently in different jurisdictions. In one jurisdiction, defense attorneys may routinely approach prosecutors with an offer from their client. In another jurisdiction, the prosecutor may make the initial offer. In a study of dialogues between prosecutors and defense attorneys, it was found that out of fifty-two cases studied, twenty-seven were settled when one party took a position (made an offer) with which the other aligned (Maynard, 1982). Another twenty-one cases were settled when, after both parties advanced a position, one of them aligned with the other's. Only three cases were settled by compromise between the two parties' positions.

Some cities have used *criminal bench trials* in which the state promises to drop charges or reduce sentences if defendants waive their right to a jury trial (New York City Criminal Justice Agency, 1992). While this practice has been challenged as unconstitutional, it continues to be used in a limited number of jurisdictions, where it has significantly shortened case-processing time.

Extensive studies of plea bargaining have been made in jurisdictions such as El Paso, New Orleans, Seattle, Tucson, and Norfolk (McDonald, 1985). It has been found that many local and state jurisdictions regularly violate defendants' constitutional rights and that these violations occur with little or no resistance from the defendants themselves. In many jurisdictions, defendants merely sign a waiver or a plea agreement initialing each right waived. A standard plea agreement form used by judges in criminal district courts in New Orleans is shown in figure 8.2.

While federal district judges are prohibited from participating in plea bargaining negotiations, this is not necessarily the case in state and local jurisdictions. In Tennessee, all state trial judges follow the federal rules rigidly and have adopted them into their rules of criminal procedure. In other states and jurisdictions where plea bargaining occurs, however, trial judges sometimes take part in plea bargaining proceedings (Ryan and Alfini, 1978; Alschuler, 1979). In spite of the obvious "conflict of interest" problems created by such judicial participation, these jurisdictions continue to condone it.

The Pros and Cons of Plea Bargaining

What are the pros and cons of plea bargaining for U.S. courts at all levels? On the positive side, plea bargaining (1) saves a defendant time and money for attorney fees; (2) saves the state the time and expense of a trial proceeding; (3) makes it possible for prosecutors and defense attorneys to handle more cases annually and to dispose of more cases with results favorable to both sides; (4) permits the state to devote more time and attention to more serious cases; and (5) increases the likelihood of leniency toward the defendant in exchange for cooperating with the government (Roberts, 1994; Stitt and Chaires, 1993).

On the negative side, critics argue that plea bargaining (1) deprives a defendant of the right to due process; (2) shortchanges the justice system by depriving society of just and equitable retribution against offenders who are offered leniency when their punishments should be more severe; (3) results in implied coercion from prosecutors through overcharging; (4) involves self-incrimination in direct violation of the Fifth Amendment; (5) is a violation of attorneys' code of professional ethics; and (6) often induces innocent defendants to plead guilty, known as *false convictions* (Holmes, Hosch, and Daudistel, 1993; Sanborn, 1993; Virginia State Crime Commission, 1994b).

Among other states and jurisdictions, Alaska has banned plea bargaining (Marenin, 1995). For the most part this has effectively eliminated sentence bargaining, in which the prosecutor could offer a reduced sentence or no sentence at all. Alaska currently follows what is known as presumptive sentencing, where statutes prescribe a specific range of imprisonment for each offense. For example, a conviction for some offense might carry a five-year prison term. The judge is permitted to vary this term between four and six years, depending upon the circumstances of the particular case. A mitigating circumstance might be that the person is elderly (Kerstetter, 1990). An aggravating circumstance might be that serious bodily harm was inflicted during the commission of the crime or that a firearm was used (Acker and Lanier, 1993).

However, Alaska prosecutors have sidestepped the plea bargaining ban by negotiating with defense attorneys about the nature of charges against their clients. Aggravated assault and battery might be reduced to simple assault, for example, if the defendant pleads guilty to that particular offense. Thus, charge bargaining continues in many jurisdictions, including Alaska, and little if anything can be done about it. The types and numbers of charges brought against a particular defendant are ordinarily within the discretionary powers of prosecutors and police.

In all plea agreement hearings, a judge assesses the fairness of the agreement. Various studies of this process show disparities regarding judicial supervision of the plea agreement proceeding. Having defendants sign a form such as that shown in figure 8.2, for instance, is an *insuf-*

Figure 8.2 Guilty Plea Acceptance Form for New Orleans, Louisiana: Alternative Procedure for Accepting Guilty Pleas Used by Local Judges

CRIMINAL DISTRICT COURT
PARISH OF ORLEAN
STATE OF LOUISIANA
SECTION "D"

STATE OF LOUISIANA

vs.

_____

JUDGE: <u>FRANK A. MARULLO, JR.</u>

NO. _____

VIO: _____

<u>PLEA OF GUILTY</u>

I, _____, defendant in the above case informed the Court that I wanted to plead guilty and do plead guilty to the crime of _____ and have been informed and understand the charge to which I am pleading guilty. (_____)

The acts which make up the crime to which I am pleading have been explained to me as well as the fact that for this crime I could possibly receive a sentence of _____. (_____)

I understand that in pleading guilty in this matter I waive the following rights:

(1) To a trial by either a judge or a jury and that further the right to a trial by judge extends until the first witness is sworn, and the right to a trial by jury extends until the first juror is sworn, and if convicted the right to an appeal.
Please specify: Judge trial or Jury trial   (_____)

(2) To face and cross-examine the witnesses who accuse me
of the crime charged.   (_____)

(3) The privilege against self-incrimination or having to take
the stand myself and testify.   (_____)

(4) To have the Court compel my witness to appear and testify.   (_____)

I am entering a plea of guilty to this crime because I am, in fact, guilty of this crime. I have not been forced, threatened, or intimidated into making this plea, nor has anyone made me promises in order that I enter a plea. I am fully satisfied with the handling of my case by my attorney and the way in which he has represented me. I am satisfied with the way the Court has handled this matter. (_____)

_____
DEFENDANT

_____
JUDGE

_____
ATTORNEY FOR DEFENDANT

DATE: _____

NOTE: Defendant is to place his initials in the blocks provided for same.
Defendant is to block out Judge trial or Jury trial as it applies.

Highlight 8.7. An Example of Plea Bargaining: The Case of Adrian Alex

Donald Jerome, thirty-one, the manager of a convenience store in Devils Lake, North Dakota, was shot in the back of the head during an armed robbery on December 14, 1995. Charged with murder and armed robbery and waived to criminal court to be tried as adults were Marlon Comes, fifteen, Wayne Greywater, sixteen, and Adrian Alex, seventeen.

All three teenagers originally entered pleas of not guilty to the murder and robbery charges. Prosecutors indicated they would seek the maximum penalty of life in prison without the possibility of parole for all three defendants. Suddenly, in June 1996, one of the suspects changed his mind and decided to plead guilty.

Adrian Alex had cooperated with police from the beginning, according to Ramsey County state's attorney, Lonnie Olson. Alex gave incriminating details of his and his two associates' involvement in the crime. He spelled out how the robbery was to progress and how they would handle the store clerk.

Alex plea bargained with the prosecution. In exchange for the prosecutor's *not* seeking the maximum penalty for Alex, Alex agreed to testify against the other two teenagers at their subsequent trial. Olson said, "Now that he has changed his plea to guilty, he no longer can invoke the Fifth Amendment privilege against self-incrimination. And so upon trial for either of the other defendants, it is anticipated we would call him as a witness." The sentence for Alex will likely be a certain number of years, with the possibility of parole.

Should murderers be allowed to plea bargain in order to escape harsh penalties for their crimes? What benefits accrue to prosecutors when plea bargains such as this one are worked out? Does society benefit? How will this plea bargain affect the trial of the other two defendants? Should they also be allowed to plea bargain if they decide to change their pleas?

Source: Adapted from Associated Press, "One of Three Charged with Clerk Murder Pleads Guilty," *Minot (N.D.) Daily News,* May 16, 1996, p. A5.

---

ficient guarantee that they fully realize the rights being relinquished. Furthermore, that particular form has no provision for determining the factual basis for the original guilty plea. Finally, defendants are signing away their right to an appeal. This is in spite of the fact that certain procedural irregularities might occur that would otherwise void the guilty plea.

There is a nationwide trend toward greater use of plea bargaining, particularly in felony cases. In California, for example, approximately 70 percent of convicted felony offenders are placed on probation rather than incarcerated (Petersilia, 1985b). Thus, probation is used increasingly as an incentive for alleged offenders to plead guilty (Roberts, 1994). Many of the offenses committed by defendants who are eventually placed on probation rather than incarcerated are nonviolent and petty crimes such as theft or burglary.

In crimes involving armed robbery, forcible rape, and homicide, the likelihood of probation is remote. Much of what happens to offenders when they enter the criminal justice system depends on what is occurring in other parts of the system, especially corrections. When prisons are overcrowded and cannot accommodate growing numbers of convicts, different sentencing alternatives must be considered. The plea bargain phase considers such factors as well as the offender's age and prior record and the seriousness of the crime. If these pretrial alternatives fail, if the defendant persists in pleading not guilty, and if the prosecution persists in pursuing criminal charges, a trial is held. This will be discussed in chapter 9.

Summary

Prosecutors perform many functions, including representing the state when persons are charged with criminal offenses. Prosecutors initially screen cases to determine which ones have prosecutive merit. Like detectives, they evaluate the sufficiency of evidence against the accused and determine the probability of the defendant's guilt or innocence. Prosecutors also represent the state before the grand jury and present evidence of an alleged offender's guilt. They also present the case for the government in a formal trial.

Defense attorneys confer with the prosecution and determine the nature of the case against the accused. They attempt to prevent prosecution of their clients. They also confer with prosecutors and perhaps work out plea agreements that are acceptable to all concerned.

Several alternatives to criminal court proceedings that occur in the pretrial phase are police cautioning, transferral of a criminal case to a civil court if possible, and pretrial diversion for those who qualify. These serve to prevent the taint of criminal prosecution and possible conviction. Finally, plea bargaining may occur.

Plea bargaining is an attempt by the prosecution to secure a guilty plea from a defendant in exchange for certain concessions, including a reduced sentence, a reduction in charges, or probation. Plea bargaining is used at the federal, state, and local levels. The process of plea bargaining varies from one jurisdiction to the next. In some states, such as Alaska, plea bargaining has been banned. It has both proponents and critics. It is seen largely as a time-saving device by prosecutors and defense attorneys alike, but others regard plea bargaining as a threat to a defendant's right to due process under the Constitution.

Between 80 and 90 percent of all criminal convictions are obtained through plea bargaining. At the federal level, strict safeguards govern the conduct of district judges in approving plea agreements. Much variation occurs at the local and state levels regarding this process, however. This chapter examined some of the major uses of plea bargaining as well as some of its strengths and weaknesses.

Key Terms

Charge-reduction bargaining
Discovery
Exculpatory evidence
Expungement orders
Implicit plea bargaining
Inculpatory evidence
Judicial plea bargaining
Malicious prosecution
Overcharging
Plea bargaining
Police cautioning
Pretrial diversion
Public defenders
Screening
Sentence recommendation plea bargaining

Questions for Review

1. What is plea bargaining? Is it used in all states and jurisdictions?
2. What is pretrial diversion? Do all persons who request pretrial diversion get it? Why or why not?
3. What constitutional amendments come into play when a person enters a plea of guilty?
4. Why does a prosecutor screen cases?
5. What is overcharging? What are some of the functions of overcharging?
6. What is police cautioning? Give two examples of circumstances in which police cautioning might be used?
7. What was the significance of *Gideon v. Wainwright*?
8. Are indigent defendants entitled to an attorney if they cannot afford one? What has the Supreme Court ruled on this issue?
9. What is a public defender?
10. Do our state and federal prison policies affect the plea bargaining process? Explain.

Suggested Readings

Flango, Victor E. *Habeas Corpus in State and Federal Courts.* Williamsburg, VA: National Center for State Courts, 1994.

Freedman, Warren. *The Constitutional Right to a Speedy and Fair Criminal Trial.* New York: Quorum Books, 1989.

McDonald, William F. (ed.). *The Defense Counsel.* Beverly Hills, CA: Sage, 1983.

McDonald, William F. *Plea Bargaining: Critical Issues and Common Practices.* Washington, DC: U.S. Government Printing Office, 1985.

Pohlman, H.L. *Constitutional Debate in Action: Criminal Justice.* New York: HarperCollins, 1995.

U.S. General Accounting Office. *Federal Criminal Justice: Cost of Providing Court-Appointed Attorneys Is Rising, But Causes Are Unclear.* Washington, DC: U.S. General Accounting Office, 1995.

CHAPTER 9

Juries and Trial Procedures

A jury trial is in progress. The process of jury selection is continuing. Mary Smith is accused of murdering her husband, Tony Smith, a factory worker. Mary claims self-defense because Tony beat her frequently and had threatened her life on the night she shot him with his own handgun. Tony was asleep at the time, following a night of heavy drinking. Mary has two young children. She is unemployed but worked as a waitress for several years. Tony's family disliked Mary, even before she married Tony. They claimed she was "trash," partly because she had been married twice before. Tony carried a $200,000 life insurance policy for himself, naming Mary as his sole beneficiary. Tony had a history of spousal abuse and had previously been arrested for abusing a former wife. Mary has no record, although depositions from others suggest that she is hot-tempered and physically abusive. Neighbors say that Mary and Tony Smith fought frequently and that the children were "scared" and often ran next door seeking protection.

Jury selection is seemingly very scientific. "Let's go with the unemployed mother of three," says the defense jury consultant. "She will be sympathetic with our client, who is also an unemployed mother. Further, let's get rid of the two men, the welder and the machinist. They probably would identify with our client's dead husband, a former factory worker." The defense attorney advises the judge, "Prospective jurors number three and number six are excused. Prospective juror number eight is acceptable."

At the other end of the table, another professional jury consultant whispers to the prosecutor, "Let's excuse the woman with the three children. She will be too sympathetic with the defendant. Let's also get rid of the two women, prospective jurors one and twelve, who are housewives." The prosecutor rises and addresses the judge. "We wish to excuse prospective jurors one, eight, and twelve, your honor."

The judge says, "Very well. Prospective jurors one, three, six, eight, and twelve are hereby excused. Thank you for coming. We will now have the bailiff call the next five prospective jurors." The bailiff rises and says, "Will prospective jurors thirty-six, thirty-seven, thirty-eight, thirty-nine, and forty please take the vacated seats in the jury box?" Five persons rise from their seats and take the empty seats in the jury box. By now, after five hours of jury selection, the prosecution and defense have agreed on only seven jurors for the trial. They need to select five more. So the jury selection process continues.

This chapter is about the trial process. Different types of trial systems will be described. Many trials involve juries of one's peers. Whenever jury trials are conducted, persons from the community are selected for jury service. These persons form the pool from which the jurors will be selected. The jury selection process will be presented.

Several constitutional amendments pertain to jury trials and one's right to a trial. The Sixth Amendment guarantees all persons the right to a trial by jury. The Seventh Amendment provides that the right of trial by jury shall be preserved. And finally, the Fourteenth Amendment guarantees that no state shall make or enforce any law that deprives citizens of their rights to due process or to enjoy all privileges or immunities as citizens (see chapter 3 for a discussion of these amendments).

The chapter begins by distinguishing between bench and jury trials. Next, the process of selecting jurors is described in detail, commencing with the creation of a list of prospective jurors and continuing with a screening process known as *voir dire*. Once jury members have been selected and the trial begins, judges are bound to observe rules of criminal procedure. These rules govern the conduct of trial proceedings. Other rules, such as rules of evidence, govern the nature of evidence that may be introduced or excluded.

Trial proceedings are also accompanied by pretrial motions. Such motions will be described and explained. Both the prosecution and defense present opening statements. The government presents its case against the defendant; this is followed by the defense's case. Witnesses from both sides are called in these *adversarial proceedings*. Witnesses are cross-examined by each side to determine their veracity and reliability. When the trial is concluded, the prosecution and defense present summations or closing arguments. The jury then begins its deliberations. Juries either reach verdicts or judgments or fail to reach them. The process of jury deliberation and voting will be described. The fed-

eral and state governments have different criteria that govern jury deliberations and voting for a defendant's guilt or acquittal. These different scenarios will be described. The chapter concludes with a description of the aftermath of jury deliberations and verdicts and of the judge's role in sentencing.

Bench Trials and Jury Trials Contrasted

The system of trial by jury first appeared in the United States in 1607 under a charter granted to the Virginia Company in Jamestown by James I. However, jury trials were held as early as the eleventh century in England (Simon, 1980:5). A **criminal trial** is *an adversarial proceeding within a particular jurisdiction. In a criminal trial a judicial examination and determination of issues can be made and a criminal defendant's guilt or innocence can be decided impartially by either a judge or jury* (Black, 1990:52). Each year there are at least 500,000 criminal trials for felonies (Maguire and Pastore, 1995). The number of nonjury trials is many times higher. About 80 percent of all jury trials are civil; the rest are criminal.

In U.S. district courts, for example, 59,625 defendants were prosecuted in 1994 (Maguire and Pastore, 1995:460). Federal district judges dismissed 8,669 of these cases (14.4 percent), while 1,239 defendants were acquitted either by a judge or jury. The remaining 49,717 defendants were convicted. Of these, 91.4 percent (45,429) entered guilty pleas through plea bargaining or by pleading *nolo contendere*, or "no contest." Federal juries found guilty 3,797 of the defendants who actually went to trial, while judges found 491 defendants guilty. About 15 percent (693) of the defendants who had federal jury trials in 1994 were acquitted; 85 percent (3,797) were found guilty.

In contrast, state courts obtained 893,630 felony convictions in 1992 (Maguire and Pastore, 1995:485). About 90 percent of the convictions in both state and federal courts were reached by plea bargaining.

There are two types of trials: (1) bench trials and (2) jury trials.

Bench Trials

Bench trials, *also known as trials by the court or trials by the judge, are conducted in cases where petty offenses are involved and a jury is not permitted or defendants waive their right to a jury trial.* A judge presides, hears the evidence, and decides the case, relying on rational principles of law.

The popular television show *The People's Court* depicts bench trials. In those cases, litigants, or parties to the lawsuits, have waived their right to a jury trial and have permitted the judge to decide their case. In criminal courts, defendants often waive their right to a jury trial and permit the judge to decide their case on the basis of the evidence.

One reason for waiving one's right to a jury trial is that juries are sometimes more likely than judges to convict persons for felonies (Smith and Stevens, 1984). If the crimes alleged are especially heinous or involve emotionally charged issues, defendants will often opt for a bench trial because juries might be more persuaded by emotional appeals and arguments from prosecutors. In the early 1990s, for example, the Reverend Moon, known for his converts referred to as "Moonies," was on trial for income tax evasion. Because of the sensationalism associated with his religion and his impact on thousands of teenaged followers, his defense attorney requested a bench trial (Wettstein, 1992). Other cases involving cults accused of child abuse have also been decided by judges rather than juries, reflecting the defense's belief that judges might be more impartial in deciding the factual evidence (Wettstein, 1992).

From a purely practical standpoint, bench trials are more efficient than jury trials because judges can hear evidence and decide a case more quickly, especially considering the fact that jury selection and deliberations are avoided. In New York City, for instance, the *Misdemeanor Trial Law* took effect in 1985. The purpose of this law was to reduce jail terms for certain types of misdemeanors to *six months or less,* meaning that jury trials involving these offenses could be avoided (Dynia, 1987, 1990). Case backlogs and overall case flow were expedited. Although sentencing patterns among judges remained about the same both before and after the law went into effect, more rapid case processing was observed.

There are some negative aspects of bench trials. Some judges are influenced by extralegal factors, such as race, class, ethnicity, and/or gender (Stolzenberg, 1993; Williams, 1995a, 1995b). Judges are also influenced by their own personal feelings about the types of offenses being tried. Some judges, for instance, impose more severe sentences on those convicted of specific types of heinous offenses, such as child sexual abuse, than on those convicted of rape, aggravated assault, and murder (Champion, 1988a).

When judges decide cases on their own, they are more susceptible to corruption. Influential defendants sometimes target specific judges for bribery. In recent years, judges at the state and federal levels have been charged with corruption and of accepting bribes to render decisions favorable to their constituency. *Bribery is the giving or offering of anything to someone in a position of trust to induce that person to act dishonestly* (Driscoll, 1984). In 1987, the Pennsylvania Supreme Court temporarily suspended 15 of 105 judges who were under investigation by the FBI and other agencies for suspected bribery. *Operation Greylord,* a sting operation against corrupt judges, was begun in 1978 in Cook County, Illinois. FBI agents tapped judges' telephones, recorded conversations, and initiated fake bribery attempts to induce judges to act dishonestly in deciding cases. Over the next several years Operation Greylord succeeded in obtaining convictions against over sixty judges for various criminal misconduct charges, including bribery (Bensinger, 1988). Recommendations made by the American Bar Association following Operation Greylord included adopting new ethical requirements for judges and attorneys and implementing procedural safeguards to monitor judges' conduct.

Briefly summarizing, the major advantages of bench trials are that:

1. Case processing is expedited.
2. Cases are usually decided on the merits of the case rather than on emotionally charged appeals in the case of heinous offenses.
3. Judges can usually be dissuaded from considering such extralegal factors as defendants' appearance.
4. In complex cases, judges are often in a better

position to evaluate the sufficiency of evidence against the accused and make fairer judgments.

5. Judges are less likely than juries to be influenced by media attention given to high-profile cases.

6. Bench trials are usually cheaper than jury trials, because they don't take as long to complete.

Some of the major disadvantages of bench trials are:

1. Judges may impose more severe punishments on defendants convicted of certain types of crimes.

2. Judges acting alone are more susceptible to corruption.

3. Juries may be more favorably influenced than judges by the defendant's situation, appearance, and emotional appeal.

Jury Trials

Persons charged with felonies are guaranteed the right to a **jury trial** in the United States. This guarantee also applies to states. The landmark case of *Duncan v. Louisiana* (1968) specifies that the right to a jury trial applies only to those offenses other than petty crimes that can be punished by a prison term of *more than six months*. Other cases such as *Baldwin v. New York* (1970) and *Blanton v. City of North Las Vegas, Nev.* (1989) have upheld this standard.

In the last few decades, the number of trials by jury has increased for both major crimes and lesser offenses or misdemeanors (Maguire and Pastore, 1995). Also, criminal convictions are obtained increasingly through plea bargaining (McDonald, 1985). And in at least one major city, the number of jury trials of *all* dispositions of felony arrests has dropped to 2 percent (Hans and Vidmar, 1986:6).

Juries: Their Forms and Functions

A jury is supposed to consist of a defendant's peers. *Peers are one's equals.* This means that defendants

are entitled to a jury of their "equals" in rank and station. This concept originated with the Magna Carta (Black, 1990:855–56, 1132). Today, *to be tried by a jury of one's peers means to be tried by a jury of citizens who may or may not be of the same rank and station as the accused* (Trugman, 1986).

We have already discussed *grand juries,* or special bodies that are convened to hear evidence against defendants and issue either *no bills* or *true bills.* Distinguished from grand juries is the **petit jury**, or *body of persons who hear the facts in cases against a defendant and decide guilt or innocence.* Ordinarily, when jury trials are conducted, reference is made simply to *the jury* rather than to *the petit jury.* In this text, the term *jury* refers to any group of persons selected to hear and decide the facts in cases. Juries are also called *fact-finders* or *finders of fact.*

Veniremen Lists

For federal and state courts, jurors are selected several ways. In each federal district, a *venire* or list of persons is prepared from which a jury will be selected. *Persons selected as potential jurors are called* **veniremen.** The names are drawn from voting registration lists, tax assessor's records, lists of persons with driver's licenses, or any other public documents listing citizens who reside within a given federal district (Knowles and Hickman, 1984).

Lists of veniremen may consist of employed or unemployed persons, housewives, firefighters, doctors, lawyers, police officers, trash collectors, teachers, businesspersons, engineers, or any other occupational or professional category. The major restriction for almost every list of veniremen is that the persons selected must reside within the jurisdiction of the court where the case is tried.

The representativeness of veniremen lists has been criticized extensively (Golash, 1992; Fukurai, Butler, and Krooth, 1991; Ogletree, 1994). In many jurisdictions, veniremen lists are derived from motor/driver lists, automobile and boat registrations, hunting and fishing licenses, telephone and utility lists, and property tax rolls (Florida Senate Committee on Executive Business Ethics and Elections, 1991). Thus, persons are automatically

Highlight 9.1. U.S. Supreme Court Cases about Right to Jury Trials

Duncan v. Louisiana, 391 U.S. 145, 88 S.Ct. 1444 (1968). States must provide jury trials for defendants charged with serious offenses. Duncan was convicted of simple battery in a bench trial in a Louisiana court. The crime was punishable as a misdemeanor, with two years' imprisonment and a fine of $300. Duncan was sentenced to only sixty days and fined $150. He appealed, saying that he demanded a jury trial and that none was provided for him. The Supreme Court agreed with Duncan, saying that a crime with a potential punishment of two years is a *serious crime,* despite the sentence of sixty days imposed on Duncan.

Baldwin v. New York, 399 U.S. 66, 90 S.Ct. 1886 (1970). Baldwin was arrested and prosecuted for "jostling" (pickpocketing), a Class A misdemeanor punishable in New York by a maximum term of one year. At the time, New York law held that pickpocketing was a petty offense and did not entitle a defendant to a jury trial. Baldwin asked for and was denied a jury trial. The Supreme Court heard Baldwin's appeal and declared that petty offenses carrying a one-year sentence are *serious* and entitle the defendant to a jury trial. The wording of *Baldwin* attaches great significance to the *months* of imprisonment constituting *serious* time. The Supreme Court said that a potential sentence in excess of six months is sufficiently severe by itself to take the offense out of the category of "petty" (at 1886, 1891). The Supreme Court overturned Baldwin's conviction and sent the case back to the lower court to be tried by a jury.

Blanton v. City of North Las Vegas, Nev., 489 U.S. 538, 109 S.Ct. 1289 (1989). Melvin Blanton was charged with DUI (driving while intoxicated). Blanton requested but was denied a jury trial by the North Las Vegas, Nevada, Municipal Court. In Nevada, the maximum sentence for a DUI conviction was six months and the maximum fine was $1,000. Blanton's driver's license was suspended for ninety days and he was ordered to pay court costs and perform forty-eight hours of community service while dressed in a way that made it known that he had been convicted of DUI. Blanton appealed, contending that he was entitled to a jury trial because the offense, he alleged, was "serious" and not "petty." The Supreme Court upheld his DUI bench trial conviction, saying that the most relevant criteria for determining the seriousness of an offense is the severity of the maximum authorized penalty fixed by the legislature. Thus, any offense carrying a maximum prison term of six months or less is presumed to be petty unless it can be shown that any additional statutory penalties are so severe that they might distinguish the offense as serious. The Supreme Court further held that the $1,000 fine did not approach an earlier standard of $5,000 established by Congress in its 1982 definition of "petty" offense, Title 18, U.S.C. Section 1. Thus, *Blanton* clearly affirms the earlier holding in *Baldwin* that a defendant is entitled to a jury trial only if the possible incarceration is *more than six months.*

excluded if they do not own automobiles, boats, or telephones; if they do not own property or pay utility bills; of if they do not hunt or fish. Even sophisticated statistical techniques and sampling methods proposed by various jury selection experts have failed to yield the perfect means of obtaining representative juror pools or veniremen lists (Fukurai, Butler, and Krooth, 1991). Thus, we are left with an imperfect, yet acceptable, means of selecting jurors. The imperfect presumption is that the

jurors who decide cases are the best possible under the circumstances. Several legal challenges have been made of particular juries, however. These will be examined in a later section of this chapter.

Functions of Juries

Juries perform a number of functions including: (1) prevention of government oppression;

(2) determination of guilt or innocence of an accused; (3) representation of diverse community interests; and (4) functioning as a "buffer" between the accuser and the accused.

1. *Prevention of government oppression.* In *Williams v. Florida* (1970), the Supreme Court declared "the chief function of a jury is to safeguard citizens against arbitrary law enforcement." The Court also said one of the primary purposes of a jury trial is "to prevent oppression by Government" (*Duncan v. Louisiana,* 1968).
2. *Determination of guilt or innocence.* A jury determines the guilt or innocence of an accused on the evidence presented by the prosecution and defense. In criminal cases, the standard that decides guilt or innocence is that the jury member must believe that the defendant is guilty "beyond a reasonable doubt." In civil cases, the standard for determining fault or liability is "the preponderance of the evidence" presented by the opposing litigants.
3. *Representation of diverse community interests.* One reason for jury trials is to represent the divergent interests of the community (Middendorf and Luginbuhl, 1995). In the case of *Williams v. Florida* (1970), the Supreme Court said that the jury is a valuable safeguard against the "corrupt or overzealous prosecutor and against the compliant, biased, or eccentric judge."
4. *Functioning as a "buffer" between the accuser and the accused.* Ideally juries should represent laypersons or community participants with shared responsibilities for determining a defendant's guilt or innocence. And all juries should be free from both internal and external attempts at intimidation (Hastie, Penrod, and Pennington, 1983:5).

Numbers of Jurors

Traditionally, juries have consisted of twelve persons. In many jurisdictions, however, local courts have conducted civil and criminal trials with juries consisting of fewer than twelve persons (Simon, 1980). In many jurisdictions, it is not uncommon to conduct a trial with six jurors. In 1970, a six-member criminal court jury was challenged as unconstitutional in the case of *Williams v. Florida.* Williams was sentenced to life imprisonment for a capital offense. He appealed the verdict on the grounds that the six-person jury violated his Fifth and Sixth Amendment rights. The Supreme Court affirmed the verdict of the lower court and said "the fact that the jury at common law was composed of precisely twelve is a historical accident." Furthermore, for the Supreme Court, twelve is not a necessary ingredient in a trial by jury.

In *Williams v. Florida* (1970), the Supreme Court also observed that in some jurisdictions, juries consist of from five to twelve persons. But in the later case of *Ballew v. Georgia* (1978), the Supreme Court held that a five-member jury was unconstitutional.

Ballew operated the Paris Adult Theater on Peachtree Street in Atlanta, Georgia. In November 1973, he showed the X-rated film *Behind the Green Door.* Investigators from the Fulton County Solicitor General's Office viewed the film and obtained a warrant to seize it on the grounds that it violated obscenity laws. Ballew obtained another print of the film and continued to show it, however. Later, investigators seized the second copy of the film and arrested Ballew, charging him with two counts of distributing obscene material, a misdemeanor. It was common practice in Fulton County to conduct misdemeanor trials with five-member juries. Ballew wanted a twelve-person jury, but the court refused. He was convicted of the charges, sentenced to a year in prison, and ordered to pay a $2,000 fine (imprisonment was suspended upon payment of the fine). Ballew appealed the court's action, claiming that the five-member jury violated his constitutional right to a jury trial.

The Supreme Court held that Ballew's right to a jury trial had been violated, saying, "We readily admit that we do not pretend to discern a clear line between six members and five. But the assembled data raise substantial doubts about the reliability and appropriate representation of panels smaller than six." For the first time, the Supreme Court established a constitutional *minimum* number of jurors in any criminal case. In a test of the Court's decision, a Colorado man challenged the limit in

1981 by requesting a jury of *one* in a case involving charges of criminal mischief (Hans and Vidmar, 1986:171). The trial judge granted the defendant's motion, but before the proceedings could be completed, a Colorado appellate court overruled the trial judge and declared that six jurors was the minimum the defendant could have (Hans and Vidmar, 1986:171).

Researchers have studied closely the issue of jury size (Ford, 1986: Kerr and MacCoun, 1985; MacCoun and Tyler, 1988; Middendorf and Luginbuhl, 1995; Roper, 1986). These investigations have focused on such questions as whether smaller juries have less difficulty agreeing on guilt or innocence than larger juries and whether smaller juries are less representative of the community and more biased than larger juries.

The research findings about jury size are disappointing and inconsistent (Iowa Equity in the Courts Task Force, 1993; MacCoun and Tyler, 1988; Ogletree, 1994). Some research shows that six-person juries have fewer disagreements and "hung" outcomes (where the jury cannot reach a unanimous verdict) than twelve-person juries (Kerr and MacCoun, 1985). Other studies show few, if any, differences in agreements or disagreements in juries of different sizes (Hastie, Penrod, and Pennington, 1983; Lempert, 1975; Saks, 1977). It would seem that juries of twelve persons would more fairly represent the racial and ethnic makeup of community residents than juries of six. In fact, a strong argument favoring the greater representativeness of larger juries has been advanced:

> Suppose that 90 percent of the community holds one view and 10 percent holds a minority viewpoint. Further suppose that we draw 100 twelve-member juries and 100 six-member juries from this population randomly. Seventy-two of the 100 twelve-person juries would have at least one person with a minority viewpoint on the jury, while only 47 percent of the 100 six-person juries would have a minority representative. (Zeisel, 1971:720)

Inconsistencies regarding jury size, representativeness, and verdict findings have been explained by certain methodological problems and a lack of control over important independent variables such as types of cases deliberated, age of jurors, gender composition, and previous jury experience (Simon, 1980:76–77). Other researchers have made similar observations about juries, their size and composition, and the decision-making process (Miller, 1985; Dillehay and Nietzel, 1985).

Jury Selection

Jury Composition

It is generally assumed that the composition of a jury significantly influences the trial outcome. The problem is that experts in jury selection differ in their opinions about which juror characteristics are most important and which factors will influence a juror to decide in favor of a defendant (Hastie, Penrod, and Pennington, 1983:121; Sandys and Dillehay, 1995).

One of the more visible juror characteristics that critically affect verdicts is race. A high correlation has been found between the race of a criminal defendant and the severity of the sentence, particularly where interracial crimes are involved (e.g., white victim-black defendant)(Bullock, 1961). Also, it has been found that racial bias influences jury deliberations and verdicts, although the conclusions of this research are inconsistent (Steinberg, 1991; Trugman, 1986; Williams and McShane, 1990). Thus far, it is uncertain how racial bias influences jury verdicts, although such bias does seem to make an important difference in some cases.

One of the more extensive investigations of juror characteristics and jury verdicts has been made by Rita Simon (1980:33–34). She conducted a thorough examination of the trial procedure literature and deduced a number of "maxims" or "rules of thumb" that many lawyers follow as they impanel a jury. Some of these maxims are:

1. A young juror is more likely to return a verdict favorable to the plaintiff.
2. An older juror is more likely to be sympathetic to the plaintiff in civil personal-injury cases.
3. A male juror is more likely to return a verdict favorable to the plaintiff if she is an attractive female.
4. A female juror is more likely to return a verdict favorable to the plaintiff if he is an attractive male.

5. A woman juror is more likely to return an unfavorable verdict to another woman.
6. A juror belonging to the same fraternal organizations, union, or political party as the client or witness is more likely to return a verdict favorable to that party.
7. A juror is more likely to return a verdict favorable to the party of his or her own religion.
8. A juror of Nordic, English, Swedish, Norwegian, German, or Scottish descent is more likely to respond to an appeal based on law and order and thus to return a verdict favorable to the defendant.
9. A woman juror is more likely to be emotional and sympathetic and to return a verdict favorable to the plaintiff.
10. A juror whose age closely approximates the age of the client, lawyer, or witness is more likely to give a favorable verdict.

Several strategies have been proposed for the selection and screening of jury members. It has been suggested, based on psychological studies, that color, dress, body language, space and time usage, and speech patterns are important indicators of attitudinal dispositions and preferences favorable or unfavorable to the defendant (Rasicot, 1983). Nonverbal cues such as not looking directly at the defendant's attorney during the process of questioning jury members concerning their biases or prejudices are considered important (Suggs and Sales, 1978).

Physically Impaired Jurors

Physically impaired jurors have been selected more and more often in recent years. Deaf jurors require interpreters to convey testimony. While deaf persons cannot fully appreciate the wavering voice of a criminal defendant or the vocal inflections of critical witnesses, they can make astute observations of a witness's body language that others sometimes overlook. Selecting jurors with physical impairments that may cause them to overlook audible or visual evidence is controversial.

Jury Consultants and the Community Network Model

Some experts employ a jury selection technique known as the *Community Network Model,* which uses members of the local community or private investigators as informants for the defendant's attorney. They supply personal background information about prospective jurors whose names appear on jury lists from which the jury will be selected (Bonora and Krauss, 1979). Also, both prosecution and defense attorneys use game theory and probability theory to synthesize and analyze information about prospective jurors (Kadane and Kairys, 1979).

Recently, defense attorneys have adopted more scientific ways of selecting jury members. Often they will hire social scientists to conduct telephone surveys in the community where their client will be tried. These surveys sometimes reveal prejudicial sentiment about the case and the client. Information about age, race, and socioeconomic status can sometimes enable attorneys to envision the "ideal" juror for their client's case.

In recent years, several trial consulting firms, such as Litigation Sciences, have emerged to help lawyers choose jurors. Litigation Sciences boasts that "to date, where our advice and recommendations have been employed, our clients have achieved successful results in over 95 percent of the cases in which we have been involved" (Hans and Vidmar, 1986:90).

The Case of Joan Little

In a widely publicized 1974 trial, the work of social scientists and jury selection experts appeared to result in a verdict favorable to the defendant (McConahay, Mullin, and Frederick, 1977). Joan Little, a black prisoner in the women's section of the Beaufort County (North Carolina) Jail, was allegedly assaulted by a night jailer, Clarence Alligood. Alligood was found dead in Ms. Little's cell in the early morning hours of August 27, 1974, stabbed with an ice pick.

Ms. Little escaped from the jail and could not be found. There was much publicity about the incident, and eventually Ms. Little turned herself in to authorities. She claimed that Alligood had raped her and that she killed him in self-defense. Her attorney hired social scientists to survey local attitudes about the incident, and these researchers found that most of the Beaufort County residents questioned held racist and sexist views. The judge was persuaded to move the trial from Beaufort County to Wake County, a larger urban location. Pretrial publicity and racism were among the reasons cited by the judge for his decision.

The jury in Wake County acquitted Ms. Little of the murder charge. Defense lawyers claimed the pretrial survey was very influential in Ms. Little's acquittal. Jerry Paul, her attorney, boasted afterward that he had "bought" the verdict with a large defense fund, which was used to support the team of jury selection experts (Hans and Vidmar, 1986:90). These jury selection experts may or may not have influenced the outcome. According to Hamilton Hobgood, the trial judge, the case against Ms. Little was "one of the weakest he had seen in twenty years on the bench" (Hans and Vidmar, 1986:90).

Jury Nullification

Twenty-two years later, when sports and television personality O. J. Simpson was acquitted of double-murder charges in 1996, the press and various government spokespersons claimed that his expensive defense team had overwhelmed the jury with many experts who gave plausible reasons for Simpson's innocence. Further, some experts said that because the jury was predominantly black, it was sympathetic to Simpson, who is also black. Specifically, prosecutors Marcia Clark and Christopher Darden blamed **jury nullification** for Simpson's acquittal. *Jury nullification results when the jury acquits a defendant despite the strength of the evidence against him.* In Simpson's case, however, Simpson's defense team raised substantial doubts about his guilt that were unrelated to his race. Shoddy police procedures in collecting incriminating evidence, as well as expert testimony about how some of the blood evidence had been planted by investigating detectives, led some jurors to conclude that there was reason enough to vote for Simpson's acquittal.

Education, gender, socioeconomic status, religion, occupation/profession, political affiliation, and any number of other variables obviously influence one's opinions and decisions. Currently, little is known about the relation between jurors' characteristics and their attitudes toward criminal defendants. The most frequently examined individual difference is gender (Hastie, Penrod, and Penning-

ton, 1983:140). Even in recent years, juror attitude prediction schemes based on gender have not been reliable.

In rape cases, some studies have found female jurors to be more likely to convict than male jurors (L. S. Miller, 1985). Most of the research has been conducted with "mock trials" with college students pretending to be jurors (Hastie, Penrod, and Pennington, 1983:140). In one hypothetical rape case, different researchers got different results using the same set of facts with different jurors. In sum, few consistent differences in jury decisions can be attributed to gender (Ford, 1986). Observations and statistics compiled from a decade's worth of criminal trials reveal that traditional techniques for eliminating the influence of racial bias—assurance of a representative jury, screening out of biased jurors, and control of the content of a jury's deliberations—are largely ineffective (S. Johnson, 1985). When older studies of mock juries and racial bias are compared with later studies, the results are fairly consistent. Racial bias is pervasive in U.S. courtrooms (S. Johnson, 1985; Trugman, 1986).

Screening Jury Members

Before the trial commences, persons summoned to jury duty are gathered or sequestered either in the courtroom or in a nearby area. The bailiff usually draws prospective jurors at random and directs them to take seats in the jury box. Depending upon the judge's rules, the prosecution and defense attorneys may or may not be permitted to ask questions of specific jurors. In certain federal district courts, for instance, the prosecutors and defense attorneys submit lists of questions they would like to ask prospective jurors. The judge reviews the questions and directs them to the jury as a whole. The judge is not obligated to ask the jurors any of the questions submitted by attorneys.

In the sensational murder trials of Lyle and Erik Menendez and O. J. Simpson in California, both prosecutors and defense attorneys submitted lengthy questionnaires to prospective jurors. Based on their responses, some prospective jurors were eliminated early. Eventually, the prosecution and defense in both cases agreed on suitable juries.

Highlight 9.2. High-Profile Trials:
The Race Card—The Case of Reginald Denny

On April 29, 1992, four white officers of the Los Angeles Police Department were acquitted of beating a black motorist, Rodney King, in a traffic incident on March 3, 1991. Much of the beating was videotaped by a civilian in a nearby apartment complex. The videotaped footage seemed sufficiently incriminating. When the officers were acquitted by the all-white jury in Simi Valley, an upscale, predominantly white area north of Los Angeles, a seventy-two-hour riot erupted in South Central Los Angeles, a predominantly black area. During the riot, at least 54 persons were killed, 2,383 persons were injured, 13,379 were arrested, and $423 million in property damage was inflicted.

During the rioting, a white truck driver, Reginald Denny, was driving his truck through South Central Los Angeles on his way to work. His truck was stopped by rioters, and Denny was pulled from the truck and beaten critically. Various bystanders videotaped the beating.

Damian Williams, twenty, and Henry Watson, twenty-nine, were later arrested and charged with serious felonies and misdemeanors related to Denny's beating. The jury, consisting of four Latinos, three blacks, two whites, and two Asian-Americans, voted to convict Williams and Watson mostly on the misdemeanor charges. They were acquitted of most of the more serious felony charges.

One newsperson reported that a "brick in the head gets a slap on the wrist," referring to the fact that one of the defendants had bashed Denny's head with a brick. The jurors themselves reported that there had been a great deal of dissension in their ranks and that for a time they thought that they would not be able to agree on a verdict. During the trial, several jurors were excused. Robert Pugsley, a professor of law at Southwestern University School of Law, said, "It's a mess. And from the public's perspective, it probably looks like a bit of a circus."

Many observers saw the verdict in the Denny case as payback for the acquittal of the white police officers who beat black motorist King. It is certain that the trial was emotionally charged and that race was a key consideration in the deliberations, according to jurors who were interviewed later.

Can juries be totally objective when considering evidence in high-profile cases? Can judges control jury objectivity? Should the media be allowed to broadcast jury deliberations in sensitive cases?

Sources: Adapted from Elizabeth Gleick and Lorenzo Benet, "The Verdict," *People,* November 8, 1993, pp. 87–88; Haya El Nasser, "Alternate, Juror Have 2 Views on Denny Case," *USA Today,* October 26, 1993, p. 2A; Haya El Nasser, "Juror vs. Juror in Denny Trial," *USA Today,* October 15, 1993, p. 3A; Haya El Nasser, "Juror Furor Rattles Denny Trial," *USA Today,* October 13, 1993, p. 3A; Walter E. Williams, "Did LA Verdicts Serve Justice?" *USA Today,* October 26, 1993, p. 13A; Patricia Edmonds, "For Juries, High Anxiety: Crucial Cases Carry Weight of the World," *USA Today,* October 14, 1993, p. 4A.

The judge determines whether any prospective juror is related to any of the trial participants. The defense often wants to know if any prospective juror is a law enforcement officer or related to one, because he or she might be partial to the prosecution. And the prosecution wants to know if any prospective juror is even remotely related to or knows the defendant. While some of these prospective jurors may not be biased, their affiliations and relations with law enforcement or the defendant are usually sufficient to disqualify them if attorneys wish to eliminate them for cause as jurors.

The formal procedure whereby both prosecutors and defense attorneys address prospective jurors and inquire into their backgrounds and potential biases in the case is called the ***voir dire.*** It applies to prospective witnesses as well. *Voir dire means "to speak the truth." It signifies an attorney's inquiry into the qualifications of witnesses who may or may not be qualified to present expert testimony, or* *it may be an oral examination of prospective jurors to discover their impartiality in the pending case.*

Both the prosecution and the defense can *challenge* prospective jurors and exclude any of them from the jury for whatever reason. These are called **peremptory challenges.** *A peremptory challenge is the right to excuse a juror without having to give a reason* (Black, 1990:1136). In *all* U.S. courts, the prosecution and defense are *limited* in the number of peremptory challenges they may use; this number varies from state to state. In federal district courts, 18 U.S.C., Rule 24 (1996), provides the following numbers of peremptory challenges:

1. *Capital Cases.* If the offense charged is punishable by death, each side is entitled to twelve peremptory challenges.
2. *Felony Cases.* If the offense charged is punishable by imprisonment for more than one year, each side is entitled to five peremptory challenges.
3. *Misdemeanor Cases.* If the offense charged is punishable by imprisonment for not more than one year or by fine or both, each side is entitled to two peremptory challenges.

In all courts, attorneys for both sides may also **challenge for cause.** *Challenging a prospective juror for cause means that if the attorneys can show at least one good reason why a prospective juror should not be a part of the jury, the judge is obliged to excuse that person.* For example, if prospective white jurors in the case of a black defendant are being questioned by the defendant's attorney, any racist expression they utter or any evidence of racial prejudice on their part will be grounds to exclude them from jury service. If prospective jurors are relatives or friends of the defendant, the defendant's witnesses, or associated in any way with the court officers (e.g., judge, prosecutor, bailiff), this is good cause to excuse the prospective juror from jury duty in the pending case. Attorneys from both sides have *unlimited challenges for cause* (S. Johnson, 1985).

In 1986, however, the Supreme Court heard an appeal from a convicted offender (*Batson v. Kentucky,* 1986). James Kirkland Batson, a black, had been convicted of second-degree burglary and re-ceipt of stolen goods by an all-white jury in a Kentucky criminal court. The prosecutor had used his four peremptory challenges to excuse four prospective black jury members. Batson's attorney moved to discharge the jury before it was sworn on the ground that the prosecutor's removal of the black veniremen violated Batson's rights under the Sixth and Fourteenth Amendments. The presiding judge denied the motion and said that prosecutors and defense attorneys were entitled to use their peremptory challenges to strike "anybody they want to."

In his appeal to the Kentucky Supreme Court, Batson's attorney argued that the all-white jury had deprived Batson of a fair and impartial jury trial. The Kentucky Supreme Court, relying on an earlier U.S. Supreme Court case, upheld Batson's conviction. The earlier case, *Swain v. Alabama* (1965), also concerned a black defendant who alleged racial discrimination in his jury selection. The Supreme Court held in *Swain* that the burden of showing the discriminatory use of peremptory challenges by prosecutors was on the defendant. Furthermore, the defendant is required to show that purposeful discrimination was a systemic pattern in the jurisdiction where the trial was held. Swain was unable to meet this burden, and his conviction was upheld.

In ruling on the *Batson* case, the Supreme Court did not directly reverse the position it adopted in *Swain.* However, it did modify *Swain* by stating that a presumption of discrimination in jury selection could be raised by defendants *in their own cases* rather than requiring them to demonstrate a pattern of discrimination throughout an entire jurisdiction. Batson's case clearly pointed to the discriminatory use of peremptory challenges by the prosecutor. The Court's ruling in *Batson* was significant also because it required prosecutors instead of defendants to show the court why their use of peremptory challenges was not discriminatory once a possible discriminatory pattern of jury selection was made apparent by the defense.

It is important to understand that the *Batson* case did *not* hold that defendants have the right to a jury composed of members of their own race. Furthermore, *Batson* established that it is unnecessary for *any* jury members to share racial similarities with defendants in order for a fair and impartial jury trial to be held (Serr and Maney, 1988). But Batson had established that the jury in his trial was exclusively white because the prosecutor used his peremptory challenges to excuse the only black persons who could have been selected as jury members. Thus, Batson's conviction was reversed because his right to an impartial trial had been violated by the Kentucky court. He had been put on trial before a jury from which members of his race had been purposely excluded (see Highlight 9.3).

Ordinarily, defense and prosecuting attorneys do not have to explain their use of peremptory challenges (Steinberg, 1991; Turner et al., 1986). This privilege has seldom been questioned. But the *Batson* case no doubt will cause prosecutors to carefully consider their use of peremptory challenges. Also, a 1994 case, *J.E.B. v. Alabama*, held that the use of peremptory challenges to dismiss prospective jurors on the basis of their *gender* is also unconstitutional.

Death-Qualified Juries

In cases where the death penalty may be imposed, the composition of jury members is especially crucial. If the prosecution asks a prospective juror if he or she would be able to impose the death penalty and if the prospective juror answers no, the prosecutor may ask that the prospective juror be dismissed for cause.

Some evidence indicates that in death penalty cases, such challenges for cause result in a **death-qualified jury** that is actually biased against the defendant (Ellsworth et al., 1984; Finch and Ferraro, 1986; Williams and McShane, 1990). *Death-qualified juries are those that can impose the death penalty if warranted, despite individual jury members' feelings about the appropriateness of the death penalty or their opposition to it.* One of the earliest studies of death-qualified juries was by George Jurow in a 1971 article in the *Harvard Law Review*. This pioneering work led to various surveys that attempted to describe the characteristics of death-qualified juries. For instance, in a random survey of the opinions of 811 eligible jurors from Alameda County, California, Fitzgerald and Ellsworth (1984) found that of the 717 respondents who said they could be fair and impartial in

deciding the guilt or innocence of a capital defendant, about 17 percent said they could never vote to impose the death penalty. These researchers found that significantly more blacks than whites and more females than males are eliminated by the process of death qualification and that this biases the resulting jury against the defendant in a capital case.

Another argument is that death qualification, or determining whether a juror would vote for the death penalty, creates a set of suggestive conditions (Haney, 1984; White, 1980). A sample of persons in one study appeared to be influenced by the very process of death qualification (Haney, 1984). Subjects were led to believe that the judge, the prosecutor, and even the defense attorney were convinced of the defendant's guilt. Specifically, these subjects were led to believe that the law "disapproves" of people who oppose the death penalty, and this belief apparently led them to choose the death penalty. But other research has found that the death-qualification process has only a negligible effect on prospective jurors (Kadane, 1984). Available research suggests that there is insufficient information to show conclusively that death-qualified juries are either unconstitutional or produce pro-death-penalty attitudes among jurors. Interestingly, findings from an extensive review of the literature suggest that death-qualified juries *more often* impose life without parole than the death penalty (Finch and Ferraro, 1986).

In sum, peremptory challenges eliminate jurors who either the prosecution or defense feels do not favor his or her client. The expertise of jury consultants is relevant here, and many defense attorneys have sought their services. Each side must use its peremptory challenges wisely. The ultimate objective of both sides is to get a jury that will maximize the chances of a conviction (for the prosecution) or an acquittal (for the defense). Any prospective juror may be dismissed for *cause,* but both prosecution and defense attorneys are limited in the numbers of peremptory challenges they can utilize. However, in view of *Batson v. Kentucky* (1986), the prosecution *may* have to provide a neutral reason for excluding jurors with certain racial or ethnic characteristics.

Highlight 9.3. Some U.S. Supreme Court Cases Involving Peremptory Challenges

Griffith v. Kentucky, 479 U.S. 314, 107 S.Ct. 708 (1987). Griffith, who was black, was convicted of conspiracy to distribute marijuana with intent to distribute. During his trial in Jefferson County, Kentucky, the prosecutor used four out of five peremptory challenges to strike from jury duty four out of five prospective black jurors. Following his conviction, Griffith appealed, saying that the prosecutor had violated his right to due process. He cited *Batson v. Kentucky* (1986) and argued that it should be *retroactively applied to his case*. The Supreme Court heard his appeal and overturned his conviction, holding that the *Batson* case, prohibiting prosecutors from using their peremptory challenges to racially bias a jury pool, should be retroactively applied where a showing exists that such conduct had occurred. Thus, in Griffith's case, the factual scenario provided the basis for a retroactive application of *Batson*. The Supreme Court held that a new rule for the conduct of criminal prosecutions is to be applied retroactively to all cases, state or federal, pending, on direct review, or not yet final, with no exception for cases in which the new rule constitutes a "clear break" with the past.

Ross v. Oklahoma, 487 U.S. 85, 108 S.Ct. 2273 (1988). Ross was convicted of first-degree murder in Oklahoma. During the impaneling of a jury, a prospective juror who should have been removed for cause was not. Ross's lawyer had to use one of his peremptory challenges to excuse this particular juror. Ross's attorney regarded this as a "waste" of a perfectly good peremptory challenge that hindered his ability to mold the jury. On that basis he appealed Ross's conviction. The Supreme Court upheld Ross's conviction, holding that a failure to exclude a prospective juror for cause and causing the defense to use one of its peremptory challenges to do so does not deprive defendants of due process. Ross's right to an impartial jury was not violated when he was required to use a peremptory challenge to excuse a juror who should have been rejected for cause.

Teague v. Lane, 489 U.S. 288, 109 S.Ct. 1060 (1989). Teague, who was black, was convicted of at-

tempted murder. During jury selection, the prosecutor used all of his ten peremptory challenges to exclude blacks from the jury. Thus, Teague's conviction was decided by an all-white jury. After Teague's conviction, *Batson v. Kentucky* was decided. In an attempt to win a new trial, Teague sought to make this ruling retroactive in his case. The Supreme Court rejected his appeal, holding that Teague had failed to make a convincing case that the peremptory challenges were used in a discriminatory fashion.

Hernandez v. New York, 500 U.S. 352, 111 S.Ct. 1859 (1991). Dionisio Hernandez was accused of various crimes. During jury selection, the prosecutor used several of his peremptory challenges to strike four Latinos from potential jury duty. Defense counsel objected to these challenges, but the prosecutor cited various valid reasons for their use. Hernandez appealed his conviction, alleging that the prosecutor deliberately deprived him of a fair trial by using his peremptory challenges to eliminate Latinos. The Supreme Court upheld Hernandez's conviction, holding that the prosecutor had presented an acceptable race-neutral explanation for striking the Latino jurors. No evidence to the contrary had been presented.

Powers v. Ohio, 499 U.S. 400, 111 S.Ct. 1364 (1991). Larry Powers, a white man, was convicted of murder, aggravated murder, and attempted aggravated murder, all with firearm specifications (calling for mandatory minimum sentences). Earlier Powers had objected to the government's use of peremptory challenges to strike seven black prospective jurors. Powers appealed his conviction, alleging that his Fourteenth Amendment guarantee to equal protection was violated because of the alleged discriminatory use of peremptory challenges. In *Batson v. Kentucky* (1986) the Supreme Court had already declared it unconstitutional to use peremptory challenges to achieve a racially pure jury. In *Batson*, however, the defendant was black, and government prejudice was obvious in the use of these peremptory challenges. Powers, however, was white, and the prospective jurors who had

Highlight 9.3. Some U.S. Supreme Court Cases
Involving Peremptory Challenges *(continued)*

been excluded were black. The Supreme Court over-turned Powers's conviction on the same grounds it had cited in *Batson,* holding that criminal defendants may object to race-based exclusions of jurors effected through peremptory challenges whether or not defendants and excluded jurors share the same race.

Georgia v. McCollum, 505 U.S. 42, 112 S.Ct. 2348 (1992). McCollum was indicted on aggravated assault and simple battery. During jury selection, McCollum's attorney used his peremptory challenges to strike certain prospective jurors because of their race. The state challenged the use of these peremptory challenges, arguing that they created a biased jury as in *Batson v. Kentucky* (1986), where the prosecutor used peremptory challenges out of racial bias. The Supreme Court agreed with the state and rejected the defense attorney's use of peremptory challenges for racial purposes. Thus, *Batson* and *McCollum* establish that neither prosecutors nor defense attorneys may deliberately use their peremptory challenges to excuse prospective jurors on the basis of race.

Purkett v. Elem, __U.S.__, 115 S.Ct. 1769 (1995). Elem, a black defendant, was convicted of second-degree robbery. During jury selection, the prosecutor used one of his peremptory challenges to strike a prospective black juror. Elem appealed, alleging that this use of a peremptory challenge violated a policy set forth in *Batson v. Kentucky* (1986) that prohibited the use of peremptory challenges for racial purposes. The Supreme Court upheld Elem's conviction, holding that the prosecutor's reason for striking the black prospective juror—he had long, unkempt hair and a moustache and beard—was racially neutral. The Supreme Court held that opponents of peremptory challenges have the burden of proving purposeful discrimination. The explanations given by those exercising peremptory challenges need not be persuasive or even plausible; rather, these explanations are considered only in determining whether opponents have shown that the peremptory strikes were discriminatory. In this case, the Court ruled that the peremptory challenge had been satisfactorily explained.

The Trial Process

Trial procedures vary greatly among jurisdictions, although the federal district court format is followed most frequently by judges in state and local trial courts. Figure 9.1 follows a typical trial from the indictment stage through the judge's instructions to the jury.

Pretrial Motions

Before the start of court proceedings, attorneys for the government and/or defense may make a number of **pretrial motions,** or **motions** *in limine*. One purpose of such motions is to avoid potentially serious or embarrassing situations that may occur later during trial, such as the attempt by either side to introduce evidence that may be considered prejudicial, inflammatory, or irrelevant. In a brutal murder case, for example, it may be considered inflammatory for the prosecution to introduce photographs of a dismembered body or a mutilated corpse. The jury may be emotionally persuaded to interpret the photographs as conclusive evidence that the defendant committed the crime. Or the photographs may increase the severity of the sentence if there is additional and overwhelming evidence of the defendant's guilt.

In some instances, a defense attorney will move to *suppress* certain evidence from being introduced because it was illegally seized by police at the time the defendant was arrested (Bell, 1983). This is known as the **exclusionary rule;** it provides that *when evidence has been obtained in violation of the privileges guaranteed citizens by the Constitution,*

Figure 9.1 The Trial Process

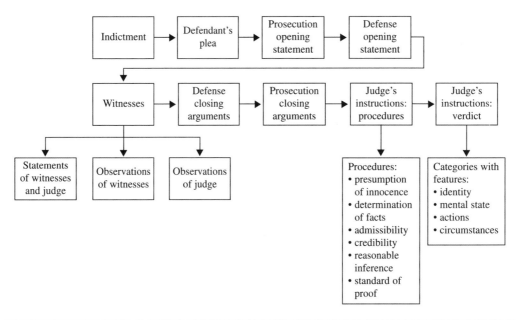

---

the evidence must be excluded at the trial (Black, 1990:564). For instance, evidence seized by police during an illegal search and seizure would fall within the exclusionary rule. The case of *Mapp v. Ohio* (1961) involved an illegal search of Ms. Mapp's premises by police officers in Cleveland, Ohio, and the illegal seizure of certain obscene materials found in a trunk in Ms. Mapp's basement. The Supreme Court overturned Ms. Mapp's conviction because of the illegal search and seizure of evidence by police.

In another case a Chinese suspect, Wong Sun, was arrested by police, charged, and convicted of violating federal narcotics laws (*Wong Sun v. United States,* 1963). Earlier, federal agents, acting on a tip and without a warrant, broke down the door of James Wah Toy's dwelling and arrested him. They searched his home for narcotics but found none. But under questioning Toy told police that Johnny Yee was selling narcotics. Yee was arrested, and narcotics were taken from his home. Yee, in turn, implicated Wong Sun, who was also arrested. All of the subsequent action against Wong

Sun stemmed from the original unlawful search of James Wah Toy's premises and from Toy's illegally obtained statements.

The Supreme Court overturned Wong Sun's conviction and declared that the statements implicating Wong Sun in narcotics sales were fruits of the poisonous tree. The **fruits-of-the-poisonous-tree doctrine** provides that *evidence that is spawned or directly derived from an illegal search or an illegal interrogation is generally inadmissible against a defendant because of its original taint* (Green, 1990).

Often, a defense attorney will file a **motion to dismiss,** *a motion designed to attack the prosecutor's evidence as insufficient or to signify the absence of a key prosecution witness upon whom a conviction depends.* Such pretrial motions are ordinarily conducted outside of the presence of the jury. The judge rules on the motions and the trial proceeds. A summary of some of the more frequent pretrial motions are:

1. *Motion for dismissal of charges* (motion seeking to throw out the case against an accused based

on the failure of the prosecution to state a sufficient case to be prosecuted; alleges critical weaknesses in the prosecution's case)

2. *Motion for discovery* (motion to seek certain documents and evidence collected by the prosecution and a list of the witnesses to be called)

3. *Motion for a bill of particulars* (motion to require the prosecutor to furnish a written statement of charges outlining the crime(s) alleged, the time and place of the crime, and other information)

4. *Motion for continuance* (motion seeking to delay trial proceedings, usually to interview additional witnesses and collect additional evidence)

5. *Motion for severance* (if more than one defendant is charged in a conspiracy or crime involving several defendants, attorneys for each client may seek to separate the cases so that each defendant can be tried separately to avoid a conflict of interest in which one defendant may tend to incriminate the others)

6. *Motion for suppression of evidence* (motion seeking to exclude incriminating evidence against the accused, such as that taken in a questionably legal search of someone's premises in violation of Fourth Amendment provisions against unreasonable searches and seizures, in the Denver, Colorado, federal trial of Timothy McVeigh, who was charged with the 1995 bombing of the Oklahoma City federal building, for example, some incriminating statements made by Terry Nichols, an alleged co-conspirator, and a receipt for bomb materials with McVeigh's fingerprint on it were the subjects of a motion to suppress by their defense attorney)

7. *Motion for determination of competency* (motion seeking to question whether the defendant is competent or sane enough to stand trial; an examination by a psychiatrist might be requested before the trial proceeds)

8. *Motion for a change of venue* (the trial of Timothy McVeigh for the 1995 bombing of the federal building in Oklahoma City was moved from Oklahoma City to Denver, Colorado, because it was believed that a Denver jury could be selected that would be less prejudicial than an Oklahoma jury)

9. *Motion of intention to provide an alibi* (motion seeking to demonstrate that the defendant could not possibly have committed the alleged offense since the defendant was at another location when the crime was committed)

Opening Arguments

Unless both the prosecution and the defense attorney agree to waive opening statements, the prosecutor makes an opening statement to the jury. Usually, this statement includes a portion of the state's theory about the case and the defendant's guilt. Often, prosecutors will tell a jury what they intend to prove and will attempt to persuade them initially to consider certain kinds of evidence to be presented later. The purpose of this outline or summary of the case is to advise the jury of the facts to be relied upon and the issues involved (Black, 1990:1091).

The court permits the defense attorney wide latitude in his or her opening statement to the jury. Basically, the defense's statement is intended to undermine the state's case against the defendant and to opine that the accused should be acquitted of all charges.

The State Presents Its Case

The prosecution begins by calling witnesses and presenting evidence that a crime has been committed and that the defendant committed it. Each witness is **sworn in** by a court officer. Being *sworn in means that a witness is obliged under the law to be truthful in all subsequent testimony given.* This stage is termed **direct examination.** *Direct examination is the question-answer exchange between the prosecutor and the prosecutor's witnesses or between the defense and the defense's witnesses.*

The defense has the right to challenge any question asked of a witness by the prosecution on direct examination. Usually, the defense attorney raises *objections* to the questions, or he or she may object to an answer given by a witness. The presiding judge rules on such objections and either *sustains* or *grants them* or *overrules* or *denies them.*

The prosecutor makes an opening statement to the jury.

The same option is available to the prosecution attorney when it is the defense's turn to present evidence. Objections may be raised at any time, and the judge sustains or overrules such objections.

The Rules of Evidence contain explicit guidelines for judges and attorneys to follow regarding what evidence is and is not admissible (Saltzburg and Redden, 1994). These rules are rather elaborate and technical. If they are not followed by the major participants in the trial, violations could be the basis for a higher court's overturning a guilty verdict. The prosecution is entitled to appeal a not guilty verdict on similar grounds, and the verdict in favor of the defendant could be reversed.

The Right of Cross-Examination

After the prosecution has questioned a witness, the defense has the right to ask the witness questions. This is known as **cross-examination.** This constitutional right to cross-examine witnesses illustrates the adversarial nature of the trial system. The defense attorney attempts to impeach or undermine the credibility of the prosecutor's witnesses (Graham, 1985). Sometimes defense attorneys can use prosecution witnesses to their own advantage and elicit statements from them that are favorable to the defendant.

Redirect Examination

Once testimony has been given by a witness, that witness may be cross-examined by the opposition. Once cross-examination has been completed, the side that called the witness initially may ask more questions. This questioning is called **redirect examination.** The purpose of redirect examination is to clarify issues that may be confusing to the jury or to enable the witness to elaborate on points the other side may have brought out that may be incriminating.

For instance, a witness may testify on behalf of the defense in a case where the defendant, Mr. X, a noted sports figure, claims to have cut his hand *after* a murder had been committed in Denver, Colorado. Some blood at the crime scene does not appear to be the victim's blood. In fact, investigators suspect that the blood is from the perpetrator, probably from a cut on his hand sustained during the murder. However, the defendant claims to have cut his hand on the day *following* the murder. The defendant claims, for instance, that he boarded an airplane on the evening of the terrible murder. Investigators have fixed the victim's time of death at about 10:00 P.M. It is known that the defendant boarded an airplane to New York at 11:30 P.M. and conversed with another passenger. The following day, the defendant is notified of the murder. He flies back to Denver on another airline. The defendant claims that when he learned of the victim's death he smashed his hand on a table in his hotel room while holding a glass. The glass shattered and cut his fingers. On the return flight to Denver, the defendant sits next to another passenger, and they converse throughout the trip.

The passenger who sat next to Mr. X on the first flight is called as a witness for the defendant. The witness is called to confirm that Mr. X *did not have a cut hand or fingers* on the flight to New York. The witness is asked some questions by the defense counsel on direct examination:

DEFENSE: Did you sit next to Mr. X on Flight 161 to New York on the evening of February 26?

WITNESS: Yes.

DEFENSE: Did you have a conversation with Mr. X during this flight?

WITNESS: Yes.

DEFENSE: Did you notice whether there were any cuts on Mr. X's hands while you were talking with him?

WITNESS: I didn't see any cuts on Mr. X's hands.

DEFENSE: Did you know Mr. X by reputation when you were sitting next to him?

WITNESS: Yes, I did.

DEFENSE: Did you make any special requests of Mr. X?

WITNESS: Yes, I asked him to autograph a pad of paper in my pocket.

DEFENSE: You asked Mr. X for his autograph?

WITNESS: Yes, I did.

DEFENSE: Did he sign something for you?

WITNESS: Yes, he signed the paper pad.

DEFENSE: Where exactly did he sign this pad, you know, did he sign it while holding it in his lap or did he write on some surface?

WITNESS: He wrote his autograph on the pull-out tray in front of my seat. He leaned over and signed my paper pad on my pull-out tray.

DEFENSE: The pull-out tray on *your* seat. OK. And therefore, this gave you a good opportunity to look closely at his hands?

WITNESS: Yes, it did.

DEFENSE: And you didn't see or notice any cuts on his hands or fingers?

WITNESS: No, I didn't.

DEFENSE: And the overhead lights were on when he gave you his autograph?

WITNESS: Yes, the lights were on.

DEFENSE: And you had a clear view of *both* of his hands?

WITNESS: Yes, he used one hand to hold the pad and the other to sign his name.

The prosecutor cross-examines the witness.

PROSECUTION: Sir, could Mr. X have been sitting in such a way so as to hide his hands from you?

WITNESS: I don't think so. We talked a lot that evening, and he was quite animated, using his hands.

PROSECUTION: But you cannot say for certain that there were *no* cuts on his hands when you were talking with him?

WITNESS: No, I can't say for certain.

PROSECUTION: And so if there *were* cuts, it is possible that you just didn't happen to see them that evening.

WITNESS: That's right. I didn't see any cuts when he gave me his autograph, but maybe I just didn't notice them.

The defense redirects.

DEFENSE: Well, you say that you can't say for sure that there were no cuts on Mr. X's hands. Is that right?

WITNESS: Yes, that's right.

The defense attorney cross-examines a prosecution witness.

DEFENSE: But suppose there was a deep gash, or perhaps even several deep gashes on Mr. X's hands? If such gashes were there, they would probably be bloody. Perhaps you would notice, for instance, if Mr. X was wearing some sort of covering to protect such cuts if they were there?

WITNESS: I didn't see any bandages.

DEFENSE: But if there was a deep cut, and if it had been made a short time before Mr. X boarded the plane, then you would probably have noticed that, wouldn't you?

WITNESS: Sure, I probably would have noticed that. We were sitting side-by-side in adjacent seats. Lights were on overhead, and I could see both of his hands.

DEFENSE: And you saw no cuts?

WITNESS: No, I saw no cuts on his hands. I think I would have seen them if there had been cuts there.

DEFENSE: Was there any blood on the paper pad where he signed the autograph?

WITNESS: No. There was no blood on the paper pad. Just his autograph.

Now suppose we have the second witness on the stand, the person who sat next to Mr. X on his return flight from New York to Denver. This witness, also called by the defense, is asked the following questions:

DEFENSE: Were you a passenger on Flight 215 from New York to Denver on the day of February 27th?

WITNESS: Yes, I was.

DEFENSE: And who did you sit next to while on the airplane, if anyone?

WITNESS: I sat next to Mr. X.

DEFENSE: Did you have a conversation with Mr. X while you flew from New York to Denver?

WITNESS: Yes, we talked with one another.

DEFENSE: Did you notice Mr. X's hands while you were talking to him?

WITNESS: Yes, I did.

DEFENSE: Was there anything unusual or extraordinary about them that you recall?

WITNESS: Yes, there was a big bandage on one of his fingers on his right hand. It looked like it was seeping with blood.

DEFENSE: You say the wound was seeping with blood?

WITNESS: That's the way it looked to me.

DEFENSE: Did Mr. X tell you how he received that wound?

WITNESS: Yes, he said he cut it on a glass in his hotel room.

DEFENSE: Did he say *when* he cut his hand?

WITNESS: Yes. He said he cut it this morning, after he received an upsetting telephone call.

The prosecution cross-examines the second witness:

PROSECUTION: When you saw this wound, you don't know precisely *when* the wound was made, do you?

WITNESS: Mr. X says it happened that morning, a few hours before the flight to Denver.

PROSECUTION: Yes, but you don't really *know for sure* when that cut was made, do you?

WITNESS: No, I don't.

PROSECUTION: It could have been the night before, couldn't it, maybe even around 10:00 P.M. at night?

WITNESS: I suppose so.

PROSECUTION: So you really don't know *when* the cut was made, and that it could perhaps have been made the night before, is that right?

WITNESS: That's right.

The defense redirects:

DEFENSE: Did you actually *see* the cut on Mr. X's hand or just the bandage covering it?

WITNESS: I saw the cut. He changed the bandage once, just before we landed.

DEFENSE: When you saw the cut, how did it look to you?

WITNESS: What do you mean?

DEFENSE: Did it look like an old cut or a new one?

WITNESS: It looked like a cut that was made fairly recently.

DEFENSE: If a cut like the one you saw had been made the night before you actually saw it, would it still be bleeding like that, as you have described?

WITNESS: I don't think so. It probably would have healed some. I don't know.

DEFENSE: And so you are saying that the cut looked entirely consistent with Mr. X's explanation that he had just cut his hand on some glass in his hotel room, is that it?

WITNESS: Yes, that's it.

As can be seen from the above exchange, each side, the defense and prosecution, attempts to use the two witnesses in ways that work to their particular advantage. The prosecution wants the jury to think that the cut occurred when Mr. X used a knife to kill the victim. The defense wants to show that there was no apparent cut when Mr. X left Denver late the evening of the murder, but that a cut *was* there when Mr. X was seen by others the following day. It if can be established that Mr. X's cut occurred the day following the murder, then it couldn't have been done when the murder was committed. The prosecution wants the jury to believe that the cut occurred during the murder, not afterward. Both the defense and prosecution are permitted to engage in redirect and recross examinations of each witness until they feel that they have adequately made their respective points. They are shaping and forming versions of the events that make a case for or against Mr. X. We might even consider redirect and recross examinations as *refinements* of witness testimony, as a way of knowing what the witness did or did not see. The jury listens and decides which version seems most believable.

Recross Examination

While some persons consider **recross examination** as prolonging an already long trial, each side is entitled to recall witnesses to the stand for further questioning. This tactic is particularly important when other witnesses bring new evidence to light. Judges may cut short extensive cross-examinations and recross examinations if they feel attorneys are merely covering information already disclosed in earlier testimony.

Impeaching Witnesses

Impeaching means to call into question the truthfulness or credibility of a witness. If either the prosecutor or defense attorney can demonstrate that a particular witness is lying or is otherwise unreliable, that witness's testimony is called into question. Jury members may disbelieve such witnesses and the evidentiary information they provide. Of course, defendants themselves are subject to impeachment if they testify.

There are several ways defense attorneys can impeach a witness. They can obtain inconsistent testimony from the witness or can get the witness to admit confusion over certain facts. Or they can introduce evidence of the untruthfulness of the witness based on previous information acquired through investigative sources. Perhaps a witness was fired from a company because of embezzle-

ment. Embezzlement is one form of dishonesty, and jurors can infer that if witnesses were dishonest in their employment, they may not be telling the truth on the witness stand. Of course, when the defense presents its witnesses, the prosecution has the right to cross-examine and can attempt to impeach the credibility of the witnesses called on the defendant's behalf.

Eyewitnesses and Expert Witnesses

There are many instances in criminal law when expert testimony is solicited (Penrod, Fulero and Cutler, 1995). Experts testify about blood samples, firearms, ballistics reports, a defendant's state of mind or sanity, and any number of other types of evidence that might link the defendant to the crime. By the same token, defense attorneys can introduce expert testimony to rebut or counter the testimony of the prosecution's experts.

An **expert witness** is called to interpret the meaningfulness of evidence presented by either the prosecution or defense (Ross, Read and Toglia, 1994) and to explain complex issues or topics (Penrod, Fulero, and Cutler, 1995).

Being an expert witness involves certain hazards or risks, however. Some expert witnesses have reported being harassed by defendants or their attorneys outside of the courtroom. Some expert witnesses, particularly forensic psychiatrists who might testify as to a defendant's sanity or criminal motives, have reported being physically assaulted or threatened (Read, Yuille, and Tollestrup, 1992). In a survey of 408 members of the American Academy of Psychiatry and the Law (representing 48 percent of the largest U.S. organization of forensic psychiatrists), 42 percent of the respondents reported harassment in some fashion from defendants, plaintiffs, victims, the press, and even judges (D. Miller, 1985). A majority of cases involving harassment involved criminal cases or cases in which the insanity defense was raised as a major issue.

Eyewitnesses are also of significant value to both prosecutors and defense attorneys (Davies et al., 1995). *They can provide opinions and interpretations of events they actually experienced, and they can describe the defendant's involvement in the crime*

Highlight 9.4. Suspected Zodiac Slayer Charged and Expert Witnesses to Testify: The Case of Heriberto Seda

A man police dubbed *the Zodiac killer* was charged with murdering three persons and attempting to murder another. For several years, New York City residents had been fearful of being the Zodiac killer's next victim. Apparently, victims were killed at random, according to their astrological signs. If you're a Cancer, you're a target. If you're a Leo, you're a target. If you're a Gemini, you're a target. It didn't make any difference to the Zodiac killer.

Seda, twenty-six, was arrested after various notes and symbols he had written were found to match those in taunting messages the Zodiac killer mailed to police. The notes berated the police methods used to search for the Zodiac killer and boasted that police would never catch him. Four men were shot by sniper fire in 1990—a Scorpio, a Gemini, a Taurus, and a Cancer. All but one died. The shootings always occurred on Thursdays and twenty-one days apart. A fifty-detective task force was created to catch the Zodiac killer. Seda was finally arrested following a police standoff, where Seda surrendered numerous weapons, some of which were linked with the murders. Seda also confessed to the crimes. Police suspect that Seda is also responsible for four other Zodiac killer-related crimes in the boroughs of Queens, Brooklyn, and Manhattan.

No doubt, expert witnesses will be very instrumental in the case against Seda. Expert witnesses will testify about the markings on bullets fired from particular weapons. Other experts will testify about DNA samples taken from envelopes on which residue of Seda's saliva was found. DNA matches have been made between the saliva on letters the Zodiac killer mailed to police and letters Seda mailed to friends and family.

Source: Adapted from Associated Press, "Suspect Charged in Zodiac Slayings" *Minot (N.D.) Daily News,* June 22, 1996, p. A2.

---

alleged. But some researchers who have explored the impact of eyewitness testimony on jury verdicts suggest strongly that any such testimony should be corroborated with additional supportive evidence in order to be more fully reliable (Jackson, 1986).

A major problem prosecutors face is getting victims or witnesses to testify in court (Davis, 1983). The courtroom is a mystery to many persons and the thought of enduring questioning on the witness stand is not especially attractive. In an effort to allay fears of victim-witnesses, various **victim-witness assistance programs** have been initiated (Finn and Lee, 1985). *Victim-witness assistance programs are services that are intended to explain court procedures to witnesses and to notify them of court dates* (Finn and Lee, 1985). Additionally, such programs permit victim-witnesses to feel more comfortable with the criminal justice system generally. One particularly important function of such programs is to help witnesses provide bet-

ter evidence in criminal prosecutions, the end result being a greater number of convictions (Finn and Lee, 1985).

Children as Eyewitnesses

One area that has received much attention in recent years is the reliability of child witnesses, especially in cases alleging child sexual abuse (Dent and Flin, 1992; McGough, 1994). The scientific study of child witnesses by psychologists in the United States began around the turn of the century. Some researchers have concluded that children are the most dangerous witnesses of all (McGough, 1994), partly because an especially traumatic event such as a rape or homicide can distort their recall impressions (Dent and Flin, 1992; Mason, 1991).

A large number of child victims of sexual abuse are under age twelve, and nearly a third are under age six (McGough, 1994). By 1994, half of all states had adopted special *hearsay* exceptions that take effect when children are giving testimony about being abused. Of primary concern to a judge and other participants in the courtroom is children's ability to distinguish between real and imagined events (Davies et al., 1995; Whitcomb et al., 1994).

Further, the parents of sexually abused children are often reluctant to allow them to testify in court. Some have suggested that children be permitted to testify in some place other than the courtroom and that their testimony be monitored through closed-circuit television (Whitcomb et al., 1994). Under the Sixth Amendment, however, defendants are entitled to confront their accusers (Ceci and Bruck, 1995; Zaragoza, 1995). Thus, at least for the present, it would seem that the use of closed-circuit television in cases such as child sexual abuse will need to be closely scrutinized by the Supreme Court before it is approved on a national scale.

To prevent distortion in the testimony of a child witness, special care should be taken to distinguish between real and imagined events.

Directed Verdict of Acquittal

At the conclusion of the state's case against the defendant, the defense attorney may make a motion to the court for a **directed verdict of acquittal.** *A directed verdict of acquittal requests the judge to dismiss the case against the defendant because the prosecution has not proved its case beyond a reasonable doubt.* Thus, the defense believes that its client has not been proved guilty and should be freed. There is no research that indicates the frequency of such requests, but they are probably made in a large number of criminal cases. If the case is being heard by a jury, the presiding judge is reluctant to grant such a motion because the jury is charged with the responsibility of determining guilt or innocence. Judges may grant such a motion, however, if they feel that the state has failed to present a convincing case of the defendant's guilt. But such motions are infrequently granted. If the case is a high-profile one, such as the trial of O. J. Simpson, the judge is even less likely to grant such a motion. Such a motion was made in Simpson's trial in early 1996 following the prosecution's case, but the presiding judge, Lance Ito, denied the motion.

The Defense and Summation

The defense attorney presents all evidence and witnesses who have relevant testimony favorable to the defendant. The prosecutor may object to the introduction of certain witnesses or to any kind of evidence the defense intends to introduce.

Defendants may or may not choose to testify in their own behalf. Their right *not to testify* is guaranteed by the Fifth Amendment, as is their right against self-incrimination. Of course, if a defendant does not testify, the jury may conclude that the defendant has something to hide. It is difficult to make the jury understand that defendants are merely exercising their rights under the Fifth Amendment and that nothing of either a positive or negative nature should be inferred from a defendant's decision not to testify. It is the responsibility of the state to prove the case against the defendant beyond a reasonable doubt. The defendant is entitled to a presumption of innocence until guilt is established by the "beyond-a-reasonable-doubt" standard.

Some persons claim that if a jury finds a defendant *not guilty* and votes for acquittal, this doesn't necessarily mean that the defendant is *innocent.* Thus, being judged not guilty is *not* equivalent to being acquitted of criminal charges. But this erroneous belief undermines the fundamental principles of the Constitution and the rights it conveys to all citizens, regardless of how guilty they *may appear* to the public or media. Therefore, if we presume that a defendant is innocent until proven guilty beyond a reasonable doubt, an acquittal causes the *presumption of innocence* to remain unchanged.

Two quite different books appeared in 1996 following the verdict in the murder trial of sports figure O. J. Simpson: *Convicted But Innocent: Wrongful Conviction and Public Policy* by Ron Huff, Arye Rattner, and Edward Sagarin, and *Guilty: The Collapse of Criminal Justice* by Harold J. Rothwax. These two books address fundamentally different views of jury voting. Jury decisions may result in *convictions of innocent persons,* or they may result in *acquittals of guilty persons.* Neither book says anything new about jury voting. Rothwax, a former judge, suggests that current laws and procedures handicap the police and prosecutors from apprehending and convicting criminals and prevent courts from resolving the primary question of whether the accused committed the crime. He explores various drastic changes in the laws so that the ends of justice might be served more effectively, through more frequent convictions and fewer reversals of convictions on technical grounds. Huff's book examines various cases in which innocent persons were convicted. Presently, we acknowledge that our legal system is flawed, and it is likely that it will always be flawed. While these two books offer criticisms of the criminal justice system that allows such events to occur, there is no foolproof way of preventing their occurrence, no matter what reforms are implemented.

Can Prosecutors Criticize Defendants for Not Testifying in Their Own Behalf?

The prosecution is forbidden from mentioning a defendant's refusal to testify to the jury (*Griffin v. California,* 1965). A statement from the prosecutor such as "Ladies and gentlemen of the jury, if this defendant were innocent, he would get up here on the stand and say so" would be improper, and the judge would order it stricken from the record. In fact, such an utterance might lead to a mistrial. Both prosecutors and defense attorneys are bound by legal ethics to comply with court rules when presenting a case or representing a client in the courtroom. But occasionally some attorneys engage in unethical conduct, either deliberately or inadvertently. Sometimes such conduct results in the judge declaring a mistrial, and the case will have to be tried again in front of a new jury.

Each side is permitted a **summation** at the conclusion of the presentation of all evidence. Ordinarily, the defense attorney first presents the final oral argument on behalf of his or her client. This is followed by the closing argument of the prosecuting attorney. Sometimes, with court consent, a prosecutor may be the first to present a portion of his or her closing argument, followed by the closing argument of the defense, followed by the remainder of the prosecutor's closing argument. The prosecutor always makes the final remarks to the jury.

Jury Deliberations

After the prosecution and defense have presented their final arguments, the judge instructs the jury on the procedures it must follow in reaching a verdict, and *the jury retires to the jury room to consider the evidence and arrive at a verdict.* The judge's instructions to the jury often include a recitation of the charges against the defendant, a listing of the elements of the crime the prosecution must prove beyond a reasonable doubt, a reminder not to draw any inferences, positive or negative, from a defendant's refusal to testify, and a charge to carefully weigh and consider the evidence and testimony of witnesses.

Again, depending upon whether the case is tried in a federal or local court, the jury's decision must either be unanimous or comply with the particular local rules governing jury verdicts. If a federal jury of twelve persons fails to reach a unanimous decision, the judge will declare a mistrial. And if one member of a federal jury becomes ill, an eleven-member jury is acceptable, with court approval, and must render a unanimous verdict as well. In states such as Louisiana and Oregon, the state rules governing jury verdicts call for 9–3 or 10–2 majority votes, respectively, in order for a defendant to be convicted of the crime alleged. In six-person jury situations, the jury must reach a unanimous decision, according to the U.S. Supreme Court.

Jury deliberations have been targeted for study by social scientists (Kerr, 1994; Kerr and MacCoun (1985). The chief difficulty confronting those interested in studying jury deliberations is that they are secret. Some investigators have participated as actual jury members in their respective jurisdictions. The insights gained through such experiences have enabled defense attorneys to present more convincing cases to juries (Greene, 1986).

Jury deliberations have often been the subject of feature films and novels. The 1957 drama *Twelve Angry Men,* starring Henry Fonda, depicted jurors' emotion and anger during a murder trial. In that film, Fonda was the lone juror voting not guilty. The remainder of the film described the jury's attempt to convince Fonda that he was wrong. As it turned out, Fonda convinced the other jurors that

they were wrong, and the defendant was acquitted. A 1996 novel by author/lawyer John Grisham, *The Runaway Jury,* gave a detailed depiction of jury deliberations, showing the interplay among jurors and the ease with which jurors' opinions are changed by particularly dominant jury members.

Jury deliberations like those depicted in *Twelve Angry Men* are not uncommon (Simon, 1980). Jurors with different opinions about particular evidence attempt to persuade the other jurors to side with them. At the outset, jurors may take an informal vote to see where they stand. More often than not, this initial ballot significantly influences the final verdict by showing where the majority of jurors stand (Kalven and Zeisel, 1966).

Hastie, Penrod, and Pennington (1983:119–20) have found that group pressure is responsible for moving minority factions in a jury into alignment with majority opinion. In jurisdictions where the majority-rule option is in effect, such as Oregon and Louisiana, agreement among jurors is achieved more rapidly than in jurisdictions requiring unanimity of opinion (Foss, 1981). Figure 9.2 illustrates jury deliberations.

Figure 9.2 Jury Deliberation

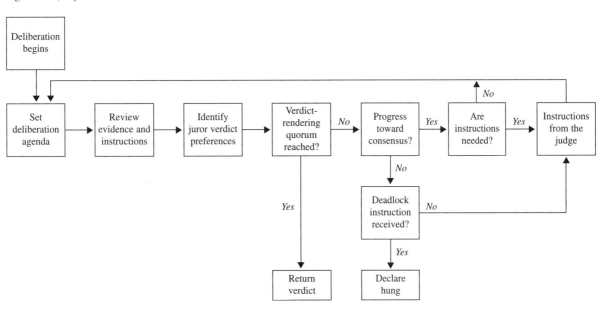

When deliberations begin, juries may or may not establish a deliberation agenda. Ordinarily, discussions take place concerning the relevance and importance of particular evidence and witness testimony. If there is an initial vote and the jury disagrees, deliberations continue until a verdict is reached. If the jury simply cannot agree, or if the required majority cannot be obtained, the judge will likely declare a mistrial.

Must the Members of a Jury Agree on a Verdict?

Jury Voting in U.S. District Courts

In federal district courts, juries consist of *twelve* persons. The judge may or may not approve the selection of several *alternate jurors.* Alternate jurors are chosen in the event that one or more of the regular jurors become ill during the proceedings. Also, during jury deliberations, if a juror cannot continue to serve, 18 U.S.C., Rule 23, provides that "if the court finds it necessary to excuse a juror for just cause after the jury has retired to consider its verdict, in the discretion of the court a valid verdict may be returned by the remaining eleven jurors" (Title 18, U.S.C., 1996). In federal courts, whether a twelve- or eleven-member jury hears a case, the decision the jury reaches must be *unanimous.* If one or more jurors persist in their disagreement with the other jurors, the result is a *hung jury* and a *mistrial* is declared. *Mistrials are erroneous, invalid, or nugatory trials* (Black, 1990:1002). This means that the entire case will have to be heard again before a new jury. Mistrials also occur during the trial, especially if irregularities jeopardize a defendant's right to a fair trial. Sometimes inadmissible evidence might be admitted erroneously. A witness may say something that might unduly bias the jury. Whenever such trial irregularities occur, the judge ordinarily grants a motion by either side for a mistrial (Hodge, 1986; Institute for Court Management, 1983).

Jury Voting in State Courts

At the local and state levels, however, the federal rule for jury agreement or unanimity does not always apply. Under existing Supreme Court guidelines, state juries may vary in size from six persons to twelve persons. The Supreme Court established the minimum number of jury members as six in the case of *Williams v. Florida* (1970). However, no such precedent has been established for upper limits of jury sizes. Thus, it is conceivable that a defendant might request a jury consisting of more than twelve persons, such as twenty-five or fifty jurors. But this would be both unconventional and in violation of state court guidelines and procedures. It would also pose severe logistical problems for courtrooms, not to mention for jurors who must reach agreement.

Six-member juries must be unanimous in their verdict (*Burch v. Louisiana,* 1979). However, if a jury consists of twelve persons, a majority verdict may be acceptable, unless unanimity is required under state or local laws. For instance, in the cases of *Apodaca v. Oregon* (1972) and *Johnson v. Louisiana* (1972), the respective defendants were convicted by a majority of jurors, but there was no unanimity of agreement. Frank Johnson was arrested, tried, and convicted of armed robbery in 1968. The twelve-person jury convicted him by a 9–3 vote (the absolute minimum majority required under Louisiana law). Robert Apodaca was convicted of assault with a deadly weapon by an 11–1 vote. (In Oregon, the minimum vote that would sustain a criminal conviction is 10–2.) Their respective appeals were heard by the Supreme Court. The Court upheld their convictions and the right of states to utilize a majority vote in jury trials. The Tennessee State Legislature has copied the Federal Rules of Criminal Procedure and elected to require their twelve-member juries to reach unanimous verdicts. In capital cases, where the death penalty may be imposed, the vote for conviction must always be unanimous.

Polling the Jurors

Once jurors have rendered their verdict, judges will frequently poll the jury by asking each juror to state in open court whether the verdict is a true reflection of his or her feelings and of how the jury voted. It is unlikely that a particular juror will tell the judge that he or she did not agree with the jury's decision. Obviously, in jurisdictions where verdicts must be unanimous, such a statement would be especially important. In states such as Louisiana and Oregon, where unanimous votes are not needed, polling individual jury members identifies the specific vote breakdown. If one or more jurors disagree with the majority in a state or federal court where the jury vote must be unanimous, judges will tell the jury to continue deliberating until they reach a verdict. If they cannot reach a verdict, a mistrial will be declared and a new trial will be scheduled.

The Selling of Jury Deliberations

The 1980s and 1990s have seen increasing interest in jury deliberations and in factual accounts of what transpires in jury rooms (Kerr, 1994). Individual jury members have exploited their jury membership for profit. This phenomenon is not peculiar to the United States. Other countries, such as Australia and Great Britain, have found that some jurors in especially high-profile cases have focused on the profit motive as a primary reason for being on the jury (Findlay and Duff, 1988).

In particularly sensational trials, jury members' opinions about jury deliberations are increasingly marketable (Kleinig, 1989). Several jurors in the murder trial of O. J. Simpson were excused when the judge learned that they were considering writing books about their experience. One former juror had been keeping a journal, which was regarded as juror misconduct. Another juror, who was excused for a different reason, eventually posed nude for *Playboy* magazine. While this is not against the law, it raises a question about her motives for becoming a juror.

When jurors in *any* trial consider profiting from their roles as jurors, it raises serious questions about their truthfulness during the *voir dire* stage of the trial. If they have hidden agendas, such as writing a book about their experiences, no laws prohibit subsequent expressions of their opinions and views. But it is juror misconduct to keep journals about their jury involvement and observations. If the prosecution or defense learned of such activities, certainly this would make the particular prospective juror suspect as an impartial finder of fact.

During the trial stemming from a highly publicized racial attack in the Howard Beach community of New York City, several jurors tried to sell their accounts of jury deliberations to the media. Some news reporters believed that such conduct was acceptable and within the boundaries of free speech. The court and prosecution took a different view and condemned those jurors who sought to profit from their experiences as jurors (Kleining, 1989).

What if persons seek to become jurors in order to advance some political view or social cause? Ideally, a jury is comprised of persons who will weigh all factual information presented by both sides in an attempt to render a fair decision. But if some jurors are sidetracked by issues not directly related to the trial, it can impair their ability to render fair judgments.

The Verdict and the Aftermath

After deliberating, the jury returns to the courtroom and delivers its **verdict** to either the judge or an officer of the court. The defendant rises and faces the jury while either the jury foreperson or the judge reads the verdict aloud. If the verdict is not guilty, the defendant is released. In some cases, acquitted defendants may be rearrested for other crimes. Ordinarily, an acquittal removes the defendant from the criminal justice system.

If the jury renders a guilty verdict, the defendant has the right to appeal. The defense attorney may again request the judge to make a directed verdict of acquittal, despite the jury's decision. The judge may, indeed, exercise this option. However, if the judge sets aside the verdict and acquits the defendant, the prosecution can appeal that decision to a higher court.

If the judge does not grant the defense attorney's request, the defendant is sentenced. The sentencing process will be examined in greater detail in chapter 10. The appeals process may take many years. In all of the Supreme Court cases described in this book, the time between the offense, the conviction, and the Supreme Court decision has been several years. Before a case gets before the Supreme Court, however, it must be reviewed by higher courts within the state jurisdiction of the original verdict. This appeals process consumes much time as well. Cases presented before the Supreme Court usually involve constitutional is-

---

Highlight 9.5. Juries Are Sometimes Wrong for the Right Reasons: The Case of Kevin Lee Green

In Santa Ana, California, in 1979, a pregnant woman was brutally raped and murdered. Her unborn baby also died as the result of the attack. But police had their man. Justice would be served! Arrested for these crimes was Kevin Lee Green, the husband of the murdered woman and the father of the unborn baby. In 1980 Green was convicted and sentenced to life imprisonment.

In June of 1996, Kevin Lee Green was brought back into court. The judge told him, "We made a mistake. You didn't kill your wife and unborn baby. Your conviction is hereby reversed and you are free to leave prison." What happened?

DNA technology has advanced to an incredibly refined stage. Now we have the technology to identify, fairly precisely, rapists who have left their semen and/or blood at the crime scene. A woman being raped might scratch her attacker. Forensics experts can recover skin scrapings from underneath her fingernails, and the rapist's DNA can be recorded. For many years after the crime, this DNA can be matched with other DNA from suspects.

A technician recording DNA samples noted that Green's DNA didn't match the rapist's DNA. In fact, a match *was* found, but it belonged to someone who was in prison for another crime. When the other man, a convicted rapist, was confronted with this new evi-

dence, he confessed to murdering Green's wife and unborn baby. Case solved!

Superior Court judge Robert Fitzgerald apologized to Green in open court. "You're about to wake up after a sixteen-year nightmare," Fitzgerald said. "I want to congratulate you on the end result, and the court, on behalf of society, apologizes to you for your incarceration. I wish you have a good and happy remainder of your life."

Circumstantial evidence led to Green's conviction for rape and murder. If DNA technology had existed in 1980, perhaps Green would have been cleared of any wrongdoing. But the system made a mistake. A prosecutor developed a convincing case, beyond a reasonable doubt in fact. The jury bought it and convicted Green. But a terrible mistake has been corrected. The question remains, how many like Green are in prison today?

What should the government do to compensate Kevin Green for his years in prison? What measures should it take to ensure him employment that suits his skills and education? Can the government adequately repay a person for sixteen years of wrongful imprisonment?

Source: Adapted from Associated Press, "Man Freed after 17 Years in Jail," *Minot (N.D.) Daily News,* June 22, 1996, p. A2.

---

sues. Were a defendant's constitutional rights violated at any stage of the criminal proceeding? Did court participants, such as the judge, make procedural errors that would invalidate the original conviction and justify a new trial?

Summary

A trial enables defendants to confront and cross-examine their accusers and to offer exculpatory evidence. A trial is an adversarial proceeding, where the prosecution attempts to establish a defendant's

guilt and the defense attempts to prove his or her innocence.

Trial procedures vary from one jurisdiction to the next. The number of jurors ranges from six to twelve. At the federal level, a verdict must be unanimous. At the state and local levels, however, a unanimous verdict may or may not be required.

Juries are made up of persons from the community or region that has jurisdiction over the crimes alleged. The selection of jury members involves questioning them concerning their possible biases or prejudices in the case before the court. Both prosecution and defense attorneys attempt to select jurors favorable to their interests. Jurors are excluded from jury duty because of illness or other compelling circumstances, and both prosecution and defense attorneys may challenge any juror for cause. Jurors may also be excluded by means of peremptory challenges, as the prosecutor and defense attorney attempt to construct the most favorable jury for their particular position. Peremptory challenges may not be used for purposes of discrimination, however.

The science of jury selection is popular. Many attorneys turn to consulting firms that specialize in selecting jury members. However, the results of studies investigating particular characteristics of jury members and their decisions have been inconsistent and disappointing. No one has been able to predict with 100 percent certainty how particular jury members will vote in a given trial.

In any trial, both the prosecution and defense have specific roles and follow established protocol in presenting their evidence and witnesses. Each side is permitted to address the jury with an opening statement. Each side is also entitled to cross-examine witnesses and to object to certain evidence. Witnesses can be reexamined in redirect and recross examinations. The process continues until both sides are satisfied that the evidence has been adequately presented.

After both sides have presented witnesses and evidence, the jury deliberates and reaches a verdict. If the jury cannot agree on a verdict as local, state, or federal law requires, the judge will declare a mistrial. This will require a new trial before a new jury. If a jury finds the defendant guilty, the judge will sentence the convicted offender, either at the conclusion of the trial or in a separate proceeding.

Key Terms

Bench trial
Challenge for cause
Criminal trial
Cross-examination
Death-qualified jury
Direct examination
Directed verdict of acquittal
Exclusionary rule

Expert witness
Eyewitnesses
Fruits-of-the-poisonous-tree doctrine
Jury deliberations
Jury nullification
Jury trial
Motions *in limine*
Motion to dismiss
Peremptory challenges
Petit jury
Pretrial motions
Recross examination
Redirect examination
Summation
Sworn in
Veniremen
Verdict
Victim-witness assistance programs
Voir dire

Questions for Review

1. What is a pretrial motion? What are some examples of pretrial motions?
2. Differentiate between a bench trial and a jury trial. Is there any evidence that a defendant is better off having a bench trial than a jury trial?
3. What is a trial? What are some of the functions of a trial proceeding?
4. Does a criminal defendant have to have a jury trial if he or she is charged with murder? Can the defendant waive his or her right to a jury trial? What constitutional amendment pertains to jury trials?
5. What is a venire? What is it used for?
6. Identify three functions of juries. What Supreme Court decision pertains to setting lower limits for jury sizes? What limit did it establish?
7. In a criminal case before a six-person jury, the jury brought back a verdict of guilty, but the vote was 5 to 1. Evaluate this verdict in view of what you have learned about jury size and unanimity among jurors.
8. On the basis of some of the research into jury size, is a twelve-member jury more representa-

tive of community interests than a six-person jury? What are some differences between juries of these sizes?

9. How are juries selected? Where do jurors come from? What criteria do courts use to prepare jury lists?

10. What are five of the "maxims" reported by Rita Simon about juror characteristics and accompanying juror attitudes?

Suggested Readings

Arrigo, Bruce A. *The Contours of Psychiatric Justice: A Postmodern Critique of Mental Illness, Criminal Insanity, and the Law.* New York: Garland, 1996.

Daley, Kathleen. *Gender, Crime and Punishment.* New Haven, CT: Yale University Press, 1994.

Epstein, Lee. *Contemplating Courts.* Washington, DC: CQ Press, 1995.

George, Jody, Deirdre Golash, and Russell Wheeler. *Handbook on Jury Use in the Federal Courts.* Washington, DC: Federal Judicial Center, 1989.

Healey, Kerry Murphy. *Victim and Witness Intimidation: New Developments and Emerging Responses.* Washington, DC: U.S. National Institute of Justice, 1995.

Huff, C. Ronald, Arye Rattner, and Edward Sagarin. *Convicted But Innocent: Wrongful Conviction and Public Policy.* Thousand Oaks, CA: Sage, 1995.

Levine, James P. *Juries and Policies.* Belmont, CA: Wadsworth, 1992.

Rothwax, Harold J. *Guilty: The Collapse of Criminal Justice.* New York: Random House, 1996.

Yanich, Danilo. *The Pace of Justice: Processing Criminal Cases in Delaware.* Newark, DE: Delaware Public Administration Institute, University of Delaware, 1990.

CHAPTER 10

The Sentencing Process

Larry Fisher, a thirty-five-year-old from Belling-ham, Washington, robbed a sandwich shop of $151. Nobody was hurt. Fisher was carrying a knife but did not use it in the robbery. Larry had had some previous trouble involving minor offenses. A few years earlier, he had taken $360 from his grandfather and $100 from a pizza parlor. The judge sentenced Larry to life imprisonment without the possibility of parole (Davis, 1994:A4).

Cheryl Richard, twenty-four, was convicted of two counts of possessing crack-cocaine pipes. Yes, pipes. Not the crack cocaine that goes with the pipes. She was eight months pregnant with her fourth child. The judge gave her the following options: "Pay a $750 fine and spend three months in jail" or "Get your fallopian tubes tied so that you can't have any more kids, stay on probation for two years, and get mandatory counseling." Cheryl elected the sentence of two years' probation, counseling, and having her fallopian tubes tied (Associated Press, 1995b:A2).

Todd Burwell, twenty-nine, was extradited in October 1993 back to Massachusetts to face charges for a murder allegedly committed in 1988. Burwell pleaded guilty to the murder and received a one-year suspended sentence. The murder? A five-month-old poodle who defecated on his carpet. He killed the dog by putting it in a trash compactor. The crime: malicious intent to kill an animal, a felony (Associated Press, 1993:A2).

Ronald Riggons, thirty-three, bit a police officer, Mason Byrd, on the finger during a scuffle when Byrd tried to arrest Riggins for being disorderly. Riggins was convicted of attempted third-degree murder and sentenced to ten years in prison. Riggins had told Byrd, "I have AIDS." Byrd had his finger treated and tested negative for HIV (Associated Press, 1995a:A2).

Debra Ann Forster, eighteen, of Mesa, Arizona, pleaded guilty in June 1988 to leaving her two sons, ages six months and eighteen months, alone in a sweltering apartment for three days. Maricopa County Superior Court Judge Lindsay Ellis Budzyn sentenced Forster as follows: Forster must use birth control for the rest of her child-bearing years. To ensure that Forster lives up to her part of the agreement, Forster must be examined monthly by a physician and must provide a report of her examination, showing that she is not pregnant, to her probation officer (*Time*, "Inconceivable Sentence").

Should Larry Fisher get a life-without-parole sentence for stealing $151? Should Cheryl Richard be required to be sterilized for possessing crack-cocaine pipes? Should Todd Burwell sustain a felony conviction for killing a five-month-old poodle? Should Ronald Riggins get ten years for biting a police officer's finger? Should Debra Ann Foster be required to remain pregnant-free and submit monthly reports to this effect to her probation officer?

The fact is that each of these punishments is a lawfully imposed **sentence** in its jurisdiction. At the time these sentences were imposed, state legislatures and the U.S. Supreme Court considered each lawful and justified. *A sentence is the judgment formally pronounced by the court or judge upon the defendant following his or her conviction in a criminal prosecution, imposing the punishment to be inflicted, usually in the form of a fine, incarceration, or probation* (Black, 1990:1362–63). Another view of sentencing is the punishment imposed for a particular offense, as prescribed by law, by a court or judge. Some of the sentences described above were *creative*, but they were lawful nevertheless. Obviously, judges can exercise some discretion in tailoring sentences to the circumstances of the offense and prior record of the offender.

This chapter examines the sentencing process. Included in this examination are discussions on the goals of sentencing, a number of sentencing issues, the defendant's rights in the sentencing process, selected variables and their influence on sentencing decisions and severity, the dangerousness of the offender, and several popular sentencing alternatives.

The sentencing process is the penalty phase of the criminal justice system. It is very controversial. In recent years, the sentencing practices of judges at the local, state, and federal levels have been widely criticized as discriminatory, unfair, inappropriate, inconsistent, and ineffective (Indermaur, 1990).

Factors such as jail and prison overcrowding;

escalating rates of recidivism; increased use of plea bargaining; and obvious gender, race, ethnic, and socioeconomic influences have led to many criticisms of the sentencing process generally and judicial sentencing practices specifically (Gray et al., 1991; Zimring and Hawkins, 1995). Some sentencing reformers favor the **selective incapacitation** of felons who pose a high risk for recidivism. *Selective incapacitation is the process of incarcerating certain offenders who are defined by various criteria as having a strong propensity to repeat serious crimes* (Champion, 1994; Spelman, 1994; Zimring and Hawkins, 1995).

Opponents of selective incapacitation argue that the process is discriminatory, results in undeserved punishment for many offenders, fails to identify the best predictors of criminal behavior, and violates the constitutional right to due process (Farrington, 1992; Gottfredson and Gottfredson, 1992; Hoffman, 1994).

The Sentencing Reform Act of 1984

Faced with a rapidly expanding prison population and the serious problem of overcrowding, Congress passed the **Sentencing Reform Act of 1984** (18 U.S.C., Sec. 3551, 1996). Amended several times in recent years, this act establishes several significant policy shifts to be implemented by federal trial judges as integral features of their sentencing practices (Jensen et al., 1991; McDonald and Carlson, 1993). For instance, Section 239 of Public Law 98–473 provides that:

> Since, due to an impending crisis in prison overcrowding, *available Federal prison space must be treated as a scarce resource in the sentencing of criminal defendants;* since, sentencing decisions should be designed to ensure that prison resources are, first and foremost, *reserved for those violent and serious criminal offenders who pose the most dangerous threat to society;* since, in cases of nonviolent and nonserious offenders, the interests of society as a whole as well as individual victims of crime can continue to be served through the imposition of alternative sentences, such as restitution and community service . . .

Federal judges, in determining the particular sentence to be imposed [should] consider *(1) the nature and circumstances of the offense and the history and characteristics of the defendant; (2) the general appropriateness of imposing a sentence other than imprisonment in cases in which the defendant has not been convicted of a crime of violence or otherwise serious offense; and (3) the general appropriateness of imposing a sentence of imprisonment in cases in which the defendant has been convicted of a crime of violence or otherwise serious offense.* (18 U.S.C., Sec. 3551, 1996:263–64; emphasis added).

This act has had mixed results. On the one hand, the wording of the act encourages judges to consider seriously various alternative sentences in lieu of incarceration, such as community service, restitution, and even probation. However, the act also provides for the establishment of *sentencing guidelines.* In fact, these U.S. Sentencing Guidelines went into effect in November 1987. Over the next several years, the guidelines significantly reduced judicial discretion in sentencing federal offenders. For instance, prior to the guidelines, each year judges sentenced about 65 percent of all convicted federal prisoners to probation. However, following the implementation of the guidelines, only about 10 percent of all convicted federal offenders were eligible for probation (Berlin, 1993; Champion, 1989b; Heaney et al., 1992). This subject will be discussed at length in the section on *presumptive sentencing* later in this chapter.

Among the factors to be considered by the federal judiciary are (1) the nature and circumstances of the offense and the history and characteristics of the defendant; (2) the need for the sentence to reflect the seriousness of the offense, to promote respect for the law, to afford adequate deterrence to criminal conduct, and to protect the public from further crimes of the defendant; (3) the kinds of educational or training services, medical care, or other correctional treatment that might be appropriate for the defendant; (4) the kinds of sentences available; and (5) the need to avoid unwarranted disparities in sentences imposed on defendants with similar records who have been found guilty of similar conduct (18 U.S.C., Sec. 3553, 1996:265).

Congress has been more sensitive to at least some of the criticisms leveled at judicial sentencing practices in recent years. For example, in several jurisdictions in the past, women have received less severe sentences than men convicted for similar offenses (Zingraff and Thomson, 1984). And quite often, black and ethnic minority defendants have received harsher sentences than whites convicted of similar crimes under similar circumstances (Clayton, 1983; Peterson and Hagan, 1984). Therefore, a major objective of sentencing legislation in the 1980s was to eliminate these sentencing disparities and create more equitable forms of sentencing (Wood and Sheehey, 1994). However, more recent evidence suggests that sentencing disparities according to gender, race, ethnicity, and other factors continue in most jurisdictions, even among the federal judiciary (Crutchfield et al., 1993; McDonald and Carlson, 1993; U.S. General Accounting Office, 1992b).

Many local and state jurisdictions are influenced by the sentencing standards and practices of federal courts. One implication of the Sentencing Reform Act of 1984 is that it has caused judges in every jurisdiction to reassess their ideas about sentencing and modify their priorities based on *which* convicted felons will pose the *least* public risk if placed on probation. About half of those released from prison each year will commit new offenses within the next three years (Maguire and Pastore, 1995:574, 578). A study of California felony probationers conducted by the Rand Corporation found that 65 percent of those placed on probation committed new offenses within the following forty months (Petersilia et al., 1985).

In 1993, for example, within the first year of being granted parole 22 percent of the parolee population had been returned to prison for violating one or more parole conditions (Maguire and Pastore, 1995). Thus, judges deciding whether to incarcerate or grant probation to convicted offenders and parole boards considering whether to grant parole must consider whether the offender is likely to reoffend in the future. (Chapter 13 gives an in-depth examination of probationers and parolees and their characteristics.) Judges must sentence offenders according to various objectives or goals. Further, judicial discretion in sentencing is influenced greatly by the type of sentencing scheme the jurisdiction uses. Therefore, it is important to consider some of the *functions* and *types* of sentencing systems.

Table 10.1
Federal Sentencing Classification of Offenses

If maximum term of imprisonment authorized is:	*Then the classification and type of offense is:*
Life imprisonment, death penalty	Class A felony
20 years or more	Class B felony
Less than 20 years but 10 or more years	Class C felony
Less than 10 years but 5 or more years	Class D felony
Less than 5 years but more than 1 year	Class E felony
1 year or less but more than 6 months	Class A misdemeanor
6 months or less but more than 30 days	Class B misdemeanor
30 days or less but more than 5 days	Class C misdemeanor
5 days or less, or no imprisonment	Infraction

Source: 18 U.S.C., Section 3559 (1986), pp. 268–69.

Functions of Sentencing

The Sentencing Reform Act of 1984 restated a number of objectives that have guided judges in sentencing defendants. Some of these objectives have been made explicit by various states and local jurisdictions, while others have been implicitly incorporated into prevailing sentencing guidelines.

The functions of sentencing are (1) to reflect the seriousness of the offense; (2) to promote respect for the law; (3) to provide just punishment for the offense; (4) to deter the defendant from future criminal conduct; (5) to protect the public from the convicted defendant; and (6) to provide the convicted defendant with education and/or vocational training or other rehabilitation. The purposes of sentencing include punishment or retribution, deterrence, custodial monitoring or incapacitation, and rehabilitation.

Reflecting the Seriousness of the Offense

Sentences should be proportional to the seriousness of the offense (Gottfredson and Gottfredson, 1992; Zimring and Hawkins, 1995). In federal district courts, offenses are designated Class A, B, C, D, and E felonies and Class A, B, and C misdemeanors. Each of these classifications carries

with it a minimum and maximum term. For example, if the maximum term of punishment is life imprisonment or if the maximum penalty is death, then the offense is a Class A felony. If the maximum term of imprisonment is between six months and one year, it is a Class A misdemeanor. These sentencing classifications are explicitly provided in 18 U.S.C., Sec. 3559 (1996). Table 10.1 shows the classifications of federal offenses.

All federal criminal statutes have accompanying penalties and variable terms of imprisonment. These felony classifications provide for imprisonment of twenty years or more, or the death penalty. But even with certain Class A and Class B felonies, particularly those with a sufficient number of mitigating circumstances, judges may impose probation. But no system thus far has totally eliminated sentencing disparity (Heaney, 1991; Rhodes, 1991).

Promoting Respect for the Law

A logical function of sentencing is to promote respect for the law. But if current **recidivism rates** are a measure of respect for the law, our sentencing practices are not successfully fulfilling this objective (Nidorf, 1995:6–7). *Recidivism rates are measured by the number of convicted offenders who are reconvicted for new offenses in proportion to the number of convicted offenders released through probation, pa-*

In 1994, Jesse Timmendequas sexually abused and then murdered seven-year-old Megan Kanka. Recidivist Timmendequas had already served six years in prison for charges of sexual molestation of a child. Campaigning by the Kanka family prompted the New Jersey legislature to enact a statute, known as Megan's Law, mandating that recently released sex offenders register with police and that the department, in turn, inform community members.

role, or sentence expiration. For example, if one hundred convicted offenders are released on parole in New Jersey in 1996 and forty of them are convicted of new crimes, the recidivism rate would be 40/100 or .40 or 40 percent. *Recidivists are convicted offenders who are subsequently reconvicted for one or more new offenses.*

Recidivism rates vary among the states and the Federal Bureau of Prisons. For example, a survey of forty-one state prison systems showed that in 1994, 34.7 percent of all new prison admissions had been convicted of a prior felony (Camp and Camp, 1995a:14). Camp and Camp (1995a:14) show that the average recidivism rate for *all* new admissions in these forty-one state systems included recidivists with prior felony convictions, with an average follow-up period of 3.6 years. This

is determined by post-release tracking. *Post-release tracking is keeping track of all offenders from their release from state or federal prisons to their next felony conviction.* This means that an average of 3.6 years passed between the time convicted offenders were released from one prison system and were admitted to a new prison system for new felony convictions. Table 10.2 shows recidivism rates for forty-one states, the percent of new admissions with prior felony convictions, and the number of years of post-release tracking.

Table 10.2 shows that for at least forty-one of the jurisdictions surveyed in 1994, post-release tracking varies from as little as 1 year in Massachusetts, New Hampshire, and Virginia to 20 years in Rhode Island. The average post-release tracking is 3.6 years. By the same token, there is considerable

Table 10.2

Forty-One Reporting State Prison Systems

What are the agencies' recidivism rates, and how many years are taken into account?
Thirty-four agencies reported that an average of 34.7 percent of 1994 admissions had served a prior felony sentence; 41 agencies reported an average recidivism rate of 35.0 percent, based on post-release tracking averaging 3.6 years.

	Percent with Priors	Recidivism	Years		Percent with Priors	Recidivism	Years
AL	23.7	27.2	3	MT	44.3	26.0	3
AZ	19.2	45.7	4.5	NE[8]	27.9	20.3	3
AR	17.1	38.0	3	NV	43.1		
CA		53.0	2	NH		49.0	1
CO[1]	21.3	37.0	3	NJ		24.0	3
CT[2]	16.4			NM	33.5	37.7	13
DE	20.7			NY	38.8	25.1	5
DC	40.5	42.1	5	NC[9]		41.0	3
FL[1,3]	50.0	25.9	2	ND	24.1	25.0	3
GA[1]	50.2	39.0	3	OH[10]	48.8	34.0	2
HI[4]		55.0	2	OK	34.9	27.1	3
ID	42.6	38.0	2	OR[11]	71.9	37.8	3
IL[5]	39.6	46.0	3	RI[12]		58.4	20
IN	25.0	25.0	3	SC[13]	56.5	35.0	3
IA	13.4	31.0	2	SD[14]		11.1	
KS[5,6]	9.1	12.0	3	TX[1,15]	28.9	43.0	3
KY		29.5	2	UT		74.0	3
LA	53.5	50.8	5	VT	12.3	35.0	3
ME	36.0			VA[16]	24.2	33.3	1
MD		44.6	3	WA		28.0	3.5
MA[5,7]	49.4	27.0	1	WI	51.6		
MI	36.1	21.4	4	WY	52.2		
MN		19.0	2	FED[17]		40.8	3
MO	23.7	23.0	4.5	Average	34.7%	35.0%	3.6

Source: Camp and Camp (1995a).
1. Prior felony served in reporting, not outside, agency.
2. Prior felony for sent. adm. only.
3. Recid. is releases FY'91–92 with 24-mo. followup.
4. Increase in adm. due to new methodology in computing status changes. Recid. rate based on no. of parole and prob. violators admitted during FY'93 and FY'94 and no. of sent. felons and sent. felon probationers released during the same FY's. Parole and prob. violators generally reincarc. for violating release conditions.
5. Inmates with prior felony est.
6. Recid. is return rate of FY'91 releases. New sent.=12% (other returns; No new sent=34%: Abscond status=5%).
7. 1-yr. follow-up study of releases from MADOC fac. in 1991. Total adm. est.
8. Prior felony excl. parole violators.
9. Recid. based on inmates released during FY'90-91.
10. Recid. based on all releases.
11. Recid. for inmates released for 1st time in 1991.
12. Years tracked is 20 year avg. 1971–1992.
13. Recid. and years based on CY'89 releases. Priors is prior convicts/commits over 90 days.
14. Inmates serving felony convictions in SD tracked forever.
15. Adm. excl. Det. Units, Transfer Units, and Out-Count Inmates.
16. Sent. adm. for inmates with >2 yr sentence. Recid. for inmates confined in the inst.
17. Recid. rate based on rearrest and/or parole revocation criterion.

variation in recidivism rates among new admissions. A low recidivism rate of 11.1 percent was observed in South Dakota in 1994, while Utah reported a high recidivism rate of 74 percent. The Federal Bureau of Prisons reported a recidivism rate of 40.8 percent. A caution is that these recidivism rates must be considered according to the length of the post-release tracking period. Thus, we might expect to observe somewhat lower recidivism rates in states that track offenders for only 1 year than in states that track offenders for 2 or more years. This is because there is greater opportunity to reoffend during longer post-release tracking periods. Interestingly, the states reported above with 1-year post-tracking periods showed recidivism rates of 27 percent, 49 percent, and 33.3 percent. For Utah, the post-release tracking period was 3 years. New Mexico had a 13-year post-release tracking period and a recidivism rate of 37.7 percent. Therefore, the recidivism rate and the duration of post-release tracking do not correlate highly, at least for these 1994 figures.

At least one view posited by experts is that greater use of early release tends to be accompanied by greater amounts of recidivism (Joo, Ekland-Olson, and Kelly, 1995). The *replacement factor hypothesis* suggests that increased levels of incarceration will actually yield a larger, more experienced criminal "workforce" and, ironically, a heightened collective potential for more crime or recidivism. Four successive cohorts of released offenders were investigated during the 1984–1987 period, including 3,547 inmates. Especially among property-offender parolees, recidivism increased dramatically. Thus, it does not appear that incarceration teaches felons respect for the law, at least the cohorts investigated in this research (Joo, Ekland-Olson, and Kelly, 1995). Even some of the more regimented and rigorous post-incarceration programs do not seem to affect recidivism rates significantly (MacKenzie and Souryal, 1994).

Providing Just Punishment for the Offense

An historical analysis of sentencing reforms in the United States suggests that determining the appropriate punishment for offenders has been at the forefront of sentencing issues for the last two centuries (Zimring and Hawkins, 1995). From 1790 to 1820, capital punishment was gradually replaced by lengthy incarceration. This was regarded as "more humane" and guaranteed "more certain" punishment (Rothman, 1983).

Between 1820 and 1900 there was a general shift in sentencing policy that reflected the sentiments of various political interest groups and concerned citizens who wanted to change the goal of sentencing from deterrence to rehabilitation (Rothman, 1983). In recent years, sentencing policy has shifted to the **justice model,** which is a legitimization of the power of the state to administer sanctions (Fogel, 1978; Gottfredson and Gottfredson, 1992). *The justice model of sentencing emphasizes punishment, fixed sentences, an abolition of parole, and an abandonment of the rehabilitative ideal.* The justice model has been applied in dealing with juvenile gangs, for instance. In 1993, a project known as *TARGET* was implemented in Orange County, California, through the joint efforts of the Westminster, California, police department and the Orange County District Attorney's Office. The project was based on selective intervention with particular gangs and intensive intervention with gang members. Of the 647 gang members identified, 77 gang leaders were selected and targeted for program intervention. With the cooperation of various social service agencies, counseling, and other forms of intervention, gang-related criminal activity was substantially reduced in Westminster (Cook, Capizzi, and Schumacher, 1994).

Some critics view the justice model as a purely symbolic sentencing reform because they believe that any policy that suggests expanding the present prison population is illogical and ignores, among other things, the fiscal crises facing federal and local government (Cavender, 1984). These critics also feel that the emphasis on "just deserts" manifested by the justice model is a convenient means for avoiding the undesirable connotation associated with retribution or societal revenge (Crocker, 1992; Texas Criminal Justice Policy Council, 1992).

Proponents of the justice model counter that it promotes more adequate standards of equality and proportionality under the law and that it neither overpunishes the poor nor overlooks the crimes of the rich. The justice model seemingly encourages

---

Highlight 10.1. What Is "Just" Punishment for Cattle Rustling in the 1990s? The Case of Roger Alan Marlow, Cattle Rustler

It happened in Colorado. And Nebraska. And Kansas. And . . . This crime is an old one—cattle rustling. In the days of the Old West, cattle rustlers were hung, usually from trees near where they were caught. Today, cattle rustlers get three years or less as a punishment for theft of property.

Roger Alan Marlow, sixty-two-years old, is a cattle thief. He began rustling cattle as a little boy. Back then, in the 1940s, Marlow stole cattle to practice his cattle roping. In his later years, Marlow would cruise by cattle ranches, stake out some cattle, and then drive his twenty-six-foot-long cattle trailer near a fence and herd cattle into it.

Not much money in cattle rustling these days, you say? Wrong! In 1994 alone, 7,448 cattle were stolen, according to the International Association of Livestock Theft Investigators. The estimated worth of 7,448 stolen cattle is $4 million.

Marlow began his serious cattle rustling in 1982. Between 1982 and 1983, he had stolen nearly four thousand cattle, netting about $1.5 million. He was "by far the smoothest I ever saw," said Texas Ranger Chumpy Cates, who once arrested Marlow in 1983. Marlow would always work alone and change tires and trailers frequently so police couldn't link him directly to the cattle thefts. He had rustled cattle about twenty times before being caught in 1983, when he served only three years as a county jail trustee (a deal arranged through a plea bargain agreement).

After his stint in jail, the Texas Rangers figured that Marlow was finished with rustling. Not so. In the 1990s, Marlow was at it again. He even acquired extra-large fuel tanks so that he could travel nonstop over great distances. His rustling escapades took him through Oklahoma, Nebraska, Kansas, Colorado, Texas, and Kentucky. Litchfield, Kentucky, was the site of his last cattle raid and also of his undoing as a rustler.

One evening in March of 1991, Marlow had staked out the cattle farm of Thomas Bratcher. While making a late-night check on the herd, Bratcher's son found some fence wire cut and several pregnant cows penned together. He notified his father, and they arranged a welcoming committee for Marlow later that evening. Marlow drove up to get the cattle at about 2:00 A.M. The farmers waited until Marlow had the cows loaded and then ordered him to surrender or they'd shoot. Marlow made a run for it, and a bit of the Old West was played out that night. The farmers opened up on Marlow's truck with their shotguns, rifles, and pistols. Marlow's truck and tires were shot full of holes, but Marlow, through some miracle of fate, escaped serious injury. He was captured, however, and the farmers turned him over to police. "It's a wonder the boys didn't kill him," says the local sheriff, Qulin Escue, who made the arrest. Marlow was convicted of cattle rustling and sentenced to three years in a federal prison.

Source: Adapted from Kevin Johnson, "Rustling King No Longer at Home on Range," *USA Today,* June 3, 1996, p. 7A.

---

equal treatment in sentencing and avoids the discriminatory and disparate nature of existing judicial sentencing practices (Humphries, 1984).

Deterring Crime

The substantial recidivism among first offenders and career criminals suggests that the threat of any sentence, even capital punishment, does not deter crime (Dickey, 1995; Spelman, 1995; Wicharaya, 1995). Experts tend to believe that imprisonment has no real deterrent effect upon inmates and that there is little hope of rehabilitating a substantial number of them (Tauro, 1983; Zimring and Hawkins, 1995).

Does selective incapacitation of recidivists keep them from committing crimes? A study of 3,552 convicted burglars was conducted in Dade County, Florida, in 1982 (McGriff, 1985). These burglars were given hypothetical sentences of one, three, and five years for their most recent felony convictions. It was determined that 5.5 percent of the burglaries would not have occurred had these felons been given an earlier one-year sentence. Furthermore, 26 percent of the burglaries would not have occurred had the felons received a five-year sentence at the time of their last felony conviction (McGriff, 1985). But 77.5 percent of these felons were first offenders and unaffected by the hypothetical sentences. Thus, it is questionable that the "gains" (i.e., an absence of burglaries) achieved through incarceration for a five-year period would seriously offset the cost of imprisoning these offenders (McGriff, 1985). The advantages of selective incapacitation have been given substantial support by various researchers (Farrington, 1992; Gottfredson and Gottfredson, 1990; Spelman, 1994).

Protecting the Public from the Convicted Offender

Imprisoning or hospitalizing felons effectively isolates them from the public. However, prisons and jails in the United States have become increasingly overcrowded with recidivists and career criminals (Gottfredson and Gottfredson, 1990), and prison construction is simply not keeping pace with the number of felony convictions. For instance, between 1990 and 1995, the national prison population increased from 773,919 to 980,513, an increase of 78.9 percent. The probation population in fifty-two reporting jurisdictions increased from 1.88 million in 1990 to 2.28 million in 1995, an increase of 82 percent (Camp and Camp, 1995a:1; 1995d:18). The number of inmates placed on parole by state and federal systems also increased from 456,803 in 1990 to 664,404 in 1995, an increase of 68.8 percent (Camp and Camp, 1995d:47; Jankowski, 1991:1–3). Furthermore, between 1983 and 1993, *every* state and federal jurisdiction experienced an increase in the prison population ranging from 27.4 percent in North Dakota to 270.6 percent in New Hampshire (Gilliard and Beck, 1994:3). Some persons are concerned that excessive use of probation and parole puts the public at a high degree of risk from increasing numbers of convicted felons who are permitted to escape the punishment of confinement.

Judges are currently concerned with the potential risk to the public created by the felons whose punishment they will decide. Judges would like to be able to use specific social and personal background criteria to determine with certainty each convict's potential for "staying clean." However, the criteria most often used by judges are frequently found to be unrelated to a convicted defendant's prospects for recidivism (Heaney, 1991; Rhodes, 1991).

Record keeping in some jurisdictions is often so unsophisticated that the same defendant goes through the justice system several times as a first offender in different parts of the state. Also, persons punished for crimes in one state may commit additional crimes in other states, which may not be detected because of faulty record keeping or cursory checks of state records. In short, it is not always easy to identify recidivists.

Attempts by criminologists and criminal justice experts to predict the dangerousness of offenders as a basis for a decision on probation have been inconclusive (Champion, 1994). Some argue against imposing a longer term of imprisonment for an offender who has been designated "dangerous" than for "nondangerous" offenders convicted of similar crimes (Fogel, 1978; Gottfredson and Gottfredson, 1990, 1992; Hoffman, 1994).

The sentencing debate centers around a choice between basing sentences on the blameworthiness of the offender's past criminal acts or on predictions of the offender's future dangerousness (von Hirsch, 1985). Some critics say that punishment ought to be person-centered, because convicted defendants are capable of choice, responsible for their own actions, and punishable according to their degree of fault (von Hirsch, 1985). But selective incapacitation on the basis of predicted dangerousness of a convicted felon is more of a custodial device for the control of undesirables and ignores the *just deserts* that ought to accrue to persons who violate criminal laws (von Hirsch, 1985).

Most states have *habitual offender statutes* that require more severe sentences for dangerous, multiple, or persistent offenders. But few state jurisdictions are enforcing such statutes (Flango, 1994b).

In a survey of all state corrections departments in 1985, for example, Hunzeker (1985) found that three states reported no inmates serving time under these statutes and that seventeen states reported fewer than 3 percent of their inmate populations consisting of these types of offenders. This would mean that most jurisdictions that have statutory mechanisms in place for incarcerating recidivists for prolonged periods refrain from doing so. A likely explanation for a state's reluctance to pursue habitual-offender charges is prison overcrowding and the mandatory prison sentences associated with an habitual-offender conviction. For example, an examination in 1988 of the convicted-offender database in Florida showed that 25,806 offenders were eligible for punishment under the state's habitual offender statute but that only 4,783 (18.5 percent) of these were actually sentenced as habitual offenders (Florida Joint Legislative Management Committee, 1992). This practice is consistent with other states' practices in regard to habitual offenders (Flango, 1994c; Hunzeker, 1985).

Providing Education and Vocational Training

Education and vocational training make up the rehabilitative function of sentencing. Some critics have observed that the rehabilitative ideal has declined as a viable correctional goal (U.S. House of Representatives Committee on the Judiciary, 1994). Alternatives to incarceration, or alternative sentencing, currently include restitution to victims, community service, or educational or vocational training (Knight, Simpson, and Dansereau, 1994; Roberts and Cheek, 1994; Williford, 1996).

When convicted offenders are sentenced to either probation, jail, or prison, they are presented with various educational and rehabilitative options, ranging from counseling for personal or social problems (Masters, 1994) to earning graduate degrees (Lanier, Philliber, and Philliber, 1994). For example, jail inmates in Jefferson County, Kentucky, have an opportunity to participate in Real Opportunities Behind Bars for Employment, or ROBBE (Tewksbury, 1994). ROBBE is a collaborative effort between the county's department of corrections and its public schools. Jail inmates may learn a variety of basic skills

as well as more traditional subjects, such as English. Involvement in this program is purely voluntary. However, over a two-year period during the early 1990s, over six hundred inmates took advantage of the program (Tewksbury, 1994).

Prison inmates in Mississippi are taught life skills to enable them to become more competitive in the job market. Life-skills subjects taught include how to look for employment and complete employment applications, how to manage finances, and how to achieve emotional and domestic stability (Wunder, 1995b:1–3). The Mississippi program is called Life Skills for Prisoners in Mississippi, or LSPM. The overall objective of the program is to enable offenders to reintegrate themselves into society, peacefully and legally, when released.

Inmates of the state prison system in Texas may participate in Operation Kick-It, which is aimed at former drug offenders. Inmates with various types of chemical dependencies, including alcoholism, are encouraged to participate. Between 1970 and 1992, recidivism rates among participants in the program were relatively low compared with those of inmates not involved in the program (Scott, Hawkins, and Farnworth, 1994). Inmates at the Dixon Correctional Institute in Louisiana, a medium-security prison, are encouraged to enroll in a program known as Community Building, which encourages them to develop reading skills. As a result, they are better able to find jobs after being released (Roberts and Cheek, 1994).

There are similar programs for parolees and probationers. In Fort Worth, Texas, probationers may become involved in Relapse Prevention Training (RPT), which provides them with drug education and instructional materials. Probationers who participated in RPT tended to have lower recidivism rates related to drug abuse compared with nonparticipants. Researchers believe that participation in RPT substantially reduces the likelihood of returning to drugs (Knight, Simpson, and Dansereau, 1994).

There are many programs that help juveniles acquire coping skills. Self-management skills are particularly important. Self-control programs in various states give juveniles practical exercises designed to help them react nonviolently to frustrating or threatening situations. Self-control is critical to avoiding delinquent acts (Williford, 1996:85–86).

A participant in the Texas program Operation Kick-It narrates his experience with drug abuse to fellow inmates.

Sentencing Systems

There are four basic kinds of sentencing systems. These vary from one state to the next and even within the same jurisdiction. The sentencing systems include: (1) indeterminate sentencing; (2) determinate sentencing; (3) mandatory sentencing; and (4) presumptive sentencing.

Indeterminate Sentencing

Indeterminate sentences *are of either specified or unspecified duration, with the final release date determined by a parole board* (Black, 1990:771). Indeterminate sentencing provides judges with maximum flexibility in imposing sentences (Tonry, 1993; Washington Indeterminate Sentencing Review Board, 1992). In the federal system, for example, a district judge may impose sentences within the minimum/maximum ranges shown in table 10.3 for various classes of felonies and misdemeanors. It is also within the judge's discretion to place a convicted offender on probation in lieu of incarceration.

Indeterminate sentencing gives parole boards considerable power in determining an offender's release date. For example, judges in Oklahoma impose fixed indeterminate sentences, which are the maximum times offenders may serve, but the parole board can release a prisoner before a third of the sentence is actually served (Koppel, 1984:9). Oregon and Wyoming have similar sentencing practices. Parole boards may award shorter sentences for *good behavior* or for participating in various types of prison activities and programs (Davis, 1990a:1–3). This is known as **good time.** *Good time is the amount of time prisoners can receive off their original sentences for every thirty days served in prison* (Austin, 1994; Chayet, 1994).

Some critics believe that indeterminate sentencing contributes to disparities in sentences, based on the defendant's socioeconomic background, ethnic and racial identity, and gender (Tonry, 1993). But in recent years, state legislatures have limited judicial sentencing discretion by creating statutes that require mandatory sentencing for various classes of offenses (Raeder, 1993).

Determinate Sentencing

In most states indeterminate sentencing schemes have been replaced by **determinate sentencing**, mandatory sentencing, or guidelines-based (presumptive) sentencing (A. R. Roberts, 1994). *A determinate sentence is one involving a sentence by the court to confinement for a fixed period of time and which must be served in full and without parole board intervention, less any "good time" earned in prison* (Black, 1990:450). In Minnesota, for example, the judge sets a determinate prison term based on sentencing guidelines that were established in 1980. Although parole has been abolished in that state, it is

Table 10.3

U.S. Sentencing Commission Sentencing Table

Offense Level	Criminal History Category					
	I 0 or 1	II 2 or 3	III 4, 5, 6	IV 7, 8, 9	V 10, 11, 12	VI 13 or more
1	0–1	0–2	0–3	0–4	0–5	0–6
2	0–2	0–3	0–4	0–5	0–6	1–7
3	0–3	0–4	0–5	0–6	2–8	3–9
4	0–4	0–5	0–6	2–8	4–10	6–12
5	0–5	0–6	1–7	4–10	6–12	9–15
6	0–6	1–7	2–8	6–12	9–15	12–18
7	1–7	2–8	4–10	8–14	12–18	15–21
8	2–8	4–10	6–12	10–16	15–21	18–24
9	4–10	6–12	8–14	12–18	18–24	21–27
10	6–12	8–14	10–16	15–21	21–27	24–30
11	8–14	10–16	12–18	18–24	24–30	27–33
12	10–16	12–18	15–21	21–27	27–33	30–37
13	12–18	15–21	18–24	24–30	30–37	33–41
14	15–21	18–24	21–27	27–33	33–41	37–46
15	18–24	21–27	24–30	30–37	37–46	41–51
16	21–27	24–30	27–33	33–41	41–51	46–57
17	24–30	27–33	30–37	37–46	46–57	51–63
18	27–33	30–37	33–41	41–51	51–63	57–71
19	30–37	33–41	37–46	46–57	57–71	63–78
20	33–41	37–46	41–51	51–63	63–78	70–87
21	37–46	41–51	46–57	57–71	70–87	77–96
22	41–51	46–57	51–63	63–78	77–96	84–105
23	46–57	51–63	57–71	70–87	84–105	92–115
24	51–63	57–71	63–78	77–96	92–115	100–125
25	57–71	63–78	70–87	84–105	100–125	110–137
26	63–78	70–87	78–97	92–115	110–137	120–150
27	70–87	78–97	87–108	100–125	120–150	130–162
28	78–97	87–108	97–121	110–137	130–162	140–175
29	87–108	97–121	108–135	121–151	140–175	151–188
30	97–121	108–135	121–151	135–168	151–188	168–210
31	108–135	121–151	135–168	151–188	168–210	188–235
32	121–151	135–168	151–188	168–210	188–235	210–262
33	135–168	151–188	168–210	188–235	210–262	235–293
34	151–188	168–210	188–235	210–262	235–293	262–327
35	168–210	188–235	210–262	235–293	262–327	292–365
36	188–235	210–262	235–293	262–327	292–365	324–405
37	210–262	234–293	262–327	292–365	324–405	360–life
38	235–293	262–327	292–365	324–405	360–life	360–life
39	262–327	292–365	324–405	360–life	360–life	360–life
40	292–365	324–405	360–life	360–life	360–life	360–life
41	324–405	360–life	360–life	360–life	360–life	360–life
42	360–life	360–life	360–life	360–life	360–life	360–life
43	life	life	life	life	life	life

Source: U.S. Sentencing Commission, *Guidelines*, 1995.

Highlight 10.2. Inmate Asks for "Longer" Sentence: The Case of Thomas Mallum

Thomas Mallum was a thirty-two-year-old inmate at the North Dakota State Penitentiary in Bismarck. He was convicted of several counts of burglary in Morton County and was serving an eighteen-month sentence. He had prior convictions, some for indecent exposure and other sex offenses. He was scheduled for release on January 7, 1996. But Mallum wanted to be kept in the state pen for a few months more. Why?

Mallum appeared before the North Dakota Parole Board in September 1995. The board turned down his request for parole. However, in January 1996, the board granted him parole. According to Mallum, he was afraid of being released penniless into frigid January North Dakota weather. He asked a judge, Thomas Schneider, to lengthen his sentence by three months so that he could be released in warmer weather. Judge Schneider denied his request, saying that the state could not lengthen Mallum's sentence unless he were convicted for a new offense.

It is not as if Mallum didn't try to get his sentence enhanced. While in prison, he exposed himself to female corrections officers to attract attention.

Mallum said of himself, "I am not dangerous. I am more of a nuisance. If I am as dangerous as they say, then why are they releasing me in the middle of winter with no protective clothing?" Good question. During the winter of 1995–1996, temperatures plummeted to –105 degrees, taking into account the wind-chill factor, and there was considerable snow. This is very inhospitable weather, especially for an ex-con with no job, no place to go, no family, and no adequate winter wear.

Should states accommodate requests like Mallum's, especially during dangerous weather? Should judges have authority to grant prisoner's requests for longer prison stays? How much does prison overcrowding affect decisions on early release? Should the weather be a serious consideration, especially in states like North Dakota that have severe winter weather?

Source: Adapted from Associated Press, "Prison Inmate Requests Longer Sentence," *Minot (N.D.) Daily News,* January 3, 1996, p. A1.

possible for a prisoner to be released before actually completing the full sentence by earning good time (D'Allessio and Stolzenberg, 1995; Stolzenberg, 1993). In fact, in jurisdictions that have implemented determinate sentencing, the average prison term has decreased by 50 percent compared with other sentencing forms (Maguire and Pastore, 1995).

In some states, such as New Mexico, the average sentence actually *served* has increased. Thus, while judges are inclined to impose shorter sentences under determinate sentencing, the sentences actually served are longer than those served under indeterminate sentencing.

One objective of determinate sentencing is to give prisoners certainty in when they will be released, and it is ideally designed to make sentencing more fair. North Carolina utilized indeter-

minate sentencing guidelines until 1981 (Clarke et al., 1983). But negative public reaction to unjustified variations in sentencing in felony cases led to North Carolina's Fair Sentencing Act. Based upon an analysis of data derived from over 15,000 felony judgments between 1979 and 1982, for instance, persons convicted of felonies statewide stood a better chance of serving time in prison after the act than before it. The actual chances that offenders would serve time in prison increased from 55 percent in 1979 to 63 percent in 1982. But interestingly, during these two years the median length of sentences decreased from sixty months to thirty-six months.

Another objective of determinate sentencing is to reduce sentencing disparities attributable to race, gender, ethnicity, socioeconomic status, and other extralegal factors (Griset, 1995). However, in states where determinate sentencing has been introduced, such as California, disparities according to race and ethnicity have continued, although more subtly than before (Zatz, 1994). In Minnesota, sentencing disparities decreased by 60 percent when more objective sentencing criteria were established in the early 1980s (Stolzenberg, 1993; D'Allessio and Stolzenberg, 1995). Nevertheless, sentencing disparities have continued in states such as New York (Griset, 1994) and Iowa (Key, 1991).

In determinate sentencing, inmate accumulation of good-time credit is very important because there is no parole board that makes decisions on early release. The use of "good time" credit under *any* sentencing method has been criticized extensively (Chayet, 1994; Texas Criminal Justice Policy Council, 1993a, 1993b). While some believe that good-time credits encourage prisoners to become rehabilitated, other experts say that no evidence exists to support such a belief (Chayet, 1994). Good-time provisions such as those used in Illinois have been applauded on other grounds, such as prison population reduction (Austin, 1994). Many of the prison reforms enacted throughout the 1990s have included reassessments of good-time credits and how they should be applied toward sentence reductions and rehabilitative programs (Texas Criminal Justice Policy Council, 1993a, 1993b; U.S. General Accounting Office, 1993).

Mandatory Sentencing

Both **mandatory sentencing** and presumptive sentencing are considered *subclasses* of determinate sentencing. There are some differences, however. *Under mandatory sentencing, the court is required to impose a prison sentence of a specified length, without the options of probation, suspended sentence, or immediate parole eligibility* (Koppel, 1984:2). This sentencing form allows the court no leeway in deciding whether or not to incarcerate a convicted defendant. Almost every jurisdiction has one or more statutes with mandatory sentencing provisions.

Hawaii's penal code was amended in 1976 to provide for the mandatory imprisonment of repeat offenders (Hawaii Crime Commission, 1984). In 1980, the Hawaii legislature enacted a mandatory

sentencing statute for all Class A felonies (e.g., murder, kidnapping, narcotics trafficking, etc.). Between 1976 and 1983, Hawaii's imprisonment rate climbed substantially, possibly as the result of this statute.

Repeat offenders are often categorized as **habitual offenders,** or career criminals. Depending upon the jurisdiction, *these are offenders with two or more previous felony convictions and who make their living from crime.* Most states, including Hawaii, have habitual offender statutes that usually provide mandatory incarceration, possibly life imprisonment, for habitual or persistent offenders.

However, there are several persistent problems with mandatory sentencing of persistent offenders. One is prison overcrowding. Mandatory incarceration may be sound in principle, but it is difficult to implement on a large scale if there is no room in prisons. One view is that mandatory minimum sentences for persistent offenders will fill prisons and jails with many low-risk offenders when this space would be better allocated to more serious, violent offenders (Campaign for an Effective Crime Policy, 1993; Shilton et al., 1994). If specific violent offenders are targeted for mandatory minimum prison terms, the costs of incarceration may be prohibitive in relation to the amount of crime controlled or prevented (Greenwood et al., 1994). Greenwood and associates (1994) have shown that as a long-term consequence, California's "three strikes and you're out" law—mandating that felons found guilty of a third serious crime can be locked up for twenty-five years to life—may reduce serious felonies committed by adults by as much as 22 to 34 percent, while the costs of incarcerating these persistent felons would cost the state an extra $4.5 billion to $6.5 billion.

Other experts suggest that mandatory sentencing may produce greater racial and gender disparities in sentencing (Schiraldi, 1994; Wallace and Wedlock, 1994). Forer (1994) says that by eliminating judicial discretion under a rationale of making sentencing more equal, more racial minorities, women, and youths will be incarcerated and for longer periods. In California, for instance, mandatory minimum sentences have caused substantial increases in the incarceration of women, especially female minorities (Bloom, Chesney-Lind, and Owen, 1994). The majority of these women are unemployed or low income, and about 80 percent have at least two dependent children.

Ideally, mandatory sentencing is reserved for the most serious violent offenders (Fischer and Thaker, 1992). In Arizona, for example, a mandatory minimum-sentencing policy has resulted in convicted offenders serving at least 75 percent of their original sentences, compared with a national average of 32 percent (Fischer and Thaker, 1992). Also in Arizona, offenders sentenced under the new mandatory minimum-sentencing policy will serve sentences that are 2.7 times longer than previous sentences. Despite the dire predictions of greater prison population growth under mandatory minimum sentencing, some jurisdictions have reported little or no change in their prison populations (Marvell, 1995). However, this "no-change" finding is explained by the fact that in most of these jurisdictions, strategic changes in incarceration policies and broader efforts to limit prison population growth have been more influential then sentencing guidelines or mandatory minimum sentencing schemes (Marvell, 1995). Greater use of jail space in these and other jurisdictions gives the appearance of little or no prison growth as well. Thus, while the incarcerated offender population grows appreciably, it may not be detected as easily in those jurisdictions where more use is made of available jail space (D'Allessio and Stolzenberg, 1995).

Interestingly, habitual offender statutes in most states are not enforced vigorously (Hunzeker, 1985, 1992). Rather, they are used as prosecutorial leverage in the plea bargaining process (Florida Joint Legislative Management Committee, 1992). It is not illegal for prosecutors to threaten to prosecute defendants on habitual offender charges if they do not plead guilty to other offenses. Of course, there must be sufficient evidence of a factual basis for the guilty plea. A judge makes this determination in a plea agreement hearing. But if all habitual offenders were convicted, the mandatory sentences of life imprisonment would soon cause problems of overcrowding beyond those already experienced in most jurisdictions (Marvell, 1995). Some judges anticipate problems of overcrowding and have been known to circumvent mandatory guidelines when sentencing offenders (D'Allessio and Stolzenberg, 1995).

Presumptive Sentencing

Another type of determinate sentencing is **presumptive sentencing.** *Presumptive sentencing is a legislature-mandated sentencing form that proposes sentences of specified lengths with limited judicial discretion to either shorten or lengthen the sentence* (Black, 1990:1363). Presumptive sentencing is also known as *guidelines-based sentencing.* Ordinarily, under presumptive sentencing, the sentence prescribed by statute must be imposed in all unexceptional circumstances. Depending on circumstances, offenders may have their sentences increased or decreased by one or more years under such a sentencing system (von Hirsch et al., 1994).

In California, for example, a judge imposes a determinate prison term based upon presumptive sentence lengths that are set by legislation (Koppel, 1984:5). There are three presumptive sentence lengths specified for each class of offense, however. The judge is obligated to impose the middle sentence length *unless* there are mitigating or aggravating circumstances, in which case the judge can impose the greater or lesser sentence length.

Most states that have instituted sentencing reforms of various kinds in recent years have changed from an indeterminate to a determinate sentencing system in which presumptive and/or mandatory sentencing provisions are included and parole discretion is eliminated or drastically curtailed (Koppel, 1984:2). California and Minnesota are examples of states that utilize presumptive sentencing provisions currently (Pranis, 1990).

In Minnesota, for instance, judges use a sentencing grid in order to determine sentence lengths. Table 10.4 shows the Minnesota Guideline Grid with presumptive sentence lengths. The guideline grid has a convicted offender's *criminal history score* across the top and *severity offense level* down the left-hand side. Where the criminal history score and severity offense level intersect determines the *number of months* judges should impose for particular offenses.

For instance, suppose a convicted offender has no criminal history or prior record. Further suppose that the offender has been convicted of theft under $2,500. At the intersection of column 0 and the row labeled "Theft Crimes ($2,500 or less)" is the number 12. This means that the judge should sentence the offender to twelve months. If the offender has a criminal history score of 3 and a severity level of IX or 9 associated with the conviction offense, then where 3 and 9 intersect shows the number of months an offender should serve. In this case, there is a *range of months*, or 189–201. Notice that 195 appears above the range of 189–201. This 195 is the *presumptive number of months a convicted offender should serve*. The lower and upper boundaries of 189 and 201 are the minimum and maximum number of months of incarceration recommended for that offense committed by an offender with that particular criminal history. Judges can impose 195 months for incarceration for that offense. Or they can move upward toward 201 or downward toward

Table 10.4

Sentencing Guidelines Used in Minnesota

The italicized numbers within the grid denote the range within which a judge may sentence without the sentence being deemed a departure. The criminal history score is computed by adding one point for each prior felony conviction, one-half point for each prior gross misdemeanor conviction, and one-quarter point for each prior misdemeanor conviction. First-degree murder is excluded from the guidelines by law and is punished by life imprisonment.

Severity Levels of Conviction Offense		*Criminal History Score*						
		0	*1*	*2*	*3*	*4*	*5*	*6 OR MORE*
Sale of simulated controlled substance	I	12	12	12	13	15	17	19 *18–20*
Theft-related crimes ($2,500 or less) *Check forgery ($200–$2,500)*	II	12	12	13	15	17	19	21 *20–22*
Theft crimes ($2,500 or less)	III	*12*	*13*	*15*	*17*	19 *18–20*	22 *21–23*	25 *24–26*
Nonresidential burglary, theft crimes (over $2,500)	IV	12	15	18	21	25 *24–26*	32 *30–34*	41 *37–45*
Residential burglary *Simple robbery*	V	18	23	27	30 *29–31*	38 *36–40*	46 *43–49*	54 *50–58*
Criminal sexual conduct, 2nd degree	VI	21	26	30	34 *33–35*	44 *42–46*	54 *50–58*	65 *60–70*
Aggravated robbery	VII	48 *44–52*	58 *54–62*	68 *64–72*	78 *74–82*	88 *84–92*	98 *94–102*	108 *104–112*
Criminal sexual conduct, 1st degree *Assault, 1st degree*	VIII	86 *81–91*	98 *93–103*	110 *105–115*	122 *117–127*	134 *129–139*	146 *141–151*	158 *153–163*
Murder, 3rd degree *Murder, 2nd degree (felony murder)*	IX	150 *144–156*	165 *159–171*	180 *174–186*	195 *189–201*	210 *204–216*	225 *219–231*	240 *234–246*
Murder, 2nd degree (with intent)	X	306 *299–313*	326 *319–333*	346 *339–353*	366 *359–373*	386 *379–393*	406 *399–413*	426 *419–433*

Note: Presumptive sentence lengths are in months.

Source: Richard S. Frase, "State Sentencing Guidelines: Still Going Strong," *Judicature* 78 (January/February 1995), p. 176.

189 if there are *aggravating* or *mitigating circumstances*. (These circumstances will be discussed in a later section of this chapter.) The judge usually has a list of factors to consider as either aggravating or mitigating. Again, if there are *no* aggravating or mitigating circumstances, judges select the presumptive sentence length of 195 months. Many states as well as the federal government have adopted sentencing guidelines. One of the most significant sentencing reforms in recent decades is the implementation of U.S. Sentencing Guidelines by the U.S. Sentencing Commission in 1987.

The U.S. Sentencing Guidelines

In November 1987, the U.S. government implemented presumptive sentencing guidelines for use by judges in all federal district courts. These guidelines were formulated by the U.S. Sentencing Commission under a mandate set forth by the Comprehensive Crime Control Act of 1984 (U.S. Sentencing Commission, 1987, 1991, 1995). While these guidelines have generated considerable controversy (Champion, 1989b), they provide federal judges with recommended sentencing ranges for those convicted of any federal crime.

Table 10.3 shows the sentencing table and guideline range recommended by the U.S. Sentencing Commission. Across the top of the table are Roman numerals ranging from I to VI. These refer to a defendant's criminal history and place offenders in one of these six categories. Down the left-hand side of the table are forty-three offense levels that reflect the seriousness of the offense.

It is beyond the scope of this text to provide a comprehensive analysis of how these guidelines were determined and how various sentencing lengths were derived. Below is some general information about how the criminal history categories across the top of the sentencing table are derived.

1. Add three points for each prior sentence of imprisonment exceeding one year and one month.
2. Add two points for each prior sentence of imprisonment of at least sixty days not counted in (1).
3. Add one point for each prior sentence not included in (1) or (2), up to a total of four points for this item.
4. Add two points if the defendant committed the instant offense while under any criminal justice sentence, including probation, parole, supervised release, imprisonment, work release, or escape status.
5. Add two points if the defendant committed the instant offense less than two years after release from imprisonment on a sentence counted under (1) or (2). If two points are added for item (4), add only one point for this item (adapted from U.S. Sentencing Guidelines, 1987:4.1).

For example, suppose an offender has been convicted of perjury in a federal district court. This offense has a base offense level of 12, meaning that the sentencing judge would move down the left-hand column to the number 12. Further suppose that the convicted offender had served a two-year sentence for forgery and was on parole when the instant offense or the new conviction offense occurred. Suppose also that the offender has been on parole for two and one-half years for the previous offense when the new conviction offense was committed. Finally, suppose the offender had been convicted of two previous felonies in the past twenty years, and in each of those cases, the offender served separate sentences of one year. We would arrive at the following criminal history score:

One prior sentence of at least one year and one month	3 points
Two prior sentences of at least sixty days' imprisonment	4 points
New conviction offense committed while on parole	2 points
Total:	9 points

The 9 points would place the offender in criminal history category VI. In table 10.3, the offense level for perjury, 12, intersects with criminal history category VI, showing a sentencing range of thirty to thirty-seven months. Thus, the federal judge would sentence the offender to thirty to thirty-seven months, and probably the middle or presumptive range of thirty-three or thirty-four months. This sentence could be lengthened or shortened, depending upon whether there are any *aggravating or mitigating circumstances*. These will be discussed in the following section.

It is clear that federal district judges have little leeway under this sentencing scheme. As will be seen later in this chapter, federal and state judges have been guilty of sentencing disparities largely attributable to extralegal and nonrational factors such as race, ethnicity, gender, and/or socioeconomic background. In fact, one reason for creating these guidelines was to reduce sentencing disparities (U.S. Sentencing Commission, 1991; von Hirsch et al., 1994).

If two twenty-five-year-old male offenders with identical criminal histories were convicted of the identical offense under very similar circumstances, and if they were both sentenced by the same judge on the same day, sentencing disparity would occur if one offender received probation while the other received two years in prison. If the offender receiving probation were white and the offender receiving two years' incarceration were black, race would conceivably be the only factor to explain the widely different sentences. Sentencing guidelines are intended to minimize these and other types of sentencing disparities.

Aggravating and Mitigating Circumstances

A violent crime is characterized by extreme physical force including murder or homicide, forcible rape or child sexual abuse, assault and battery by means of a dangerous weapon, robbery, and arson (Black, 1990:371). Sometimes these offenses are referred to as *crimes against the person*, because persons are directly involved as victims and are affected emotionally and physically by the crimes. *Nonviolent offenses include crimes such as burglary, vehicular theft, embezzlement, fraud, forgery, and larceny.* These are often referred to as *crimes against property*. Although persons are indirectly victimized or affected by such offenses, their lives and physical well-being are not directly jeopardized. Judges are more lenient in their sentencing of convicted defendants who have committed nonviolent of-

fenses compared with those felons who have committed violent acts (Daly, 1994; von Hirsch et al., 1994).

If one or more aggravating circumstances accompanied the crime, the judge is likely to "enhance" the punishment prescribed. In simple terms, this means a longer sentence, incarceration in lieu of probation, or a sentence to be served in a maximum security prison rather than a minimum- or medium-security prison facility.

Mitigating circumstances may cause the judge to be lenient with the defendant and prescribe probation rather than confinement in a jail or prison. A sentence of a year or less may be imposed rather than a five-year term.

Aggravating Circumstances

Aggravating circumstances *are those that may increase the severity of punishment*. Some of the factors considered by judges to be "aggravating" include:

1. The crime involved death or serious bodily injury to one or more victims.
2. The crime was committed while the offender was out on bail facing other criminal charges.
3. The offender was on probation, parole, or work release at the time the crime was committed.
4. The offender was a recidivist and had committed several previous offenses for which he or she had been punished.
5. The offender was the leader in the commission of the offense involving two or more offenders.
6. The offense involved more than one victim and/or was a violent or nonviolent crime.
7. The offender treated the victim(s) with extreme cruelty during the commission of the offense.
8. The offender used a dangerous weapon in the commission of the crime, and the risk to human life was high.

Mitigating Circumstances

Mitigating circumstances *are those that may lessen the severity of punishment*. Some of the more frequently cited mitigating factors include:

1. The offender did not cause serious bodily injury while committing the crime.
2. The offender did not contemplate that his or her criminal conduct would inflict serious bodily injury.
3. The offender acted under duress or extreme provocation.
4. The offender's conduct was possibly justified under the circumstances.
5. The offender was suffering from mental incapacitation or from a physical condition that significantly reduced his or her culpability in the offense.
6. The offender cooperated with authorities in apprehending other participants in the crime or in making restitution to the victims for losses suffered.
7. The offender committed the crime to provide necessities for himself or herself or for his or her family.
8. The offender did not have a previous criminal record.

If one or more mitigating circumstances are associated with the crime, the sentencing judge will be increasingly lenient in the sentence imposed. In view of the current trend toward greater use of probation, first offenders and nonviolent criminals are likely to be considered prime candidates for alternative sentencing that does not involve incarceration. But recidivists, especially those who have committed a number of violent acts and show every likelihood of continuing their criminal behavior, are likely to have their punishments enhanced (e.g., longer and more severe sentences and/or fines). These circumstances are usually outlined in documents prepared by probation officers prior to sentencing. These documents are presentence investigation reports.

The Presentence Investigation and Report

In all felony convictions in local, state, and federal trial courts, a **presentence investigation** (PSI) is conducted. *The purpose of a presentence investigation is to assist the judge in determining the most ap-propriate punishment or sentence for the convicted defendant; the investigation is usually made by a probation officer attached to the court and consists of a check of all relevant background information about a convicted defendant.* Similar investigations are conducted for all juvenile offenders as well.

A PSI report is prepared from the facts uncovered by the investigation. This report varies considerably in focus and scope from jurisdiction to jurisdiction, but it should contain at least the following items (Black, 1990:1184):

1. a complete description of the situation surrounding the criminal activity
2. the offender's educational background
3. the offender's employment history
4. the offender's social history
5. the offender's residence history
6. the offender's medical history
7. information about the environment to which the offender will return
8. information about any resources available to assist the offender
9. the probation officer's view of the offender's motivations and ambitions
10. a full description of the offender's criminal record
11. a recommendation from the probation officer as to the sentence disposition

Sometimes the PSI includes information or reports from psychiatrists or social workers and their opinions and recommendations concerning the offender. Figure 10.1 shows a U.S. Magistrate's Trial Docket Sheet for an offender who was charged with two counts of "willfully obstructing the passage of mail." In this case, bail was set at $1,000. The initials O.R. signify that the offender was released *on his own recognizance,* however, and bail was waived. Later, he entered a plea of "guilty" to the charges filed against him. An inspection of the form in figure 10.1 shows that the magistrate ordered a presentence investigation.

As a result of the investigation, the magistrate sentenced the convicted defendant to two six-month prison terms, to run concurrently. No fine was imposed. A criminal information was issued on May 19, the initial appearance occurred May 26,

Figure 10.1 United States Magistrate Trial Docket Sheet

UNITED STATES MAGISTRATE TRIAL DOCKET SHEET AO 254			FPI LC	

No.

Docket Number

OFFENSE [X] Petty [_] Minor other than Petty

DEFENDANT

Description **willfully obstructing the passage of mail**

Place

U.S.C./C.F.R. Citation

Date

Violation Notice [_] or Citation [X] Information [_] Complaint	ARREST WARRANT	Date issued	Date of Arrest
Number CR-	Date issued 5-19-	If Prosecution from Another District, Give District Name	

Date 5/26/	Tape Number (if recorded)	APPEARED: [X] Voluntarily [_] In Custody	Arresting Officer

B
A
I
L

Amount Set ▶ $ **1,000.00** O. R.

PROCEEDINGS CONTINUED

To (date): | Reason

Date **June 5, 19**	Tape Number	Verbatim Record Waived [_] (see reverse)	Testifying Officer or Complainant , **AUSA**

Attorney for U.S.

AUSA

Attorney for Defendant

[X] C.J.A.
[_] Pub. Def.
[_] Retained
[_] Waived

DEFENDANT'S CONSENT TO TRIAL BY U.S. MAGISTRATE

The United States Magistrate has explained to me the nature of the offense against the laws of the United States with which I am charged and the possible penalties if I am found guilty. He has fully informed me of my rights to counsel and to a trial before a judge of the United States District Court and of whatever right I may have to a jury trial.

I hereby waive my right to a trial before a United States District Judge and whatever right I may have to a jury trial, and I hereby consent to trial before the United States Magistrate.

(Signature of Defendant) | (Date)

PLEA	DISPOSITION
[_] Not Guilty	[_] Collateral forfeited $_____ [_] Dismissed
[X] Guilty	[_] Not Guilty
[_] Nolo Contendere	[X] Guilty

[X] Presentence Investigation Ordered

6/30/ Date (If different from plea or trial) Count I - Six months confinement; and Count II - Six months confinement to run concurrently with sentence imposed in Count I.

FINE ▶ $ **XX** | Receipt No. _____ | Date Committed to Custody **6/30/**

Date Filed	Bail Pending $	*Certified to be an accurate record of proceedings conducted before the magistrate*	

City Location of Magistrate _____

6/30/

(Magistrate or deputy clerk) | (Date)

the arraignment occurred June 5 when the guilty plea was entered, and the sentence was pronounced on June 30. At that time, the defendant was taken into custody and imprisoned, presumably for the six-month term prescribed by the sentence.

Convicted defendants don't always serve the full term prescribed by the sentencing judge. Almost every jurisdiction has a formula whereby a convict may be released after serving only a fraction of the original sentence. And as one result of court-mandated reductions in the prison population, some offenders may be released within a few weeks after being confined even if they have been sentenced to terms of one or more years. Such incidents mean that increasingly parole boards and judges are weighing a convict's potential risk to the public in deciding whether to release early.

The Convicted Offender's Version of Events and Victim Impact Statements

In most PSI reports, probation officers solicit convicted offenders' own versions of the events leading to their arrest. In these expositions offenders are sometimes able to *accept responsibility* for their crimes. In some instances, judges have been persuaded to be more lenient in their sentencing if offenders accept responsibility for their actions and appear genuinely contrite.

At the same time, many states have adopted policies that encourage victims to take an active role in the sentencing process. Victims or the families or friends of victims may make statements at an offender's sentencing hearing. They may write their version of the events and append them to PSI reports. These are known as victim impact statements. *The* **victim impact statement** *is a statement made by the victim and addressed to the judge for consideration in sentencing. It includes a description of the financial, social, psychological, and physical harm the victim has suffered because of the crime, and a statement concerning the victim's feelings about the crime, the offender, and a proposed sentence* (Erez and Tontodonato (1990:452–53). These statements usually provide judges with a clearer picture of the seriousness of the crime. If the victim impact statement is powerful enough, judges may sentence offenders to harsher prison terms than otherwise contemplated. In later sentencing hearings, victims and/or their families may appear and speak against of-

fenders. They may encourage judges to impose maximum penalties for the pain and suffering they have incurred from the offender's criminal acts.

Does the Presentence Investigation Report Influence Judges' Sentencing Decisions?

Yes and no. Judges *consider* a PSI report. Usually, probation officers who prepare such reports make a sentence recommendation, which judges may ignore. Judicial policies vary among jurisdictions about whether such reports will be prepared (Daly, 1994). In most serious felony cases in most jurisdictions, however, PSI reports will be prepared to assist judges in sentencing offenders.

Whether PSI reports are favorable to convicted offenders is not clear. Studies of federal probation officers indicate that they believe that, particularly under the new U.S. sentencing guidelines, PSI reports do not work to offenders' advantage (Lanier and Miller, 1995). PSI reports tend to include all relevant facts describing the offense. Therefore, if a weapon was used or serious injuries were inflicted, this information will be included in the report. Judges consider this information when making their sentencing decisions.

PSI reports also take a great deal of time to prepare (American Correctional Association, 1994b; Minnesota Probation Standards Task Force, 1993). State and local resources are strained to capacity as larger numbers of persons are sentenced to probation. As probation officers acquire more clients, the quality of service to new probationers declines. Perhaps the quality of the PSI reports suffers accordingly (Minnesota Probation Standards Task Force, 1993). Substantial reforms have been recommended in the sentencing process, including revamping how PSI reports are prepared and considered by judges (Wooten and Shilton, 1993). Some experts have recommended that judges pay *less* rather than *more* attention to PSI reports (Wooten and Shilton, 1993) and that the entire sentencing process be more individualized.

The Sentencing Hearing

Under Rule 32 of the Federal Rules of Criminal Procedure (18 U.S.C., 1996), the contents of a

PSI must be disclosed to defendants and their counsels, although some information is exempt from disclosure. Mental or psychological reports, interviews with family members, a personal account of the defendant's marital problems, and certain personal observations by the probation officer and the court are potentially excludable from PSIs.

Most jurisdictions hold a *sentencing hearing*, at which defendants and their attorneys can respond to the contents of the PSI report. Also, an increasing number of jurisdictions are permitting crime victims to attend sentencing hearings and provide victim impact statements either orally, in writing, or both. Evidence suggests a general increase in citizen involvement at other stages of the criminal justice process as well (Rubin, 1985a, 1985b). Of course, many jurisdictions do not allow victims to participate in the sentencing process. The nature of victim participation varies among jurisdictions, although often their participation consists of describing the personal and psychological effects of the crime and the financial costs incurred (McLeod, 1986).

Sentencing hearings also permit offenders and their attorneys to comment on the PSI report and to append any information on mitigating circumstances of the crime. The role of defense attorneys is particularly important at this stage because they can work with the probation officer who prepared the report as well as with the victims, and they can make timely legal attacks on erroneous information presented to the judge (Carroll, 1986).

After considering the contents of a PSI, the oral and written reports furnished by the victims and the offenders, and prosecution and defense arguments, judges use their best judgment in arriving at the most equitable sentence. Judges consider mitigating and aggravating circumstances of the offense; the age, psychological and physical condition, and social/educational background of the offender; and the minimum and maximum statutory penalties of incarceration and/or fines accompanying the crime.

Sentencing Issues

A variety of sentencing reforms are motivated by several issues that raise a number of moral and ethical questions. These issues pertain to (1) sentencing disparity; (2) predicting dangerousness; (3) selective incapacitation; and (4) alternative or creative sentencing.

Sentencing Disparity

Sentencing disparity takes several different forms. *Disparities in sentencing may occur when different judges within any given jurisdiction impose vastly different sentences on offenders charged with similar crimes* (Hanke, 1995). Judges may be inclined to be more lenient with female offenders than with their male counterparts (Daly and Bordt, 1995). Blacks and Hispanics may receive harsher sentences than whites convicted of the same kinds of offenses (Lopez, 1995; Williams, 1995a). Older offenders may receive more lenient sentences than younger offenders (Smykla and Selke, 1995; Tonry, 1995).

Promoters of sentencing reforms have been quick to point out these sorts of deficiencies in our sentencing system (Tonry, 1995). As discussed earlier, many states are switching from indeterminate to determinate sentencing. Such a change is almost always accompanied by reductions in sentencing disparities attributable to race, ethnicity, gender, or socioeconomic status. The influence of race, ethnicity, gender, and socioeconomic status on sentencing severity and sentencing disparities generally has been investigated extensively.

Race and Ethnicity

Different jurisdictions report variations in sentencing attributable to race. For example, a study of 183 defendants in Leon and Gadsden County Circuit Courts in Tallahassee and Quincy, Florida, revealed that black appellants sentenced in excess of the recommended maximum sentence were more likely than whites to have the trial court's recommendation affirmed on appeal (Williams, 1995a). Thus, at least in these jurisdictions, appellate decision making is far from "routine."

An investigation of sentencing disparities among 685 white and black women in Alabama during the period 1929–1985 showed that whites who killed interracially were likely to have lighter sentences (of one to five years) than blacks who killed interracially. Black women who killed interracially tended to receive moderate to heavy sentences (six to ten or eleven to twenty years); (Hanke, 1995). Also, a sample of 755 defendants prosecuted for burglary and robbery was studied. In Tucson, being Hispanic had no effect on the type of adjudication received, the verdict, or sentence severity. However, in El Paso, Hispanic defendants were more likely than whites to receive less favorable pretrial release outcomes, to be convicted in jury trials, and to receive more severe sentences when they were found guilty at trial (LaFree, 1985). Interviews with DA's and other officials in both cities indicated that these disparities may be partially attributable to greater language difficulties in El Paso, different mechanisms for providing attorneys to indigent defendants, and differences between established Hispanic-Americans in Tucson and less well-established Mexican-American citizens and Mexican nationals in El Paso (LaFree, 1985).

Despite the increasing attention given to sentencing disparities and the reforms established to correct them, there is considerable evidence that disparities based on race and ethnicity are growing rather than diminishing (Tonry, 1995). Blacks are overrepresented at virtually every stage in the criminal justice system, and they are increasingly included in incarcerated populations. Scholars report that such disproportionate representation of blacks is due to greater offending rates of blacks, and such reports are supported by the literature (Tonry, 1995). However, at the root of such disproportionate representation of blacks and other minorities in the criminal justice system are poverty and unemployment (Tonry, 1995). It has been recommended, for instance, that judges take into account special circumstances when sentencing minority offenders. With more honest sentencing policies, fewer sentencing disparities attributable to race or ethnicity should occur (Tonry, 1995).

Sentencing disparities attributable to race are particularly noticeable in the South (Clayton, 1983). It has been shown, for instance, that of 21,169 felons convicted in Georgia during the years 1973–1980, blacks tended to receive longer sentences than whites (Clayton, 1983). As a matter of fact, sentences for blacks were an average of 2.5 years longer than sentences for whites convicted of the same crimes. Similar disparities are pervasive in capital cases (Sorensen and Wallace, 1995).

Gender

Do women tend to receive more lenient sentences than men? A study of 1,027 male and female offenders convicted of theft, forgery, or drug law violations in Minneapolis between 1972 and 1976 revealed that women receive more lenient sentences than men convicted of similar offenses (Kruttschnitt, 1984). Women also received more lenient treatment related to pretrial release. And in a related study of 1,558 convicted males and 1,365 convicted females in Minneapolis between 1965 and 1980, it was found that women were more likely than men to receive pretrial release and were apt to receive less severe sentences for similar offenses (Kruttschnitt and Green, 1984).

Other research has been largely supportive of the Minnesota study. For example, Daly and Bordt (1995) conducted an extensive statistical review of the literature on sentencing disparity to determine whether "sex effects" favoring women over men in sentencing exist. Over half of the fifty studies surveyed indicated that such effects do indeed exist. Both older and more recent data sets reveal similar findings.

Investigations have also been made of the relation between gender and the application of the death penalty in capital cases. Both surveys of citizens and the actual use of capital punishment in selected states reveal that females convicted of capital crimes are far less likely to receive the death penalty than men convicted of capital crimes committed under similar circumstances (Daly and Bordt, 1995; Farnworth and Teske, 1995; Sandys and McGarrell, 1995). Further, citizens surveyed tended to favor more lenient treatment for females convicted of capital offenses (i.e., life-without-parole sentences as opposed to death sentences). Farnworth and Teske (1995) suggest that gender differentiation in the use of the death penalty can be explained by the *chivalry hypothesis,* which posits that decision makers or judges will tend to treat female offenders with chivalry during sentencing and that judges will be inclined to dispense *selective chivalry* toward white females compared with other females or with minorities of either gender. Data from 9,866 felony theft cases and 18,176 felony assault cases from California courts in 1988 show that females with no prior record were more likely than males to have the charges against them reduced. Also, female offenders were more likely than males to receive probation (Farnworth and Teske, 1995).

As more states adopt sentencing reforms, there will be fewer sentencing disparities between jurisdictions. Also, judges seem to favor greater uniformity in their sentencing practices. In the future, the adoption of consistent sentencing standards will gradually eliminate gender, ethnic, or racial discrimination in sentencing.

Socioeconomic Status

Socioeconomic status plays a significant part in explaining sentencing disparities. Offenders with limited resources cannot afford private counsel, and less experienced public defenders are often appointed to defend them. Further, the sentencing guidelines in many states tend to overpenalize street crimes, which are most often committed by those with lower socioeconomic status.

There is considerable evidence of sentencing disparities attributable to socioeconomic status. Studies of sentencing patterns in southeastern states have shown that there is an inverse relation between socioeconomic status and sentence length (D'Allessio and Stolzenberg, 1993). Of 2,760 convicted offenders, those of lower socioeconomic status drew longer sentences than those of higher socioeconomic statuses. Thus, it was concluded that this extralegal factor was significant in explaining differential sentence lengths of offenders, after controlling for criminal history and conviction offense (D'Allessio and Stolzenberg, 1993). Other research has supported the idea that those with lower socioeconomic status are disenfranchised by the criminal justice system. However, higher socioeconomic status may work against certain types of offenders. A survey showed that white-collar offenders sentenced in seven district courts tended to receive imprisonment more often than comparable offenders of lower statuses. Furthermore, the sentences imposed on white-collar offenders were longer (Weisburd, Waring, and Wheeler, 1990). The general consensus seems to be that offenders of lower socioeconomic status will tend to receive harsher and longer sentences than offenders of higher socioeconomic statuses, although there are always exceptions.

Predicting Dangerousness

Judges and parole boards are increasingly concerned about making good sentencing and early-release decisions. It is frequently important for judges to know whether offenders will pose a risk to others and whether certain offenders will be more likely to reoffend than other offenders. Therefore, in recent years several investigators have attempted to devise prediction schemes that would permit judges and other officials to predict a convicted defendant's **dangerousness.** *Dangerousness is the propensity for offenders, particularly violent offenders, to commit new offenses when freed from incarceration.* Judges don't want to make bad decisions. When probationers commit new and violent offenses, it implies that sentencing judges exercised poor judgment in releasing them. In all fairness to these judges, it is impossible to forecast with absolute certainty *which* offenders will reoffend.

Early attempts to predict the incidence of violent behavior among samples of convicted felons were unsuccessful, inconclusive, and highly inaccurate (Monahan, 1984). Behavioral scientists and mental health professionals were initially involved in attempts to identify personality traits or behavioral patterns indicative of dangerousness (Wilbanks, 1985). Much of this early research was conducted in Canada. For example, a 1978 investigation of 598 criminal defendants in Toronto failed to accurately predict which offenders would be more dangerous than others if released (Menzies, Webster, and Sepejak, 1985). Psychiatrists were better than social workers, nurses, psychologists, and corrections personnel at predicting an offender's potential dangerousness. But, unimpressively, psychiatrists' predictions were only 40 percent accurate.

Thirty-one states currently have laws permitting officials to detain criminal defendants on the basis of the defendant's perceived "dangerousness" (Gottlieb and Rosen, 1984). These include South Dakota, Tennessee, Utah, Vermont, Virginia, Washington, Wisconsin, Arkansas, Arizona, Georgia, Florida, Delaware, Colorado, and Hawaii. The "dangerous-tendency" test used legally is the propensity of a person (or an animal) to inflict injury (Black, 1990:394; *Frazier v. Stone*, 1974).

Different jurisdictions interpret dangerousness differently. In twenty-one states, for example, dangerousness is defined as a history of prior criminal involvement (Gottlieb, 1984). This history may include a prior conviction, probation or parole status, or a pending charge at the time of arrest. In seven states, the type of crime with which the offender is charged defines dangerousness (e.g., a violent crime such as aggravated assault, robbery, or homicide). And in twenty-three states, judicial discretion determines dangerousness (Gottlieb, 1984).

Attempts to predict dangerousness have not improved over time. Some researchers and theorists argue that all offenders who have committed the same or similar offenses should be treated similarly (Griffith, 1985; Wright, Clear, and Dickson, 1984). In short, is it ethical or moral to incapacitate certain defendants charged with armed robbery and deemed dangerous and yet release others charged with the same offense but not deemed dangerous?

Dangerousness or risk forecasts have been conducted for different phases of the criminal justice process. For instance, studies of pretrial bail decision making have failed to prove the utility of instruments such as the Vera Institute Scale, a device intended to predict more likely candidates for bail (Cuvelier and Potts, 1993). Even instruments designed to predict the future conduct of delinquents have been somewhat unsuccessful. Barry Krisberg et al. (1993) studied populations of incarcerated juveniles in fourteen state jurisdictions, profiling their characteristics and the screening instruments used to classify and place them. They found that at least a third of all youths examined either did not require incarceration or did not require the level of incarceration they received. Thus, risk prediction devices were found to overpredict, generating many needless secure placements of juveniles when probation would have been more suitable.

A prediction device that has been used extensively and successfully by the U.S. Parole Commission is the Salient Factor Score (SFS) (Hoffman, 1983). The SFS is an actuarial device that assesses parole success. Using factors such as offense severity and offender characteristics, the SFS suggests a range of months to be served, assuming appropriate conduct from the offender while incarcerated. The SFS has been used since 1972 and has been revised several times in recent years. In August 1981, a six-item predictive device designated SFS 81 was established (Hoffman, 1983). This device emphasizes the extent and recency of an offender's criminal history, and, as such, it appears somewhat compatible with the "just deserts" approach to corrections (Hoffman, 1983).

Peter Hoffman (1994) has followed up by studying three samples of prisoners released by the U.S. Parole Commission. The samples consisted of 3,955 prisoners released during 1970–1972, 2,339 prisoners released during 1978, and 1,092 prisoners released in 1987. Files were obtained from the Federal Bureau of Prisons and U.S. Parole Commission records. Hoffman says that the SFS 81 has retained a fairly high predictive accuracy over a seventeen-year period, during which three separate samples of offenders were released. Further, the SFS 81 continues to reveal statistically significant distinctions between prisoners likely or unlikely to reoffend. It should be noted that in view of the large samples studied by Hoffman, the requirements for significant differences among inmates who do or do not recidivate are not rigorous. For instance, prediction accuracy of 30 or 40 percent may be judged as significant. This means that the instrument predicts correctly in 30 or 40 percent of all cases examined. But this also means that the instrument does not predict correctly in 60 to 70 percent of the cases. Depending upon the length of the follow-up period, recidivism rates among parolees in federal and state jurisdictions are about 65 percent, meaning that 65 percent of all of those granted early release from prison will reoffend, usually within a three-year follow-up period (Maguire and Pastore, 1995).

Given the flaws in our ability to forecast future dangerousness or risk to society, some observers have favored rejecting risk prediction instruments outright. Since this is unlikely, the next best alternative is to devise more equitable sentencing schemes that utilize fairer prediction criteria.

Some authorities contend that *all* felons who have been convicted of violent offenses should serve a term in jail or prison (Conrad, 1985). Of course, decisions to incarcerate violent felons could take into account mitigating or aggravating circumstances and exceptional factors. Favoring a "just desert" view of sentencing that holds that punishment should be based on the gravity of the crime, von Hirsch (1985) argues that persons should be punished according to their *degree of fault* rather than selectively incapacitated according to flawed dangerousness prediction devices.

Selective Incapacitation

Closely related to predictions of dangerousness is selectively incapacitating certain offenders who are likely candidates for recidivism (Gottfredson and Gottfredson, 1990; Spelman, 1988). *In* **selective incapacitation,** *offenders prone to recidivism or who have prior criminality are given relatively long prison sentences* (Zimring and Hawkins, 1995). In 1982, the Rand Corporation in Santa Monica, California, devised a classification scheme that would enable criminal justice practitioners to determine which offenders should be selectively incapacitated and which ones should be sentenced to alternative correctional programs (Greenwood, 1982; Wilson, 1983).

The rise of selective incapacitation as the official justification for incarceration during the 1970s and 1980s was primarily due to disenchantment with other penal purposes rather than to any intrinsic merits (Zimring and Hawkins, 1995). But the promise of selectively incapacitating certain types of offenders and thus using prison resources more wisely and reducing crime has not been fulfilled. For example, a study of 6,000 California prison inmates during the 1960s and all persons whose first arrests were in California in 1980 (157,936) reveals that the prediction models used to forecast future criminal behaviors of these persons were weak and had relatively low predictive power (Gottfredson and Gottfredson, 1992). A decline in offenses was most often related to the aging of the growing offender population rather than to any specific crime control strategy based on prediction devices and selective incapacitation. Considerably more research is needed before selec-

tive incapacitation becomes a significant crime prevention technique (Farrington, 1992).

Generally, selective incapacitation as a crime control strategy is fraught with theoretical, methodological, and ethical problems (Spelman, 1994). Some researchers argue that the incapacitation of certain offenders will simply result in their replacement by newly recruited criminals (Champion, 1994). Also, how much predictive error should be permitted in incapacitation decisions? Of course, the issue of fairness is increasingly important, especially as states move toward more determinate and presumptive sentencing forms. How will judges justify assigning certain offenders to alternative sentencing programs and prescribing incapacitation for other offenders who have similar criminal histories and have committed similar offenses?

It has been suggested by some researchers that we must be willing to sacrifice our concern for justice in the interests of crime prevention and support predictive sentencing (von Hirsch, 1984). But many doubt that predictive sentencing and selective incapacitation are ethical because of a tendency of forecasts of criminality to overpredict and because of the potential for meting out undeserved punishment to certain offenders (von Hirsch, 1984). Despite these pitfalls, some experts believe that selective incapacitation has considerable potential for alleviating prison overcrowding, although the problems of prediction measures are certainly acknowledged (Spelman, 1994).

Alternative, or Creative, Sentencing

A prevailing view of sentencing equates punishment and control with incarceration (Gottfredson and Gottfredson, 1992; Zimring and Hawkins, 1995). In recent years, however, several proposals advanced and adopted in some jurisdictions favor various alternative sentencing forms (Czajkoski and Wollan, Jr., 1986; Miller, 1986; Smith, 1984).

Sometimes referred to as creative sentencing, **alternative sentencing** offers offenders, especially those who have committed relatively minor or nonviolent offenses, an opportunity to serve their sentences outside prison. *Usually, alternative sentencing involves some form of community service,* *some degree of restitution to victims of crimes, active involvement in educational or vocational training programs, or affiliation with some other "good works" activity* (Czajkoski and Wollan, 1986).

The goals of alternative sentencing are twofold. First, it is aimed at helping certain types of offenders avoid imprisonment. Imprisonment means associating with other criminals, and labeling theorists consider imprisonment an important contributing factor to a person's self-concept as a criminal. Second, it is perceived as a viable means of reducing prison overcrowding and cutting certain costs associated with corrections (Harris, 1984; Wallace and Clarke, 1986:1).

Some of the criticisms leveled at alternative, or creative, sentencing are that it restores to judges the power that they formerly enjoyed under indeterminate sentencing systems. Not all judges favor creative sentencing, and such sentencing alternatives may increase the potential for various kinds of judicial abuse (American Bar Association, 1994; McGarrell and Sabath, 1994).

Czajkoski and Wollan, Jr. (1986:228) describe the judge, for instance, who considered the case of a woman who was convicted for a marijuana offense. The judge placed the woman on probation, but he also set as one of the conditions of probation that she be sterilized (the woman had a number of illegitimate children). Of course, the sterilization had nothing to do with the marijuana offense, but as Czajkoski and Wollan point out, "The judge must have had in mind some benefit to the community by reducing the number of illegitimate children and welfare recipients" (Czajkoski and Wollan, Jr., 1986:228). This extreme example serves to illustrate the types of judicial excesses that *might* occur.

One alternative sentencing program that has had modest success is the Client Specific Planning (CSP) Program administered by the Indiana Sentencing Resource Center (McGarrell and Sabath, 1994). Public defenders in various Indiana communities prepare client-centered investigations and recommend non-incarcerative sentences instead of imprisonment. The CSP program has helped many convicted offenders become successfully rehabilitated. Some of the more successful alternative-to-incarceration programs have incorporated certain educational and vocational ele-

ments, where convicted offenders can learn new skills and improve their ability to find jobs (Fort, 1991; Mack, 1992; Steen, 1991; Texas Office of the State Auditor, 1993).

In view of prison overcrowding, it is likely that we will continue to see the development and promotion of alternative sentencing programs such as those operating in North Carolina and Florida. The recurring question is: How can we identify offenders who will be most responsive to sentencing alternatives (Farrington, 1992; Smykla and Selke, 1995)? Many of these programs are fairly new, and more data are needed before we can assess their true impact on crime trends, recidivism rates, and offender rehabilitation (Gray et al., 1991; Spelman, 1988).

Life-Without-Parole Sentences and Capital Punishment

No other issue in sentencing has been debated as vigorously as **capital punishment**, *or the death penalty* (Bedau, 1992; Galliher, Ray, and Cook, 1992; New York State Division of Criminal Justice Services, 1982; Sandys and McGarrell, 1994; Van den Haag and Conrad, 1983), which is exacted for offenses such as murder. In many jurisdictions, if a defendant is found guilty of a capital offense, a separate jury decision is often required to establish the actual punishment. This is referred to as a *bifurcated trial*.

Bifurcated Trials

The **bifurcated trial** *is a two-stage proceeding consisting of a first phase, when guilt is established, followed by a second stage, when punishment is decided.* All capital cases, where prosecutors seek the death penalty against one or more defendants, are bifurcated trials. Usually the issue to be decided is whether the convicted offender should receive the death penalty or life without the possibility of parole. This decision by the jury is based upon whether there are factors that justify the death penalty or argue against it. The bifurcated trial became common practice following the case of *Gregg v. Georgia* (1976) (see Highlight 10.4).

Highlight 10.3. Brothers Sentenced to Life Without Parole: The Case of Erik and Lyle Menendez

On a balmy summer evening in Beverly Hills, California, in 1989, Jose Menendez, a popular entertainment executive, and his wife, Kitty, were cut down by shotgun fire while sitting in their living room watching television. The assailants reloaded and pumped eighteen shotgun shells into the bodies. Police suspected mob retaliation.

The Menendez's two sons, Lyle and Erik, twenty-one and nineteen years old, stood to inherit $14 million from their deceased parents' estate. At the time, nobody suspected them. They had perfect alibis—they were out watching a movie.

Many months later during a session with a psychological counselor, Erik Menendez broke down and confessed to the murders of his parents. A girlfriend of the psychologist overheard the conversation and reported it to the police. Lyle and Erik Menendez were later arrested on suspicion in the double homicide. More evidence surfaced that deeply incriminated them in their parents' deaths.

At their first trial, the brothers contended that they were put in fear of their lives by their parents. Jose Menendez allegedly had homosexual relations with both of his sons. The trial brought out much to indicate severe child sexual abuse. After a mistrial was declared, the Menendez brothers were tried again. This time, the verdict was guilty. On July 2, 1996, the judge, Stanley Weisberg, imposed two sentences of life without the possibility of parole for both brothers. The sentences were to run consecutively to ensure that the offenders would be imprisoned for life.

The trials of two sons for the murders of their parents divided the nation. Many believed that the sons had been abused by their father and that the murders were therefore somewhat justified. However, a majority of people believed that there was substantial premeditation. The sons had driven 120 miles south to San Diego, where they purchased shotguns and ammunition using fictitious drivers' licenses. The weapons they used, as well as their bloody clothing, were never recovered. The crime was all but perfect, with the exception of the counseling session with the psychologist.

Whether the act was premeditated, the conclusion played out as though it had been. The brothers asked to be housed in the same penitentiary. The prosecutor for Los Angeles County, David Conn, said that he was pleased with the sentences because the consecutive terms imposed by the judge (instead of concurrent terms) would send a strong and symbolic message against the horrors of the killings.

In situations of suspected child sexual abuse where the abused kills the abuser, what should the penalty be? Should such abuse mitigate the punishments imposed?

Source: Adapted from Associated Press, "Menendez Brothers Sentenced to Life," *Minot (N.D.) Daily News,* July 3, 1996, p. A7.

Prior to 1972, a majority of states had an assortment of capital punishment laws established for special classes of violent offenders. Death penalties were imposed in various states for the murder of police officers, aggravated rape, kidnapping, and other serious offenses. However, in *Furman v. Georgia* (1972) the Supreme Court declared the death penalty unconstitutional because it was applied in an arbitrary and capricious manner. In that landmark case, the Supreme Court heard appeals that would eventually affect three separate cases—a murder case from Georgia and two rape cases from Georgia and Texas. In all three of these cases, the offenders had been convicted and sentenced to death.

While the convicts appealed their cases on the grounds that the death penalty constituted "cruel and unusual punishment" under the Eighth and Fourteenth Amendments, there were other factors relevant to the issue of the death penalty. The offenders were black, and a disproportionate number of black convicts in capital cases involving crimes

Highlight 10.4. The Twentieth Anniversary of the Death Penalty's Reinstatement: The Death Penalty in Retrospect

In *Furman v. Georgia* (1972), the Supreme Court decided to suspend the death penalty in Georgia, largely because of the racially discriminatory manner in which it was being applied. Many blacks were being executed for noncapital offenses, such as rape and aggravated assault, while whites convicted of the same offenses drew prison terms of varying lengths. Thus, there was clear evidence that the application of the death penalty, at least in Georgia, was too random, arbitrary, and racially influenced.

Erroneously termed a "ban on capital punishment," the *Furman* case caused other states to review their death penalty procedures to see if they were similar to *Furman*. Every state temporarily suspended the death penalty for legislative review.

In *Gregg v. Georgia* (1976), the Supreme Court declared that Georgia had established an equitable method of applying the death penalty. (Troy Leon Gregg was a twenty-seven-year-old drifter convicted of murdering two Florida hitchhikers.) One feature of the new process was a two-phase bifurcated trial procedure. In the first phase, the jury would decide a defendant's guilt. If the jury delivered a "guilty" verdict, it would meet again to consider sentencing.

In the sentencing stage, prosecutors and defense attorneys present aggravating and mitigating circumstances. Aggravating circumstances include whether there was more than one victim, whether a murder was committed with extreme cruelty, whether there was torture. Mitigating circumstances include whether the offender helped police capture others involved and whether he or she was a first offender. If aggravating circumstances outweigh mitigating ones, the jury would vote for the death penalty. If mitigating circumstances outweigh the aggravating ones, the jury would recommend life imprisonment or life without parole.

Many opponents of capital punishment recycle the standard arguments that the death penalty doesn't deter murderers from committing murder, that the United States is one of the few countries in the world barbaric enough to have a death penalty, that the death penalty is cruel and unusual punishment, that it costs more to execute someone than to support them during life imprisonment, and that some convicted murderers are later found to be innocent.

However, an even more vocal majority reject these arguments, saying that whether the death penalty deters is irrelevant. The death penalty is the punishment prescribed for the crime. Persons who murder others should themselves be executed if the circumstances warrant. This is the reason for bifurcated trials.

Outspoken supporters of capital punishment include Lynne Abraham, America's deadliest district attorney, according to Philadelphia defense lawyers. Abraham says that people are tired of running away from their neighborhoods and of little girls being raped and murdered and dumped in the bushes. They're tired of whining, complaining criminals.

Jane Brady, Delaware's attorney general, says that "some people would ask for ten minutes alone in a room with a killer . . . others would ask that he suffer torture and agony for days. But we as a country set up rules and lawyers as a means of moderation."

Between 1976 and 1996, 331 persons were executed in U.S. prisons. In mid-1996, over 3,000 inmates were on death row awaiting execution. In 1996, capital punishment was legal in thirty-eight states. Surveys show consistently that over two-thirds of U.S. citizens favor the death penalty instead of life sentences.

If you were opposed to the death penalty, what would you say to the grieving parent who has lost a loved one to murder? Is the death penalty cruel and unusual punishment? Should the standards and policies of other countries influence whether the United States has the death penalty?

Source: Adapted from Associated Press, "Death Penalty: A Right to Kill?" *Minot (N.D.) Daily News,* July 2, 1996, p. A6.

other than murder were being executed in Georgia and other jurisdictions.

The Supreme Court reversed their convictions and held that "the imposition and carrying out of the death penalty in these cases constitutes cruel and unusual punishment in violation of the Eighth and Fourteenth Amendments." The Court also concluded that capital punishment is unconstitutional whenever it is imposed discriminatorily against certain identifiable classes of people. Justice Douglas indicated that "it would seem to be incontestable that the death penalty inflicted on one defendant is 'unusual' if it discriminates against him by reason of his race, religion, wealth, social position, or class, or if it is imposed under a procedure that gives room for the play of such prejudices." Not only was the death penalty declared to be "cruel and unusual punishment" in that instance, but it was also declared to be discriminatory because it was selectively applied to certain offenders and not to others.

This decision caused many states to reexamine their death penalty provisions. No executions were carried out for several years while state legislators examined the various implications of the Supreme Court's holding in *Furman*. Some states considered the Supreme Court action to be the equivalent of abolishing the death penalty, although this was neither the intent nor the result of *Furman*.

In 1976, however, the Supreme Court ruled on another significant case pertaining to the death penalty issue. In the case of *Gregg v. Georgia* (1976), Troy Leon Gregg, a white male, was charged with committing armed robbery and murder. Gregg and a companion, Floyd Allen, allegedly were hitchhiking north in Florida on November 21, 1973. They were picked up by Fred Simmons and Bob Moore. Along the way, Simmons and Moore picked up another hitchhiker, Dennis Weaver, who rode with them to Atlanta. Later that evening, they stopped to rest along the highway. The next morning, the bodies of Simmons and Moore were found along the Georgia highway. The other hitchhiker, Weaver, read about the incident in the newspapers and went to the police. The next afternoon, Gregg and Allen, while in Simmons's car, were arrested in Asheville, North Carolina. In a search incident to their arrest, a .25-caliber pistol was found in Gregg's pocket. This was later confirmed to be the weapon used to kill Simmons and Moore.

Gregg was convicted, and a separate jury hearing considered the issue of his punishment in accordance with the newly revised Georgia law in view of *Furman v. Georgia* (1972). Gregg appealed to the Supreme Court on the grounds that the death penalty violated his Eighth and Fourteenth Amendment rights. In this particular case, the Supreme Court held that Gregg's rights had *not* been violated and that the death sentence had not resulted from prejudice or any other arbitrary factor. Furthermore, the Court held that the penalty was not excessive or disproportionate to the penalty applied in similar cases. Thus, in four short years, the Supreme Court had made two important rulings affecting the application of the death penalty. Of course, all states were obligated to examine closely their death penalty provisions and determine whether they complied with the new Supreme Court guidelines.

The Primary Functions of a Bifurcated Trial

The bifurcated trial permits an examination and consideration of any aggravating or mitigating factors that might increase or decrease the severity of a sentence. If a defendant is convicted of capital murder, the jury has an opportunity to consider factors that might cause them to recommend a life sentence rather than the death penalty. If the murder is especially heinous and if there are other aggravating factors that tend to outweigh any mitigating factors, the jury can return a decision to impose the death penalty. The jury's decision is determined by specific aggravating and mitigating factors. Extralegal factors, such as the offender's or victim's race, gender, socioeconomic status, or ethnicity, are not proper objects of a jury's deliberations. Judges may or may not accept the jury's decision. Thus, a judge may impose a sentence of life or life without parole even though the jury has recommended the death penalty. However, it is rare for judges to impose sentences different from those recommended by the jury.

The Unconstitutionality of Mandatory Death Penalties

At one time, applications of the death penalty were often mandatory for noncapital offenses, such as rape or assault. We have already seen that race might impact unfavorably on a jury's decision to impose the death penalty for convicted minority offenders prior to *Gregg v. Georgia* (1976). In other cases, such as the killing of a police officer during the commission of a felony, various state statutes provided for mandatory death penalties. The problem with mandatory death penalties was that they did not include any provision for weighing aggravating or mitigating circumstances.

Instrumental in abolishing the mandatory death penalty was *Woodson v. North Carolina* (1980). Woodson and others were convicted of first-degree murder. Although Woodson was a lookout and did not participate in the actual murder, under a North Carolina felony-murder statute, the death penalty for such an offense was mandatory. The Supreme Court overturned Woodson's sentence, declaring that *mandatory death penalty statutes are unconstitutional,* mainly because they preclude the consideration of aggravating and mitigating circumstances.

How Many Inmates Are on Death Row?

Table 10.4 shows the status of the death penalty as of December 31, 1994 (Stephan and Snell, 1996:1). Fourteen states do not have the death penalty. At the end of 1994, there were 2,890 prisoners on death row. Texas had 394 inmates on death row, the largest number of any state. California and Florida had 381 and 342 death row inmates respectively.

During 1994, thirteen states executed 31 prisoners (Stephan and Snell, 1996:1). Of those executed, 20 were white and 11 were black. These prisoners spent an average of ten years and two months on death row. Of the 2,890 persons under sentence of death, 1,645 were white, 1,197 were black, 23 were Native American, 17 were Asian American, and 8 were "Other." Hispanic inmates accounted for 224 of those on death row, or about 8.4 percent of inmates with a known ethnicity. Forty percent of the inmates on death row had been on probation or parole at the time they committed their capital offenses. Sixty-six percent had prior felony convictions.

The death penalty was resumed in 1977. Between January 1, 1977, and December 31, 1994, a total of 4,557 persons entered state or federal prisons under sentence of death. The preferred

---

Table 10.4

Status of the Death Penalty, December 31, 1994

Executions during 1994		Number of prisoners under sentence of death		Jurisdictions without a death penalty
Texas	14	Texas	394	Alaska
Arkansas	5	California	381	District of Columbia
Virginia	2	Florida	342	Hawaii
Delaware	1	Pennsylvania	182	Iowa
Florida	1	Illinois	155	Maine
Georgia	1	Ohio	140	Massachusetts
Idaho	1	Alabama	135	Michigan
Illinois	1	Oklahoma	129	Minnesota
Indiana	1	Arizona	121	New York
Maryland	1	North Carolina	111	North Dakota
Nebraska	1	Tennessee	100	Rhode Island
North Carolina	1	Georgia	96	Vermont
Washington	1	23 other jurisdictions	604	West Virginia
				Wisconsin
Total	31	Total	2,890	

Source: Stephan and Snell (1996).

method of execution among the states is lethal injection, with twenty-seven states authorizing such a procedure. Other execution methods used by the states and federal government include electrocution (twelve states), hanging (four states), lethal gas (seven states), and firing squad (one state). Between 1930 and the end of 1994, 4,116 persons had been executed, 257 of them between January 1, 1977, and December 31, 1994 (Stephan and Snell, 1996:10). Table 10.5 shows the distribution of executions from 1930 through 1994.

Reasons for Supporting the Death Penalty

The primary reasons for applying the death penalty in certain capital cases are threefold: (1) retribution; (2) deterrence; and (3) just deserts.

The Death Penalty Is Retribution

Retribution is defended largely on the basis of the philosophical "just deserts" rationale (Bohm, 1992). Offenders should be executed because they did not respect the lives of others. Death is the "just deserts" for someone who inflicted death on someone else.

Some experts regard retribution as the primary purpose of the death penalty (Bohm, Clark, and Aventi, 1990, 1991; Haas, 1994). For example, in a study of the opinions of a sample of residents in Seattle, Washington, Warr and Stafford (1984) found that the respondents were most likely to choose retribution as the main purpose of punishment when given a choice between incapacitation, rehabilitation, specific or general deterrence, or retribution. However, these researchers caution that no single adjective adequately describes public opinion about the specific purpose of capital punishment. There are minorities of citizens who endorse each of these views. Currently, no single dominant ideology of punishment now exists nationwide.

Theoretically, retribution serves abstract societal interests and has historically been used to justify the nature and severity of punishments imposed on criminals. However, the value of capital punishment as a sound retributive form continues to be debated (Bedau, 1992; E. Miller, 1990).

Table 10.5

Number of Persons Executed, by Jurisdiction, 1930–1994

State	Number Executed	
	Since 1930	Since 1977
U.S. total	4,116	257
Georgia	384	18
Texas	382	85
New York	329	
California	294	2
North Carolina	269	6
Florida	203	33
Ohio	172	
South Carolina	166	4
Mississippi	158	4
Louisiana	154	21
Pennsylvania	152	
Alabama	145	10
Arkansas	127	9
Virginia	116	24
Kentucky	103	
Tennessee	93	
Illinois	92	2
New Jersey	74	
Missouri	73	11
Maryland	69	1
Oklahoma	63	3
Washington	49	2
Colorado	47	
Indiana	44	3
Arizona	41	3
District of Columbia	40	
West Virginia	40	
Nevada	34	5
Federal system	33	
Massachusetts	27	
Connecticut	21	
Oregon	19	
Iowa	18	
Utah	17	4
Delaware	16	4
Kansas	15	
New Mexico	8	
Wyoming	8	1
Montana	6	
Nebraska	5	1
Idaho	4	1
Vermont	4	
New Hampshire	1	
South Dakota	1	
Alaska	0	
Hawaii	0	
Maine	0	
Michigan	0	
Minnesota	0	
North Dakota	0	
Rhode Island	0	
Wisconsin	0	

Source: Stephan and Snell (1996), p. 10.

289

The Death Penalty Deters Others from Committing Murder

The value of the death penalty as a deterrent is also frequently questioned. A study of homicide rates in Illinois during a forty-eight-year period (1933–1980) revealed that average homicide rates for three different periods did not fluctuate noticeably. These periods included (1) years when the death penalty was allowed; (2) years when the death penalty was allowed but not carried out; and (3) years when the death penalty was abolished (Decker and Kohfeld, 1984).

Other investigations into the deterrent value of capital punishment have been conducted in New York, Chicago, and Washington, D.C. (Bailey, 1983, 1984; Scarfone, 1986). Most of the investigators categorically conclude that the death penalty fails to deter people from committing murder.

For instance, Forst (1983) examined the deterrent effect of the death penalty by examining 1960 data from a cross-section of states. Variables Forst considered in his analysis included (1) the probability of execution if convicted, (2) the rate at which murderers are convicted, (3) the average prison term served by persons convicted of homicide, (4) the proportion of nonwhites who commit homicide, (5) the median family income of people who commit homicide, (6) the proportion of males who commit homicide, and a host of other factors. None of Forst's results showed that execution deters homicides.

Bailey (1984) conducted a time-series analysis of the deterrent effect of the death penalty in Washington, DC, for the periods 1890–1950, 1890–1955, 1890–1960, 1890–1965, and 1890–1970. His findings gave absolutely no support to the hypothesis that the death penalty deters homicides, regardless of how execution rates or murder rates were measured. In fact, Bailey found that murder rates and execution rates were *positively related* for these time periods. In other words, more executions were associated with more homicides.

Opponents of the death penalty argue that *no* criminal act justifies capital punishment (Bedau, 1992). They further contend that even if capital punishment were an effective deterrent to criminality, it should be abolished. Van den Haag and Conrad (1983) have challenged abolitionists to demonstrate the validity of such arguments, however. In the final analysis, neither position can be proven conclusively (Reiman, 1985).

The Death Penalty Is "Just Deserts" for Commission of a Capital Offense

The "just-deserts" philosophy argues that the death penalty is just punishment for murderers. The Supreme Court has indirectly validated this reasoning by refusing to declare the death penalty cruel and unusual punishment (Haas, 1994). Some authors have viewed Supreme Court decisions about the death penalty and its application to those as young as sixteen as well as the mentally retarded as vengeance (Miller, 1990). Further supporting this notion of vengeance is the fact that victim-impact statements and testimony are increasingly allowed in sentencing hearings for offenders who face the death penalty (Haas, 1994).

It has been found that people's opinions on the death penalty depend on their knowledge of capital punishment and its application (Bohm, Clark, and Aveni, 1990, 1991). Research examining the opinions of a sample of undergraduate students at a medium-sized university in northeastern Alabama during 1985–1987 found that knowledge about the death penalty did little to change students' views about whether it should be applied. Race and gender were closely associated with changed opinions, however. It was found that blacks and females were more likely to change their opinions about the death penalty once they learned more about it. Whites tended to favor the death penalty, and acquiring more information about it did little or nothing to change their opinions one way or another (Bohm, Clark and Aveni, 1991).

Reasons for Opposing the Death Penalty

The Death Penalty Is Barbaric

Hugo Bedau (1992) says that the death penalty is barbaric. There are other ways of punishing capital offenders. The United States is one of the few civilized countries of the modern world that still use the death penalty. Opponents of the death penalty include not only close friends and family members of offenders (Dicks, 1991) but also family members of victims.

The Death Penalty Is Unfair and May Be Applied Erroneously

Some convicted murderers on death row awaiting execution have been freed because of new evidence that proved them innocent. This is why Bedau (1992) and the American Civil Liberties Union are strong opponents of the death penalty. They and others propose an outright ban on the death penalty because of the mere possibility that some persons sentenced to death are innocent. A study by Michael Radelet, Hugo Bedau, and Constance Putnam (1992) showed that over four hundred persons have been wrongly convicted of capital crimes and sentenced to death. Evidence eventually used to free these persons included the confessions of the real perpetrators, reversals on appeal, and unofficial judgments that crimes did not occur (e.g., missing bodies eventually discovered and found not to have been murdered).

The Death Penalty Is Nothing More Than Sheer Revenge

Haas (1994) and others argue that by condoning the death penalty, the Supreme Court has sanctioned vengeance, which is an unacceptable justification for capital punishment. It is unlikely that persons who are retarded or intellectually disabled can reach the level of culpability necessary to trigger the need for the death penalty. They cannot engage in "cold calculus" to weigh committing the crime against the potential death penalty used to punish it (Miller, 1990).

The Death Penalty Is More Costly Than Life Sentences

Many opponents of capital punishment argue that executing prisoners is more costly than imprisoning them for life (Bedau, 1992; Bohm, 1992; Simons et al., 1995). However, a key reason for the high cost of executing prisoners is that they have been entitled to file endless appeals and delay the imposition of their death sentences (Costanzo and White, 1994). In 1996, Congress acted to limit the number of appeals inmates on death row can file. Thus, it is expected that in the future the length of

time between conviction and the imposition of the death penalty will be greatly abbreviated. This shorter period of time will decrease the expense of death penalty appeals and undermine this particular argument.

A study of the cost of imposing the death penalty compared with the costs of incarcerating offenders for life was conducted in North Carolina (Cook and Slawson, 1993). The study found that capital cases tend to be litigated more thoroughly than other types of cases. Bifurcated trials cost about $55,000 more than noncapital murder trials. A direct appeal in a death penalty case costs about $7,000. Further, an inmate who is executed after serving ten years on death row costs the Department of Corrections $166,000 *less* than an inmate who serves a "life" term and is then paroled after twenty years. Therefore, the extra costs of litigating death penalty cases and housing offenders on death row are far less than the costs of housing offenders who are eventually paroled. In some respects, this finding undermines the argument that capital punishment is more costly than sentences of life imprisonment.

The Death Penalty Is Still Applied Arbitrarily Despite Efforts by Legislatures and Congress to Make Its Application More Equitable

Evidence suggests that bifurcated trials have decreased but not eliminated racial and ethnic bias in death penalty applications (Bohm and Vogel, 1994; Simmons et al., 1995). While some experts argue that some races and ethnic categories have higher rates of capital murder and thus are disproportionately represented on death row, other experts say that the death penalty continues to be applied in a discriminatory manner in many jurisdictions (Baird and Rosenbaum, 1995; Costanzo and White, 1994; Simmons et al., 1995).

The Death Penalty Does Not Deter Others from Committing Murder

The literature strongly supports the idea that the death penalty apparently has no discernable deterrent effect. People will commit murder anyway, even knowing that there is a chance they may be caught and executed for the crime (Decker and

Kohfeld, 1990). Comparisons of jurisdictions that do and do not apply the death penalty show few, if any, differences in murder rates (Cheatwood, 1993; Godfrey and Schiraldi, 1995). Thus, the argument goes, if capital punishment fails to deter capital murder, it should be abolished (Bedau, 1992; Cochran, Chamlin, and Seth, 1994).

Most People in the United States Are Against the Death Penalty

Bedau (1992) has suggested that there is growing lack of public support for the death penalty. However, several national surveys show that over 75 percent of those interviewed support the death penalty and its application (Haas, 1994; Simmons et al., 1995). Certainly a knowledge of the death penalty and its deterrent and retributive effects makes a difference in whether persons support or oppose its use (Bohm, 1991; Bohm, Clark, and Aventi, 1990; Bohm and Vogel, 1994). Increasing rates of street crime, especially violent street crimes resulting in the deaths of innocent victims, trigger pro-capital-punishment sentiments in a frightened public. The debate continues (Baird and Rosenbaum, 1995).

Death Penalty Appeals

All sentences where the death penalty is imposed are subject to an automatic appellate review, although some offenders attempt to waive their right to such a review (Goodpaster, 1983). The purpose of the automatic review is to allow a higher court to determine whether the lower court adhered to proper procedures in arriving at a guilty verdict and whether the circumstances of the case warrant the death penalty. Were the defendants' rights observed at all stages of the trial (Haas, 1994; Simmons et al., 1995)?

Condemned offenders who appeal their death sentences usually do so by filing habeas corpus petitions. These petitions challenge three things: (1) the fact of confinement; (2) the nature of confinement; and (3) the length of confinement. The "fact of confinement" challenge is very broad. It may seek to address virtually every point of the offender's processing—the collection of evidence,

the offender's booking and initial appearance, the trial, and the sentencing. Any irregularities in the trial record—for instance, the questionable admission of evidence—may be challenged. Thus, capital offenders are at liberty to address any and all issues that might cause their death sentences to be reversed or reduced to life or life without parole.

For state prisoners, state appellate courts are normal avenues for lodging appeals. If these appeals are eventually exhausted by an unfavorable ruling by the state supreme court, prisoners can take their cases directly to the Supreme Court. Most of these appeals are never heard, primarily because there is not enough evidence to warrant a court hearing. In most of the appeals that it does hear, the Supreme Court upholds the original death sentence. This does not prevent prisoners from filing new appeals with different challenges to the factual basis for their conviction. This is one reason why it takes many years to carry out a death sentence. As we have seen, the average time between sentencing an offender to death and actually carrying out the sentence is a little over ten years (Stephan and Snell, 1996:1). This length of time will be shortened by restrictions that in 1996 were placed on the number of appeals condemned persons may file.

Will the U.S. Supreme Court Ever Resolve the Death Penalty Debate?

It is unlikely that any Supreme Court decision will resolve the capital punishment debate. Several alternatives to the death penalty have been recommended by various criminal justice researchers, such as commutation of a death sentence to life imprisonment (Cheatwood, 1985) or imposing solitary confinement for life (Snellenburg, 1986).

Some prisoners have even volunteered to be executed rather than languish in prison during prolonged appeals. One such prisoner was Gary Gilmore. In *Gilmore v. Utah* (1976), Gary Gilmore, a convicted murderer, was ordered executed in Utah after being convicted of capital murder. Shortly thereafter, Gilmore waived his rights to appeals in favor of a speedy execution. Several of his friends interceded and moved for a *stay of execution*, which was granted. Gilmore promptly sought to have the stay of execution *terminated*. The Supreme Court removed the stay of execution, saying that whenever a convicted murderer under sentence of death makes a *knowing and intelligent waiver* of any and all federal rights that he or she might have asserted, he or she is entitled to terminate a stay of execution despite objections of family members or friends. Thus, death row inmates may intelligently and knowingly waive their rights to appeal a death sentences over objections from friends and relatives. Gilmore was executed by firing squad on January 17, 1977.

Despite the Supreme Court's prohibition of the discriminatory application of the death penalty in capital cases, discrimination continues. In South Carolina, for example, it was found that during the years 1977–1981, the race of the victim was significantly related to the decision to seek the death penalty even when several legally relevant factors were taken into account. Black killers of whites were more likely, and black killers of blacks less likely, to be recommended for the death penalty (Paternoster, 1984).

But it is difficult to convince the Supreme Court that racial factors are responsible for the disproportionate number of blacks on death row. The Court has reviewed several allegations that race affects the imposition of the death penalty. In 1987, after finding that while there was indeed disproportionate representation of blacks on death rows throughout the United States, there was no evidence that this was legally relevant (*McCleskey v. Kemp*, 1987). In the *McCleskey* case, the Supreme Court rejected a challenge of Georgia's death penalty on grounds of racial discrimination. McCleskey, a black man, was sentenced to death for murdering a police officer during a grocery store robbery in 1978. During his appeal, he introduced statistical evidence that showed that more blacks than whites receive the death penalty. The U.S. Supreme Court rejected McCleskey's claim that disproportionality of executions by race is unconstitutional. Georgia's death penalty, the Supreme Court said, was not arbitrary and capricious, nor was it applied in a discriminatory manner, regardless of statistical evidence to the contrary.

Summary

This chapter has described the sentencing process. The Sentencing Reform Act of 1984 was a major attempt to provide greater consistency of sentences and alternatives to incarceration. Judges now have greater latitude to impose alternative sentences on low-risk offenders. Most states have followed suit in reforming their sentencing practices.

Some of the functions of sentencing are to promote respect for the law, to provide a "just" punishment for the offense, to deter the offender from future criminal conduct, to protect the public against the actions of the offender, and to provide the offender with the means to become rehabilitated through vocational or educational training.

There are several sentencing systems. Indeterminate sentencing gives judges broad discretionary powers in determining sentence length and severity. Parole boards usually determine when a prisoner should be paroled. Determinate sentencing involves a fixed term of confinement without parole board intervention. Mandatory sentencing requires that the offender be incarcerated for a specified length of time. Presumptive sentencing is a statutory form of sentencing that specifies normal sentence lengths but permits judges to shorten or lengthen sentences, depending upon mitigating or aggravating circumstances.

Current sentencing issues include sentencing disparity, where defendants receive more or less severe sentences depending upon their gender, race, ethnic background, or socioeconomic status. Another issue is predicting an offender's dangerousness. A third issue pertains to selectively incapacitating offenders. Finally, alternative sentencing is used as a means of alleviating prison overcrowding and removing low-risk, nonviolent offenders from prisons.

In capital cases, those in which the death penalty may be imposed, most jurisdictions have a bifurcated trial, where juries establish guilt and determine punishment in two separate hearings. All death sentences are automatically appealed, although the success rate of such appeals is quite low.

Key Terms

Aggravating circumstances
Alternative sentencing
Bifurcated trial

Capital punishment
Dangerousness
Determinate sentencing
Good time
Habitual offenders
Indeterminate sentences
Justice model
Mandatory sentencing
Mitigating circumstances
Presentence investigation
Presumptive sentencing
Recidivism rates
Selective incapacitation
Sentence
Sentencing disparity
Sentencing Reform Act of 1984
Victim impact statement

Questions for Review

1. Differentiate between indeterminate and determinate sentencing. Which sentencing system gives the judge more flexibility in the sentence he or she can impose on an offender?
2. What are two reforms suggested by the Sentencing Reform Act of 1984?
3. What are four functions of sentencing?
4. How does prison overcrowding influence a judge's decision whether to incarcerate an offender?
5. Differentiate between aggravating and mitigating circumstances, or factors. List three aggra-

vating and three mitigating factors. How does a judge utilize these factors in sentencing?
6. Differentiate between mandatory and presumptive sentencing.
7. What are the minimum and maximum sentence lengths for Class B, Class C, and Class E felonies?
8. On the basis of recidivism figures, what can be said about the ability of sentencing to promote respect for the law?
9. Discuss two studies that detected sentencing disparities. How are sentencing disparities being eliminated or reduced?
10. Identify and discuss briefly two studies involving sentencing disparities based on race. What were some of the basic findings?

Suggested Readings

American Correctional Association. *Classification: A Tool for Managing Today's Offenders.* Laurel, MD: American Correctional Association, 1993.

Bohm, Robert M. (ed.). *The Death Penalty in America: Current Research.* Cincinnati, OH: Anderson, 1991.

Johnson, Robert. *Death Work: A Study of the Modern Execution Process.* Belmont, CA: Wadsworth, 1990.

Wekesser, Carol (ed.). *The Death Penalty: Opposing Viewpoints.* San Diego, CA: Greenhaven Press, 1991.

CHAPTER 11

Correctional Institutions: Forms and Functions

Robert James Howard, a convicted kidnapper, was sentenced to ten years in a federal prison. Howard's first request when placed in the prison was for candles, candleholders, incense, a gong, a black robe, a chalice, and a short wooden staff for his satanic worship services. Howard wanted to practice destruction rituals, which he described as a way to visualize people's deaths, thus purging anger toward them without killing them. He wanted to perform ten rituals a month, between 2:00 A.M. and 5:00 A.M., and on Halloween. He said the rituals would help him cope with such things as his father's death the previous year. His request was refused, and Howard appealed to a U.S. District Court. On the basis of his First Amendment rights, Howard was permitted to conduct his satanic rituals after all, despite the prison warden's protests that some of the items Howard requested could be used as weapons (Associated Press, 1994c).

Correctional officers at the Allegheny County Jail in Pittsburgh, Pennsylvania, held target practice in the woods near the jail. A hunter came across the area and discovered large photographs of five black persons; the photos were riddled with bullet holes. Concerned, the hunter turned the photos over to police, who questioned the owner of the property. The owner turned out to be Charles Kainz, fifty-four, a guard at the Allegheny County Jail. Kainz explained to police that the photos were of actual inmates in the jail and that they had been used for target practice. Further investigation revealed that one of the photos was of Harold Cook, an inmate who was suing the jail for making him and five other inmates take off their clothes and scrub the floor following a food fight in the jail dining room. The newspaper published an article about the incident. The prisoners were furious. The warden was "fit to be tied" about the target practice and said, "It's just not the way to run an institution. It will not be condoned." Although Charles Kainz denied involvement, he was reprimanded, and the guards' union has filed a grievance for the reprimand (Associated Press, 1995c).

The prison system in Puerto Rico has paid at least $38 million in fines as the result of inmate overcrowding. Nearly $1 million every two weeks is being assessed because of a class action suit filed by inmates who were forced to sleep on window ledges, stairs, and in other unsuitable locations ("Noteworthy," 1991).

Satanic worship by inmates, using inmate photographs for target practice, and a prison system paying out millions for chronic overcrowding say much about the nation's prison and jail systems. Prison and jail overcrowding is a persistent problem. Issues of prisoners' rights absorb considerable court time as inmates seek to improve the quality of their lives behind bars. In the midst of massive sentencing reforms and more "truth in sentencing," the burden in the criminal justice system has shifted toward corrections as the primary offender manager. This responsibility is overwhelming. Further, corrections is the last in line for funding. In short, corrections is in trouble, and the situation is getting worse (Clear, 1994).

This chapter is about **corrections,** particularly that aspect that deals with prisons and jails. *Corrections is the aggregate of programs, services, facilities, and organizations responsible for the management of both adults and juveniles who have been accused, convicted, or adjudicated of criminal offenses or infractions.*

The term *corrections* is laden with overtones of punishment and reformation. These connotations have fostered numerous myths about what corrections is and does. Ideally, criminals assigned to correctional agencies are "corrected," which means they are punished and reformed. Yet much of the correctional field is unrelated to punishment or reformation. In fact, some experts question whether *any* correctional institution corrects or reforms (Walker, 1989b; Martinson, 1974; White, 1989). However, this view has been challenged by those who believe that rehabilitation occurs more frequently than is believed (Palmer, 1992). Although prisons and jails are the most visible correctional institutions, the vast majority of correctional personnel, agencies, and organizations are less obvious and blend in with many other community agencies and organizations (Cronin, 1994). While both institutional and community corrections are included under the larger term *corrections,* this chapter will focus solely on *institutional corrections,* which is limited to prisons and jails.

First, a brief history of corrections in the United States will be presented. Several important correctional goals will be identified and discussed. Next, prisons and jails will be defined and distinguished. Each will be examined in some detail, paying particular attention to the goals, functions, and problems associated with prison and jail operations. The chapter concludes with an examination of women and special-needs offenders in prisons and jails. At least one important fact will be learned from reading this chapter. Corrections doesn't necessarily correct. There are many difficult problems that corrections faces daily, and these problems are intensifying rather than diminishing.

The History of Prisons in the United States

Prisons have existed for all recorded time. The first prison systems in the United States were patterned after early British penal models and performed similar functions (Harding, et al., 1985; American Correctional Association, 1983). *Gaols* (pronounced: jails) were established in 1166 by the Assize (Constitution) of Clarendon under Henry II (American Correctional Association, 1983:3).

Devices to restrain prisoners called **body belts,** large belts worn about the waist with wrist restraints at the center of the abdomen, originated in the Middle Ages and are still used in state and federal prisons (Prison Reform Trust, 1984). In fact, prison statistics show that between 1981 and 1982, a 35 percent increase in the use of body belts in United States prisons occurred (Prison Reform Trust, 1984).

Debtors' Prisons

In the Middle Ages in England and Scotland, there was little planned imprisonment. Clothing and feeding outlaws was considered wasteful, and capital and brutal corporal punishments were administered freely as the most common punishment methods (Cameron, 1983). Debtors' prisons were abundant, and if debtors couldn't pay their debts, they were imprisoned until the debt could be paid, either by family members or friends. Many debtors died in these prisons (Harding et al., 1985). Prisons were places to confine society's undesirables. The practice of incarcerating debtors continues, despite the fact that indebtedness has been decriminalized. For instance, *bad-check laws* result in the jailing of numerous poor people for checks written on insufficient funds (Smith, 1989).

Religious Influence on Prison Growth

Religious organizations influenced the growth and purpose of prisons. Following the Reformation in the sixteenth century, the Church of England frequently used prisons to punish "offenders against morality" together with debtors and secular offenders (Cameron, 1983; Harding et al., 1985). As Great Britain expanded her domination of the colonies and established economic enterprises throughout the world, British penal policy included transporting large numbers of prisoners to remote penal colonies, such as Australia, for cheap labor and general economic exploitation (Smith, 1983).

During the sixteenth and seventeenth centuries, Scottish and English prisons were gradually transformed into industrial centers. Powerful mercantile interests established some of the first formal houses of correction (Dobash, 1983). The work performed in these early correctional institutions was intended to achieve several objectives, including improving prisoners' "social and moral habits, developing industrial skills, and producing marketable goods to defray confinement costs" (Dobash, 1983). These mercantile interests created the need for trained labor and skilled craftsmen in houses of correction. The Bridewell workhouse was constructed in 1557 to employ and house London's riffraff (American Correctional Association, 1983:4).

Banishment, *the physical removal of undesirables to a remote location,* was once a popular method of punishing serious offenders. Between 1788 and 1868, 160,000 English prisoners were exiled to Africa and Australia (American Correc-

tional Association, 1983:7; Hughes, 1987). Australia in 1788 was considered the "end of the world," and Britain's exile policy was labeled "the long enterprise of social excretion" (Hughes, 1987). Political dissidents as well as the most violent offenders were dispatched in this fashion. Only moral reformers and the development of a comprehensive penitentiary system in England terminated the Australian experiment. Banishment was also practiced in other societies, such as China (Waley-Cohen, 1991). Interestingly, a form of parental banishment exists today, as some youths are banished from their homes and ordered never to return for failure to conform to societal or school rules. While such banishment is not as severe as that practiced in Australia, it nevertheless functions according to the same principle of isolating and rejecting those who exhibit chronic misconduct (Borgman, 1986).

The Great Law of Pennsylvania

During the colonial period of the United States, religious interest profoundly influenced corrections programs (Evans, 1982). In 1682, **William Penn,** a Quaker who deplored the miserable conditions of Pennsylvania's penal system, caused to be enacted the **Great Law of Pennsylvania.** Penn, who had once been imprisoned himself for religious beliefs that were contrary to those of the Church of England, was sensitive to the plight of prisoners. Penn's law eliminated branding irons, gallows, and stocks and pillories, replacing them with fines and a more humane standard of imprisonment.

Penn also ordered each county in Pennsylvania to construct jails for offenders who violated local laws (Dunn and Dunn, 1982). Several of the other colonies eventually established county jails as well. The county jail concept continues in the United States.

The Walnut Street Jail

When Penn died in 1718, the humane measures he established in houses of corrections died with him. His successors replaced his policies with previous correctional philosophies, which stressed harsh, corporal treatment and public punishment. However, in 1787, a decade after the Revolutionary War, Penn's Quakers reestablished his correctional ideas and created the Philadelphia Society for Alleviating the Miseries of Public Prisons. This was followed a few years later by Pennsylvania legislative action in 1790 which created the **Walnut Street Jail** in Philadelphia.

The Walnut Street Jail is important because it represented *the first meaningful attempt to classify and segregate offenders according to the types of crimes they committed and the seriousness of their offenses* (American Correctional Association, 1983). Violent offenders were isolated from others and confined in separate cells. Nonviolent offenders were permitted limited movement in common social areas and could interact with other prisoners. Offenders were also segregated by gender. In addition to pioneering the classification of prisoners, the Walnut Street Jail introduced the idea of **solitary confinement,** a concept that is the standard for today's penitentiary system (Rogers, 1993). Solitary confinement today is used in many prison systems. *Its uses include punishment, prison security for especially dangerous prisoners, and isolation from others who might adversely influence those isolated.* If some crime arises out of a social context, that context can be removed while offenders are in isolation (Franke, 1992).

An early pioneer who influenced the design and operation of Walnut Street Jail was **Benjamin Rush** (1745–1813). Dr. Rush was a prominent physician, political leader and member of both Continental Congresses, and a signer of the Declaration of Independence. He believed that prison systems should contain areas where prisoners could grow food and exercise. He believed also that punishment should reform the offender, prevent further crimes, and remove those offenders from society who are unfit to live with others (American Correctional Association, 1983:30).

Penal developments in the United States from 1790 to 1914 can be divided into six distinct periods: (1) the post-revolutionary period, 1790–1812; (2) the recession following the War of 1812; (3) the Jacksonian period, 1812–1837; (4) the midcentury period, 1837–1860; (5) the post-bellum South, 1865–1890; and (6) the industrial Northeast, 1865–1914 (Adamson, 1984). Changes in economic

conditions and in the labor supply were closely linked with these stages. General economic changes had a profound impact on prison policies during the nineteenth century, and prison discipline and labor varied according to the periods described (Adamson, 1984).

Following the example set by Philadelphia with the Walnut Street Jail, New York State established correctional programs that eventually led to the construction of several state prisons. In 1797, Newgate Prison was constructed in New York City. It incorporated several of the penal concepts from Pennsylvania prison systems. In 1816, New York began the construction of Newgate Prison at Auburn (American Correctional Association, 1983:48). Newgate Prison was the first true colonial prison for the long-term punishment of serious offenders (Durham, 1990; Rawlings, 1992).

Auburn State Penitentiary and the Tier System

The Auburn State Penitentiary was another "first" in U.S. prison development. Architecturally, Auburn State Penitentiary introduced the **tier system** of cell blocks to alleviate some of the overcrowding typical of other prisons. At Auburn, cells were placed on five floors. Also, the Auburn State Penitentiary adopted a **congregate system,** where prisoners could work and eat together in large work and recreational areas. At night, prisoners were isolated from one another in solitary cells, however.

The **Auburn system** became a popular penitentiary model because it enabled prisoners to produce goods that benefited the prison system. The Auburn model was also important because it established separate confinement for various classifications of offenders beyond the classificatory criteria developed at the Walnut Street Jail. Prisoners who could not conform to prison norms or who were unruly were placed in long-term solitary confinement. Less dangerous prisoners were permitted to work at various skilled and semiskilled jobs. Most prisoners were permitted recreation and opportunities to associate with one another daily in the prison yard. Later, other states such as Vermont, New Hampshire, Massachusetts, Ohio, Georgia, and Kentucky built similar correctional facilities. In some respects, the Auburn system created the maximum, medium, and minimum security prison conditions that are found in penitentiaries today.

The national prison population in 1840 was 4,000 prisoners, or about 24 prisoners for every 100,000 persons in the population. In 1850, there were 7,000 prisoners, or 30 per 100,000. In 1860, there were 19,000 prisoners, or about 60 per 100,000. By 1870, this figure had reached 33,000 prisoners, or about 83 prisoners per 100,000 population. Thus, between 1860 and 1870 the prison population increased by 72 percent. Drastic measures became necessary to provide suitable facilities for this growing number of prisoners (American Correctional Association, 1983:63).

The American Correctional Association

In 1870, the National Prison Association was founded, and Rutherford B. Hayes (who would become president of the United States) was chosen as its first president. This association eventually became the **American Correctional Association (ACA)** (American Correctional Association, 1983:73). The goals of the ACA include formulating national correctional philosophy, designing and implementing standards for correctional services and methods for measuring compliance, and providing publications, training, and technical assistance to correctional institutions.

Elmira Reformatory and the Era of Prison Reform

New York State continued its penal innovations by establishing a reform-oriented prison, **Elmira Reformatory** in Elmira, New York, in 1876 (American Correctional Association, 1983). Constructed in a social environment of widespread opposition to corporal punishment and to harsh, violent prison practices, this new prison paralleled developments in England that emphasized prisoner reform and rehabilitation (Glenn, 1984). Priority was given to prisoner educational development and vocational

training. An inmate's good behavior and work output could mean more privileges and early release through parole (American Correctional Association, 1983). Among the early advocates of these penal philosophies were Robert Vaux (1786–1836) and his brother, Richard Vaux (1816–1895). These men belonged to the Philadelphia Prison Society, and their ideas influenced penal philosophy for more than a century.

Hailed by some corrections officials as an example of the new penology and of scientific reform, Elmira Reformatory, under the direction of Superintendent **Zebulon Brockway** (1827–1920), stressed individualized treatment, indeterminate sentencing, and parole. But historical records and eyewitness accounts of Brockway's methods suggest that Elmira Reformatory was unsuccessful in achieving its goals (Pisciotta, 1983). Some evidence indicates that Brockway's staff used severe, sometimes brutal, corporal punishment as a way of coercing conformity to reformatory norms and maintaining order (Pisciotta, 1983).

One-fourth of the states copied the Elmira Reformatory model between 1876 and 1920. During the "Lawless Decade" of the 1920s, prisons became increasingly overcrowded, and some of the educational and vocational programs could no longer operate effectively. More penitentiaries were built between 1920 and 1935, but these facilities were primarily custodial rather than rehabilitative.

The Federal Bureau of Prisons

On May 14, 1930, the **Federal Bureau of Prisons** was created. *It was charged with managing and regulating all federal penal and correctional institutions and providing safe and suitable quarters for all persons convicted of offenses against the United States.* It also provided technical assistance to state and local governments so that they could improve their correctional systems. The first federal penitentiary was built at Leavenworth, Kansas, in 1895; it was one of five established by the time the Bureau of Prisons was created. Although it is more than one hundred years old, Leavenworth continues to house federal prisoners.

Among the other functions of the Bureau of Prisons was the "protection, instruction, and discipline of all persons charged with or convicted of offenses against the United States" (18 U.S.C., Sec. 4042, 1996). The Bureau of Prisons interpreted this charge as a mandate to rehabilitate prisoners, besides furnishing them with vocational and educational training. Several new treatment-oriented programs were implemented at several federal penitentiaries over the next twenty years, including group therapy, individualized psychological counseling, encounter groups, and mental health assistance (U.S. Federal Bureau of Prisons, 1993). Today, goals of the Federal Bureau of Prisons include population management, human resource management, security and facility management, correctional leadership and effective public administration, inmate programs and services, and building partnerships with external organizations and agencies (U.S. Federal Bureau of Prisons, 1994; U.S. House of Representatives Committee on the Judiciary, 1994).

Between 1950 and 1966, over one hundred riots occurred in state and federal prisons. (Useem, Camp and Camp, 1993). One major contributing factor was prison *overcrowding,* although the lack of professional leadership and professional programs, inadequate staffing and financial support, and enforced idleness also contributed to prisoner unrest (American Correctional Association, 1983:209). While numerous reforms have been introduced over the years, prisons and jails still have similar problems (Harlow, 1994). The Federal Bureau of Prisons reports, for instance, that prison space is being expanded to cure overcrowding. However, rising inmate populations in future years will revive the issue of overcrowding. Thus, some experts see the problem of overcrowding as never-ending (U.S. General Accounting Office, 1993). Some types of problems have escalated. For instance, 186 prison riots were reported in twenty-one U.S. jurisdictions in 1993 alone (Lillis, 1994:7). The Texas Department of Corrections reported 103 of these riots.

Correctional Goals

The major goals of corrections include (1) retribution, (2) deterrence, (3) rehabilitation, (4) reintegration, and (5) isolation and incapacitation.

Retribution

Depriving offenders of freedom is a major function of corrections (Cragg et al., 1992). Incarceration is a form of retribution. Early prison reforms stressed rehabilitation through individualized treatment and therapy, but there is evidence that these values are being abandoned in favor of a more primitive purpose—punishment (Palmer, 1992). However, inmates seem to be coping more effectively with imprisonment by adjusting to it and even resisting it (Meisenhelder, 1985). Public opinion about the retribution function of correctional institutions is mixed (Clear, 1994), but some critics say that the public wants the protection of society rather than retribution as a goal of corrections (Michigan Council on Crime and Delinquency, 1993).

Deterrence

Another goal of corrections is to encourage offenders not to commit crimes in the future. However, corrections does not appear to be a significant deterrent to future crimes. It has been shown that each year about 60 percent of all those admitted to prisons are recidivists (Maguire and Pastore, 1995). Coupled with earlier research on recidivism, these figures do not support the idea that incarceration is a deterrent to crime.

For example, an investigation was conducted of a sample of 1,806 federal prisoners released in 1970. The study showed that during the following five-year period, half of these parolees committed new crimes for which they were incarcerated (Hoffman and Beck, 1985). **Recidivism** *was defined as a new sentence of imprisonment exceeding one year for offenses committed during the follow-up period*. It is likely that some of these recidivists were ex-prisoners who had been returned to prison several times for two or more criminal offenses. Not much has changed between 1970 and the mid-1990s. In 1993, for instance, about half of all federal and state parolees violated one or more conditions of their parole and were either returned to prison or placed in a more intensive supervision program (Maguire and Pastore, 1995:578). Further, about 60 percent of all new federal and state prison admissions were recidivists who had been convicted earlier for one or more offenses (Maguire and Pastore, 1995). This pattern continued throughout 1994 (Camp and Camp, 1995a).

Recidivism rates are high among the states. For instance, a study of 3,257 persons released from Delaware prisons between 1980 and 1982 disclosed that more than half (51.4 percent) were rearrested, and almost 75 percent of these rearrests occurred within the first year following their release (Delaware Executive Department, 1984). It is important to note, however, that rearrests do not necessarily result in **reconvictions.** *Reconvictions are defined as convictions for new offenses other than the original conviction offenses.* If a probationer or parolee commits and is convicted of a new crime, such as burglary, while on probation or parole, this is a reconviction.

In the Delaware sample, officials measured recidivism by rearrests. *Being taken into custody on suspicion of committing a crime constitutes a rearrest.* Rearrests do not mean that someone is guilty of a crime. Many persons who are rearrested are never charged. Many persons who are charged are never convicted. Thus, a rearrest is often investigatory and goes no further than questioning a probationer or parolee. It is difficult to compare statistical information from different studies on recidivism because the same term is used in several different contexts. For example, recidivism has been defined as "return to prison" in a North Carolina study (Clarke and Crum, 1985) and a "violation of one or more parole conditions" in an Iowa investigation (Boudouris, 1983). The most frequent meaning of the term *recidivist is the convicted offender who commits a new crime and is convicted of it* (Matthews, Boone, and Fogg, 1994:10–17).

Further, *increasing* the penalties for committing crimes doesn't seem to deter criminals. Drug use is at an all-time high. Interdiction efforts by various law enforcement agencies have reduced the flow of drugs from other countries into the United States, but there is a pervasive drug problem. One way of attacking the drug problem is to penalize severely those who deal drugs. Several important laws were enacted in the late 1980s and early 1990s to make drug trafficking an offense punishable by life without parole and possibly death. However, a study of the effectiveness of these increased sanctions has shown that greater penalties for drug trafficking are generally ineffective (Cavanaugh, Boyum, and Nambiar, 1993). Research on the impact of increased penalties for drug-related crimes upon the number of offenses is ambiguous at best.

Rehabilitation

A key objective of most prison reforms is rehabilitation, which was one of several objectives of Auburn State Penitentiary, New York, in 1816 and of Elmira Reformatory in 1876. Inmates received vocational training and attended educational programs. While critics have concluded that the rehabilitative ideal of correctional institutions is ineffective, some analysts believe that the work ethic in prisons gives inmates work skills and dignity (Michigan Council on Crime and Delinquency, 1993).

The policy of paying prisoners a reasonable wage for work performed is one recommended policy (Cullen and Travis, 1984). The argument is that current "get tough on crime" crusades will continue in the absence of alternative reforms that will mitigate the consequences of current correctional policies, which only seem to contain large numbers of offenders. Employing offenders may be a way of transforming them into productive citizens and may counter the negative effects of idleness and boredom that are often associated with prison and jail problems (Claggett et al., 1992). Thus, it has been recommended that in order to promote more effective rehabilitation, corrections adopt several new and innovative practices to help prisoners acquire coping skills and manage their behavior.

The prison reform movement has greatly improved the quality of correctional education (Muth and Gehring, 1986). Programs for female prisoners have included classes in child rearing and maternal bonding (Virginia Department of Corrections, 1995). Programs for male offenders have included ways of dealing with drug or alcohol abuse. Specific therapies are provided to help mentally ill inmates cope once they are released from prison. A combination of prison and community mental health programs provide an array of helpful social and psychological services for such offenders, which has reduced their recidivism rates significantly (Poole and Slavick, 1995; Ventura and Cassel, 1994).

Prisoner response to educational programs has been favorable (Wunder, 1995b). Education is a direct path to self-improvement, and studies show that prisoners develop more positive self-images through their participation in education programs. In the Mississippi state prison system, for example, prisoners are given both vocational and educational training to improve their employability and reduce recidivism (Wunder, 1995b). A key factor in ex-offender employment may not be skills or training, but rather a stable employment record (Williford, 1996:85), which can be acquired through the development of a more favorable self-image, self-esteem, and improved communication skills, work habits, and cognitive abilities. A liberal arts education for prisoners is one way of developing these characteristics. But prison and jail overcrowding undermines the efforts of prison educators to offer the kinds of individualized instruction inmates need (Denham, 1996:66–68).

An educational program known as Read Out was implemented in 1990–1991 at the Rio Cosumnes Correctional Center in Sacramento County, California (Denham, 1966). During the 1993–1994 operational year of Read Out, the center had sixteen teachers. Services were extended to 1,572 inmates, 692 of whom earned time off of their original sentences. The inmates were also granted 2,587 days of leave from the center. The center awarded 202 G.E.D. certificates to inmates, together with twenty-five high school diplomas (Denham, 1996:67). Inmates who participated in the literacy program also showed marked improvement in their reading levels. The center also offered job readiness and job placement programs, together with vocational educational guidance.

Reintegration

Reintegration is closely related to rehabilitation as a correctional goal. As inmates prepare for reentry into their communities, the transitions require significant adjustments to diminish the effects of confinement and rigid compliance to

Programs educating inmate parents in child care and permitting them to raise their children in prison are the offspring of the prison reform movement.

prison rules and regulations (Washington State Department of Corrections, 1993).

Some prisons gradually move their inmates to living quarters that do not have the stigma of the traditional prison environment, such as locked cells and bars. Typical cells in the Special Offender Center, a maximum security facility in Monroe, Washington, include flowers in the windows, a television set, and a radio. The center also has a small library (American Correctional Association, 1983:252). And the North Carolina Central Prison in Raleigh, North Carolina, looks more like a large private college or motor lodge than a prison (American Correctional Association, 1983:249).

Often, reintegration of inmates being released from long-term prisons is facilitated by networking with various community agencies and services. Assistance with housing and employment and other forms of support and counseling are recommended (National Association for the Care and Resettlement of Offenders, 1993; Washington State Department of Corrections, 1993). Day reporting centers for low-risk offenders are often established. Day reporting centers are operated primarily during daytime hours for the purpose of providing diverse services to offenders and their families. They are highly structured nonresidential programs utilizing supervision, sanctions, and services coordinated from a central focus. Offenders live at home and report to these centers regularly. These centers provide services that might include employment assistance, family counseling, and educational/vocational training. The centers may also be used for supervisory and/or monitoring purposes. Modification of clients' behavior is a key goal of such centers (Diggs and Pieper, 1994). Thus, close links with a supportive community environment enable many parolees and probationers to remain crime free and to establish stable employment and families (Johnson et al., 1994).

Isolation and Incapacitation

The custodial goal of corrections is to isolate inmates from the general public. Isolating offenders is the most direct form of crime control (Institute for Rational Public Policy, Inc., 1991). Isolation is most frequently used for extremely dangerous and violent offenders. During the 1980s, Charles Manson, convicted of the murder of Sharon Tate and others in California, became eligible for parole. However, public sentiment, usually expressed through the media, strongly opposed Manson's parole. By 1996, Manson's efforts to secure early release through parole had been unsuccessful. In cases such as Manson's, a crucial question is the potential dangerousness of the inmate and the degree of public risk incurred if parole is granted. Most offenders are eventually returned to society, however, and their isolation is temporary. A relatively small number of extremely dangerous criminals serve life terms or are executed.

In the mid-1980s and early 1990s, various researchers examined what effect jailing offenders had on community crime rates. Shinnar and Shinnar (1975) estimated that the average criminal committed ten crimes per year (Wilson, 1983:148). Basing these estimates on a complex statistical model, the Shinnars concluded that in a city such as New York, crimes such as robbery would be reduced by 80 percent each year for each year these offenders were incarcerated.

Eventually, research interest was directed at studying offenders who committed disproportionately large numbers of crimes. On the basis of self-reports of over 2,200 inmates in California, Michigan, and Texas prisons, the Rand Corporation found that a small core of offenders in each state committed from eight to twenty-three times more crimes than the average inmate in the entire sample (Greenwood, 1982). Self-reports are disclosures by inmates about the number of crimes they committed per year while free and for which they were not apprehended. The small core of criminals were labeled as *career offenders, chronic offenders,* or *persistent offenders.*

Interestingly, some of this research was stimulated, in part, by two earlier investigations by Marvin Wolfgang and his associates (Wolfgang, Figlio, and Sellin, 1972; Wolfgang, 1983). Popularly known as the *Philadelphia Birth Cohort Study,* this research involved the identification of 9,945 boys born in Philadelphia in 1945. This *cohort* was tracked until 1963, when all boys reached age eighteen. Furthermore, Wolfgang selected a 10 percent sample of these eighteen-year-olds and continued to monitor their progress until they reached age thirty in 1975. Wolfgang also investigated a second birth cohort of infants born in Philadelphia in 1958. This cohort included 28,338 children—13,811 males and 14,527 females. Thus, the second cohort was not only larger than the first but was also considered more representative because of the inclusion of females. As well as insightful, the findings from both cohorts were similar in several respects.

Wolfgang found that for the 1945 cohort, one-third of the boys had had some contact with police or had acquired records of delinquency by age eighteen. Perhaps the most important finding was that 6 percent (627 out of 9,945 boys) had committed about 52 percent of all offenses among the entire cohort, including 82 percent of all robberies, 73 percent of all rapes, and 71 percent of all homicides. In his follow-up of these chronic offenders, he found that by age thirty, many of these subjects continued their former offending rates and accounted for a disproportionately large share of crimes.

Wolfgang's preliminary investigation of the 1958 cohort of 28,338 boys and girls showed that by 1976, when these subjects reached age eighteen, a chronic-offender aggregate had been identified. While the proportion of delinquent youths was about the same as in the 1945 cohort, about 7.5 percent of the entire sample were identified as chronic offenders, accounting for 61 percent of all offenses, including 76 percent of all rapes, 61 percent of all homicides, and 73 percent of all robberies (Wolfgang, 1983). Less than one percent of all females in the 1958 cohort were identified as chronic offenders. One of the more significant differences, however, was that the 1958 cohort had a rate of violent offenses three times larger than that of the 1945 cohort. These findings suggest that the nature of delinquency has changed or is changing and that the change is toward increased violence among juveniles. However, no satisfactory explanation has been provided that reliably accounts for such differences between the two cohorts (Tracy, Wolfgang, and Figlio, 1985).

Wolfgang and others studied a more recent birth cohort from Puerto Rico in 1970 (Nevares et al., 1990). This longitudinal study involved 24,669 males and females born in 1970 who, before reaching age eighteen, had at least one recorded arrest or were officially recorded as status offenders in the Greater San Juan Metropolitan Area. Data were gathered from court and police records. Wolfgang and his associates found that 25 percent of all offenses in the 1970 cohort were committed by known drug users. Overall, the offending rate of the cohort increased until age sixteen and then declined appreciably. Compared with the former 1945 and 1958 cohorts, both delinquency and recidivism rates were lower.

The idea that a small core of offenders, both juvenile and adult, accounts for a disproportionately large share of criminal behavior has prompted interest in *selective incapacitation,* or the selective and longer incarceration of those believed to be most likely to commit new crimes (Gottfredson and Gottfredson, 1992; Zimring and Hawkins, 1995). However, selective incapacitation has been criticized on moral, legal, methodological, and practical grounds (von Hirsch, 1985; Gottfredson and Gottfredson, 1988). Sentencing certain offenders differently than other offenders convicted of similar crimes raises the question of fairness. Is it

fair to penalize certain offenders more harshly on the basis of what they might do in the future? (von Hirsch, 1985). Are our predictive instruments sophisticated enough to identify offenders who will reoffend? Can we be certain that those who are treated more leniently and sentenced to probation will not reoffend?

Efforts at targeting those offenders who are "high risks" and "low risks" have been unsuccessful (Champion, 1994), although some experts believe that despite its limitations, selective incapacitation is a viable strategy for reducing crime (Spelman, 1994). Methodological problems undermine our attempts to devise predictive scales that accurately forecast behavior, suggesting that some people will be punished unjustly. The use of such predictive tools by judges raises legal issues that are beyond the scope of this book. However, changing sentencing procedures such as the use of presumptive sentencing schemes by the federal government and states such as Minnesota are narrowing judicial sentencing options. Questions of predicted dangerousness or potential public risk are irrelevant if sentencing tables are used to determine jail terms. Nevertheless, a substantial number of states continue to use indeterminate sentencing. In those jurisdictions, at least, selective incapacitation of certain offenders continues to be a viable option for the judiciary.

Jails and Prisons: Some Preliminary Distinctions

By the end of 1994, there were 980,513 convicts sentenced to terms of one year or longer in state and federal prisons (Camp and Camp, 1995a:1). In 1994, there was an average daily population of 562,715 inmates in city and county jails (Camp and Camp, 1995b:46). Official figures from the Bureau of Justice Statistics for 1994 show 490,442 jail inmates (Maguire and Pastore, 1995:533). This is a 21 percent population increase over the 1990 figure of 405,320 inmates (Maguire and Pastore, 1995:533).

Prisons and penitentiaries are designed to house more serious felony offenders. Usually, convicted offenders who have been sentenced to imprisonment for a year or longer will serve that time in a prison or penitentiary. Prisons are self-contained units, usually covering substantial acreage and surrounded by high fences, walls, and guard towers. Prisons are financed by state or federal government taxes and are operated by civil employees and administrators.

Jails are city- or county-operated, and they are usually administered as part of a police department facility. Jails house less serious offenders, including misdemeanants (Perkins, Stephan, and Beck, 1995). Jails also accommodate federal or state prisoners transferred from overcrowded federal and state prisons. Some jails house these prisoners through contractural agreements with state or federal authorities. Those arrested by local police are initially detained in city or county jails. Also, those awaiting trial or who cannot afford bail are placed in jail rather than in prisons or penitentiaries. Table 11.1 shows the changing number of inmates in state and federal prisons between 1925 and 1993.

Between 1983 and 1993, inmate populations in state and federal penitentiaries more than doubled. State prisons are currently operating at 115 percent of their rated capacities, while federal prisons are operating at 125 percent of their rated capacity (Camp and Camp, 1995a:36–37). Texas prisons were the most crowded, with its prison system operating at 129.6 percent of its rated capacity. Only six states in 1996 had inmate populations at or under their rated capacities. In short, most state and federal prisons are overcrowded.

Jails are almost as overcrowded. In 1994, jails were operating at 97 percent of their rated capacities (Maguire and Pastore, 1995:533). Table 11.2 shows the number of jail inmates, average daily inmate population, and rated capacity of jails from 1983 to 1994. Jail overcrowding peaked in 1989 with a jail inmate population of 108 percent of rated capacity. Court-ordered reductions of populations in both jails and prisons have eased this overcrowding somewhat, and new jail and prison construction has helped as well. However, the problem of overcrowding is persistent, and construction of new jails and prisons does not seem to be an effective long-term remedy (Mauer and Young, 1992; Texas Criminal Justice Policy Council, 1993b).

Jails

Jails, or gaols, were inspired by England's Henry II (1154–1189). In sixteenth century England, county sheriffs and justices of the peace in local jurisdictions were charged with the responsibility of building and maintaining jails to imprison local offenders (Wayson et al., 1977:3–4).

The inhabitants of these *houses of correction* originally were petty offenders and vagrants. Keepers were hired by sheriffs to watch the inmates. Keepers rarely received a salary, however. Rather, they obtained funds for maintaining inmates from the inmates themselves, from friends of inmates, or from inmate begging.

> The schedule of payments under this much criticized . . . system was not uniform . . . but varied with the dreadfulness of events and the prisoner's social station. Beds, mattresses, bedclothes . . . [and other items] were each assigned a price; more striking however, were the charges for admission to the jail and discharge (even if the prisoner was acquitted. (Wayson et al., 1977:3)

In the colonies in 1642, the General Assembly of Virginia initiated an administrative pattern that describes current jail systems in the United States (Wayson et al., 1977:4). Six counties in Virginia were required to build jails for the general detention of prisoners awaiting monthly court sessions in Jamestown. Of course, the previously discussed Walnut Street Jail built in Philadelphia in 1790 is recognized as the first "modern" jail facility.

Jails in the United States house both short-term offenders and those awaiting trial. Some jails have contracted with state and federal governments to house some of their inmate overflow who may require only short-term incarceration. Also detained in these jails are those arrested for petty offenses who cannot post bond. Jails also hold convicted offenders who have been sentenced to less than a year. Jails hold mostly young males with poor education, the mentally ill, the retarded, and public inebriates. A majority of those admitted to jail remain there less than three weeks (Perkins, Stephan, and Beck, 1995).

Jails in the United States have been called "fes-

Table 11.1

Number and Rate (per 100,000 Resident Population of Each Sex) of Sentenced Prisoners in the United States, 1925–1993, in State and Federal Institutions on December 31, 1993

Year	Total	Rate	Male		Female	
			Number	Rate	Number	Rate
1925	91,669	79	88,231	149	3,438	6
1926	97,991	83	94,287	157	3,704	6
1927	109,983	91	104,983	173	4,363	7
1928	116,390	96	111,836	182	4,554	8
1929	120,496	98	115,876	187	4,620	8
1930	129,453	104	124,785	200	4,668	8
1931	137,082	110	132,638	211	4,444	7
1932	137,997	110	133,573	211	4,424	7
1933	136,810	109	132,520	209	4,290	7
1934	138,316	109	133,769	209	4,547	7
1935	144,180	113	139,278	217	4,902	8
1936	145,038	113	139,990	217	5,048	8
1937	152,741	118	147,375	227	5,366	8
1938	160,285	123	154,826	236	5,459	8
1939	179,818	137	173,143	263	6,675	10
1940	173,706	131	167,345	252	6,361	10
1941	165,439	124	159,228	239	6,211	9
1942	150,384	112	144,167	217	6,217	9
1943	137,220	103	131,054	202	6,166	9
1944	132,456	100	126,350	200	6,106	9
1945	133,649	98	127,609	193	6,040	9
1946	140,079	99	134,075	191	6,004	8
1947	151,304	105	144,961	202	6,343	9
1948	155,977	106	149,739	205	6,238	8
1949	163,749	109	157,663	211	6,086	8
1950	166,123	109	160,309	211	5,814	8
1951	165,680	107	159,610	208	6,070	8
1952	168,233	107	161,994	208	6,239	8
1953	173,579	108	166,909	211	6,670	8
1954	182,901	112	175,907	218	6,994	8
1955	185,780	112	178,655	217	7,125	8
1956	189,565	112	182,190	218	7,375	9
1957	195,414	113	188,113	221	7,301	8
1958	205,643	117	198,208	229	7,435	8
1959	208,105	117	200,469	228	7,636	8

(continued next page)

Table 11.1 *(continued)*

Number and Rate (per 100,000 Resident Population of Each Sex) of Sentenced Prisoners in the United States, 1925–1993, in State and Federal Institutions on December 31, 1993

Year	Total	Rate	Male Number	Male Rate	Female Number	Female Rate
1960	212,953	117	205,265	230	7,688	8
1961	220,149	119	212,268	234	7,881	8
1962	218,830	117	210,823	229	8,007	8
1963	217,283	114	209,538	225	7,745	8
1964	214,336	111	206,632	219	7,704	8
1965	210,895	108	203,327	213	7,568	8
1966	199,654	102	192,703	201	6,951	7
1967	194,896	98	188,661	195	6,235	6
1968	187,914	94	182,102	187	5,812	6
1969	196,007	97	189,413	192	6,594	6
1970	196,429	96	190,794	191	5,635	5
1971	198,061	95	191,732	189	6,329	6
1972	196,092	93	189,823	185	6,269	6
1973	204,211	96	197,523	191	6,004	6
1974	218,466	102	211,077	202	7,389	7
1975	240,593	111	231,918	220	8,675	8
1976	262,833	120	252,794	238	10,039	9
1977[a]	278,141	126	267,097	249	11,044	10
1977[b]	285,456	129	274,244	255	11,212	10
1978	294,396	132	282,813	261	11,583	10
1979	301,470	133	289,465	264	12,005	10
1980	315,974	138	303,643	274	12,331	11
1981	353,167	153	338,940	302	14,227	12
1982	394,374	170	378,045	336	16,329	14
1983	419,820	179	402,391	352	17,429	14
1984	443,398	188	424,193	NA	19,205	NA
1985	480,568	200	458,972	NA	21,296	NA
1986	522,084	216	497,540	NA	24,544	NA
1987	560,812	228	533,990	NA	26,822	NA
1988	603,732	244	573,587	NA	30,145	NA
1989	680,907	271	643,643	NA	37,264	NA
1990	739,980	292	699,416	NA	40,564	NA
1991	789,610	310	745,808	NA	43,802	NA
1992	846,277	330	799,776	NA	46,501	NA
1993	910,080	350	859,227	NA	50,853	NA

Source: Maguire and Pastore (1995), p. 540.
a. Custody counts.
b. Jurisdiction counts.

Table 11.2

Number of Jail Inmates, Average Daily Population, and Rated Capacity by Legal Status and Sex, United States, 1983–1994

| | One-day counts | | | | | Average daily population[a] | | | | | Rated capacity of jails | Percent of rated capacity occupied[c] |
| | All inmates | Adults | | | Juvenile[b] | All inmates | Total | Adults | | Juvenile[b] | | |
		Total	Male	Female				Male	Female			
1983	223,551	221,815	206,163	15,652	1,736	227,541	225,781	210,451	15,330	1,760	261,556	85%
1984	234,500	233,018	216,275	16,743	1,482	230,641	228,944	212,749	16,195	1,697	261,432	90
1985	256,615	254,986	235,909	19,077	1,629	265,010	263,543	244,711	18,832	1,467	272,830	94
1986	274,444	272,736	251,235	21,501	1,708	265,517	264,113	243,143	20,970	1,404	285,726	96
1987	295,873	294,092	270,172	23,920	1,781	290,300	288,725	264,929	23,796	1,575	301,198	98
1988	343,569	341,893	311,594	30,299	1,676	336,017	334,566	306,379	28,187	1,451	339,633	101
1989	395,553	393,303	356,050	37,253	2,250	386,845	384,954	349,180	35,774	1,891	367,769	108
1990	405,320	403,019	365,821	37,198	2,301	408,075	405,935	368,091	37,844	2,140	389,171	104
1991	426,479	424,129	384,628	39,501	2,350	422,609	420,276	381,458	38,818	2,333	421,237	101
1992	444,584	441,781	401,106	40,674	2,804	441,889	439,362	399,528	39,834	2,527	449,197	99
1993[d]	459,804	455,500	411,500	44,100	4,300	466,140	462,800	418,200	44,600	3,400[e]	475,224	97
1994	490,442	483,717	434,838	48,879	6,725	479,757	NA	NA	NA	NA	504,324	97

Source: Maguire and Pastore (1995), p. 532.

Note: Data for 1983, 1988, and 1993 are from the National Jail Census. Data for 1984–87, 1989–92, and 1994 are from the Annual Survey of Jails taken during noncensus years. Both the censuses and the surveys are conducted for the U.S. Department of Justice, Bureau of Justice Statistics by the U.S. Bureau of the Census. The data from the annual surveys are estimates and therefore are subject to sampling variation. A jail is defined as a locally administered confinement facility that holds inmates beyond arraignment, usually for more than 48 hours, and is administered and staffed by municipal or county employees. Excluded from the censuses and surveys were temporary holding facilities, such as physically separate drunk tanks and police lockups, and other holding facilities that did not hold persons after they were formally charged in court. Also excluded for all years were Connecticut, Delaware, Hawaii, Rhode Island, and Vermont because these States have integrated jail-prison systems. Alaska also was excluded as an integrated system; however, beginning in 1988, five locally operated jails in Alaska were included.

a. Based on the average daily population for the year ending on the reference date of each census or survey. The average daily population is the sum of the number of inmates in a jail each day for a year, divided by 365.

b. Juveniles are persons defined by State statute as being under a certain age, usually 18, and subject initially to juvenile court authority even if tried as adults in criminal court. In 1994, the definition was changed to include all persons under age 18.

c. The number of inmates divided by rated capacity times 100. This ratio may include some inmates not in physical custody, but under the jurisdiction of a local jail, such as inmates on electronic monitoring, under house arrest, or in day reporting or other community supervision programs.

d. Detailed data for 1993 were estimated and rounded to the nearest 100.

e. Counts for 1993 differ from previous counts because juveniles tried or awaiting trial as adults were included.

tering sores," "cesspools of crime," "teeming houses of horror," and "the ultimate ghetto" (Thompson, 1986:205). Much of the blame for such labels is attributed to their unique political nature (Thompson, 1986:205). Thompson (1986:206–8) says that our jails are faced with numerous problems. A majority of jails in the United States are old, many having been built in the nineteenth century. Also, these facilities are poorly designed; staffed by poorly trained, underpaid, and low status personnel; and have little public sympathy or support (Mays, 1992). Jails rely heavily upon county sheriffs for administrative leadership and on county government for financial support (Florida Legislative Advisory Council, 1993).

The U.S. Jail Population

In 1982, the Bureau of the Census began a national survey of jails for the Bureau of Justice Statistics. In 1978, a complete enumeration of jails was conducted by the Bureau of Justice Statistics. These surveys are now conducted every five years. A 1993 Census of Jails was conducted. This census showed that there were 3,304 jails in the United States. A subsequent 1994 survey showed that there were 2,981 jail facilities (Perkins, Stephan, and Beck, 1995). These discrepancies are explained by the fact that not everyone agrees on how jails should be defined. Facilities such as drunk tanks and lockups (police-holding areas for persons who are not formally charged with crimes) are counted as jails in some but not all surveys. Privately operated jails or jail-prison facilities operated by state prison systems may or may not be included. For instance, in 1993, seventeen jails were operated by private corporations, while another seven jail facilities were maintained by the Bureau of Prisons. The 1993 jail census did not include state-operated jail facilities in Alaska, Connecticut, Delaware, Hawaii, Rhode Island, and Vermont. Further, jail demolition and new jail construction change the actual number of jails (Higgins, 1996:8).

Jail Inmate Characteristics

Of the 490,442 jail inmates described in official sources in 1994, 90 percent were male. Blacks made up 44 percent of all jail inmates, while His-

panics contributed another 15.4 percent. About 48 percent of all adult inmates were unconvicted and were either on trial or awaiting trial. Less than 1 percent (6,725) of all jail inmates were juveniles under eighteen years of age awaiting transfer to juvenile facilities.

Between 1983 and 1993, the jail inmate population more than doubled. The following factors are responsible for this increase (Perkins, Stephan, and Beck, 1995:2):

1. An increase in adult arrests.
2. A growth in the number of jail admissions.
3. An increase in the number of felons sentenced to local jails.
4. An increase in the number of inmates charged with or convicted of drug offenses.
5. More inmates held in jails because of crowded state or federal prison facilities.

Jail Functions

Jails have the following functions:

1. receive individuals pending arraignment and hold them awaiting trial, conviction, or sentencing;
2. readmit probation, parole, and bail-bond violators and absconders;
3. temporarily detain juveniles pending transfer to juvenile authorities;
4. hold mentally ill persons pending their movement to appropriate health facilities;
5. hold individuals for the military, for protective custody, for contempt, and for the courts as witnesses;
6. release convicted inmates to the community upon completion of sentence;
7. transfer inmates to federal, state, or other authorities;
8. house inmates for federal, state, or other authorities because of crowding of their facilities;
9. relinquish custody of temporary detainees to juvenile and medical authorities; and
10. sometimes operate community-based programs with electronic monitoring or other types of supervision (Perkins, Stephan, and Beck, 1995:2).

Jails Described

Jails are less complex than prisons, though they have many of the same features as prisons, such as cells for solitary confinement and areas segregated according to the type of inmate incarcerated. However, jail administrators have different kinds of problems compared with those that confront prison administrators. The cost of maintaining inmates varies among jails, depending upon the quality of facilities provided. The average cost of maintaining a jail inmate per day is $47, or about $17,155 per year. The lowest cost per inmate per day is in Decatur, Georgia, and Taylor, Texas, with a cost of $15 per inmate, or $5,475 per year. The highest cost per inmate per day is in Suffolk, New York, with a cost of $110.28 per inmate per day, or $40,252 per year (Camp and Camp, 1995b: 33–34). Inmate-to-staff ratios range from 2.4 to 4.6 inmates for every correctional officer.

Because of the short-term nature of a jail inmate's confinement, little concern is given to inmate adjustment problems. Group counseling and therapy are rare. Jails are short-term custodial institutions primarily operated for cities and counties. Therefore, there is little justification for reform or rehabilitation programs. Nevertheless, in 1994, 73 percent of all jails had either educational or vocational training programs for interested inmates (Camp and Camp, 1995b:71). Further, over 98 percent of all jails had medical services.

Jails have no guard towers or close supervision of inmate activities. Most jails do not have outside recreational yards, although many jails have recreational areas where prisoners can watch television or play cards. Often, these areas are dayrooms.

Inmates are not paroled from jails. When inmates have served their time, they are released without supervision. However, judges may impose short-term sentences for felons and assign them temporarily to jails. The remainder of their sentences are served on parole. Occasionally, state or federal prisoners convicted of felonies or several misdemeanors are housed temporarily in jails rather than prisons. In 1994, 24 percent of all jails in jurisdictions with large jail populations held inmates from state and federal institutions to alleviate overcrowding.

Ironically, transferring state and federal prisoners to local jail facilities has created overcrowding in many local jails. Between 1983 and 1994, jail space increased by 93 percent (Perkins, Stephan, and Beck, 1995). Even with this additional space from new jail construction and remodeling, jail overcrowding continues to be near chronic.

Court-Ordered Jail Reforms

Some of the overcrowding problem has been attributable to court-ordered jail reforms (Harris et al., 1991; Thompson and Mays, 1991; DiIulio, 1990). Many jails have been declared unfit for inmates because of fire hazards, low health and safety standards, and other problems. In 1990, 28 percent of all large jails (100 inmates or more) in the United States were under court order to limit their inmate populations (Welsh, 1993:90). Welsh (1993) suggests that such court-ordered jail reforms have affected police citation and arrest policies. In some states, such as California, jails have taken advantage of a California penal code provision permitting arresting officers to issue citations to certain types of offenders at station houses and release these offenders on their own recognizance rather than jail them. Further, jail officials can issue early-release orders or jail citations. *A jail citation is a document authorizing the early release of pretrial detainees and other misdemeanants, provided the released inmates sign a written promise to appear later in court.* Although controversial, the use of jail citations in California and other jurisdictions with serious overcrowding is becoming increasingly common.

Jail Inmate Diversity

In 1991, a survey was conducted of 505 jurisdictions that included a description of about 81 percent of all jail inmates. The survey showed that the jail population was 41.1 percent white, 43.4 percent black, and 14.2 percent Hispanic (Kerle, 1993:5). Such diversity of inmates has caused critics to question whether jails are primarily designed for law enforcement (since they are operated by sheriffs) or whether they are a major corrections component. The lack of inmate programs and other facilities, together with poorly trained guards, suggests that they are neither. However, they serve both law enforcement and corrections

---

Highlight 11.1. Inmates Escape Because of Upside-Down Jail Door

The Perry County Jail in New Augusta, Mississippi, was being improved. Among other improvements was the installation of a new jail door. Unfortunately, the door was installed upside-down.

The upside-down door caused the lock to malfunction. During the evening hours, several inmates opened the door latch and made their escape. Jailers discovered the faulty door installation, but only after many of the chickens had flown the coop. "This is simply the fault of the installer," said Sheriff Carlos Herring. "There's nothing for me to do now but get another welder down here and turn the thing back over."

What security improvements should be made to guard against this type of error, considering the court-ordered jail improvements underway in numerous jurisdictions throughout the United States?

Source: Adapted from Associated Press, "Inmates Escape after Jail-Door Installer Didn't Know Which End Was Up," *Minot (N.D.) Daily News,* January 11, 1996, p. A2.

---

functions to a limited degree (e.g., detention and isolation, deterrence and retribution).

Jails and the Nation's Rabble

John Irwin (1985) has made one of the more insightful analyses of jails. Although Irwin studied only San Francisco jails, he believes his conclusions may apply to most jails in the United States. First, Irwin found that jail clientele are quite different from inmates in prisons. Jail inmates are largely noncriminals. Second, Irwin discovered that jails receive and confine mostly detached and disreputable persons, or "rabble" (Irwin, 1985:xiii). Third, he concluded that by arresting and holding "rabble" in jails, society inadvertently increases their number and holds people in a rabble status (Irwin, 1985:xiii). Jails continue to lack mental health services and other client-specific programs for inmates with special problems (Thompson and Mays, 1991).

In view of Irwin's generalizations about jails and their inmates, it is understandable why politicians and others have neglected jails. Jails have been ignored by various improvements primarily because of the inmates they accommodate—society's undesirables, the unemployed, and minorities. Most inmates have little or no political power or influence. Citizens are not supportive of programs designed to help them. Irwin believes that there is a large and persistent rabble population, and that jails exist primarily to control them. In recent years, however, jail inmate litigation has increased. The Supreme Court has gradually acquired a better understanding of jails and jail problems. Particularly, the high court has mandated substantial jail improvements and reductions of inmate populations. In the next section, several common problems of jails will be described.

Selected Jail Problems

Incidence of Assaults and Deaths in Jails

While jails are ordinarily short-term facilities, inmate subcultures nevertheless develop that influence the lives of most other inmates. When more experienced inmates enter a jail, they assess their length of stay and readapt quickly to the prevalent inmate subculture (Garofalo and Clark, 1985). In many jails, sexual assaults similar to those in prisons occur (Travisono et al., 1986). In fact, because of inadequate staffing and housing patterns, sexual assaults occur more frequently in jails than in prisons (Mays, 1992). In 1994, there were 123 deaths from natural causes. However, 83 prisoners died of AIDS, 7 were murdered by other jail inmates, 4 died during escapes or assaults, and 9 others died from accidents or other causes (Camp and Camp, 1995b:61).

In past years, observers described Chicago's Cook County Jail as the "worst jail they have ever seen" (Davidson, 1968). Inmate and guard brutality were commonplace, and homosexual rape, narcotics addiction, administrative corruption, and ineptitude were prevalent. One problem was the "barn boss" system, where certain inmates, because of their wealth, race, or social status, dominated large numbers of other inmates and even some jail guards.

Highlight 11.2. Jail Problems: Neglect, Neglect, and More Neglect

In 1990, a jury in Los Angeles awarded $2.5 million to the family of Stanley Malinovitz, thirty-eight, who died from a blood clot in his lung on January 28, 1984. Malinovitz had been arrested earlier for "bizarre behavior" that included shoving an elderly woman to the ground in a shopping mall. While in jail, Malinovitz was strapped to a jailhouse cot for at least forty hours. His cries for help went unanswered. Three days following his arrest, he was found naked and dazed, lying face down in a court holding cell. A municipal court judge ordered jailers to take Malinovitz to County-USC Medical Center for treatment. Instead, the deputies took him to the Men's Central Jail, where they strapped him to a cot for another three days. Counsel for Los Angeles County allege that deputies never received an order from the court directing them to take Malinovitz to a hospital. He died while in the jail's custody.

You know that there is going to be an overcrowding problem. You don't need to be a rocket scientist. Between 1983 and 1988, local jails added 5.3 million square feet of new housing space. This was a 44 percent increase in jail space. However, the jail inmate population grew by 54 percent during the same five-year period. Yes, you know there is going to be an overcrowding problem.

In Spotsylvania, Virginia, on Labor Day weekend of 1995, Allen Wilhelm, twenty-five, was stopped by police officers and arrested for driving with a suspended driver's license. He was placed in a courthouse holding cell and forgotten by a court bailiff for the weekend. After five days without food, Wilhelm's cries were heard by a passing secretary.

Earlier, Wilhelm's father had asked various court personnel where his son was. Nobody knew. The previous Thursday, the judge had ordered Wilhelm jailed for two days for the driving conviction. The jail was supposed to be the Rappahannock Regional Jail, about ten miles from the courthouse. But Wilhelm was never transferred. Instead, he was placed in an eight-by-twelve-foot cell with running water and a toilet but no bedding. A Commonwealth Attorney, William F. Neely, said he did not believe any law had been violated. The bailiff, Steve Coleman, was fired for forgetting to call a deputy sheriff to pick up Wilhelm for the transfer. The happy ending is that Wilhelm didn't die in the holding cell. It is not known whether the county was sued for its negligence in handling Wilhelm.

On September 14, 1991, four inmates of the Taney County Jail in Forsyth, Missouri, died of smoke inhalation when a fire from an adjacent shed sent thick smoke billowing into the jail. Thirteen other inmates were hospitalized in serious condition. The inmates were trapped in their cells behind electronically locked doors that failed to operate because of a short circuit.

Sources: Adapted from Associates Press, "Man Held in Jail 5 Days Without Food," *Minot (N.D.) Daily News,* September 7, 1995:A2; *Corrections Digest,* "Jury Awards $2.5 Million to Family of Man Who Died in L.A. Jail," *Corrections Compendium,* 15:18; *New York Times,* "4 Prisoners Trapped in Their Cells, Are Killed by Smoke from Fire at Missouri Jail," September 15, 1991:18; Michael Welch, "Distortions and Myths Surrounding Jail Conditions and Detention," *American Jails,* 7:55–60.

Another problem with jails is the lack of trained jail personnel. Many local jails are supervised by part-time employees with little or no corrections experience (DiIulio, 1990). Voluntary reserve police officers sometimes perform routine guard duty and inspect packages brought to inmates. Some jails use sheriff's deputies as guards when deputies have failed to perform adequately on patrol. Other jails use rookie deputies as jailers while they are on probationary status. Such inexperienced jail staff aggravate existing jail problems (Harris et al., 1991; Thompson and Mays, 1991).

Probationers and Pretrial Detainees

Many jail inmates are there unnecessarily. A study of 20,797 booking records of the Milwaukee County Jail in 1983 showed that many of the inmates were housed there temporarily while waiting to be transferred to the Milwaukee House of Corrections (Wood, Verber, and Reddin, 1985). Many of those arrested and processed were probationers and parole violators who committed technical infractions not ordinarily requiring incarceration. Some offenses, such as disorderly conduct, shoplifting, and possession of small amounts of marijuana, are treated as ordinance violations in the suburbs but are jailable offenses in the city. Also, suspects charged with nonviolent property crimes were also jailed unnecessarily prior to trial. One recommendation is the use of community service in lieu of confinement (D'Allessio, 1993; Perkins, Stephan, and Beck, 1995).

In 1994, average length of stay in city and county jails for pretrial detainees was about 67 days. Sentenced offenders were held for an average of 144 days before being transferred to state prisons, which were also overcrowded (Camp and Camp, 1995b:59).

Jail Suicides

Jail suicides pose a major problem for jail administrators. Considering the short-term nature of confinement, authorities cannot explain why certain inmates commit suicide. In 1994, there were fifty-nine jail suicides reported in 136 jail systems (Camp and Camp, 1995b:61). Inmate suicides accounted for 20.7 percent of all jail inmate deaths.

Studies of jail suicides show no particular racial, ethnic, age, gender, or socioeconomic patterns (Burks and DeHeer, 1986). Suicides occur most often within the first few weeks of incarceration, however, and there is a noticeable decline in suicide rates the longer inmates are incarcerated (Kennedy, 1994). Of the four hundred fifty or so custodial suicides per year in all types of incarcerative facilities, no significant differences are found attributable to race, age, location of suicide, or reason for arrest, when the suicide cases were compared with the general arrest trends for the state (Kennedy, 1994). One unsettling fact is that such custodial suicides are thus very unpredictable. It is also a fact that many custodial suicides occur because of inadequate personnel (Wooldredge and Winfree, 1992). There simply are not enough jail officers to watch inmates twenty-four hours a day.

Attempts have been made to isolate specific suicide risk factors that might enable jail officers to predict which inmates are prone to suicide. For instance, it has been found that the chances of suicide are greater for inmates placed in isolation (Kunzman, 1995:90–91). Other variables associated with jail suicides are significant losses; worries about personal problems; prior use of drugs and/or alcohol; committing a shocking crime; signs of hopelessness and depression; prior suicide attempts; and expressions of anxiety, fear, anger, embarrassment, or shame (Kunzman, 1995:91). Perhaps the best way to prevent jail suicides would be to devise more effective ways to screen new jail inmates. No method of prediction is foolproof, however.

The Prospects for Jail Improvements

Much of jail overcrowding can be eased through better planning. Greater use of probation after sentencing, especially for minor offenses, will ease the jail population to some degree. More efficient bail systems can decrease jail populations as well, particularly if booking for petty or minor offenses occurs without formal incarceration.

Jail improvements are closely linked with political interests and community administrative policies. Determining the appropriate jail size is not the technical problem many persons believe it to be. Rather, it is more a matter of public policy (Mays, 1992). Obviously, communities will have to appropriate more money before jails can acquire better equipment, including better bedding, food, and clothing.

It is difficult to forecast jail trends (Thompson, 1986; Thompson and Mays, 1991). Law enforcement officials, judges, district attorneys, public defenders, and probation officials determine who goes to jail and for how long. Court-ordered reductions in jail populations help alleviate overcrowding, but most jails are operating at an average of 102 percent of their maximum inmate capacity.

As court dockets become crowded and state and federal prisons exceed their rated capacities, district attorneys increasingly consider probation for less violent felony offenders. In Tennessee, Mississippi, Texas, and California, no inmates may be put in the state prison unless an equal number of inmates are released. The prison populations of these states cannot be exceeded for any reason. This shifts the responsibility of deciding who goes to prison to district attorneys and judges. The same holds true for jails and jail populations. Policy changes about who is confined for how long must be made if significant reductions in existing jail populations are to occur (Harris et al., 1991).

Direct Supervision and Regional Jails

A major improvement in inmate management has been the creation of the direct supervision jail. *Direct supervision jails are constructed in a modular fashion so that supervising jail officers can watch all inmates in a given module. The primary objective of such jails is to ensure staff, inmate and public safety by effectively controlling and surveilling inmate conduct* (Perroncello, 1995:38–39).

In podular direct supervision jails, also known as *new generation jails,* cells surround a common dayroom. Inmates are continuously supervised by an officer who can observe all cell fronts and dayroom activities. The pod officer is directly responsible for inmate discipline. Pod officers make most inmate management decisions (Zupan, 1991). Previous jail designs have been linear, with long cell blocks where most inmates could not be observed directly. Thus, there was greater opportunity for inmate misconduct, such as sexual or physical assault. In direct supervision jails, there is direct contact between the pod officer and inmates, because pod officers are located in an octagonal control room with a 360-degree field of vision (Nelson and Davis, 1995:11–12).

Another major jail development has been the creation of regional jails. *Regional jails are state-funded facilities designed to house inmates from adjacent counties on a short-term basis. These jails comply with both state and federal guidelines for prisoner care, health, safety, and custody.* West Virginia operates several regional jails, replacing many of the smaller locally operated jails, which were old and failed to comply with court-ordered improvements. Several counties in and around regional jails house offenders there at a specified cost per prisoner per day. Each county contributes to the cost of inmate maintenance (Gardner, 1992).

Among the advantages of regional jails is that they may engage in contractual arrangements with private vendors for various goods and services (Bernsen, 1996:54). Further, they are self-sufficient regarding laundry services and other chores that can be performed locally. Because of the consolidation of services, regional jails can retain full-time counselors and medical personnel on a twenty-four-hour basis. Twelve regional jails were planned for the early 1990s, each of which would house various numbers of inmates. The first regional jail in West Virginia had a capacity of 125. Vocational and educational programs were established in this regional ultra-modern jail, the Mineral County Detention Center in Keyser, West Virginia (Grimes, 1989:31–32).

Prisons

In 1994, there were seventy-eight federal correctional institutions (Camp and Camp, 1995a:34–35). In 1994, there were 1,449 federal and state prison facilities in the United States (Camp and Camp, 1995a:34–35). By 1994, there were over 94,827 inmates in federal penitentiaries (Maguire and Pastore, 1995:537). This was 18 percent more than in 1993 (Maguire and Pastore, 1995:533). Table 11.3 shows the distribution of state and federal prisoners for 1994 as well as projected prison populations through the year 2000. Table 11.3 also shows prison capacities for

Table 11.3

Number of Inmates, Design Capacity, and Prison Population Projections in State and Federal Correctional Facilities, by Sex and Jurisdiction, United States, 1994 (Population figures, 1994; Projections 1996, 1998, 2000)

Jurisdiction	1994 adult prison population	Adult prison capacity	Prison population projections								
			1996			1998			2000		
			Total	Male	Female	Total	Male	Female	Total	Male	Female
Alabama	19,270	17,300	21,260	19,888	1,372	23,310	21,786	1,524	25,359	23,682	1,677
Alaska	3,329	3,312	3,757	3,504	253	4,785	4,463	322	5,623	5,244	379
Arkansas	8,345[a]	8,014	9,719	NA	NA	10,919	NA	NA	12,119	NA	NA
California	126,412	72,853	150,866	141,376	9,490	189,996	178,416	11,580	232,770	219,146	13,624
Colorado	10,005[b]	9,062	11,403	10,644	759	13,232	12,322	910	15,455	14,374	1,081
Connecticut	14,519	13,363	(c)	X	X	X	X	X	X	X	X
Delaware	4,460	4,205	4,869	NA	NA	4,987	NA	NA	5,088	NA	NA
District of Columbia	10,982[d]	11,098	11,834	11,065	769	12,745	11,917	828	13,125	12,272	853
Florida	56,851	56,877	(c)	X	X	X	X	X	X	X	X
Hawaii	1,859	1,647	2,034	1,943	91	2,083	1,987	96	2,105	2,002	103
Idaho	2,928	2,519	2,930	2,709	221	3,341	3,054	287	3,712	3,339	373
Illinois	35,614	26,527	41,726	39,762	1,964	46,105	43,835	2,270	51,216	48,633	2,583
Indiana	14,975	13,169	15,102	14,231	871	15,491	14,604	887	16,086	15,147	939
Iowa	5,343	3,603	(c)	X	X	X	X	X	X	X	X
Kansas	6,322	6,607	6,650	6,317	333	6,632	6,300	332	NA	NA	NA
Kentucky	10,869	10,600	12,320	11,561	759	13,811	12,943	868	15,227	14,284	943
Louisiana	15,723[e]	16,094	28,000[f]	NA	NA	31,000[f]	NA	NA	34,000[f]	NA	NA
Maryland	20,942	19,876	23,458	22,285	1,173	24,990	23,740	1,250	25,599	24,319	1,280
Massachusetts[g]	10,704	7,876	11,399	9,680	622	12,468	10,584	672	13,403	11,431	707
Michigan	37,928	38,621	41,623	NA	NA	44,991	NA	NA	NA	NA	NA
Minnesota	4,432	4,232	5,172	4,900	272	5,449	5,159	290	5,558	5,267	291
Mississippi	11,260	9,705	11,222	10,410	812	12,090	11,223	867	12,973	12,051	922
Missouri	17,708[h]	17,492	19,088	17,998	1,090	21,157	19,947	1,210	23,432	22,082	1,350
Montana	1,366	956	1,298	1,256	42	1,169	1,118	51	NA	NA	NA
Nebraska	2,557	2,103	2,904	2,707	197	3,187	2,977	210	NA	NA	NA
New Hampshire	2,056	1,667	(c)	X	X	X	X	X	X	X	X
New Jersey	24,160	13,869	26,260	NA	NA	28,660	NA	NA	NA	NA	NA
New Mexico	3,809	3,630	4,198	3,968	230	4,621	4,363	258	5,199	4,911	288
New York	66,814	51,057	68,900	65,250	3,650	73,700	69,900	3,800	77,750	73,800	3,950
North Carolina	22,746	20,420	30,751	NA	NA	30,761	NA	NA	30,761	NA	NA
North Dakota	586	613	589	NA	NA	589	NA	NA	589	NA	NA
Ohio	41,402	23,266	43,253	40,490	2,763	44,733	41,987	2,746	46,483	43,610	2,873
Oklahoma	13,272	13,496	18,290	16,522	1,768	19,419	17,541	1,878	20,223	18,267	1,956
Oregon	6,795	6,517	7,472	NA	NA	9,764	NA	NA	13,116	NA	NA
Pennsylvania	27,823[i]	21,550	27,919	26,353	1,566	27,549	26,001	1,548	27,686	26,142	1,562
Rhode Island	3,079	3,438	3,181	NA	NA	3,248	NA	NA	3,337	NA	NA
South Carolina	17,363	16,310	(c)	X	X	X	X	X	X	X	X
South Dakota	1,726	1,491	1,723	NA	NA	1,779	NA	NA	1,822	NA	NA
Tennessee	17,600[j]	12,654	18,418	NA	NA	19,720	NA	NA	19,961	NA	NA
Texas	96,977	98,844	152,875	NA	NA	187,964	NA	NA	206,162	NA	NA
Utah	3,490	3,216	3,796	NA	NA	4,360	NA	NA	NA	NA	NA
Vermont	1,278	941	1,367	1,337	30	1,503	1,463	40	1,640	1,590	50
Virginia	20,503	14,292	31,703	30,147	1,556	38,050	36,175	1,875	40,984	38,754	2,230
Washington	10,840	7,790	11,879	11,129	750	13,136	12,331	805	14,121	13,285	836
West Virginia	1,975	1,900	(c)	X	X	X	X	X	X	X	X
Wisconsin	1,054	7,230	11,515	11,075	440	13,453	12,972	481	15,012	14,500	512
Wyoming	1,062	1,126	(k)	1,107	X	(k)	1,195	X	(k)	1,269	X
Federal Bureau of Prisons[l]	94,827	66,900	114,579	105,942	8,637	125,536	116,028	9,508	133,534	123,396	10,138

Source: Corrections Compendium (Lincoln, NE: Cega Publishing, 1995), pp. 6–11.

Note: This information was collected through a survey of the 50 States, the District of Columbia, and the Federal Bureau of Prisons conducted in October 1994. The data were collected through January 1995. Arizona, Georgia, Maine, and Nevada did not respond to the survey. Responding agencies generally reported prison population counts for a single day in the fourth quarter of 1994. The Source presents the information as submitted by the responding agencies. No attempt is made by the Source to verify the information received.

a. Excludes county jail contracts.
b. Includes community, off grounds, escapees, and jail backlog.
c. No population projections are computed by the Department of Corrections.
d. Includes some Federal Bureau of Prisons inmates.
e. Excludes 7,938 State inmates held in parish prisons.
f. Includes State inmates held in parish prisons.
g. Projections include some county, Federal, and interstate prisoners.
h. Includes 551 inmates in community programs.
i. Includes community placements.
j. Includes 12,568 held in State institutions, 1,733 held in local jails awaiting transfer, and 3,299 locally-sentenced felons.
k. Projections for males only.
l. Capacity figure does not include contract facility population; however, projections include both Bureau facilities and contract facilities.

each of these state and federal jurisdictions. Only ten states had prison inmate populations below their maximum capacities. All other cases, prisons were overcrowded (Maguire and Pastore, 1995:537). Unofficial estimates are that 980,513 inmates were being confined in state and federal prisons on January 1, 1995 (Camp and Camp, 1995a:1). California held the most prison inmates, with 126,412, followed by Texas, with 96,977 inmates. North Dakota had the fewest prisoners, with 586 inmates.

Prisoner Characteristics

In 1994, 94.4 percent of all inmates were male, and 5.6 percent were female. Black inmates made up 38 percent of state and federal prisoners, with white inmates accounting for 48.5 percent, Hispanic inmates for 8.3 percent, Asian inmates for 0.6 percent, Native American inmates for 2.9 percent, and "Other" for about 1.6 percent (Camp and Camp, 1995a:4–5). Racial and ethnic diversity among prison inmates varies by state. For instance, a study of the 1991 inmate population in New York reported that 82.7 percent of all inmates were either black or Hispanic (Toure, 1994). Other prison populations, such as that of North Dakota, is over 95 percent white (Maguire and Pastore, 1995).

The average age of all prison inmates for 1994 was 30.6 years, while prisoners 50 years old or older made up 6.1 percent of the prison population (Camp and Camp, 1995a:13). About 9 percent of all state and federal prison inmates were serving life sentences, with about another 16 percent serving sentences of twenty or more years (Camp and Camp, 1995a:18–19).

Types of Prisons

State and federal prisons and penitentiaries are classified as **maximum, medium,** and **minimum security prisons.** Within state prisons and federal penitentiaries are areas that are classified similarly.

Security Classifications

These security classifications pertain to the *level or degree of custody.* Maximum-security prisons

maintain prisoners in the highest degree of custody, and inmate supervision by guards is intensive. In 1994, about 11 percent of all prison inmates were confined in maximum-security prisons (Camp and Camp, 1995a:23). *Medium-security custody* provides for intensive supervision of offenders. Prisoners' access to prison amenities is limited, but not as limited as in maximum-security prisons. About 41.4 percent of all inmates are classified as medium security (Camp and Camp, 1995a:23). Minimum-security prisons permit inmates considerable freedom of movement, and their activities are casually supervised by guards. About 26.7 percent of all inmates are classified as minimum-security (Camp and Camp, 1995a:23).

The U.S. Bureau of Prisons labels prisons with a scale ranging from Level 1 through Level 6. Level 1 designates an honor farm or minimum-security camp facility, while Level 6 describes a maximum-security penitentiary, or a maxi-maxi penitentiary, such as the U.S. Penitentiary at Marion, Illinois (Berkey, 1987; Olivero and Roberts, 1990). Marion Federal penitentiary inmates consider themselves the "baddest of the bad" (Holt and Phillips, 1991). Marion had a rated inmate capacity of 713 in 1995, although only 661 were housed there (American Correctional Association, 1995:490).

Most inmates in state and federal prisons are classified as either medium- or minimum-security risks. Usually, prisoners are assigned to different types of prisons or prison areas according to the seriousness of their conviction offense, their propensity for violence or escape, and/or the availability of particular programs. Nonviolent prisoners are sentenced to minimum-security prisons, while violent offenders (e.g., those convicted of homicide, robbery, or aggravated assault) are housed in maximum-security facilities (A. Roberts, 1994).

Maximum-Security Prisons

In maximum-security prisons inmates are isolated from one another in single cells and are monitored constantly by prison guards. Inmates are restricted to their immediate security housing area, and their privileges, including visits from family and friends, are severely limited. Although maximum-security prisons provide educational programs and other activities, they make no pretense

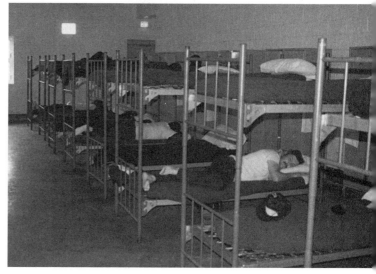

(Top) A typical cellblock in a maximum security prison.
(Bottom left) A cell in a medium-security prison.
(Bottom right) Sleeping quarters in a minimum security prison.

about the fact that they exist to control and contain dangerous offenders.

Alcatraz, located on an island in San Francisco Bay, was once considered the epitome of maximum-security prisons. Constructed in 1934, Alcatraz (also known as "The Rock") was one of the most feared federal prisons in the nation. The primary aims of Alcatraz were discipline and punishment. Inmates were not allowed to read newspapers, watch television, or listen to radios. Escape from Alcatraz was almost impossible. Escapees who managed to get as far as the bay were drowned by the strong currents. Only eight persons ever escaped from Alcatraz; three of these were never recaptured (Carney, 1979:104–105). The movie *Escape from Alcatraz* is a semifictionalized account of their escape.

About fifteen hundred prisoners were housed at Alcatraz during the years 1934–1963. Because of escalating prison costs and declining health standards, Alcatraz was closed on March 21, 1963, with an inmate population of 260 (Bennett, 1970:114). Other well-known maximum-security prisons include San Quentin and Folsom prisons in California, Marion Federal Correctional Center in Illinois, Sing-Sing and Attica in New York, and the federal penitentiaries at Atlanta, Georgia, and Leavenworth, Kansas.

One problem with maximum-security prisons is inmate idleness (Chilton and Nice, 1993). Visits to eight maximum-security prisons in New York revealed that thirty-one hundred inmates, or 24 percent of the state's prison population, were idle most of the time. About fifteen hundred inmates in six of these facilities were assigned to menial, unproductive jobs (Steelman, 1984).

During the late 1980s, numerous complaints and litigation by inmates of the Texas Department of Correction's twenty-seven maximum-security units prompted Texas officials to implement several important reforms. Besides providing prisoners with more opportunities for self-improvement, the department established new institutional controls, thus fostering a safer inmate environment. Over time, inmate assaults drastically declined and prisoners acquired a feeling of safety (Crouch and Marquart, 1990).

Medium-Security Prisons

Medium-security prisons offer prisoners dormitory-like accommodations. Direct supervision of inmates is limited, except in their particular areas of assignment. There are main perimeters where inmates may move, and all inmates are eligible for day and night recreational activities. Prisoners may also be eligible for assignments outside the main perimeter. Rules of visitation are relaxed, and prisoners may move about freely without much monitoring by guards.

Minimum-Security Prisons

Minimum-security prisons are designed for nonviolent offenders who have either low or no potential for violent behavior. Housing is similar to a typical small efficiency apartment. Supervision by guards is unobtrusive. Inmate privileges are extensive, and family visits, even conjugal visits, are sometimes permitted. Minimum-security inmates are eligible for a variety of work tasks outside the prison. One positive feature of minimum-security prisons is that they allow inmates to develop higher self-esteem. Minimum-security facilities maximize trust between prison officials and inmates. Self-esteem is particularly important for prison counseling and rehabilitation programs to be successful (del Carmen et al., 1990; Vicary and Good, 1983).

Inmate Classification

Prison administrators must determine where each new inmate should be housed. Prisoners differ greatly in their potential for violence as well as in the crimes they have committed. Some prisoners have histories of escapes or attempts to escape, records of assaults against other prisoners and correctional officers, and a pattern of previous institutional violence. Prisoners who are violent and dangerous should be placed in different security levels and segregated from one another.

Some prisoners are persistent troublemakers, others are retarded or otherwise vulnerable to attack and exploitation. Some offenders need to be placed in protective custody. Police officers sentenced to prison are generally segregated from other inmates because of the fear of reprisal. Isolation and segregation are also used to punish unruly inmates (Hardyman, 1993; McGee, Warner, and Harlow, 1985).

California prisons have a variety of custody levels, including Maximum A Custody, Maximum B Custody, Close A Custody, Close B Custody, Medium A Custody, Medium B Custody, Minimum A Custody, and Minimum B Custody. These prisons also use a system of letter classification to designate special types of offenders, such as "N" for narcotics offenders, "R" for sex offenders, and "S" for persons who must not have cellmates (Champion 1994). Prisoners entering the California prison system are classified at the Reception Guidance Center, which tries to determine which inmates are most violent and which are most likely to attempt to escape.

Psychological assessment inventories are often used to predict inmates' success at adapting to prison and their propensity toward violence. None of these devices has been foolproof, however, although some measures have helped authorities identify the most pathological offenders (Champion, 1994).

The Minnesota Multiphasic Personality Inventory (MMPI) is a popular psychological predictive instrument used by some researchers to predict dangerousness and propensity to escape (Bohn, Carbonell, and Megargee, 1995). The MMPI consists of over five hundred true-false statements; various combinations of statements form "subscales" of selected personality characteristics.

The **Megargee Inmate Typology** measures inmates' adjustment to prison life (Megargee and Carbonell, 1985). Using items from the MMPI, Megargee established ten prisoner types or classifications that can be used to predict inmate dangerousness or violent behavior. The typology has been used in several prisons for separating inmates into different custody levels, such as maximum or minimum security. For example, 120 inmates at a federal prison in Springfield, Missouri, were given Megargee's and Bohn's MMPI-based classification scale and classified according to various adjustment levels (Bohn, Carbonell, and Megargee, 1995). One sample consisted of 57 general-population inmates, while the 63 other inmates were selected from the U.S. Medical Center Mental Health Unit at the prison. The prisoners from the mental health unit were receiving counseling and being taught coping skills to deal with their aggressiveness and other psychological problems. The typology showed significant differences between the two subsamples. The inmates from the general prisoner population tended to have lower adjustment ratings than inmates from the mental health unit. These researchers believe that at least in this instance, the MMPI-based instrument was useful in distinguishing different levels of adjustment.

Megargee examined the interrelationships between a number of popular adjustment scales. Using 1,214 inmates from the Federal Correctional Institute at Tallahassee, Florida, Megargee and Carbonell (1985) correlated eight MMPI subscales with six criteria for adjustment to prison, including Panton's Adjustment to Prison (revised), Religious Identification, Homosexuality, Habitual Criminalism and Parole Violation, Beall and Panton's Escape, Clark's Recidivism, and Wattron's Prison Maladjustment. Megargee and Carbonell found no significant correlations among the scales, indicating that they had little practical predictive value. In contrast, between 1986 and 1988, Van Voorhis examined several similar scales (e.g., the Quay AIMS, the Megargee MMPI, the Jesness I-level, and the Megargee Work Adjustment and Prison Adjustment (Van Voorhis, 1993). She found that the scales tended to differentiate between inmates previously diagnosed with character and adjustment disorders and those with better adjustment and conduct evaluations. Thus, Van Voorhis's research indicates that such measures can effectively classify inmates.

In 1984, the South Carolina Department of Corrections began using the Adult Inmate Management System (AIMS) to comply with a court order to come up with an effective internal classification structure (Leeke and Mohn, 1986; Travisono, et al., 1986). AIMS divided prisoners into three groups, alphas, betas, and gammas, according to their aggressiveness. While approximately 70 percent of all inmates have violent offense records, AIMS has reduced violence by 18 percent. In fact, one maximum-security facility had a lower "protective custody" population than any other prison in the state (Leeke and Mohn, 1986).

Women in U.S. Prisons and Jails

Female prisoners have seldom exceeded 7 or 8 percent of the total prison population. In 1994, there were 50,853 female inmates of state and federal prisons, representing about 6 percent of all inmates. This is over four times the number of female inmates incarcerated (12,331) in 1980. By comparison, the male prison population increased from 303,643 inmates in 1980 to 859,227 inmates in 1994 (Maguire and Pastore, 1995:540). Between 1980 and 1994, the population of male inmates increased by 183 percent, while the population of female inmates increased by 312 percent. In 1994, females made up about 7.5 percent of the federal prison population and about 5.6 percent of the state prison population. Table 11.1 shows the rate per 100,000 of females in federal/state prisons for the years 1925–1993.

Until 1790, male, female, and juvenile prisoners were confined together in large rooms (Dobash, 1983; American Correctional Association, 1983). In 1790, the Walnut Street Jail in Philadelphia implemented the first segregation of offenders according to gender as well as other criteria (e.g., seriousness of offense, type of crime).

During the next thirty years conditions in women's prisons did not improve. In 1819, the New York Society for the Prevention of Pauperism characterized the women's quarters at the Bellevue Penitentiary as "one great school of vice and desperation, replete with prostitutes, vagrants, lunatics, thieves, and those of a less heinous character" (Freedman, 1981:7). What troubled the New York Society was that women outside of prison did not seem to care about the terrible conditions being endured by women inside the prison (Freedman, 1981:7).

Even in more "modern" prison facilities, such as the New York State Penitentiary at Auburn, which was constructed between 1816 and 1820, the well-known tier system and more individualized prisoner accommodations failed to improve the treatment of female inmates. At Auburn, unlike male inmates, women did not have separate cells. Instead they were lodged together in one large attic room where they were left unattended. Their windows were sealed to prevent communication with men (Freedman, 1981:15). While there were never any more than thirty women at Auburn, their living conditions were characterized by overcrowding, immobilization, and neglect

(Freedman, 1981:15). Between 1790 and 1870, female inmates of most penal facilities in the United States received worse care than male prisoners (Rafter, 1983).

One instance of the scandalous conditions at Auburn involved a young woman, Rachel Welch, who became pregnant "while serving a punishment sentence in a solitary cell" (Freedman, 1981:15). Welch was flogged brutally by a prison guard (possibly the one who fathered her child), and she died shortly after childbirth. Her death had no influence on a grand jury convened to investigate her death, but in 1832 public uproar led to the appointment of a matron to oversee the women's quarters and to replace male guards (Freedman, 1981:15–16).

The Women's Reform Movement

The Women's Reform Movement began during the 1820s in England and the United States with small groups of women, frequently affiliated with one religious faith or another, visiting prisons to offer charitable aid to female inmates. Reflecting the strong Quaker tradition of concern for prisoners, Elizabeth Gurney Fry (1780–1845) emerged as the mother of women's prison reform.

Fry was a minister. In that capacity, she frequently visited London's Newgate Gaol to convert inmates to the Quaker faith through prayer (Freedman, 1981:23). However, she soon realized that the female inmates needed better food, clothing, and other amenities that the jail did not provide. With the permission of prison authorities, she conducted an experiment in prison reform for women by founding the Ladies Association for the Improvement of the Female Prisoners at Newgate. This association established the workshops, Bible classes, and self-administered inmate monitoring system that enabled women to look after each other (Freedman, 1981:23). To culminate her important reform work, in 1827 she published a treatise outlining her observations and recommendations entitled *Observations in Visiting, Superintendence, and Government of Female Prisoners*. This work was significant because it elaborated on the principles that would later dominate women's prison reform in the United States. (Freedman, 1981:23).

Prisons for Women

The Dedham Temporary Asylum for Discharged Female Prisoners in Massachusetts, which operated from 1864 to 1909, functioned in much the same way as halfway houses (Bularik, 1984). It was a privately controlled facility that provided individualized attention and assistance to women who had recently been discharged from prison. There were several similar institutions in the United States prior to the creation of prisons exclusively for women (Bularik, 1984).

Historians disagree about the first exclusively women's prison in the United States. Zebulon Brockway, the first superintendent of the Elmira, New York, Reformatory, helped establish a "House of Shelter" exclusively for female offenders in 1869. He hired Emma Hall, a Detroit school teacher, to serve as matron from 1869 to 1874 (Freedman, 1981:50–51). Michigan historians have labeled this "House of Shelter" as "America's first women's reformatory" (Freedman, 1981:50–51). However, Freedman (1981:50–51) says that the House of Shelter was not technically a prison but rather the first penal institution where women had complete control and authority over female inmates.

The Women's Prison in Indiana, constructed in 1873, is usually considered the first prison facility exclusively for women. One of its major objectives was to instill feelings of motherhood and sobriety in the women it housed (Clark, 1995). The Bedford Hills Reformatory for Women was constructed in New York in 1901, and in 1933, women at Auburn began to be housed in a separate prison known as Westfield State Farm (Carney, 1979:201). Federal female prisoners were originally housed in the Women's Reformatory in the District of Columbia until 1927, when the first federal reformatory for women was opened in Alderson, West Virginia. California did not establish a separate women's prison until 1936 (Carney, 1979:201–202).

Characteristics of Female Prisoners

Between 1980 and 1993, the population of male offenders in U.S. prisons increased by 183 percent. During the same period, the population of female prisoners increased by 312 percent (Maguire and Pastore, 1995:540). Additionally, in 1983, sixteen states had female inmate populations of 500 or more. By 1994, twenty-seven states, the District of Columbia, and the federal system had female inmate populations of five hundred or more (Gilliard and Beck, 1994:4–5).

One important cause of the growth of the female inmate population has been the shift to more objective, guidelines-based presumptive sentencing schemes. Under earlier sentencing methods, judges were paternalistic toward female offenders and sentenced disproportionately fewer women to jail or prison than men, controlling for other relevant factors (e.g., prior record, age, seriousness of conviction offense).

In Oklahoma, the rate of female incarcerations has been more than twice that of male incarcerations for several years. In 1993, women made up 12.4 percent of the inmate population in Oklahoma (Sandhu, Al-Mousleh, and Chown, 1994). This is about twice the national average.

Glick (1978) described several demographic and social characteristics of female prisoners in the United States. Over two-thirds of the female inmates were under thirty years old. In 1978, about 50 percent of all female prisoners were black, a significant overrepresentation of black inmates compared with their representation in the overall population. By 1983, the female inmate population was 38 percent black and 50 percent white (Ryan, 1984). Between 1975 and 1983, the average age and educational level of female offenders remained the same. In 1994, the average age of female offenders was 31.8, compared with the average male inmate age of 30.6 (Camp and Camp, 1995a:12–13). By 1994, the female inmate population was 49.4 percent black and 37 percent white (American Correctional Association, 1995:xxvi). Table 11.4 shows a profile of female state and federal prison inmates and several relevant sociodemographic characteristics.

Of all incarcerated female felons in 1978, 43 percent were serving time for violent offenses, while the rest were confined for property crimes and drug offenses (Glick, 1978). Property crime by females increased significantly between 1978 and 1983, however (Ryan, 1984). By 1994, only 32 percent of all female prison inmates were serving

Table 11.4

Characteristics of Female Prison Inmates

Characteristic	Percentage	Characteristic	Percentage
Offense		**Education**	
Violent	32.2%	8th grade or less	16.0
Property	28.7	Some high school	45.8
Drugs	32.8	High school graduate	22.7
Public order	5.7	Some college or more	15.5
Other	.6		
		Pre-Arrest Employment	
Race/Ethnicity		Employed	46.7
White/non-Hispanic	36.2	Part-time	11.0
Black/non-Hispanic	46.0	Full-time	35.7
Hispanic	14.2	Unemployed	53.3
Other	3.6	Looking	19.2
		Not looking	34.1
Marital Status			
Married	17.3	**Age**	
Widowed	5.9	17 or younger	.1
Divorced	19.1	18–24	16.3
Separated	12.5	25–34	50.4
Never married	45.1	35–44	25.5
		45–54	6.1
		55 or older	1.7

Source: Snell and Morton (1994), pp. 2–3.

sentences for violent crimes. However, about 33 percent of the female inmates were convicted of drug offenses, while 33 percent were convicted of property crimes (Maguire and Pastore, 1995:553). Thus, the profile of female offending changed dramatically during the 1980s and 1990s.

Some investigators suggest that this increase in drug and property offending by women is attributable to the passivity of drug dealing, the ease with which drugs may be acquired, and the nonconfrontational nature of property crimes such as theft or shoplifting. Treatment programs have been tailored for this type of offender in various jurisdictions, such as Detroit (Haaga, Scott and Hawes-Dawson, 1992).

An interesting characteristic of female prisoners is that over 70 percent are mothers (Quinlan et al., 1992). Most often they are single, primary parents (Clark, 1995; Humphrey and Gohlke, 1993). In many prisons, women are incarcerated while in the early stages of pregnancy. All prisons have medical services for pregnant women, and services are provided for child care until the mothers are released (Quinlan et al., 1992).

Aggressiveness in female inmates is less widespread than it is among male inmates (Kruttschnitt and Krmpotich, 1990). The few studies that have examined this phenomenon conclude that fewer than one-fourth of the female inmates studied tended to be aggressive and assault other inmates. In this respect, then, female prisons could be characterized as more stable environments than men's prisons and prison culture.

The Outlook for Women's Prisons

Since the 1870s the philosophy of women's prisons has been to promote a more humane envi-

Highlight 11.3. Prison and Motherhood: The Bedford Hills, New York, Nursery Program and Inmate No. 91G2130

Christine Thompson, twenty-six, has been arrested at least thirteen times for various offenses, including drug possession and theft. In 1991 she was convicted of forgery and attempted burglary and sentenced to two to ten years. She was confined at the maximum-security prison for women at Bedford Hills, New York. After serving about a year of this sentence she was placed on work release, a program that permitted her to work at a job during daytime hours. At night, she returned to the prison. While on work release, she was caught smoking crack cocaine. Her work release was cancelled. Eventually, she was paroled. As one condition of her parole she was to participate in a drug treatment program. While on parole in 1994, she was turned in by her husband and mother for smoking crack cocaine. She had not been attending the drug treatment program. At the time, she was pregnant with her second child.

Her daughter, Elissa, was born November 22, 1994, in the Bedford Hills prison hospital. Earlier in October, Christine had been admitted to the Bedford Hills nursery program, which was designed to teach pregnant inmates parenting skills.

The Bedford Hills nursery program is housed in a converted ward of an old hospital at New York State's maximum-security prison for women. The facility enables female inmates to keep their babies while incarcerated. Christine Thompson said, "Seeing my baby and everyone else's baby every day made a difference. It made me realize how special life is and how precious life is. Because I was Elissa's sole caregiver, it made me feel very needed, very wanted, very loved and special. If it weren't for her, who knows?"

On May 26, 1995, Christine was paroled from Bedford Hills. Today she lives in Hudson, New York, where she holds down two jobs, in a hospital and in a clothing store. She also cares for her daughter and her eight-year-old son, Eddie, while trying to rebuild her marriage.

Should pregnant inmates be allowed to keep their babies while incarcerated? Of what therapeutic value is the Bedford Hills nursery program? Is a prison an appropriate place to raise a child?

Source: Adapted from Kathy Willens, "Prison Nursery: Woman Allowed to Keep Baby While in Prison Says Program Set Her Straight," *Minot (N.D.) Daily News*, September 5, 1995, p. A5.

ronment (Wooldredge and Masters, 1993). Many women's prisons permit inmates to wear their own clothes rather than uniforms, and women are more likely to be housed in rooms rather than cells. They are also permitted to furnish their rooms with personal items (Hunter, 1985). However, guards conduct frequent headcounts and regulations are rigidly enforced. Thus, these prisons attempt to achieve a delicate balance between security and humanity (*Corrections Compendium*, 1991a).

Some critics say that women ought to be housed in cells like men and subjected to similarly harsh conditions. However, most women's prisons have been patterned after early reformatories, and most prison programs continue to perpetuate structurally induced sexism (Fox, 1984).

A study of the women's facility in Bedford Hills, New York, during the 1970s showed that although the prison physically resembled a college campus, there were hostile relationships between administrators, guards, and inmates (Fox, 1984). Fox suggests that this may have been because of the large influx of younger, more assertive, and more aggressive women into the prison. Furthermore, many of the older administrators were replaced with less experienced managers who instituted internal reforms that made the prison more like a men's prison. Fox (1984) says that equality of treatment has been interpreted to mean similarity of treatment, and therefore the new measures created undesirable prison conditions for women as well as for men.

Incidents with inmates in 1983–1984 prompted a study of female inmates at the Bayview Correctional facility in New York. The study showed that Bayview was never intended to be a correctional facility (Potler, 1985). Bayview was converted into a medium-security women's facility in 1979, and no significant structural changes have been made since then. It had numerous physical problems, including faulty wiring, lack of adequate fire and safety protection, lack of adequate ventilation, and numerous unsanitary conditions (Potler, 1985). Furthermore, while it eased overcrowding in other women's facilities in New York, Bayview became overcrowded. Insufficient staffing, medical care, and vocational/ academic programs for inmates were cited as reasons for inmate discontent. Members of the Bayview Advisory Board were persuaded to make improvements in each of these problem areas as a way of restoring prison order (Potler, 1985).

One problem affecting both men's and women's prisons is that they are sexually segregated. Some critics have advocated coed prisons as a means of reducing homosexuality, lesbianism, and aggravated sexual assaults that are common features of the prison environment.

In 1971, the first sexually integrated prison in the United States was established in Fort Worth, Texas. Called the Federal Correctional Institution, it is strictly a minimum-security prison (Smykla, 1980:41). It has a low rate of recidivism, a more natural environment where males and females can mingle in more relaxed social settings, and lower rates of sexual assaults. Smykla (1980:45) says that its major disadvantage is the guards' lack of control over the sexual activities of inmates. Although the rules permit hand holding and limited kissing, some prisoners engage in sexual intercourse in areas known to be frequently unsupervised. Birth control pills are issued to female inmates on request.

Some experts say that women are exploited by males. Therefore, female inmates may need time away from men to discover themselves and develop a realistic understanding of their own needs. One superintendent of a women's correctional facility interprets the establishment of **co-correctional prisons** as an effort to ease overcrowding in men's prisons. She says that one gets a very strong impression—even though it cannot be verified—that institutions are being sexually integrated to please male egos or to smooth the operation of men's institutions rather than to meet the unique and special needs of the female offender (Schweber, 1984).

Alaska has developed a **coordinate model** *in which neighboring female and male prisons share facilities and programs* (Schweber, 1984). Schweber (1984) says that women in co-correctional facilities are under more intense surveillance for possible sex code *violations* than they would be in sexually segregated institutions. She thinks that Alaska's model permits the break up of female prisons into smaller administrative units, giving officials more flexibility in safeguarding and promoting the interests of female inmates. Such a program offers women a greater range of educational programs and other services not otherwise provided in strictly segregated institutions.

To some degree, women's institutions have benefited from stereotypical attitudes about prison operations because their facilities have often been targeted for experimental "change" programs of various kinds (Hunter, 1985:134). Also, lawsuits filed by female prisoners have resulted in new programs like those offered to male inmates. However, correctional officials in some jurisdictions have taken steps to drastically modify and curtail the operation of coed prisons (Snell and Morton, 1994). In 1988, for instance, the Federal Bureau of Prisons terminated their coed prison programs and instead took action to provide equivalent services in women's correctional institutions.

Subsequent investigations of coed prisons have yielded positive results. During 1984–1986, Mahan (1989) studied a large federal co-correctional facility in Forth Worth, Texas. The population of 856 inmates was about 60 percent female. A survey of both staff and inmates showed that the presence of female inmates tended to generate a "calming atmosphere" (p. 233) on the male inmates. In addition to generating better behavior among both male and female inmates, the co-correctional facility countered the traditional destructiveness of other prison environments by providing inmates with diverse educational and vocational opportunities. Some inmates reported higher self-esteem following their incarceration. One negative outcome was five pregnancies while women were confined. Thus, sexual contact has not been prevented, regardless of rules and supervision.

Experts say that the growing female inmate population will require additional facilities, expansion of existing facilities, and additional programs and services (Nesbitt, 1992:5). Gender-specific vocational and educational programs should be established. Female inmates desire greater privacy than male inmates, and this need should be addressed in planning for future prisons. Special medical and health care planning will be needed. Greater attention should be given to visitation and child care (Nesbitt, 1992:5–6). Additionally, women's prisons are required to house women at all levels of security. In men's institutions, security classification is more specialized. Thus, women's prison administration will have to consider the special management needs of female inmates, especially those that emphasize family interactions (Kiser, 1991).

Summary

Correctional programs in the United States began in the 1790s and early 1800s with the creation of facilities such as the Walnut Street Jail in Philadelphia and the New York Penitentiary in Auburn. Politicians and prison reformers such as William Penn and Benjamin Rush were instrumental in promoting corrections policies that eventually led to the upgrading of prisons and jails for the next century.

The Auburn system introduced the tier concept and helped alleviate prison overcrowding as well as promoting more individualized inmate treatment. In 1876, New York Reformatory in Elmira, under the direction of Superintendent Zebulon Brockway, promoted individualized treatment even further and fostered indeterminate sentencing and parole programs.

In 1930, the Federal Bureau of Prisons was established, and significant developments in penal reform followed. Programs became increasingly treatment-oriented rather than custodial. Many state prison systems tended to copy the federal system.

The major goals of corrections are punishment, deterrence, rehabilitation, and reintegration, although critics question the degree to which these various goals have been achieved. Prisons are classified as maximum-, medium-, or minimum-security institutions. Inmates are classified according to the seriousness of their offenses and the types of crimes they committed. Psychological scales are often used to arrive at these classifications. Among the problems associated with prisons are violence and inadequacy of leadership. The architectural influence on prison operation is also an important area of concern.

While prisons house long-term offenders, jails house inmates for less than one year or those awaiting trial. Sometimes prisoners from state or federal prisons are transferred to jails through contractual arrangements as a way of alleviating overcrowding. Jail problems include overcrowding, prisoner suicides, and a general lack of programs to help inmates improve their educational or social development. Current trends favor greater use of probation and less use of jails as temporary holding facilities for booking and bail.

Women's prisons have recently received considerable attention from corrections personnel. A women's prison reform movement has been successful in improving the conditions of women's prisons generally and providing women with necessary services. Women's prisons provide temporary shelter and custody of inmates' children. Women who are pregnant when they enter prison, also receive medical services. Efforts are continuing to make women's prisons more hospitable and successful at rehabilitating inmates. Co-correctional or coed institutions aimed at reducing sexual aggressiveness among both men and women in prison have been established in several states, but the results of such programs are so far inconclusive.

Key Terms

American Correctional Association (ACA)
Auburn system
Banishment
Body belts
Zebulon Brockway

Co-correctional prisons
Congregate system
Coordinate model
Corrections
Elmira Reformatory
Federal Bureau of Prisons
Great Law of Pennsylvania
Megargee Inmate Typology
Maximum, medium, and minimum security
    prisons
William Penn
Recidivism
Reconvictions
Benjamin Rush
Solitary confinement
Tier system
Walnut Street Jail

Questions for Review

1. Differentiate between jails and prisons. What types of prisoners are each designed to accommodate?
2. What was the first jail in the United States? Why was it important as an instrument of prison reform?
3. What was significant about the New York Penitentiary in Auburn? How did the prison in Elmira, New York, improve on Auburn's correctional goals?
4. What are four correctional goals? Are United States prisons and jails achieving these goals?
5. What evidence is there that imprisonment does not deter crime?
6. What sorts of prison activities might be part of a rehabilitation program? Do jails have similar programs?

7. List three types of prisons and differentiate between them.
8. Describe some inmate classification systems. Are these systems helpful in assigning prisoners to one type of prison or another?
9. When did jails originate? What were their original functions? In what ways have their functions changed?
10. What are new generation or direct-supervision jails? What are some of their advantages over linear jails?

Suggested Readings

Durham, Alexis M. III. 1994. *Crisis and Reform: Current Issues in American Punishment.* Boston: Little, Brown.

Flowers, R. Barri. 1995. *Female Crime, Criminals, and Cellmates: An Exploration of Female Criminality and Delinquency.* Jefferson, NC: McFarland & Co.

Houston, James G. 1996. *Correctional Management: Functions, Skills, and Systems.* Chicago: Nelson-Hall.

Irwin, John and James Austin. 1994. *It's About Time: America's Imprisonment Binge.* Belmont, CA: Wadsworth.

Murphy, Jeffrie G. 1995. *Punishment and Rehabilitation.* 3d ed. Belmont, CA: Wadsworth.

Silberman, Matthew. 1995. *A World of Violence: Corrections in America.* Belmont, CA: Wadsworth.

Tipp, Stacey L. (ed.). 1991. *America's Prisons: Opposing Viewpoints.* San Diego, CA: Greenhaven Press.

Welch, Michael. 1996. *Corrections: A Critical Approach.* New York: McGraw-Hill.

CHAPTER 12

Corrections Operations and Issues

On September 2, 1993, the Federal Correctional Institution in Sheridan, Oregon, was racked by inmate rioting. Prisoners set fire to their mattresses and other prison property and broke numerous windows in adjacent office buildings. Property damage was estimated at $185,000. Although prison administration defended the integrity of their staff and maintained that the prison was adequately funded, the prison has come under recent attack. Congresswoman Elizabeth Furse complained to Attorney General Janet Reno that the prison was seriously overcrowded and that staffing for the prison was underfunded. Correctional officers voiced their own complaints through their local union president, Manny Borquez, who said that overcrowding together with inadequate personnel can lead to open season on officers. "Let us not wait for an officer to get injured . . . before we react and get more staff" (*Corrections Compendium*, 1993a).

An Illinois Task Force on Crime and Corrections has issued a warning that the state's prisons are becoming increasingly dangerous for both inmates and staff members because of severe overcrowding. Solutions may not be easy, since inmates are already double-celled, and early-release policies are being implemented. In 1991, the Illinois prison system, which was designed to hold twenty thousand inmates, was housing thirty thousand (*Corrections Compendium*, 1992a).

Alvin J. Bronstein, director of the ACLU Prison Project, says that forty states, including the District of Columbia, Puerto Rico, and the Virgin Islands, are under court order to reduce prison overcrowding and/or to remedy unconstitutional conditions. Conditions in the prison systems targeted by courts were found to violate the Eighth Amendment's ban against cruel and unusual punishment. Additionally, inmates are filing increasing numbers of lawsuits against all prison systems. At the root of most of these lawsuits is overcrowding (*Corrections Compendium*, 1992b).

One barometer of the effectiveness of prison operations is the number of inmates filing lawsuits against their prison systems alleging civil rights violations or challenging the quality and length of their incarceration and treatment. In 1960, two thousand petitions from state and federal prisoners and jail inmates were filed in U.S. district courts. In 1970, sixteen thousand petitions were filed. In 1985, twenty-two thousand prisoners filed petitions in U.S. district and appeals courts (Hunzeker and Conger, 1985). In 1994, over thirty-five thousand lawsuits were filed by inmates against prison systems (Camp and Camp, 1995a:6–7). Thus, we are in the midst of a prisoner *litigation explosion.*

Many problems prisoners cite in their petitions are traceable to prison administration and policy decisions (Suchner and Thomas, 1989; Thomas, 1991a, 1991b). Other problems are grounded in conflicts between inmates and prison staff. Petitions allege a variety of problems, including inadequate food and medical care, staff brutality, gang rape or assault, few or no recreational opportunities, too-severe punishment and prison rules, racism, exploitation of prison labor, inadequate or nonexistent vocational and educational programs, overcrowding, violations of health and safety standards, and lost or stolen property (Hanson and Daley, 1995).

This chapter describes corrections operations and types of offenders. First, we look at prisoner culture. Different kinds of offenders are described. Next, we examine procedures for recruiting and training correctional staff. This discussion includes a description of corrections personnel. Closely associated with the management of corrections institutions is the movement to privatize prison management.

A discussion of issues that often trigger inmate litigation follows. These issues include prison and jail overcrowding, prison labor, vocational and educational programs for inmates, racism, private prisons, prison architecture and design, prisoners' rights and jail house lawyers, prison violence, and the death penalty.

Prison Culture and Types of Offenders

Prison culture is as diverse as life in the community. But there are some important differences that make prison culture unique. The most important difference is that the prison population consists exclusively of criminals. Another distinction is that strict rules require inmates to adhere to a high standard of conformity (Steinke, 1991). Depending upon the type of prison and facilities available, inmates may be segregated from one another. With few exceptions, most prisons segregate inmates according to gender and do not permit any type of contact with the opposite sex. When chronic overcrowding becomes problematic for any prison system, optimum conditions for prison violence are fostered (Braswell and Miller, 1989; Braswell and Montgomery, 1994; McCorkle, Miethe, and Drass, 1995).

The Inmate Code

Every prison has an inmate subculture, including an **inmate code** by which most inmates live. These inmate codes are different from prison rules enforced by guards (Hunt et al., 1993). Prisoners develop a social hierarchy based upon several criteria. These include physical strength, race or ethnicity, and political power. Bartering or informal exchange takes place not only between prisoners but also between prisoners and prison staff (Hewitt, Poole, and Regoli, 1984). These bartering systems promote stability and make supervising prisoners less stressful.

Some evidence suggests that whether inmates adopt the inmate code (that is, become prisonized) depends on race or ethnicity and on whether inmates have had drug or alcohol dependencies (Winfree et al., 1994). A study of seventy-two inmates in a medium-security state-operated prison in the Southwest revealed that the rate of prisonization was greater for minority inmates as well as for those with drug dependencies. Nonminorities were less likely to adopt inmate codes and to be dependent upon other inmates (Winfree et al., 1994). Thus, inmates who become a part of the therapeutic community and receive counseling and treatment for their chemical dependencies seem less likely to adopt inmate codes and are more easily resocialized to noncriminal behaviors in long-term rehabilitation programs (Peat and Winfree, 1992).

Highlight 12.1. Prison Escapes: The Case of the Unauthorized Furlough

The Missouri River Correctional Center (MRCC) in Bismarck, North Dakota, was the scene of an escape over the weekend of June 22–23, 1996. Three inmates, Christopher Lockwood, twenty-one, Joshua Sailor, nineteen, and Tim Cominghay, nineteen, walked away from the facility following a visitor's session on Friday afternoon. The MRCC is a minimum-security facility designed to house offenders who are nearing their release dates. Inmates are given a high amount of trust because they have too much to lose by running away, according to officials who operate the center.

Cominghay's fiancée was visiting from Fargo, about 150 miles from Bismarck. She agreed to meet him outside the facility later Friday evening. When Cominghay walked off the grounds, Sailor and Lockwood followed him. Sailor and Lockwood bought some liquor and went on a joyride with the man who brought Cominghay's fiancée to Bismarck while Cominghay and his fiancée went to a motel.

They were caught as Cominghay was trying to carry Sailor, who was too drunk to walk, back to his room at MRCC. Only a conscientious guard who spotted the pair stood in the way of a perfect weekend. Two of the inmates were sent to the nearby state penitentiary to await charges of escape. No doubt they will be reincarcerated on the new charges, and it will be several years before they are again considered for release. Elaine Little, director of the North Dakota Department of Corrections, said that there had been no escapes such as this for the preceding two years.

What should state policies be regarding inmates about to be released? Should there be unmonitored housing, such as the MRCC, where prisoners can leave the premises without much difficulty? How much trust should the state place in them?

Source: Adapted from Associated Press, "Three Inmates Leave Minimum Security Center," *Minot (N.D.) Daily News,* June 25, 1996, p. B4.

Inmate Rule Breaking and Officer-Inmate Interactions

In 1983, a study of 391 inmates and 44 guards at the Federal Correctional Institution in Fort Worth, Texas, examined rule breaking and correctional officer/inmate interactions pertaining to rule violations (Hewitt, Poole, and Regoli, 1984). It was determined that rule breaking is more widespread than official records indicate. Both guards and inmates said that many rule infractions observed by correctional officers were never reported. Correctional officers said that they did not report these rule violations because they wanted to preserve stability among the inmates.

In a study of 809 infraction reports completed by correctional officers between 1987 and 1988 at a medium-security California prison, violent incidents accounted for about 50 percent of all infractions. There were 82 assaults against prison staff, 128 assaults against other inmates; 53 incidents of self-inflicted violence; and 153 incidents of violence toward property. Violence toward other inmates occurred most often in areas where prisoners were allowed to congregate (Steinke, 1991). Violence toward oneself or against property seldom occurred outside of cell or dormitory areas.

Indications are that inmate violence is becoming increasingly severe as prisoners replace fists with weapons and assaults are more likely to result in death than in injury (Buchanan, Unger, and Whitlow, 1988).

Inmate Classification and Program Placements

Efforts by wardens and others to classify inmates according to custody levels and programs are not always successful and sometimes create problems. One study investigated the classification process at a large, state maximum-security prison in the Midwest during 1974–1976 (Webb, 1984). Although appropriate inmate placement was the stated goal of the Reception and Classification unit of the prison, the unit's real goal was to process offenders as rapidly as possible. Organizational goals were seemingly irrelevant. The unit wanted to appear efficient and to maintain their administrative authority.

The same study showed that informal groups of inmates contributed to extensive rule-breaking (Webb, 1984). Prisoners who did not become gang members were frequent victims of assault, robbery, sexual abuse, and extortion. Black inmates not affiliated with gangs were frequently victimized as well. In recent years, however, black gangs have formed in most prisons as a means of self-protection. These gangs compete with other gangs for prison privileges and power.

Later efforts to classify inmates have had mixed results. In 1983, for example, the Nevada Department of Prisons devised the *Prisoner Classification System;* in 1987 it applied this classification to one thousand prisoners. The classification system was considered successful because it significantly improved prisoner safety and led to more efficient inmate management. Escapes, suicides, and complaints about misclassification declined sharply (Austin and Chan, 1989).

Usually, the less restrictive the classification (e.g., minimum-security compared with maximum- or medium-security), the more privileges available. Thus, inmates enjoy the most freedom and privileges under a minimum-security classification. If inmates feel that they have been overclassified, perhaps as maximum-security instead of medium- or minimum-security, they may file suit or lodge a complaint with the prison administration (Suchner and Thomas, 1989; Thomas, 1991a, 1991b). Developing effective prisoner classification systems is a continuing problem (Rudman and Berthelsen, 1991; Washington State Legislative Budget Committee, 1983).

An example of a prison classification instrument is the one used by the Alaska Department of Corrections, shown in figure 12.1 The form is filled out by correctional staff. An inmate's background and criminal history make up a score, which is then used to place the inmate in one custody level or another. Depending upon the score, the prison superintendent can either approve or override the recommended security level. An override may result in the security level being upgraded or downgraded. Usually, these placement forms are supplemented with actual interviews with inmates. Once the form has been completed and a recommendation has been made, the prisoner signs the form. Thus, an inmate knows his security level and the reasons for this decision. Placement decisions are appealable, and placement and security level status are reassessed regularly, such as every six months or year.

Not all prison classification instruments are equally reliable (Champion, 1994). The Nebraska Department of Corrections has devised the *Inmate Classification Model,* which has been used more or less successfully to place inmates (Proctor, 1994). This instrument uses five classification variables and six demographic variables. While the Nebraska Department of Corrections makes objective classification decisions on the basis of scores derived from this instrument, experts have found that the device fails to predict offenders' institutional adjustment problems. Thus, the device needs additional modification and improvement to make it more valid for this purpose (Proctor, 1994). Instruments used by other systems, such as the Federal Bureau of Prisons, have had better success at forecasting potential inmate adjustment problems (Van Voorhis, 1994).

Various dimensions of inmate environments have been described by researchers (Marquart and Roebuck, 1986; Webb, 1984; Zamble and Porporino, 1988). Environmental factors such as privacy, safety, structure, support, emotional feedback, social stimulation, activity, and freedom have been assessed by instruments such as the *Prison Environment Inventory* (Wright, 1993). Many maximum-security prisons lack several of these environmental features. Inmate idleness, for instance, is frequently associated with rioting and unrest (Steelman, 1984). However, in prisons that provide opportunities for self-advancement and improvement, more positive prison adjustments are associated with prisoners who take advantage of these opportunities (Wright, 1993). Further, these inmates seem less likely to be influenced by inmate codes that are generally disruptive and troublesome for prison systems.

Figure 12.1 Alaska Department of Corrections Classification Form for Sentenced Prisoners

STATE OF ALASKA   DEPARTMENT OF CORRECTIONS

Classification Form for Sentenced Prisoners

(1) _____   (2) _____
    Institution   Prisoner Name

(3) _____   (4) _____
    Date   Date of Birth

(5) _____   (6) _____
    Type of Case: Regular or Exception   OBSCIS Number

SECTION A   **SECURITY SCORING**

1. *Type of Detainer:*
   0 = None   3 = Class C Felony   7 = Unclassified or
   1 = Misdemeanor   5 = Class B Felony   Class A Felony   [   ]

2. *Severity of Current Offense:*
   1 = Misdemeanor   3 = Class C Felony   7 = Unclassified or
   2 = Felony   5 = Class B Felony   Class A Felony   [   ]

3. *Time to Firm Release Date:*
   0 = 0-12 months   3 = 60-83 months
   1 = 13-59 months   5 = 84 + months
   [   ] 3   Firm Release Date

4. *Type of Prior Convictions:*
   0 = None   1 = Misdemeanor   3 = Felony   [   ]

5. *History of Escapes or Attempted Escapes:*

	None	+15 Years	10-15 Years	5-10 Years	-5 Years	
Minor	0	1	1	2	3	
Serious	0	4	5	6	7	[ ]

6. *History of Violent Behavior:*

	None	+15 Years	10–15 Years	5-10 Years	-5 Years	
Minor	0	1	1	2	3	
Serious	0	4	5	6	7	[ ]

7. SECURITY TOTAL   [   ]

8. *Security Level:*
   Minimum = 0-6 points   Medium = 7-13 points   Maximum = 14-36 points

---

SECTION B   **CUSTODY SCORING**

1. *Percent of Time Served:*
   3 = 0 thru 25 %   5 = 76 thru 90%
   4 = 26 thru 75%   6 = 91 plus %   [   ]

2. *Involvement with Drugs and/or Alcohol:*
   2 = Current   3 = Past   4 = Never   [   ]

Figure 12.1 Alaska Department of Corrections Classification Form for Sentenced Prisoners *(continued)*

3. *Mental/Psychological Stability:*
   2 = Unfavorable   4 = No referral or favorable   [   ]

4. *Type Most Serious Disciplinary Report:*
   1 = Major   3 = Low Moderate   5 = None
   2 = High Moderate   4 = Minor   [   ]

5. *Frequency of Disciplinary Reports:*
   0 = 5 + Reports   2 = 1 Report
   1 = 2 - 4 Reports   3 = None   [   ]

6. *Responsibility Prisoner Has Demonstrated:*
   0 = Poor   2 = Average   4 = Good   [   ]

7. *Family/Community:*
   3 = None or Minimal   4 = Average or Good   [   ]

8. CUSTODY TOTAL: [   ]

9. *Custody Change Scale:*

Prisoner's Present Security Level	Consider Custody Increase if Points	Continue Present Custody if Points	Consider Custody Decrease if Points
Minimum	11-19 Points	20-22 Points	23-30 Points
Medium	11-19 Points	20-24 Points	25-30 Points
Maximum	11-19 Points	20-27 Points	28-30 Points

10. _____   _____
   PRESENT CUSTODY   RECOMMENDED CUSTODY

11. *Administrative/Program Considerations:*
   1. Release Plans   4. Education   7. Overcrowding
   2. Medical   5. Special Treatment   8. Judicial Recommendation
   3. Psychiatric   6. Ethnic/Cultural   9. Residence Consideration

12. *Explanation:* _____
_____

SECTION C   **INSTITUTION ACTION**

1. Recommendation/Justification _____

2. Recommendation based on: _____Points Total   _____ Management Override

3. Community Custody Provisions (if applicable): _____
_____
_____

4. Date of Next Review: _____

(continued next page)

Figure 12.1 Alaska Department of Corrections Classification Form for Sentenced Prisoners *(continued)*

5. Chair Person: _____

    Member: _____

    Member: _____

6. Superintendent's Action (if applicable): _____Approve   _____Disapprove

Comments: _____
_____
_____

COPY RECEIVED

_____   _____

PRISONER SIGNATURE   DATE

Notice to Sentenced Prisoners:

(1) The sentenced prisoner designation is without administrative appeal;
(2) Classification Committee action not referred to or modified by the Superintendent may be appealed only to the Superintendent, and no higher;
(3) Classification Committee action referred to or modified by the Superintendent, except for transfer, may be appealed to the Regional Director in accordance with 760.01, Appeal Procedures;
(4) Classification Committee action regarding transfer may be appealed directly to the Deputy Commissioner for Operations in accordance with 760.01, Appeal Procedures;
(5) Forms to facilitate an appeal will be provided by institutional staff upon request by the prisoner;
(6) An appeal must be routed through the institutional staff member designated for the purpose of receiving and forwarding classification appeals; and
(7) Any classification action may be commenced pending an appeal, except a transfer to an out-of-state facility.

Mentally Ill and Retarded Inmates

Prison culture is affected not only by violent offenders but also by large numbers of mentally ill or retarded inmates. Surveys of prisons have found numerous inmates who are mentally ill and should be hospitalized rather than imprisoned (Austin et al., 1990). A study of forty-eight state prison systems in 1984 showed that thirteen thousand inmates incarcerated for one or more years were either mentally retarded or mentally ill and in need of clinical treatment or hospitalization (Denkowski and Denkowski, 1985).

Sex Offenders and Drug/Alcohol Dependent Inmates

Sex offenders and narcotics addicts are sometimes diverted from prison to treatment programs or hospitalization. The Sex Offender Treatment and Evaluation Project established in California in 1984 has rehabilitated many incarcerated sex offenders (Prentky, 1994). The program treats sex offenders over a twenty-two-month period. It is especially helpful to inmates during the two years before their parole. Participation in this program was voluntary. A major incentive to participate was the possibility of being transferred from the strict prison environment to a less formal hospital setting for treatment. Still, program officials said that too few inmates volunteered for the program.

An evaluation of seventy sex-offender treatment programs in Minnesota reported that 2,600 sex offenders were treated in 1992 (Minnesota Program Evaluation Division, 1994). These were counseled mostly as outpatients. About half of these offenders were successfully rehabilitated. One problem with these Minnesota programs was that consistent standards have not been developed whereby reliable assessments of program effectiveness can be made. Thus, not all offenders diagnosed as sex offenders actually received treatment, while those who did receive treatment and did not successfully complete their programs continued to be monitored during variable probation periods. Similar programs in other states have had more success, especially when family and other support systems can be integrated into the treatment (Skolnik et al., 1991).

Selection and Recruitment of Correctional Staff

Competent and qualified correctional staff is very important for the proper management and administration of prisons and jails. In recent years, the hiring of correctional officers has become increasingly selective (*Corrections Compendium,* 1994:8). It has generally been found that the more competent the prison or jail staff, the less inmate unrest and complaints. Studies tend to show that correctional officers who believe that they have the confidence and support of their prison or jail administration tend to perform better. Corrections officers who have greater levels of work satisfaction tend to perform better, have less labor turnover, and have greater organizational commitment (Kerce, Magnusson, and Rudolph, 1994; Stohr et al., 1994; U.S. Federal Bureau of Prisons, 1993).

Many prisons and jails use a *control model* based upon rigid routinization of work tasks and compliance with bureaucratic rules. Emphasis is upon demonstrating respect for rules and authority and upon the tight control of inmate time and activities (Stohr et al., 1994:475). Under an *employee investment model,* the emphasis shifts toward investment in staff training that prepares correctional officers for a wider range of responsibilities and duties. They get training in communication skills as well as in ethics, leadership, and interpersonal problem solving. One result of using an employee investment model is that staff can generally cope better with inmate problems and incidents. While prison and jail overcrowding continues to aggravate social conditions among inmates, a better-trained staff does much to alleviate some inmate complaints. Therefore, it is important to select competent staff and train them in ways that will maximize their effectiveness (Stohr et al., 1994:495–96).

A better-trained correctional staff will be able to minimize certain kinds of inmate problems. Under some conditions, untrained or undertrained staff may be at risk of losing their lives. For instance, a correctional officer at the Maximum Security Unit in Tucker, Arkansas, was killed by inmates while he was overseeing a routine shower call. Two inmates who were showering got into a fight in which a shank or plastic knife was used as a weapon. When the officer, Scott Turner, intervened, he was fatally stabbed (Dallao, 1996:69). Turner was actually working a shift for another correctional officer, Scott Grimes. When interviewed about the incident, Scott Grimes said, "If I wouldn't have taken off, it would have been me. The only difference is that I wouldn't have died to save an inmate. That's where Scott was more of a man than I am. He died for a man doing life without parole; now his kids are doing life without him" (Dallao, 1996:69).

Additionally, better correctional officers have the flexibility and patience needed to manage certain types of special-needs offenders (Turner, 1994:134). Increasing numbers of elderly inmates often require special treatment. Corrections officers must become more sensitive to these problems and develop strategies to deal with them (Aday, 1994:47–49).

Overcoming Stereotyping

Over the years, corrections has had to contend with adverse stereotyping by various sources, including the media. Stereotyping of corrections work suggests that it is performed by persons with limited intellectual skills and low educational levels; also only males are fit for corrections work, and female officers cannot cope with the stress and demands of dealing with violent inmates. In hopes of overcoming such adverse stereotyping, some jurisdictions offer workshops and other educational opportunities to corrections staff. For instance, the Handlon Training Unit in Michigan has helped corrections officers learn to identify problems in the workplace, including incidents related to race, gender, and organization.

The workshops provide participants with positive experiences and strategies for dealing with these types of problems. They emphasize communication among people from different departments and who perform different types of correctional work. Group discussions are encouraged so that problems can be brought out into the open and aired. In one instance, a black supervisor and a white corrections officer who had a long-running disagreement pledged to begin a new relationship in an effort to resolve their prior problems. In follow-up workshops results are evaluated and group members report on their learning experiences. Participants are very positive about the workshops' effects on work environments (Brown, 1991:1, 5).

Population Characteristics of Corrections Personnel

Demographic Characteristics

The 1994 survey of forty-two state and federal correctional systems describes the employment status of 155,245 corrections officers (*Corrections Compendium*, 1994:8). Of these, 18 percent were female, up from 11 percent in 1984. The greatest proportion of female corrections personnel was found in Mississippi (44 percent), followed by Nevada (33 percent), Louisiana (32 percent), and the District of Columbia (30 percent). The lowest proportion of female corrections officers was found in Montana (9.5 percent) and Indiana (11 percent) (*Corrections Compendium*, 1994:9–10). Between 1992 and 1994, there was an increase in the total number of corrections officers of 16,532, or 12.5 percent. The American Correctional Association reports that in 1995 there were 219,821 corrections officers in state and federal prison systems (American Correctional Association, 1995:xliv–xlv). In 1995, the total number of *both* staff and corrections officers employed by state and federal departments of corrections was 365,755 (Camp and Camp, 1995a:68).

Many corrections officers are recruited directly from criminal justice programs at colleges and universities. Recent criminal justice graduates often have field experience. Perhaps they have interned as correctional officers with agencies near their schools. One provision of the Crime Bill passed by Congress in 1994 was additional money to recruit more qualified corrections personnel. The Crime Bill offered educational grants to induce police officers and corrections officers to acquire college degrees as well as forgivable loans to attract college-educated individuals into police and correctional work. While a direct correlation between a college degree and correctional officer effectiveness has yet to be shown, some experts believe that money is well spent on educating correctional officers. Certainly, additional education cannot hurt one's job performance (Taylor, 1995). More education is also equated with the increasing professionalism of corrections work.

Labor Turnover

Turnover rates among correctional officers during their first year on the job have averaged about 12 percent (Camp and Camp, 1995a:79). In 1995, the highest turnover rate, 32 percent, occurred among correctional officers in the Arkansas Department of Corrections. The Federal Bureau of Prisons had a turnover rate of 6 percent that same year (Camp and Camp, 1995a:79).

Salaries

One reason for labor turnover among corrections officers is low pay. While the range of salaries among corrections officers varies greatly, in 1995 the average entry-level salary was $19,907. Following a six- to thirteen-month training period, corrections officers averaged $20,215 per year. Following their probationary periods, corrections officers averaged an annual salary of $21,589, while the average maximum salary was $31,447. The highest maximum salary was $56,016 in the Alaska Department of Corrections. The lowest maximum salary was in South Carolina, at $16,558. In 1995, entry-level salaries in South Carolina were only $15,310; thus the difference between entry-level pay and maximum salary in that state is small (Camp and Camp, 1995a:80–81). In 1995 the maximum salary for Federal Bureau of Prisons corrections officers was $35,067. Other states with high salaries were New Jersey ($48,661), California ($46,020), Pennsylvania ($42,062), and New York ($40,419). States paying maximum salaries of $25,000 or less included Maine ($21,944), Mississippi ($24,690), Montana ($17,424), New Mexico

($24,183), South Carolina ($16,558), Tennessee ($21,804), and Texas ($24,324) (Camp and Camp, 1995a:80–81). These relatively low salaries make it difficult to attract and retain high-quality corrections personnel.

Many corrections officers enter the field only temporarily. Those who leave corrections often earn more money in the private sector. Furthermore, private-sector occupations are less dangerous. Some state corrections officers use these jobs to qualify for more lucrative federal positions. Thus, many federal corrections officers have first been state corrections officers.

Correctional Administration

Administrative personnel earn considerably more per year than corrections officers—sometimes in excess of $100,000 (American Correctional Association, 1995). In 1995, directors of adult correctional agencies averaged $81,106 per year. These directors' average length of service is about three years (Camp and Camp, 1995a:68–69). For wardens, the average salary in 1995 was $70,645, with a maximum salary of $123,100 and a minimum of $27,492 (Camp and Camp, 1995a:68). Table 12.1 summarizes some of the major sociodemographic characteristics of corrections officers.

Recruitment Practices

Selection Criteria

Selection criteria in many states include civil service examinations and high school diplomas. Because of the nature of corrections work, several psychological assessment measures used to recruit police officers are also used to recruit corrections officers. Officers are selected on the basis of physical attributes (e.g., size, strength, gender), security considerations, personal background data (e.g., prior criminal record, veteran status), and various psychological and personality assessment measures (Friend et al., 1993). Some research has generated a lengthy list of traits that seem associated with effective correctional officers. Presumably, if one acquires more of these traits, one will become a more effective correctional officer. However, psychological tests have not highly correlated specific traits

Table 12.1

Sociodemographic Characteristics of U.S. Corrections Officers, 1995

Characteristic	Percent	Average
Gender		
Male	69.2%	
Female	30.8	
Race/Ethnicity		
White	66.9	
Nonwhite	33.1	
Training Periods		
Shortest		6 months
Longest		13 months
Salary		
Entry level		$19,907
After training		$20,215
After probation		$21,589
Maximum salary		$31,447
Training Hours		224 hours

Sources: Camp and Camp (1995a); *ACA Directory 1995* (1995); *Corrections Compendium* (1994a).

with effectiveness as a corrections officer (Heper, Skok, and McLaughlin, 1990).

Currently, only scattered efforts have been made to improve the recruitment and selection requirements for correctional officers. Superintendents, wardens, and other administrators of penal institutions have expressed comparatively little interest in developing ways of retaining competent correctional officers and reducing labor turnover.

Computers and Correctional Work

Local jails and state and federal prisons have computerized their operations to such a degree that many employees need sophisticated computer training. Doing background checks of arrestees; keeping track of inmates' movements, custody levels, and infractions in large prison systems; and all other forms of paperwork are more easily maintained and accessed by computer. The transition to using computers can be traumatic. Nevertheless, more sophisticated computer training is strongly recommended for those contemplating careers in corrections (Lieberg, 1996:23–26).

Racial and Ethnic Diversity in Recruiting

Some believe that diversifying the work force would smooth relations between inmates and staff, primarily by reducing interpersonal friction. Some evidence of the success of this strategy has been provided by the New York Department of Correction in Westchester County (Friend et al., 1993).

Inadequacies of State In-Service Correctional Training

Many critics consider the kind of training corrections officers receive to be inadequate. For instance, preservice training hours are as low as 70 in Maine and 40 in Vermont. Maine also has the lowest amount of inservice training, with 4 hours. Michigan has the most preservice training—640 hours. However, Michigan also has 40 hours of inservice training, which seems about average for most other states (Camp and Camp, 1995a:85). Other states with high amounts of preservice training are Connecticut (471 hours), Utah (440 hours), and Alabama (400 hours).

Learning to Avoid Manipulation by Inmates

One problem confronting all corrections personnel who work in prisons is their likelihood for being manipulated by inmates. The American Correctional Association and other agencies have attempted to educate and help corrections officers resist inmates' demands (McGuire and Priestley, 1985). Many guards are unskilled at managing potentially hazardous guard-inmate encounters. Although there are materials to educate and inform officers about how to deal effectively with such problems, many guards either ignore this information or treat it lightly (McGuire and Priestley, 1985).

Job Burnout and Stress

Because of the hazards of correctional work, especially supervising inmates in maximum-security prisons, many correctional officers have high stress levels and experience job burnout (American Correctional Association, 1994b; Stohr, Lovrich and Wilson, 1994; Stohr et al., 1994). A study of 258 Alabama correctional officers in 1984 showed that emotional exhaustion and depersonalization, char-

acteristics of job burnout, were highly correlated with the officers' perceived work stress, role conflict, lack of support from administration, lack of job satisfaction, and age (Lindquist and Whitehead, 1986). The Maslach and Jackson twenty-two-item Human Services Survey was used to measure job burnout. Most officers reported administrative practices and policies rather than interactions with inmates to be most responsible for their high burnout levels. In fact, these corrections officers said that they had greater feelings of personal accomplishment through their various inmate contacts.

However, a 1983 survey of 250 correctional staff in a large state prison in the South showed that officers believed that job dangerousness and stress were the primary causes of their job burnout (Cullen et al., 1985). Although supervisory support lessened stress and job dissatisfaction, an officer's educational level was also important. More-educated correctional officers had greater job dissatisfaction and stress than less-educated officers. Female corrections officers exhibited greater stress levels than male officers.

In 1989–1990, a survey and organizational profile was conducted of 147 employees of five direct-supervision jails. Questions covered sociodemographic variables as well as attitudinal dimensions. The organizational settings varied in the degree to which they encouraged employee involvement in the decision making process. Some settings that practiced participative management reported higher levels of job satisfaction than settings with lower amounts of employee participation in decision making. Further, involvement in decision making correlated highly with lower stress levels and improved work performance (Stohr, Lovrich, and Wilson, 1994). Organizations with greater employee involvement and participative management had less turnover. Similar findings have been reported in other correctional settings (Beavon et al., 1993; Cornelius, 1994).

Women in Corrections

Women were first employed in prisons as matrons. One result of the women's movement was the hiring of women as wardens and guards (Parisi, 1984). Through public employee unionism and equal opportunity laws, women were eventually hired as correctional officers in prisons for males as well as for females, although there was substantial resistance to such change (Parisi, 1984; Rison, 1994).

In 1995, women made up 31 percent of all correctional officers in the United States (Camp and Camp, 1995a:68–69). Between 1978 and 1988, the presence of women in the correctional work force increased dramatically (Morton, 1991) as has the sophistication of correctional institutions for women.

For many years, women have been subjected to discrimination in correctional work. Stereotypical notions about female inadequacies and their inability to handle serious disturbances have made it difficult for women to enter the corrections field in large numbers (Morton, 1991). One major obstacle women have had to overcome is informal resistance among male administrators and officers (Farkas, 1992). Males in correctional work tend to have stereotypical notions of women as corrections officers (Morton, 1991).

Among the reasons given by corrections authorities for their reluctance to hire female officers is that women will not be able to back up male officers when serious inmate disturbances occur. Other reasons are that women use more sick leave, are reprimanded more frequently than men, and are less competent. Interestingly, police chiefs and sheriffs give the same reasons for not wanting to hire women as law enforcement officers. However, in an investigation of records of 386 female correctional officers in California prisons in 1982, researchers found no significant differences between men and women on any performance indicator related to correctional work (Holeman and Krepps-Hess, 1983).

The same study found that female officers were younger than male officers and that they were more likely to belong to an ethnic minority and to be single. More women than men had bachelor's degrees. Some inmates said that female guards invaded their privacy; however, other inmates said that female officers improved the prison environment. Most female officers and about two-thirds of the inmates said that female officers did not en-

danger the lives of either male officers or other prisoners. A majority of male officers said that female officers backed them up satisfactorily (Holeman and Krepps-Hess, 1983). The Supreme Court has upheld the employment of female personnel as prison guards and has denied relief to inmates seeking policy changes because of the violence they believe results from the presence of female officers (*Yusuf Asad Madyun v. Thompson*, 1981).

Women often seek supervisory or mid-level management positions after serving as corrections officers for several years (Rison, 1994). In contrast, men tend to aspire to administrative positions (Chapman et al., 1983). Subsequent investigations suggest that women entering the correctional field will increasingly seek administrative positions (American Correctional Association, 1992; Price and Sokoloff, 1995; Walters, 1993b).

Female corrections officers in jails are more discriminated against than their counterparts in prisons, although this discrimination is gradually declining. On-site visits to 554 jails between 1979 and 1984 showed much gender stereotyping on the part of sheriffs and jail administrators (Kerle, 1985). Local government officials claimed that women "lacked experience in supervising male prisoners and could not relate to male inmates' problems" (Kerle, 1985). In most of the jails investigated, female officers were employed as matrons for female inmates. There were also significant wage discrepancies between male and female guards. While it is likely that there will be greater employment equity for women in the future, it is also likely that court action may be necessary. Currently, administrators are the main barriers to women who are interested in jail employment (Kerle, 1985).

In the 1990s, studies of male correctional officers' attitudes toward their female counterparts showed some significant shifts (Walters, 1993a, 1993b). A study of 178 male corrections officers in four prisons showed prevalent "pro-woman" attitudes. The quality of the relationships between male and female co-workers was reported as favorable. The same study asked both male and female officers about job satisfaction levels and its primary sources. Male officers with longer service reported greater job satisfaction and lower stress than male officers with shorter service. Both male and female officers reported that job satisfaction derived from their working relationship with other officers, although women said that they were particularly satisfied because of the security levels in the prisons where they worked (Walters, 1993a, 1993b). Other researchers have reported similar findings (American Correctional Association, 1992; Robinson et al., 1992).

Female correctional officers also report a greater preference for counseling roles as well as a more punitive orientation toward inmates, at least in some of the corrections facilities in Wisconsin (Farkas, 1992). However, female officers in other correctional settings have said that if they have support from their peers, they are less inclined to regard their work as stressful and unrewarding (Van Voorhis et al., 1991).

One important influence on the trend toward greater numbers of women in correctional roles is privatization of prison and jail management and operation.

Privatization of Management and Prison Design

Prisoners' petitions filed with U.S. district courts have reported dissatisfaction with physical conditions of jails and prisons, including unhygienic living quarters, segregation of prisoners from inmates with AIDS, inadequate recreational areas, fire hazards, and overcrowding (*Harris v. Anglina County, Tex.,* 1994; *Walker v. Shansky,* 1994; *Wilson v. Seiter,* 1990; *Harmon v. Ohio Dept. Of Corr.,* 1991; *Lopez v. Robinson,* 1990; *Goss v. Sullivan,* 1993). Many lawsuits alleging various types of misconduct have been filed against prison officials and administrators as well (*Campbell v. Grammar,* 1989; *Richardson v. Van Dusen,* 1993; *Risdal v. Martin,* 1993; *Brown v. Doe,* 1992).

Some analysts believe that if prisons were administered properly, they would generate fewer complaints from inmates. Administrative style is important to creating or eliminating many correctional problems. Four types of prison management models have been described: (1) the authoritarian

model, (2) the bureaucratic lawful model, (3) the shared-powers model, and (4) the inmate control model (Barak-Glantz, 1985).

The authoritarian model prevailed during the nineteenth century. The main features of this model are one-person rule and repressive social control. The bureaucratic lawful model was especially popular immediately after World War II. Each correctional institution established formal chains of command comparable to those in governmental departments. The objective of this model was to "rationalize" prison life by creating principles, rules, and regulations. Wardens relinquished power through bureaucratization as supervisors at different levels of prison administration acquired more decision-making power through decentralization.

In the shared-powers model, which was popular during the 1960s, prisoners are given limited power and influence over prison operations. This model is characterized by a rehabilitative and democratic philosophy, the recognition of prisoners' right to form group associations, and overt confrontation between custodial staff and administration (Barak-Glantz, 1985:48). Inmate government councils were created that increasingly challenged almost every prison policy.

In the early 1970s, prisoners' unions were formed in several state prisons. The goals of the California Union, a major inmate union, offer insights into the amount of control inmates have acquired. These goals are: (1) to abolish the indeterminate sentence system and all its ramifications; (2) to establish workers' rights for the prisoners, including the right to organize and bargain collectively; and (3) to restore prisoners' civil and human rights (Irwin and Holder, 1973; Barak-Glantz, 1985:50).

In California and some other states, gangs based on race and ethnicity wield considerable power over other inmates and prison guards. At San Quentin and Soledad, an inmate organization called the Mexican Mafia is so powerful that it controls administrative affairs such as job classification, housing assignments, and even decisions about freedom of movement (Barak-Glantz, 1985:54). Because of these powerful inmate gangs and organizations, correctional classification committees often screen incoming convicts' credentials to determine whether they will be compatible with existing gangs. "The chances of a member of the Nuestra Familia [another Mexican-American mafia-type rival gang] avoiding physical harm or even surviving at San Quentin are not very great. Unfortunately, the gangs have virtually *taken over* the prison and now contribute overtly to its management" (Barak-Glantz, 1985:54).

In recent years, *private, profit-centered corporations have attempted to finance and operate local jails and state prisons. This is called* **privatization of prison management.** Skyrocketing building and maintenance expenses have forced many jail and prison administrators to explore various financing alternatives. Between June 30, 1994, and June 30, 1995, the population of state and federal inmates increased by 89,707 (Marvell, 1996:1–5; Wees, 1996b:9) while the number of beds increased by only 86,117 (Camp and Camp, 1995a:45). Thus, it is evident that prison space is not keeping pace with prison population growth. This statement holds for virtually every growth period since 1975.

During the 1980s, annual budgets for prison construction averaged $7 billion (Wees, 1996b). In the 1990s, California alone has averaged $5.2 billion per year for additional prison construction (Wees, 1996b:9). The National Institute of Justice estimates that correctional institutions require sixty-two months to construct and that the average cost per single-occupancy cell is $50,000 (Camp and Camp, 1995a). However, the average cost of prison space varies and must be measured according to whether the bed space is for a minimum-, medium-, or maximum-security inmate. The cost of minimum-security space averaged $32,356 in 1995, while costs for medium- and maximum-security bed space were $54,133 and $79,958 respectively (Camp and Camp, 1995a:47). The most frequently constructed prison space was for medium-security inmates (Camp and Camp, 1995a:40).

Can corporations with only private financial backing operate prisons and jails economically and profitably? Currently, there are no clear answers to this question. Some experts say that overcrowding, the lack of prison space, the high cost of prison construction, and the use of emergency powers to reduce overcrowding (e.g., court-mandated reductions in inmate populations) foster competition among private interests and could thus reduce prison costs (Marvell, 1994, 1996).

The success of privatizing prison ownership and management may be illustrated by correctional agencies that currently use private services and programs. New Mexico awarded a contract to the Corrections Corporation of America (CCA), a private corporation, to design, site, finance, construct, and operate a two-hundred-bed, multisecurity-level facility for the state's entire population of female offenders. On June 5, 1989, the Western New Mexico Correctional Facility transferred all of its female inmates to the CCA-operated New Mexico Women's Correctional Facility in Grants, New Mexico. A study was conducted to compare the quality of services and confinement in the CCA-operated facility with those of publicly operated prison facilities throughout New Mexico. On the basis of eight crucial dimensions of prison quality—security, safety, order, care, activity, justice, conditions, and management—a Prison Quality Index was devised. This index showed that the CCA-operated facility clearly outperformed its governmental counterparts in nearly every dimension (Logan, 1992:601–3). While this study by itself does not prove conclusively that private prison ownership and management is consistently more effective in delivering quality services to inmates, it does suggest that privatization should be explored as a remedy to prison and jail overcrowding (California State Senate, 1994; Durham, 1994; Etheridge and Marquart, 1993; Shichor, 1993).

No laws forbid the private ownership and management of correctional institutions (Durham, 1994; Shichor, 1993). Some critics believe that the privatization of correctional institutions is most useful for inmates with special needs, including the physically handicapped, those in protective custody or administrative segregation, and the elderly (Heard, 1993). However, the aging prison population is not as problematic as once predicted (Durham, 1994; Heard, 1993).

The American Civil Liberties Union (ACLU) opposes the privatization of prisons because it believes that privatization will limit prisoners' rights unless strong measures are taken to guarantee adequate prison standards (Florida Advisory Council on Intergovernmental Relations, 1993). Some experts say that privatization will not necessarily reduce prison and jail costs (Kratcoski, 1994). Another fear is that privatization will result in the construction of large numbers of prisons and that incarceration will dramatically increase (Immarigeon, 1985). This fear appears to be groundless, however. Interestingly, private prisons presently accommodate less than *2 percent* of all state and federal prison inmates (Wees, 1996b:10). Thus, there has been no massive increase in incarceration attributable to "growing" prison privatization, despite the dire forecasts of some prison experts.

Accountability is an important issue for many correctional critics (Mays and Gray, 1996). Who will monitor the actions and policies of administrators of private prisons? Many of these administrators have been recruited from state and federal prisons. They are often retired or former wardens or associate wardens or have served in some other prison capacity. It is believed that conflicts may arise between private prison managers and politicians, judges, activists, labor leaders, journalists, academics, and the public (Mays and Gray, 1996). There is little reason to believe that private prison managers will be able to avoid the pressures experienced by public prison administrators.

Also, there is an inherent conflict between an entrepreneur's interest in maximizing profits from prison operations by maximizing inmate populations and government efforts to provide alternatives to incarceration for low-risk offenders (Etheridge and Marquart, 1993). Again, there are no definite answers about how the privatization of correctional institutions will affect inmates (Mays and Gray, 1996).

Several states are attempting to lower their construction costs by adopting economical construction designs developed by prison architects. Pinellas County, Florida, near the Tampa Bay area, is one of the fastest growing regions in the state (Florida Advisory Council on Intergovernmental Relations, 1993). In order to reduce jail construction costs, Pinellas County officials have adopted a "precast" modular building design. The concrete building units are cast at a plant and then transported to the construction site. Figure 12.2 shows the floor plan of Pinellas County Jail's two main housing wings. The modular design reduced construction costs by nearly 10 percent, or $1.2 million

(DeWitt, 1986). Louisiana is also experimenting with such housing (Kyle, 1995).

Modular jail designs have several advantages, including better use of correctional officers, more opportunities to monitor inmates' activities, and improved security for guards. Existing jails will be substantially modified in the future to meet the needs of a growing population of inmates. For example, in 1994, the Niagara County Jail in Lockport, New York, coped with serious overcrowding by using modular prefabricated jail components (Beilein and Krasnow, 1996:128). The jail had a rated capacity of 204 inmates, although the average inmate population was between 260 and 300. A local planning and design firm proposed building several low-cost predesigned pods, or housing units. Each unit consisted of four triangular pods radiating from a central core. These pods contained fifty-six precast concrete cells, divided evenly on two levels and placed along the sides and diagonal of the pod. Each pod contained a multipurpose room, an interview room, toilets, and a janitor's closet. The units came fully equipped with stainless steel bathroom facilities and electrical connections. The cells had few joints and were considered very secure. Thus, they provided additional cell space at lower cost, with the advantage of secure units and quality management (Beilein and Krasnow, 1996:130–31). An added advantage was short construction time—twenty-four to twenty-seven months, compared with thirty-six months for more conventional cells.

Both local and federal authorities are exploring new jail and prison designs to minimize construction costs. One important implication is the likelihood that lawsuits alleging violations of health and safety codes and other related conditions of confinement will decrease (Collins, 1994). The savings in construction costs make these prefabricated units attractive to jail and prison officials at all levels of government (Bogard et al., 1993; U.S. Genera; Accounting Office, 1992a).

Selected Corrections Issues

Prisoners do not forfeit all of their constitutional rights as the result of being imprisoned (*Cook v.*

Figure 12.2 Floor plan of Pinellas County Jail

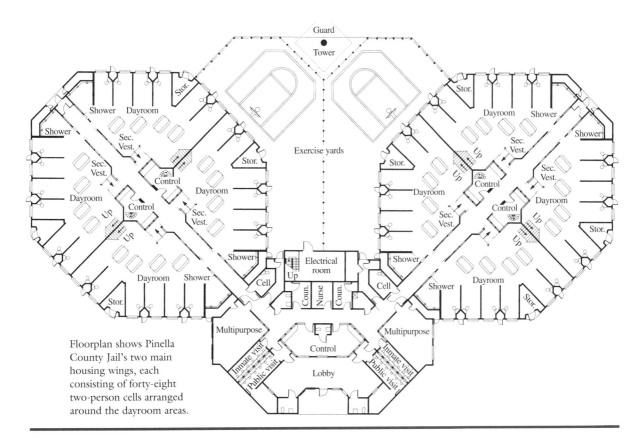

Floorplan shows Pinella County Jail's two main housing wings, each consisting of forty-eight two-person cells arranged around the dayroom areas.

City of New York, 1984; Palmer, 1996). In 1967, the President's Commission on Law Enforcement and Administration of Justice recommended the establishment of specific inmate grievance procedures in all state and federal prisons (Miller, 1983). By the end of 1982, *all* state prisons had administrative inmate grievance systems whose purpose was to act as a buffer between prisoners and the courts and thus avert legal action by means of internal administrative remedies. However, the system turned out not to work that way (Turner, 1985).

One consequence of the Commission's action was a noticeable increase in the number of petitions filed by state and federal inmates against prison administrators and others alleging civil rights violations and other complaints. For the twelve-month period ending June 30, 1985, for example, twenty-two thousand prisoner petitions had been filed in U.S. district and appeals courts (Hunzekar and Conger, 1985). In 1993, thirty-five thousand prisoner petitions were filed in federal courts, an increase of 59 percent (*Corrections Today,* 1995:32). These suits have alleged every conceivable violation of inmates' rights (Collins, 1995).

Because many lawsuits filed by jail and prison inmates are frivolous and/or without merit, much valuable court time has been consumed with various types of actions, such as *habeas corpus* petitions and Title 42, Section 1983 civil rights actions (Maahs and del Carmen, 1996:53–54). In an effort to restrict the rising number of petitions filed by inmates, the Supreme Court and Congress have moved to limit both the number and types of petitions inmates may file. In 1996, President Bill

Clinton signed the Prison Litigation Reform Act, which prohibits federal courts from ordering improvements in prisons or jails unless the court finds that an inmate's federal rights have been violated (*Criminal Justice Newsletter,* 1996:1). Earlier in 1995, the Supreme Court ruled that inmates have only a limited right to challenge disciplinary measures they may be subjected to (*Corrections Today,* 1995:32). Further, Congress has also moved to limit the number of *habeas corpus* appeals that inmates who have been sentenced to death may file (Call, 1995; Maahs and del Carmen, 1996). Despite these restrictions, the number of lawsuits inmates file continues to be high (*Corrections Today,* 1995:32).

Following is a discussion of several issues that have spawned lawsuits from inmates or have created conditions that inmates find objectionable. Among the issues raised by prisoners are (1) prison and jail overcrowding; (2) prison labor; (3) vocational and educational training programs; (4) racism; (5) prisoners' rights; (6) violence; and (7) the death penalty.

Prison and Jail Overcrowding

It has been predicted that the population of state and federal prisons will increase by 43 percent by the year 2002 (Wees, 1996a:1). Overcrowding in correctional institutions is correlated with several other administrative problems (Call, 1995a), such as increased rates of natural and violent deaths, suicides, psychiatric commitments, disciplinary infractions, and reconvictions (Glaser, 1994; Vaughn, 1993).

Most prisoner grievances are directly or indirectly connected with overcrowding. Factors contributing to overcrowding are judicial discretion in sentencing, statutory constraints limiting the flexibility of probation and parole programs, staff shortages, and poor prison administration (Shelden and Brown, 1991; Vaughn, 1993). Although there is considerably less overcrowding in women's prisons than in men's, overcrowding is a persistent problem there as well (Snell and Morton, 1994).

Prison and jail overcrowding has been challenged in court as "cruel and unusual punishment"

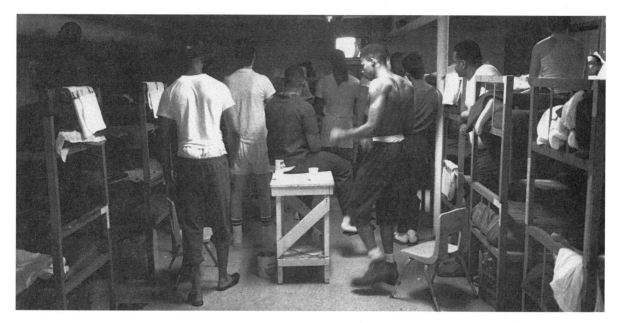

With approximately seventeen people per cell, Somerset County Jail in Sommerville, New Jersey, was at 500 percent capacity early in 1990. Most prisoner grievances in American jails and prisons are directly or indirectly connected with overcrowding.

in violation of the Eighth Amendment (Palmer, 1996). Presented here are three landmark cases involving prison and jail overcrowding: *Bell v. Wolfish* (1979), *Rhodes v. Chapman* (1981), and *Ruiz v. Estelle* (1982).

While awaiting trial, Louis Wolfish was housed at the Federal Metropolitan Correctional Center in New York. The building was fairly new, and each room was designed to accommodate one prisoner. However, an increase in the number of detainees prompted officials to place two persons in each room. This is known as **double-bunking,** and it became one of the major issues in the lawsuit filed by Wolfish. He also complained of body cavity searches following visits with friends and relatives and of the prohibition against receiving packages from outside the institution.

The government argued that all conditions of pretrial detention at its correctional facility were justified in order to ensure security, internal order, discipline and the detainee's presence at trial. In *Bell v. Wolfish,* the Supreme Court upheld the constitutionality of double-bunking (American Correctional Association, 1983:221). Applied to pretrial detainees, this decision was again upheld in a 1983 New Jersey case, *Union County Jail Inmates v. DuBuono.* The court said that the overcrowded county jail would pass constitutional muster upon full implementation of recommendations by the Commissioner of the New Jersey State Department of Corrections to double-bunk the cells, allow inmates at least one hour of recreation a day, provide clean clothing weekly, and medically screen all new inmates.

Kelly Chapman was an inmate of the Southern Ohio Correctional Facility (maximum-security) at Lucasville, Ohio. Although this facility was fairly new, because of overcrowding fourteen hundred prisoners out of twenty-three hundred were double-bunked in sixty-three-square-foot cells. In what became known as the "one man, one cell" case, Chapman argued that two persons per cell violated his constitutional right against cruel and unusual punishment. In *Rhodes v. Chapman,* the Supreme Court disagreed, ruling in an 8–1 decision that prison overcrowding is not unconstitutional. Justice Powell declared that "the Constitution does not mandate comfortable prisons. . . . To the extent that prison conditions are restrictive and even harsh, they are part of the penalty that criminal offenders pay for their offenses against society."

The *Ruiz v. Estelle* case involved a class action suit filed by Ruiz and other inmates against the Texas Department of Corrections (Estelle was then the director of the prison system). Among other things, the suit alleged violations of prisoners' constitutional rights relating to prison overcrowding, health care, guard brutality, and an abusive building-tender system (i.e., using dominant/aggressive inmates to work with regular staff guards to control other inmates) (Marquart, 1986:17).

The Fifth Circuit Court of Appeals held that the overcrowding in the Texas Department of Corrections "was of such a magnitude as to amount to severe punishment." While this may seem to contradict the Supreme Court's earlier decisions in *Bell v. Wolfish* and *Rhodes v. Chapman,* the Fifth Circuit declared that "although the Supreme Court stated that there was no 'one man, one cell' principle lurking in the due process clause, the Court specifically reserved judgment on cases that present *different facts*" (emphasis added).

This decision caused massive changes within the Texas correctional system (Maahs and del Carmen, 1996). One change was to establish selective early release procedures for inmates with good records, particularly those who had little or no history of alcohol or drug abuse (Maahs and del Carmen, 1996). Another change was the passage of the Prison Management Act and the implementation of the Texas Prison Management Plan in 1985. While the 1986 Texas prison population was approximately 41,000 it was projected that *an additional 6,000 cells* would be needed between 1987 and 1992 at a cost of $200 million (Martinez and Fabelo, 1985). This estimate was incredibly off the mark. By the end of 1992, the Texas prison inmate population was *61,178,* an increase of over 20,000 inmates since 1986 (Gilliard, 1993:4). By the end of 1995, Texas had the second-largest inmate population in the United States, with 97,650 inmates (Camp and Camp, 1995a:3). Thus, the Texas inmate population grew by 53 percent between 1987 and 1992 and by 144 percent between 1987 and 1995. This dramatically illustrates the glaring gap between what experts *predict will happen* and *what actually happens* regarding prison inmate statistics. Because we cannot accurately predict the growth of the prison population, we also cannot predict how many new jails and prisons will be needed to accommodate tomorrow's inmate populations.

Besides Texas, states with serious overcrowding problems include Connecticut, Oklahoma, Maryland, Louisiana, Tennessee, Massachusetts, Illinois, Maine, Pennsylvania, Oregon, Washington, New Jersey, Rhode Island, and California. The Committee on Prison Overcrowding in Maryland had labeled Maryland's current level of prison overcrowding "intolerable" (Maryland Criminal Justice Coordinating Council, 1984).

Affecting prison overcrowding in many states are determinate and mandatory sentencing, which have removed the power to parole from parole boards and imposed sentences of specific lengths without time off for "good behavior" (Call, 1995b; D'Allessio and Stolzenberg, 1995).

Several solutions to overcrowding have been proposed. Alternative sentencing is used in some jurisdictions, such as Oregon and California (Vaughn, 1993). Work camps, work release, and a statewide probation department are used in Iowa, Kansas, Minnesota, Rhode Island, and other jurisdictions (D'Allessio and Stolzenberg, 1995; Jones, 1990; Key, 1991; Rhode Island Governor's Commission to Avoid Future Prison Overcrowding, 1993).

The short-term nature of a jail inmate's confinement has caused some authorities to believe that jail overcrowding is easier to control than prison overcrowding. California has experimented with single-bed cells, double-bed cells, eight-bed cells, and sixteen-bed dormitories (Thompson and Mays, 1991). While jail administrators oppose large cells, a dormitory-style arrangement reduces jail costs and is likely to reduce inmate stress.

Jail overcrowding results also from the classification methods used to determine an inmate's length of stay (Champion, 1994; Thompson and Mays, 1991). A study of Colorado jails showed that misclassifications of inmates caused hundreds to be needlessly imprisoned (Brennan, 1985). In California and several other states, 90 percent of all jail bookings involve pretrial defendants. Many of these can be safely released on their own recognizance with effective supervisory measures (Perkins, Stephan, and Beck, 1995).

Prison Labor

All states have prison industries (Grieser, 1989). In 1983, Florida operated seventeen industries; on average, each state operated five industries. The number of inmates employed in prison industries has ranged from 4,200 in Texas to 52 in Vermont. By 1994, 70,000 inmates were employed in state and federal correctional industries throughout the United States, and another 340,000 offenders worked in other correctional programs (Camp and Camp, 1995c).

License Plates and Chain Gangs

Many people associate prison labor and industries with the manufacture of automobile license plates. Although this form of prison labor is about a century old, it is still common in prisons (Wunder, 1994:9). In 1911, the Iowa state prison system pioneered the use of inmate labor to manufacture license plates. In 1915 and 1916 New Jersey and New York instituted similar programs. Today, prison inmates manufacture garments, soap, mattresses, signs, and agricultural products, as well as license plates (Wunder, 1994:9). Nearly 70 percent of all prison industries are self-supporting. One of the most thriving industries is in Iowa, where inmates use telephones to encourage state tourism (Wunder, 1994:9).

Another stereotype of prison labor is men in striped uniforms chained together and breaking rocks along roadsides. These chain gangs were used extensively in the early 1900s and then abandoned. In the 1990s, several states revived their use. Alabama, Georgia, and Florida have experimented with bringing back chain gangs as a means of subjecting inmates to hard labor (and hard punishment) (Crist, 1996:178). Senator Charlie Crist of Florida sponsored legislation that in December 1995 made Florida the third state to reinstate chain gangs. Crist says that "the prison system I envision is self-sustaining, where inmates can grow their own food, do their own carpentry and plumbing, and handle the upkeep of the prison; but I believe that convicted criminals should also work on our highways and byways, in visible places where would-be criminals can see the price of committing crime" (Crist, 1996:178). Prisoners have since filed several lawsuits against the state of Florida and other jurisdictions alleging that chain gangs are a form of cruel and unusual punishment.

The Sky Is Falling! No, It Isn't!

Over the years, many prison reformers have feared exploitation of inmates by private enterprise through the use of prison labor to produce goods. Also, some labor and business groups are concerned that cheap prison labor will result in unfair competition (Greiser, 1989). In 1929, congressional reaction to these complaints led to the passage of the **Hawes-Cooper Act of 1929.** *This act provided that any and all prison-made goods transported from one state to another should be regulated by the commerce laws of the importing state.* In 1940, the Sumners-Ashurst Act was passed by Congress. This act made it a federal criminal offense for common carriers to violate state statutes created as the result of the Hawes-Cooper Act. As a result, thirty states passed laws restricting the transportation of prisoner-made goods. For many years, these laws effectively discouraged prison industry (U.S. House of Representatives Committee on the Judiciary, 1994). However, the fears of the private sector proved to be unfounded (Altemose, 1996; Crist, 1996).

In 1979, the Prison-Industries Enhancement Act was passed, which repealed earlier federal laws restricting the movement of prison-made goods in interstate commerce and thus revitalized prison labor and industry. New federal and state statutes have also provided that prisoners be paid reasonable wages for their work.

UNICOR

Federal Prison Industries, or **UNICOR,** *is a profitable, government-owned corporation that employs thousands of prisoners and markets numerous prisoner-made products to a variety of federal agencies* (Ingley, 1996a; U.S. General Accounting Office, 1985). Audits and evaluations of UNICOR show that customers are satisfied with these products and that the pricing seems competitive with that of similar goods produced by privately owned industries and corporations. In 1995, gross sales of prison-industry goods were $1.2 billion, which would rank them within the top third of the Fortune 500 if they were included (Verdeyen, 1995:108). UNICOR alone has a large budget at its disposal, at $405 million (Wunder, 1994:10).

Besides contributing to the economy, prison labor fulfills other important functions. One major benefit to prisoners is that it reduces idleness, which has been a major cause of inmate unrest. Another benefit is that it enables inmates to acquire work skills they can use after they are released. Prison labor is also believed to have rehabilitative value, because it restores a prisoner's self-esteem and sense of pride (Grieser, 1989; U.S. General Accounting Office, 1985).

Inmates as Telephone Operators

Inmate labor is not restricted to state or federal prisons. At least seventy-four jail jurisdictions have industries run by inmates, resulting in less idleness, facilitation of management, job training, and significant cost reductions as major benefits (U.S. House of Representatives Committee on the Judiciary, 1994). For example, at the Montgomery County Jail in Dayton, Ohio, inmates answer all of the incoming telephone calls (Olin, 1995:68). This program involves minimal training, yet it provides offenders with an opportunity to learn about telephone courtesy and computer operations. There are built-in safeguards, however, so that prisoners cannot change any information in the main system (Olin, 1995:68). Inmates also are assigned tasks such as cleaning the grounds and taking care of the shrubbery and flowers. Thus, more than a few inmates are given the opportunity to acquire work responsibilities with a minimum of close supervision. Ultimately, this improves prisoners' chances of being rehabilitated. The savings to Montgomery County Jail between June 1993 and May 1995 was estimated at $955,968 (Olin, 1995:72). Similar results have been reported in other jurisdictions, such as the Jefferson County Jail in Texas (Altemose, 1996).

A study by Abt Associates for the National Institute of Justice shows how interested private industry is in participating in prison work programs

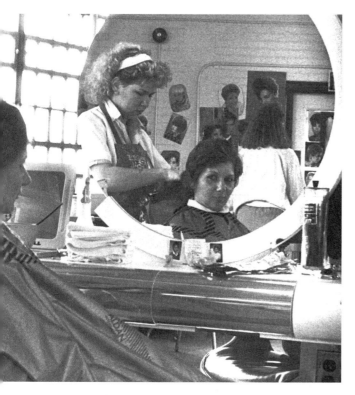 

Correctional educational and vocational training programs are many and varied. Male and female prisoners learn skills that may become careers.

(Mullen, 1986:2). "The aggressive participation of private industry in organizing institutions as places of work might go far toward achieving Chief Justice Burger's vision of prisons as 'factories with fences' instead of warehouses with walls." So far, little has been done to privatize prison labor (Mullen, 1982:2). Prisoners' labor unions will no doubt play a significant role if and when correctional institutions become privatized on a large scale.

Vocational Training and Educational Programs

Correctional education is largely an outgrowth of the prison reform movement (Berlew et al., 1994; Duguid, 1990). Prison reformers such as Zebulon Brockway (Elmira Reformatory) and Austin MacCormick (*The Education of Adult Prisoners,* 1931) helped develop educational reforms in many prisons and jails (Muth and Gehring, 1986).

Not everyone supports educational reforms in prisons, however. For example, 566 correctional practitioners were surveyed to determine how they felt about formal accreditation of inmate educational programs. While most practitioners believed that accreditation helped prepare inmates for emergencies and that the effectiveness of programs and operations had improved, 57 percent also believed that the programs had had little or no positive effect on the incidence of riots or other disturbances. In fact, 50 percent of the respondents believed that accreditation had been disruptive to prison routine and operations (Farkas and Fosen, 1983).

Some authorities say that vocational/educational programs can easily be financed with the prisoners' own money (Denham, 1996). At any given time, there are 200,000 prisoners serving multiyear sentences. About the same number are

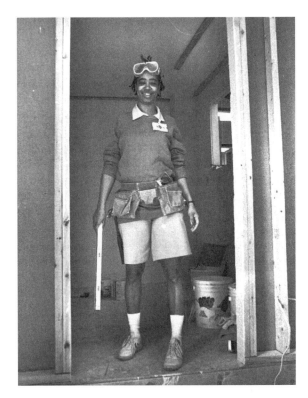

Training in metal working and the building trades may pay off when a prisoner reenters society.

serving short-term sentences. Most of these inmates have at least $500 in their prison accounts, from which they may draw modest sums for monthly purchases. The aggregate savings is estimated to be $200 million annually. Currently, those accounts draw no interest. However, interest from such accounts invested in a national education money management fund could yield as much as $20 million annually to defray the costs of educating inmates. Allowing inmates themselves to help determine program objectives and spending patterns, as well as advisory boards made up of education professionals and specialists, has been suggested.

Some experts believe that improving a prisoner's education can help him cope with the stress and strain associated with overcrowding (Lawrence, 1995). In fact, prisoner participation in educational programs has been associated with more positive feelings among inmates. Further-

more, these inmates report fewer headaches and stress (Lawrence, 1995).

Some prison programs help inmates acquire master's degrees and become involved in professional activities outside their prisons. A master's degree in sociology was established in 1984 at the SUNY College at New Palz for prisoners at the maximum-security men's prison in Napanoch, New York (Lanier, Philliber, and Philliber, 1994). Inmates became involved in conferences and publications and in developing prison programs. At one point, there were seventy-two students in four cohorts, and most earned degrees. Other prison educational programs resulted in improved self-esteem, and social competence among inmates (Parker, 1990). Generally, educational programs in both juvenile and adult prisons and jails have benefited a majority of the participants (Berlew et al., 1994; Correctional Educational Association, 1988).

Racism in U.S. Prisons

The U.S. prison system is considered by some as a "bastion of racism" (Frazier, 1995). The number of blacks and other people of color who are "warehoused" in prisons is alarming. Black persons are incarcerated ten times more often than whites. Prisoners who file lawsuits in U.S. district courts frequently allege racism. Black and other minority inmates report discriminatory or differential treatment in prisons and jails similar to what they experience outside of prison (Goetting, 1985).

Although race has figured prominently in assorted prison problems, more general issues of civil rights for all minorities have been the basis for inmate litigation (Frazier, 1995). Prison administrators are increasingly sensitive to civil rights issues. The Supreme Court has frequently ruled against prisoners' claims of discrimination, and it has stated more than once that "federal courts cannot undertake to review every official action taken against a prisoner which results in such prisoner being treated differently from any other prisoner" (*Beatham v. Manson*, 1973).

The Mississippi State Prison system has seen an inordinate amount of conflict (Taylor, 1993). A 1975 case involving a black inmate's allegations of discrimination is typical of lawsuits filed by inmates in recent years. In *Gates v. Collier* (1975), the Mississippi prison administration was found innocent of any unconstitutional discrimination. The Supreme Court declared that "evidence established that racial discrimination at the penitentiary had, for all practical purposes, been eliminated." With all due respect to the wisdom of the Supreme Court, Marquart's and Roebuck's (1986) experiences as prison guards lead one to doubt that racial discrimination in that Mississippi penitentiary, or in any other state prison for that matter, has been completely eliminated.

The significance of the *Gates* case lies not in the decision itself but rather in the "fortitude demonstrated in seeing the [Court] orders through" (Hopper, 1985). Court action occurred during a period when the public wanted more criminals to be incarcerated. As a result of this court action, Mississippi shifted its correctional practices toward the construction of larger "brick and mortar" prisons, thereby dispensing with its old system, which consisted of smaller, more informal, prison units.

Simply stating that some inmates receive more favorable treatment than others does not justify a claim of racial discrimination (*Fowler v. Graham,* 1979). In order for any court to interpret an administrative policy or action as discriminatory, clear and convincing proof must support these allegations. The 1967 President's Commission on Law Enforcement and Administration of Justice opened a Pandora's box of prisoner complaints when it mandated the establishment of inmate grievance systems in all state and federal prisons. Although some prisoners file multiple suits or nuisance suits, it is believed that most inmates do not abuse the system through repeated filings (Palmer, 1996).

Prisoners' Rights and Jailhouse Lawyers

The advancement of prisoners' rights through formal inmate grievance procedures has become an increasingly important correctional issue (Palmer, 1996). While inmates filed over thirty-five thousand lawsuits in federal courts in 1993, very few of those suits resulted in awards of monetary damages (*Corrections Today*, 1995:32).

Much prisoner litigation is directed at improving the prison environment and general prison conditions (Palmer, 1996). However, state prisoners are currently obligated to exhaust all state remedies before filing petitions in federal courts for relief. An Indiana case is relevant here. In *Owen v. Kimmel* (1982), a prisoner asserted a claim under Title 42 U.S.C., Sec. 1983 (1996) that prison officials unlawfully confiscated a piece of his furniture during a **shakedown.** *Shakedowns are intensive searches of inmate cells for the purpose of discovering weapons or contraband.* The district court remanded the case to the Indiana prison for disposition through the administrative grievance procedure.

As we have seen earlier, prisoners do not lose all their rights as the result of being incarcerated (Palmer, 1996). In fact, inmates must be granted access to a law library as a part of their right to petition the courts (*Ganey v. Edwards,* 1985). In an Illinois case, an inmate was segregated from other

A Native American sweat lodge has been constructed on the grounds of the North Dakota State Penitentiary in observance of inmate religious rituals.

inmates and had no direct access to a law library (*Walters v. Thompson*, 1985). He had to rely exclusively on inmate clerks who had little or no legal experience, formalized training, or supervision by attorneys, and he was restricted to three hundred pages of photocopied material per year. Furthermore, he was denied telephone access to outside legal counsel. The court ruled that his constitutional rights had been flagrantly violated.

States have the obligation to provide prisoners either with adequate law library facilities or with someone trained in the law (*Lewis v. Faulkner,* 1983). The Supreme Court has declared it to be unconstitutional if a prison law library fails to meet the minimum standards set by the American Bar Association and the American Association of Law Libraries (*Bouiles v. Ricketts,* 1981). In one case, a prisoner's access to the prison law library was so limited that a federal appellate court declared that his constitutional rights were violated (*Borning v. Cain,* 1985).

Computerization of Legal Materials and Law Libraries for Prisoners

In the mid 1990s, many prison systems were able to acquire rather extensive prison libraries and legal materials through CD-ROM disks. Today, portable technology and stand-alone computer systems can make a variety of legal materials available to inmates. Law books are continually being revised and updated, as are major sources of case materials, such as the *U.S. Code* and *Supreme Court Reporter.* Reporters (compilations of cases) from individual states as well as the federal government are now available on CD-ROM, and direct access to this information by inmates is increasingly easy.

In the past, prison law libraries were notorious for having to replace crucial pages torn from legal volumes by inconsiderate inmates. This replacement was costly. But with computer access to the same material, these types of problems can be avoided. Further, the space requirements for legal books are greatly diminished. For instance, it takes about forty-five feet of shelf space to house the Maryland Statutes (Vogel, 1996:100). Other state statutes require even more shelf space. Computerized access to these same legal materials assures that prisoners will always have the most recent updates of legal information. They may also access on-line services, such as legal libraries at major universities. The costs to various prisons are relatively low compared with the costs of maintaining legal materials in law libraries. Vogel (1996:101) notes that CD-ROM disks and computer data bases have the following advantages:

1. The law library is brought to the user (e.g., inmates in lockdown units).
2. One resource can be used by several inmates at a time.
3. There is no need to purchase duplicate copies of titles.
4. Less research time is needed.
5. They occupy less space—one CD-ROM disk may contain 200,000 or more pages, or a hundred volumes.
6. Easy-to-use, menu-driven software allows users to search according to a specific word, subject area, court jurisdiction, historical sequence, and current and previous court rulings.

7. Legal practice forms can be printed out through word processing software.

Inmate Responsibilities for Observing Prison Protocol

In *Skelton v. Pri-Cor, Inc.* (1991), prison authorities refused an inmate access to legal materials in the law library because he failed to fill out a request form. The inmate sued the prison, alleging that he should not have to fill out the request form and that his access to the courts was being denied. However, a federal appellate court held that the requirement to fill out a request form to use the law library did not violate the inmate's rights and that such a form was reasonably related to a legitimate penological interest in prison security. This lawsuit illustrates the petty nature of many lawsuits filed by inmates. The suit itself is a diversion from prison routine and monotony. The courts would consider such a suit as frivolous (Maahs and del Carmen, 1996).

Jailhouse Lawyers

Prisoners often become proficient at learning the law and understanding the constitutional rights to which they are entitled. These inmates are often called jailhouse lawyers. One of the most famous jailhouse lawyers was Caryl Chessman, author of *Cell 2455, Death Row.* Chessman was sentenced to death for committing a number of violent offenses in the hills of Hollywood, California in the 1950s. His legal expertise, acquired in prison while awaiting the gas chamber, won him one reprieve after another through appeals based upon legal technicalities. After many years, however, his appeals were exhausted, and he was executed.

One purpose of an inmate grievance procedure is to give inmates an outlet for their frustrations when they feel their rights have been infringed upon (Maahs and del Carmen, 1996). Such alternative dispute resolution diverts many prisoners from court litigation, because inmate councils can satisfactorily arbitrate many inmate grievances.

Inmates' grievances and the lawsuits inmates file influence the courts, politicians, and prison administrations in various ways. In New Mexico, for example, prisoner litigation brought about major changes in prison conditions, including the hiring of a new

warden (Thompson and Mays, 1991). Also, prisoner litigation in Alabama has stimulated numerous prison reforms in recent years (Yarborough, 1984). Even though *Gates v. Collier* (1975) did not prove charges of racial discrimination in Mississippi prisons, that state has made considerable improvements in its state prison system (Palmer, 1996).

Prison Violence

Between 1971 and 1983, 247 prison riots in U.S. prisons caused over $60 million in damages (Montgomery, 1984). These riots were attributable to overcrowding, poorly trained correctional officers, racism, poor food, escape attempts, power blackouts, drinking, rumors, gang warfare, inmates attacking staff, staff attacking inmates, arson, medical maltreatment, shakedowns, heat, demonstrations, and even a lack of boats to transport inmates' visitors (Montgomery, 1984). Racial tension was cited as a major cause of most of these incidents. Security problems have been blamed for other prison riots (Sachs et al., 1984).

An example of a major prison riot occured at the maximum-security federal prison in Marion, Illinois, in 1983. In October 1983, violence erupted at the Marion penitentiary, and two correctional officers were killed by prisoners in the Control Unit (Mauer, 1985). Ordinarily, this would be considered just another prison riot such as those occurring during the 1970s and 1980s in other prisons throughout the United States. However, this particular penitentiary was considered an ideal model of prison planning.

The penitentiary was constructed in 1963 and functioned as the maximum confinement facility—a maxi-maxi prison—for federal inmates who were considered incorrigible, vicious, and unmanageable. Later, it housed escape artists, gang leaders, and other hardened criminals. There were no newspapers, no entertainment visits from outside groups, and little or no vocational training. Six months' of hearings and a review by a panel of experts are required before inmates are confined there (Satchell, 1980). Currently Marion only receives inmates transferred from other institutions.

The Control Unit is a solitary confinement

area for nonconformist inmates. It holds sixty inmates, and prisoners must remain in their cell twenty-three hours a day. The remaining hour is for showering only, and this is a suspendable privilege if certain rules are violated. Prisoners must submit to frequent rectal searches for contraband and weapons (Ward and Breed, 1985). Such conditions create a great deal of tension and resentment among inmates.

As a result of the deaths of the two correctional officers, a **lockdown** was imposed. *Lockdowns are complete removals of prisoner privileges and permanent confinement in cells.* Among the factors responsible for the violence at Marion were the mental stresses of solitary confinement, antagonism between correctional officers and inmates, forced rectal searches, and the lack of graded confinement units that would function as behavioral incentives for inmates (Ward and Breed, 1985).

The most common form of prison violence is male rape (American Correctional Association, 1990; Dumond, 1992). Prison violence, whether it involves sexual assaults or assaults against corrections officers, is strongly associated with poor prison management and low inmate control (American Correctional Association, 1990; Austin et al., 1990; Braswell, Montgomery, and Lombardo, 1994; McCorkle, Miethe, and Drass, 1995).

Prison violence, particularly sexual violence and aggression, has been linked to racial differences and violent subcultures in the inmates' communities. Some studies of sexual violence in prisons find that the targets of sexual aggression are white while the sexual aggressors are black (American Correctional Association, 1990, Dumond, 1992). One explanation that has been suggested is that blacks hate whites and seek to victimize them whenever possible (Braswell, Montgomery, and Lombardo, 1994; McCorkle, Miethe, and Drass, 1995). However, there is little evidence for this view. Another theory is that much prison violence is caused by those who were a part of violent subcultures in their communities. Thus, their prison violence is merely a continuation of how they learned to cope with violence from others in their community (McCorkle, Miethe, and Drass, 1995).

A New Mexico State Penitentiary cellblock in the aftermath of thirty-six hours of rioting in 1980.

The Death Penalty

The controversy over capital punishment, as well as its pro's and con's, has already been discussed in chapter 10. From the standpoint of correctional management and inmate control, imposing the death penalty is particularly cumbersome. The strange paradox is that while the number of inmates on death row increases annually, so does reluctance to execute them (Keve, 1992). The

Highlight 12.2. Viewing Executions: The Children of Victims Watch the Execution of Steven Keith Hatch

In 1979, Steven Hatch and a friend, Glen Burton Ake, posed as lost motorists and entered the home of Richard and Marilyn Douglass in McAlester, Oklahoma. At gunpoint, they hog-tied Richard, a minister, and his wife as well as their children, Brooks Douglass and his sister, Leslie Frizzell. After making the Douglasses reveal where they kept their cash, credit cards, and jewelry, the intruders shot the couple to death. Both Hatch and Ake attempted to rape Frizzell, who was twelve at the time. They then shot Brooks and Leslie in the back and left them for dead. The children survived and were able to identify their parents' murderers, who were apprehended.

In 1996, Hatch, forty-two, was executed by lethal injection. At his execution were Brooks Douglass, now a state senator, and his sister, Leslie Frizzell. They were accompanied by their three uncles. Senator Douglass, a death penalty proponent, said at the execution, "Leslie and I have again witnessed the taking of a life. The first time we did, we were young people who were present when our mother and father were viciously killed. It is the end of a very long ordeal that has dominated our lives."

Showing absolutely no remorse, Hatch issued a statement proclaiming, "Be stronger than those who sit in judgment and prey upon you, for they are weak with lies and deception. They're evil and barbaric and politicians." Both Douglass and his sister were unmoved by Hatch's last words. Hatch's accomplice, Ake, had earlier won a new trial and received consecutive life sentences for the crimes.

Should executions be publicized and televised? Would such an event deter potential murderers? What satisfaction would victims and/or their families and friends derive from being present at the execution of the person who murdered their loved ones?

Source: Adapted from Associated Press, "Children of Victims Watch Execution," *Minot (N.D.) Daily News,* August 10, 1996, p.A11.

Supreme Court reviews capital cases automatically (Nagel, 1990). Further, insistence on using newly discovered evidence to prove a defendant's innocence creates emotionally charged scenarios that disturb prosecutors and the government generally, because the government is often reluctant to admit that it might have convicted an innocent defendant of a capital crime (U.S. Senate Committee on the Judiciary, 1994).

One controversial issue relating to the death penalty is whether victims of the condemned offender should be permitted to watch the execution. Further, some experts believe that opening executions to the public would deter potential murderers. However, there is no strong evidence that would support such a view (Stack, 1994; Stack and Goetting, 1995). Some studies have shown *increases* in homicides during periods when executions were highly publicized (Stack, 1994). This is known as the *brutalization effect—executions legitimize lethal vengeance because they devalue human life and demonstrate that it is appropriate to kill those who have gravely offended* (Cochran, Chamlin, and Seth, 1994). Generally, research shows that executions have little or no effect on the murder rate. Thus, the death penalty neither deters nor promotes murders. But then, deterrence is only one argument in favor of capital punishment. For those who support the death penalty, retribution and justice are more compelling arguments (Costanzo and White, 1994; Simmons et al., 1995).

Enter Buddha and Hollywood

On August 8, 1996, Si Fu William Frank Parker was executed by lethal injection for killing his ex-wife's parents in 1984 because he believed that they had broken up his marriage (Associated Press, 1996:A11). During his stay on death row, Parker converted to Buddhism and wrote to various Hollywood personalities in hopes that they could help him avoid execution. At the last minute, movie star Richard Gere attempted to intervene on his behalf. The Arkansas Department of Corrections refused Gere permission to see Parker, claiming that it didn't have sufficient time to do a background check on Gere. Also, Parker's mother, Janie Parker, was prevented from seeing her son in his last hours. She was stopped on her way into the prison carrying several cans of beer and a pistol in her purse. "I forgot I had it in my damn purse," she told reporters. "You never know when [your car] might break down and someone try to kill you!"

While a majority of the public seems in favor of the death penalty, it is unclear whether the public wants to be able to view executions. Some experts say that if the public knew how traumatic executions are, most would not want to view them. Knowing about executions and how they are conducted might cause some persons who are in favor of the death penalty to oppose it (Bohm and Vogel, 1994).

Death Penalty Appeals

The process of appealing death sentences is slow. There is often a delay of ten or more years before a death sentence is actually carried out (Acker and Lanier, 1995). This is partly because *all* death sentences are *automatically appealed* whether or not the convicted offender wishes it. Usually, however, defendants and their attorneys try to have death sentences overturned or set aside in favor of a less severe sentence, such as life without parole. The long-term thinking of offenders sentenced to death is that changing their sentence to life without parole *may* eventually lead to simply a *life* sentence. *A life sentence does not guarantee that an offender will be incarcerated for the rest of his or her life.* Often, a life sentence results in incarceration for a fixed period of years, such as seven, before parole is granted. On the other hand, parole may never be granted, but at least a life sentence makes it possible.

The snail's pace of the appeals process has angered many lawmakers and the public. In John Wayne Gacy's case, for instance, there was a fifteen-year delay between conviction, the death sentence,

and Gacy's actual execution. Even up to the last minute of his life, John Gacy believed that his death sentence would somehow be overturned and that he would be spared by some court.

In June 1996, the Supreme Court voted unanimously to support congressional action to speed up the execution process by limiting the number of appeals condemned prisoners can file. Some inmates have filed hundreds of appeals in a year. These jailhouse lawyers, or "frequent filers," are the target of tightened restrictions on state prisoners who seek relief from federal district courts.

Summary

Prison culture is diverse. It is unique because it is a population made up entirely of criminals. This environment creates many problems for prison administrators. Prison subcultures and informal inmate codes dominate internal prison affairs.

An important influence on prison/jail operations is the quality of prison/jail staff. Different jurisdictions offer different training and preparation for correctional work. Jail staff are less adequately trained than prison staff. Currently, recruitment practices often result in employees who lack the skills to deal with prisoners. One factor contributing to high turnover among jail and prison personnel is burnout or stress. However, more selective recruitment will probably result in employees who are better able to cope with the demands of correctional work. While women have been underrepresented in corrections work, in recent years their numbers have increased.

One option in prison and jail management is the privatization of prison operations. Private enterprise promises more cost-effective prison operations. However, some government officials and concerned citizens fear that private ownership and operation of prisons may violate prisoners' rights and create conflicts of interest. Contemporary issues in corrections include overcrowding, the exploitation of prison labor by private industry, racism, the inadequacy of prison vocational/technical and/or educational programs, and prisoner rights. Efforts are underway to remedy these problems. Increasing numbers of prisoners are learning about their constitutional rights and are filing record numbers of lawsuits in state and federal courts.

Key Terms

Double-bunking
Hawes-Cooper Act of 1929
Inmate code
Jailhouse lawyers
Lockdown
Prison culture
Privatization of prison management
Shakedown
UNICOR

Questions for Review

1. Are the problems created by jail overcrowding identical to those created by prison over-crowding? Why or why not?
2. How are prison environments similar to "out-side" environments? In what ways are they different?
3. What are some of the grounds on which prisoners file lawsuits against jail and prison administrators?
4. What evidence suggests the existence of a "prison culture"?
5. How do selection and recruitment methods employed by state agencies affect prisoner-staff relationships?
6. What are some general characteristics of corrections personnel?
7. What reasons do corrections personnel cite for job burnout and stress leading to labor turnover?
8. What proportion of the correctional staff in prisons and jails in the United States consists of

women? What appear to be the prospects for women in corrections work? What are some obstacles to women's employment as corrections officers?
9. What is meant by the "privatization of prison management"? Discuss briefly the pros and cons of the privatization of prison management.
10. Identify and discuss briefly four different kinds of prison management models. Which one is most popular today from the material you have read?

Suggested Readings

American Correctional Association. 1993. *Standards for Administration of Correctional Agencies.* Laurel, MD: American Correctional Association.

Collins, William C. 1993. *Correctional Law for the Correctional Officer.* Laurel, MD: American Correctional Association.

Coyne, Randall and Lyn Entzeroth. 1994. *Capital Punishment and the Judicial Process: Cases and Materials.* Durham, NC: Carolina Academic Press.

del Carmen, Rolando V., Susan E. Ritter, and Betsy A. Witt. 1993. *Briefs of Leading Cases in Corrections.* Cincinnati, OH: Anderson.

DiIulio, John J. Jr. 1990. *Courts, Corrections, and the Constitution.* New York: Oxford University Press.

Hartjen, Clayton A. and Edward E. Rhine (eds.). 1992. *Correctional Theory and Practice.* Chicago: Nelson-Hall.

Selke, William L. 1993. *Prisons in Crisis.* Bloomington: Indiana University Press.

Taylor, William Banks. 1996. *Brokered Justice: Race, Politics, and Mississippi Prisons, 1798–1992.* Columbus: Ohio State University Press.

CHAPTER 13

Probation, Parole, and Intermediate Punishments

James J. Brown, #155413, South Carolina State Park Correctional Center, serving a six-year sentence. Age at time of arrest: fifty-five. Charges: Possession of PCP, carrying concealed firearm; resisting arrest; eluding police; menacing. Background: Rock 'n' roll singer. Hit songs: "I Feel Good," "Poppa's Got a Brand New Bag." Parole eligibility date: 1992 (Stanley, 1989).

Lt. Col. Oliver North. Charges: Perjury in Iran-Contra affair. Two-year suspended sentence; probation; fined $150,000; 1,200 hours of community service (Sachs, 1989).

Rob Lowe, actor. Charges: Sexual exploitation of underage girl. Diverted to twenty hours of community service. No conviction (Sachs, 1989).

Linda Siefer, Ottawa, Ohio. Charges: Stealing $411,000 from Catholic Church collection plates. Convicted and sentenced to one and one-half years; six-month parole to follow jail term (Associated Press, 1996).

Mitzi Jean Horton, Roanoke, Virginia. Age: thirty-one. Charges: Locking her employer in her car trunk for two days. Convicted of abduction and robbery. Sentenced to twelve years. Eligible for parole after two years (Associated Press, 1996).

Each of the scenarios describes situations involving probation, parole, parole eligibility, or diversion from the criminal justice system. The crimes vary in seriousness, as do the punishments. This chapter is about probation and parole and the supervision of clients sentenced to these programs.

According to the U.S. Department of Justice, in January 1993, 2,843,445 adults were under some form of probation supervision in the United States, an increase of 1 percent over the previous year (Maguire and Pastore, 1995:524–25). By 1995, the number of probationers was 2,282,168, according to the Criminal Justice Institute (Camp and Camp, 1995d:18–19). The drop in number between 1993 and 1995 does not mean that the use of probation is declining. Rather, there are different reporting sources for this information, and the sources do not always survey the same number of agencies from all jurisdictions. In fact, the use of probation is continually growing.

According to the Criminal Justice Institute, 664,404 persons comprised the parolee population in 1995 (Camp and Camp, 1995d:48). This was an increase of about 6 percent over 1994. Again, it should be noted that these figures are less than those arrived at by Bureau of Justice Statistics.

As more offenders are diverted from incarceration through alternative sentencing practices, as court-ordered prison population reductions occur, and as prisoners are released through parole, the pressure on already overworked probation and parole workers increases (Champion, 1996). Because many of the agencies that monitor parolees also supervise probationers, and because these agencies share several common problems, both probation and parole will be examined in this chapter (American Correctional Association, 1986).

Several key functions of probation and parole programs will be identified. Current methods of recruiting and retaining probation and parole officers will be described. Some of the more popular monitoring methods will be examined, including halfway houses and electronic devices. Finally, recidivism will be discussed as a method of evaluating the effectiveness of probation and parole programs.

Probation and Parole Distinguished

Probation *is serving a portion or all of a sentence imposed in lieu of incarceration;* **parole** *refers to serving some of an imposed prison sentence outside of prison under the supervision of designated officials.*

Probation is a sentence that does not involve confinement. The sentencing court retains the authority to modify the conditions of probation or to resentence the offender if the offender violates the conditions. Probation should not involve or require suspension of any other sentence (Allen, Eskridge, Latessa, and Vito, 1985:36).

Probation and parole are also differentiated by the authorities who oversee probationers and parolees. In the case of probation, judges impose the conditional release when they sentence offenders.

In contrast, parole is controlled by a **parole board.** *Parole boards are usually governor-appointed bodies that evaluate those parole-eligible inmates and decide whether to grant parole.* A paroled offender is conditionally released from a confinement facility before his or her sentence has expired and placed under the supervision of a parole agency (Allen, Eskridge, Latessa, and Vito, 1985:293).

On January 1, 1995, of all convicted offenders under some form of supervision, probationers accounted for 59 percent, prisoners accounted for 27 percent, and parolees accounted for 14 percent (Camp and Camp, 1995d:4). Nearly three-fourths of all convicted offenders are under some form of supervision, either as probationers or parolees. These persons are often supervised by officers designated as either **probation officers** or **parole officers,** or "POs."

The History of Probation and Parole in the United States

Probation

Probation in the United States began largely through the efforts of **John Augustus** of Boston, Massachusetts (Allen, Eskridge, Latessa, and Vito, 1985:40). Much like a bailbondsman, Augustus acted as a guarantor or surety for various offenders. Acting on his own, Augustus would appear in court and offer to supervise alleged offenders until their cases were heard. Usually, judges hearing the case would be so impressed with the offenders' "improvement" that they would impose only nominal fines rather than prison terms. Between 1841, when he started this practice, and his death in 1859, Augustus obtained probation for 1,956 men and women (Allen, Eskridge, Latessa, and Vito, 1985:40).

For the most part, Augustus assisted *first-offenders, those who had never been convicted of criminal offenses.* Augustus conducted something like a presentence investigation by researching the offender's background and determining the "previous character of the person, his age, and influences by which he would be surrounded" (Allen, Eskridge, Latessa, and Vito, 1985:41).

In 1901, New York State enacted a statutory probation provision whereby offenders could be closely supervised by responsible officials. James Bronson Reynolds, an early prison reformer, founded the University Settlement, a private probationary facility designed to alleviate some of the harshness and inequities inherent in severe penal sanctions (Lindner and Savarese, 1984). However, the settlement lacked a clearly defined purpose, specific goals, or particular implementation methods, and thus it lost a considerable amount of credibility with the public (Lindner and Savarese, 1984).

Parole

The origins of parole in the United States are disputed. It *is* generally agreed that parole, or at least an early version of it, existed in eighteenth-century Spain, France, England, and Wales (Bottomley, 1984; Hughes, 1987). The number of British convicts sentenced to death or convicted of serious offenses created prison overcrowding. In the eighteenth-century, Britain had no penitentiaries (Hughes, 1987; Evans, 1982), and so excess prisoners were exported to the American colonies. After the Revolutionary War, this option no longer existed.

Seeking new places to send its criminals, England chose Australia, one of several remote English colonies to which small numbers of offenders had already been sent (Fogel, 1979:4–5). English convicts were exported to Australia on a large scale beginning in 1788 (Hughes, 1987). The English government intended that these transportees, many of whom had been convicted of minor theft, become builders and farmers. However, they were highly unsuccessful at these trades (Hughes, 1987). It became apparent that officials needed prisons to house some of their prisoner-transportees. One such outpost was established 1,000 miles off the coast of Australia on Norfolk Island. Another was built on Van Diemen's Land.

Alexander Maconochie

In 1836, the private secretary to the lieutenant governor of Van Diemen's Land was a former officer of the Royal Navy and a social reformer, **Alexander Maconochie** (1787–1860). In 1840, Maconochie was appointed superintendent of the penal colony at Norfolk Island. When he arrived to assume his new duties, he was appalled by what he found. Prisoners were lashed repeatedly and tortured frequently by other means.

Maconochie's penchant for humanitarianism and his leniency toward prisoners made him unpopular with both his superiors and other penal officials. For instance, Maconochie believed that confinement ought to be *rehabilitative,* not *punitive*. Also, he felt that prisoners ought to be granted *early release from custody* if they behaved well and did good work while confined. Thus, he gave prisoners *marks of commendation* and authorized early release of some inmates who demonstrated a willingness and ability to behave well. This indeterminate sentencing was subsequently adopted in the United States. Maconochie's downfall at Norfolk Island occurred largely because of a report he filed condemning the English penal system generally and disciplinary measures used by the island penal colony specifically. In 1844, he was relieved of his duties and sent back to England.

During the next five years, Maconochie was transferred from one desk job to another, although he continued to press for penal reforms. Eventually he was reassigned, probably as a probationary move by his superiors, to the governorship of the new Birmingham Borough Prison. His position there lasted less than two years. His superiors dismissed him for being too lenient with prisoners.

Maconochie's efforts at prison reform did not end with this dismissal. In 1853, he successfully lobbied for the passage of the *English Penal Servitude Act,* which established several rehabilitative programs for inmates and abolished the practice of transporting prisoners to Australia. Because of these significant improvements in British penal policy and the institutionalization of early-release provisions, Maconochie is called the father of parole.

Tickets of Leave

Impressed with Maconochie's work, Sir Walter Crofton, a prison reformer and director of Ireland's prison system during the 1850s, copied Maconochie's three-stage intermediate system and thereby enabled Irish prisoners to earn early conditional release. Crofton, also known as the father of parole in various European countries, modified Maconochie's plan. Under Crofton's system, prisoners were: (1) strictly imprisoned for a time; (2) transferred to an "intermediate" prison for a short period, where they could participate in educational programs and perform useful and responsible tasks to earn good marks; and (3) given tickets of leave that authorized their release from prison under the limited supervision of local police.

Released prisoners were required to submit monthly reports of their progress to police, who helped them find work. A study of 557 prisoners during that period showed that only 17 had their tickets of leave revoked for various infractions (Clear and Cole, 1986:372). Thus, Walter Crofton pioneered what later came to be several major functions of parole officers: to help released prisoners find jobs, to visit parolees regularly, and to supervise parolees' activities (Cole, 1986:595).

The United States Connection

The United States connection with the European use of parole allegedly occurred in 1863, when Gaylord Hubbell, the warden at New York's Sing Sing Prison, visited Ireland and conferred with Crofton about his penal innovations and parole system (Clear and Cole, 1986:372). When the National Prison Association convened in Cincinnati, Ohio, in 1870, an important part of its agenda was a discussion of the Irish parole system. Attending that meeting were Crofton, Hubbell, and other reformers and penologists. The meeting resulted in the Declaration of Principles, which promoted an "indeterminate sentence" and a classification system based largely on Crofton's work (Clear and Cole, 1986:372–73).

Parole Means Trust

Parole involves a degree of trust. The government says to an incarcerated offender, "You have behaved well in prison, and if you comply with certain conditions and regulations, we will release you from incarceration into the community under supervision." The expectation is that the parolee will abide by the terms of early release until the full sentence has been served.

Early release is a type of sentence **commutation**. *Commutation of a sentence means to change or reduce its severity.* Those who have been sentenced to death may have their death sentences commuted to life imprisonment. In the case of inmates, commutation may be parole.

Zebulon Brockway

Zebulon Brockway became superintendent of the New York State Reformatory at Elmira in 1876. He was instrumental in passing the first indeterminate sentencing law in the United States (Smykla, 1981:139–40). He is also credited with introducing the first good-time system, in which an inmate's sentence is reduced by the number of good marks earned. When this system was shown to be moderately effective, several other states patterned their own early-release standards after it.

"Good-Time" Credit

Early release occurred much earlier than good-time release, or parole, although authorities dispute its true origin. Dressler (1969) claims parole was officially established in Boston by Samuel G. Howe in 1847. From 1790 to 1817, convicts were obligated to serve their entire sentences in prison.

In 1817, New York adopted a form of commutation that became known as "good time." By accumulating enough good time, an inmate could earn early release (Davis, 1990a). This good-time early release was essentially *an executive decision to release inmates before they served their full sentences in order to alleviate overcrowding.* The unofficial practice of parole, therefore, preceded the unofficial practice of probation by several decades. Officially, however, true parole resulted from the ticket-of-leave practice and was first adopted by Massachusetts in 1884. In 1878, Massachusetts also became the first state to implement probation (Shane-DuBow, Brown, Olsen, 1985:4–5). Today, most states have parole programs, although in many jurisdictions, the sentencing schemes have been modified in favor of guidelines-based or presumptive sentencing. Thus, parole is less of an option today than it was in the 1980s or early 1990s.

Some Functions of Probation and Parole

The primary functions of probation and parole are (1) to reduce and control crime; (2) to rehabilitate and reintegrate offenders; (3) to reduce prison populations; and (4) to punish and deter offenders.

Crime Reduction and Control

Crime reduction and control as probation/parole functions stem directly from probationers' and parolees' close supervision by their POs (Klofas and Stojkovic, 1995). Jurisdictions with large numbers of probationers have difficulty supervising these offenders closely because there simply aren't enough POs (Mauer and Huling, 1995). In many cases, probationers/parolees mail in a form to the probation office weekly or monthly. This form is usually a checklist on which the offenders report any law infractions, their most recent employment record, and other information. They may also pay pre-established fees to defray a portion of their probation costs and maintenance (Parent, 1989a). Because this information is self-reported, much of it is subjective. It is difficult if not impossible to verify the truth of the statements without some alternative supervisory scheme (Petersilia, 1994). Most of the time, probation agencies simply do not have the resources to check this self-reported information. Often offenders are brought to the attention of POs only if they are rearrested within the jurisdiction supervising them.

Standard probation/parole offers little by way of true crime control, since there is minimal contact between offenders and their POs. However, it is believed that even standard probation/parole offers some measure of crime control by extending to probationers/parolees a degree of trust as well as minimal behavioral restrictions (Byrne and Brewster, 1993; Clear, 1993). It would be a mistake to believe that no monitoring occurs under standard probation/parole supervision. POs are obligated to make periodic checks of offenders' workplaces, and conversations with employers disclose much about how offenders are managing their time.

However, because of limited probation/parole department resources, these checks are fairly superficial activity (Merlo and Benekos, 1992).

Offender Rehabilitation and Reintegration

One obvious benefit for probationers and parolees is that they avoid the criminogenic environment of incarceration (Mauer and Huling, 1995). Offenders on probation/parole usually maintain jobs, live with and support their families, engage in vocational/technical training or other educational programs, receive counseling, and lead otherwise normal lives (Lovell, 1985). While minimum-security prisons and some jails do afford prisoners opportunities to learn skills and to participate in programs designed to rehabilitate them, the therapeutic value of these programs is nothing like that of remaining free.

The effectiveness of probation/parole under intensive supervision is illustrated by a New Jersey experiment. As participants in the New Jersey Intensive Supervision Program, officials accepted 226 convicted felons from 18,000 applicants (Pearson, 1985). During a fourteen-month period (1983–1984), offenders maintained regular contact with POs either by telephone or in person. Only 29 out of the 226 clients were returned to prison, and only one of these was incarcerated for a new felony conviction. Similar patterns have been observed in other communities (American Correctional Association, 1993b; Champion, 1988c; Petersilia, 1987a; Petersilia et al., 1985; Petersilia, Turner, and Peterson, 1986).

It is difficult to make the transformation from prison life to community life, especially for inmates who have been incarcerated for several years. Prison life is highly regulated and bears no resemblance to life on the outside. The community reintegration function of probation/parole is most closely associated with its rehabilitative aim (Dickey and Wagner, 1990; Ellsworth, 1990a, 1990b, 1990c).

Some offenders reintegrate more easily into their communities than others. For instance, sex offenders often find that communities into which they

---

Highlight 13.1. When Should Inmates Be Paroled? The Case of Robert Chambers

The media dubbed it the "Preppy Murder Case." In 1988, Robert Chambers, a young man with a promising future, choked Jennifer Levin to death, allegedly during "rough sex." Chambers's past was not entirely clean. He admitted to cocaine addiction, was a suspect in several apartment burglaries and credit card thefts, and was under indictment for burglary. When Chambers was tried for Levin's murder, the jury deliberated too long, according to the prosecutor, who then offered a plea bargain: Admit to manslaughter and burglary and be sentenced to 5 to 15 years. Chambers accepted the plea bargain and after five years of confinement became eligible for parole in 1994. Although he was a model prisoner, the parole board rejected his release. In the future, Chambers will regularly appear before the parole board to be reconsidered for release.

What standards should be used to determine whether inmates who have committed violent crimes should be paroled? Should the parole system be abolished? If you were a parole board member, how would you decide whether Chambers was eligible for parole?

Source: Adapted from Alice Vachss, "How to Keep Dangerous Criminals Behind Bars," *Parade*, September 25, 1994, p. 4–5.

---

have been released have been advised by the authorities of their presence. Further, many sex offenders must undergo continuing psychiatric treatment while on parole. These negative labels that sex offenders acquire significantly hinder their community reintegration, even though many are fully rehabilitated before their release (Walsh, 1990).

The Reduction of Prison Populations

One purpose of probation and parole is to reduce prison and jail populations. However, each year between 1925 and 1993, both prison and jail populations increased annually (Maguire and Pastore, 1995:533, 540). The number of probationers and parolees has also increased (Maguire and Pastore, 1995; Petersilia et al., 1985:2). As described in earlier chapters, prison and jail construction costs have escalated to the point that programs in lieu of incarceration are gradually gaining acceptance (Pennsylvania Economic League, 1993).

Selected programs aimed at reducing prison overcrowding include Florida's Community Con-

trol Program. This program was implemented in 1983 as the result of the Correctional Reform Act of that year (Florida Probation and Parole Services, 1984). One of the major goals of the Community Control Program was to "help reduce prison overcrowding." But between 1984 and 1985, Florida's prison population increased by 6 percent. Of course, it might be that if such a program had not been in place by 1983, by the end of 1985, the population of Florida's prisons would have been considerably higher. Only 93 of the first 1,886 prison and jail probationers had had their probation revoked by the end of 1984. By 1995, Florida prisons were slightly under full capacity at 99.2 percent (Camp and Camp, 1995a:36).

Many judges favor probation over incarceration, as long as probationers have adequate supervision. A study of 254 Texas district court judges, for instance, found that most judges would be more likely to use probation and diversion in lieu of sentences of jail terms if offenders have adequate supervision and basic probation services (Fields, Field, and Williams, 1983). However, paroling large numbers of convicted felons might create a "revolving door" effect. Successive cohorts of Texas parolees were investigated in 1984, 1985,

1986, and 1987. It was discovered that while paroling inmates did lessen prison overcrowding, many of the offenders recidivated fairly soon after their release. Thus, overcrowding became a problem once again (Joo, 1993).

Under determinate and mandatory sentencing, parole boards do not determine a prisoner's early release. Critics of parole boards cite high rates of recidivism among parolees, although there is little evidence that a parole board's decisions are any worse than a judge's on who should be placed on probation and who should be incarcerated. No sentencing system is more or less fair, predictable, or confusing than parole (Florida Senate Committee on Corrections, Probation and Parole, 1993). Some authorities advocate the preservation of parole board authority to commute sentences while also advocating the establishment of consistent and fair parole guidelines (Simon, 1993).

Punishment and Deterrence

Both the courts and parole boards define probation and parole as a *continuation of punishment,* although it may appear to community residents that probationers and parolees have unlimited freedom to go where they please. However, *all probationers and parolees participate in programs and must follow program requirements.* These requirements are not always apparent to the community.

First, POs can recommend that an offender's program be revoked if the offender violates any of the program's conditions. For instance, filing a late monthly report is a technical violation. Being absent from work without a legitimate excuse might also violate probation/parole requirements. Other punishments might not involve direct or frequent contact with POs. For example, judges may order convicted offenders to make **restitution** to victims to pay for damages and medical bills sustained through whatever crime was committed. **Community service** may be required (such as was the case with actor Rob Lowe and Lt. Col. Oliver North), and supervisors may be asked to report on the quality of the offender's work. And, of course, offenders may be fined. A portion of an offender's wages may be garnished by the court as payment for fines

or victim compensation. Obviously, offenders must maintain regular employment in order to pay these court-imposed fines. While these are certainly punishments, they may not be necessarily severe or cause undue hardships for offenders.

The deterrent value of probation/parole is usually measured by offenders' rates of recidivism. Recidivism rates of offenders on standard probation, which often offers little or no supervision, are frequently higher than those of offenders who are more intensively supervised. Even more disturbing is the fact that over the years there has been a substantial rise in the use of felony probation. Thus, PO caseloads now involve more dangerous offenders who are more likely to reoffend (Johnson and Jones, 1994).

Experts disagree about the deterrent effect of probation. Almost all studies of probation and its effects cite some program failures. This causes skeptics to take a dim view of probation and even to consider it unworkable as a rehabilitative strategy (Martinson, 1974). However, others have pointed to "probation as the one correctional treatment program that seems to work" (Walker, 1989b). Probationers' *recidivism rates* are consistently lower than those of jailed offenders. Therefore, one important factor to consider is the cost effectiveness of different correctional options as measured by the amount of new crime. Alternative community programs that emphasize restorative justice and restitution to victims seem more effective than those involving minimal client supervision (Bazemore and Maloney, 1994). A balanced approach is encouraged, which emphasizes community safety, offender accountability through community service, offender rehabilitation, and victim compensation. Further, more intensive supervision of probationers and parolees encourages greater program compliance and less recidivism (Fulton, Stone, and Gendreau, 1994).

Generally, probation programs are less costly than incarceration. Offenders on probation also exhibit less recidivism than convicts released from prisons. Viewed from this perspective, probation functions as a deterrent. However, some critics say that if probation and parole were done away with today, the crime rate in the United States would

Table 13.1

Types of Felony Sentences Imposed by State Courts, by Offense, 1992

Most Serious Conviction Offense	Total	Percent of Felons Sentenced to Incarceration			
		Total	Prison	Jail	Probation
All offenses	100%	70%	44%	26%	30%
Violent offenses	100%	81%	60%	21%	19%
Murder[a]	100	97	93	4	3
Rape	100	87	68	19	13
Robbery	100	88	74	14	12
Aggravated assault	100	72	44	28	28
Other[b]	100	68	39	29	32
Property offenses	100%	66%	42%	24%	34%
Burglary	100	75	52	23	25
Larceny[c]	100	65	38	27	35
Fraud[d]	100	52	31	21	48
Drug offenses	100%	70%	42%	28%	30%
Possession	100	62	33	29	38
Trafficking	100	75	48	27	25
Weapons offenses	100%	66%	40%	26%	34%
Other offenses[e]	100%	65%	35%	30%	35%

Source: Langan and Graziadei (1995).

Note: For persons receiving a combination of sentences, the sentence designation came from the most severe penalty imposed—prison being the most severe, followed by jail, then probation. Prison includes death sentences. Data on sentence type were available for 886,359 cases.

a. Includes nonnegligent manslaughter.

b. Includes offenses such as negligent manslaughter, sexual assault, and kidnaping.

c. Includes motor vehicle theft.

d. Includes forgery and embezzlement.

e. Composed of nonviolent offenses such as receiving stolen property and vandalism.

probably go up by only about 2 percent. This 2 percent would consist of probation and parole administrators and line staff who turned to crime only because they could find no other suitable employment (Callanan, 1987:16). This remark underscores the current lack of consensus about how probation functions in relation to courts and criminal defendants.

A Profile of Probationers and Parolees

What are the criminal histories of probationers and parolees? Are these offenders dangerous? What types of crimes have they committed? What are their conviction offenses? Is it reasonable for the government

to loose upon the public thousands of convicted felons annually, with minimal supervision?

The profile of probationers and parolees is changing annually. Each year, the probation population includes increasing numbers of felony offenders (Gottfredson and Gottfredson, 1988), and the seriousness of their offenses is intensifying. Tables 13.1 and 13.2 show the conviction-offense profiles of probationers and parolees for 1992.

Table 13.1 shows the percentage breakdown of the types of felony sentences imposed on 886,359 persons in state courts in 1992. It can be seen that probation was used, on the average, about 30 percent of the time. About 19 percent of those convicted of *violent offenses* were placed on probation. About 34 percent of those convicted of *property offenses* were placed on probation. About 30 percent of all convicted drug offenders received

Table 13.2

Entries to Parole Supervision from Prisons in Thirty-Six States by Offense, Sex, Race, and Hispanic Origin, United States, 1992[a]

Most Serious Offense	All Entries	Sex		Race[b]			Hispanic
		Male	Female	White	Black	Other[c]	
Number of parole entries	176,564	160,602	15,864	72,111	86,717	1,674	29,350
All offenses	100%	100%	100%	100%	100%	100%	100%
Violent offenses	25.2	26.2	14.7	23.6	26.7	32.1	22.7
Homicide	2.7	2.6	3.4	2.7	2.7	4.4	2.3
Murder and nonnegligent			*				
manslaughter	1.7	1.6	1.9	1.5	1.8	2.3	1.5
Murder	1.1	1.1	1.2	1.0	1.2	1.7	0.7
Nonnegligent manslaughter	0.6	0.5	0.7	0.4	0.6	0.7	0.8
Negligent manslaughter	1.0	1.0	1.5	1.3	0.9	2.0	0.7
Unspecified homicide	0.0	0.0	0.0	0.0	0.0	0.0	(e)
Kidnaping	0.4	0.4	0.2	0.5	0.3	1.0	0.3
Rape	1.7	1.8	0.2	2.1	1.4	2.3	1.4
Other sexual assault	2.5	2.7	0.3	4.1	1.3	3.2	2.1
Robbery	10.7	11.2	5.6	7.0	13.7	7.9	10.1
Assault	6.6	6.8	4.3	6.4	6.8	11.6	6.0
Other violent	0.6	0.6	0.8	0.8	0.5	1.7	0.5
Property offenses	32.7	32.4	36.3	38.2	29.6	36.4	23.8
Burglary	14.8	15.7	5.8	17.9	12.4	17.9	13.2
Larceny-theft	8.4	7.7	15.6	9.1	8.6	8.4	4.8
Motor vehicle theft	2.7	2.9	1.0	3.1	2.4	3.6	3.0
Arson	0.6	0.6	0.8	0.9	0.4	0.3	0.3
Fraud	3.9	3.1	12.0	5.0	3.5	3.2	1.1
Stolen property	1.6	1.6	0.9	1.3	1.7	1.6	1.1
Other property	0.7	0.7	0.3	0.8	0.6	1.4	0.3
Drug offenses	31.1	30.1	41.3	23.3	35.4	15.0	43.4
Possession	8.2	7.8	11.3	4.9	10.4	3.5	7.0
Trafficking	19.3	18.8	23.7	14.3	21.3	8.5	30.8
Other drug	3.7	3.4	6.3	4.1	3.7	3.0	5.6
Public-order offenses	9.8	10.1	6.2	13.2	7.4	15.2	8.4
Weapons	2.2	2.4	0.6	1.5	2.6	1.8	2.5
Driving while intoxicated	3.7	3.9	1.3	7.0	1.2	8.4	5.0
Other public-order	3.9	3.8	4.2	4.7	3.6	5.0	1.0
Other offenses	1.2	1.2	1.4	1.7	0.8	1.2	1.6

Source: Maguire and Pastore (1995).

a. Detail may not add to total because of rounding.

b. Includes persons of Hispanic origin.

c. Includes American Indians, Alaska Natives, Asians, and Pacific Islanders.

probation, while 34 percent of those convicted of weapons offenses received probation. Thus, probation is used less for violent offenders and more for property offenders. It should be noted that jail terms were relatively short and were almost always *split sentences*—that is, a jail term followed by a probationary term (Langan and Graziadei, 1995).

Table 13.2 shows conviction offenses for those paroled during 1992. Those convicted of property offenses were most likely to receive parole (32.7 percent), followed by drug offenders (31.1 percent), violent offenders (25.2 percent), and offenders of public order (9.8 percent) (Maguire and Pastore, 1995:579). In 1992, about 91 percent of all parolees were male, while 49 percent were black and 40.8 percent were white. If these figures are typical of state and federal jurisdictions generally, *no* crime category is excluded from consideration for probation or parole. About 3 percent of all convicted murderers received probation or parole. Less than 5 percent of those paroled in 1992 were rapists, while about 13 percent of those convicted of rape received probation (Langan and Graziadei, 1995:2; Maguire and Pastore, 1995:579).

Ordinarily, first-offenders, low-risk offenders, property offenders, and nonviolent offenders are prime candidates for some form of probation. Who gets probation and who gets jail or prison often depends on the jurisdiction. Those states without serious overcrowding are able to accommodate more offenders who commit serious crimes. However, in states such as California, Texas, Louisiana, and Tennessee, serious overcrowding forces judges and others to consider alternatives to incarceration.

Probation and Parole Decision Making

Probation decisions are made on the basis of several factors. One method of determining who receives probation is to examine criteria associated with a high likelihood of incarceration. Joan Petersilia (1985b:4) has reported a high statistical correlation between prison sentences and the following offender characteristics:

1. having two or more current convictions;
2. having two or more prior convictions as an adult;
3. being on parole or probation when arrested;
4. being a drug addict;
5. being armed;
6. using a weapon; and/or
7. seriously injuring the victim.

It would seem, therefore, that those most likely to receive probation are those without prior criminal records, those not addicted to drugs or alcohol, those whose offenses did not involve injury to victims, and those not using weapons during the commission of their offenses. At extreme ends of a continuum of offender dangerousness might be first-offenders and recidivists (Fulton, Stone, and Gendreau, 1994).

Selecting and Training Probation and Parole Officers

In 1958, the National Probation and Parole Association recommended that all probation and parole officers have at least a bachelor's degree from an accredited college or university and perhaps an additional year of graduate study (Allen, Latessa, Eskridge, and Vito, 1985:144). By 1990, forty-five states and the District of Columbia required all entry-level personnel working as probation or parole officers have a bachelor's degree, preferably in a behavioral science (Davis, 1990b:7).

Characteristics of Probation and Parole Officers

Although there is little comprehensive information about POs, surveys have been conducted in recent years that depict the characteristics of those performing various correctional roles. These surveys indicate a gradual move toward greater professionalization of corrections officers. One indication of this has been the movement toward accreditation and the establishment of accreditation programs through the American Correctional Association (ACA) and the American Probation and Parole Association (APPA).

The ACA was established in 1870, with Rutherford B. Hayes as its first president. Since its inception, the ACA has advocated general improvements and reforms throughout all phases of corrections, including the professionalization of POs. The ACA sponsors training seminars and educational programs throughout the United States. Those who belong to the ACA or to a similar organization, such as the APPA, receive current information about parole and probation innovations and programs. Many officers attend annual meetings of the associations, where they learn much from other POs and corrections professionals. While membership in these or similar organizations is not contingent upon being up-to-date in the correctional field, it at least shows support for these organizations and their goals. One goal is to upgrade the selection and training requirements of correctional officers, including POs.

The *Corrections Compendium* (1990) conducted a survey of parole officers in 1990, while the American Correctional Association solicited information from its probation and parole officer membership in 1994. The ACA boasts a membership of about a third of all correctional personnel nationwide. Over ten thousand ACA members provided information about their ages, educational levels, and other pertinent information concerning the positions they hold. Table 13.3 summarizes selected socioeconomic and job-related characteristics for these responding POs.

A majority of POs are male, white, possess bachelor's degrees, and have nine to twelve years' experience, in contrast to the high rate of turnover that some researchers have noted among POs. One reason for this apparent discrepancy may be that those belonging to the American Correctional Association are perhaps more committed to their work, as evidenced by their membership in this voluntary professional association. Average PO annual salaries in 1994 ranged from $12,768 to $41,215, which are slightly higher than those reported by Shirley Davis in 1990 ($12,768–$34,560).

The proportion of women in the *Corrections Compendium* survey is actually larger than the proportion of women in corrections generally. As we have seen, about 21 percent of all corrections officers are women, according to ACA figures for 1994 (American Correctional Association, 1994a:xliv–xlv). Women pursuing careers as POs have voiced the opinion that they must constantly prove themselves to their male co-workers

Table 13.3

Summary Characteristics for Probation and Parole Officers in the United States.

Characteristic	Percentage/Median	
	ACA	*CC*
Age	34	36
Gender		
Male	64.4%	74.6%
Female	35.6%	25.4%
Educational Level	B.S.	B.S.
Length of Experience	9–11 yrs	11–12 yrs
Salary (Average Annual)	$16,135–	$12,768–
	$41,215	$34,560
Cultural Background		
Caucasian	82.4%	80.2%
Black	9.6%	12.3%
Hispanic	4.1%	5.0%
Other	3.9%	2.5%

Sources: "Survey I: Fourteen State Systems Reduce Correctional Officer Positions," *Corrections Compendium,* 17:7–20, 1990; *Corrections Today,* "Survey," 1994.

(Hunter, 1986). This greater aggressiveness among female POs *may* manifest itself in part through membership in professional associations such as the ACA or APPA.

The median educational level of most POs in the sample is a bachelor's degree. However, a majority of state systems, twenty-nine, require a bachelor's degree as the minimum educational level for entry-level positions as parole officer. In many states, however, the entry-level requirements for PO positions are less stringent. In 1990, sixteen jurisdictions required a bachelor's degree or "equivalent experience," whatever that may be (Su Davis, 1990b:7). Davis (1990b:7) notes, however, that in at least forty-two of the systems surveyed, applicants for PO work had more than the minimum entry-level requirements.

Considering the relatively low salaries of POs, their higher median ages, and their comparatively lower educational levels, it is understandable that they have been criticized for lacking professionalism (Lawrence, 1984). This problem is explained, at least in part, by the lack of professional identity of PO work, the lack of a recognized professional school that prepares leaders in the field of probation, and the lack of nationally recognized scholars or administrators who can be called eminent leaders in probation or parole (Lawrence, 1984).

What Do POs Do?

Most studies of correctional personnel have focused on prison and jail correctional officers, their behaviors and backgrounds, and their work orientations (Crank, 1996). Findings of later investigations of POs are consistent with those of earlier investigations, suggesting that POs continue to have negative self-images and impressions (Lawrence, 1984). This means that despite definite gains in the selection, recruitment, and professionalization of POs, little has caused them to improve their attitudes about their work roles and relationships with offender-clients. The highest labor turnover among POs usually occurs during the early years of their employment (Brown, 1987; Maryland Department of Budget and Fiscal Planning, 1986). Those anticipating a career change will probably not join professional organizations because they may conclude that membership will not help them advance in other professions. While the membership fees of these organizations are modest, those electing not to join may feel that their money is best spent elsewhere.

The duties of POs are diverse (Ring, 1989: 43–48). Burton, Latessa, and Barker (1992:277–80) have listed twenty-three legally prescribed functions of POs. These include supervising, surveilling, investigating cases, assisting in rehabilitation, developing and discussing conditions of probation, counseling, visiting homes and working with clients, making arrests, making referrals, writing presentence investigation reports, keeping records, performing court duties, collecting fines, supervising restitution, serving warrants, maintaining contacts with courts, recommending sentences, developing community service programs, assisting law enforcement officers and agencies, assisting courts in transferring cases, enforcing criminal laws, helping clients find jobs, and initiating program revocations.

The idea that a college graduate makes a better probation or parole officer is widely held in criminal justice circles. However, there is little evidence that older probation and parole officers with less education are less effective at their jobs than younger, more educated officers (Allen, Eskridge, Latessa, and Vito, 1985:148). While it is important that officers be familiar with the variety of treatment and educational programs available to offenders, the need for officers to possess formal college degrees has not been demonstrated by any administration or agency. While it might be helpful for officers to be able to recognize the behavioral symptoms of drug abuse, alcoholism, or mental disturbance, they often gain this knowledge from workshops, seminars, and in-service sessions. Again, the issue of college education as a prerequisite for probation or parole officer work is unresolved.

One unintended consequence of requiring probation and parole officers to have college degrees is that it places greater social distance between them and their clients. Generally, convicted felons lack formal educational training and certain communicative skills. More highly educated probation and parole officers may have greater difficulty relating to such clients, which may hinder rather than facilitate the counselor role that these officers perform.

Probation and parole work is stressful. Heavy caseloads (i.e., the number of parolees and/or probationers assigned each officer) and officers' constant exposure to different and often hazardous situations create feelings of job stress and burnout (Whitehead and Lindquist, 1985). In a study of 108 Alabama POs conducted in 1984, for example, over half reported high job stress, and 20 percent believed they were burned out by their jobs (Whitehead and Lindquist, 1985). In this study, burnout and stress were explained by heavy work loads and the strain of officer-client contacts. Other similar reports suggest that although certain aspects of PO work are stressful, their capacity to help others enables many POs to adjust to such stress and turns their work and PO-client contacts into positive experiences (Beto and Brown, 1996:50; Clayton, 1996).

In order for probation and parole officers to spend at least one hour a month in face-to-face contact with their clients, they should have fewer than thirty clients at any given time. In reality, many officers have far more than that. Also, the effectiveness of probation and parole programs depends on caseloads of between twenty and thirty clients for each officer. But caseloads of three hundred or four hundred clients per officer are not uncommon in some jurisdictions. When caseloads become unwieldy, it is difficult for POs to give clients the individualized attention they require. The corrections system is blamed when clients commit serious offenses while on probation or parole. However, jurisdictions such as Texas are trying new organizational strategies, with favorable results. Working in more positive environments with motivated administrators can do much to improve PO morale as well as productivity and quality of work (Telecky, 1996:26–27).

Many POs experience conflict between their role as a treatment resource and that as a supervisor (Sigler and McGraw, 1984). A 1978 study of 113 Alabama POs examined the influence of policy changes that required all officers to participate in mandatory firearms training. This caused many officers to reevaluate their roles and see themselves more as law enforcement officers than as treatment/rehabilitation-oriented helpers (Sigler and McGraw, 1984). Nevertheless, many POs consider the needs of society, the court, and offenders as paramount, and they are able to realize substantial professional growth from their experiences (Cosgrove, 1994:29–30). Commitment to their jobs and effective communication skills also help POs see their work favorably (Beto and Brown, 1996:50–52).

In 1981, the National Institute of Corrections (NIC) responded to the need for greater professionalism and training among POs by sponsoring a series of training programs in various jurisdictions. The American Correctional Association was selected to administer some of these programs and eventually founded the Development of Correctional Staff Trainers Program, which provided comprehensive, experience-based training for more than one thousand trainers and other professionals between 1981 and 1985 (Taylor, 1985:24). By 1985, over six thousand individuals had enrolled in ACA correspondence courses and participated in related programs, seminars, and workshops on a variety of correctional topics. Enrollment in these training programs has grown considerably (American Correctional Association, 1989a, 1992).

These programs and workshops stress legal liabilities of POs and other types of corrections officers as well as skills in managing and supervising clients. Additionally, programs and coursework are offered for managing stress, crisis intervention and hostage negotiations, proposal and report writing, legal issues training, managing community corrections facilities, dealing with the mentally ill offender, and suicide prevention. By 1985 more than six hundred agencies and institutions were seeking accreditation or reaccreditation so that they could foster greater professionalization among prospective PO recruits.

Recruiting Women in PO Roles

Although women comprise only 5.9 percent of the incarcerated offender population and only 18 percent of the probation/parole population, females in various correctional fields are currently underrepresented (American Correctional Association, 1994a:xxvi). Only about 21 percent of the correctional officers in the United States are women (American Correctional Association, 1994a). Many of the women employed in correctional positions perform clerical and staff work and/or deal primarily with female or juvenile offenders (Holeman and Krepps-Hess, 1983).

Most studies of women in all types of corrections work have focused upon the role of women as prison or jail matrons (Zupan, 1986; Hunter, 1986; Carlen and Davis, 1987; Kerle, 1985). Although the greatest opposition to the idea of women entering the correctional field has been found among male officers, few significant differences have actually been observed in the effectiveness of male and female correctional officers (Chapman et al., 1983).

One barrier to the recruitment of women into corrections, especially as correctional officers, is the legal obstacle of guarding offenders' right to privacy (Jurik, 1985). For the most part, the privacy issue is moot in PO work. Nevertheless, women must contend with male POs as they seek to perform similar work roles. Evidence suggests that each year greater numbers of women are being recruited into correctional work and that greater numbers are carrying out PO and other mainline correctional work (Shawver, 1987).

Intermediate Punishments for Probationers and Parolees: Community Corrections

Community Corrections Defined

One reason community corrections is difficult to define is that different segments of our society view it differently (Siedschlaw, 1990). **Community corrections** refers to *any community-based program that supervises convicted offenders, either by city, county, state or federal authority; that provides various services to client/offenders; that monitors and furthers client/offender behaviors related to sentencing conditions; that heightens client/offender responsibility regarding payment of fines, victim compensation, community service, and restitution; and that provides for a continuation of punishment through more controlled supervision and greater accountability* (Duffee and McGarrell, 1990; Reeves, 1992).

Minimum-custody inmates become involved in a community work project.

Community Corrections Acts

A community corrections act enables jurisdictions to establish local community corrections agencies, facilities, and programs. A generic definition of a community corrections act is *a statewide mechanism through which funds are granted to local units of government to plan, develop, and deliver correctional sanctions and services. The overall purpose of this mechanism is to provide local sentencing options in lieu of imprisonment in state institutions* (McManus and Barclay, 1994:12).

The aim of community corrections acts is to make it possible to divert certain prison-bound offenders into local, city- or county-level programs where they can be treated and helped rather than imprisoned. Usually, offenders who qualify for community corrections programs are low-risk nonviolent, nondangerous offenders (*Corrections Compendium*, 1991b:15). Community corrections acts also target incarcerated offenders who pose little or no risk if released into the community under close supervision. Thus, community corrections acts alleviate prison and jail overcrowding by diverting jail- or prison-bound offenders to community programs.

Components of Community Corrections Programs

Community-based corrections programs are locally operated services offering minimum-security, limited release, or work release alternatives to prisoners about to be paroled (Jones, 1990). For example, in 1978, Iowa passed legislation establishing a locally administered community-based corrections program (Jones, 1990). The Kansas community-based corrections provides four types of programs: (1) pretrial release and release-on-own-recognizance or release with services; (2) presentence investigation; (3) probation; and (4) residential treatment facilities. Kansas has found community-based adult corrections programs to be inexpensive and effective at reducing recidivism among parolees.

In 1982, Virginia operated six community-based work release units that maintained an average daily work release population of 314 inmates (Orchowsky, Merritt, and Browning, 1994). Offenders placed on work release are permitted to hold regular jobs in the community during the daytime but must return and spend evenings and nights at the community-based facility. Assignments to Virginia work release programs according to race have been about fifty-fifty. One significant outcome of Virginia's work release units is that inmates have been able to contribute substantially to the support of their families or dependents. About 14 percent of the program's cost was defrayed by monies inmates paid to the center.

Aims of Community Corrections

An extensive examination of various state statutes pertaining to community corrections has identified at least seven major goals: (1) to rehabilitate offenders; (2) to provide custody and/or supervision for offenders requiring it; (3) to provide an opportunity for offenders to reintegrate themselves into the community; (4) to enable offenders to provide restitution to victims; (5) to provide employment training to offenders; (6) to reduce prison overcrowding; and (7) to continue punishment of offenders (Johnson et al., 1994). The primary purpose of community-based correctional programs is to help probationers reintegrate into their communities, although parolees are assisted by such programs as well (Racine, Vittitow, and Riggs, 1984). It is not so much that probationers (in contrast with parolees) have lost touch with their communities through incarceration but rather that they have the opportunity of avoiding confinement and remaining within their communities to perform productive work to support themselves and others and to repay victims for losses suffered (Fields, 1994).

Duffee and McGarrell (1990) note that community corrections programs can also be distinguished according to the controlling authority. They categorize such programs as *community-run* (locally operated, but lacking state funding and other external support); *community-placed* (located in communities but not networking with any community agency); and *community-based* (locally operated but also financially supplemented from outside sources. These are programs that network with other community agencies and the criminal justice system). Community-based correctional programs vary considerably among states (Harris, Jones and Funke, 1990). However, in recent years, different jurisdictions have made efforts to network with one another as a means of disseminating in-

formation and sharing results of particular community corrections programs (Faulkner, 1994:23).

The term *community corrections* is often used in a general way to refer to a range of punishments known as *intermediate punishments.* As has been indicated, intermediate punishments are sanctions ranging between incarceration and standard probation on the continuum of criminal penalties (McCarthy, 1987a:1). The term may refer to any of several programs designed to closely control or monitor offenders. Because there are several types of intermediate punishments, the term is widely applied, correctly or incorrectly, to a variety of community-based programs involving nonincarcerative sanctions.

Key distinguishing features of intermediate punishments are the high degree of monitoring and control of offenders by program staff. Other characteristics include *curfews,* where offenders must observe time guidelines and be at particular places at particular times, and *frequent monitoring and contact* with program officials (Reeves, 1992). The amount and type of monitoring or contact varies with the program, although daily visits by a probation officer to an offender's workplace or home are not unusual. One semantic problem is that the intensity of monitoring or officer-offender contact depends on the jurisdiction. Intermediate punishments are intended for prison- or jail-bound offenders. Offenders who are probably going to receive probation anyway are the least likely candidates for intensively supervised programs. However, judges often assign low-risk probation-bound offenders to these programs anyway. This tends to defeat the goals of such programs, because they are intended for offenders who would otherwise occupy valuable prison or jail space. Cluttering intensive supervision programs with offenders who don't need close supervision, referred to as "net-widening" (Jones, 1990), is a waste of money, time, and personnel. It is believed that intensive monitoring and control fosters a high degree of compliance with program requirements and deters offenders from committing new crimes.

Intermediate Punishments as Distinguished from Community Corrections

Several states have **intermediate punishment programs** for probationers and parolees (Mc-

Carthy, 1987a). Because these programs are most often community-operated and are often similar to projects and programs sponsored by community corrections acts, the two are often considered synonymous (Cromwell and Killinger, 1994).

One form of intermediate punishment consists of intensive supervision programs. These programs enable low PO caseloads and intensive supervision of offenders through frequent visits or telephone communication (Orchowsky, Merritt, and Browning, 1994). Furlough programs, halfway houses, and work release are utilized as ways of easing parolees who have been or are about to be released from prison, back into society.

Intensive Supervision Programs

Intensive supervision programs (ISP) *are intended to increase the surveillance and supervision of probationers or parolees. ISP involves more frequent drug and alcohol checks, curfew monitoring, more frequent face-to-face contact between clients and their POs, and generally heightened accountability.* Thus, POs may contact a client's employer frequently to determine whether the client is performing satisfactorily. Random spot checks might be conducted of a client's premises to determine whether illegal contraband is present.

Not all offenders need to be placed in ISP. Most offenders, in fact, can function well with minimal supervision. However, some serious offenders need more frequent monitoring (English, Chadwick, and Pullen, 1994). They lack self-control, are prone to violence, and are generally difficult to manage. Community agencies, judges, and correctional institutions, including parole boards, try to determine which offenders are most in need of ISP. Often, paper-and-pencil instruments are used to assess their needs as well as the potential risk if they are allowed to remain free (Runda, Rhine, and Wetter, 1994).

Decisions about parole-eligible inmates or decisions about which offenders ought to be placed on probation involve some educated guesswork on the part of sentencing judges and parole boards (Metchik, 1992; Runda, Rhine, and Wetter, 1994). A number of risk assessment devices have been de-

veloped in recent years as objective methods of determining which offenders pose the greatest risk to the public (Virginia Commission on Sentencing and Parole Reform, 1995). *A risk assessment device is a way of predicting whether offenders will violate the terms of their parole or probation and recidivate.*

The utility of several parole-success predictors has been examined (Gottfredson and Gottfredson, 1985). A study of forty-five hundred offenders released from federal prisons between 1970 and 1972 showed that while there was a high correlation among the various measures examined, variables ordinarily associated with predicting recidivism, including present and previous offenses, were of little more help in predicting actual recidivism than the statistical prediction devices that were tested. Other studies examining ways of predicting successfulness of parole have also found inconsistent and disappointing results (Baird, 1992).

Massachusetts has devised a risk/need classification system in order to differentiate the degree of supervision required in any given offender's case (Brown and Cochran, 1984). Having a prior record, being educationally disadvantaged, coming from a disorganized family structure, and having a history of substance abuse are used as predictors of subsequent criminal behavior. In 1982, a sample of 1,963 adults and juveniles in Massachusetts were placed under the risk/need supervision program. Those offenders designated as higher risk upon their initial assessment were more likely to commit new offenses, while those scoring low on the risk scale had considerably lower recidivism rates. This suggests that the program and risk/needs classification system is workable, at least in that jurisdiction (Brown and Cochran, 1984). A risk/needs assessment used by the Kansas Department of Corrections is shown in figure 13.1

Perhaps the most important influence on the success or failure of an intensive supervision program is the size of an officer's workload or the number of cases assigned to him or her (Schumacher, 1985; Steppe, 1986). As a result of the Correctional Reform Act of 1983, Florida created the Community Control Program, which was designed to provide work programs for probationers and parolees and to reduce caseloads to fewer than twenty per officer—an ideal number in view of the original objectives of probation and parole programs generally (Florida Probation and Parole Services, 1984). During its first year of operation, the Community Control Program had 1,886 clients. Only ninety-three revocations have occurred, with forty-

one of these being for new crimes and fifty-two for technical violations (e.g., failure to communicate with PO at regular intervals, leaving the immediate jurisdiction temporarily). The program is considered successful in that 72 percent of the cases are classi-

---

Figure 13.1 Kansas Department of Corrections Parolee Risk and Needs Assessment Coding Form

NAME _____   NUMBER _____

ASSESSMENT DATE _____ _____ _____   TYPE OF ASSESSMENT _____
                  MO   DA   YR

ACTION CODE: [   ]   DISTRICT [   ]   PO NO. _____

Risk Assessment			**Needs Assessment**		
Pts	Item	Code	Pts	Item	Code
[ ]	1. Severity Level I Offense	[ ]	[ ]	17. Academic/Vocational	[ ]
[ ]	2. # Prior Periods Prob/Par Sup	[ ]	[ ]	18. Employment	[ ]
[ ]	3. Attitude	[ ]	[ ]	19. Financial Management	[ ]
[ ]	4. Age 1st Felony Conviction	[ ]	[ ]	20. Marital Family	[ ]
[ ]	5. # Prior Felony Convictions	[ ]	[ ]	21. Companions	[ ]
[ ]	6. Convictions Certain Offenses	[ ]	[ ]	22. Emotional Stability	[ ]
[ ]	7. # Prior Prob/Par Revocations	[ ]	[ ]	23. Alcohol Usage	[ ]
[ ]	8. Alcohol Usage Problems	[ ]	[ ]	24. Other Drug Usage	[ ]
[ ]	9. Other Drug Usage	[ ]	[ ]	25. Mental Ability	[ ]
[ ]	10. # Address Changes	[ ]	[ ]	26. Health	[ ]
[ ]	11. % Time Employed	[ ]	[ ]	27. Sexual Behavior	[ ]
[ ]	12. Social Identification	[ ]	[ ]	28. Officer Impression	[ ]
[ ]	13. Problem Interpersonal Rel.	[ ]	[ ]	29. Needs Total	[ ]
[ ]	14. Use of Community Resources	[ ]	[ ]		
[ ]	15. Response to Supervision	[ ]	[ ]		
[ ]	16. Risk Total	[ ]			

Decision

30	Supervision Determination	[ ]
31	Override	[ ]
32	Supervision Level Assigned	[ ]

33 Next Assessment Date _____ _____
                          MO   YR

_____

ASSESSMENT COMPLETED BY: Signature

Distribution

Original—Data Entry

Copy—PO File

Copy—Deputy Secretary if Override Required

---

fied as bona fide diversions from prison (Florida Probation and Parole Services, 1984).

In an experiment with intensively supervised pretrial release programs in Miami, Florida; Portland, Oregon; and Milwaukee, Wisconsin, between 1980 and 1984, 3,226 persons were randomly assigned to a variety of pretrial release alternatives, including (1) release on own recognizance, (2) bail or citation, or (3) supervised release (Austin, Krisberg, and Litsky, 1984). Over 98 percent of those under supervised pretrial release appeared in court later, while failure-to-appear statistics for those who were released on their own recognizance or released on bail or citation were much higher.

Women under intensive supervised probation or parole have a much better record than men. Women are less likely than men to be charged with new offenses. One explanation for this gender difference may be that probation and parole officers are reluctant to report women because of their family-based obligations and because officers feel their offenses to be "minor problems" (Norland and Mann, 1984).

Helping POs supervise various offenders are paraprofessionals and community volunteers (Latessa, Travis, and Allen, 1983). In a 1979 national survey, questionnaires mailed to all fifty-two state parole field supervision departments revealed that volunteer and paraprofessional programs were widely accepted. Although the qualifications for paraprofessionals were more stringent than those for volunteers, both groups received favorable marks from reporting agencies.

Furloughs

Furloughs *are authorized, unescorted leaves from confinement granted for specific purposes and for designated time periods* (Marlette, 1988, 1990; McCarthy and McCarthy, 1991). Forty prison systems granted more than 230,960 furloughs in 1990. This was 15 percent more than the estimated 200,000 furloughs granted in 1987 and 35 percent more than the 170,000 granted in 1988 for all systems (Davis, 1991:10). Rates of absconding are quite low, about one-half of one percent (Smith and Sabatino, 1989; 1990). Furloughs may be granted

to prisoners for periods ranging from twenty-four hours to several weeks and are similar to leaves enjoyed by military personnel. In 1986, states granting the largest numbers of furloughs were North Carolina and Oklahoma (American Correctional Association, 1987:xvi–xvii). By 1994, the number of furloughs had increased to 16,201 (American Correctional Association, 1994a:xxviii–xxix). This is an increase of 131 percent during the period 1986 to 1994.

Florida and Rhode Island became the largest grantors of furloughs, with 7,729 and 5,705, respectively. (The furloughs reported by Davis (1991) are *multiple furloughs* granted to the same offenders during their final months of incarceration in different state and federal facilities. The later figures reported by the ACA are the numbers of the same individuals granted multiple furloughs by any given state or federal system.)

Furloughs originated in 1918 in Mississippi. By 1970, about half the states had furlough programs (Marley, 1973). In those days, prisoners who had completed two or more years of their original sentences were considered eligible for furloughs. These furloughs usually involved conjugal visits or ten-day visits with families during the Christmas holiday. Furloughs were believed valuable for preparing offenders for permanent reentry into their communities. In 1990, forty-six states and the federal government had furlough programs (Davis, 1991:10).

Furloughs are an outgrowth of work-release programs. Typically, furloughed inmates have served a significant portion of their sentences and are eligible to be considered for parole. The successfulness of an inmate's furlough figures prominently in a parole board's decision whether to release early. Thus, offenders who comply with furlough requirements have an advantage over those who were not furloughed.

While furloughs have many of the same characteristics as work release programs, they are used only about a third as much as work release. The length of furloughs varies by jurisdiction. Most furlough programs range from twenty-four to seventy-two hours, although some programs may grant inmates two weeks or more of freedom for special activities (McCarthy and McCarthy, 1991).

The Goals of Furlough Programs

Furlough programs have several goals. Offenders are given a high degree of trust by prison officials and are permitted leaves to visit their homes and families. Such furloughs benefit both prisoners and their families because they permit family members to get used to the presence of the offender after a long absence. As a type of study release, prisoners may participate in educational programs outside of prison. They can arrange for employment or they can participate in vocational training for short periods. In Illinois, for instance, furloughs may be granted for the following reasons: to make contacts for employment; to visit close relatives; to obtain

---

Highlight 13.2. On Ohio Furloughs: The Case of Furloughs for Lifers

In 1992, the Ohio Department of Corrections indefinitely suspended the use of furloughs. Furloughs are unescorted leaves that are available to inmates who are parole-eligible and within a year or less of being freed. Their intent is to help inmates become reintegrated into society.

Home furloughs up to three days long are usually granted so that inmates may attend funerals, visit a dying family member, or strengthen family ties. Only inmates who have exhibited exemplary behavior for at least two years are eligible for furlough. What went wrong in Ohio?

Lt. Governor Mike DeWine received a telephone call from Riggie Wilkinson, director of the State Department of Rehabilitation and Correction. Wilkinson reported to DeWine that eleven inmates presently on furlough had been convicted of murder and were currently serving sentences of life without parole. Hamilton County prosecutor Joseph Deters hit the ceiling when he heard about it. "Does the governor know this?" he demanded. "It is hard to believe they're letting people like this out on home furloughs."

Wilkinson told DeWine and Deters that the number of inmates eligible for home furloughs had been reduced from eighty in 1988 to eleven in 1991. Wilkinson said, "It's been a successful system because we haven't had a major catastrophe. They've all behaved well. We parole murderers all the time. Everybody gets out." When DeWine heard about it, *all* furloughs were cancelled indefinitely, until the policy for furlough-granting could be investigated more thoroughly.

In early 1991, then-U.S. Attorney Dick Thornburgh announced a 53 percent decline in furloughs.

He said that the new furlough policy was to "crack down" on violent and white-collar crime committed by furloughees. Then-Bureau of Prisons director J. Michael Quinlan said in response that "the new restrictions have made an already conservative furlough program even more conservative."

Then-president George Bush also bashed the furlough program issue in an August 1991 speech before the Fraternal Order of Police. Bush had earlier capitalized on the furlough issue during his presidential campaign against Governor Michael Dukakis of Massachusetts. Under Dukakis's administration, a life-without-parole inmate, Willie Horton, committed several violent assaults during a furlough. The assaults were blamed on a lax furlough program. Bush said, "We've tightened the furlough review process for inmates, restricting the already limited furlough opportunities for federal offenders."

The American Correctional Association countered this negative publicity by noting that incidents such as those involving Willie Horton are exceptional. It adopted a resolution stating that furloughs have been very effective in helping prepare inmates for release as well as easing prison overcrowding.

When should prisoners be granted furloughs? What guidelines would you establish to regulate who does and does not receive furloughs?

Sources: Adapted from *Corrections Digest,* "Furloughs Suspended in Ohio," *Corrections Compendium,* 17 (1992):18; *On the Line,* "New Policy Reduces Furloughs for Federal Prison Inmates," *Corrections Compendium,* 16 (1991):15; *Corrections Digest,* "Back to Willy Horton," *Corrections Compendium,* 16 (1991):17.

medical or psychiatric services; to visit seriously ill relatives or attend the funerals of close relatives; to appear before study groups; to make contacts for discharge; and to secure a residence upon release.

Furloughs also provide officials with an opportunity to evaluate offenders and determine how they adapt to living with others in their community. Thus, the furlough is a type of test to determine, with some predictability, the likelihood that inmates will conform to society's rules if they are eventually released through parole. For some prisoners, furloughs function as incentives to conform to prison rules and regulations, because only prisoners who have demonstrated that they can control their behaviors in prison will be considered for furlough. Most prisoners selected for furlough are nearing the end of their sentences and will eventually be paroled or released anyway. They are good risks because their likelihood of absconding while on furlough is quite remote.

The Functions of Furlough Programs

Furloughs are intended to accomplish certain functions. These include (1) to rehabilitate and reintegrate the offender; (2) to develop the offender's self-esteem and sense of self-worth; (3) to allow the offender to pursue vocational/educational programs; and (4) to help the parole boards determine when the inmate is ready to be released.

Offender Rehabilitation and Reintegration

A study of a furlough program established by the Oahu Community Correctional Center showed that between 1977 and 1983, ninety-eight inmates were granted furloughs. Of these furloughs, 68 percent were successful. Offenders who failed their furloughs either were returned to prison because of new criminal convictions or were terminated from the program because of technical violations of the program (Uriell, 1984).

The Development of Self-Esteem and Self-Worth

Furloughs seem to instill in inmates feelings of self-esteem and self-worth. Again, the element of trust plays an important role in enabling those granted furloughs to acquire trust for those who place trust in them. While it is not possible to mea-

sure the development of self-esteem and self-worth, many of those granted furloughs report that they believe they have benefited from their temporary release experiences.

Opportunities to Pursue Vocational/Educational Programs

Furloughs permit inmates to participate in programs not available to them in prisons or jails. Thus, if inmates wish to take courses in typing, art, automobile repair, social science, or related areas, furloughs permit them to pursue such courses. Sometimes these furloughs are called study release because they involve a program of study designed for the offender's specific needs.

Helping Parole Boards Determine When Inmates Ought to Be Released

A key function of furloughs is to alert parole boards as to which inmates are most eligible to be released and who will likely be successful while on parole (Milling, 1978). For example, Connecticut's use of its furlough program for this purpose has an 80 percent success rate. In that jurisdiction, inmates are granted furloughs if they are within sixty days of being paroled. They are limited to three-day furloughs, during which they can make home visits, obtain required medical treatment or psychological counseling, participate in special training courses, and perform work or other duties (Milling, 1978).

Who Qualifies for Furlough Programs?

Most furloughs are restricted to the following types of inmates: those in minimum custody; those who have served a fixed amount of their sentences and are within some fixed time of release; those who have been approved by a committee that reviews all furlough applications; those who have a clean institutional record and a stable home situation; and those whose crimes were nonviolent. Exclusions commonly include those who have committed notorious or heinous crimes, crimes of violence, or sex offenses (Smith and Milan, 1973).

The Declining Use of Furloughs

Not all states have furlough programs. One reason is that under certain types of sentencing systems, any sort of temporary release is not permitted. Under an indeterminate sentencing scheme, authorities have considerable latitude to grant furloughs or work releases to inmates who have shown that they can conform to the institutional rules (Harer and Eichenlaub, 1992).

There has been a general shift toward determinate and presumptive sentencing schemes, which permit little variation from judges' sentences. Thus, in some jurisdictions statutory prohibitions make it difficult if not impossible to operate furlough or work release programs (*Corrections Compendium,* 1993b; Davis, 1991).

The reduction of furlough and work release programs nationally has lessened inmates' incentive to abide by institutional rules, although some incentive to conform continues to exist because of good time credits, which may be applied to an offender's original sentence. Another reason for the reduction of these programs is lack of funds. In view of diminished resources and unenthusiastic response from the public and corrections officials to furlough programs and other temporary release options, these alternatives are less prevalent than in past years.

Halfway Houses

A **halfway house** is a *transitional residence for inmates who have been released from prison* (Wilson, 1985:152). Ordinarily, these homes offer food, clothing, and temporary housing for parolees recently released from prison. A released offender may be assigned to one of these homes for a short period. In many jurisdictions, released offenders move into these homes voluntarily. Halfway houses greatly help former inmates make the transition from rigid prison life to community living (Miller, 1977).

More than any other parole program, the halfway house eases the transition prisoners must make from the unique custodial world of prisons and jails to the outside community. Halfway houses furnish not only living accommodations and food but also provide job placement services, group and/or individual counseling, medical assistance, placement assistance in vocational/technical training programs, as well as numerous other opportu-nities for self-development (Donnelly and Forschner, 1987; National Office for Social Responsibility, 1987).

Halfway House Origins

The concept of a halfway house probably originated in England during the early 1800s. The first formal recommendation for a halfway house in the United States occurred in 1817 in Pennsylvania (McCarthy and McCarthy, 1991). A Pennsylvania prison riot had stirred the legislature to think of various prison reforms, including housing provisions for ex-convicts who were often poor and could not find employment or adequate places to live. These proposals were never implemented, because the public feared criminal contamination— that if ex-offenders lived together, their criminality would spread like a disease (McCarthy and McCarthy, 1991).

For the next one hundred fifty years, sponsorship of halfway houses stemmed primarily from private and/or religious sources. In 1845, the Quakers opened the Isaac T. Hopper Home in New York City. This was followed by the Temporary Asylum for Disadvantaged Female Prisoners established in Boston in 1864 by a reformist group (Wilson, 1985:153). In 1889, the House of Industry was opened in Philadelphia, and in 1896, Hope House was established in New York City by Maud and Ballington Booth. After receiving considerable financial support from a missionary religious society called the Volunteers of America, the Booths were able to open additional Hope Houses, or Hope Halls, in Chicago, San Francisco, and New Orleans (Wilson, 1985:153).

The International Halfway House Association

One of the most significant events that sparked the growth of state-operated halfway houses was the creation of the International Halfway House Association (IHHA) in Chicago in 1964. The growth in the number of halfway houses during the next decade was phenomenal. Between 1966 and 1982, the number of halfway houses operating in the United States and Canada rose from forty to eighteen hundred (Wilson, 1985:154). Although some researchers reported that as many as twenty-

Highlight 13.3. Halfway Houses and Missed Opportunities: The Case of Charles Rill

Since 1995, the Salvation Army has operated a halfway house in Mandan, North Dakota. The halfway house, known as *Freedom House,* serves sixteen clients at any given time. Freedom House provides shelter and supervision for parolees who must make the often difficult transition from the strict regimentation of prison to life on the outside.

Wayne Junkert is the on-site assistant director of Freedom House. According to Junkert, Freedom House screens its clients, who are also screened by the prison system before being paroled. Junkert says that Freedom House maintains a Christian environment and imposes several important regulations, including remaining drug- and alcohol-free and observing curfew. Clients at Freedom House perform weekly chores and earn some time away from the home. Clients can also *lose* some time away from the home because of failure to conform to Freedom House rules. Greg Odell, executive director of Freedom House, says that "accountability is a big deal here."

North Dakota pays Freedom House $25 per day per client to defray operating costs. One of Freedom House's clients is Charles Rill, a six-foot, two-inch, 210-pound athlete who was originally convicted of carrying a handgun and aggravated assault. While imprisoned, Rill enrolled in various self-help programs, but not because of their rehabilitative value. Rill attempted to exploit the system. He "went through the motions," but he couldn't escape his internal rage.

When he was placed in Freedom House, his outlook changed, and he wanted to succeed. One of his dreams was to play college football. In the spring of 1996, Rill applied to a Virginia university, where he was accepted. His dream was finally realized. He credits Freedom House with giving him this chance to change his life.

Freedom House expects its clients to perform weekly chores. They may hold outside jobs, although they are not required to do so. The Salvation Army owns a strip mall where the halfway house is located. Therefore, it can place many Freedom House clients in useful jobs. The Salvation Army also operates a thrift shop and a laundromat, where some of the Freedom House clients are employed. One of the fringe benefits to the state is that Freedom House helps alleviate overcrowding at the nearby state penitentiary.

Should halfway houses be located in every community? Should potential halfway house clients be screened, or should any parolee be admitted? What screening mechanisms should be used to protect the public from potentially dangerous parolees and halfway house clients?

Source: Adapted from Associated Press, "Salvation Army Halfway House Provides Many Missed Opportunities," *Minot (N.D.) Daily News,* May 7, 1996, p. B3.

---

three hundred halfway house facilities with over one hundred thousand beds operated in 1981 (Gatz and Murray, 1981).

Halfway House Variations

Because there are so many different government-sponsored and private agencies claiming to be halfway houses, it is impossible to devise a definition of halfway house that fits all jurisdictions (Berger, 1994). The level of custody for clients ranges from simple shelter on a voluntary basis to mandatory confinement with curfew. Halfway houses also provide many different services, including alcohol- or drug-related rehabilitation facilities with some hospitalization on the premises, minimal or extensive counseling services, and/or employment assistance (McCarthy and McCarthy, 1991). Also, offenders serviced by halfway house programs range from probationers and pre-releasees to parolees and others assigned to community service with special conditions (Klein-Saffran, 1993).

Some idea of the variation among halfway houses can be gleaned by the following. Brooke House, established in 1965 in Massachusetts, accepts prereleasees from federal institutions and state prison parolees. It employs reality therapy and emphasizes job placement, improved work habits, and sound financial planning (Berger, 1994; Tonry and Hamilton, 1995). Halfway house residents are often subject to prescreening, which may include psychological tests and other forms of evaluation to determine a client's suitability for the program (Motiuk, Bonta, and Andrews, 1986).

The Dreyfous House

In 1973, Dreyfous House in New Orleans was established for emotionally disturbed youths. However, strong community opposition to Dreyfous House resulted in its termination in 1975 (Slotnik, 1976). In San Mateo, California, El Camino House was established for ex-mental patients (Richmond, 1970). El Camino House's program has two purposes—to provide a performance-oriented culture for residents and to use community housing as post-halfway houses with built-in followup. These programs serve El Camino House's overall goal of preparing severely disturbed psychiatric patients for more independent living (Richmond, 1970). Other halfway houses include the Ralph W. Alvis House; the Bridge Home for Young Men; the Denton House; Fellowship House; Fresh Start, Inc.; the Helping Hand Halfway Home, Inc.; Talbert House; and Vander Meulen House, located in Ohio (Seiter, Petersilia and Allen, 1974).

The Functions of Halfway Houses

The major functions of halfway houses overlap some of those associated with other programs for parolees. These include (1) parolee rehabilitation and reintegration into the community; (2) providing food and shelter; (3) providing job placement, vocational guidance, and employment assistance; (4) providing client-specific treatments; (5) alleviating jail and prison overcrowding; (6) supplementing supervisory functions of probation and parole agencies; and (7) monitoring probationers, work/study releasees, and others by means of special conditions.

Parolee Rehabilitation and Reintegration into the Community

The administrative personnel of halfway houses as well as the professional and paraprofes-

sional staff members help offenders with specific problems they might have, such as alcohol or drug dependencies. Many parolees work out a plan for themselves before their parole date. This plan is scrutinized by parole board members, and a PO often helps the parolee prepare the plan.

Providing Food and Shelter

Some parolees have accumulated savings from working in prison industries, while other parolees have no operating capital. Thus, halfway houses furnish offenders with a place to stay and regular meals while they look for jobs and participate in self-help programs.

Providing Job Placement, Vocational Guidance, and Employment Assistance

Almost every halfway house assists offenders by providing job leads and putting them in touch with prospective employers. Some halfway houses lend offenders money, which must be repaid when the offender has found work and stabilized his or her life. Although women make up only about 4 percent of the entire inmate population of prisons and jails, some halfway houses serve only female offenders.

Alleviating Jail and Prison Overcrowding

Halfway houses alleviate jail and prison overcrowding by housing probationers and other inmates who may be paroled to them for brief transitional periods (Vaughn, 1993). In a 1990 survey of fifty state correctional facilities, Vaughn found that most were operating at 122 percent of their rated capacity—in other words, 613,046 inmates were being housed in facilities designed to accommodate 501,070. While the Supreme Court has said that prison life doesn't have to be comfortable, a major concern of prison administrators is to alleviate overcrowding. "Back-end" techniques, such as parole to reliable halfway houses, does much to alleviate such overcrowding in the short-term (Vaughn, 1993).

Supplementing Supervisory Functions of Probation and Parole Agencies

One latent function of halfway houses is to supervise and control probationers and parolees. These supervisory functions are ordinarily performed by POs. The job of halfway house staff is to counsel clients, not control their behavior. Other functions of POs include ensuring that victims receive restitution where parolees have been required to pay it (South Carolina State Reorganization Commission, 1990).

Monitoring Probationers, Work/Study Releases, and Others by Means of Special Conditions

Halfway houses are intended to serve as transitional community residences where parolees can adjust to life on the outside. Occasionally, a condition of parole is to live in a halfway house for a predetermined period. The offender benefits by being provided basic necessities such as food, clothing, and shelter as well as jobs that help defray the costs of maintaining these homes.

In 1994, nearly twenty thousand parolees were assigned to state-operated or private-contract community homes (American Correctional Association, 1994a:xxviii–xxix). Costs of operating a majority of these halfway houses range from $15 to $25 per day per resident, with the state providing about 75 percent of the funding and city/county monies providing the remainder (Wilson, 1985:158–59).

Client-Specific Treatments

Offenders with special needs or problems (e.g., sex offenders, drug addicts, alcoholics, or mentally retarded clients) benefit from halfway houses by having access to special treatment programs. They may receive counseling, medical treatment, or other services custom-designed for their particular needs. If these offenders were released from jail directly to the street, the transition might be too traumatic, and they might revert to old habits or dependencies.

Some halfway houses are designed specifically for mentally ill or developmentally disabled offenders (Lippold, 1985:46). In Washington State, the Department of Corrections began compiling records of mentally retarded inmates in 1977. As a result, special offender needs were targeted and authorities were able to establish several residential placement programs in various communities (Lippold, 1985:46). Two halfway houses were opened in 1980–1981 in the Tacoma area. These large,

older homes in a residential neighborhood were called the Rap House and the Lincoln Park House (Lippold, 1985:82).

Co-Correctional Halfway Houses

Co-correctional halfway houses serve the needs of both male and female adult offenders. One of these is the Cope House, a nonprofit, community-based correctional agency whose primary function is to rehabilitate and reintegrate adult offenders (Donnelly and Forschner, 1987:7). It was founded in 1975 in Cincinnati, Ohio. Between January 1980 and December 1982, researchers studied the characteristics of 417 Cope House clients as well as factors seemingly associated with their success or failure in the program (Donnelly and Forschner, 1987:10). Cope House has four or five full-time professional staff, seven part-time employees, and a twenty-two-bed capacity. The clientele consist primarily of federal, state, and county pre-releases. Chronic and violent offenders, rapists, psychotics, the severely retarded, arsonists, and severe drug and alcohol abusers are not admitted.

When clients enter Cope House, an interviewer administers a standard intake questionnaire. Cope House programming centers around a behavioral contract called the Mutual Agreement Plan (MAP), modeled after that used by the Massachusetts Halfway House Association. This contract is client-oriented and focuses on employment, educational training, housing, and social services (Donnelly and Forschner, 1987:8). During the study period most of the women in Cope House were misdemeanants, whereas the men had been convicted primarily of felony offenses. This could be the reason that 82 percent of the females and 58 percent of the males successfully completed the program.

Work Release

Work release *is any program that allows inmates to work in their communities with minimal restrictions and supervision, pays them the prevailing minimum wage, and requires them to spend their nonworking hours in a secure facility* (adapted from McCarthy and McCarthy, 1991). The first use of work release in the United States took place in Vermont in 1906, when sheriffs, acting on their own authority, assigned inmates to jobs in the community (Busher, 1973). In 1913 Wisconsin's legislature became the first to authorize work release, and by 1975, all states and the federal system had initiated some form of work-release program (Rosenblum and Whitcomb, 1978). In those days, passes issued to certain low-risk inmates by county sheriffs permitted them to work in the community during daytime hours. However, the inmates were obligated to return to jail at a particular time. Work release is also known as day pass, day parole, temporary release, and work or education furlough.

The increase in the popularity of work release has been substantial (Smith and Sabatino, 1989, 1990). In 1986, about 10 percent of Florida's total inmate population—2,873—were involved in work release programs. Other states with large numbers of work releasees include North Carolina (1,852), California (1,254), Alabama (1,179), and New York (1,086). At that time there were about 17,000 work releasees in the entire country. By 1994, there were 24,492 work releasees in the United States—an increase of 44 percent. Forty-three state and federal correctional systems had work release programs, and thirty-one had educational release programs (American Correctional Association, 1994:xxviii–xxix). In 1994, New York had the largest number of work releasees—5,500. Florida had about 2,100 work releasees, followed by Alabama (1,800), California (1,300), and South Carolina (1,025).

The Goals of Work Release

The goals of work release programs are to:

1. reintegrate offenders into the community;
2. give offenders an opportunity to learn and/or practice new skills;
3. provide offenders with the means to make restitution to victims of crimes;
4. give offenders a chance to help support themselves and their families;
5. help authorities predict the likelihood that offenders can be successfully paroled; and
6. improve offenders' self-images by allowing them to work in a nonincarcerative environment and to assume full responsibility for their conduct.

This North Carolina minimum-security inmate cooks for a Raleigh, North Carolina, restaurant while waiting to be paroled.

Other benefits accruing to offenders and the community are that prisoners are not idle and not exposed to the continuous moral decay associated with incarceration; that prisoners pay confinement costs and can support their families; and that prisoners can receive rehabilitative treatment and possibly work to pay back victims (Eilers, 1994; Humphrey, 1992; New York State Department of Correctional Services, 1993). Some experts suggest that work release facilitates the reintegration of offenders into their communities through the responsibilities and trust they are given by the system. Inmates subject to high-security supervision and incarceration seem more inclined to reoffend when released then those who have participated in work release programs (Stevens, 1994).

Selecting Work Releasees

Not all inmates are eligible for work release. Long-term inmates who have committed serious crimes are often automatically excluded from work release because of their risk to the community. Statutory provisions in several states specify the minimum amount of time inmates must serve before applying for work release. Of course, an advantage of being able to participate in work release is that inmates who have successfully completed work release programs stand a much better chance of being paroled than those who have not been selected. In short, they have proven themselves capable of living and working on the outside and are not considered potentially troublesome.

Parole boards in most jurisdictions are increasingly sensitive about their parole decisions because of lawsuits against parole boards that have released dangerous offenders who have subsequently injured community residents (Benson, 1988; *Division of Corrections v. Neakok*, 1986). An Alaska court held that the state has a special obligation to control dangerous parolees and to protect anyone who might be endangered by a parolee. The significance of this decision is that the court extended the state's liability to anyone in the community, thus rejecting the findings of other courts that required the threat of harm to be directed at specific, identifiable persons before parole authorities could be held liable for negligent supervision (Benson, 1988). This same concern applies to work releasees.

Alternatives to Officer Surveillance

Home Confinement, or House Arrest

The late 1980s saw a proliferation of house arrest/home incarceration/home confinement/home detention programs, primarily because of jail and prison overcrowding and the increasing availability of reliable electronic monitoring equipment (Huff, 1990). **House arrest,** or **home confinement,** is *an intermediate punishment that confines offenders to their residences during evening hours, curfews, and/or on weekends* (Brown and Elrod, 1995). Gowen (1995) adds that house arrest is a sentence in which the court orders offenders to remain confined to their own residences. They are usually allowed to leave their residences for medical reasons or employment. As further punishment they may be required to perform community service or to pay victim restitution or probation supervision fees.

Home confinement is not new. In the 1600s, Galileo, the astronomer, was forced to live out the last eight years of his life under house arrest. In 1917, Czar Nicholas II of Russia was detained under house arrest until his death. During Czar Nicholas II's reign, Lenin was placed under house arrest for a short time (Meachum, 1986:102).

In 1971, St. Louis became the first city to use house arrest but limited it to juvenile offenders. Since then house arrest for both adults and juveniles has become widespread in many jurisdictions, including Washington, DC; Baltimore; Newport News; San Jose; and Louisville (Ball, Huff and Lilly, 1988:34).

House Arrest in Florida

In 1983, incarceration of offenders in their own homes was implemented in Florida (Blomberg, Waldo, and Burcroff, 1987:171). Home incarceration has also been called house arrest, community control, or home confinement. Home incarceration is usually though not always accompanied by some form of surveillance such as electronic monitoring systems (Blomberg, Waldo, and Burcroff, 1987:169).

The Florida program has involved at least 5,000 offenders, making it the largest program of its type in the country (Blomberg, Waldo, and Burcroff, 1987:171). Three categories of offenders are eligible for home incarceration in Florida: (1) those guilty of nonforcible felonies; (2) probationers charged with technical or misdemeanor violations; and (3) parolees charged with technical or misdemeanor violations—in short, low-risk offenders (Blomberg, Waldo, and Burcroff, 1987:172).

Conditions of Home Confinement Programs

Florida statutes governing the home incarceration program require that offenders (1) report to the home confinement officer regularly; (2) perform a substantial amount of public service work without pay; (3) remain confined to their residence when not working at a regular job; (4) make periodic restitution payments to victims; (5) maintain a daily log of their activities; (6) participate in self-help programs, and (7) submit to urinalysis or blood specimen tests to determine the presence of alcohol or drugs (Blomberg, Waldo, and Burcroff, 1987:172). Thus far, the program in Florida appears successful. However, one criticism is that those considered for home confinement would probably not be incarcerated anyway. Thus, the idea that Florida is freeing up jail and prison space may be illusory. In effect, Florida may simply be widening the net rather than decreasing prison and jail overcrowding.

The Goals of Home Confinement

The goals of home confinement programs include the following:

1. To continue the offenders' punishment while permitting them to be confined to their personal residences
2. To enable offenders to hold jobs and earn a living while caring for their families and/or making restitution to victims
3. To reduce jail and prison overcrowding
4. To provide a means for ostracism while ensuring public safety
5. To reduce the costs of supervising offenders
6. To foster rehabilitation and reintegration by controlling offenders' behavior in the community

Electronic Monitoring

Electronic monitoring *is the use of telemetry devices to verify that offenders are at certain places at certain times* (Schmidt and Curtis, 1987:137). Offenders must wear electronic devices such as wristlets or anklets during the course of their sentence. The punishment for tampering with a telemetry device is being returned to prison or jail (Bellassai and Toborg, 1990). In 1987, only 800 offenders were under some type of electronic monitoring program in the United States. By 1992, that figure was estimated to be approximately 70,000 (Lilly, 1992:500).

The First Commercial Use of Electronic Monitoring

Electronic monitoring devices were first used on a commercial basis in 1964 as an alternative to incarcerating mental patients and certain parolees (Gable, 1986). In subsequent years, electronic monitoring was extended to include monitoring office work, testing employees for security clearances, and many other applications (U.S. Congress Office of Technology Assessment, 1987a, 1987b). The feasibility of using electronic devices to monitor probationers was investigated by various researchers during the 1960s and 1970s. New Mexico officially sanctioned its use for criminal offenders in 1983 (Schmidt, 1986). In the next few years, Florida, California, and Kentucky experimented with electronic monitoring devices (Smykla and Selke, 1995).

In 1983, Second Judicial District judge Jack Love of New Mexico implemented a pilot project

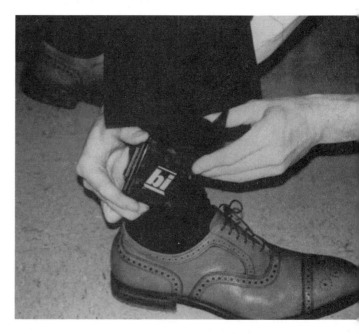

An electronic monitoring device verifying the wearer's location may be used for offenders who are confined to their homes.

to electronically monitor persons convicted of drunk driving and various white collar offenses. The New Mexico Supreme Court approved the project subject to offenders' voluntary consent as a condition of their probation and as long as their privacy, dignity, and families were protected (Houk, 1984). Offenders were required to wear anklets or wristlets that emitted electronic signals that could be intercepted by probation officers conducting surveillance operations.

Following the New Mexico experiment, other jurisdictions began using a variety of electronic monitoring systems for supervising parolees, probationers, inmates, and pretrial releasees (Cooprider and Kerby, 1990; English, Chadwick, and Pullen, 1994; Rohn and Ostroski, 1991). Both praised and condemned by criminal justice practitioners, electronic monitoring seems to be the most cost-effective solution to the problems of prison overcrowding and the management of PO caseloads (Corbett and Marx, 1991; Quinn and Holman, 1991). Until the advent of electronic monitoring devices, the idea of confining convicted offenders to their homes was simply unworkable, unless a jurisdiction was willing to pay for continuous monitoring by a probation officer.

Types of Electronic Monitoring Equipment

There are four general categories of electronic monitoring equipment. Two of these include devices that use telephones at the monitoring location and two include radio signal-emitting systems in which radio signals are received either by portable or stationary units.

Continuous signalling devices use a miniature transmitter strapped to the offender. The transmitter broadcasts an encoded signal, which is picked up by a receiver-dialer in the offender's home. The signal is relayed to a central receiver over telephone lines. While the uses of these monitoring devices are potentially unlimited and obviously not restricted to probationers, thus far, probationers have been most likely to participate in electronic monitoring programs. In most cases, electronic monitoring systems are combined with home confinement programs. By 1987, the following states were using a combination of home confinement and electronic monitoring for supervising many of their probationers: California, Colorado, Idaho, Illinois, Kentucky, Michigan, New

Jersey, New Mexico, New York, Oklahoma, Oregon, Utah, and Virginia (Blomberg, Waldo, and Burcroff, 1987: 170).

Programmed contact devices are similar to the continuous signal units, except that a central computer calls at random hours to verify that offenders are where they are supposed to be. Offenders answer the telephone and their voices are verified by computer. Some offenders have attempted to beat these electronic devices by using call forwarding and tape-recorded messages. In some instances, these efforts have been successful at deceiving the machines.

Cellular telephone devices are transmitters worn by offenders that emit a radio signal, which is received by a local area monitor. Such systems can monitor as many as twenty-five offenders simultaneously. Finally, continuous signalling transmitters, also worn by offenders, send out a continuous signal. Using a portable receiver unit, a probation officer can drive by an offender's home and verify the offender's presence. All of these devices are tamper-resistant (some claim to be tamperproof), and stiff penalties are usually imposed on offenders who tamper with their electronic anklets or wristlets (Rasmussen and Benson, 1994).

Combining Home Confinement with Electronic Monitoring

Although home confinement and electronic monitoring can be used independently of each other, it is increasingly common to see them used together in a single probationer/parolee program (Brown and Elrod, 1995; Champion, 1994). Influenced significantly by the Palm Beach County Sheriff's Department's use of house arrest, officials in Kenton County, Kentucky, decided to experiment with a similar program in their own jurisdiction. In late 1984, the court had ordered the county jail to reduce overcrowding, and electronic monitoring coupled with house arrest offered one feasible solution to the problem.

Participation in the program was strictly voluntary, and it was aimed especially at misdemeanor offenders who posed little risk to the community (Lilly, Ball, and Wright, 1987:190). However, a substantial number of offenders selected to participate had prior records, including some serious offenses. Subsequently, thirty-five offenders became program participants. According to Lilly (1985), the home incarceration program had three objectives: (1) to protect the citizenry at minimal expense; (2) to reduce jail overcrowding; and (3) to help offenders reintegrate into their communities through job training, employment, and restitution.

Lilly, Ball, and Wright (1987:191–92) have presented some evidence of the cost-effectiveness of electronic monitoring programs. With the costs of hardware, computer training, salaries for monitoring personnel, and other expenditures, the total expense for the project was $42,568. The program lasted from May 1, 1985, through mid December, 1986. It served thirty-five offenders and amounted to 1,720 person-days of home incarceration with electronic monitoring. The cost of maintaining thirty-five offenders in the Kenton County Jail during this same period at the rate of $26 per day would have been $44,720, or over $2,100 more than home incarceration. These researchers caution that the operational figures are misleading, because additional funds were not required to pay the program's administrative assistant and the probation or parole officers involved. Furthermore, new offenders entering the program would lead to more significant savings, because the direct costs of monitoring equipment and operator training had already been defrayed by the first wave of participants.

A concern of both officials and researchers was that home incarceration with electronic monitoring might serve to widen the net by imposing the program on offenders who might otherwise receive standard probation (Petersilia, 1986b:53–54). Although the sample of offenders was small, it was determined that 96 percent of these participants had prior convictions in Kentucky, while 80 percent had prior jail time. Most offenders involved probably would not have received standard probation, according to officials interviewed. Thus, net-widening did not occur (Lilly, Ball, and Wright, 1987:196).

Although the study was short-term, recidivism was extremely low. Only two participants in the program were convicted of new offenses, rendering a recidivism rate of 5.7 percent (Lilly, Ball, and Wright, 1987:196). Again percentages and/or trends must be interpreted cautiously because of the small sample. These researchers concluded that

the Kenton County project was quite economical and that it placed no additional financial burden on Kentucky taxpayers. Nearly 65 percent of the participants maintained their jobs and supported their families, thus preventing problems of nonsupport. Improved equipment and greater skill at solving some of the electronic problems encountered in the first phase of the program led these researchers to believe that home incarceration with electronic monitoring is an economical and practical long-term alternative to incarceration (Langan, 1994; Rackmill, 1994).

Recidivism among Probationers and Parolees

Some experts have adopted a "nothing works" attitude toward many of the innovative treatment programs designed to rehabilitate and/or reintegrate offenders (LeClair, 1990; Orsagh and Marsden, 1985). This is because recidivism rates among probationers and parolees are fairly high, regardless of the type of program implemented. While this overstates the case against efforts at rehabilitation, it does cause practitioners to closely examine rehabilitative schemes, probation/parole programs, and other efforts aimed at reducing recidivism.

Lack of education, having a prior record, and the seriousness of the offense committed seem most indicative of future crimes. Race, gender, age at leaving school, being employed at time of offense, and marital status do not seem to have much predictive value regarding recidivism. A fourteen-state study of recidivists during the late 1970s showed that they shared several common characteristics regarding offenses committed (Wallerstedt, 1984). Property offenders were more likely than violent offenders to recidivate within three years (36.8 percent compared with 31.5 percent). The median recidivism rate for burglary offenses in the reporting states was 43.2 percent, while the median recidivism rate for violent offenders was 34.8 percent (Wallerstedt, 1984). Also, the younger the offender at the time of parole, the greater is his or her likelihood of being returned to prison before the end of a three-year follow-up.

A study of 2,072 prisoners released from the Texas Department of Corrections in 1983 showed that race had little to do with recidivism and that females recidivated less often than males (Eissenberg, 1985b). Subsequent studies showed that those with higher recidivism rates also had prior offenses, prior offenses as juveniles, problems with drug abuse and alcoholism, and assaultive tendencies (Van Stelle, Mauser, and Moberg, 1994).

Between 1984 and 1987, 3,547 paroled property offenders in Texas were investigated to determine their recidivism rate. Texas prisons were severely overcrowded, and the Texas Department of Corrections was desperate for solutions. Early release of certain inmates through parole seemed to be one way to alleviate overcrowding. Property offenders were targeted for early release first, because they posed the least risk to the public. However, it was found that there was extensive recidivism among these property offenders. The expanded use of early release for these offenders—that is, releasing them even earlier than their original early-release dates under their original sentences—was believed the cause (Joo, Ekland-Olson, and Kelly, 1995).

Of 9,549 offenders released from North Carolina state prisons between 1979 and 1980, 33 percent returned to prison within thirty-six months (Clarke and Crum, 1985). While several of the services described earlier in this chapter (e.g., intensive supervised release, furloughs, halfway houses) appear to decrease rates of recidivism, no program seems to reduce it more than the traditional probation/parole methods used by supervisory agencies in recent years. Even the amount of time an offender serves in prison does not appear to affect recidivism rates appreciably (U.S. General Accounting Office, 1985).

Much work needs to be done to devise more effective strategies for dealing with released offenders. Individualized attention and supervision are helpful. Halfway houses, properly administered and operated, also help rehabilitate (Orchowsky, Merritt, and Browning, 1994; Van Stelle, Mauser, and Moberg, 1994). Efforts to reintegrate offenders with drug and/or alcohol problems must be even more intensive than those in existing programs (Hepburn and Albonetti, 1994).

Using furloughs to restore an offender's pride and to demonstrate trust is instrumental in putting the criminal in the right frame of mind to be rehabilitated. But it may eventually come down to the fact that for some offenders, nothing works. Ageing helps reduce criminality, but new crime control methods are needed to help younger offenders quit crime. Perhaps the new technology described here, such as electronic monitoring, house arrest, and intensive supervised probation/parole, can be an effective deterrent (Joo, 1993; Piehl, 1992). Especially critical to success during parole or probation is steady employment. States that provide effective placement services in conjunction with other programs will do much to curtail recidivism (Texas Criminal Justice Policy Council, 1992).

Summary

In 1995 nearly 3 million offenders were on probation and parole in various jurisdictions in the United States. These probationers and parolees are supervised by POs under a variety of probation/parole programs. Prison overcrowding and crowded court dockets are causing courts and prison officials to reevaluate their sentencing and early release priorities.

Probationers are not incarcerated but serve their sentences under some form of supervision. Parolees have had their sentences shortened and serve the remainder of their time under supervision similar to that of probationers. Parole originated in the early 1820s as a way of alleviating prison overcrowding. In the early days, prisoners were required to serve their entire sentences in prison.

The goals of probation and parole are to reduce crime, rehabilitate offenders, and alleviate prison overcrowding. It is questionable whether these objectives have been realized in all jurisdictions. Most states require POs to have at least a bachelor's degree. Some states have no educational requirements, and New Jersey requires only a valid driver's license. The years 1960 to 1990 saw major changes in ways of recruiting probation and parole officers.

Key Terms

John Augustus
Community corrections
Community service
Commutation
Electronic monitoring
Furloughs
Halfway house
Home confinement
House arrest
Intensive supervision programs (ISP)
Intermediate punishment programs
Alexander Maconochie
Parole
Parole board
Parole officers
Probation
Probation officers
Restitution
Work release

Questions for Review

1. Differentiate between probation and parole. How many probationers are there in the United States?
2. Do all states have minimum educational requirements for persons wishing to do probation or parole work? Do any states require educational attainment beyond the bachelor's degree?
3. What are the duties of parole/probation officers?
4. What were the "unofficial" and "official" origins of probation in the United States?
5. What was the original reason for instituting parole in U.S. prisons? About when did parole first occur in the United States?
6. How does "good time" affect a prisoner's sentence?
7. Does the use of probation reduce crime? Why or why not?
8. Are there any programs that *always* reduce recidivism among probationers and parolees?
9. Why do you think that there has been a systematic increase in the parolee population, the probationer population, *and* the prison population?

Suggested Readings

Abadinsky, Howard. 1994. *Probation and Parole: Theory and Practice.* 5th ed. Upper Saddle River, NJ: Prentice-Hall.

Champion, Dean J. 1996. *Probation, Parole, and Community Corrections.* 2d ed. Upper Saddle River, NJ: Prentice-Hall.

Cromwell, Paul F. and George G. Killinger. 1994. *Community-Based Corrections: Probation, Parole, and Intermediate Sanctions.* 3d ed. St. Paul, MN: West.

McShane, Marilyn D. and Wesley Krause. 1993. *Community Corrections.* New York: Macmillan.

Smykla, John Ortiz and William Selke (eds.). *Intermediate Sanctions: Sentencing for the 1990s.* Cincinnati, OH: Anderson.

CHAPTER 14

The Juvenile Justice System

The Case of the Homicidal Twelve-Year-Old. Two children, a twelve-year-old girl and her cousin, a seven-year-old boy, lived with their grandmother in a neighborhood of small, family-owned businesses and houses in Orlando, Florida, home of Disneyworld. The girl got mad at her cousin for tattling to their grandmother about something she had done. She put a plastic garbage bag over the boy's head, attempting to smother him. She told police later that if the plastic bag didn't kill the boy, she would have used a knife to finish him off. The boy pulled off the bag and ran away. Police were notified, and an investigation led to the arrest of the girl. She was charged with attempted murder. As an afterthought, the girl wrote, "I'm sorry" in big letters in her notebook. Her notebook also contained an incriminating confession, detailing her plans to smother the boy. The girl was held in a local detention center pending a juvenile court appearance. Her name was not disclosed because of her age (Associated Press, 1996b).

What types of punishment should be imposed on such a young child? Should children suspected of serious crimes be tried as adults? Can juvenile courts do anything to prevent such occurrences?

The Case of the Sixth Grade Poisoners. Sondra Haile, fifty-four, taught a class of thirty students at Lucerne Valley Middle School in Lucerne Valley, California. Several of her students were getting failing marks. One afternoon a group of her sixth-graders approached her. One of them said, "Watch out! Someone put something in your Gatorade!" Sondra looked at her lunch box and at her Gatorade container, which had been sitting on her desk. Nothing looked amiss. Nevertheless, Sondra took the Gatorade to the Lucerne Valley Police Department and had it tested. It contained enough rat poison to kill a horse. Apparently, the perpetrators had laced her Gatorade with the poison while she was away from her room. As the result of an investigation, two girls, ages eleven and twelve, were charged with felony food poisoning, while two boys, also eleven and twelve, were charged with being accessories after the fact. At least fifteen students saw what happened, according to police, because the four pupils put the rat poison in Ms. Haile's Gatorade in full view of the class. The boys stashed the empty rat poison box under a vent cover in the classroom (Associated Press, 1996g).

Should these children be charged as adults for attempted murder? What should be their punishment if they are judged delinquent or convicted of criminal charges? What does trying to poison their teachers for failing grades say about the students?

The Case of Federico Cruz. Federico Cruz, a sixteen-year-old high school dropout from Sparta, Michigan, had a history of criminality. On April 29, 1996, Federico decided to kill someone. He followed a young man walking along a nearby railway. First, he assaulted the man with a blunt instrument and then bludgeoned him to death. He then decapitated the man and dumped the body in a swamp a few hundred yards from his own home. He took the man's head home with him, wrapped in a plastic bag. In the privacy of his bedroom, Federico cut the man's head numerous times with a large knife. He cut out the man's brain and probed it with the tip of the knife. Finally, he put the man's head and brain back into a plastic bag and set it outside on a porch. He was arrested a few days later and charged with the man's murder. How did police know that he was the killer? Wearing a black sweatshirt, a blue bandanna across his face, dark glasses, a black ski hat, and black leather gloves, he had videotaped himself removing the man's brain and examining it. Later, during the same videotaping, Cruz removed his dark glasses and bandanna, clearly revealing his face to the camera. Next, he invited some high school friends over to watch the video. A father of one of the boys heard about the video, retrieved it from the Cruz home, and turned it over to police. Cruz confessed to the murder and showed police where to find the body. Cruz continually referred to the body as "Eddie" on the videotape, although police could not determine the man's identity from his fingerprints. Federico gave no explanation to police about why he killed the unidentified man, except that it was "something to do" (Associated Press, 1996h).

Did Federico Cruz know the man he killed? No. Had the man harmed him in any way? No. This heinous crime is without a motive. What should authorities do with Cruz? Should he be hospitalized to determine whether he is mentally ill? Should he be executed? Could this crime have been prevented, because Cruz had a prior criminal record? We have no answers to these questions.

Each of these stories describes an incident that must be resolved by the juvenile justice system. Each case has individual and emotional dimensions, and each must be decided on its own merits. Both the victims and the victimizers reflect a portion of the American social fabric that we are attempting to understand. This chapter is about juvenile offenders, who they are, how they are processed, and what happens to them.

Under the common law, persons under the age of seven cannot be punished for violating criminal laws (Black, 1990:778). In most jurisdictions children between the ages of seven and eighteen are considered **juveniles,** *persons who have not achieved the age of majority or their eighteenth birthday* (Black, 1990:778). In a third of the states, the upper age limit for juvenile status is either sixteen or seventeen. According to the federal Juvenile Justice and Delinquency Prevention Act of 1974, juveniles are persons who have not attained their eighteenth birthday (18 U.S.C. Sec. 5031, 1996). Federal law defines juvenile delinquency as the violation of a law of the United States by a person prior to his or her eighteenth birthday that would have been a crime if committed by an adult.

Although there are significant variations between the adult and juvenile justice systems, juveniles face many of the same kinds of processes that adults must go through when arrested for any offense. For example, when youthful offenders are apprehended for alleged law violations, they may be taken to jail, where their age and identity can be determined. Depending upon the offense(s) alleged, they may be released into the custody of their parents or detained in a juvenile facility. They may be subject to court proceedings, formally charged with an offense, and appear before a juvenile judge or referee. An attorney may defend them. They may be sentenced, depending upon applicable statutes and juvenile provisions, and they will ultimately enter some agency associated with juvenile corrections.

This chapter is about that large, bureaucratic apparatus dealing with juvenile offenders known as the juvenile justice system. All jurisdictions have juvenile justice systems, although the systems vary in complexity. Juvenile offenders in New York City are processed differently than those in a small farming community in Idaho. Generally, the juvenile justice system deals with juvenile delinquency.

Juvenile Delinquency

Juvenile Delinquency Defined

Because different jurisdictions define *juvenile* differently, it is difficult to construct a definition of juvenile delinquency that applies to all jurisdictions. Generally, *juvenile delinquency is any illegal behavior or activity committed by a person who is within a particular age range that subjects him or her to the jurisdiction of a juvenile court or its equivalent.* Viewed another way, **delinquency** *is any act committed by a minor child that would be considered a crime if an adult committed it.* Thus, if a fourteen-year-old boy robbed a convenience store, shot a rival gang member, raped a girl, or stole some items from a department store, each of these *acts* would be considered *delinquent acts,* because adults would be charged with *crimes* if they did the same thing.

In legal phraseology, juveniles are referred to as infants. *A delinquent child is an infant of not more than a specified age who has violated criminal laws or engages in disobedient, indecent, or immoral conduct, and is in need of treatment, rehabilitation, or supervision* (Black, 1990:428). Such acts include violations of state or local civil or criminal statutes, running away from home, being beyond the control of parents or guardians, or being habitually truant from school or repeatedly violating school rules (Black, 1990:428).

Status Offenses

Status offenses *are violations of statutes or ordinances by minors that if committed by adults would not be considered either felonies or misdemeanors.* Some communities have ordinances im-posing curfews on people under a given age. A minor who is on the streets after the curfew is a status offender. An adult would not be penalized for being on the streets after a curfew for minors. An example of a status offense for an adult might be vagrancy (Black, 1990:548).

Other status offenses are running away from home, being incorrigible at either home or school, being habitually truant from school, violating liquor laws, smoking on school grounds, loitering, or violating a court order (Little Hoover Commission, 1990; Texas Bill Blackwood Law Enforcement Management Institute, 1994). These infractions place the juvenile within the jurisdiction of the juvenile court. But these activities are not in the same category as delinquent offenses. Committing robbery or burglary are much more serious offenses than violating curfew or being truant from school.

Deinstitutionalization of Status Offenses and Net Widening

In 1974, the U.S. Office of Juvenile Justice and Delinquency Prevention promoted a Congressional Act aimed at narrowing the range of juvenile offenses considered delinquent (Hahn, 1984:182). It encouraged all jurisdictions to consider delinquent only those acts that violated federal, state, or local criminal laws. While some jurisdictions have changed their definition of delinquent conduct, many still combine status and delinquent offenders into one catch-all category for legal processing. Thus, in many jurisdictions status offenders are subject to secure confinement, just as delinquent youths might be securely confined. In other jurisdictions, such as Hawaii, juvenile crime problems are appropriately handled by the Youth Gang Response System, a collaboration between state and county agencies that emphasizes programs and community services (Chesney-Lind and Matsuo, 1995). Noncriminal cases involving status offenders are ordinarily diverted from the juvenile justice system as a means of separating nonserious from serious offenders.

Delinquent offenses are inherently more serious than status offenses. Thus, it would seem to make sense to separate such youths from those who commit status offenses through some type of official juvenile treatment policy. However, the idea of differentiating status offenses from delinquent offenses and treating each class of offender differently is controversial.

Eliminating status offenses from the delinquency category and removing juveniles from or precluding their confinement in juvenile correction facilities is referred to as the **deinstitutionalization of status offenses.** Some authorities believe that failing to remove status offenders from juvenile court jurisdiction and subjecting them to custodial confinement harden them and increase their likelihood of committing more serious criminal acts (Land, McCall, and Parker, 1994). Other authorities say that deinstitutionalizing status offenses is pointless and that recidivism rates will remain unaffected, regardless of how status offenses are treated legally (Florida Governor's Juvenile Justice and Delinquency Prevention Advisory Committee, 1994; Krause and McShane, 1994). Some of the more rural states, such as North Dakota, Montana, and Wyoming, continue to process both status and delinquent offenders together in their juvenile courts. In many instances, both juvenile delinquents and status offenders are incarcerated for varying periods in secure juvenile facilities (Champion, 1992).

Status Offending and Career Escalation

The main reason for juvenile courts to retain jurisdiction over status offenders rests on the assumption that delinquent career escalation might occur and that status offenders, if left untreated, will progress to more serious offenses. But this argument is challenged by research showing that no escalation occurs in those jurisdictions where deinstitutionalization has been implemented (Rojek and Erickson, 1982). However, just because escalation does not occur does not necessarily mean that *no* future offenses will be committed. Rather, it means only that the subsequent offenses are no more serious than earlier ones. Further, comparative studies of delinquents and status offenders show few differences in their personal and family backgrounds. Status and delinquent offenders seem to have similar assertiveness levels, self-concepts, and family histories. Delinquents tend to

have more exposure to violence, and more than a few delinquents have been physically and sexually abused (Ford and Linney, 1995).

Other studies have shown that *some* career escalation occurs among status offenders, although we don't know how much of this is due to associations with delinquents (Rankin and Wells, 1985; Thornberry, Loeber, and Huizinga, 1991; Tontondonato, 1986). It is generally accepted that the earlier the onset of status or delinquent offending, the more likely it is to continue (Elliott, 1994; LeBlanc, Cote and Loeber, 1991; Thornberry, Loeber, and Huizinga, 1991). Some studies suggest that not all status offenders are alike, that delinquent offenders differ considerably in their recidivism as either property or violent offenders, and that numerous complex factors complicate accurate predictions of career escalation (Shelden, Horvath, and Tracy, 1989; Towberman, 1992). Still other research suggests that both status and delinquent offenders will usually outgrow their youthful misconduct (Henretta, Frazier and Bishop, 1986; Rutherford, 1992).

Deinstitutionalization of Status Offenders

The deinstitutionalization of status offenders, (removing them from secure institutions), referred to as DSO, was begun in Connecticut in the 1970s (Altschuler and Luneberg, 1992). Available data for 1977 suggests that the primary impact of the DSO program was the diversion of status offenders from the state's only secure facility for juveniles at Long Lane (Logan and Rausch, 1985). The overall detention rate for the juvenile facility remained relatively unaffected, however.

Divestiture and Its Impact

In 1978, Washington passed a divestiture law that removed status offenders from the jurisdiction of juvenile courts. An analysis of 3,200 juveniles in Yakima and Seattle both before and after the legislation showed, however, that deinstitutionalization of status offenders did not remove large numbers of status offenders from control of juvenile court (Castellano, 1986). Police officers merely relabeled youths apprehended for various offenses as delinquent and processed them differently than in the prereform period. Such relabeling created the impression that delinquent acts had more than doubled within a short time. This is a good illustration of how police officers may create crime waves or eliminate them, depending upon the labels they apply to offenses.

An extensive analysis of studies investigating the impact of deinstitutionalizing status offenders has indicated that DSO may have little or no impact on recidivism (Schneider, 1984b). However, no adequate test of this particular relationship has been conducted (Schneider, 1984b:427). While public confinement of status offenders has declined considerably since the mid 1970s, private confinement of status offenders has increased during the same time period. Several states, such as Massachusetts and Rhode Island, have contracted with private providers of children's services to confine runaways and other status offenders (Keating, 1984).

DSO and Net Widening

DSO has resulted in the following: (1) **net widening,** *or pulling into the juvenile justice system youths who otherwise would not have been involved;* (2) labeling youths as delinquent who before would have been classified as status offenders; (3) no reduction in the overall rate of secure confinement for status offenders (taking into account combined private and public confinement figures); and (4) a general inadequacy of services and juvenile facilities (Schneider, 1984b:411).

How Much Juvenile Delinquency Is There?

How do we know how much juvenile delinquency or status offending there is in the United States? Measuring the true amount of delinquency is the equivalent of measuring the true amount of adult crime. The *Uniform Crime Reports* has numerous methodological inadequacies. The current delinquency figures for the United States significantly underestimate the true amount of delinquency. Police officers exercise considerable discretion in determining whether a minor should be arrested for particular offenses. Police often regard many juvenile acts as trivial, and they release youths with a stern warning (Harris, 1986:105;

Reiss, 1971). If these same youths who *could have been* arrested *had been* arrested and booked, delinquency rates would obviously be much higher than those currently reported.

In 1993, those under age eighteen accounted for 17.1 percent of all offenses charged or about 2.1 million out of 11.8 million reported offenses (Maguire and Pastore, 1995:383). Persons under age fifteen accounted for about 6 percent of these crimes. Considering index offenses only, persons under age eighteen accounted for 18.5 percent of all violent crimes, including murder and nonnegligent manslaughter, forcible rape, robbery, and aggravated assault. Persons under eighteen also accounted for 33.3 percent of all property crimes, such as burglary and motor vehicle theft (Maguire and Pastore, 1995:384).

In 1993, the most common felonies committed by persons under age eighteen were larceny and burglary/theft; the third most frequent felony was motor vehicle theft. This pattern was the same for those under age fifteen. There were 85,354 curfew or loitering law violations involving persons under eighteen in 1993, and 152,132 runaways were reported. Twenty-two percent of all liquor law violations involved persons under eighteen (Maguire and Pastore, 1995:384).

The Use of Self-Reports

One method of obtaining a more accurate picture of the amount of delinquency in the United States is **self-report surveys** (Rowe and Osgood, 1984; Giordano, Cernkovich, and Pugh, 1986). *In a self-report survey, researchers ask adolescents or minors directly about various types of offenses they have committed, regardless of whether they have been arrested for and/or charged with committing those offenses.* For example, we might enter a random cross-section of high schools or junior high schools and ask all students to respond anonymously to questions about crimes they may have committed. These responses are tabulated and compared with official estimates of delinquency such as figures reported in the *Uniform Crime Reports.*

The National Youth Survey Project has used self-reports of delinquency extensively (Elliott et

---

Highlight 14.1. Teen Crime Trends:
Crime Is Rising among Teens

During 1995, serious crime in the United States fell for the fourth consecutive year. Experts believe that the "crime wave" of the 1980s has come to an end. The most significant declines are:

Homicide: −8%	Assault: −3%
Rape: −8%	Burglary −5%
Robbery: −7%	Car theft: −6%

Crime fell substantially in the nine largest cities. For instance, in New York, homicides declined by 25 percent to 1,170 in 1995, while Chicago boasted an 11 percent decline in homicides, to 824. The Clinton administration has cited the Crime Bill as a major causal factor here, according to unofficial sources. More police officers placed on city streets have a deterrent effect, according to Clinton administration officials. U.S. Attorney General Janet Reno has said, "We will continue to put more cops on the beat, get guns off the street, and put violent criminals behind bars."

Some experts, such as James Fox at Northeast-ern University in Boston, say that the 1995 crime statistics show both good and bad trends. For instance, homicides committed by youths age fourteen to seventeen rose 22 percent during 1995, while homicides among adults declined by 18 percent for the same period. Professor Fox says, "The bad news is that we have 39 million kids under ten years of age now. They'll be teenagers before you can say 'juvenile crime wave.' If current trends persist, there will likely be a bloodbath that will make 1995 look like the good old days." Other experts share his pessimism.

How reliable are crime statistics? Do we really know much about crimes that go unreported? What cautions might we observe when interpreting crime trends?

Source: Adapted from Kevin V. Johnson, "Homicide, Rape, Robbery: The Numbers Are Fewer," *USA Today,* May 6, 1996, p.9A.

---

al., 1983). Between 1976 and 1980, a survey of a national probability sample of 1,725 adolescents between the ages of eleven and seventeen disclosed the extent of their delinquent behavior. Males committed delinquent acts more often than females. Urban youths were more likely to report delinquency than rural youths. Generally, the study showed higher rates of delinquency among those surveyed than official estimates through other sources. Most of those surveyed were involved in some delinquent activity in each of the years between 1976 and 1980. However, serious and violent offenses accounted for only a small proportion of offenses reported (Elliott et al., 1983).

One flaw of self-reporting delinquency is that juveniles may exaggerate or fantasize about their exploits (Farrington and Tarling, 1985). One survey of teenage smoking behavior among 4,300 students in grades seven through twelve in Muscatine, Iowa, showed a discrepancy between self-reported behavior and actual behavior when validated independently by certain biochemical methods (Akers et al., 1983). For the offense of smoking, a biochemical measure of smoking (salinary thiocyanate) can be used in conjunction with self-reports to minimize the effects of the deliberate "faking" of responses.

Regardless of the weaknesses of self-reporting, it is a legitimate alternative to the official measuring of juvenile crimes (Curry and Spergel, 1992; Gold and Osgood, 1992; Krueger et al., 1994). It may also be used to chart the potential effectiveness of different kinds of delinquency programs. For instance, in the late 1970s, various jurisdictions established the federally funded Juvenile Restitution Initiative (Griffith, 1983). Participating juvenile delinquents were surveyed in six-month intervals between 1980 and 1983 to determine whether making restitution to their victims had any effect on their behaviors or attitudes. Sites such as

Washington, DC, Clayton County, Georgia, Ada County, Idaho, Oklahoma County, Oklahoma, and Dane County, Wisconsin, were surveyed. Self-report information showed that groups that made restitution had lower rates of self-reported reoffending than groups that did not participate in the project (Elliott, 1994).

The Juvenile Justice System

The first juvenile court in the United States was created in Illinois in 1899 under the Illinois Juvenile Court Act (U.S. General Accounting Office, 1995). Prior to 1899, other states attempted to establish ways of dealing with juvenile offenders. In 1874, Massachusetts enacted a statute establishing "children's tribunals" for dealing with "children charged with crimes" (Hahn, 1984:5). New York passed a similar law in 1892. And in 1899, the same year the Illinois Act was passed, Colorado enacted an education law that was an informal version of today's juvenile court (U.S. General Accounting Office, 1995).

Before these developments, juvenile matters were processed in courts of chancery or equity. These courts were created in the twelfth century by the king of England and were presided over by chancellors or judges appointed by the king. Matters before courts of chancery involved property boundary disputes, trespass, dispute resolution in business transactions, and, of course, matters pertaining to children.

Such courts operated under common law and the doctrine of *parens patriae*, which means "parent of the country" (Black, 1990:1114). The king, through his agents or chancellors, oversaw the welfare of his subjects, especially minors. Several jurisdictions in the United States today have chancery courts that resolve juvenile matters. Many other jurisdictions, however, have courts of limited jurisdiction that handle only juvenile problems.

An Overview of the Juvenile Justice System

The juvenile justice system is made up of a more or less integrated network of agencies, institutions, organizations, and personnel that process juvenile offenders. This network is made up of law enforcement agencies, prosecutors, and courts; corrections, probation, and parole services; and public and private community-based treatment programs. This definition is qualified by the phrase "more or less integrated" because the concept of juvenile justice means different things to the states and to the federal government. Also, in some jurisdictions, the diverse components of the juvenile justice system are closely coordinated, while in other jurisdictions, they are loosely coordinated at best.

The Origins and Purposes of Juvenile Courts

Juvenile courts are a relatively recent U.S. creation. However, modern U.S. juvenile courts have various less formal European antecedents. The age of seven was used in Roman times to separate infants from older children, who were accountable to the law for their actions. During the Middle Ages, English common law established under the monarchy adhered to the same standard. In the United States, several state jurisdictions consider all children below the age of seven not accountable for any criminal acts.

Juvenile Reforms

Reforms in the American colonies relating to the treatment and/or punishment of juvenile offenders occurred slowly. Shortly after the Revolutionary War, religious interests in the United States made various proposals to improve the plight of the oppressed, particularly those who were incarcerated. In 1787, the Quakers in Pennsylvania established the *Philadelphia Society for Alleviating the Miseries of Public Prisons*. This largely philanthropic society comprised of prominent citizens and religious leaders was appalled at conditions in prisons and jails. Male and female offenders, old and young alike were housed in common quarters and treated poorly. In 1790, the Society's efforts were rewarded by the opening of the Walnut Street Jail in Philadelphia. This jail had considerable historical significance for corrections as well as for juvenile offenders. As one of its major innovations, during evening hours women and children were maintained in separate rooms apart from adult male offenders.

The *New York House of Refuge* was established in New York City in 1825 by the Society for the Prevention of Pauperism (Cahalan, 1986:101). This institution was largely devoted to managing status offenders, such as runaways and incorrigible children, who received compulsory education and other forms of training and assistance. However, the strict, prison like regimen of this organization was not entirely therapeutic. Many of the youthful offenders sent to such institutions, including the House of Reformation in Boston, were the offspring of immigrants.

Ex parte Crouse

Until the late 1830s, authority over children was divided unequally among parents, the church, and the state. In 1838, a court decision vested juvenile authorities with considerable parental power. *Ex parte Crouse* (1838) involved a father who sought custody of his daughter from the Philadelphia House of Refuge. The girl had been committed to that facility by the court because she was declared unmanageable. She was not given a jury trial but was arbitrarily committed by a judge. A higher court rejected the father's claim that parental control of children is exclusive, natural, and proper. It upheld the power of the state to exercise necessary reforms and restraints to protect children from themselves and their environments. While this decision was applicable only to Pennsylvania citizens and their children, other states took note of it and sought to invoke similar controls over errant children in their jurisdictions. In effect, children (at least in Pennsylvania) were temporarily deprived of any legal standing to challenge decisions made by the state in their behalf. This was the general state of juvenile affairs until the post–Civil War period known as Reconstruction. Considerable family migration toward large cities occurred after the Civil War. New York, Philadelphia, Boston, and Chicago were centers where fragmented families attempted to find work.

Quite often, both parents had to work, and such work involved extended working hours (e.g., sixteen-hour work periods). This meant that while parents worked, increasing numbers of children roamed city streets unsupervised. Religious organizations subsequently intervened to protect unsupervised youths from the perils of life in the streets. Believing that these youths would subsequently turn to lives of crime as adults, many reformers and philanthropists sought to "save" them from their plight. Thus, in different cities throughout the United States, various groups were formed to find and control these youths by offering them constructive work programs, healthful living conditions, and above all, adult supervision. Collectively, these efforts became widely known as the child-saving movement. Child-savers came largely from the middle and upper classes, and their assistance to youths took many forms. Food and shelter were provided to children who were in trouble with the law or who were simply idle. Private homes were converted into settlements where social, educational, and other important activities could be provided for needy youths.

The Advent of Reform Schools

Prior to the Civil War, reform schools proliferated. One of the first state-operated reform schools was established in Westboro, Massachusetts, in 1848 (U.S. Department of Justice, 1976). By the end of the century, all states had reform schools. All of these institutions were characterized by strict discipline, absolute control over juvenile behavior, and compulsory work at various trades. Another common feature was that they were controversial.

Early Children's Tribunals

While Illinois is credited with establishing the first juvenile court system in the United States, an earlier juvenile justice apparatus was created in Massachusetts in 1874. Known as the children's tribunal, this was used exclusively to deal with children charged with crimes; it was kept separate from the system of criminal courts for adults (Hahn, 1984:5). In 1899, Colorado implemented an education law known as the Compulsory School Act.

Dependent and Neglected Children

During the 1880s, relatively few legal challenges of state authority over juveniles were lodged by parents. But in 1870, an Illinois case made it possible for special courts to dispose of juvenile matters, thus representing an early recognition of certain minimal rights children might have. Daniel O'Connell, a youth who was declared vagrant and in need of supervision, was committed to the Chicago Reform School for an unspecified period. O'Connell's parents challenged this court action, claiming that his confinement for vagrancy was unjust and untenable. At the time, Illinois law vested state authorities with the power to commit any juvenile to a state reform school as long as they provided "reasonable justification." In this instance, vagrancy was a reasonable justification. The Illinois Supreme Court distinguished between misfortune (vagrancy) and criminal acts in arriving at its decision to reverse Daniel O'Connell's commitment. In effect, the court nullified the law by declaring that the state could not commit youths to reform school if their "offense" was simple misfortune. The court reasoned that the state's interests would be better served if juveniles committed to reform schools were limited to those guilty of more serious criminal offenses rather than those who were victims of misfortune.

The First Juvenile Court

Three decades later, on July 1, 1899, the Illinois legislature established the first juvenile court by passing the *Act to Regulate the Treatment and Control of Dependent, Neglected, and Delinquent Children*, or the Juvenile Court Act. This act provided for limited courts of record, where notes might be taken by judges or their assistants, to reflect judicial actions against juveniles. The jurisdiction of these courts, subsequently designated as "juvenile courts," would include all juveniles under the age of sixteen who were found in violation of any state or local law or ordinance. Also, provision was made for the care of dependent and/or neglected children who had been abandoned or who otherwise lacked proper parental care, support, or guardianship. No minimum age was specified that would limit the jurisdiction of juvenile court judges. However, the act provided that judges could impose secure confinement of juveniles ten years of age or over by placing them in state-regulated juvenile facilities such as the state reformatory

or the State Home for Juvenile Female Offenders. Judges were expressly prohibited from confining any juvenile under twelve years of age in a jail or police station. Extremely young juveniles would be assigned probation officers to temporarily look after their needs and placement. Between 1900 and 1920, twenty states passed similar acts to establish juvenile courts. By the end of World War II, all states had juvenile court systems. However, these court systems varied considerably.

Differences Between Juvenile and Criminal Courts

This section describes several major similarities in and differences between juvenile and criminal courts. The diversity among juvenile courts precludes blanket generalizations about them. Generally, the following statements apply to juvenile and criminal courts.

1. Juvenile courts hold civil proceedings exclusively for juveniles, whereas criminal courts hold proceedings for alleged violators of criminal laws. In criminal courts, alleged criminal law violators are primarily adults, although some juveniles may be tried as adults in criminal courts.
2. Juvenile proceedings are informal, whereas criminal proceedings are formal. Many juvenile courts attempt to avoid the formal trappings that characterize criminal proceedings.
3. In most states, juveniles are not entitled to a trial by jury, unless the juvenile judge approves.
4. Both juvenile and criminal proceedings are adversarial. Juveniles may or may not wish to retain or be represented by counsel. Today, the juvenile codes in most states provide for public defenders for juveniles if they are indigent and cannot afford to hire private counsel.
5. Criminal courts are courts of record, whereas juvenile proceedings may or may not maintain a running transcript of proceedings.
6. The standard of proof used for determining guilt in criminal proceedings is "beyond a reasonable

doubt." Judges in juvenile courts use the same standard for juvenile delinquents who face possible commitment to secure juvenile facilities. In other court proceedings that do not lead to commitment, the court uses the civil standard of "preponderence of the evidence." (Some states, particularly rural states like North Dakota, continue to commit status offenders to secure youth facilities together with juvenile delinquents.)

7. The range of penalties juvenile judges may impose is more limited than in criminal courts. Both juvenile and criminal courts can impose fines, restitution, community service, probation, and other forms of conditional discharge. Juvenile courts can also impose stays in secure or nonsecure facilities, group homes, and camps/ranches. Long terms of commitment to secure facilities are also within the purview of juvenile court judges. In most criminal courts, penalties may include life imprisonment or the death penalty.

These comparisons show that the actions of criminal courts are more serious and have more significant long-term consequences for offenders than actions taken by juvenile courts. However, juvenile courts do have the power to place juveniles in secure confinement for lengthy periods. Table 14.1 summarizes some of the differences between the treatment of juveniles and adults relating to delinquency and crime.

Strong rehabilitative orientations drive juvenile courts in most jurisdictions, despite a general "get-tough" movement that developed during the 1980s and 1990s, while criminal courts are seemingly adopting more punitive sanctions for adult offenders. Many critics see juvenile courts moving toward a "just deserts" philosophy in the treatment and adjudication of juveniles. However, many youth are still subject to treatment-oriented nonsecure alternatives rather than custodial options. Furthermore, overcrowding is a chronic problem in many juvenile facilities. Thus, correctional facilities for juveniles mirror many of the same problems as those for adults. Thus, it is in the best interests of the state to provide alternatives to incarceration for both adult and juvenile offenders.

Parens Patriae

Cases in juvenile courts have always been given considerable latitude. The freedom to act in a child's behalf is rooted in the largely unchallenged doctrine of *parens patriae.* The *parens patriae* doctrine received formal recognition in U.S. courts in the case of *Ex parte Crouse* (1838).

Components of *Parens Patriae*

The key components of *parens patriae* that have contributed to its persistence as a dominant philosophical perspective in the juvenile justice system are as follows:

1. *Parens patriae* encourages informal handling of juvenile matters as opposed to more formal and criminalizing procedures.
2. *Parens patriae* vests juvenile courts with absolute authority to do what is best for youthful offenders (e.g., provide support services and other forms of care).
3. *Parens patriae* strongly encourages benevolent and rehabilitative treatments to help youths overcome their personal and social problems.
4. *Parens patriae* avoids the effects of adverse labeling that might result from formal court proceedings.
5. *Parens patriae* means state control over juvenile life chances.

An example of *parens patriae* is the interaction of police officers with juveniles during the 1940s, 1950s, and 1960s. Whenever juveniles were apprehended by police officers, they were eventually turned over to juvenile authorities or taken to *juvenile halls* for further processing. Juveniles were *not* advised of their right to an attorney, to have an attorney present during any interrogation, and to remain silent. They were subject to lengthy interrogations by police, without parental notification and consent or legal counsel. Juveniles had virtually *no* assurance of the constitutional rights that apply to adults. *Due process* simply did not apply to juveniles.

Since juvenile proceedings in most jurisdictions were quite informal, frequent and obvious abuses of judicial discretion occurred because of

Table 14.1

Comparison of Juvenile and Adult Rights Relating to Delinquency and Crime[a]

Right	Adults	Juveniles
1. "Beyond a Reasonable Doubt" standard used in court	Yes	Yes
2. Right against double jeopardy	Yes	Yes
3. Right to assistance of counsel	Yes	Yes
4. Right to notice of charges	Yes	Yes
5. Right to a transcript of court proceedings	Yes	No
6. Right against self-incrimination	Yes	Yes
7. Right to trial by jury	Yes	No in most states
8. Right to defense counsel in court proceedings	Yes	No
9. Right to due process	Yes	No*
10. Right to bail	Yes	No, with exceptions
11. Right to cross-examine witnesses	Yes	Yes
12. Right of confrontation	Yes	Yes
13. Standards relating to searches and seizures:		
a. "Probable cause" and warrants required for searches and seizures	Yes, with exceptions	No
b. "Reasonable suspicion" required for searches and seizures without warrant	No	Yes
14. Right to hearing prior to transfer to criminal court or to a reverse waiver hearing in states with automatic transfer provisions	NA	Yes
15. Right to a speedy trial	Yes	No
16. Right to *habeas corpus* relief in correctional settings	Yes	No
17. Right to rehabilitation	No	No
18. Criminal evidentiary standards	Yes	Yes
19. Right to hearing for parole or probation revocation	Yes	No
20. Bifurcated trial, death penalty cases	Yes	Yes
21. Right to discovery	Yes	Limited
22. Fingerprinting, photographing at booking	Yes	No, with exceptions
23. Right to appeal	Yes	Limited
24. Waivers of rights		
a. Adults	Knowingly, intelligently	
b. Juveniles		Totality of circumstances
25. Right to hearing for parole or probation revocation	Yes	No, with exceptions
26. "Equal protection" clause of Fourteenth Amendment applicable	Yes	No, with exceptions
27. Right to court-appointed attorney if indigent	Yes	No, with exceptions
28. Transcript required of criminal/delinquency trial proceedings	Yes	No, with exceptions
29. Pretrial detention permitted	Yes	Yes
30. Plea bargaining	Yes, with exceptions	No, with exceptions
31. Burden of proof borne by prosecution	Yes	No, with exceptions**
32. Public access to trials	Yes	Limited
33. Conviction/adjudication results in criminal record	Yes	No

a. Compiled by author

* Minimal, not full, due process safeguards assured

** Burden of proof is borne by prosecutor in twenty-three state juvenile courts, while the rest make no provision or mention of who bears the burden of proof.

the absence of consistent guidelines whereby cases could be adjudicated. Juvenile POs might casually recommend to judges that particular juveniles "ought to do a few months" in an industrial school or other secure detention facility, and the judge might be persuaded to adjudicate these cases accordingly. However, several forces at work during the 1950s and 1960s eventually made juvenile courts more accountable for specific adjudications of youthful offenders. One of these forces was increased parental and public recognition of and concern for the license taken by juvenile courts in administering the affairs of juveniles. The abuse of judicial discretion was becoming increasingly apparent. Additionally, there was a growing disenchantment with the rehabilitative ideal, although this disenchantment was not directed solely at juvenile courts. Rogers and Mays (1987:383) note that "disaffection during the 1960s and 1970s with the juvenile court was typical of the disenchantment then with many of society's institutions."

One juvenile justice expert, Barry Feld (1988), says that the juvenile court as originally envisioned by Progressives was procedurally informal, characterized by individualized, offender-oriented dispositional practices. However, the contemporary juvenile court has departed markedly from this Progressive ideal. Today, juvenile courts are increasingly criminalized, featuring an adversarial system and greater procedural formality. This formality effectively inhibits any individualized treatment these courts might contemplate, and it has increased the perfunctory nature of sentencing juveniles adjudicated as delinquent.

The shift from *parens patriae,* state-based interests to a "due process" juvenile justice model occurred gradually during the 1970s. The shift did not make *parens patriae* disappear, however. Rather, it signified a general abandonment of most of these *parens patriae* elements. Decision making relative to youthful offenders became more rationalized, and the philosophy of "just deserts" increasingly influenced the disposition of juvenile cases. This shift resulted in less discretionary authority among juvenile judges, since they began to decide each case more on the basis of the seriousness of the offense than on the individual characteristics of the youthful offender.

Arrests and Other Options

In most cases, police officers need little justification to apprehend juveniles or *take them into custody.* There is little uniformity among jurisdictions in how an "arrest" is defined. There is even greater ambiguity about what constitutes a juvenile arrest. Technically, an arrest is the legal detainment of a person to answer for criminal charges or (infrequently at present) civil demands (Rush, 1994:18). Arrests of juveniles are more serious than simply taking them into custody.

Since any juvenile may be taken into custody on any pretext, all types of juveniles may be temporarily detained at police headquarters or at a sheriff's station, department, or jail. Suspected runaways, truants, or curfew violators may be taken into custody for their own welfare or protection, not necessarily for the purpose of facing subsequent charges (Texas Bill Blackwood Law Enforcement Management Institute, 1994). It is standard police policy in most jurisdictions for officers and jailers to turn juveniles over to the appropriate agencies as soon as possible after these youths have been taken into custody. If a youth's alleged offenses are serious, he or she may be placed in detention temporarily, before being brought before a juvenile court judge (Schwartz and Barton, 1994). The first screening of juveniles before further proceedings take place is called *intake* (Altschuler, 1991).

Intake Screenings and Detention Hearings

Intake or an intake screening is the second major step in the juvenile justice process. It is a more or less informally conducted screening procedure in which intake POs or other juvenile court functionaries decide whether detained juveniles should be (1) unconditionally released from the juvenile justice system, (2) released to parents or guardians subject to a subsequent juvenile court appearance, (3) released or referred to one or more community-based services or resources, (4) placed in secure detention subject to a subsequent juvenile court appearance, or (5) waived or transferred to the jurisdiction of criminal courts.

During intake hearings, POs have virtually unbridled discretion regarding a youth's chances in the system. No constitutional provisions require states to conduct such hearings, apart from certain state-mandated hearings that must precede formal adjudicatory proceedings held before juvenile judges (Wadlington et al., 1983). Intake officers seldom hear legal arguments or evaluate the sufficiency of evidence for or against youths. These proceedings usually result in *adjustments,* where intake officers adjust the particular matter informally to almost everyone's satisfaction. Dougherty (1988:78) notes that while intake officers might advise juveniles and their parents that they *may* have attorneys present during such proceedings, these officers also indicate that the presence of attorneys may "jeopardize" the "informal" nature of these proceedings and any possible "informal" resolution of the case that might be made. Thus, parents and youths are tacitly discouraged from having legal counsel at this critical screening stage (Guggenheim, 1985).

Petitions and Adjudicatory Proceedings

Considerable variation exists among jurisdictions in how juvenile court proceedings are conducted. Increasingly, juvenile courts are emulating criminal courts in many respects (Krisberg, 1988). Most of the physical trappings are present, including the judge's bench, tables for the prosecution and defense, and a witness stand. In some jurisdictions, such as Ocean County, New Jersey, however, these facilities are being redesigned to appear less courtlike and threatening (Kearney, 1989). Manuals are available that catalog various pleadings defense attorneys may enter in juvenile courtrooms, and there is growing interest in the rules of juvenile court procedure (Volenik, 1986). Further, there appears to be more interest in holding juveniles accountable for their actions than there was in past years (Feld, 1987).

Delinquency Petitions

Prosecutors either file petitions or act on the petitions filed by others (Laub and MacMurray, 1987). *Petitions are official documents filed in juvenile courts on the juvenile's behalf, specifying reasons for the youth's court appearance. These documents assert that juveniles fall within the categories of dependent or neglected, status offender, or delinquent, and the reasons for such assertions are usually provided* (Rogers and Mays, 1987:571). In many jurisdictions, filling a petition formally places the juvenile before the juvenile judge. But juveniles may come before juvenile judges in less formal ways. Those able to file petitions against juveniles include their parents, school officials, neighbors, or any other interested party. The legitimacy and factual accuracy of petitions are evaluated by juvenile court judges.

The Discretion of Juvenile Court Judges

In most jurisdictions, juvenile judges have almost absolute discretion in how their courts are conducted. Juvenile defendants may or may not be granted a trial by jury, if one is requested. Few states permit jury trials for juveniles, according to legislative mandates. After hearing the evidence presented by both sides, the juvenile court judge decides or *adjudicates* the matter. An **adjudication** is *a judgment or action on the petition filed with the court.* If the petition alleges delinquency, the judge determines whether the juvenile is or is not delinquent. If the petition alleges that the juveniles involved are dependent, neglected, or otherwise in need of care by agencies or others, the judge decides the matter. If the adjudicatory proceeding fails to support the facts alleged in the petition, the case is dismissed and the youth is freed. If the adjudicatory proceeding supports the allegations, the judge must adjudicate the youth as either a delinquent, a status offender, or someone in need of special treatment or supervision. The juvenile court judge then has several options for disposing of the case. The judge may order a predispositional report to be prepared by a juvenile probation officer, or he or she may declare the juvenile to be an adult and *transfer* or *waive* the youth to a criminal court for processing.

Transfers, Waivers, and Certifications

Transfers, also known as waivers and certifications, are *transferrals or shifts of jurisdiction over certain types of cases from juvenile courts to criminal* courts (Champion, 1989a). These terms will be used interchangeably throughout this chapter. Youths who are subjected to waivers are *not* tried as juveniles (Mays and Houghtalin, 1992). Rather, they are redefined and classified as adults and eventually tried in criminal courts. Only a small proportion of juveniles each year are subject to criminal court transfers. Preliminary determinations are made of crime seriousness, the youth's characteristics, such as age and other factors associated with the type of crime committed, and the amount or degree of the victim's injuries.

There are four types of waivers. These include (1) **prosecutorial waivers,** (2) **judicial waivers,** (3) **demand waivers,** and (4) **legislative waivers.**

Prosecutorial Waivers

When offenders are screened at intake and referred to the juvenile court for possible prosecution, prosecutors in various jurisdictions conduct further screenings. They determine which cases merit further action and formal adjudication by judges. Not all cases sent to prosecutors by intake POs automatically result in subsequent formal juvenile court action. In an Oregon case, for instance, a juvenile who had recently turned eighteen was charged with armed robbery. The prosecutor in the case believed the charge to be serious enough to warrant transferring the juvenile to criminal court. Further, the youth had an extensive record of delinquency. The Oregon Court of Appeals rejected the youth's appeal, and he was tried as an adult in criminal court (*State ex rel. Juvenile Dept. v. George,* 1993).

Judicial or Discretionary Waivers

Most waivers from juvenile to criminal court result from direct judicial action. *Juvenile judges in most jurisdictions may take independent action and waive certain juveniles to criminal court jurisdiction.* Judicial waivers are also known as *discretionary waivers,* because judges exercise their discretion when transferring jurisdiction over these juveniles to criminal court judges (Virginia Commission on Youth, 1993).

Demand Waivers

In some jurisdictions juveniles may ask for demand waivers. *Demand waivers are demands by ju-*

veniles to have their cases transferred from juvenile courts and tried in criminal courts. Why would they want to do this? Most jurisdictions do not provide jury trials for juveniles in juvenile courts as a matter of right. However, about a fifth of the states have legislatively provided for jury trials for juveniles at their request, depending upon the nature of the charges. The rest of the states grant jury trials for juveniles only at the discretion of the juvenile judge (Mays and Houghtalin, 1992). Most juvenile judges are not inclined to grant jury trials to juveniles. Thus, if juveniles (1) are in a jurisdiction where they are not entitled to a jury trial, (2) face serious charges, and (3) believe that their cases would be heard more impartially by a jury in a criminal courtroom, they may use a demand waiver to have their cases transferred to criminal court, where they *will be entitled to a jury trial.* The constitutions of nearly forty states, including Oregon, do not permit juveniles to have jury trials in juvenile courts (*State ex rel. Juvenile Dept. v. Jackson,* 1993).

Legislative or Automatic Waivers

Automatic transfers, or *legislative waivers, are statutorily prescribed actions that provide for a specified list of crimes to be excluded from the jurisdiction of juvenile courts, where offending juveniles are within a specified age range, and where the resulting action gives criminal courts immediate jurisdiction over the juveniles.* By the mid 1980s, thirty-six states excluded certain types of offenses from juvenile court jurisdiction. These offenses ranged from traffic or fishing violations to rape or murder (U.S. Department of Justice, 1988:79). Also, many state jurisdictions, such as Washington, New York, and Illinois, have made provisions for automatic transfers of juveniles to criminal court (Sagatun, Mc-Collum and Edwards, 1985).

Waiver Hearings

All juveniles are entitled to waiver hearings prior to being transferred to criminal court (*Kent v. United States,* 1966). Waiver hearings are normally conducted before the juvenile judge. These hearings are to some extent evidentiary, since a case must be made for why criminal courts should have jurisdiction in any specific instance. Usually, juveniles with lengthy prior records, several previous

---

Highlight 14.2. Stabbing Death Results in Youth Transfers to Criminal Court: The Murder at Gordon's Holiday Spot Motel

In Minot, North Dakota, three adults and a seventeen-year-old were arrested in early January of 1996 for the murder of Curt "Scott" Sieglin, forty-six, the manager of Gordon's Holiday Spot Motel. Sieglin's body had multiple stab wounds, which coroners said were "defense" wounds received when he attempted to fend off his attackers. An undetermined amount of cash and checks were missing from the cash register, which was left open.

The break in the case came when authorities investigated a former employee of the motel, a seventeen-year-old unnamed juvenile. The juvenile, who had moved to Bismarck, had worked at the motel with Sieglin during the Thanksgiving holidays. When questioned by police in Bismarck, the youth implicated three others, including Scott Kyle Clark, eighteen, Jason Gregory Morrell, eighteen, and James Alexander Fannin, twenty-two. These suspects made

incriminating statements about one another, according to police sources. The unnamed juvenile was scheduled to be transferred to criminal court to stand trial on murder charges.

Police believed that the unnamed juvenile told the older suspects about the motel and the available cash. Actually, the murder-robbery netted the suspects only about $300. No motive other than robbery was provided.

The get-tough movement is steadily gaining support. Juveniles are being transferred to criminal court at younger ages. Are transfers effective deterrents to juvenile delinquency?

Source: Adapted from Kent Olson, "Four Arrested in Stabbing Death," _Minot (N.D.) Daily News,_ January 7, 1996, p. A1.

---

referrals, and/or one or more previous adjudications as delinquent are more apt to be transferred (Dundes, 1994). While the offenses alleged are most often crimes, they are not always very serious (Podkopacz, 1994). In some instances, chronic, persistent, or habitual status offenders have been transferred, particularly if they have violated specific court orders to attend school, participate in therapeutic programs, perform community service, make restitution, or engage in some other constructive enterprise (Sickmund, 1994).

Where jurisdictions use automatic or legislative waivers, _reverse waiver hearings_ are conducted. These hearings seek to restore the original jurisdiction over the case to the juvenile court, if a juvenile defendant wishes to seek such jurisdiction. For _both_ waiver and reverse waiver hearings, defense counsel and the prosecution attempt to make a case for their desired action. A waiver or reverse waiver hearing can result in a juvenile having his or her case decided

either in criminal courts, where criminal penalties can be imposed, or in juvenile court, where judicial dispositional options are more restricted. New York, for example, has special sentencing guidelines that criminal court judges must follow in cases where juveniles have been transferred to criminal court and convicted of crimes. New York law provides that youths thirteen to sixteen years old must receive specific sentences for specific crimes, such as murder, arson, kidnapping, burglary, rape, and robbery. These sentences range from three to fifteen years, depending upon the offense.

Prevention and Diversion

There are three stages in the juvenile justice system. These involve (1) prevention and diversion, (2) the juvenile court, and (3) juvenile corrections. The phase of the juvenile justice process concerned with prevention and diversion involves decisions by both police officers and juvenile intake personnel. If a law enforcement officer arrests a juvenile suspect instead of warning and releasing her or him, one of four things happens. First, the parents or guardians of the arrested youth are notified. If the offense is a status offense rather than a criminal act, the youth may be counseled and released to his or her parents.

A second option is to refer or divert juveniles to community resources such as residential treatment centers where they can receive group therapy or counseling services (Pierce, 1985). Several states have agencies that deal with special juvenile problems. Missouri's Division of Family Services handles a large number of juvenile referrals and devises particular residential treatment programs for low-risk juvenile offenders prior to any formal court action (Pierce, 1985). If a youth succeeds in either of these two alternatives (i.e., counseling and release or referral and diversion), he or she avoids further contact with the juvenile justice system.

If the alleged offense is more serious, however, two remaining options are available. First, *a citation and referral to juvenile intake and release to parents* may be recommended. This procedure is a temporary release of the juvenile to his or her parents or guardians and is tantamount to bail for adult offenders. The juvenile will reappear at a later date and face an intake screening, at which the juvenile's alleged offense will be more closely examined. The second, more severe option is to *transport the youth to juvenile hall or another shelter* for secure detention. These options are followed in a number of jurisdictions, including Chicago; Lancaster County, Nebraska; Philadelphia; and Lake County, Indiana (Butts and Gable, 1992; Johnson and Secret, 1990; Natalini, 1985; Stewart, Vockell, and Ray, 1986).

As a result of the Juvenile Justice and Delinquency Prevention Act of 1974, several improvements in juvenile detention have been made. Better services and facilities have been provided in many jurisdictions (Florida Advisory Council on Intergovernmental Relations, 1994). The average length of juvenile detention, previously as much as thirty days or longer in some jurisdictions, has been shortened. Also, most jurisdictions now separate juveniles from adult offenders. Some states continue to engage in controversial juvenile detention practices, however (Champion, 1989a; Florida Advisory Council on Intergovernmental Relations, 1994; Virginia Commission on Youth, 1994).

Juveniles are eventually classified in a subsequent **intake screening.** *An intake screening is a critical phase in which a juvenile probation officer or other official makes a determination whether to release juveniles into their parents' custody, detain juveniles in formal detention facilities for a later court appearance, or release them to parents pending a later court appearance.*

Intake screenings are important because they enable a probation officer to examine closely the facts or circumstances associated with the juvenile's alleged offense. Do the parents appear responsible and capable of controlling the youth's behavior? Does the seriousness of the offense warrant further legal action? Does the youth appear to be the victim of child abuse? Is the youth mentally retarded? Are there community resources that can meet the juvenile's needs as an alternative to court action? Most probation officers try to keep the juvenile out of the juvenile justice process. At this stage the officer predicts whether the juvenile offender will be a risk to society. As is the case with any behavioral prediction, there will always be errors of judgment.

Diverting juvenile offenders from further involvement in the juvenile justice system is seen by some as a way of helping juveniles avoid being labeled as delinquents and ultimately of reducing adult criminal justice costs (Lieb, Fish, and Crosby, 1994; Miller, 1991). For example, in 1974, the Youth Section of the Dallas Police Department established a diversion program to combat 50 percent recidivism rates among juveniles (Williams, 1984). Between 1975 and 1982, the program serviced 19,745 youths, and the recidivism rate dropped to 21 percent (Williams, 1984).

In 1981, the New Orleans district attorney's office implemented a juvenile diversion program targeted at first-offender juvenile felons (Litton and Marye, 1983). Some of the services the program provided included intensive counseling, parent involvement, restitution to victims, and the use of certain community services. While the project did not fully realize its goals, 80 percent of the participants did not recidivate within one year of their release from the program (Litton and Marye, 1983).

Critics of diversion claim that often such programs result in net-widening (Schneider, 1984b; Miller, 1991). For instance, between 1977 and 1981, the Status Offender Service Unit in St. Louis, Missouri, resulted in net-widening as increasing numbers of juveniles were referred to juvenile court by police and other authorities (Decker, 1985). But given police officers' predominant values, it is unrealistic to expect them to support a true diversion program enthusiastically (Decker, 1985). Apparently, police officers want to retain their discretionary powers regarding status offenders and do not want a Status Offender Service Unit telling them how to handle juveniles in the field. One unfortunate consequence of the Status Offender program in St. Louis was the abuse of police discretion at the expense of the status offenders the program was designed to help. Police officers began arresting and detaining juveniles for relatively minor offenses that prior to the establishment of the Status Offender Service Unit would have drawn only verbal warnings and token "wrist slaps." Similar actions by police have been observed in other jurisdictions (Websdale, 1991).

Intake screening of juvenile cases results in one of three kinds of dispositions. First, juveniles may be released to their parents or referred to the appropriate community services. No further contact with the juvenile justice system takes place. Second, juveniles may be released into the custody of their parents prior to a possible court appearance at a later date. Third, the juvenile may be detained in an appropriate juvenile shelter, possibly even a jail, until a formal **detention hearing** can be held.

A detention hearing is a judicial or quasi-judicial proceeding held to determine whether or not it is appropriate to continue to hold or detain a juvenile in a shelter facility (Black, 1990:450). Detention hearings are similar to adult preliminary hearings. The court determines whether there is a factual basis for the offenses alleged and probable cause. If there are insufficient grounds to hold juveniles, they are released. But if probable cause is established, the court will usually issue a detention order and the ju-

venile will be held in a juvenile shelter or other facility until an adjudication hearing can be held.

Juvenile Corrections

The different custodial options for juvenile court judges are of two general types: (1) *nonsecure facilities*, and (2) *secure facilities*. Nonsecure custodial facilities permit freedom of movement within the community. Youths are generally free to leave the premises, although they must observe various rules, such as to observe curfew, to avoid alcoholic beverages and drugs, and to participate in specific programs tailored to their particular needs. These types of nonsecure facilities include foster homes, group homes and halfway houses, camps, ranches, experience programs, and wilderness projects.

Nonsecure Facilities

Foster Homes

When a juvenile's natural parents are considered unfit or the juvenile is abandoned or orphaned, foster homes are often used for temporary placement. Youths placed in foster homes are not necessarily law violators. They may be *children in need of supervision (CHINS)* or *persons in need of supervision (PINS)* (*Matter of Zachary "I,"* 1993). A foster home provides a substitute family. A stable family environment is believed to be beneficial in many cases where youths have no consistent adult supervision or are unmanageable or unruly in their own households. In 1990, approximately four thousand youths were under the supervision of foster homes in state-operated public placement programs (American Correctional Association, 1991). Rogers and Mays (1987:429) indicate that many of those assigned to foster homes are dependent, neglected, or abused. Youths placed in foster homes are usually in the ten- to fourteen-year-old range.

Foster home placements are often useful when youths have been apprehended for status offenses. Most people who accept youths into their homes have been investigated by state or local authorities to determine their fitness as foster parents. Socioeconomic factors and home stability are important considerations. Foster parents are often middle-aged and middle-class and have above-average educational backgrounds. Despite these positive features, foster homes are unlikely to provide the intense adult supervision required by more hard-core juvenile offenders. Further, foster parents are often unable to furnish the quality of special treatments that might improve the youth's chances of rehabilitation or societal reintegration. Most foster parents simply are not trained as counselors, social workers, or psychologists. For many nonserious offenders, however, a home environment, particularly a stable one, has certain therapeutic benefits.

Group Homes

Placing youths in group homes is considered an intermediate option. Group homes are publicly or privately administered community-based operations (Simone, 1984:110). Usually, group homes have counselors or residents who act as parental figures for groups of ten to twenty youths. *Family group homes* are actually family-operated and are thus in a sense an extension of foster homes. Group homes offer nonsecure supervision of juvenile clients. Nearly four thousand youths were in state-sponsored group homes during 1990 (American Correctional Association, 1991).

Group homes require juvenile clients to observe the rights of others, refrain from drugs, participate in various vocational or educational training programs, attend school, participate in therapy or receive prescribed medical treatment, and observe curfew. Urinalysis or other tests may be conducted randomly to see whether juveniles are consuming drugs. Youths committing one or more violations may be reported to juvenile judges, who retain dispositional control over the youths. Assignment to a group home is usually for a limited period.

Group homes provide youths with the companionship of other juveniles and enable them to share problems through group discussions. Staff are available to help youths get jobs, resolve problems at school, and cope with difficult interpersonal relationships. However, group homes are sometimes staffed by community volunteers with little training or experience in helping juveniles deal with their problems. Certain risks and legal liabilities may be incurred by giving bad advice or in-adequate assistance. Currently, group homes are only lightly regulated. Training programs for staff are scarce in most jurisdictions, and there are few standards relating to the qualifications and training of staff. Therefore, group homes vary considerably in the quality of the services they render.

Camps, Ranches, Experience Programs, and Wilderness Projects

Camps and ranches, or "camp ranches," are nonsecure facilities that are sometimes referred to as wilderness projects or experience programs. A less expensive alternative to detaining even chronic juvenile offenders is requiring them to participate in experience programs. *Experience programs include a wide array of outdoor programs designed to improve a juvenile's sense of self-worth, self-concept, pride, and trust* (McCarthy and McCarthy, 1991).

Hope Center Wilderness Camp

An example of a fairly successful wilderness experiment is the *Hope Center Wilderness Camp* in Houston, Texas (Claggett, 1989). This camp houses an organized network of four small, interdependent groups of twelve teenagers each. The camp's goals are to provide quality care and treatment in a nonpunitive environment, with specific emphases on health, safety, education, and therapy. Emotionally disturbed youths whose offenses range from truancy to murder participate in the program. Informal therapy offered by the camp includes "aftertalk" (informal discussions during meals), "huddle up" (a group discussion technique), and "pow wow" (a nightly gathering around the fire). Special nondenominational religious services are conducted. Participants learn survival skills such as how to cook meals outdoors and how to camp. Follow-ups by camp officials show that participants have a recidivism rate of only about 15 percent (Claggett, 1989).

Project Outward Bound

Project Outward Bound is one of more than two hundred programs of its type in the United States today. Outward Bound, first introduced in Colorado in 1962, emphasizes personal survival in the wilderness. During a three-week period, youths participate in various outdoor activities, including rock climbing, solo survival, camping, and long-range hiking (McCarthy and McCarthy, 1984: 319). Program officials are not concerned with equipping juveniles with survival skills *per se* but rather hope to instill them with self-confidence and self-assurance so that they can cope with problems in their communities.

Homeward Bound

The goal of *Homeward Bound,* established in Massachusetts in 1970, is to provide juvenile boys with a sense of maturity and responsibility through the acquisition of survival skills and wilderness experiences. A six-week training program promotes endurance, physical fitness, and community service (McCarthy and McCarthy, 1984:318–19). Additionally, a release program for those who complete the program successfully offers instruction in ecology, search and rescue, and overnight treks.

At the end of the program, the boys prove their survival skills during a three-day, three-night trip to the wilderness. In 1973, recidivism rates among participants were lower than those for boys who had been institutionalized in industrial or reform schools (Willman and Chun, 1974).

Although these programs serve only a few juveniles and some authorities question their value in deterring delinquency, some evidence suggests that wilderness experiences lower the recidivism rate more than institutionalization in industrial schools under close custody and monitoring (McCarthy and McCarthy, 1984:319).

Secure Facilities

Short-Term and Long-Term Facilities

Like prisons or penitentiaries for adults, juvenile facilities are either short-term or long-term. These terms are ambiguous as they pertain to facilities for juveniles. Technically, short term confinement facilities, sometimes referred to as detention, are designed to accommodate juveniles on a temporary basis—about thirty days, on average. These juveniles are awaiting a juvenile court adjudication, subsequent foster home or group home placement, or transfer to criminal court. Sometimes youths will be placed in short-term confinement because

their identity is unknown and it is deemed best not to confine them in adult lock-ups or jails. When juveniles are placed in short-term facilities, they are considered to be held in detention. Juveniles placed in long-term facilities may be confined for several days or years, although the average duration across *all* categories of juvenile offenders is about six or seven months (Maguire and Pastore, 1995). Most juvenile court judges regard incarceration as a last resort. By far the most frequently used sanction against juveniles is probation.

The Legal Rights of Juveniles

Historically, the fate of juvenile offenders has been at the whim of juvenile court judges, referees, intake officers, chancellors, and a host of other authorities. The state has traditionally functioned under the *parens patriae* doctrine in looking after the interests of minors. For many decades, the idea of applying constitutional laws to juveniles was unthinkable.

There was no concentrated effort to investigate juveniles' constitutional rights until the mid 1960s. At the beginning of this century, efforts to establish a juvenile justice system were sporadic, and only a few jurisdictions, such as Illinois, New York, and Massachusetts, made significant attempts to develop formal, consistent mechanisms of dealing with juvenile offenses.

Juvenile delinquency was not recognized as a national social problem until well into the 1950s, although some people, including J. Edgar Hoover, had attempted to sound the alert as early as 1943 (Gilbert, 1986). An analysis of the cultural history of the United States reveals that the public "discovered" delinquency during the two decades following the end of World War II (Gilbert, 1986). Films such as *Rebel Without a Cause, Blackboard Jungle,* and *Twelve Angry Men* in the 1950s portrayed America's youth as violent, gang-affiliated, immoral, and intent on disrupting cultural value systems. Stereotypical notions of juveniles were fostered in part during the post-World War II period when both parents often worked outside the home and teenagers often had little or no adult supervision (Gilbert, 1986).

Highlight 14.3. Attorneys for Kids?
The Case of a Call for Justice in Juvenile Courtrooms

Few experts believed that it would ever come to this. Thousands of juvenile defendants are increasingly in need of legal counsel. Juvenile court judges are meting out increasingly severe punishments in response to escalating juvenile violence. The "get-tough" movement has finally made it to juvenile court.

According to the Call for Justice report, juvenile defendants in all parts of the country regularly appear in juvenile courts either without legal counsel or with overworked and underpaid counsel whose effectiveness is questionable. Although most juvenile courts are empowered to provide indigent juveniles with counsel, thousands of juveniles appear each year without counsel. Thus, their freedom is jeopardized to a great degree by the simple absence of counsel.

The Call for Justice report was funded in 1992 by the Office of Juvenile Justice and Delinquency Prevention. It was prepared by the American Bar Association and two advocacy organizations, the Youth Law Center and the Juvenile Law Center in Philadelphia. Robert Schwartz, principal investigator with the Juvenile Law Center, said that the "next few years will be telling. Youth face the prospect of much longer sentences, mandatory minimum sentences, and time in adult jails or prisons. . . . The need for access to

quality defense attorneys for juveniles has never been greater." Other experts agree with Schwartz (American Bar Association, 1994).

The facts are that in many cases, juvenile defense lawyers work at least 500 cases at a time. Often, children in juvenile court meet their counsels for the first time when they sit down at the counsel table during detention hearings. The strain of defending so many youths at once is so great that most lawyers work in that field for less than two years. Thus, most lawyers who represent juvenile clients are inexperienced. There are serious gaps in the training of juvenile counsel, say various reports. About half of all public defender offices lack the resources to send even new lawyers to training programs so that they can master the unique problems that emerge in juvenile court proceedings.

Should attorneys be required in *all* juvenile court proceedings? What are the implications of the greater formalization of juvenile courts? Should one court handle both adult and juvenile cases?

Source: Associated Press, "Report: Children Need Legal Representation," *Minot (N.D.) Daily News,* January 1, 1996, p. A5.

Between 1912 and 1940, the U.S. Children's Bureau formulated delinquency policy (Rosenthal, 1983). During these years, many interested parties, including a number of child welfare reformers, enthusiastically supported the juvenile court as the most appropriate prevention and treatment structure for delinquents (Rosenthal, 1983). However, during the 1930s, a general disenchantment with juvenile court emerged. This was accompanied by the increased use of psychological treatment methods associated with some of our current juvenile rehabilitation programs (Rosenthal, 1983). According to some writers, we are now in the midst of an era of juvenile justice reform (Feld, 1993a, 1993b; Reddington, 1992).

Between 1960 and 1970, the Supreme Court

settled three important cases dealing with the constitutional rights of juveniles. Sometimes referred to as the "big three" cases of the juvenile justice system, these included (1) *Kent v. United States* (1966), (2) *In re Gault* (1967), and (3) *In re Winship* (1970). *In re* means "in the matter of" or "in the affair of." The expression is applied to cases that have no adversary party and is frequently used in lawsuits in which a juvenile's rights are at issue.

Kent v. United States *(1966)*

Kent was a sixteen-year-old resident of the District of Columbia who was charged with robbery, rape, and burglary. Acting on its own authority, the juvenile court waived the matter to an adult court, which tried Kent. It is significant that if Kent had been tried as a juvenile, his maximum punishment would have been five years' incarceration in a juvenile secure facility. Being tried as an adult, however, Kent faced the maximum sentence of the death penalty if convicted. Although the District of Columbia statutes provided for a waiver hearing in juvenile remand motions, there was no hearing in Kent's case. Kent was ultimately convicted.

Kent appealed the juvenile court's decision to waive him to the jurisdiction of an adult court to the Supreme Court. The Court concluded that Kent had been deprived of his "rights to due process" under the Constitution. He was entitled to a waiver hearing under the law and did not receive one. The Supreme Court reversed Kent's conviction and took the liberty of being openly critical of the juvenile court process generally. It said:

> While there can be no doubt of the original laudable purpose of juvenile courts, studies and critiques in recent years raise serious questions as to whether actual performance measures well enough against theoretical purpose to make tolerable the immunity of the process from the reach of Constitutional guarantees applicable to adults. . . . There is evidence, in fact, that there may be grounds for concern that the child *receives the worst of both worlds; that he gets neither the protections accorded to adults nor the solicitous care and regenerative treatment postulated for children.* (Emphasis added)

Kent is significant in part because it successfully challenged juvenile court discretion to make arbitrary decisions affecting juveniles. Clearly, there were statutes in effect governing the conduct of the court concerning a waiver hearing. But the court acted in a cavalier and indifferent fashion and ignored the statute. Although the Supreme Court decision pertained strictly to the right of juveniles to a waiver hearing, the groundwork had been laid for subsequent decisions.

Many scholars have attempted to determine the Supreme Court's true intent in the Kent case. It has been concluded that the *Kent* criteria are intended to assure that only the most serious cases will be transferred to adult court (Dawson, 1992). In actual practice, however, the criteria were more

closely related to prosecutors' decisions in selecting cases for transfer motions than to the transfer decisions made by juvenile court judges. *Kent* limited judicial discretion to finding required facts and reviewing potential abuses of prosecutorial discretion (Dawson, 1992).

In re Gault *(1967)*

Gerald Gault was a fifteen-year-old residing in Gila County, Arizona. One day, he and another boy allegedly made an obscene telephone call to Mrs. Cook, a neighbor. Mrs. Cook complained to the police, who arrested Gault. An investigation of Gault's juvenile record disclosed that he was serving six-months' probation for stealing a wallet.

Gault was immediately removed to a children's home in the county. His parents were not immediately notified of his apprehension or confinement. A day later, they were advised that a police officer had filed a petition with the juvenile court alleging Gault's delinquency. The day after Gault's arrest and detention, Gault, his mother, and the arresting officer appeared before the judge, who interrogated Gault about the alleged obscene telephone call. Mrs. Cook was not present. Gault was then sent back to the detention facility and released a few days later.

Gault's mother soon received a letter from the court advising that a hearing on Gault's delinquency would be held in a few days. The hearing eventually was held, again with Mrs. Cook absent. No transcript of the proceedings was made, and the investigating juvenile officer testified that Gault had admitted making the obscene telephone call. At no time was Gault advised of his "rights" or told that he could remain silent. When the proceedings ended, Gault was judged by the court to be a juvenile delinquent and sentenced to the Arizona State Industrial School until he was twenty-one. This meant that he would have to serve five or six years in secure confinement. An adult convicted of making an obscene telephone call would have received a maximum $50 fine and no more than two months in jail.

Mrs. Gault hired an attorney, who petitioned the Arizona Supreme Court to overturn the decision of the juvenile court. The Arizona Supreme Court upheld the juvenile court's decision. The case eventually came before the U.S. Supreme Court. Specifically, Gault's appeal alleged that his basic due-process rights had been violated, that he had not received a timely notice of charges against him, that he had not been informed of his right to counsel, that he had not had the opportunity to confront and cross-examine his accuser (Mrs. Cook), that he had been denied a transcript of the proceedings, and that he had not been advised of his right against self-incrimination or his right to an appellate review.

The Supreme Court reversed the Arizona decision and set forth specific constitutional rights for all juveniles. Essentially, the Court declared that the Fourteenth Amendment due-process provision applies to juveniles as well as to adults. It held that all juveniles have the right to adequate written notice of charges against them, the right to representation by counsel, the privilege against self-incrimination, and the right to confront witnesses, particularly when charged with acts that if committed by adults would be criminal and involve possible incarceration.

While the Supreme Court decision in Gault's case pertained to the adjudicatory hearing or trial phase of the juvenile justice process, an extension of the Court's decision has been made applicable to other phases of the juvenile justice process as well as the arrest stage and detention hearing. This case became the most significant decision affecting juveniles' constitutional rights (Feld, 1991).

Analysts and experts such as Barry Feld have suggested that *Gault* permanently changed juvenile court proceedings. Specifically, it changed the juvenile court from a benevolent, therapeutic institution to a scaled-down criminal court. Proceedings in juvenile courts have come to resemble those in criminal courts. Both judicial and legislative changes have altered the juvenile court's jurisdiction over noncriminal status offenders and serious young offenders: the former are diverted from the system, while the latter are transferred to adult criminal courts. Thus, the juvenile courts increasingly punish youths for their offenses rather than treat their "real needs" (Feld, 1993a, 1993b).

In re Winship *(1970)*

Winship was a twelve-year-old boy who was found guilty of larceny under a New York Family Court Act. In Winship's case, the court relied upon the "preponderance of the evidence" against him rather than the standard of "beyond a reasonable doubt" that otherwise would be applicable in a criminal case. Until Winship's case was heard by the Supreme Court, three standards of proof had been acceptable in various state and local juvenile courts. These were proof of delinquency (1) "beyond a reasonable doubt," (2) by "clear and convincing" evidence, and (3) by a "preponderance of the evidence." The Supreme Court heard Winship's appeal and reversed the New York court on the grounds that the "beyond a reasonable doubt" standard had not been employed in deciding Winship's delinquency (Nathan, 1984). The Court further declared that:

> When one assesses the consequences of an erroneous factual determination in a juvenile delinquency proceeding in which a youth is accused of a crime, I think it must be concluded that, while the consequences are not identical to those in a criminal case, the differences will not support a distinction in the standard of proof. First, and of paramount importance, a factual error here, as in a criminal case, exposes the accused to a complete loss of his personal liberty through a self-imposed confinement away from his home, family, and friends. And, second, a delinquency determination, to some extent at least, stigmatizes a youth in that it is by definition bottomed on a finding that the accused committed a crime.

Other Precedent-Setting Juvenile Cases

Several other Supreme Court cases have defined juveniles' constitutional rights. Following *In re Winship* (1970), the Supreme Court heard the case of *McKeiver v. Pennsylvania* (1971). McKeiver was a juvenile who appealed to the Supreme Court on the grounds that he had been denied a trial by jury. The Supreme Court declared that McKeiver did not have an absolute right to a trial by jury. Justice Blackmun observed that the mandatory jury trial might "remake the juvenile proceeding into a formal adversary proceeding, thus ending [juvenile courts'] aim for an intimate, informal protective proceeding" (Vorenberg, 1981:118). *McKeiver* did not absolutely eliminate the possibility that a juvenile could be tried by a jury. Some jurisdictions currently offer jury trials to juveniles charged with particularly serious offenses. In other words, the juvenile's right to a trial by jury is purely discretionary.

In *Breed v. Jones* (1975), Breed was a juvenile who was declared delinquent in an adjudicatory proceeding in a California juvenile court. Later, he was remanded to the California Superior Court and tried as an adult for the same offenses alleged in his earlier adjudicatory hearing. He was convicted and sentenced.

The Supreme Court concluded that he had been placed in double jeopardy as the result of the adjudicatory hearing and the conviction for the same offense in an adult court. Declaring that his Fifth Amendment rights had been violated, the Court overturned his conviction.

In 1984, the Supreme Court decided *Schall v. Martin*. This case questioned the right of New York juvenile officials to detain an accused prior to trial in violation of the due process clause of the Fourteenth Amendment (Nathan, 1984). The Court held that in this matter, pretrial detention did not violate the accused's right to due process under the law. However, in order to justify a juvenile's detention, the state must demonstrate that there is a serious risk that the juvenile might commit further crimes before the return date. Within the context of fundamental fairness, the New York statute authorizing pretrial detention for certain juveniles was compatible with protecting both the juvenile and society (Arthur, 1987; Jackson, 1987).

One particularly sensitive area of concern to juveniles is their Fourth Amendment right against unreasonable search and seizure while in school. In the past, some school officials have acted haphazardly in conducting warrantless searches of school lockers, desks, and other storage places. In 1985, search and seizure actions of school officials were challenged in *New Jersey v. T.L.O.*

While the Supreme Court upheld a student's right against unreasonable search and seizure, it held in that case that a student's rights are diminished while he or she is under the school-student relationship (Dunaway, 1985). It held that school officials, as agents of the state, are authorized to conduct reasonable searches without warrant, provided that a reasonable suspicion exists that a crime has been committed or that illegal contraband is being secreted by a particular student. Blanket locker searches violate students' Fourth Amendment right against unreasonable searches and seizures, however.

How well do juveniles understand their legal rights? Several studies have examined this question in some detail, and the results are somewhat disappointing. For example, Lawrence (1984) studied a small sample of forty-five juveniles who had appeared before the juvenile court of "a major metropolitan area in the southwestern United States." Through questionnaires and interviews with the juveniles, attorneys, and juvenile probation officers, Lawrence discovered that probation officers themselves are often the major source of juveniles' legal information. But generally, the juveniles interviewed tended to have a very poor understanding of their legal rights. More than a fourth did not remember or understand the police *Miranda* warning. This raises some serious questions about a juvenile's capacity to make intelligent and informed decisions about waiving his or her rights and consenting to police interrogations (Lawrence, 1984).

If juveniles are arrested and asked to waive their rights and submit to police interrogation, under what circumstances is it valid to accept a juvenile's waiver of these rights (e.g., to an attorney or to refuse to answer any questions)? Custodial interrogations involve a number of rights important to adults. Should these same rights be extended to juveniles?

The Supreme Court has provided a "totality of circumstances" test of the validity of juvenile waivers of their constitutional rights in the case of *Fare v. Michael C.* (1979). In this case, in the absence of parental guidance or consent a juvenile disclosed some incriminating information about an offense (Shaffner, 1985). But the Supreme Court ruled that considering the "totality of circumstances" surrounding the juvenile's waiver of his constitutional rights, his disclosures were admissible in court. In short, considering all circumstances, he knowingly gave up his right to remain silent and to meet with an attorney before questioning. Currently, appellate courts use the totality of circumstances test in determining the permissibility of juveniles' admissions and confessions.

A 1982 California case concerned whether a parent can be separated from a juvenile suspect prior to a confession (Gonzalez, 1982). *In re Myron* (1982) concerned a juvenile who was arrested and read his rights in the presence of his mother. Myron said that he understood his rights and would speak to the officers. At that point, he seemed uneasy with his mother in the room, and the officers asked her to leave. After she left, Myron made a full confession of his crime. Later, Myron appealed on the grounds that the separation from his mother made the confession inadmissible in court. But a higher California court rejected his appeal, holding that "the purpose of a parent's presence, when requested, is to assist the juvenile in understanding his or her rights and in making a decision to waive those rights" (Gonzalez, 1982). Once that decision had been made, the parent's presence is no longer necessary or essential to the protection of the juvenile's rights.

The American Bar Association established a Juvenile Justice Standards Project in the early 1980s (Feld, 1993a). This project has resulted in the ABA's recommendation that the rights of minors can best be protected legally by legislative action in each state to delimit specific juvenile court jurisdiction to a narrow set of problem areas. There appears to be a trend toward granting greater autonomy to juveniles in legal matters (Green, 1984). Courts have increasingly requested guidance concerning the maturity and capacity of juveniles in such matters as their right to choose parents, to act as witnesses, and to choose medical interventions (Green, 1984; Ream, 1985).

Selected Issues in Juvenile Justice

Some of the major issues confronting the juvenile justice system have already been discussed. A continuing issue is whether status offenses ought to be deinstitutionalized and separated from the jurisdiction of the juvenile court. Another issue is whether diverting juvenile offenders to community projects and services should be an alternative to adjudication and secure confinement.

Each of these issues is warmly disputed. Court officials and judges are often reluctant to relinquish control over status offenders (Schneider, 1984a). By the same token, some researchers argue that status offenders are in a different class than juveniles who commit misdemeanors and felonies. They conclude that as a result, status offenders should be handled differently to avoid tainting them with the term "juvenile delinquent" (Rankin and Wells, 1985; Bortner, Sunderland, and Winn, 1985).

Diversion is viewed as too lenient on juvenile offenders and as not necessarily living up to its rehabilitative potential (Polk, 1984). Some critics say that it causes a certain amount of net-widening (Decker, 1985). The "just deserts" proponents favor making juvenile offenders go through the rigors of the juvenile justice system to "teach them a lesson" and to make them more accountable to their victims. Those in favor of diversion argue that by avoiding formal contact with the juvenile justice system, juveniles who commit minor or status offenses will be less likely to be labeled as delinquent or to develop unfavorable delinquent self-definitions (Miller, 1991).

A third issue involves waiving a juvenile to the jurisdiction of an adult court. The primary reason for transferring a juvenile's case to an adult court is that the juvenile is not amenable to treatment in the juvenile justice system (Champion and Mays, 1992). In an adult court, a juvenile offender is subject to more severe penalties for particularly serious offenses. But again, for a variety of reasons both financial and social, not everyone is in favor of motions to transfer juveniles from juvenile court jurisdiction (Feld, 1993a).

Additional concerns of the juvenile justice system are (1) female delinquency; (2) juvenile violence and violent offenders; (3) juvenile drug and alcohol use and abuse; (4) the state of juvenile corrections; (5) parole for juveniles; (6) rehabilitation alternatives; (7) delinquency prevention; and (8) the death penalty for juveniles. While this list is not exhaustive, it does include some of the primary areas of interest to researchers.

Table 14.2

Chronological Summary of Major Events in Juvenile Justice[a]

Year	Event
1791	Bill of Rights passed by U.S. Congress
1825	New York House of Refuge established
1839	*Ex parte Crouse* establishes right of juvenile court to intervene in parent-child matters
1841	John Augustus initiates probation in Boston
1853	New York Children's Aid Society established
1855	Death penalty imposed on ten-year-old, James Arcene, in Arkansas for robbery and murder; earliest juvenile execution was of Thomas Graunger, sixteen, for sodomizing a horse and cow in 1642
1866	Massachusetts statute passed giving juvenile court power to intervene and take custody when parents are unfit
1868	Fourteenth Amendment passed by U.S. Congress, establishing right to due process and equal protection under the law
1874	Massachusetts establishes first Children's Tribunal to deal with youthful offenders
1889	Indiana establishes children's guardians to have jurisdiction over neglected and dependent children
1889	Hull House established in Chicago by Jane Addams to assist unsupervised children of immigrant parents
1899	Compulsory School Act, Colorado; statutory regulation of truants
1899	Illinois Act to Regulate the Treatment and Control of Dependent, Neglected and Delinquent Children; first juvenile court in United States established
1901	Juvenile court established in Denver, Colorado
1907	Separate juvenile court with original jurisdiction in juvenile matters established in Denver, Colorado
1912	Creation of U.S. Children's Bureau, charged with compiling statistical information about juvenile offenders; existed from 1912 to 1940
1918	Chicago slums studied by Shaw and McKay; delinquency related to urban environment and transitional neighborhoods
1938	Federal Juvenile Delinquency Act
1966	*Kent v. United States* establishes juvenile's right to hearing before transfer to criminal court, right to assistance of counsel during police interrogations, right to reports and records relating to transfer decision, and right to reasons given by judge for transfer
1967	*In re Gault* establishes juvenile's right to an attorney, right to notice of charges, right to confront and cross-examine witnesses, and right against self-incrimination
1970	*In re Winship* establishes juvenile's right to criminal court standard of "beyond a reasonable doubt" when loss of freedom is a possible penalty
1971	*McKeiver v. Pennsylvania* establishes that juvenile's right to a trial by jury is not absolute
1974	Juvenile Justice and Delinquency Prevention Act
1974	Office of Juvenile Justice and Delinquency Prevention established, instrumental in promoting deinstitutionalization of status offenses
1975	*Breed v. Jones* establishes that double jeopardy exists if juvenile is adjudicated as delinquent in juvenile court and tried for same offense later in criminal court; prohibits double jeopardy
1982	*Eddings v. Oklahoma* establishes that death penalty applied to juveniles was not "cruel and unusual punishment" *per se*
1984	*Schall v. Martin* establishes the constitutionality of the preventive detention of juveniles
1985	*New Jersey v. T.L.O.* establishes lesser standard of search and seizure on school property; searches and seizures permissible without probable cause or warrant
1988	*Thompson v. Oklahoma* establishes that the death penalty applied to juveniles convicted of murder who were under age sixteen at time of murder is cruel and unusual punishment
1989	*Stanford v. Kentucky* and *Wilkins v. Missouri* establish that the death penalty is not cruel and unusual punishment applied to juveniles convicted of murder who were aged sixteen or seventeen at the time the murder was committed

a. Compiled by author

Female Delinquency

Interest in female delinquency has risen sharply in recent years among justice professionals (Caspi et al., 1993; Sommers and Baskin, 1994; Vacho et al., 1994). Some say this is because of the allegedly growing numbers of female delinquents or greater involvement of females in delinquent activities. The women's movement supposedly has generated several significant changes in both the quality and quantity of female juvenile offenses (Culliver, 1993).

The alleged increase in female delinquency is also linked to allegations that juvenile delinquency is increasing generally. A national crackdown on juvenile delinquency has been justified by the Office of Juvenile Justice and Delinquency Prevention, which cites statistical compilations of delinquency rates in various jurisdictions. For example, the Maryland Department of Corrections established an "SOS" ("See Our Side") juvenile "aversion" program to curb the "rising tide of crime" among juveniles (Mitchell and Williams, 1986). In Prince George's County, Maryland, juvenile delinquency purportedly rose 26 percent between 1981 and 1983, and alarmists reacted by formulating SOS. There is likely to be significant variations in reported delinquent behavior among jurisdictions. However, on a national scale, little evidence supports the conclusion that juvenile delinquency is increasing. During the period 1985–1995, the proportion of juvenile delinquency has remained fairly constant (Maguire and Pastore, 1995). A fourth of all juvenile delinquency is attributable to females (Camp and Camp, 1995c).

Some say that reports of the rising number of female delinquents are pure fiction (Culliver, 1993). Political policy changes and the election of so-called law and order district attorneys do much to influence juvenile arrest statistics and trends (Chesney-Lind, 1993). In Philadelphia, three political-legal periods have been identified between 1960 and 1980. Between 1960 and 1967, a "paternalistic" philosophy prevailed, during which female delinquents were harshly treated by juvenile courts "for their own good." Between 1968 and 1976, a "due process" orientation stimulated by *In re Gault* (1967) emphasized the legal rights of juveniles. The third period, 1977–1980, was a "law

and order" phase during which the juvenile court adjusted to the new conservatism of the 1970s (Sommers and Baskin, 1994). Thus, growing female delinquency may be largely illusory and more a function of legal and political shifts rather than of growing numbers of females committing delinquent acts (Chesney-Lind, 1993).

However, other evidence suggests that female delinquency is increasing (Calhoun, Jurgens and Chen, 1993). The new generation of female delinquents appears to be emulating the types of offenses committed by male delinquents. Greater numbers of females are involved in armed robbery, gang activity, drug trafficking, burglary, weapons posses-

A young woman in an isolation cell. A fourth of all juvenile delinquency is attributable to females.

Highlight 14.4. Delinquency and Female Teenagers: The Case of the High School Girl Burglars

In March of 1996, four teenage girls were arrested for committing a string of daytime burglaries in Albuquerque, New Mexico. The four girls attended Moriarty High School in Albuquerque and were considered well-behaved. They attended classes daily, and their grades were above average. But they had a dark side that was hidden from others.

During the afternoons, the girls would skip their classes and set about burglarizing homes. The police know that they burglarized at least four homes. What they don't know is how many other homes the girls may have burglarized.

The girls were arrested when items taken during some of the burglaries were discovered in their possession. When they were arrested, the girls had jewelry, thirteen handguns, stereos, and other valuables, said Ronnie Sparks, a spokesperson for the Bernalillo County Sheriff's Department. One fifteen-year-old girl was charged with twenty-nine felony counts and

was placed in the county Juvenile Detention Center to await an adjudicatory hearing. A sixteen-year-old suspect was charged with nineteen felony counts and released into the custody of her parents.

Is delinquency among teenage girls rising? Is there a new female crime wave in the United States? How should these girls be punished if adjudicated delinquent or convicted? What responsibility should the parents bear for the behavior of their daughters? What is the liability and responsibility of school officials? Can school officials do a better job of keeping track of students on campus during school hours? Ultimately, who is to blame for these girls' behavior?

Source: Adapted from Associated Press, "Police Say High School Girls Linked to String of Burglaries," *Minot (N.D.) Daily News,* March 22, 1996, p. A2.

---

sion, aggravated assault, and prostitution (Calhoun, Jurgens and Chen, 1993). The changing community structure has contributed to growing female delinquency (Figueira-McDonough, 1992).

The typical female juvenile offenses include primarily (1) property crimes such as shoplifting, (2) sex offenses such as prostitution, and (3) various status violations including runaway behavior and truancy (Culliver, 1993). Violent offenses such as aggravated assault among female juveniles are more frequent than reported, however (Chesney-Lind, 1993; Sommers and Baskin, 1994).

Juvenile Violence and Violent Offenders

The *National Crime Victimization Survey* and the *Uniform Crime Reports* indicate that violent juvenile crime increased between 1975 and 1995. In 1995, juveniles accounted for 18.5 percent of all

arrests for violent crime and for 34 percent of all arrests for property crime. This represents a significant downward trend compared with 1975 (Maguire and Pastore, 1995:384). In 1996, U.S. Attorney General Janet Reno announced that for the first time in many years, juvenile violence had declined. However, she urged the public not to be overly optimistic (Reno, 1996:3).

Perhaps the incidence of juvenile violence that peaked in 1995 partially accounts for the increased frequency of remand or waiver motions by prosecutors to pass certain violent juvenile offenders along to adult courts. These actions are usually based on the theory that if these juveniles are not punished severely, they will progress to more violent crimes or repeat their previous violent behaviors (Walker, 1995). But studies of juvenile violence reveal that often these youths do not repeat their violent offenses. Usually, these offenses have been triggered by family incidents, abuse of drugs and/or alcohol, or psychological disorders and can be dealt with therapeutically (Lewis et al., 1994; Sheley and Wright, 1995).

Juvenile Drug and Alcohol Use and Abuse

About a fourth of all liquor law violations in 1995 were committed by persons under eighteen. About 12 percent of all drug arrests in 1985 involved juveniles (Maguire and Pastore, 1995:384). The rising incidence of drug and alcohol abuse among juveniles is disturbing to the public as well as to professionals who investigate this phenomenon (Gray and Wish, 1993; Jackson, 1994; Milin et al., 1991). Particularly troubling is that juveniles who receive individualized treatment and are placed on probation have a high rate of recidivism, particularly regarding their abuse of drugs and alcohol (Archibald, Brown, and Cicchetti, 1992). Further, youths involved in drug and alcohol abuse often use weapons as a means of self-defense when carrying out their illegal business (Rasmussen and Benson, 1994a; Sheley, 1994; Sheley and Wright, 1995).

Juvenile drug and alcohol abuse is not the specialty of any particular racial or ethnic group. Many juvenile detainees who have participated in exploratory experiments have come from diverse backgrounds, ethnicities, and races (Gray and Wish, 1993). Many of those detained tested positive for at least one type of drug. A study of 248 black juveniles in an Ohio facility found, for example, that 90 percent of the participants had used some illicit mood-altering substance (Jackson, 1994). Use of such substances has been associated with a high rate of attention deficit disorder among youths in elementary and secondary schools (Milin et al., 1991).

There is some evidence that at least in some jurisdictions, police officers who take juveniles into custody are influenced by racial factors. For instance, a study of 126 male police officers in five different metropolitan areas of Georgia showed that black juveniles tended to be charged with more serious offenses than white juveniles whenever drugs or alcohol were involved (Sutphen, Kurtz, and Giddings, 1993).

Suggestions to reduce recidivism among alco-

hol- and drug-dependent juveniles include (1) encouraging practitioners to pay special attention to the juvenile's prior record, school involvement, and peer relations; and (2) expanding offender management strategies through collaborative researcher-practitioner efforts to pursue innovative program development and evaluation (Archibald, Brown, and Cicchetti, 1992).

The State of Juvenile Corrections

Incarceration or secure confinement is the most severe form of punishment for juvenile offenders (Human Rights Watch, 1995). Fines, restitution, and various rehabilitative strategies not involving incarceration certainly affect one's propensity to commit further delinquent activities. But deprivation of freedom is threatening to anyone, especially juvenile offenders (Schwartz and Hsieh,1994).

Like adult corrections, juvenile corrections involves an array of programs and alternatives ranging from diversion and supervised probation to secure confinement. One problem many jurisdictions face is where to confine juvenile offenders. Until recently, most jurisdictions confined juvenile offenders in adult jails or other adult facilities. In many instances, no attempt was made to separate adult and youthful offenders. Currently, most jurisdictions have separate juvenile facilities, although many of them fall far short of their intended aim of rehabilitating juvenile offenders (Schwartz and Hsieh, 1994).

Many juvenile detention centers and secure confinement facilities are overcrowded. Each year approximately 500,000 juveniles enter some form of detention (Maguire and Pastore, 1995). Most of these juveniles are not held for prolonged periods. In fact, nearly 90 percent are released to parents or guardians shortly after being taken into custody. In 1991, about 57,000 youths were being held in public juvenile facilities (Maguire and Pastore, 1995:531). In 1995, there were about 79,237 youths in thirty-five public juvenile agencies (Camp and Camp, 1995c:19). And despite federal and state initiatives to remove juveniles from adult jails and lockups, several thousand juveniles enter these jails annually. In fact, between 1983 and 1994, the number of juveniles in jails increased from 1,760 to over 3,400 (Maguire and Pastore, 1995:533).

In response to overcrowding, the use of probation and parole has been increasing. Another controversial strategy is the privatization of juvenile corrections facilities (Schwartz and Hsieh, 1994). Several jurisdictions have engaged in a limited amount of juvenile facility contracting involving private organizations such as the Correction Corporation of America (Field, 1987). Such private enterprises have somewhat eased overcrowding in secure confinement facilities (Minnesota Correcions Crowding Task Force, 1993).

Intermediate Punishments

Intensive supervised probation (ISP) programs, also known as intensive probation supervision (IPS) programs, have become increasingly popular ways of managing nonincarcerated offenders (Snyder and Marshall, 1990). Since the mid 1960s, these programs have been aimed primarily at adult offenders, and in recent years, they have been designed for juvenile offenders as well (Armstrong, 1988:342). *Intensive supervised probation is a highly structured supervision program for either adult or juvenile offenders that serves as an alternative to incarceration and provides an acceptable level of public safety* (adapted from a definition by Armstrong, 1988:343). Some researchers argue that the effectiveness of ISP depends on how well supervising POs manage certain risk control factors rather than on the intensity with which they monitor clients (Sontheimer and Goodstein, 1993: 197–98, 222–25).

ISP Programs and Their Characteristics

About one-third to one-half of all jurisdictions have ISP programs for juveniles (Weibush, 1990). Like adult ISP programs, juvenile ISP (JISP) programs are ideally designed to manage detention-bound youths and are considered acceptable alternatives to incarceration. According to Armstrong (1988:342), this is what JISP programs were always meant to be. Armstrong differentiates JISP programs from other forms of standard probation by citing obvious differences in the amount of officer/client contact during the probationary period. For example, standard probation entails no more than two face-to-face officer/client contacts per month, whereas JISP programs can necessitate face-to-face meetings two or three times per week, once per week, or four times per week (Armstrong, 1988:346).

While ISP programs have their differences (Wiebush, 1990:26), many juvenile ISP programs share similarities:

1. Recognition of the shortcomings of traditional responses to serious and/or chronic offenders (e.g., incarceration or out-of-home placement).
2. Severe resource constraints within jurisdictions that compel many probation departments to adopt agency-wide classification and workload deployment systems that target a disproportionate share of resources for the most problematic juvenile offenders.
3. The goal of reducing incarceration in juvenile secure detention facilities and thus reduce overcrowding.
4. The tendency to include aggressive supervision and control elements as a part of the "get tough" movement.
5. The goal of rehabilitating youthful offenders.

The following are basic characteristics of JISP programs:

1. Low officer/client caseloads (i.e., thirty or fewer probationers).
2. High levels of offender accountability (e.g., victim restitution, community service, payment of fines, partial defrayment of program expenses).
3. High levels of offender responsibility.
4. High levels of offender control (home confinement, electronic monitoring, frequent face-to-face visits by POs).
5. Frequent checks for arrests, drug and/or alcohol use, and employment/school attendance (drug/alcohol screening, coordination with police departments and juvenile halls, teachers, family) (Armstrong, 1988:342–43; Wiebush, 1990).

The Ohio Experience

Wiebush (1990) has described the Ohio Experience, a program that targets juveniles with a high propensity to recidivate as well as more serious felony offenders who are detention-bound. Youths begin the program with a five-day detention, followed by two weeks of house arrest. Later, they must observe curfews, attend school and complete schoolwork satisfactorily, report daily to the probation office, and submit to periodic urinalysis. Counselors and surveillance staff monitor each youth's progress sixteen hours a day, seven days a week. Weibush says that although the program as it is carried out in Delaware, Ohio, has a rather strict approach, it embodies rehabilitation as a primary program objective. The Delaware program has about a 40 percent rate of recidivism, which although high is better than the 75 percent rate of recidivism among the general juvenile court population of high-risk offenders in other Ohio jurisdictions.

Program officials in Lucas County select clients from those already in detention and who are considered high-risk offenders. Lucas County officials wished to use this particular selection method in order to avoid any appearance of "net-widening" that their JISP program might generate. The Lucas program is similar to the Delaware program in its treatment and control approaches. However, the Lucas program obligates offenders to perform up to one hundred hours of community service. House arrest, curfew, and other requirements of the Delaware program are also found in the Lucas program. The successfulness of the Lucas program has not been evaluated fully, although it did appear to reduce institutional commitments by about 10 percent between 1986 and 1987.

Each of these programs has required enormous investments of time and energy by high-quality staff, according to Wiebush. Further, each program has illustrated how to use community resources to further its objectives and best serve juvenile clients. However, Wiebush says that what is good for Ohio probationers and parolees may not necessarily be good for offenders in other jurisdictions. Nevertheless, these programs function as potential models for programs in other jurisdictions.

Community-based programs are particularly advantageous for youths because they enable them to get help and treatment while remaining in the community. Altshuler and Armstrong (1990:170) suggest that community-based correctional programs and other probationary programs involving intensive supervision can help youths most if they follow five important guidelines:

1. To prepare youths for gradually increased responsibility and freedom.
2. To help youths become involved in the community and to help the community interact with them.
3. To work with youths and their families, peers, teachers, and employers to identify the qualities necessary for success.
4. To develop new resources and supports where needed.
5. To monitor and test youths concerning their abilities to interact.

Electronic Monitoring for Juvenile Offenders

Charles (1989a) describes an electronic monitoring program for juvenile offenders in Allen County, Indiana. Known as the Allen County, Indiana, Juvenile Electronic Monitoring Program Pilot Project, or EMP, this program began as an experimental study in October 1987 through May 1988, a span of nine months. At the time the study started, the probation department had twenty-five POs who were appointed by the court and certified by the Indiana Judicial Conference. During 1987, the court referred 2,404 juveniles to the probation department. About 34 percent of these were female offenders. During that same year, 167 youths were incarcerated in secure facilities for delinquents at a total cost of $1.5 million.

Charles (1989b:152–53) says that because of fiscal constraints, Allen County placed only six juveniles in the electronic monitoring program. However, two of these youths soon recidivated and were dropped from the program. The remaining four youths remained in the program. The juvenile judge in these cases had sentenced each youth to a six-month probationary period with electronic monitoring. Each youth wore a conspicuous wristlet, which became a symbol of court sanctions. Like the proverbial string around one's finger, the

Highlight 14.5. Juvenile Probation Work Release and Compulsory School Attendance: Time Off for Good Behavior?

A fourteen-year-old joyrider from Evanston, Wyoming, borrowed a neighbor's car one New Year's Eve and crashed it into a fence while drunk. Investigating police found a pipe and drug residue in the boy's pockets. The boy was transferred to criminal court, where he pled guilty and was convicted of joyriding. Instead of sentencing the youth to a year in jail or the Wyoming State Penitentiary, the judge, Thomas Mealey, gave the youth six months in the county jail. But Judge Mealey added a unique provision. The six-month sentence would be reduced by one day for each day the boy attended school. The youth agreed.

The boy's schedule requires a wake-up call at 6:00 A.M., breakfast, and a bus ride from the jail to school. The bus returns the youth to jail at 3:00 P.M. At the jail, the youth receives counseling or has recreation time. So far, the plan is working out well.

One reason for Mealey's sentence was his earlier experience with a sixteen-year-old. While taking his son to school every day, Mealey would wave at a boy he had represented while a lawyer. The boy hung out in the neighborhood, was expelled from school, and ultimately became involved in drugs. With friends he would stake out homes and burglarize them. Following a conviction for these offenses, he served time in the Wyoming State Penitentiary. Mealey was so affected by this unfortunate outcome that he vowed to try to make a difference in the lives of youths if he ever had the chance. His position as judge for Uinta County, Wyoming, gives him the perfect opportunity to intervene in cases that he feels merit it.

Jack Greene, director of Professional Development for the American Correctional Association, praises Mealey's work but says of his sentencing of the fourteen-year-old, "This is unique. I think it would be a model that every community and every jail would have to evaluate on their own."

Spokespersons for Uinta County say that Judge Mealey's arrangement with the fourteen-year-old has not been adopted as an official program and may never happen again, at least partly because of understaffing. There is simply not enough staff to maintain such a program and supervise it properly. But authorities believe the rehabilitative value of such a program should be promoted and funded by county and state residents. It pays off, according to officials. "When he [the fourteen-year-old] first came here, he had a very bad attitude, his behavior was very poor; his temper was violent, and he wasn't very cooperative. Over a period of time, his attitude has got a lot better, a lot more positive, and it's my understanding that he's getting A's and B's in school," says Uinta County Sheriff Forrest Bright. The American Civil Liberties Union has no objections to the program, as long as the fourteen-year-old is housed separately from adult inmates. Officers working at the jail have also helped the juvenile with his homework.

Essentially, Judge Mealey's sentence was not entirely new. It is very similar to the concept of adult study release, in which inmates are permitted some free time during each week to attend classes at nearby high schools, colleges, universities, or technical schools. Prison and jail authorities believe that such work/study release experiences further the rehabilitative goal of corrections. Usually, only those inmates who pose the least amount of community risk are permitted to enroll in such programs.

Should work or study release be required of all youths who are judged delinquent and sentenced to secure confinement? Do such programs mean that the system is "too lenient"? What are the success rates of such programs in other jurisdictions? What criteria should be used for selecting juveniles for such programs?

Source: Associated Press, "Student Splits Time Between Jail and School," *Minot (N.D.) Daily News,* April 6, 1996, p. A12

wristlets were a constant reminder that the juveniles were on probation. Further, these electronic devices became reminders to others to help the youths avoid activities that might violate conditions of the program.

Although Charles's research had only a few participants, his findings suggest that the program would also succeed with larger groups of offenders. Each juvenile was interviewed at the conclusion of the program. All reported that their wristlets were continuous reminders of their involvement in the probation program. However, they didn't feel as though program officials were spying on them. One of the youths compared his experience with electronic monitoring with his previous experience of being supervised by a PO. He remarked that when he was under the supervision of the PO, he could do whatever he wished, and there was little likelihood that his PO would ever find out about it. However, while he was wearing the wristlet he was always under the threat of being discovered by the computer or by the surveillance officer.

Another interesting phenomenon was that the wristlet enabled certain offenders to avoid peer pressure to "hang out" with their friends. Since they had wristlets, they had good excuses to return home and not violate their curfews. Also, the families of these juveniles took a greater interest in them and their program. In short, the program was considered successful, at least for these four youths. Parents who were also interviewed at the conclusion of the program agreed that the program and monitoring system had been quite beneficial for their sons. While electronic monitoring for juveniles is still in the early stages of experimentation, Charles (1989b) believes that it is a cost-effective alternative to incarceration.

Home Confinement for Juvenile Offenders

Home confinement for juveniles is often supplemented by electronic monitoring (Schlatter, 1989). Relatively little is known about the extent to which home confinement is used as a sentencing alternative. However, home confinement may be redundant, since curfew for juvenile offenders means home confinement anyway, especially during evening hours. As a day sentence, home confinement for juveniles would probably be counterproductive, because they are often obligated to finish their schooling as a condition of probation.

Boot Camps

Boot camps are highly regimented, military-like, short-term correctional programs (90–180 days) that impose strict discipline, physical training, and hard labor. When successfully completed, boot camps provide for transfers of participants to community-based facilities for nonsecure supervision. By 1993, over half the states had boot camps (Florida Office of Program Policy Analysis, 1995; Virginia State Crime Commission, 1993). In 1995, there were thirty-five federal and state boot camps with a total of 9,304 inmate-clients. Of these, 626 were females and 455 were juvenile offenders distributed among nine locally operated programs (Bourque, Han, and Hill, 1996:3). Some experts approve of boot camps as the latest correctional reform (Florida Advisory Council on Intergovernmental Relations, 1994). Other professionals are skeptical about their potential for success (Lieb, Fish, and Crosby, 1994). Much depends upon how particular boot camps are operated and for how long.

Boot camps were officially established in 1983 by the Georgia Department of Corrections Special Alternative Incarceration (SAI), although the general idea for boot camps originated in the late 1970s, also in Georgia (Parent, 1989b).

The Rationale for Boot Camps

Boot camps, also known as **shock incarceration,** are an alternative to long- term traditional incarceration. Austin, Jones, and Bolyard outline a brief rationale for boot camps:

1. A substantial number of youthful first-time offenders now incarcerated will respond to a short but intensive period of confinement followed by a longer period of intensive community supervision.
2. These youthful offenders will benefit from a military-type atmosphere that instills a sense of self-discipline and physical conditioning that were lacking in their lives.
3. These same youths need exposure to relevant educational and vocational training, drug

Girls at a New Jersey boot camp playing hockey. Physical education activities are part of the daily schedule at these facilities.

treatment, and general counseling services so that they can develop more positive values and become better prepared to get jobs.

4. Boot camp costs less than a traditional criminal justice sanction that imprisons the offender for a substantially longer period of time (Austin, Jones, and Bolyard, 1993:1).

Boot Camp Goals

Boot camps have several general goals. These goals include: (1) rehabilitation/reintegration; (2) discipline; (3) deterrence; (4) relief of prison and jail overcrowding; and (5) vocational, educational, and rehabilitative services.

1. *Provide rehabilitation and reintegration.* In 1986, the Orleans (Louisiana) Parish Prison System established a boot camp program called *About Face* (Caldas, 1990). This program sought to improve offenders' sense of purpose, self-discipline, self-control, and self-confidence through physical conditioning, educational programs, and social skills training, all within the framework of strict military discipline (Caldas, 1990). One early criticism of this program was that the staff lacked experience. Over time, however, this criticism was minimized (Caldas, 1990; MacKenzie, 1990, MacKenzie and Shaw, 1993:463–66).

2. *Provide discipline.* Certain boot camps must deal with juvenile offenders who usually resist authority and refuse to listen or learn in traditional classroom or treatment environments (Taylor, 1992:122). Physical conditioning and structure are most frequently stressed in these programs, but most boot camps also include literacy training, academic and vocational education, intensive value clarification, and resocialization (MacKenzie and Shaw, 1993).

3. *Promote deterrence.* The sudden immersion into a military-like atmosphere is frightening to many participants, and the rigorous approach to formal rules and authority is also challenging

(Shaw and MacKenzie, 1991). Latessa and Vito (1988) cite low recidivism rates among clients as evidence of the deterrent value of such programs. Other experts concur that boot camps and shock incarceration deter crime. Mack (1992:63–65) reports that of the many clients who have participated in the *Rikers Boot Camp High Impact Incarceration Program (HIIP)*, only 23 percent have recidivated, compared with the 28 percent rate of recidivism of those released from traditional incarceration. While the difference in these rates is not substantial, it does say something about the potential deterrent value of boot camp programs.

4. *Ease prison and jail overcrowding.* Besides serving as an alternative to incarceration, boot camps are believed to have a long-term impact on jail and prison overcrowding. This is theoretically possible because of the low recidivism rates among boot camp participants (MacKenzie and Souryal, 1991).

5. *Provide vocational, educational, and rehabilitative services.* An integral feature of *most* boot camp programs is some form of educational and/or vocational training (MacKenzie, Shaw, and Gowdy, 1993; Parent, 1989b). A New York Shock Incarceration program enables participants to work on GEDs and provides instruction in the basics (New York State Department of Correctional Services, 1989, 1990, 1991). Educational training is also a key feature of Louisiana's *IMPACT*, or *Intensive Motivational Program of Alternative Correctional Treatment* (Piquero and MacKenzie, 1993). As an alternative to traditional incarceration, boot camps do much to promote greater social and educational adjustment for clients re-entering their communities (Osler, 1991).

Profiling Boot Camp Participants

Depending on the program, participants may or may not be able to enter or withdraw from boot camps voluntarily. Most boot camp participants are prison-bound youthful offenders convicted of less serious, nonviolent crimes, who have never been incarcerated (Parent, 1988a; 1989b). However, different programs have different requirements (MacKenzie, Shaw, and Gowdy, 1993:1–3). Participants may be referred to these programs by judges or corrections departments, or they may volunteer.

They may or may not be accepted, and if they complete their programs successfully, they may or may not be released under supervision.

The Camp Monterey Shock Incarceration Facility (New York State Department of Correctional Services)

New York State's boot camp has the following features:

- It accommodates 250 participants in minimum-security institution.
- It has 131 staff members, 83 of whom hold custody positions.
- Participants are screened and must meet statutory criteria; three-fourths of applicants volunteer; one-third of applicants are rejected.
- Inmates form platoons and live in open dormitories.
- Completing the program successfully leads to parole board releases to an intensive probation program called "aftershock."
- Participants have physical training, drill, and eight hours daily of hard labor.
- Inmates must participate in therapeutic community meetings, basic education courses, individual counseling, and recreation.
- All must participate in alcohol and substance abuse treatment programs.
- Participants take part in job-seeking skills training and re-entry planning.

The Oklahoma Regimented Inmate Discipline Program (RID)

The Oklahoma RID program has the following features:

- A 145-bed facility at the Lexington Assessment and Reception Center; also houses six hundred long-term general population inmates as medium security.
- Offenders screened according to statutory criteria and may volunteer.
- Inmates live in single or double-bunk cells.
- Strict discipline, drill, physical training; housekeeping and institutional maintenance.
- Six hours daily of educational/vocational programs.

Standing in line and at attention in the mess hall of a New York shock prison, inmates are not permitted to talk to one another.

- Drug abuse programs, individual and group counseling.
- After completing the program, participants are resentenced to intensively supervised probation or "community custody," perhaps beginning at a halfway house.

The Georgia Special Alternative Program (SAI)

This program has the following characteristics:

- Program for male offenders.
- Judges control selection process, and SAI is a "condition of probation"; if successful, boot camp graduates are released, since judges do not ordinarily re-sentence them to probation.
- Physical training, drill, hard work; two exercise and drill periods daily, with eight hours of hard labor in between.
- Participants perform limited community services.
- Little emphasis on counseling or treatment.
- Drug abuse education and information about sexually transmitted diseases.
- Inmates are double-bunked in two twenty-

five-cell units at Dodge, and at Burris, one hundred inmates are single-bunked in four twenty-five-cell units (MacKenzie, Shaw, and Gowdy, 1993).

Because many of these boot camp programs have been active only since the late 1980s or early 1990s, research about their effectiveness is sparse. However, indications are that boot camps generally help reduce recidivism. Some states, such as Georgia, report relatively high rates of recidivism, whereas New York and Oklahoma have much lower recidivism rates. Besides reducing recidivism, boot camps might also save taxpayers money over time. In some states, the cost of operating boot camps is considerably less than that of traditional incarceration.

Parole for Juveniles

Parole for juveniles is similar to parole for adults. Juvenile offenders may be released before they have served full sentences. Generally, parole is a conditional supervised release from incarceration granted to youths who have served a portion of their original sentences (Altschuler and Armstrong, 1993).

Purposes of Parole for Juveniles

The general purposes of parole are:

1. To reward good behavior during incarceration.
2. To alleviate overcrowding.
3. To permit youths to reintegrate into their communities and enhance their chances of being rehabilitated.
4. To deter youths from offending by providing continued supervision by parole officers.

Some authorities also believe that the prospect of earning parole induces conformity to institutional rules. Also, some experts see parole as a continuation of the juvenile's punishment, because parole programs are usually conditional (e.g., dependent upon observance of curfew, school attendance, staying out of trouble, periodic drug and alcohol urinalyses, participation in counseling programs, and vocational and educational training).

The American Correctional Association (1994a:xxxvi) reports that in 1994, over 11,700 juveniles were in nonsecure, state-operated halfway houses and other community-based facilities and that about 15,000 youths were under other forms of state-controlled supervision as parolees.

Characteristics of Juvenile Parolees

Some studies of juvenile parolees indicate that most are black males between seventeen and nineteen years of age (Maguire and Pastore, 1995). *Juvenile Offender Laws* in states such as New York consider thirteen-, fourteen-, fifteen-, and sixteen-year-olds charged with certain felonies to be adults. Thus, they may be tried and convicted as adults. When they are released from institutionalization, they are placed under adult parole supervision. Many jurisdictions that do not have Juvenile Offender Laws have waiver or transfer provisions for juveniles charged with serious crimes.

Juvenile parolees participate in many of the same programs as youthful probationers. Many jurisdictions have intensively supervised probation programs for both probationers and parolees. Fur-

ther, juvenile parole officers often supervise both types of offenders.

In 1990, the Office of Juvenile Justice and Delinquency Prevention (OJJDP) conducted research aimed at formulating guidelines for intensive supervision parole programs for juveniles (Altschuler and Armstrong, 1990). They wanted to identify youths who might benefit the most from a parole program as well as the most effective methods for supervising offenders. Among their chief aims was to reduce and even eliminate recidivism among youthful parolees. While it is unrealistic to expect that any program will eliminate recidivism, it is possible to target certain features of programs that appear to reduce it among specific populations, including juvenile parolees. It is hoped that the efforts of the OJJDP will eventually yield more successful strategies for managing an especially troublesome population of offenders.

Juvenile Parole Policy

Between November 1987 and November 1988, Ashford and LeCroy (1993:186) undertook an investigation of the various state juvenile parole programs. They sent letters and questionnaires to all state juvenile jurisdictions; the response rate was 94 percent, with forty-seven states responding. As a result of their survey, they were able to develop a typology of juvenile parole. They discovered eight different kinds of juvenile parole:

1. *Determinate parole* (the length of parole is closely linked with the period of commitment specified by the court; paroling authorities cannot extend the length of confinement beyond that prescribed by the judge; juvenile can be released before serving the full sentence).
2. *Determinate parole set by administrative agency* (a parole release date is set immediately after the youth's arrival at the secure facility).
3. *Presumptive minimum with limits on the extension of the supervision period for a fixed length of time* (a minimum confinement period is specified, and the youth must be paroled after that date except in cases of bad conduct).
4. *Presumptive minimum with limits on the extension of supervision for an indeterminate period* (parole should end after fixed period of time;

parole period is indeterminate; PO may extend the parole period at his or her discretion; parole can last until the youth reaches the age of majority and leaves the jurisdiction of the juvenile court.

5. *Presumptive minimum with discretionary extension of supervision for an indeterminate period* (same as number 4 except that PO has discretion to extend parole indefinitely).

6. *Indeterminate parole with a specified maximum and a discretionary minimum length of supervision* (follows Model Juvenile Court Act of 1968, which provides limits for confinement but allows parole board to specify length of confinement and period of supervised release within these limits).

7. *Indeterminate parole with legal minimum and maximum periods of supervision* (the parole board can parole youths at any time within minimum and maximum confinement periods; more liberal than numbers 1 and 2).

8. *Indeterminate or purely discretionary parole* (the length of parole is unspecified; youths may remain on parole until they reach the age of majority; youths may be released from parole at any time during this period) (Ashford and LeCroy, 1993:187–91).

The most popular parole type is number 8; the least popular is number 1.

Juvenile Rehabilitation

The problem of finding the right rehabilitative program for juveniles is closely associated with other corrections issues. Many experimental programs have been tested over the years. Most have not achieved their original, optimistic goals. Three primary/secondary-school law-related curriculum projects were undertaken between 1979–1983 in California, Michigan, and North Carolina. One of the goals was to instruct students on law-related topics, personal responsibilities and the rights of others, and constitutional rights and guarantees. However, the teachers in these programs did not have the technical knowledge or expertise to present these topics effectively. The lesson objectives were vague, teachers were complacent, and no outside legal consultants were used. The programs failed to have a positive effect on the juvenile participants (Barton and Butts, 1991).

Some consideration has been given to "wilderness experience" programs as ways of curbing recidivism among delinquents (McCord, 1995; Thompson, 1991). But a general lack of coordination between program planners/coordinators and program staff has frequently led to disappointing results.

Some researchers argue that the most promising intervention strategies for dealing with "chronic" juvenile offenders should do the following: (1) provide opportunities for youths to overcome adversity and experience success; (2) facilitate bonds of affection and mutual respect between juveniles and their guardians or parents; (3) provide frequent, timely, and accurate feedback for both positive and negative behavior; (4) reduce or eliminate negative role models and peer support for negative attitudes or behavior; (5) require that juveniles recognize and understand thought processes that rationalize negative behavior; (6) create opportunities for juveniles to discuss family matters and early experiences in a relaxed, nonjudgmental atmosphere; and (7) adapt the sequence and amount of exposure to program components to the needs and capabilities of each youth (Montgomery and Torbet, 1994; Steiger and Dizon, 1991).

Often, the policies that confine juveniles for greater periods of time don't decrease recidivism. Furthermore, graduates of traditional training schools continue to commit many crimes (Thompson, 1991). Finally, much criminal behavior among juveniles is traceable to inadequate schools and other community resources (Steiger and Dizon, 1991).

Delinquency Prevention

The first community-based delinquency-prevention program in the United States was the **Chicago Area Project,** implemented by Clifford Shaw in 1934. The project originally targeted juveniles with high delinquency potential: lower class, inner-city youths and slum/ghetto dwellers (Shaw,

1929; Shaw and McKay, 1972). Rates of truancy were high, and juvenile crime flourished. The Chicago Area Project provided a variety of services to inner-city youth, including several juvenile recreational centers and some supervisory staff. But Shaw's focus upon such a limited sector of society was criticized by much of the social-scientific community. The primary criticism was that he had failed to recognize that delinquency was also prevalent in other socioeconomic strata and in suburban areas and that these areas also deserved attention. In spite of this criticism, however, Shaw's work has been considered successful at reducing delinquency in selected urban areas (Brantley, Sorrentino, and Torok, 1994).

Several delinquency prevention programs have focused on exposing elementary and secondary school students to anti-delinquency messages (Borduin et al., 1995; Virginia Commission on Youth, 1995). In some instances, school authorities have identified particularly troublesome juveniles as prime candidates for juvenile delinquency. These students have been subjected to certain educational experiences by local police, probation officers, and other authorities. The programs that seem most effective at preventing delinquency involve diversion of juvenile offenders to supervised, community-based services (Baker, Pollack and Kohn, 1995; DeJong, 1994). Preventing delinquency is worthwhile, but a consistent educational program for this purpose with a high success rate has yet to be identified. Currently, educational efforts along these lines are aimed at helping juveniles reduce their vulnerability to certain crimes.

A lawyer volunteer serves as a tutor/mentor at Chicago's Cabrini Green housing project. One-on-one relationships between concerned adults and juveniles with high delinquency potential are instrumental in delinquency prevention.

The Death Penalty for Juvenile Offenders

In April, 1995, there were 3,009 prisoners on death row in thirty-seven states and the federal government, an increase of 5.7 percent since April of 1994 (Camp and Camp, 1995a:33). At any given time, it is difficult to affix a particular number to how many juveniles are on death row. According to the government, in 1993 there were fourteen youths under age twenty on death row and seventy-three youths between the ages of twenty and twenty-four (Maguire and Pastore, 1995:591). Because the length of time between the imposition of death sentence and its execution is often ten or more years, it follows that many of the youths in their twenties were convicted as teenagers.

The First Juvenile Execution in the United States

The first recorded execution of a juvenile occurred in 1642. Thomas Graunger, a sixteen-year-old, was convicted of bestiality after being caught sodomizing a horse and a cow. The youngest age at which the death penalty was imposed is ten. This poorly documented case involved a ten-year-old convicted of murder in Louisiana in 1855. A more celebrated case was that of James Arcene, who was ten years old when he robbed and murdered his victim in Arkansas in 1885. He was finally arrested at age twenty-three and executed (Streib, 1987:57). Through 1993, Georgia led all states in executions with 383 since 1930. Texas and California follow Georgia. Thirteen states have never executed juveniles (Maguire and Pastore, 1995).

What Does the Supreme Court Say about Executing Juveniles?

In two landmark cases presented below (*Stanford v. Kentucky* [1989] and *Wilkins v. Missouri* [1989]), the Supreme Court has declared that death penalty may be applied to anyone convicted of a capital offense if he or she was sixteen or older at the time of the crime.

Arguments For and Against the Death Penalty

Opponents of capital punishment argue even more vehemently against executing youthful offenders. While 76 percent of U.S. citizens surveyed are pro-capital punishment, considerably fewer are in favor of executing juveniles (Sandys and McGarrell, 1995). One reason often given is the belief that youths *may* be rehabilitated over time, whereas older offenders are less likely to be responsive to rehabilitative strategies.

Those favoring the death penalty say it is "just" punishment and a societal revenge for the life taken or the harm inflicted by the offender. Fundamentalist religious groups tend to favor the death penalty, often because it is consistent with biblical practices (Grasmick, Bursik, and Blackwell, 1993). Some proponents of capital punishment believe that it is more economical than lifetime confinement, that it may be administered "humanely" through lethal injection, and that it deters capital crimes. Opponents say it is cruel and unusual punishment, that it does not deter murderers, that it is barbaric and uncivilized, that other countries do not impose it for any type of offense, regardless of its seriousness, and that it makes no sense to kill in order to send a message not to kill (Amnesty International, 1991).

For juveniles, these arguments are supplemented by the one that age is a mitigating factor. Researchers in two experiments conducted with 172 undergraduates and 174 adults in a large community asked whether capital punishment ought to be imposed on persons in particular age ranges. About 75 percent of participants opposed the death penalty for youths age thirteen to fifteen; 65 percent opposed the death penalty for persons aged sixteen to eighteen; and 60 percent *favored* the death penalty for persons twenty-five years old or older (Finkel et al., 1994). While these findings do not necessarily typify U.S. public opinion, they do indicate what the prevailing sentiment might be relative to juvenile executions. Other studies have found similar results (Skovron, Scott, and Cullen, 1989).

In any capital conviction, the offender is entitled to a bifurcated trial in which guilt is established first and then the punishment is decided, taking into account mitigating or aggravating circumstances. Was the crime especially brutal? Did the victim suffer? Was the murderer senile or mentally ill? Or was the murderer a juvenile? Some say that the death penalty should not be applied to juveniles under any condition, but least of all when youth is combined with these and other mitigating factors, such as substance abuse, indigence, mental retardation, psychological disturbances, and "troubled" family history and social background (Robinson and Stephens, 1992).

Early English precedent and common law assumed that those under age seven were incapable of formulating criminal intent. A presumption exists that between ages seven and twelve, the child is capable of formulating criminal intent, and in every jurisdiction, the prosecution has the burden of establishing beyond a reasonable doubt that the youth did so in this particular case.

There are always at least two sides in a murder case. The victim's survivors demand justice, and the justice they usually want is the death of the murderer—"an eye for an eye." But family members cannot help but feel compassion for the killer. Someone they love is about to lose his or her life. But hadn't the person taken someone else's life? But does taking the life of the murderer bring back the dead victim or fulfill some lofty social purpose? The arguments are endless.

In 1977, in Fort Jackson, South Carolina, a seventeen-year-old mentally retarded youth and a sixteen-year-old companion were living with a twenty-two-year-old soldier in a rented, run-down house. Alcohol, THC, PCP, marijuana, and other

---

Highlight 14.6. Teen Gangs and Disney-Inspired Hate Crimes: The Case of the Lords of Chaos

In Fort Myers, Florida, there was a teenage "militia" known as the Lords of Chaos. The Lords of Chaos organized in April of 1996 under the leadership of eighteen-year-old Kevin D. Foster. Some of the gang's members referred to Foster as "God." According to police investigators, the Lords of Chaos were consumed with blood lust and the desire to commit arson. According to a gang member who was interviewed following his arrest, the gang had a "master plan" that included stealing costumes from nearby Disney World and going on a shooting spree that would target black victims. There is no doubt that the gang would have put their plan into effect, according to Sheriff John McDougall. "It was consuming them. They couldn't get enough."

The Lords of Chaos shot and killed Mark Schwebes, the thirty-two-year-old Riverdale High School band director, who was killed by a blast from a twelve-gauge shotgun when he answered his door on May 2, 1996. Earlier, he had questioned his alleged killers when he saw them with a can of gasoline. Apparently suspecting that Schwebes would tell police, the Lords of Chaos killed him.

The gang members also confessed to various crimes, including the burning of a church and restaurant, a carjacking at another restaurant, and the burning of an abandoned Coca-Cola bottling plant. The arson and carjacking were a part of the gang's initiation rites for new members, according to various gang members. According to police, gang members called themselves a militia, although none of them knew what a militia was.

What is the best way to combat hate crimes that target specific ethnic groups or races? What types of interventions are most effective in discouraging the formation of such gangs? How prevalent are such gangs throughout the United States? Is there an epidemic of gang activity? Should gang members receive the death penalty if convicted of murder?

Source: Adapted from Associated Press, "'Blood Lust': Police Say Florida Teen Gang Consumed by Hate, Murder and a Desire for Arson," *Minot (N.D.) Daily News,* May 6, 1996, p. A6.

---

drugs were readily available. On October 29, after drinking heavily and consuming drugs, the three decided to look for a girl to rape. They drove to a baseball park in nearby Columbia and parked next to a seventeen-year-old boy and his fourteen-year-old girlfriend. On orders from the soldier, the seventeen-year-old shot the boy three times with a high-powered rifle, killing him instantly. Then they drove off with the girl to a secluded area where each raped her repeatedly. Finally, they shot her and mutilated her body.

The three were soon arrested. The sixteen-year-old agreed to testify against the soldier and the seventeen-year-old in exchange for a lighter sentence. Both the soldier and the seventeen-year-old eventually entered guilty pleas and were sentenced to death. After lengthy appeals, the soldier

was executed on January 11, 1985. On January 10, 1986, James Terry Roach, who had killed the boy and girl and mutilated the girl's body, was electrocuted. Justice was served. Or was it? A crowd outside the prison cheered on hearing that Roach had been executed. As he was strapped into the electric chair, Roach, his hands shaking, read his last letter: "To the families of the victims, my heart is still with you in your sorrow. May you forgive me just as I know that my Lord has done." Two one-minute surges of electricity hit him, and he was pronounced dead at 5:16 A.M. (Streib, 1987:125–27). The minimum ages for the death penalty are shown in table 14.3

Until recently, the Supreme Court has consistently refused to become embroiled in the "capital punishment for juveniles" issue, although it has

Table 14.3

Minimum Ages for Death Penalty in Selected States in 1987 Prior to *Thompson v. Oklahoma* (1988), *Wilkins v. Missouri* (1989), and *Stanford v. Kentucky* (1989)[a, b]

Age	States
16	Alabama, Arkansas, Idaho, Indiana, Kentucky, Louisiana, Mississippi, Missouri, Montana, Nevada, North Carolina, Utah, Virginia
17	Georgia, New Hampshire, Texas
18	California, Colorado, Connecticut, Illinois, Nebraska, New Jersey, New Mexico, Ohio, Oregon, Tennessee
No Minimum[b]	Arizona, Delaware, Florida, Maryland, Oklahoma, Pennsylvania, South Carolina, South Dakota, Washington, Wyoming

a. Compiled by the author.

b. The Supreme Court has ruled that it is unconstitutional to impose the death penalty on juveniles who committed their crimes when they were younger than sixteen years of age.

heard several death penalty cases involving juveniles in past years. One frequently cited case is *Eddings v. Oklahoma* (1982). The case raised the question of whether the death penalty as applied to juveniles was "cruel and unusual" punishment as defined by the Eighth Amendment. In its ruling, the Court did not say that the death penalty for juveniles was "crual and unusual punishment," but it also did not say that it wasn't. What it said was that the *youthfulness of the offender is a mitigating factor of great weight that must be considered*. Thus, many jurisdictions were left to make their own interpretations of the high court opinion.

If any trend is apparent regarding the death penalty for juveniles it is that many jurisdictions are moving away from executing juveniles under eighteen. Courts and juries almost always consider an offender's youth to be a mitigating factor, and public sentiment seems to favor abolishing the death penalty for all juveniles (Streib, 1987:50–51). Female juveniles are almost never executed. Only .06 percent of all executions in the United States have involved female juveniles (Streib and Sametz, 1989).

Most people maintain a strong belief that juve-

nile courts and corrections must make substantial efforts to rehabilitate juveniles rather than incarcerate or execute them. For example, a study conducted by Amnesty International examined attitudes toward the death penalty among a sample of 1,400 Florida residents (Amnesty International, 1991). While the survey disclosed overwhelming support for the death penalty, it also disclosed that most respondents considered the death penalty to be inappropriate for juveniles. Where should states draw the line concerning the minimum age at which someone can be put to death?

Landmark Juvenile Death Penalty Cases

In recent years the Supreme Court has decided several cases involving executions of juveniles. These cases are especially significant in that they provide a legal foundation for such executions. The cases include *Eddings v. Oklahoma* (1982), *Thompson v. Oklahoma* (1988), *Stanford v. Kentucky* (1989), and *Wilkins v. Missouri* (1989). As a prelude to discussing these cases, it should be noted that until 1988, sixteen states had established minimum ages for executing juveniles under eighteen. The ages ranged from ten (Indiana) to seventeen (Georgia, New Hampshire, and Texas). *Thompson v. Oklahoma* raised the minimum age for juvenile executions in all states to sixteen. The following year, the Supreme Court upheld the death sentences of a sixteen-year-old and a seventeen-year-old.

1. *Eddings v. Oklahoma* (1982). On April 4, 1977, Monty Lee Eddings and several other companions ran away from their Missouri homes. In a car owned by Eddings's older brother, they drove as far as the Oklahoma Turnpike. Eddings had several firearms in the car, including rifles that he had stolen from his father. At one point, Eddings lost control of the car and was stopped by an Oklahoma State Highway Patrol officer. When the officer approached the car, Eddings stuck a shotgun out of the window and killed the officer. When Eddings was subsequently apprehended, he was waived to criminal court on a prosecutorial motion. Efforts by Eddings's attorney to oppose the waiver failed. In a subsequent bifurcated trial, the trial judge considered both aggravating and mitigating circumstances, including Eddings's youthfulness,

mental state, and potential for treatment. However, the judge did not consider Eddings's "unhappy upbringing and emotional disturbance" sufficient to offset the aggravating circumstances. Eddings's attorney filed an appeal, which eventually reached the Supreme Court. Although the Oklahoma Court of Criminal Appeals reversed the trial judge's ruling, the Supreme Court reversed the Oklahoma Court of Criminal Appeals. The issue pivoted on whether the trial judge erred by refusing to consider Eddings's "unhappy upbringing and emotionally disturbed state." The trial judge had previously acknowledged Eddings's youth as a mitigating factor. Eddings's age, sixteen, was significant precisely because the majority of justices did not consider it to be so. Rather, they focused on the discussion of mitigating circumstances outlined in Eddings's appeal. Oklahoma was therefore in the position of lawfully imposing the death penalty on a juvenile who was sixteen years old at the time he committed murder.

2. *Thompson v. Oklahoma* (1988). William Wayne Thompson was convicted of murdering his former brother-in-law, Charles Keene. Keene had been suspected of abusing Thompson's sister. In the evening hours of January 22–23, 1983, Thompson and three older companions left his mother's house, saying "We're going to kill Charles." Early the following morning, Thompson and his associates beat Charles to death with fists and weapons, including a length of pipe. Thompson later told others, "We killed him. I shot him in the head and cut his throat in the river." Thompson's accomplices told police shortly after their arrest that Thompson had shot Keene twice in the head and then cut his body in several places (e.g., throat, chest, and abdomen), so that, according to Thompson, "the fish could eat his body."

Because Thompson was fifteen at the time of the murder, juvenile officials transferred his case to criminal court. This transfer was supported, in part, by an Oklahoma statutory provision indicating that there was "prosecutive merit" in pursuing the case against Thompson. The defendant's youthfulness, among other factors, was introduced as a mitigating circumstance; aggravating factors, such as the "especially heinous, atrocious, and

cruel" manner in which Keene had been murdered, were also presented. Thompson was convicted of first-degree murder and sentenced to death. Thompson's appeal eventually reached the Supreme Court. In a vigorously debated opinion, the Court overturned Thompson's death sentence, saying in its conclusory data that

> petitioner's counsel and various *amici curiae* have asked us to "draw the line" that would prohibit the execution of any person who was under the age of eighteen at the time of the offense. Our task, today, however, is to decide the case before us; we do so by concluding that the Eighth and Fourteenth Amendments prohibit the execution of a person who was under sixteen years of age at the time of his or her offense. (108 S.Ct. at 2700)

Accordingly, Thompson's death penalty was reversed. This Supreme Court decision effectively established a minimum age of sixteen for exacting the death penalty. This decision awaited subsequent challenges, however.

3. *Stanford v. Kentucky* (1989). Kevin Stanford was seventeen when, on January 17, 1981, he and an accomplice repeatedly raped and sodomized and eventually shot to death twenty-year-old Baerbel Poore while robbing the gas station in Jefferson County, Kentucky, where Poore worked as an attendant. Stanford later told police, "I had to shoot her [since] she lived next door to me and she would recognize me. . . . I guess we could have tied her up or something or beat [her up] . . . and tell her if she tells, we would kill her." A corrections officer who interviewed Stanford said that after Stanford made that disclosure, "He [Stanford] started laughing." The jury found him guilty of first-degree murder, and the judge sentenced him to death. In an opinion that addressed the issue of the "minimum age for the death penalty," the Supreme Court decided this case and the case of Heath Wilkins as follows.

4. *Wilkins v. Missouri* (1989). On July 27, 1985, Heath Wilkins and his accomplice, Patrick Stevens, entered a convenience store in Avondale, Missouri, with the intention of robbing it. Their plan was to kill "whoever was behind the counter"

because "a dead person can't talk." Accordingly, they stabbed Nancy Allen Moore, a twenty-six-year-old mother of two, who fell to the floor. When Stevens had difficulty opening the cash register, Moore, mortally wounded, offered to help him. Wilkins stabbed her three more times in the chest, two of the knife wounds penetrating her heart. Moore began to beg for her life, whereupon Wilkins stabbed her four more times in the neck, opening up her carotid artery. She died shortly thereafter. The robbery netted Stevens and Wilkins $450 in cash and checks, a few bottles of liquor, cigarettes, and rolling papers. Wilkins was convicted of first-degree murder and sentenced to death.

The U.S. Supreme Court heard both Wilkins's and Stanford's cases simultaneously, because the overriding issue was whether the death penalty was cruel and inhumane when applied to sixteen- and seventeen-year-olds. Although several justices dissented from the majority view, the Supreme Court upheld the death sentences of Stanford and Wilkins, concluding that "we discern neither a historical nor a modern societal consensus forbidding the imposition of capital punishment on any person who murders at sixteen or seventeen years of age. Accordingly, we conclude that such punishment does not offend the Eighth Amendment's prohibition against cruel and unusual punishment" (109 S.Ct. at 2980). Thus, this crucial opinion underscored age sixteen as the minimum age at which the death penalty may be administered.

The issue of sentencing juveniles to death has been vigorously debated (Finkel et al., 1994; Robinson and Stephens, 1992; Sandys and McGarrell, 1995; Seis and Elbe, 1991), without apparent consensus. Arguments favoring the death penalty for juveniles stress holding youthful offenders accountable for their crimes and the justice of capital punishment when capital crimes have been committed. Arguments opposing the death penalty for juveniles are often emotionally laden or address issues related only remotely to the death penalty issue (Grasmick, Bursik, and Blackwell, 1993). For instance, some argue that juveniles are more amenable to treatment and rehabilitation and thus that they should be given another chance (Wilson, 1983). Whatever the appeal of such an argument,

the Supreme Court has, at least for the time being, resolved the age/death penalty issue with some degree of finality. Factors other than age will therefore have to be cited as mitigating in cases that involve the death penalty.

Currently, only a few juveniles are on death row. Because of the declining frequency with which juveniles have been executed in recent years, the death penalty issue as it applies to juveniles does not seem as strongly debated as it once was. There will always be many people who oppose the death penalty for any reason (Gewerth and Dorne, 1991). But it is doubtful that major changes will be made in how the death penalty is applied to juvenile offenders, unless the composition of the Supreme Court changes significantly (Bieler, 1990). While public sentiment is not always easy to measure, there seems to be strong sentiment in favor of harsher penalties for juvenile offenders. This doesn't necessarily mean the death penalty or life imprisonment, but it does mean tougher laws and law enforcement where juveniles are concerned.

Summary

The juvenile justice system parallels the criminal justice system in several respects. Juveniles are arrested and booked. Depending upon the seriousness of the offense, they may be released to the custody of their parents or detained. Minor offenses are "status" offenses, in contrast with more serious violations, which are the equivalent of felonies or misdemeanors.

The true amount of juvenile delinquency in the United States is unknown. Juveniles under age eighteen are believed to account for about 31 percent of all index offenses reported by the *Uniform Crime Reports*. Self-reporting of delinquent acts not detected by police shows that delinquency is much higher than official figures suggest.

The juvenile justice system consists of prevention and diversion, the juvenile court, and juvenile corrections. An intake hearing is held prior to a formal adjudication that a juvenile is delinquent. Some juveniles accused of more serious crimes are detained for adjudication, while others are placed on bond and/or released to the custody of parents. In some cases, a prosecutor may move to waive the juvenile to the jurisdiction of an adult court. This recommendation is usually, though not always, reserved for the most serious crimes or violent offenders. The juvenile court is a formal proceeding in which a juvenile is adjudicated as either delinquent or nondelinquent. Adjudication as delinquent results in a number of correctional alternatives, ranging from a verbal warning to community service to formal secure confinement for a specified period.

The Supreme Court decisions *In re Gault* (1967) and *Kent v. United States* (1966) established that juveniles have many rights equivalent to those of adults, including the right to counsel, the right to confront witnesses, and the right to due process.

Problems facing juvenile justice include the deinstitutionalization of status offenses, remanding juveniles to the jurisdiction of the criminal court, the female juvenile offender, the use and abuse of drugs and alcohol among juvenile offenders, juvenile violence, the effectiveness of various non-incarcerative alternatives for rehabilitating juveniles, the adequacy of detention and secure-confinement facilities for juveniles, the effectiveness of diversion programs, and delinquency prevention.

Key Terms

Adjudication
Chicago Area Project
Deinstitutionalization of status offenses
Delinquency
Demand waivers
Detention hearing
Intake screening
Judicial waivers
Juveniles
Legislative waivers
Net widening
Parens patriae
Prosecutorial waivers
Self-report surveys
Shock incarceration
Status offenses
Transfers

Questions for Review

1. Who are juveniles? Is there a consistent definition of *juvenile* in all jurisdictions? What are some different definitions that can be listed?
2. Define juvenile delinquency. Differentiate between status offenses and delinquency.
3. What is meant by the deinstitutionalization of status offenses? Is everyone in favor of the deinstitutionalization of status offenses? Why or why not? What are some of the arguments favoring or opposing the deinstitutionalization of status offenses?
4. How much juvenile delinquency is there in the United States? According to the best estimates, what is the amount of delinquency as measured by arrest figures in the *Uniform Crime Reports*?
5. What is a self-report survey? What is its purpose? How is it different from official delinquency reports?
6. What are the three major components of the juvenile justice system? Briefly describe the functions of each.
7. What is the doctrine of *parens patriae*? What is the origin of this doctrine?
8. What is an intake screening? What is its purpose? What are three alternatives that may occur as the result of an intake screening?
9. What is meant by adjudication? What does an adjudication hearing accomplish?
10. Identify three major Supreme Court cases having to do with the legal rights of juveniles. Identify the major issue(s) involved in each of these cases.

Suggested Readings

Albanese, Jay S. 1993. *Dealing with Delinquency: The Future of Juvenile Justice*. 2d ed. Chicago: Nelson-Hall.

Bynum, Jack E. and William E. Thompson. 1996. *Juvenile Delinquency: Sociological Approach*. 3d ed. Needham Heights, MA: Allyn and Bacon.

Clement, Mary. 1996. *Juvenile Justice System: Law and Process*. Newton, MA: Butterworth/Heinemann.

Dorne, Clifford and Kenneth Gewerth. 1996. *American Juvenile Justice: Cases, Legislation and Comments*. Bethesda, MD: Austin and Winfield.

Forst, Martin L. 1995. *The New Juvenile Justice*. Chicago: Nelson-Hall.

Sanders, William B. 1994. *Gangbangs and Drive-Bys*. Hawthorne, NY: Aldine de Gruyter.

Schwartz, Ira M. and William H. Barton (eds.) 1996. *Reforming Juvenile Detention: No More Hidden Closets*. Columbus: Ohio State University Press.

Whitehead, John T. and Steven P. Lab. 1996. *Juvenile Justice: An Introduction*. Cincinnati, OH: Anderson.

Glossary

ABA model   A configuration of court structure and judicial selection established by the American Bar Association.

Acceptance of responsibility   A genuine admission or acknowledgment of wrong-doing; in federal presentence investigation reports, for example, convicted offenders may write an explanation and apology for the crime(s) they committed. A provision that may be considered in deciding whether leniency should be extended to offenders during the sentencing phase of their processing.

Accountability   Responsibility of either adults or children for their actions, criminal or delinquent; may involve restitution to victims, community service, or other forms of compensation to manifest one's acceptance of responsibility.

Acquittal   Any judgment by the court, considering a jury verdict or judicial determination of the factual basis for criminal charges, where the defendant is declared not guilty of the offenses alleged.

Actus reus   Criminal or overt act.

Adjudication hearing   Formal proceeding involving a prosecuting attorney and a defense attorney where evidence is presented and the juvenile's status or condition is determined by the juvenile court judge.

Aggravating circumstances   Statutory listing of factors that intensify the punishment of convicted offenders.

Aggravating factors   Events about crime that may intensify the severity of punishment, including bodily injury or death to victim; brutality of an act.

Alibi   Defense to a criminal allegation that places an accused individual at some place other than the crime scene at the time the crime occurred.

Alternative sentencing   When the judge imposes a sentence other than incarceration; often involves good works such as community service, restitution to victims, and other public service activity. Also called "creative sentencing."

American Correctional Association   Established in 1870 to disseminate information about correctional programs and correctional training; designed to foster professionalism throughout correctional community.

Appearance   Act of coming into a court and submitting to the authority of that court.

Appellant   Person who initiates an appeal.

Appellee   Party who prevails in lower court, who argues on appeal against reversing the lower court's decision.

Arraignment   Official proceeding in which the defendant is formally confronted by criminal charges and enters a plea; a trial date is established through the arraignment proceeding.

Arrest   Taking persons into custody and restraining them until they can be brought before the court to answer the charges against them.

Arrestee   Person who is arrested.

Arrest rate   The number of arrests as a percentage of crimes known to the police.

Arrest report   Document prepared by an arresting officer describing the arrested person and the events and circumstances leading to the arrest.

Arrest warrant   Document issued by a court ordering law officers to arrest a specific individual.

Attachment of rights   Any phase of criminal processing, from arrest through conviction and sentencing, where a person's due process rights become relevant.

Auburn system   The system used in a prison constructed in Auburn, New York, in 1816. The Auburn prison pioneered use of "tiers" where inmates were housed on different floors or levels, usually according to their offense seriousness; introduced "congregate system," where prisoners had opportunities to "congregate" with one another for work, dining, recreation; and introduced stereotypical "striped" prison uniforms for prisoners. Prison system developed in New York during the nineteenth century that stressed congregate working conditions. Form of imprisonment in the 1820s that depended upon mass prisons, where prisoners were held in congregate fashion.

Augustus, John (1785–1859) Originated probation in the United States in 1841; considered first informal probation officer; Boston shoemaker and philanthropist, active in reforming petty offenders and alcoholics charged with crimes; assumed responsibility for them and posted their bail while attempting to reform them; considered successful.

Bail Surety provided by defendants or others to guarantee their subsequent appearance in court to face criminal charges; available to anyone *entitled* to it. Not everyone is entitled to bail; bail is denied when suspects are considered dangerous or likely to flee. *See also* Preventive detention; *also see United States v. Salerno* in list of cases.

Bail Bond A written guarantee, often accompanied by money or other securities, that the person charged with an offense will remain within the court's jurisdiction to face trial at a time in the future.

Bailiff Court officer who maintains order in the court while it is in session. The bailiff oversees the jury during a trial proceeding. Sometimes the bailiff has custody of prisoners while they are in the courtroom; also known as a messenger.

Bail Reform Act of 1984 Act to revise bail practices and to assure that all persons, regardless of their financial status, shall not needlessly be detained to answer criminal charges. This does not mean that all persons are entitled to bail regardless of their alleged offense. Some persons charged with murder and other egregious offenses are not entitled to bail by legislative provision.

Banishment Physical removal of undesirables, criminals, political and religious dissidents to remote locations; practiced by England until 1800. Popular sites for banishment included the American colonies and Australia.

Behavioral approach Type of police discretion typified by a blend of sociology, psychology, and political science; a developmental scheme whereby police officers attempt to negotiate their way through each public encounter.

Bench trial Tribunal where guilt or innocence of defendant is determined by the judge rather than a jury.

Bench warrant Document issued by a judge and not requested by the police demanding that a specified person be brought before the court without undue or unnecessary delay.

Beyond a reasonable doubt Standard used in criminal courts to establish guilt of criminal defendant.

Bifurcated trial Tribunal in capital cases where the jury is asked to make two decisions. The first decision is to determine guilt or innocence of defendant; if guilty, the jury meets to decide punishment which may include the death penalty.

Body Belt Restraining device worn by prisoners, with wrist restraints at the center, over the abdomen.

Booking Process of making a written report of an arrest, including the name and address of the arrested person, the alleged crime, arresting officer, place and time of arrest, physical description of suspect, photographs, sometimes called "mug shots," and fingerprints.

Brockway, Zebulon First superintendent of New York State Reformatory at Elmira in 1876; arguably credited with introducing the first "good time" system in United States whereby inmates could have their sentences reduced or shortened by the number of good marks earned through good behavior.

"Broken windows" approach Form of police patrol stressing better communication with citizens. Foot patrols, team policing, and other "back to the people" programs are consistent with this patrol form. The term is used to describe the role of the police as maintainers of community order and safety.

Bureau of Alcohol, Tobacco and Firearms Agency created to oversee alcohol manufacture, firearms regulation, and tobacco production and to prevent illegal practices relating thereto.

Bureau of Justice Statistics Bureau created in 1979 to distribute statistical information concerning crime, criminals, and crime trends.

Burnout Psychological phenomenon measured by the Maslach Burnout Inventory; characterized by a loss of motivation and commitment related to task performance. The MBI tests the degree of commitment to the job and the loss of motivation to be successful.

California Youth Authority Major incarcerative facility for juveniles age seventeen to twenty-five in California; houses both short- and long-term violent and property offenders; provides therapeutic milieu within which offenders can become rehabilitated.

Capital punishment Imposition of the death penalty for the most serious crimes; may be administered by electrocution, lethal injection, gas, hanging, or shooting.

Career offender Those offenders who earn their living through crime. Usually, offenses occur over the lifetime of the offender.

Caseload   Refers to the number of persons who have criminal charges filed against them in a particular court; court docket schedules trials on each case; cumulative cases is the caseload for a judge. Also, in probation/parole, the number of clients a probation or parole officer is assigned according to some standard such as a week, month, or year; caseloads vary among jurisdictions.

Cash bond   Cash payment for situations where charges are not serious and the scheduled bail is low. Defendants obtain release by paying in cash the full amount, which is recoverable after the required court appearances are made.

Cause   *See* Challenge for cause.

Central Intelligence Agency   Under the National Security Act of 1947, an organization created to investigate matters of national security; also known as the CIA; headquartered in Langley, Virginia.

Challenge for cause   Dismissal of a prospective juror because the juror has biases for or against the defendant or is related to court officers, law enforcement officers, defense counsel, the defendant, or the defendant's family.

Charge   A formal allegation filed by a prosecutor that a specific person has committed a specific offense.

Charge reduction bargaining   Negotiation process between prosecutors and defense attorneys involving dismissal of one or more charges against a defendant in exchange for a guilty plea to remaining charges. The prosecutor downgrades the charges in return for a plea of guilty from the defendant.

Child abuse   Any form of physical, moral, mental, or sexual abuse or exploitation, negligent treatment, or maltreatment of a child under the age of eighteen by a person who is responsible for the child's welfare.

Chronic offender   Person who persists in committing crimes; may be violent or property offenses; the person is a habitual offender.

Circuit courts of appeal   Originally, courts that were held by judges who heard cases periodically in various communities; however, it now refers to courts with several counties or districts within their jurisdiction.

Citizen's arrest   Apprehension of a criminal suspect by a private citizen unaffiliated with any law enforcement agency.

Co-correctional prison   Penal facility where male and female prisoners live, supervised by female and male staff; prisoners participate in all activities together but do not share the same quarters.

Common law   Authority based on court decrees and judgments which recognize, affirm, and enforce certain usages and customs of the people; laws determined by judges in accordance with their rulings.

Community-based corrections   Locally operated services offering minimum-security, limited release, or work release alternatives to prisoners about to be paroled; may also serve probationers.

Community Dispute Resolution Program   A civil alternative to legal action; a mechanism within a community where a criminal case has been changed to a civil proceeding, where the victim and perpetrator can work out a mutually convenient resolution of differences; includes restitution to victims.

Community policing   A philosophy rather than a specific tactic. A proactive, decentralized approach designed to reduce crime, disorder, and fear of crime by intensely involving the same officer in a community for a long term so that personal links are formed with residents.

Community service   An alternative sanction requiring offenders to work in the community at such tasks as cleaning public parks or working with handicapped children in lieu of an incarcerative sentence; reimbursing a victim through money received from the offender's work.

Complaint   Written statement of essential facts constituting the offense alleged made under oath before a magistrate or other qualified judicial officer.

Concurrent jurisdiction   Where offender may be held accountable in several different jurisdictions simultaneously or in courts in the same jurisdiction.

Congregate system   Introduced at Auburn State Penitentiary in New York; prisoners could work and eat together in common work and recreational areas; prisoners segregated at night.

Control beats   Police patrol style, originating in the early 1900s, designed to bring officers into closer physical contact with area residents; beats arranged for small geographical areas of neighborhoods or cities that are patrolled by individual officers, usually on foot.

Conviction   Judgment of a court, based on a jury or judicial verdict, or on the guilty plea of the defendant, that the defendant is guilty of the offenses alleged.

Coordinate model   Neighboring female and male prisons sharing common facilities and programs, such as certain Alaskan prisons.

Corrections   The aggregate of programs, services, facilities, and organizations responsible for the management of people who have been accused or convicted of criminal offenses.

Counsel   A lawyer who represents a party in either a civil or criminal matter.

Courts   Public judiciary bodies that apply the law to controversies and oversee the administration of justice.

Court clerk   Court officer who may file pleadings, motions, or judgments, issue process, and keep general records of court proceedings.

Court of civil appeals   Any appellate court hearing cases appealed from lower courts, where only noncriminal issues are involved; any court hearing a tort action.

Court of criminal appeals   Any appellate court hearing criminal cases appealed from criminal courts, superior courts, or circuit courts (in selected states, such as Tennessee).

Court of record   Any court where a written record is kept of court proceedings.

Court reporter   Court official who keeps a written word-for-word and/or tape-recorded record of court proceedings. *See* Transcript.

Creative sentencing   A broad class of punishments as alternatives to incarceration that are designed to fit the particular crimes; may involve community service, restitution, fines, becoming involved in educational or vocational training programs, or becoming affiliated with other "good works" activity.

Crime   Act or omission prohibited by law by one who is held accountable by that law; consists of legality, *actus reus, mens rea,* consensus, harm, causation, and prescribed punishment.

Crime control model   A model of criminal justice that emphasizes containment of dangerous offenders and societal protection. A criminal justice system that assumes that freedom is so important that every effort must be made to repress crime. It emphasizes efficiency and the capacity to apprehend, try, convict, and dispose of a high proportion of offenders.

Crime prevention   Any overt activity conducted by individuals or groups to deter persons from committing crimes; may include "target hardening" by making businesses and residences more difficult targets for burglary; may include neighborhood watch programs, where neighborhood residents keep watch during evening hours for suspicious persons or automobiles in residential areas; may include equipping homes and businesses with devices to detect crime.

Crime(s) against persons   Violent crimes, including all crimes committed in the victim's presence (includes murder, rape, robbery, aggravated assault).

Crime(s) against property   Nonviolent or passive crimes, where no physical harm is inflicted upon victims (includes vehicular theft, burglary, and larceny).

Criminal justice system   An interrelated set of agencies and organizations designed to control criminal behavior, to detect crime, and to apprehend, process, prosecute, punish, and/or rehabilitate criminal offenders. The processual aspect suggests that the interrelatedness implied by "system" may not be strong; e.g., perhaps many judges do not contact jail or prison officials to inquire whether there is sufficient space whenever offenders are sentenced to jail or prison terms.

Criminology   The study of crime; the science of crime and criminal behavior, the forms of criminal behavior, the causes of crime, the definition of criminality, and the societal reaction to crime. An empirical social-behavioral science that investigates crime, criminals, and criminal justice.

Cross-examination   Questioning of one side's witnesses by the other side, either the prosecution or the defense.

Cruel and unusual punishment   Prohibited by Eighth Amendment of U.S. Constitution; unspecified by U.S. Supreme Court; subjectively interpreted on case-by-case basis. In some states, the electric chair has been determined to be "cruel and unusual" punishment for purposes of administering the death penalty, whereas lethal injection has not been determined to be cruel and unusual.

Deadly force   Any force used by law enforcement officers or any other person (as in citizen's arrests), that may result in death or great bodily harm, to apprehend those suspected of or engaging in unlawful acts. *See* Fleeing felon rule.

Death row   Arrangement of prison cells where inmates are housed who have been sentenced to death.

Decriminalization   Legislative action whereby an act or omission, formerly criminal, is made noncriminal and without punitive sanctions; usually occurs through legislative action.

Defendant   Person against whom a criminal proceeding is pending.

Defense   A response by defendants in criminal law or civil cases; may consist only of a denial of the factual allegations of the prosecution (in a criminal case) or of the plaintiff (in a civil case). If the defense offers new factual allegations in an effort to negate the charges, this is called an affirmative defense.

Defense attorney   A lawyer who represents a client accused of a crime.

Defense-of-life standard   Criteria by which law enforcement officers decide whether to use deadly force in effecting the arrest of criminal suspects. Involves deciding whether an officer's life or the lives of others are in jeopardy as the result of a suspect's actions. Standard established in *Tennessee v. Garner* (1985).

Defenses to criminal charges   Includes claims based upon personal, special, and procedural considerations that defendants should not be held accountable for their actions, even though they may have acted in violation of the criminal laws.

Deinstitutionalization Providing programs in community-based settings instead of institutional ones.

Deinstitutionalization of status offenses (DSO) Movement to remove nondelinquent juveniles from secure facilities. Eliminating status offenses from the delinquency category and removing juveniles from or precluding their confinement in juvenile correction facilities. Also, the process of removing status offenses from the jurisdiction of juvenile court.

Delinquent, delinquent child Child who has committed an offense that would be a crime if committed by an adult; in some states, status offenses are considered delinquent conduct and subject to identical punishments, including incarceration. Infant of not more than a specified age who has violated criminal laws or engages in disobedient, indecent or immoral conduct, and is in need of treatment, rehabilitation, or supervision.

Delinquent act, delinquency Any act committed by a juvenile that would be a crime if committed by an adult. Any act committed by an infant of not more than a specified age who has violated criminal laws or engages in disobedient, indecent, or immoral conduct, and is in need of treatment, rehabilitation, or supervision; status acquired through an adjudicatory proceeding by juvenile court.

Department of Justice, U.S. Organization headed by the attorney general of United States; responsible for prosecuting federal law violators; oversees Federal Bureau of Investigation and the Drug Enforcement Administration.

Department of Treasury Agency that oversees the Bureau of Alcohol, Tobacco, and Firearms, U.S. Customs Service, Internal Revenue Service, and the Secret Service.

Detention Period of temporary custody of juveniles before their case dispositions.

Determinate sentencing Sanctioning scheme where court sentences an offender to incarceration for a fixed period, which must be served in full and without parole intervention, less any "good time" earned in prison.

Deterrence Action that is designed to prevent crime before it occurs by threatening severe criminal penalties or sanctions. May include safety measures to discourage potential lawbreakers such as elaborate security systems, electronic monitoring, and greater police officer visibility. Andenaes (1975) defines deterrence as *influencing by fear*, where fear is of apprehension and punishment. Potential offenders do not have to actually receive punishment to be deterred; rather, the potential or threat of punishment may bring about the desired outcome.

Deviance Conduct that departs from accepted codes expected by society or from a particular group; also includes illegal behavior prohibited by statute.

Direct examination Questioning of one's own (prosecution or defense) witness during a trial.

Discovery Procedure whereby the prosecution shares information with the defense attorney and defendant. Specific types of information are made available to the defendant before a trial, including the results of any tests conducted, psychiatric reports, transcripts or tape-recorded statements made by the defendant; also known as "Brady materials" after a specific court case.

Diversion Removing a case from the criminal justice system, while a defendant is required to comply with various conditions such as attending a school for drunk drivers, undergoing counseling, performing community service, or other condition; may result in expungement of record. A pretrial alternative to prosecution; conditional removal of the prosecution of a case prior to its adjudication, usually as the result of an arrangement between the prosecutor and judge.

Double-bunking Placing two or more inmates in a cell originally designed to accommodate one inmate.

Dropsy testimony Perjured testimony by police officers in an attempt to solidify a weak case. Defendants are often alleged to have "dropped" drugs on the ground during automobile stops for traffic violations, hence, dropsy testimony. More prevalent after the exclusionary rule became a search and seizure standard following the case of *Mapp v. Ohio* (1963).

Drug Enforcement Administration (DEA) Agency established to investigate violations of all federal drug trafficking laws; regulates the legal manufacture of drugs and other controlled substances.

Due process Basic constitutional right to a fair trial; presumption of innocence until guilt is proven beyond a reasonable doubt; the opportunity to be heard, to be aware of a matter that is pending, to make an informed choice whether to acquiesce or contest, and to provide the reasons for such a choice before a judicial official. Actual due process rights include timely notice of a hearing or trial that informs the accused of charges; the opportunity to confront one's accusers and to present evidence on one's own behalf before an impartial jury or judge; the presumption of innocence under which guilt must be proved by legally obtained evidence and the verdict must be supported by the evidence presented; the right of accused persons to be warned of their constitutional rights at the earliest stage of the criminal process; protection against self-incrimination; assistance of counsel at every critical stage of the criminal process; and the guarantee that individuals will not be tried more than once for the same offense.

Duress Affirmative defense used by defendants to show lack of criminal intent, alleging force, psychological or physical, from others as the stimulus for otherwise criminal conduct.

Electronic monitoring The use of electronic devices that emit electronic signals. These devices, anklets or wristlets, are worn by offenders, probationers, and parolees. The purpose is to monitor an offender's presence in a given environment where the offender is required to remain or to verify the offender's whereabouts.

Element of the offense Any conduct, circumstance, condition, or state of mind that in combination with other conduct, circumstances, conditions, or states of mind constitutes an unlawful act.

Elmira Reformatory The first true reformatory built in 1876. The first superintendent was Zebulon Brockway, a rehabilitation and reformation advocate, who promoted educational training and cultivation of vocational skills. He believed in prisoner reformation. Questionably successful as a reformatory.

Employee assistance program Program used by some police departments to assist police officers or their family members with problems such as drug abuse, alcoholism, drugs, or emotional difficulties; uses counselors.

Entrapment Activity of law enforcement officers who suggest, encourage, or aid others in the commission of crimes that would ordinarily not have occurred without officer intervention, encouragement, or assistance. Defense used by defendants to show that an otherwise criminal act would not have occurred without police intervention, assistance, and/or encouragement.

Excessive bail Bond set unreasonably high so that offenders cannot secure their freedom prior to their trials; e.g., requiring a shoplifter to post $1 million bond to obtain his or her release for a temporary pretrial period.

Excessive force Any exceptional force extending beyond what is necessary to disable suspects or take them into custody through arrest.

Exclusionary rule Rule that provides that where evidence has been obtained in violation of the privileges guaranteed by U.S. Constitution, such evidence may be excluded at the trial.

Exculpatory evidence Any information that tends to exonerate a person of allegations of wrongdoing. An alibi showing that the person was elsewhere when the crime was committed would be exculpatory.

Excuse A defense to a criminal charge in which an accused person maintains he lacked the intent to commit the crime.

Exigent circumstances Circumstances where quick action is necessitated, such as searches for drugs and other contraband that might be destroyed easily; exception to the exclusionary rule.

Expert witness Sometimes called "hired guns"; witnesses who have expertise or special knowledge in a relevant field pertaining to the case at trial, for example, a psychiatrist might be an expert witness in a case where the defense alleges insanity. A witness who is qualified under the Federal Rules of Evidence to offer an opinion about the authenticity or accuracy of reports or who has special knowledge that is relevant to the proceeding.

Expungement orders Juvenile court orders to seal juvenile records.

Eye witness Witness who actually saw the crime committed.

False arrest Unlawful physical restraint of someone by a law enforcement officer. May include confinement or brief detention in a jail for no valid legal reason. Innocent persons accused of shoplifting may be arrested in a store and detained by store private security personnel is one type of false arrest. A police officer may arrest a motorist for no valid reason, if, for instance, the motorist is a minority or says something that may offend the officer but that is insufficient to warrant arrest.

False negatives Offenders who are predicted to be nonviolent or not dangerous according to various risk or dangerousness prediction devices but who turn out to be dangerous or pose serious public risk.

False positives Offenders who are predicted to be dangerous or who pose serious public risk according to various prediction devices and instruments but who are not dangerous and do not post public risks.

Federal Bureau of Investigation (FBI) Established in 1908 through the Department of Justice Appropriation Act. Investigative agency that enforces all federal criminal laws and compiles information for the *Uniform Crime Reports* annually. The enforcement arm of the Department of Justice that investigates over two hundred different kinds of federal law violations, maintains extensive files on criminals, and assists other law agencies (the acronym FBI also stands for fidelity, bravery, and integrity).

Federal Bureau of Prisons Established in 1930; charged with providing suitable quarters for prisoners and safekeeping of all persons convicted of offenses against the United States. Also contracts with local jails and state prisons for confinement of federal prisoners where there are insufficient federal facilities in the geographical area where the persons were convicted.

Federal district court Basic trial court for the federal government. Tries all criminal cases and has an extensive jurisdiction. District judges are appointed by the president of United States with the advice, counsel, and approval of the Senate.

Felony Crime punishable by incarceration, usually in a state or federal prison, for a period of one year or longer.

Filings The commencement of criminal proceedings by entering a charging document into a court's official record.

Fines Financial penalties imposed at time of sentencing convicted offenders. Most criminal statutes contain provisions for the imposition of monetary penalties as sentencing options.

Fleeing felon rule Rule rendered unconstitutional by the U.S. Supreme Court in 1985 whereby law enforcement officers were permitted to use deadly force to apprehend felons who attempt to escape apprehension (see *Tennessee v. Garner*, 1985).

Foot patrol Originating in Flint, Michigan, and elsewhere, foot patrols have been moderately successful in bringing community residents into closer touch with patrolling officers. Officers patrol on foot, presumably to bring them in touch with citizens. *See also* Community policing.

Fruits of the poisonous tree doctrine U.S. Supreme Court decision in *Wong Sun v. United States* holding that evidence that is spawned or directly derived from an illegal search or an illegal interrogation is generally inadmissible against a defendant because of its original taint; if the tree is tainted, so is the fruit.

"Funnelling effect" The reduction occurring between the number of crimes committed annually and the number of arrests, prosecutions, and convictions. Only about 25 percent of all arrests in the United States result in convictions annually.

Furlough An unescorted or unsupervised leave granted to inmates for home visits, work, or educational activity; temporary release program; authorized, unescorted leaves from confinement granted for specific purposes and for designated time periods, usually from 24 to 72 hours, although they may be as long as several weeks or as short as a few hours; first used in Mississippi in 1918.

General jurisdiction Power of a court to hear a wide range of cases; may hear both civil and criminal matters.

Golf cart patrol Combined with *sector patrolling* patrols on golf carts have been instrumental in bringing police officers closer to community residents.

"Good faith" exception An exception to the exclusionary rule where police officers wish to conduct search and seizure on the basis of a faulty warrant; acting in "good faith" presumably excuses conduct.

Good marks Marks obtained by prisoners in nineteenth century England; prisoners were given credit for participating in educational programs and other self-improvement activities.

"Good time" The amount of time deducted from the period of incarceration of a convicted offender; calculated as so many days per month on the basis of good behavior while incarcerated.

"Good time" credits Credits earned by prisoners for good behavior; introduced in early 1800s by British penal authorities, including Alexander Maconochie and Sir Walter Crofton.

"Good-time" laws Laws that allow a reduction of a portion of a prisoner's sentence for "good behavior" while in prison.

Grand jury Investigative bodies whose numbers vary among states. Duties include determining probable cause regarding commission of a crime and returning formal charges against suspects. *See* True bill, No true bill.

Great Law of Pennsylvania Established by William Penn in 1682, this law was designed to ban branding, stocks and pillories, and other forms of corporal punishment. It was later repealed when Penn died, and corporal punishments were restored. The original intent of the law was to make prison and jail conditions more humane.

Habeas corpus Writ meaning "produce the body"; used by prisoners to challenge the nature and length of their confinement.

Habeas corpus petition Petition filed, usually by inmates, challenging the legitimacy of their confinement and the nature of their confinement. A document that commands authorities to show cause why an inmate should be confined in either a prison or jail; means literally "you should have the body" or "produce the body." It may also challenge the nature of confinement. A written order by the court to any person, including a law enforcement officer, directing that person to bring the named individual before the court so that it can determine if there is adequate cause for continued detention.

Habitual offender Variously defined in different states; any person who has been convicted of two or more felonies and may be sentenced under the Habitual Offender statute for an aggravated or longer prison term.

Halfway house Community-based centers or homes operated either by the government or privately and which are designed to provide housing, food, clothing, job assistance, and counseling to ex-prisoners and others; publicly or privately operated facilities staffed by professionals, para-professionals, or volunteers; designed to assist parolees make the transition from prison to the community.

"Hands-off" doctrine or policy   Doctrine practiced by state and federal judiciary until the 1940s whereby matters pertaining to inmate rights were left up to jail and prison administrators to resolve; considered "internal" matters, where no court intervention was required or desired. In juvenile matters, this doctrine was typical of the U.S. Supreme Court's view of appeals stemming from juvenile court decisions; the tendency was to let juvenile courts manage themselves until *Kent v. United States.*

Harmful error   Errors made by judges that may be prejudicial to a defendant's case; may lead to reversals of convictions against defendants and to new trials.

Harmless error   Errors of a minor or trivial nature and not deemed sufficient to harm the rights of parties in a legal action. Cases are not reversed on the basis of harmless errors.

Hate crimes   Crimes committed against victims of specific ethnic or racial categories.

Hawes-Cooper Act of 1929   This Act provided that any and all prison-made goods transported from one state to another should be regulated by the commerce laws of the importing state.

Highway patrol   State law enforcement agency whose primary function is to enforce motor vehicle laws on state and interstate highways.

Holding   The legal principle drawn from a judicial decision; whatever a court, usually an appellate court, decides when cases are appealed from lower courts. When an appellate court "holds" a particular decision, this may be to uphold the original conviction, set it aside, or overturn in part and uphold in part.

Home confinement   Also called "house arrest" and "home incarceration"; intended to house offenders in their own homes with or without electronic devices; reduces prison overcrowding and prisoner costs; intermediate punishment involving the use of offender residences for mandatory incarceration during evening hours after a curfew and on weekends.

Hot pursuit   Circumstance involving chase of suspects by law enforcement officers. Often used to justify searches and seizures when suspect is eventually apprehended.

House arrest   *See* Home confinement.

Ignorance or mistake   A weak defense to a crime charge; similar to mistake of fact.

Immigration and Naturalization Service (INS) Congressionally created service to regulate entry into the United States of aliens and given powers to expel aliens considered a threat to the United States.

Impanel   To select and swear in a jury in a civil or criminal case.

Impeach, impeachment   Attempt by prosecution or defense to question the credibility or veracity of each other's witnesses.

Implicit plea bargaining   When a defendant pleads guilty with the expectation of receiving a more lenient sentence. *See also* Plea bargaining.

Indeterminate sentencing   A period set by judges between the earliest date for a parole decision and the latest date for completion of the sentence. In holding that the time necessary for treatment cannot be set exactly, the indeterminate sentence is closely associated with rehabilitation.

Index offenses   Specific felonies used by the Federal Bureau of Investigation in the *Uniform Crime Reports* to chart crime trends. There are eight index offenses listed prior to 1988 (aggravated assault, larceny, burglary, vehicular theft, arson, robbery, forcible rape, murder).

Indictment   A charge or written accusation found and presented by a grand jury that a particular defendant probably committed a crime.

Industrial school   A secure facility designed for juvenile delinquents where the principal functions are to equip youths with employable work skills.

In forma pauperis   "In the manner of a pauper"; refers to waiver of filing costs and other fees associated with judicial proceedings in order to allow indigent persons to proceed with their case.

Information   Sometimes called criminal information; written accusation made by a public prosecutor against a person for some criminal offense, without an indictment; usually restricted to minor crimes or misdemeanors.

Initial appearance   Formal proceeding during which the judge advises the defendant of the charges, including a recitation of the defendants' rights and a bail decision.

Inmate   Prisoner of jail or prison.

Inmate classification   Method of assigning prisoners in either jails or prisons to one level of custody or supervision or another; may be paper-pencil administered or through judgment of prison or jail administrators.

Innovations Project   Project implemented by Ninth Circuit Court of Appeals where cases are presented without oral argument; submission-without-argument program, streamlining case processing and backlogs.

In re   "In the matter of"; refers to cases being filed on behalf of juveniles who must have an adult act on their behalf when filing motions or appeals.

Intake   Process of screening juveniles who have been charged with offenses.

Intake decision Review of a case by a court (juvenile or criminal) official; screening of cases includes weeding out weak cases. In juvenile cases, intake involves the reception of a juvenile against whom complaints have been made; the decision to proceed or dismiss the case is made at this stage.

Intake officer Officer who conducts screening of juveniles. Dispositions include release to parents pending further juvenile court action, dismissal of charges against juvenile, detention, or treatment by some community agency.

Intake screening A critical phase where a determination is made by a juvenile probation officer or other official whether to release juveniles to their parents' custody, detain juveniles in formal detention facilities for a later court appearance, or release them to parents pending a later court appearance.

Intensive supervised probation/parole (ISP) No specific guidelines exist across all jurisdictions, but ISP usually means lower case loads for probation officers, less than ten clients per month, regular drug tests, and other intensive supervision measures.

Intermediate punishments Punishments involving sanctions existing somewhere between incarceration and probation on a continuum of criminal penalties; may include home incarceration and electronic monitoring.

Internal Revenue Service (IRS) Agency charged with monitoring and collecting federal income taxes from individuals and businesses.

Intoxication Defense used by defendants to explain otherwise criminal conduct; does not overcome *actus reus* but may be used as a mitigating circumstance to account for otherwise violent behavior; may be used to rebut presumption of premeditation.

Jails City or county operated and financed facilities to contain those offenders who are serving short sentences or are awaiting further processing. Jails also house prisoners from state or federal prisons through contracts to alleviate overcrowding, witnesses, juveniles, vagrants, and others.

Jailhouse lawyer Inmate in a prison or jail who becomes skilled in the law; may assist other prisoners in filing suits against prison or jail administration.

Joint trial calendar Method of case processing used by judges in certain jurisdictions. Several judges may share a common court calendar; objective is to try all cases on the calendar within a specified period. All judges share responsibility for clearing the calendar.

Judicial adjuncts Lawyers and others who assist courts and judges on a temporary basis in minor offense cases; maintain law practice while performing these temporary duties.

Judicial plea bargaining Recommended sentence by the judge, who offers a specific sentence and/or fine in exchange for a guilty plea. *See also* Plea bargaining.

Judicial waiver Decision by a juvenile judge to waive juvenile to jurisdiction of criminal court.

Jurisdiction The power of a court to hear and determine a particular type of case. Also refers to the territory within which a court may exercise authority, such as a city, county, or state.

Jury The trier of fact in a criminal case; the defendant's peers called to hear the evidence and decide the defendant's guilt or innocence; varies in size among states.

Jury deliberations Discussion among jury members concerning the weight and sufficiency of witness testimony and other evidence presented by both the prosecution and defense; an attempt to arrive at a verdict.

Jury nullification Jury that refuses to accept the validity of evidence at trial and acquits or convicts for a lesser offense; e.g., although all of the elements for murder are proved, a jury may acquit a defendant who killed his or her spouse allegedly as an act of mercy killing.

Jury trial Trial where guilt or innocence of a defendant is determined by a jury instead of by the judge.

Just deserts Correctional model stressing equating punishment with the severity of the crime; based on Cesare Beccaria's ideas about punishment.

Justice model Philosophy that emphasizes punishment as a primary objective of sentencing, fixed sentences, abolition of parole, and abandonment of the rehabilitative ideal.

Juvenile delinquent Any minor who commits an offense that would be a crime if committed by an adult.

Juvenile delinquency The violation of criminal laws by juveniles; any illegal behavior or activity committed by persons who are within a particular age range and which subjects them to the jurisdiction of a juvenile court or its equivalent.

Kales plan 1914 version of the Missouri Plan, where a committee of experts creates a list of qualified persons for judgeships and makes recommendations to the governor. *See* Missouri Plan.

Kansas City Preventive Patrol Experiment Experiment conducted in early 1970s in Kansas City; showed no relation between crime and the intensity of police patrolling in various city areas; controversial study.

Law The body of rules of specific conduct prescribed by existing, legitimate authority, in a particular jurisdiction, and at a particular point in time.

Law enforcement The activities of various public and private agencies at local, state, and federal levels that are designed to ensure compliance with formal rules of society that regulate social conduct.

Law enforcement agency (agencies) Local, state, or federal agencies and personnel who uphold the laws of their respective jurisdictions.

Law Enforcement Assistance Administration (LEAA) An outgrowth of the President's Crime Commission during the period 1965 to 1967, a time of great social unrest and civil disobedience, when racial and political tensions were exceptionally high. Created by Congress in 1968 and terminated in late 1970s. Designed to provide resources, leadership, and coordination to state and local law enforcement agencies to prevent and/or reduce adult crime and juvenile delinquency. Allocated millions of dollars to researchers and police departments over the next decade for various purposes; many experiments were conducted with these monies, many of which led to innovative patrolling strategies in different communities.

Law enforcement officer An employee of a local, state, or federal governmental agency sworn to carry out law enforcement duties; a sworn employee of a prosecutorial agency who primarily performs investigative functions.

Law of precedent Rulings made in the past that govern how judges should decide cases with similar factual scenarios; customary law, where custom prevails rather than written statutory law. *See also Stare decisis.*

Legislative waiver Provision that compels a juvenile court to remand certain youths to criminal courts because of specific offenses that have been committed or alleged.

Legislature That segment of government responsible for the consideration, drafting, and enactment of the law, e.g., U.S. Congress, state legislatures, county commissioners, and city councils.

Lockdown Complete removal of inmate privileges and permanent confinement in cells; usually follows a prison riot or other serious prison disturbance.

Maconochie, Alexander (1787–1860) Prison reformer former superintendent of the British penal colony at Norfolk Island and governor of Birmingham Borough Prison; known for humanitarian treatment of prisoners and issuance of "marks of commendation" to prisoners that led to their early release; considered the forerunner of indeterminate sentencing in the United States.

Mala in se Illegal acts that are inherently wrong; crimes that are intrinsically evil or wrong, including murder, rape, or arson.

Mala prohibita Illegal acts that have been codified or reduced to writing; offenses defined by legislatures as crimes. Many state and federal criminal statutes are *mala prohibita*.

Mandatory sentencing Sentencing where the court is required to impose an incarcerative sentence of a specified length, without the option for probation, suspended sentence, or immediate parole eligibility.

Maximum-security prisons Prisons where inmates are maintained in the highest degree of custody and supervision. Inmates are ordinarily segregated from one another and visitation privileges are restricted.

Maxi-maxi prison(s) Prisons such as the federal penitentiary at Marion, Illinois, where offenders are confined in individual cells with limited freedom daily; confinement in individual cells may be up to twenty-three hours per day; continuous monitoring and supervision; no more than three prisoners per guard.

Medium-security prisons Prisons where some direct supervision of inmates is maintained; prisoners are eligible for recreational activities; visitation privileges are more relaxed.

Megargee Typology Measure of inmate adjustment to prison life devised from items from the Minnesota Multiphasic Personality Inventory, a psychological personality assessment device; permits classification of prisoners into different risk levels.

Mens rea Intent to commit a crime; "guilty mind."

Metropolitan Police of London A police agency of London organized in 1829 by Sir Robert Peel, a prominent British government official; duties emphasized close interaction with the public and maintenance of proper attitudes and temperament.

Minimum-security prisons Prisons where inmates are permitted extensive freedoms and activities and have little supervision by correctional officers. Designated for nonviolent, low-risk offenders who are housed in efficiency apartments; inmates permitted family visits and considerable inmate privileges.

Ministation Small suburban police station, usually staffed by officers twenty-four hours a day; no provisions for detention of arrestees; assists in promoting better police-community relations.

Minnesota Multiphasic Personality Inventory (MMPI) Personality assessment measure that assesses a number of personality traits including anxiety, authoritarianism, and sociability.

Minnesota sentencing grid Sentencing guidelines established by Minnesota legislature in 1980 and used by judges to sentence offenders. Grid contains criminal history score, offense seriousness, and presumptive sentences to be imposed. Judges may depart from guidelines upward or downward depending upon aggravating or mitigating circumstances.

Minor   A person under the age of consent.

Miranda warning   Warning given to suspects by police officers advising suspects of their legal rights to counsel, to refuse to answer questions, to avoid self-incrimination, and other privileges.

Misdemeanor   Crime punishable by fines and/or imprisonment, usually in a city or county jail, for periods of less than one year.

Missouri Plan   Method of selecting judges where merit system for appointments is used; believed to reduce political influence in the selection of judges.

Mistake   Affirmative defense used by defendants to account for criminal conduct, where belief is that the law violation was accidental or that knowledge of the law was absent.

Mistrial   A trial that cannot stand, that is invalid. Judges may call a mistrial for reasons such as errors on the part of prosecutors or defense counsel, the death of a juror or counsel, or the inability of a jury to reach a verdict.

Mitigating circumstances   Circumstances about a crime that may lessen the severity of the sentence imposed by the judge; cooperating with police to apprehend others involved, youthfulness or old age of defendant, mental instability, and having no prior record are considered mitigating circumstances.

Money laundering   Process whereby money derived from illegal activities and placed in secret bank accounts is subsequently transferred as "legal funds" to U.S. banks or institutions.

Motion for summary judgment   Decisions by judges who have read the plaintiffs' version and defendants' version of events in actions filed by inmates, where a conclusion is reached holding for the defendants or plantiffs.

Motion *in limine*   A pretrial motion; purpose is generally to obtain judicial approval to admit certain items into evidence that might otherwise be considered prejudicial or inflammatory.

Motion to dismiss   Motions granted by judges when inmates who file petitions fail to state a claim upon which relief can be granted; court has read inmate claim and decided no basis exists for suit.

Mules   Name given to couriers and smugglers of drugs and other illegal contraband, especially from other countries into the United States. "Mules" often swallow large quantities of heroin or cocaine in glassine envelopes in an originating country; after crossing U.S. borders, they defecate and the illegal contraband is retrieved. Mules are paid nominal amounts for such smuggling.

Municipal liability theory   Theory that says a city is liable when its police officers or other agents act to cause unreasonable harm to citizens; theory whereby city assumes responsibility for the actions of its employees, including the police.

Mushrooms   Term given by youth gang members to innocent victims who are either injured or killed by random bullets in gang wars or simple drive-by shootings. The term comes from a popular video game, *Centipede*, where the object of the game is to "kill" or "mash" mushrooms that grow into threatening enemies. Whenever gang members discuss how many rival gang members were shot, they may say, "We got a few mushrooms too," meaning that they hurt or killed innocent bystanders during their gang activity.

National Crime Information Center (NCIC)   Center established by the FBI in 1967; central information source for stolen vehicles, accident information, stolen property, arrested persons, fingerprint information, criminal offenses, and criminal offenders and their whereabouts.

National Crime Victimization Survey   Published in cooperation with the United States Bureau of the Census as the *National Crime Survey*, a random survey of 60,000 households, including 127,000 persons twelve years of age or older; includes 50,000 businesses. Measures crime committed against specific victims interviewed and not necessarily reported to law enforcement officers. In 1991 the survey became known as *National Crime Victimization Survey* to reflect more accurately the nature of the data collected.

National Incident-Based Reporting System (NIBRS)   A reporting system in which the police describe each offense in a crime incident together with the data describing the offender, victim, and property.

National Institute of Justice   Institute created in 1979 to provide for and encourage research to improve federal, state, and local criminal justice systems, to prevent or reduce incidence of crime, and to identify effective programs.

Necessity   A condition that compels someone to act because of perceived needs; an affirmative defense, e.g., when someone's automobile breaks down during a snowstorm and an unoccupied cabin is nearby, breaking into the cabin to save oneself from freezing to death is acting out of "necessity" and would be a defense to "breaking and entering" charges.

Negligence   Liability accruing to prison or correctional program administrators and POs as the result of a failure to perform a duty owed clients or inmates or the improper or inadequate performance of that duty; may include negligent entrustment, negligent training, negligent assignment, negligent retention, or negligent supervision (e.g., providing POs with revolvers and not providing them with firearms training).

Negligent assignment   When correctional officers or probation/parole officers or other staff members are assigned to a position for which they are unqualified.

Negligent entrustment   When administrators fail to monitor guards entrusted with items they are unfamiliar with using, such as firearms.

Negligent hiring and selection   Basis for civil lawsuit when incompetent persons have been selected to perform important tasks, such as police work, and when injuries to victims are caused by such incompetent persons.

Negligent retention   When officers determined to be unfit for their jobs are kept in those jobs by administrators.

Negligent training   Basis for civil lawsuit when clear duty to train employees (e.g., to use firearms) is lacking.

Net widening   Pulling anyone into a program who would not otherwise be targeted for such a program; also known as "widening the net." Under ordinary conditions, when police officers confront adults or juveniles on the street, the officers may be inclined to issue verbal warnings and release them. However, if a community program is created that caters to particular kinds of clients, police officers may arrest these same adults and juveniles and involve them in these community programs, simply because the programs are there. Thus, some persons are brought into community programs needlessly.

No bill   *See* No true bill.

Nolle prosequi   An entry made by the prosecutor on the record in a case and announced in court to indicate that the charges specified will not be prosecuted; in effect, the charges are thereby dismissed.

Nolo contendere   Plea of "no contest" to charges; the defendant does not contest the facts, although issue may be taken with the legality or constitutionality of the law allegedly violated; treated as a guilty plea.

No true bill   Grand jury decision that insufficient evidence exists to establish probable cause that a crime was committed and a specific person committed it.

Organizational approach   Type of police discretion whereby police administrators create for officers a list of priorities and clarify explicitly how police should handle encounters with citizens.

Organized crime   Those self-perpetuating, structured associations of individuals and groups combined for the purpose of profiting in whole or in part by illegal means, while protecting their activities through a pattern of graft and corruption.

Overcrowding   Condition that exists when the number of prisoners exceeds the space allocations for which the jail or prison is designed; often associated with double-bunking or putting two prisoners in a cell.

Overlapping jurisdiction   Situation where two or more levels of government (e.g., county, city, state, federal) have general authority to act when crimes are committed; e.g., robbing a U.S. Post Office in a city, located in a particular county and state, would invite multiple actions from different agencies. In these cases, federal jurisdiction would have primacy because of the nature of the business robbed.

Pardon   Unconditional release of an inmate, usually by the governor or chief executive officer of jurisdiction.

Parens patriae   "Parent of the country"; refers to the doctrine whereby the state oversees the welfare of youth; originally established by king of England and administered through chancellors.

Parole   The status of an offender conditionally released from a confinement facility prior to the expiration of the sentence and placed under the supervision of a parole agency.

Parole officer   Correctional official who supervises a parolee.

Pat down   Search of a criminal suspect by a law enforcement officer wherein the outer clothing of suspect is patted or felt to determine whether suspect is carrying a dangerous weapon.

Peel, Sir Robert (1788–1850)   British Home Secretary who in 1829 founded the Metropolitan Police of London, one of the first organized police forces in the world.

Penitentiary   Interchangeably used with *prison* to refer to those long-term facilities where high custody levels are observed; solitary confinement or single-cell occupancy, where prisoners are segregated from one another during evening hours.

Penn, William   Established the "Great Law of Pennsylvania"; Quaker, penal reformer, and founder of Pennsylvania; abolished corporal punishments in favor of fines and incarceration; used gaols or jails to confine offenders.

Pennsylvania System   Devised and used in the Walnut Street Jail in 1790 to place prisoners in solitary confinement; predecessor to modern prisons; used silence to increase penitence and prevent cross-infection of prisoners; encouraged behavioral improvements.

Peremptory challenges   Rejection of a juror by either prosecution or defense where no reason needs to be provided for excusing the juror from jury duty. Each side has a limited number of these types of challenges; the more serious the offense, the more peremptory challenges are given the defense and prosecution.

Persistent offender Habitual criminal who commits felonies or misdemeanors and has a high recidivism rate.

Plaintiff The person or party who initiates a legal action against someone or some party in a civil court.

Plain view Evidence rule that authorizes officers conducting a search to seize any contraband or illegal substance or item that is in plain view or in the immediate vision of officers.

Plain view doctrine Evidentiary doctrine whereby evidence may be introduced in a trial, where the evidence seized was in plain view or within the immediate visual range of officers; evidence may be used whether the original search was lawful or unlawful.

Plea, initial The first plea entered in response to a given charge entered in a court record by or for a defendant.

Pleas Answers to charges by the defendant. Pleas vary among jurisdictions; not guilty, guilty, *nolo contendere*, not guilty by reason of insanity, and guilty but mentally ill are alternative pleas.

Plea bargaining A preconviction bargain or agreement between the state and the accused whereby the defendant exchanges a plea of guilty or *nolo contendere* for a reduction in charges, a promise of sentencing leniency, or some other concession from full, maximum implementation of the conviction and sentencing authority of the court; includes implicit plea bargaining, charge reduction bargaining, sentence recommendation bargaining, and judicial plea bargaining.

Police cautioning Verbal warning by law enforcement officer to person who may have committed or attempted to commit a crime.

Police-community relations A generic concept including any program designed to promote or make more visible law enforcement strategies that are aimed at crime prevention and control and where varying degrees of proactive citizen involvement are solicited.

Police corruption Misconduct by police officers in the form of illegal activities for economic gain and accepting gratuities, favors, or payment for services that police are sworn to carry out as a part of their peace-keeping role; not applied to officer conduct while off duty.

Police discretion Choices by police officers to act in given ways in citizen-police encounters; selection of behaviors from among alternatives.

Police personality A psychological orientation toward citizens based upon the isolation of law enforcement work. Law enforcement personnel tend to exhibit similar characteristics, including a distrust of public and citizen motives. A working personality that deals with catching criminals; especially, being suspicious of certain types of events.

Police presence The presence of police officers in places of business for the crime deterrent effect it affords.

Police professionalism Increasing formalization of police work, and the rise in public acceptance of the police which accompanies it; a well-focused code of ethics, equitable recruitment and selection practices, and informed promotional strategies among many agencies.

Post-conviction relief Term applied to various mechanisms whereby offenders may challenge their conviction after other appeal attempts have been exhausted.

Pound model Plan of court organization with three tiers: supreme court, major trial court, and minor trial court.

Predicting dangerousness Use of instruments that purport to estimate an offender's chances of posing serious public risk if released from custody; any device or instrument that purports to predict an offender's future dangerousness.

Preliminary examination *See* Preliminary hearing.

Preliminary hearing Hearing by magistrate or other judicial officer to determine if person charged with a crime should be held for trial; proceeding to establish probable cause; does not determine guilt or innocence.

Preponderance of evidence Standard used in civil courts to determine defendant or plaintiff liability.

Presentence investigation Examination of convicted offender by a probation officer; usually requested or ordered by the court. Background information is obtained, including a victim impact statement; facts in the case are included; prior arrests, jobs and educational history of defendant are listed.

Presentence investigation report (PSI) Report filed by probation or parole officer appointed by court; contains background information, socioeconomic data, and demographic data relative to defendant. Used to influence the sentence imposed by a judge; also used by the parole board in considering an inmate's early release.

Presentment An accusation, initiated by the grand jury on its own authority, from the members' own knowledge or observation; functions as an instruction for the preparation of an indictment.

Presumptive sentencing Statutory sentencing form that specifies normal sentences of particular lengths with limited judicial leeway to shorten or lengthen the term of the sentence.

Pretrial diversion A procedure whereby criminal defendants are diverted to a community-based agency for treatment or are assigned to a counselor for social and/or psychiatric assistance.

Pretrial motion Made by either defense or prosecution prior to trial; usually pertains to introduction or exclusion of specific evidence. *See* Motion *in limine*.

Preventive detention Constitutionally approved method of detaining those charged with crimes when the likelihood exists that, if released, they either pose a serious risk to others or will flee the jurisdiction to avoid prosecution.

Preventive patrol Scheme by police officers inspired by the belief that high police officer visibility will effectively deter crime.

Prima facie **case** A case in which there is enough evidence to warrant the conviction of a defendant if properly proved in court, unless contradicted; a case that meets the evidentiary requirements for a grand jury indictment.

Prison State or federally operated facility to house long-term offenders; usually designed to house inmates serving incarcerative terms of one or more years. These are self-contained facilities that are sometimes called "total institutions."

Prison and jail construction Enterprises where buildings are established to confine criminals; projects undertaken to meet growing needs of overcrowded prisons and jails.

Prison culture Communication among jail and prison inmates using special language to convey ideas not ordinarily intended by traditional language usage; ways of behaving by which inmates establish a pecking order based on strength and the ability to provide scarce goods.

Private police All nonpublic law enforcement officers including guards, watchmen, doorkeepers, crossing guards, bridge tenders, private detectives, and investigators.

Privatization Trend in prison and jail management and correctional operations in which private interests are becoming increasingly involved in the management and operations of correctional institutions.

Proactive beats Aggressive patrolling by police officers in neighborhoods, particularly in high-crime neighborhoods; one type of beat used in the Kansas City Preventive Patrol Experiments.

Probable cause Reasonable suspicion or belief that a crime has been committed and a particular person committed it.

Probation An alternative sentence to incarceration where the convict stays under state's authority; involves conditions; authority is retained by the sentencing court to modify the conditions of sentence or to resentence the offender if the offender violates the conditions. Such a sentence should not involve or require suspension of the imposition or execution of any other sentence.

Probationer Convicted offender sentenced to a nonincarcerative alternative including supervised release in the community, restitution, community service, fines, or other conditions.

Probation officer Professional person who supervises probationers.

Probation revocation Process of declaring that a sentenced offender violated one or more terms of a probation program imposed by the court or probation agency. If probation involved a suspended prison or jail sentence, the revocation may mean that the original sentence is invoked and the individual is sent to prison or jail.

Procedural law Division of law that sets forth the rules governing the method of enforcing the laws of crime and punishment.

Property crime Felony that is nonviolent and does not result in physical injury to victims; involves criminal acts against property including but not limited to larceny, burglary, and vehicular theft.

Prosecution Carrying forth a criminal proceedings against a person, culminating in a trial or other final disposition such as a plea of guilty in lieu of trial.

Prosecutor Court official who commences civil and criminal proceedings against defendants; represents state interests or government interests, prosecutes defendants on behalf of the state or government.

Prosecutorial waiver Authority of prosecutors in juvenile cases to have those cases transferred to the jurisdiction of criminal court.

Protection of property Affirmative defense to offset the allegation that an individual has committed a crime. The defense alleges that the individual acted to ensure that possessions would not be destroyed; in the process, certain elements of a crime were present, such as window-breaking.

Provo Experiment Community-based delinquency rehabilitation program in Provo, Utah, designed to curb recidivism through group therapy and other group activities.

Public defender Attorneys appointed by the court to represent indigent defendants.

Randolph Plan *See* Virginia Model.

Reactive beats Police activity occurring in response to a stimulus, such as a reported crime incident or notification that a crime has been committed; type of experimental beat used in the Kansas City Preventive Patrol Experiment.

Reasonable doubt Standard used by jurors to decide if the prosecution has provided sufficient evidence for conviction. Jurors vote for acquittal if they have reasonable doubt that the accused did not commit the crime.

Reasonable suspicion Warranted suspicion (short of probable cause) that a person may be engaged in criminal conduct.

Recidivism   Has many definitions; most frequently used definitions are rearrest, reconviction, and reincarceration of previously convicted felons or misdemeanants.

Recross examination   Opposing party's requestioning of a witness following questions from counsel who called the witness originally.

Rehabilitation   Correcting criminal behavior through educational and other means; usually associated with prisons.

Released on own recognizance (ROR)   Used in connection with bail determination in initial appearance proceedings, preliminary examinations, and arraignments.

Reversible error   Error committed by a judge during a trial that may result in the reversal of a conviction of a defendant.

ROR   *See* Release on own recognizance

Rules of criminal procedure   Rules established whereby a criminal case is conducted; law enforcement officers, prosecutors, and judges use rules of criminal procedure in discretionary actions against suspects and defendants.

Rush, Dr. Benjamin (1745–1813)   Quaker penal and religious reformer and physician; helped organize and operate the Walnut Street Jail for the benefit of prisoners; encouraged humane treatment of inmates.

Scale of patrol   The scope of a police officer's routine geographical patrol responsibilities.

Screening   Procedure used by a prosecutor to define which cases have prosecutive merit and which ones do not. Some screening bureaus are made up of police and lawyers with trial experience.

Search and seizure   Legal term contained in the Fourth Amendment of the U.S. Constitution referring to the searching for and carrying away of evidence by police during a criminal investigation.

Search incident to an arrest   Authority of arresting law enforcement officer to search immediate areas within control of an arrestee. If the suspect is arrested in his or her living room, police authority does not extend to searches of areas not immediately within the control of the arrestee, such as an attic or back porch, detached garage, or basement. Officers must have a search warrant to search further.

Search warrant   An order of the court directing law enforcement officers to search designated places for specific persons or items to be seized.

Selective incapacitation   Selectively incarcerating individuals who show a high likelihood of repeating their previous offenses; based on forecasts of potential for recidivism; includes but is not limited to dangerousness; process of incarcerating certain offenders who are defined by various criteria as having a strong propensity to repeat serious crimes. Based on a belief that offenders who are recidivists or who have prior criminality should be incapacitated with relatively long prison sentences.

Self-defense   Affirmative defense whereby defendants explain otherwise criminal conduct by showing necessity to defend themselves against aggression.

Self-reports   Any information disclosed by a study in which persons disclose things that they have done, such as crimes, which may or may not have been detected by police.

Sentence   Penalty imposed upon a convicted person for a crime; may include incarceration, fine, or both, or some other alternative. *See also* Determinate sentencing; Indeterminate sentencing; Mandatory sentencing; Presumptive sentencing.

Sentence recommendation bargaining   The prosecutor proposes a sentence in exchange for a guilty plea. *See also* Plea bargaining.

Sentencing disparity   Inconsistency in sentencing of convicted offenders, where those committing similar crimes under similar circumstances are given widely disparate sentences by the same judge; usually based on gender, race, ethnic, or socioeconomic factors.

Sentencing guidelines   Instruments developed by the federal government and states to assist judges in assessing fair and consistent lengths of incarceration for various crimes and past criminal histories; referred to as presumptive sentencing in some jurisdictions.

Sentencing hearing   Optional hearing, held in many jurisdictions, at which defendants and victims can hear the contents of presentence investigation reports prepared by probation officers. Defendants and/or victims may respond to the report orally, in writing, or both. The hearing precedes sentence imposed by a judge.

Sentencing memorandum   Court decision that furnishes a ruling or finding and orders to be implemented relative to a convicted offender. Does not necessarily include reasons or rationale for the sentence imposed.

Sentencing Reform Act of 1984   Act that provided federal judges and others with considerable discretionary powers to provide alternative sentencing and other provisions in their sentencing of various offenders.

Shakedown   Intensive search of inmate cells for the purpose of discovering weapons or contraband. Also a form of police corruption where money or valuables are extorted from criminals by police officers in exchange for the criminals not being arrested.

Shock probation   Sentencing offenders to prison or jail for a brief period, primarily to give them a taste or "shock" of prison or jail life, and then releasing them into the custody of a probation or parole officer through a resentencing project.

Solitary confinement Placement of a prisoner in a cell where no communication with others is permitted. Originated in the Walnut Street Jail in Philadelphia, Pennsylvania, in late 1700s.

Speedy trial As defined by federal law and applicable to federal district courts, the defendant must be tried within 100 days of an arrest. Every state has speedy trial provisions that are within reasonable ranges of the federal standard. Originally designed to comply with the Sixth Amendment of the U.S. Constitution. The longest state speedy trial provision is in New Mexico, 180 days.

Speedy Trial Act Compliance with the Sixth Amendment provision for citizens to be brought to trial without undue delay from thirty to seventy days from the date of formal specification of charges, usually in an arraignment proceeding.

Staff brutality Actions by prison or jail officers or guards whereby prisoners are subjected to unwarranted and unjustified physical attacks or intentional inflictions of emotional distress.

Stare decisis Legal precedent. Lower courts must follow precedents established in higher courts in particular legal matters and cases. Principle whereby lower courts issue rulings consistent with those of higher courts, where the same types of cases and facts are at issue. The principle of leaving undisturbed a settled point of law or a particular precedent.

State highway patrol State law enforcement agency whose principal functions are the prevention, detection, and investigation of motor vehicle offenses and the apprehension of motor vehicle traffic offenders.

Status offender Any juvenile who has been adjudicated by a judicial officer of a juvenile court as having committed a status offense, which is an act or conduct that is an offense only when committed or engaged in by a juvenile.

Status offense Any act committed by a juvenile that would not be a crime if committed by an adult (e.g., runaway behavior, truancy, and curfew violation).

Statute of limitations Period of time after which a crime that has been committed cannot be prosecuted. No statute of limitations exists for capital crimes such as murder.

Statutes Laws passed by legislatures. Statutory definitions of criminal offenses are embodied in penal codes.

Statutory law Authority based on enactments of state legislatures; laws passed by legislatures.

Stop and frisk When police officers who are suspicious of individuals run their hands lightly over suspects' outer clothing to determine if the persons possess a con-

cealed weapon; also called a "pat-down" or "threshold inquiry." A stop and frisk is intended to stop short of any activity that would be considered a violation of the Fourth Amendment clause pertinent to reasonable searches and seizures.

Stress The body's nonspecific response to any demand placed upon it. Police stress is negative stress accompanied by an alarm reaction, resistance, and exhaustion; negative anxiety that is accompanied by an alarm reaction, resistance, and exhaustion; such anxiety contributes to heart disease, headaches, high blood pressure, and ulcers; factors that cause stress. Stressors include boredom, constant threats to officer health and safety, responsibility for protecting the lives of others, and the fragmented nature of police work.

Substantive law Body of law that creates, discovers, and defines the rights and obligations of each person in society; prescribes behavior.

Summation Closing argument of defense and prosecuting attorneys in a civil or criminal case.

Summons Same form as a warrant, except that it commands a defendant to appear before the magistrate at a particular time and place.

Superior court The court of record or trial court.

Take into custody The physical apprehension by a police action of a child engaged in status offending or delinquent conduct.

Target hardening Making residences, businesses, and people less susceptible to breaking and entering through better security measures.

Team policing When investigative teams of police officers, detectives, and other personnel are assigned to a particular community area to work as a team in solving crimes that occur in that area.

Tennessee v. Garner (1985) U.S. Supreme Court case prohibiting the use of fleeing felon rule and the application of deadly force for fleeing felons who pose little or no risk to police officers or others. The standard for using deadly force as set forth by this case is that deadly force can be used if the life of the officer or someone else's life is in jeopardy as a result of the actions of the suspect.

Texas model Also known as the "traditional" model of state court organization; includes two supreme courts—one for civil appeals and one for criminal appeals; has five tiers, with district, county, and municipal courts.

Tier system Method of establishing various floors for cells where prisoners of different types can be housed; started at Auburn State Penitentiary in 1816.

Tort A private or civil wrong or injury, other than

breach of contract, for which the court will provide a remedy in the form of an action for damages. A violation of a duty imposed by law; existence of a legal duty to a plaintiff, breach of that duty, and damage as a result of that breach.

Totality of circumstances   Exception to exclusionary rule whereby officers may make warrantless searches of property and seizures of illegal contraband on the basis of the entire set of suspicious circumstances.

Traditional model   *See* Texas Model.

Transfer   Action whereby juveniles are remanded to the jurisdiction of criminal courts; also known as certification and waiver. Proceeding to determine whether juveniles should be certified as adults for purposes of being subjected to jurisdiction of adult criminal courts where more severe penalties may be imposed.

True bill   Grand jury decision that sufficient evidence exists that a crime has been committed and a specific suspect committed it; a charge of an alleged crime; an indictment.

Unconstitutionally vague laws   A term used by the U.S. Supreme Court to declare a particular law lacking in specificity and failing to describe specific actions or behaviors that are prohibited, such as municipal vagrancy laws.

UNICOR   Federal prison industry that manufactures goods for profit. Workers are prisoners who are paid a prevailing wage; considered a rehabilitative tool.

Uniform Crime Reports   Annual publication by Federal Bureau of Investigation that describes crime from all reporting law enforcement agencies in the United States. New format in 1988 identifies incident-based reporting compared with other reporting schemes used in past years.

United States Customs Service   Agency authorized to conduct searches and inspections of all ships, aircraft, and vehicles entering U.S. borders.

United States Marshals Service   One of oldest federal agencies. Duties of U.S. Marshals include executing warrants from federal district courts, investigating and arresting dangerous fugitives, providing security for federal courts and judiciary, suppressing riots on federal lands or federal prisons, and escorting missile convoys.

United States Secret Service (USSS)   Agency under the control of the Department of the Treasury; investigates electronic fund transfer fraud and counterfeiting and protects presidents and other government figures.

United States Sentencing Guidelines   Rules implemented by federal courts in November 1987 obligating federal judges to impose presumptive sentences on all convicted offenders; based upon offense seriousness and offender characteristics. Judges may depart from guidelines only by justifying their departures in writing.

United States Supreme Court   Highest appellate court in United States; consists of nine justices; resolves controversies between states; determines resolution of all federal questions.

Unreasonable force   Physical power used by law enforcement officers that exceeds whatever is necessary to subdue an arrestee or someone who is taken into custody.

Venire   List of prospective jurors made up from registered voters, vehicle driver's licenses, tax assessors' records. Persons must reside within particular jurisdiction where jury trial is held.

Veniremen   Persons summoned to jury duty in a given jurisdiction.

Venue   The geographical area from which the jury is drawn and in which the trial is held in a criminal action.

Venue, change of   Refers to relocating a trial from one site to another, usually because of some pretrial publicity that makes it possible that a jury might be biased and a fair trial will be difficult to obtain.

Verdict   In criminal proceedings, the decision made by a judicial officer in a court trial that defendants are either guilty or not guilty of the offense(s) for which they have been tried.

Victim   Person who has suffered death, serious physical, mental suffering, or loss of property resulting from actual or attempted criminal actions committed by others.

Victim assistance program   One of many programs in various states seeking to compensate victims of crimes for their losses.

Victim Compensation Act   A law requiring offenders to make financial restitution to victims.

Victim compensation program   Any plan for assisting crime victims in making social, emotional, and economic adjustments.

Victim impact statement   Information or version of events filed voluntarily by a victim of crime and appended to the presentence investigation report as a supplement for judicial consideration in sentencing an offender; describes injuries to victims resulting from convicted offender's actions.

Victimization   Basic measure of the occurrence of a crime; a specific criminal act affecting a specific victim.

Victimless crime   Crime in which there are no apparent victims or victims are willing participants in the criminal activity; includes gambling and prostitution.

Victimology   A criminological subdiscipline that examines the role played by the victim in a criminal incident and in the criminal process.

Victim-witness assistance programs   Programs available to prospective witnesses to explain court procedures and inform them of court dates; assist witnesses in providing better testimony in court.

Victim's Bill of Rights Entitlements established by New York State Compensation Board outlining specific rights of crime victims; rights include victim notification of offender status and custody, case disposition, and incarceration-nonincarceration details.

Violent crime Law violation characterized by extreme physical force including murder or homicide, forcible rape or child sexual abuse, assault and battery by means of a dangerous weapon, robbery, and arson.

Virginia Plan Scheme deriving from England's royal court system involving superior and inferior courts; also called the Randolph Plan.

Voir dire "To speak the truth"; applied to the interrogation process whereby jurors are questioned by either the judge or by the prosecution or defense attorneys to determine their biases and prejudices.

Vollmer, August Chief of Police of Berkeley, California, who professionalized policing by recommending educational training for police officers; relied heavily on academic specialists in various forensics areas. Pioneered informal academic regimen of police training, including investigative techniques, photography, fingerprinting, and anatomy, among other academic subject areas.

Volunteer lawyer judges Part-time lawyers who function as judges and decide minor cases. The intent is to reduce case load and volume of petty cases in certain courts or jurisdictions.

Waiver motion or hearing Motion by prosecutor to transfer a juvenile charged with various offenses to a criminal or adult court for prosecution. Waiver motions make it possible to sustain adult criminal penalties.

Walnut Street Jail Considered the first American prison seeking to correct offenders; built in 1776 in Philadelphia, Pennsylvania. One of first penal facilities that segregated female from male offenders and children from adults; introduced solitary confinement of prisoners; separated prisoners according to their offense severity; operated on the notion that inmates could perform useful services to defray the costs of confinement. This jail operated one of first prison industry programs. Inmates even produced much of their own food through gardening.

Warrant A written order directing a suspect's arrest and issued by an official with the authority to issue the warrant; commands suspect to be arrested and brought before the nearest magistrate.

Warrant, arrest Document issued by a judge that directs a law enforcement officer to arrest a person who has been accused of an offense.

Warrant, bench Document issued by a judge directing that a person who has failed to obey an order or notice to appear be brought before the court without undue delay.

Warrant, search Document issued by a judge directing law enforcement officers to conduct searches of specified property or persons at a specific location, to seize property or persons if found, and to account for the results of the search to the issuing judge.

Warrantless search Examination of a dwelling unit, a person, or an automobile without obtaining a search warrant from a magistrate or judge.

White-collar crime Law violation committed by those persons of higher socioeconomic status in the course of their businesses, occupations, or professions; a banker who embezzles is a white-collar criminal.

Wickersham Commission Commission established in 1929 to investigate police agencies and the state of training and education among police officers; generally critical of contemporary methods of police agency organization and operation.

Wickersham Reports Conclusions published by the National Commission on Law Observance and Enforcement, chaired by George W. Wickersham.

Without undue delay Standard used to determine whether a suspect has been brought in a timely manner before a magistrate or other judicial authority after arrest. The definition of undue delay varies among jurisdictions; circumstances of arrest, availability of judge, and time of arrest are factors that determine reasonableness of delay.

Witnesses Persons who see an event or thing, such as a crime being committed or persons fleeing, or who have expert knowledge relevant to a case.

Work release Community-based program whereby persons about to be paroled work in the community at jobs during the day and return to a jail facility at night; any program that provides for prison labor in the community under conditions of relaxed supervision and for which prisoners are paid adequate wages.

Working personality Term used by Jerome Skolnick to describe characteristics of police officers. He believed that police officers have similar and distinctive cognitive tendencies and behavioral responses, including a particular "life style."

Writ A document issued by a judicial officer ordering or forbidding the performance of a specific act.

Writ of *certiorari* "To be more fully informed"; an order of a superior court requesting that the record of an inferior court (or administrative body) be brought forward for review or inspection.

References

Abernathy, Alexis D. and Christopher Cox (1994). "Anger Management Training for Law Enforcement Personnel." *Journal of Criminal Justice,* 22:459–466.

Abraham, Henry J. (1968). *The Judicial Process.* 2d ed. New York: Oxford University Press.

Acker, James R. and Charles R. Lanier (1993). "The Dimensions of Capital Murder." *Criminal Law Bulletin,* 29:379–417.

Acker, James R. and Charles R. Lanier (1994). "In Fairness and Mercy: Statutory Mitigating Factors in Capital Punishment Laws." *Criminal Law Bulletin,* 30:299–345.

Acker, James R. and Charles R. Lanier (1995). "Statutory Measures for More Effective Appellate Review of Capital Cases." *Criminal Law Bulletin,* 31:211–258.

Adams, Kenneth (1983). "The Effect of Evidentiary Factors on Charge Reduction." *Journal of Criminal Justice* 11:525–537.

Adamson, Christopher (1984). "Toward a Marxian Penology: Captive Criminal Populations as Economic Threats and Resources." *Social Problems,* 31:435–458.

Aday, Ronald H. (1994). "Golden Years Behind Bars: Special Programs and Facilities for Elderly Inmates." *Federal Probation,* 58:47–54.

Aday, Ronald H. (1994). "Aging in Prison: A Case Study of New Elderly Offenders." *International Journal of Offender Therapy and Comparative Criminology,* 38:79–91.

Administrative Office of the United States Courts (1994). *Annual Report to the Director, 1994.* Washington, DC: U.S. Government Printing Office.

Aho, James A. *This Thing of Darkness: A Sociology of the Enemy.* Seattle, WA: University of Washington Press.

Aikman, Alex B. (1986). "Volunteer Lawyer-Judges Bolster Court Resources." *NIJ Reports,* 195:2–6.

Akers, Ronald L. et al. (1983). "Are Self-Report Studies of Adolescent Deviance Valid? Biochemical Measures, Randomized Response, and the Bogus Pipeline in Smoking Behavior." *Social Forces,* 62:234–251.

Albanese, Jay S. (1988). *The Police Officer's Dilemma: Balanc-ing Peace, Order, and Individual Rights.* Buffalo, NY: Great Ideas Publishing.

Albanese, Jay S. (1989). *Private Security and the Public Interest.* Buffalo, NY: Great Books Publishing.

Albanese, Jay S. (ed.) (1995). *Contemporary Issues in Organized Crime.* Monsey, NY: Criminal Justice Press.

Alexander, Charles C. (1995). *The Ku Klux Klan in the Southwest.* Norman, OK: The University of Oklahoma Press.

Alexander, Rudolph Jr. (1991). "A Curious Legal Anomaly: Female Inmates Could Have the Right to Vote—But Not Male Inmates." *Criminal Justice Policy Review,* 5:335–346.

Alexander, Rudolph Jr. (1992). "Cruel and Unusual Punishment: A Slowly Metamorphosing Concept." *Criminal Justice Policy Review,* 6:123–135.

Alfini, James J. (1981). "Mississippi Judicial Selection: Election, Appointment, and Bar Anointment." In *Courts and Judges,* James A. Cramer (ed.). Beverly Hills, CA: Sage.

Allen, Craig M. (1991). *Women and Men Who Sexually Abuse Children: A Comparative Analysis.* Orwell, VT: Safer Society Press.

Allen, Craig M. and Chung M. Lee (1992). "Family of Origin Structure and Intra-Extrafamilial Childhood Sexual Victimization of Male and Female Offenders." *Journal of Child Sexual Abuse,* 1:31–45.

Allen, Harry E., Chris Eskridge, Edward Latessa, and Gennaro F. Vito (1985). *Probation and Parole in America.* New York: Macmillan.

Allen, Ronald J. (1991). "Supreme Court Review," *Journal of Criminal Law and Criminology,* 81:727–1001.

Alpert, Geoffrey P. (1991). "Hiring and Promoting Police Officers in Small Departments—The Role of Psychological Testing." *Criminal Law Bulletin,* 27:261–269.

Alpert, Geoffrey P. and Patrick R. Anderson (1986). "The Most Deadly Force: Police Pursuits." *Justice Quarterly,* 3:1–14.

Alpert, Geoffrey P. and William C. Smith (1991). "Beyond City Limits and into the Woods: A Brief Look at the Policy Impact of *City of Canton v. Harris* and *Wood v. Ostrander*." *American Journal of Police,* 10:19–40.

Alpert, Geoffrey P. and William C. Smith (1994). "How Reasonable Is the Reasonable Man? Police and Excessive Force." *Journal of Criminal Law and Criminology,* 85:481–501.

Alschuler, Albert W. (1975). "The Prosecutor's Role in Plea Bargaining." *University of Chicago Law Review,* 36:50–59.

Alschuler, Albert W. (1979). "Plea Bargaining and Its History." *Law and Society Review,* 13:211–245.

Altemose, J. Rick (1996). "Inmates at Work: Jefferson County's Positive Production Program." *American Jails,* 10:37–50.

Altschuler, David M. (1991). *The Supervision of Juvenile Offenders in Maryland: Policy and Practice Implications of the Workload Study.* Baltimore, MD: Institute for Policy Studies, Johns Hopkins University.

Altschuler, David M. and Troy L. Armstrong (1990). "Intensive Parole for High-Risk Juvenile Offenders: A Framework for Action." Unpublished paper presented at the American Society of Criminology meetings, Baltimore, MD (November).

Altschuler, David M. and Troy L. Armstrong (1991). "Intensive Aftercare for the High-Risk Juvenile Parolee: Issues and Approaches in Reintegration and Community Supervision in Juvenile Probation and Parole." In *Intensive Interventions with High-Risk Youths: Promising Approaches,* Troy L. Armstrong (ed.) Monsey, NY: Criminal Justice Press.

Altschuler, David M. and Troy L. Armstrong (1993). "Intensive Aftercare for High-Risk Juvenile Parolees: Program Development and Implementation in Eight Pilot Sites." Unpublished paper presented at the annual meeting of the American Society of Criminology, Phoenix, AZ, (October).

Altschuler, David M. and William V. Luneburg (1992). "The Juvenile Justice and Delinquency Prevention Formula Grant Program: Federal-State Relationships in a Quasi-Regulatory Context." *Criminal Justice Policy Review,* 6:136–158.

American Bar Association (1971). *Standards Relating to the Prosecution Function and Defense Function.* Washington, DC: American Bar Association Commission on Standards of Judicial Administration.

American Bar Association (1975). *Standards Relating to Trial Courts.* Washington, DC: American Bar Association Commission on Standards of Judicial Administration.

American Bar Association (1985). *A Comprehensive Perspective on Civil and Criminal RICO Legislation and Litigation.* Washington, DC: American Bar Association.

American Bar Association (1994). *Just Solutions: A Program Guide to Innovative Justice System Improvements.* Chicago: American Bar Association and American Judicature Society.

American Correctional Association (1983). *The American Prison: From the Beginning . . . A Pictorial History.* Laurel, MD: American Correctional Association.

American Correctional Association (1986). "Probation and Parole: Today's Challenges: Future Directions." *Corrections Today,* 48:4–87.

American Correctional Association (1987). *Directory.* Laurel, MD: American Correctional Association.

American Correctional Association (1989a). *Correctional Officer Resource Guide.* Laurel, MD: American Correctional Association.

American Correctional Association (1989b). *Emerging Technologies and Community Corrections.* Laurel, MD: American Correctional Association.

American Correctional Association (1990). *Causes, Preventive Measures, and Methods of Controlling Riots and Disturbances in Correctional Institutions.* Laurel, MD: American Correctional Association.

American Correctional Association (1991). *Vital Statistics in Corrections.* College Park, MD: American Correctional Association.

American Correctional Association (1992). *The Effective Correctional Officer.* Laurel, MD: American Correctional Association.

American Correctional Association (1993a). *Classification: A Tool for Managing Today's Offenders.* Laurel, MD: American Correctional Association.

American Correctional Association (1993b). *Community Partnerships in Action.* Laurel, MD: American Correctional Association.

American Correctional Association (1993c). *Female Offenders: Meeting Needs of a Neglected Population.* Laurel, MD: American Correctional Association.

American Correctional Association (1993d). *Juvenile and Adult Correctional Departments, Institutions, Agencies and Paroling Authorities: United States and Canada.* College Park, MD: American Correctional Association.

American Correctional Association (1994a). *Directory: Juvenile and Adult Correctional Departments, Institutions, Agencies, and Paroling Authorities.* Laurel, MD: American Correctional Association.

American Correctional Association (1994b). *Field Officer Resource Guide.* Laurel, MD: American Correctional Association.

American Correctional Association (1995). *ACA Directory 1995.* Laurel, MD: American Correctional Association.

American Judicature Society (1983). *Report of the Committee on Qualification Guidelines for Judicial Candidates.* Chicago: American Judicature Society.

American Law Institute (1962). *Model Penal Code Official Draft.* Washington, DC: American Law Institute.

American Law Institute (1975). *A Model Code of Pre-Arraignment Procedure.* Philadelphia, PA: American Law Institute.

Amnesty International (1991). *United States of America: The Death Penalty and Juvenile Offenders.* New York: Amnesty International.

Anderson, Wayne, David Swenson, and Daniel Clay (1995). *Stress Management for Law Enforcement Officers.* Englewood Cliffs, NJ: Prentice-Hall.

Anechiarico, Frank (1984). "Suing the Philadelphia Police: The Case for an Institutional Approach." *Law and Policy,* 6:231–250.

Annest, Joseph L., James A. Mercy, and Delinda R. Gibson (1995). "National Estimates of Nonfatal Firearms-Related Injuries." *Journal of the American Medical Association,* 273:1749–1754.

Appier, Janis Marie (1993). "Gender and Justice: Women Police in America, 1910–1946." Unpublished doctoral dissertation. Riverside, CA: University of California, Riverside.

Archibald, Matthew E., Marjorie E. Brown, and Carmen A. Cicchetti (1992). *Juvenile Delinquency: A Study of Massachusetts Juvenile Probationers.* Boston: Massachusetts Trial Court.

Armstrong, Troy L. (1988). "National Survey of Juvenile Intensive Probation Supervision, Part I." *Criminal Justice Abstracts,* 20:342–348.

Arthur, John A. and Charles E. Case (1994). "Race, Class and Support for Police Use of Force." *Crime, Law and Social Change,* 21:167–182.

Arthur, Kevin F. (1987). "Preventive Detention: Liberty in the Balance." *Maryland Law Review,* 85:510–569.

Asdigian, Nancy L., David Finkelhor, and Gerald Hotaling (1995). "Varieties of Nonfamily Abduction of Children and Adolescents." *Criminal Justice and Behavior,* 22:215–232.

Ash, Philip, Karen B. Slora, and Cynthia F. Britton (1990). "Police Agency Officer Selection Practices." *Journal of Police Science and Administration,* 17:258–269.

Ashford, Jose B. and Craig Winston LeCroy (1993). "Juvenile Parole Policy in the United States: Determinate Versus Indeterminate Models." *Justice Quarterly,* 10:179–195.

Assister, Alison and Carol Avedon (eds.) (1993). *Bad Girls and Dirty Pictures: The Challenge to Reclaim Feminism.* Boulder, CO: Pluto Press.

Associated Press (1993). "Man Sentenced in Puppy Strangling." *Minot (ND) Daily News,* October 31, p. A2.

Associated Press (1994a). "Dancing in the Dark Can Get You Arrested in Iowa." *Minot (ND) Daily News,* March 31, p. A3.

Associated Press (1994b). "Death Row Defenders: Funds for Nation's Death Row Defender System Endangered." *Minot (ND) Daily News,* May 6, p. A6.

Associated Press (1994c). "A Right to Rituals? 'We Should Give the Devil His Due': Judge Allows Satanism Behind Bars," *Minot (ND) Daily News,* October 18, p. A4.

Associated Press (1995a). "HIV-Positive Man Sentenced to 10 Years for Biting Officer." *Minot (ND) Daily News,* March 24, p. A2.

Associated Press (1995b) "Woman Chooses Sterilization Over Jail." *Minot (ND) Daily News,* February 12, p. A2.

Associated Press (1995c). "Inmates' Mug Shots Used for Target Practice, Guard Reprimanded." *Minot (ND) Daily News,* November 19, p. A2.

Associated Press (1996a). "Children of Victims Watch Execution." *Minot (ND) Daily News,* August 10, p. A11.

Associated Press (1996b). "Girl Tells Police She Tried to Smother 7-Year-Old Cousin with Plastic Bag." *Minot (ND) Daily News,* June 9, p. A2.

Associated Press (1996c). "Judge Rules on Jones Accusations Against President Clinton." *Minot (ND) Daily News,* May 12, p. A2.

Associated Press (1996d). "Man with HIV Sentenced to 90 Years for Sexually Assaulting Step-Grandson." *Minot (ND) Daily News,* February 3, p. A2.

Associated Press (1996e). "McVeigh, Nichols Transferred to Denver." *Minot (ND) Daily News,* March 31, p. A4.

Associated Press (1996f). "Ruling to Speed Appeal Process." *Minot (ND) Daily News,* June 29, p. A2.

Associated Press (1996g). "Students Charged in Poison Plot." *Minot (ND) Daily News,* May 16, p. A2.

Associated Press (1996h). "Teen Decapitated Victim, Made Video." *Minot (ND) Daily News,* May 1, p. A2.

Associated Press (1996i). "Woman Gets Jail Sentence for Stealing from Church." *Minot (ND) Daily News,* May 18, p. A6.

Associated Press (1996j). "Woman Gets 12 Years for Locking Boss in Car Trunk." *Minot (ND) Daily News,* May 23, p. A2.

Attorney General's Advisory Commission (1973). *The Police in the California Community.* Sacramento: State of California Attorney General's Advisory Commission on Community-Police Relations.

Austin, James (1994). *The Case for Shorter Prison Terms: The Illinois Experience.* San Francisco, CA: National Council on Crime and Delinquency.

Austin, James and Luiza Chan (1989). *Evaluation of the Nevada Department of Prisons Prisoner Classification System.* San Francisco: National Council on Crime and Delinquency.

Austin, James, Michael Jones, and Melissa Bolyard (1993). *The Growing Use of Jail Boot Camps: The Current State of the Art.* Washington, DC: U.S. Department of Justice, Office of Justice Programs.

Austin, James, Barry Krisberg, and Paul Litsky (1984). *Evaluation of the Field Test of Supervised Pretrial Release: Final Report.* San Francisco, CA: National Council on Crime and Delinquency.

Austin, James et al. (1990). *Reducing Prison Violence by More Effective Inmate Management: An Experimental Field Test of the Prisoner Management Classification (PMC) System.* San Francisco: National Council on Crime and Delinquency.

Austin, Thomas L. and Donald C. Hummer (1994). "'Has a Decade Made a Difference?': Attitudes of Male Criminal Justice Majors towards Female Police Officers." *Journal of Criminal Justice Education,* 5:229–239.

Bachman, Ronet (1994a). *Elderly Crime Victims.* Washington, DC: U.S. Department of Justice.

Bachman, Ronet (1994b). *Violence and Theft in the Workplace.* Washington, DC: Department of Justice.

Bachman, Ronet and Linda E. Saltzman (1995). *Violence Against Women: Estimates from the Redesigned Survey.* Washington, DC: U.S. Department of Justice.

Bailey, William C. (1983). "Disaggregation in Deterrence and Death Penalty Research: The Case of Murder in Chicago." *Journal of Criminal Law and Criminology,* 74:827–859.

Bailey, William C. (1984). "Murder and Capital Punishment in the Nation's Capital." *Justice Quarterly,* 1:211–233.

Baird, Christopher (1992). *Validating Risk Assessment Instruments Used in Community Corrections.* Madison, WI: National Council on Crime and Delinquency.

Baird, Robert M. and Stuart E. Rosenbaum (1995). *Punishment and the Death Penalty: The Current Debate.* Amherst, NY: Prometheus Books.

Baker, Keith, Marcus Pollack, and Imre Kohn (1995). "Violence Prevention through Informal Socialization: An Evaluation of the South Baltimore Youth Center." *Studies on Crime and Crime Prevention,* 4:61–85.

Baker, Ralph and Fred A. Meyer, Jr. (1980). *The Criminal Justice Game: Politics and Players.* North Scituate, MA: Duxbury.

Bales, John P. and Timothy N. Oettmeier (1985). "Houston's DART Program: A Transition to the Future." *FBI Law Enforcement Bulletin,* 54:13–17.

Ball, Richard A., R. Huff, and J. Robert Lilly (1988). *House Arrest and Correctional Policy: Doing Time at Home.* Beverly Hills, CA: Sage.

Bannister, Jonathan (1991). *The Impact of Environmental Design upon the Incidence and Type of Crime.* Edinburgh, SCOT: Central Research Unit, Scottish Office.

Barak-Glantz, Israel L. (1985). "Toward a Conceptual Schema of Prison Management Styles." *Prison Journal,* 10:279–291.

Barker, Thomas and David L. Carter (1986). *Police Deviance.* Cincinnati, OH: Pilgrimage Press.

Barker, Thomas, Ronald D. Hunter, and Jeffrey P. Rush (1994). *Police Systems and Practices: An Introduction.* Upper Saddle River, NJ: Prentice-Hall.

Barlow, David E. and Melissa Hickman Barlow (1994). "Cultural Diversity Rediscovered: Developing Training Strategies for Police Officers." *Justice Professional,* 8:97–116.

Barnes, Arnold and Paul H. Ephross (1994). "The Impact of Hate Violence on Victims: Emotional and Behavioral Responses to Attacks." *Social Work,* 39:247–251.

Barton, William H. and Jeffrey A. Butts (1991). "Intensive Supervision Alternatives for Adjudicated Juveniles." In *Intensive Interventions with High-Risk Youths: Promising Approaches in Juvenile Probation and Parole,* Troy L. Armstrong (ed.). Monsey, NY: Criminal Justice Press.

Bastian, Lisa (1995). *Criminal Victimization 1993.* Washington, DC: U.S. Department of Justice.

Bayley, David H. (1984). "Learning the Skills of Policing." *Law and Contemporary Problems,* 47:35–60.

Bayley, David H. (1985). *Patterns of Policing: A Comparative International Analysis.* New Brunswick, NJ: Rutgers University Press.

Bazemore, Gordon and Dennis Maloney (1994). "Rehabilitating Community Service: Toward Restorative Service Sanctions in a Balanced Justice System." *Federal Probation,* 58:24–35.

Beare, Margaret E. (1995). "Money Laundering: A Preferred Law Enforcement Target." In *Contemporary Issues in Organized Crime,* Jay Albanese (ed.). Monsey, NY: Criminal Justice Press.

Beavon, Daniel J.K. et al. (1993). "Research on Staff Issues." *Forum on Corrections Research,* 5:16–24.

Becker, Harold K. and Jack E. Whitehouse (1980). *Police of America: A Personal View, Introduction, and Commentary.* Springfield, IL: Charles C. Thomas.

Bedau, Hugo Adam (1992). *The Case Against the Death Penalty.* Washington, DC: American Civil Liberties Union, Capital Punishment Project.

Beehr, Terry A., Leanor B. Johnson, and Ronie Nieva (1995).

"Occupational Stress: Coping of Police and Their Spouses." *Journal of Organizational Behavior,* 16:3–25.

Beha, James A. (1977). "Testing the Functions and Effects of the Parole Halfway House: One Case Study." *Journal of Criminal Law and Criminology,* 67:335–350.

Beilein, Thomas and Peter Krasnow (1996). "Jail Prototype Leads to Faster Construction, Lower Costs." *Corrections Today,* 58:128–131.

Belknap, Joanne and Jill Kastens Shelley (1993). "The New Lone Ranger: Policewomen on Patrol." *American Journal of Police,* 12:47–75.

Bell, Bernard P. (1983). "Closure of Pretrial Suppression Hearings: Resolving the Fair Trial/Free Press Conflict." *Fordham Law Review,* 51:1297–1316.

Bell, Daniel J. and Sandra L. Bell (1991). "The Victim-Offender Relationship as a Determinant Factor in Police Dispositions of Family Violence Cases: A Replication Study." *Policing and Society,* 1:225–234.

Bellassai, John P. and Mary A. Toborg (1990). "Electronic Surveillance of Pretrial Releasees in Indianapolis." Unpublished paper presented at the annual meetings of the American Society of Criminology, Baltimore, MD (November).

Benedict, Laura Wolf, and Richard I. Lanyon (1992). "An Analysis of Deceptiveness: Incarcerated Prisoners," *Journal of Addictions and Offender Counseling,* 13:23–31.

Bennett, Brad R. (1992). "Transforming Police Leadership in the 90's." *Journal of Contemporary Criminal Justice,* 8:257–264.

Bennett, Laurence A. (1970). "The Study of Violence in California Prisons: A Review with Policy Implications." In *Prison Violence,* A.K. Cohen, G.F. Cole, and R.C. Bailey (eds.). Lexington, MA: Heath.

Bensinger, Gad J. (1988). "Operation Greylord and Its Aftermath." *International Journal of Comparative and Applied Criminal Justice,* 12:111–118.

Bensinger, Gad J. (1992). "Hate Crimes: A New/Old Problem." *International Journal of Comparative and Applied Criminal Justice,* 16:115–123.

Benson, James (1988). "Damage Suits by Crime Victims Against State Agencies Arising from the Negligent Supervision of Parolees." Unpublished paper presented at the Academy of Criminal Justice Science meetings, San Francisco, CA (April).

Berger, Garry A. (1994). "Pre-Sentence Halfway House Residents: Are They Entitled to Credit Toward Subsequent Prison Sentences?" *Columbia Journal of Law and Social Problems,* 27:191–224.

Berkey, Francine Roussell (1987). *The Farm: An Organizational Analysis of the Wyoming State Honor Farm.* Ann Arbor, MI: University Microfilms International.

Berkson, Larry C. (1977). "The Emerging Ideal of Court Unification." *Judicature,* 60:372–382.

Berkson, Larry C. and Susan Carbon (1978). *Court Unification: History, Politics, and Implementation.* Washington, DC: U.S. National Institute of Law Enforcement and Criminal Justice.

Berlew, Kathleen et al. (1994). *Final Report and Recommenda-*

REFERENCES

tions of the Governor's Select Committee on Corrections. Columbus, OH: Ohio Governor's Select Committee on Corrections.

Berlin, Eric P. (1993). "The Federal Sentencing Guidelines' Failure to Eliminate Sentencing Disparity: Governmental Manipulations Before Arrest." *Wisconsin Law Review,* 1:187–230.

Bernsen, Herbert L. (1996). "St. Louis County, Missouri, Justice Center." *American Jails,* 10:53–60.

Best, Joel (1990). *Threatened Children: Rhetoric and Concern About Child Victims.* Chicago: University of Chicago Press.

Beto, Dan Richard and Melvin Brown, Jr. (1996). "Success in the Organization: A Primer for Probation Officers Seeking Upward Mobility." *Federal Probation,* 60:50–54.

Bharam, Durga M. (1989). "Statute of Limitations for Child Sexual Abuse Offenses: A Time for Reform Utilizing the Discovery Rule." *Journal of Criminal Law and Criminology,* 80:842–865.

Biderman, A.D. and J.P. Lynch (1991). *Understanding Crime Incidence Statistics: Why the UCR Diverges from the NCS.* New York: Springer-Verlag, Research in Criminology Series.

Bieler, Glenn M. (1990). "Death Be Not Proud: A Note on Juvenile Capital Punishment." *New York Law School Journal of Human Rights,* 72:179–213.

Bittner, Egon (1970). *The Functions of the Police in Modern Society: A Review of Background Factors, Current Practices, and Possible Role Models.* Chevy Chase, MD: National Institute of Mental Health.

Bittner, Egon (1985). "The Capacity to Use Force as the Core of the Police Role." In *Moral Issues in Police Work,* F.A. Elliston and M. Felberg (eds.). Totowa, NJ: Rowman and Allanheld.

Bizzack, John W. (1993). *Professionalism and Law Enforcement Accreditation: The First Ten Years.* Lexington, KY: Autumn House.

Black, Henry Campbell (1990). *Black's Law Dictionary.* St Paul, MN: West Publishing Company.

Blankenship, Michael B., Jerry B. Spargar, and W. Richard Janikowski (1994). "Accountability v. Independence: Myths of Judicial Selection." *Criminal Justice Police Review,* 6:69–79.

Blomberg, Thomas G., Gordon P. Waldo, and Lisa C. Burcroff (1987). "Home Confinement and Electronic Surveillance." In *Intermediate Punishments: Intensive Supervision, Home Confinement, and Electronic Surveillance.* Belinda R. McCarthy (ed). Monsey, NY: Criminal Justice Press.

Bloom, Barbara, Meda Chesney-Lind, and Barbara Owen (1994). *Women in California Prisons: Hidden Victims of the War on Drugs.* San Francisco: Center on Juvenile Crime and Criminal Justice.

Blumstein, Alfred, Jaqueline Cohen, and Richard Rosenfeld (1991). "Trend and Deviation in Crime Rates: A Comparison of the UCR and NCS Data for Burglary and Robbery." *Criminology,* 29:237–263.

Blunt, Robert C. (1976). "Developments in the Law of Expunction of Arrest Record Entries." *FBI Law Enforcement Bulletin,* 45:24–27.

Bock, Alan W. (1995). *Ambush at Ruby Ridge: How Government Agents Set Randy Weaver Up and Took His Family Down.* Irvin, CA: Dickens Press.

Bogard, David M. et al. (1993). "Architecture, Construction and Design." *Corrections Today,* 55:74–128.

Boggess, Scott and John Bound (1993). *Did Criminal Activity Increase During the 1980s? Comparisons Across Data Sources.* Ann Arbor, MI: Population Studies Center, University of Michigan, Research Report No. 93–280.

Bohm, Robert M. (1986). "Crime, Criminal and Crime Control Policy Myths." *Justice Quarterly,* 3:193–214.

Bohm, Robert M. (ed.) (1991). *The Death Penalty in America: Current Research.* Cincinnati, OH: Anderson Publishing Company.

Bohm, Robert M. (1992). "Retribution and Capital Punishment: Toward a Better Understanding of Death Penalty Opinion." *Journal of Criminal Justice,* 20:227–236.

Bohm, Robert M., Louise J. Clark, and Adrian F. Aventi (1990). "The Influence of Knowledge on Reasons for Death Penalty Opinions: An Experimental Test." *Justice Quarterly,* 7:175–188.

Bohm, Robert M., Louise J. Clark and Adrian F. Aventi (1991). "Knowledge and Death Penalty Opinion: A Test of the Marshall Hypotheses." *Journal of Research in Crime and Delinquency,* 28:360–387.

Bohm, Robert M. and Ronald E. Vogel (1994). "A Comparison of Factors Associated with Uninformed and Informed Death Penalty Opinions." *Journal of Criminal Justice,* 22:125–143.

Bohn, Martin J., Joyce L. Carbonell, and Edwin I. Megargee (1995). "The Applicability and Utility of the MMPI-Based Offender Classification System in a Correctional Mental Health Unit." *Criminal Behaviour and Mental Health,* 5:14–33.

Bond, James E. (1981). *Plea Bargaining and Guilty Pleas.* New York: Clark Boardman.

Bonifacio, Philip (1991). *The Psychological Effects of Police Work: A Psychodynamic Approach.* New York: Plenum.

Bonora, B. and E. Krauss (1979). *Jury Work: Systematic Techniques.* Washington, DC: National Jury Project.

Boostrom, Ron (ed.) (1995). *Enduring Issues in Criminology.* San Diego, CA: Greenhaven Press.

Borduin, Charles M. et al. (1995). "Multisystemic Treatment of Serious Juvenile Offenders: Long-Term Prevention of Criminality and Violence." *Journal of Consulting and Clinical Psychology,* 63:569–578.

Borgman, Robert (1986). "'Don't Come Home Again': Parental Banishment of Delinquent Youths." *Child Welfare,* 65:295–304.

Bork, Michael V. (1994). *Federal Judicial Caseload: A Five-Year Review, 1989–1993.* Washington, DC: Administrative Office of the United States Courts.

Bortner, M.A., Mary L. Sunderland, and Russ Winn (1985). "Race and the Impact of Juvenile Deinstitutionalization." *Crime and Delinquency* 31:35–46.

Bottomley, A. Keith (1984). "Dilemmas of Parole in a Penal Crisis." *The Howard Journal of Criminal Justice,* 23:24–40.

Bourdouris, James (1983). *The Recidivism of Releasees from the Iowa State Penitentiary at Fort Madison.* Des Moines, IA: Iowa Division of Adult Corrections.

Bourque, Blair B., Mel Han, and Sarah M. Hill (1996). *A National Survey of Aftercare Provisions for Boot Camp Graduates.* Washington, DC: U.S. Department of Justice.

Bradley, Craig M. (1993a). "The Court's 'Two-Model' Approach to the Fourth Amendment: *Carpe Diem!" Journal of Criminal Law and Criminology,* 84:429–461.

Bradley, Craig M. (1993b). *The Failure of the Criminal Procedure Revolution.* Philadelphia: University of Pennsylvania Press.

Bradley, J.M. (1986). "Training Doesn't Have to Be Expensive to Be Good." *FBI Law Enforcement Bulletin,* 55:11–14.

Brand, Richard F. and Ken Peak (1995). "Assessing Police Training Curricula: 'Consumer Reports'." *Justice Professional,* 9:45–58.

Brandl, Steven G. and Frank G. Horvath (1991). "Crime Victim Evaluation of Police Investigative Performance." *Journal of Criminal Justice,* 19:109–122.

Brantley, Alan C., Anthony Sorrentino, and Wayne C. Torok (1994). "Focus on Gangs." *FBI Law Enforcement Bulletin,* 63:1–17.

Braswell, Michael C. and Larry S. Miller (1989). "The Seriousness of Inmate Induced Prison Violence: An Analysis of Correctional Personnel Perceptions." *Journal of Criminal Justice,* 17:47–53.

Braswell, Michael C. and Reid H. Montgomery, Jr., (1994). *Prison Violence in America.* 2d ed. Cincinnati, OH: Anderson Publishing Company.

Braswell, Michael C., Reid H. Montgomery Jr., and Lucien X. Lombardo (eds.) (1994). *Prison Violence in America.* 2d ed. Cincinnati, OH: Anderson Publishing Company.

Bratton, William J. (1995). *Police Strategy No. 7: Rooting Out Corruption, Building Organizational Integrity in the New York Police Department.* New York: New York City Police Department Internal Affairs Bureau.

Brennan, Tim (1985). *Offender Classification and Jail Crowding: Examining the Connection Between Poor Classification and the Problem of Jail Crowding.* Boulder, CO: HSI.

Brennan, William J. Jr. et al. (1994). "Symposium on Capital Punishment." *Notre Dame Journal of Law Ethics and Public Policy,* 8:1–419.

Brewer, Neil and Carlene Wilson (eds.) (1995). *Psychology and Policing.* Hillsdale, NJ: Lawrence Erlbaum.

Brewton, Pete (1992). *The Mafia, CIA and George Bush: The Untold Story of America's Greatest Financial Debacle.* New York: S.P.I. Books.

Broderick, John J. (1987). *Police in a Time of Change.* Prospect Heights, IL: Waveland Press.

Broderick, Vincent L. et al. (1993). "Pretrial Release and Detention and Pretrial Services." *Federal Probation,* 57:4–79.

Brody, Arthur L. and Richard Green (1994). "Washington State's Unscientific Approach to the Problem of Repeat Sex Offenders." *Bulletin of the American Academy of Psychiatry and the Law,* 22:343–356.

Brown, Lee P. (1984). "Strategies to Reduce the Fear of Crime." *Police Chief,* 51:45–46.

Brown, M. Craig and Barbara D. Warner (1992). "Immigrants, Urban Politics, and Policing in 1900." *American Sociological Review,* 57:293–305.

Brown, Marjorie E. and Donald Cochran (1984). *Executive Summary of Research Findings from the Massachusetts Risk/Need Classification System, Report #5.* Boston, MA: Office of the Commissioner on Probation.

Brown, Michael P. and Preston Elrod (1995). "Electronic House Arrest: An Examination of Citizen Attitudes." *Crime and Delinquency,* 41:332–346.

Brown, M.K. (1981). *Working the Street: Police Discretion and the Dilemmas of Reform.* New York: Russell Sage Foundation.

Brown, Paul W. (1987). "Probation Officer Burnout: An Organizational Disease/An Organizational Cure, Part II." *Federal Probation,* 51:17–21.

Brown, Richard Maxwell (1994). *No Duty to Retreat: Violence and Values in American History and Society.* Norman, OK: University of Oklahoma Press.

Brown, Robert (1991). "Training to Stop Stereotypes." *Corrections Compendium,* 16:1, 5.

Brown, S.E. and Ron E. Vogel (1983). "Police Professionalism." *Journal of Crime and Justice,* 6:17–37.

Brzeczek, Richard J. (1985). "Chief-Mayor Relations: The View from the Chief's Chair." In *Police Leadership in America: Crisis and Opportunity,* W.A. Geller (ed.). New York: Praeger.

Buchanan, Cathy and Peter R. Hartley (1992). *Criminal Choice: The Economic Theory of Crime.* St. Leonards, New South Wales: Center for Independent Studies.

Buchanan, Robert A., Cindie A. Unger, and Karen L. Whitlow (1988). *Disruptive Maximum Security Inmate Management Guide.* Washington, DC: U.S. National Institute of Corrections.

Buikema, Charles, Frank Horvath, and Minot Dodson (1983). "Security Regulation: A State-by-State Update." *Security Management* 28:39–48.

Bularik, Mary J. (1984). "The Dedham Temporary Asylum for Discharged Female Prisoners, 1864–1909." *Historical Journal of Massachusetts,* 12:28–35.

Bulkley, Josephine A. and Mark J. Horwitz (1994). "Adults Sexually Abused as Children: Legal Actions and Issues." *Behavioral Sciences and the Law,* 12:65–87.

Bullock, H. (1961). "Significance of the Racial Factor in the Length of Prison Sentences." *Journal of Criminal Law, Criminology and Police Science* 52:411–417.

Bumby, Kurt M. (1993). "Reviewing the Guilty but Mentally Ill Alternative: A Case of the Blind 'Pleading' the Blind." *Journal of Psychiatry and Law,* 21:191–200.

Bureau of Justice Assistance (1992). *Drugs, Crime and the Justice System.* Washington, DC: U.S. Department of Justice.

Bureau of Justice Statistics (1992). *State and Local Police Departments, 1990.* Washington, DC: U.S. Department of Justice.

Burks, David N. and Dean DeHeer (1986). "Jail Suicide Prevention." *Corrections Today,* 48:52–88.

Burns, T.B. and Sandra Pomainville (eds.) (1995). *Criminal Intelligence Service Canada 1995 Annual Report on Eastern European Organized Crime*. Ottawa, CAN: Criminal Intelligence Service Canada.

Bursik, Robert J., Jr., and Harold G. Grasmick (1993). "The Use of Multiple Indicators to Estimate Crime Trends in American Cities." *Journal of Criminal Justice*, 21:509–516.

Burstein, Karen S., David B. Kopel, and Christopher D. Ram (1995). "Guns at Home, Guns on the Street: An International Perspective." *New York Law School Journal of International and Comparative Law*, 15:217–343.

Burton, Bob (1984). *Bounty Hunter*. Boulder, CO: Paladin Press.

Burton, Velmer S., Jr., Edward J. Latessa, and Troy Barker (1992). "The Role of Probation Officers: An Examination of Statutory Requirements." *Journal of Contemporary Criminology Justice*, 8:274–282.

Busher, Walter (1973). *Ordering Time to Serve Prisoners: A Manual for the Planning and Administering of Work Release*. Washington, DC: U.S. Government Printing Office.

Butts, Jeffrey and Jeffrey Gable (1992). *Juvenile Detention in Cook County and the Feasibility of Alternatives*. Pittsburgh, PA: National Center for Juvenile Justice.

Buzawa, Eve, Thomas Austin, and James Bannon (1994). "The Role of Selected Sociodemographic and Job-Specific Variables in Predicting Patrol Officer Job Satisfaction: A Reexamination Ten Years Later." *American Journal of Police*, 13:51–75.

Bynum, Timothy (1977). "An Empirical Exploration of the Factors Influencing Release on Recognizance." Unpublished doctoral dissertation, Florida State University. Ann Arbor, MI: University Microfilms International.

Byrne, James M. and Mary Brewster (1993). "Crime Control Policy and Community Corrections Practice: An Assessment of Gender, Race, and Class Bias." Unpublished paper presented at the annual meetings of the American Society of Criminology, Phoenix, AZ (October).

Cahalan, Margaret W. (1986). *Historical Corrections Statistics in the United States, 1850–1984*. Washington, DC: U.S. Department of Justice.

Caldas, Stephen J. (1990). "Intensive Incarceration Programs Offer Hope of Rehabilitation to a Fortunate Few: Orleans Parish Prison Does an 'About Face.'" *International Journal of Offender Therapy and Comparative Criminology*, 34:67–76.

Calhoun, George, Janelle Jurgens, and Fengling Chen (1993). "The Neophyte Female Delinquent: A Review of the Literature." *Adolescence*, 28:461–471.

California State Senate (1994). *Curbing the Cost of Incarceration in California*. Sacramento, CA: California State Senate.

Call, Jack E. (1995a). "Prison Overcrowding Cases in the Aftermath of *Wilson v. Seiter*." *Prisoner Journal*, 75:390–405.

Call, Jack E. (1995b). "The Supreme Court and Prisoners' Rights." *Federal Probation*, 59:36–46.

Callahan, Lisa A., Margaret A. McGrevy, and Carmen Cirincione (1992). "Measuring the Effects of the Guilty but Mentally Ill (GBMI) Verdict." *Law and Human Behavior*, 16:447–462.

Callahan, Thomas J. (1987). "Probation and Parole: Meeting the Future Head-on." *Corrections Today*, 48:16–20.

Cameron, Joy (1983). *Prisons and Punishment in Scotland from the Middle Ages*. Edinburgh: Canongate.

Camp, Damon D. (1993). "Out of the Quagmire after *Jacobson v. United States* (1992: Toward a More Balanced Entrapment Standard." *Journal of Criminal Law and Criminology*, 83:1055–1097.

Camp, George M. and Camille G. Camp (1995a). *The Corrections Yearbook: Adult Corrections*. South Salem, NY: Criminal Justice Institute, Inc.

Camp, George M. and Camille G. Camp (1995b). *The Corrections Yearbook: Jail Systems*. South Salem, NY: Criminal Justice Institute, Inc.

Camp, George M. and Camille G. Camp (1995c). *The Corrections Yearbook: Juvenile Corrections*. South Salem, NY: Criminal Justice Institute, Inc.

Camp, George M. and Camille G. Camp (1995d). *The Corrections Yearbook: Probation and Parole*. South Salem, NY: Criminal Justice Institute, Inc.

Campaign for an Effective Crime Policy (1993). *Evaluating Mandatory Minimum Sentences*. Washington, DC: Campaign for an Effective Crime Policy.

Caringella-MacDonald, Susan (1990). "State Crises and the Crackdown on Crime Under Reagan." *Contemporary Crises*, 14:91–118.

Carlen, Pat and J. Nanette Davis (1987). "Women in the Health, Welfare, and Criminal Justice Systems." *Contemporary Crises*, 10:361–443.

Carney, Louis P. (1979). *Introduction to Correctional Science*. New York: McGraw-Hill.

Carp, Robert A. and Ronald Stidham (1993). *Judicial Process in America 2/e*. Washington, DC: Congressional Quarterly, Inc.

Carroll, John L. (1986). "The Defense Lawyer's Role in the Sentencing Process: You've Got to Accentuate the Positive and Eliminate the Negative." *Mercer Law Review*, 37:981–1004.

Carter, David L. and Allen D. Sapp (1991). *Police Education and Minority Recruitment: The Impact of a Collect Requirement*. Washington, DC: Police Executive Research Forum.

Carter, Martha (1995). *Cost of the Death Penalty: An Introduction to the Issue*. Lincoln, NE: Legislative Research Division, Nebraska Legislature.

Casarez, Nicole B. (1995). "Furthering the Accountability Principle in Privatized Federal Corrections: The Need for Access to Private Prison Records." *University of Michigan Journal of Law Reform*, 28:249–303.

Cascardi, Michele and Dina Vivian (1995). "Context for Specific Episodes of Marital Violence: Gender and Severity of Violence Differences." *Journal of Family Violence*, 10:265–293.

Caspi, Avshalom et al. (1993). "Unraveling Girls' Delinquency: Biological Dispositional, and Contextual Contributions to Adolescent Misbehavior." *Development Psychology,* 29:19–30.

Castellano, Thomas C. (1986). "The Justice Model in the Juvenile Justice System: Washington State's Experience." *Law and Policy* 8:479–506.

Castellano, Thomas C. (1988). "The Justice Model in the Juvenile Justice System: Washington State's Experience." *Law and Policy* 8:479–506.

Catanzaro, Raimondo (1992). *Men of Respect: A Social History of Sicilian Mafia.* New York: Free Press.

Catanzaro, Raimondo (1994). "Violent Social Regulation: Organized Crime in the Italian South." *Social and Legal Studies,* 3:267–279.

Caudell-Feagan, Linda S. (1993). "Federal Detention: The United States Marshals Service's Management of a Challenging Program." *Federal Probation,* 57:22–27.

Cavanaugh, David P., David Boyum, and Jyothi Nambiar (1993). *Relations Between Increases in the Certainty, Severity and Celerity of Punishment for Drug Crimes and Reductions in the Level of Crime.* Washington, DC: BOTEC Analysis Corporation.

Cavender, Gray (1984). "A Critique of Sanctioning Reform." *Justice Quarterly,* 1:1–16.

Ceci, Stephen J. and Maggie Bruck (1995). *Jeopardy in the Courtroom: A Scientific Analysis of Children's Testimony.* Washington, DC: American Psychological Association.

Cecil, Joe S. (1985). *Administration of Justice in a Large Appellate Court: The Ninth Circuit Innovations Project.* Washington, DC: Federal Judicial Center.

Champagne, Anthony (1988). "Judicial Reform in Texas." *Judicature,* 72:146–159.

Champion, Dean J. (1987). "Felony Offenders, Plea Bargaining, and Probation." *The Justice Professional,* 2:1–18.

Champion, Dean J. (1988a). "Private Counsels and Public Defenders: A Look at Weak Cases, Prior Records, and Leniency in Plea Bargaining." *Journal of Criminal Justice,* 17:253–263.

Champion, Dean J. (1988b). "The Severity of Sentencing: Do Federal Judges Really Go Easier on Elderly Offenders?" In *Older Offenders: Perspectives in Criminology and Criminal Justice,* Belinda McCarthy and Robert Langworthy (eds.). New York: Praeger.

Champion, Dean J. (1988c). *Felony Probation: Problems and Prospects.* New York: Praeger.

Champion, Dean J. (1989a). "Teenage Felons and Waiver Hearings: Some Recent Trends, 1980–1988." *Crime and Delinquency,* 35:577–585.

Champion, Dean J. (ed.) (1989b). *The U.S. Sentencing Guidelines: Implications for Criminal Justice.* New York: Praeger.

Champion, Dean J. (1992). *A Five-State Analysis of Attorney Involvement in Juvenile Cases.* Pittsburgh, PA: National Center for Juvenile Justice.

Champion, Dean J. (1994). *Measuring Offender Risk: A Criminal Justice Sourcebook.* Westport, CT: Greenwood Press.

Champion, Dean J. (1996). *Probation, Parole and Community Corrections.* Upper Saddle River, NJ: Prentice-Hall.

Champion, Dean J. and G. Larry Mays (1991). *Juvenile Transfer Hearings: Some Trends and Implications for Criminal Justice.* New York: Praeger.

Chapman, Jane Roberts et al. (1983). *Women Employed in Corrections.* Washington, DC: U.S. Government Printing Office.

Charles, Michael T. (1989a). "The Development of a Juvenile Electronic Monitoring Program." *Federal Probation,* 53:3–12.

Charles, Michael T. (1989b). "Electronic Monitoring for Juveniles." *Journal of Crime and Justice,* 12:147–169.

Chayet, Ellen F. (1994). "Correctional 'Good Time' as a Means of Early Release." *Criminal Justice Abstracts,* 26:521–538.

Chayet, Ellen F. et al. (1989). *Classification for Custody and the Assessment of Risk in the Colorado Department of Corrections.* Newark, NJ: Rutgers School of Criminal Justice.

Cheatwood, Derral (1985). "Capital Punishment and Corrections: Is There an Impending Crisis?" *Crime and Delinquency,* 31:461–479.

Cheatwood, Derral (1993). "Capital Punishment and the Deterrence of Violent Crime in Comparable Counties." *Criminal Justice Review,* 18:165–181.

Chesney-Lind, Meda (1993). "Girls, Gangs and Violence: Anatomy of a Backlash." *Humanity and Society,* 17:321–344.

Chesney-Lind, Meda and Wayne Matsuo (1995). *Juvenile Crime and Juvenile Justice in Hawaii.* Philadelphia, PA: Center for the Study of Youth Policy, University of Pennsylvania.

Chilton, Bradley S. (1993). "Reforming Plea Bargaining to Facilitate Ethical Discourse." *Criminal Justice Policy Review,* 5:322–334.

Chilton, Bradley S. and David C. Nice (1993). "Triggering Federal Court Intervention in State Prison Reform." *Prison Journal,* 73:30–45.

Claggett, Arthur F. (1989). "Effective Therapeutic Wilderness Camp Programs for Rehabilitating Emotionally-Disturbed, Problem Teenagers and Delinquents." *Journal of Offender Counseling, Services, and Rehabilitation,* 14:79–96.

Claggett, Arthur F. et al. (1992). "Corrections—Innovative Practices, Inmate Behavior Dynamics, Policy Analysis, Personnel." *Journal of Offender Rehabilitation,* 17:1–211.

Clark, Judith (1995). "The Impact of Prison Environment on Mothers." *Prison Journal,* 75:306–329.

Clarke, David C. (1994). *An Evaluation of the Department's Policy on Criminal Aliens: Four Year Post-Release Follow-Up of Criminal Aliens Released in 1988.* Albany, NY: New York State Department of Correctional Services.

Clarke, Ronald V. and David Weisburd (1994). "Diffusion of Crime Control Benefits: Observations on the Reverse of Displacement." In *Crime Prevention Studies,* Vol. 2, Ronald V. Clarke (ed.). Monsey, NY: Criminal Justice Press.

Clarke, Stevens H. and Larry Crum (1985). *Returns to Prison in North Carolina.* Chapel Hill, NC: Institute of Government, University of North Carolina, Chapel Hill.

Clarke, Stevens H. et al. (1983). *North Carolina's Determinate Sentencing Legislation: An Evaluation of the First Year's Experience.* Chapel Hill, NC: Institute of Government, University of North Carolina.

Clayton, Obie Jr. (1983). "Reconsideration of the Effects of Race in Criminal Sentencing." *Criminal Justice Review,* 8:15–20.

Clayton, Susan (1996). "Young Probation/Parole Officer Toughens with Experience." *Corrections Today,* 58:85–88.

Clear, Todd R. (1993). "Thinking about Community Corrections." Unpublished paper presented at the annual meeting of the American Society of Criminology, Phoenix, AZ (October).

Clear, Todd R. (1994). *Harm in American Penology: Offenders, Victims and Their Communities.* Albany, NY: State University of New York Press.

Clear, Todd R. and George F. Cole (1986). *American Corrections.* Belmont, CA: Brooks/Cole.

Cleary, Jim and Michelle Powell (1994). *History, Issues and Analysis of Pretrial Release and Detention: A Policy Analysis.* St. Paul, MN: Minnesota House of Representatives Research Department.

Cochran, John K., Mitchell B. Chamlin, and Mark Seth (1994). "Deterrence or Brutalization? An Impact Assessment of Oklahoma's Return to Capital Punishment." *Criminology,* 32:107–134.

Coddon, R.E. (1985). "*Tennessee v. Garner:* Comment." *Law Focus,* 1:14–16.

Cohen, Fred (1972). "Police Perjury: An Interview with Martin Garbess." *Criminal Law Bulletin,* 8:363–375.

Cohen, Howard (1985). "A Dilemma for Discretion." In *Police Ethics: Hard Choices in Law Enforcement,* W.C. Heffernan and T. Stroup (eds.). New York: John Jay.

Cohn, Bob (1991). "There Goes the Judge: Why Bush's Appeals-Court Nominee Was Rejected." *Newsweek,* April 22, 1991: 31.

Cole, George F. (1970). *The American System of Criminal Justice.* North Scituate, MA: Duxbury.

Cole, George F. (1975). *The American System of Criminal Justice.* North Scituate, MA: Duxbury.

Coleman, John L. (1995). *Operational Mid-Level Management for Police.* 2d ed. Springfield, IL: Charles C. Thomas.

Collins, James J. et al. (1993). *Law Enforcement Policies and Practices Regarding Missing Children and Homeless Youth: Research Summary.* Washington, DC: U.S. Office of Juvenile Justice and Delinquency Prevention.

Collins, William C. (1994). *Jail Design and Operation and the Constitution: An Overview.* Boulder, CO: U.S. National Institute of Corrections.

Collins, William C. (1995). "A History of Recent Corrections Is a History of Court Involvement." *Corrections Today,* 57:112–150.

Colorado Office of State Auditor (1993). *Community-Based Corrections System Performance Audit.* Denver, CO: Colorado Office of State Auditor.

Colquhoun, P. (1806/1969). *1796–1806 Treatise on the Police in the Metropolis.* Reprint, Montclair, NJ: Patterson-Smith.

Connelly, Peter J. (1983). "Alibi: Proof of Falsehood and Consciousness of Guilt." *Criminal Law Quarterly,* 25:165–178.

Conner, G. (1986). "Use of Force Continuum." *Law and Order,* 34:18–60.

Conrad, John (1985). *The Dangerous and the Endangered.* Lexington, MA: Lexington Books.

Conti, Samuel D. et al. (1985). *Hudson County (NJ) Criminal Justice Project Evaluation.* North Andover, MA: National Center for State Courts.

Cook, James L., Michael Capizzi, and Michael Schumacher (1994). "TARGET: A Multi-Agency Model to Reduce Gang Crime." *Police Chief,* 61:110–113.

Cook, Philip I. and Donna B. Slawson (1993). *The Costs of Processing Murder Cases in North Carolina.* Durham, NC: Terry Sanford Institute of Public Policy, Duke University.

Cooprider, Keith W. and Judith Kerby (1990). "A Practical Application of Electronic Monitoring at the Pretrial Stage." *Federal Probation,* 54:28–35.

Corbett, Ronald P. Jr. and Ellsworth A. L. Fersch (1985). "Home as Prison: The Use of House Arrest." *Federal Probation,* 49:13–17.

Corbett, Ronald P. Jr. and Gary T. Marx (1991). "Critique: No Soul in the New Machine: Technofallacies in the Electronic Monitoring Movement." *Justice Quarterly,* 8:399–414.

Cordner, Gary W. and Donna C. Hale (eds.) (1992). *What Works in Policing? Operations and Administration Examined.* Cincinnati, OH: Anderson Publishing Company.

Cordner, Gary W. and Dennis J. Kenney (eds.) (1996). *Managing Police Organizations.* Cincinnati, OH: Anderson Publishing Company.

Corey, David Michael (1988). "The Psychological Suitability of Police Officer Candidates." Unpublished doctoral dissertation, The Fielding Institute. Ann Arbor, MI: University Microfilms International.

Cornelius, Gary F. (1994). *Stressed Out: Strategies for Living and Working with Stress in Corrections.* Laurel, MD: American Correctional Association.

Corrado, Michael Louis (ed.) (1994). *Justification and Excuse in the Criminal Law: A Collection of Essays.* New York: Garland.

Correctional Educational Association (1988). *Learning Behind Bars: Selected Educational Programs from Juvenile, Jail and Prison Facilities.* Laurel, MD: Correctional Educational Association.

Corrections Compendium (1991a). "Camp to Open for Children of Incarcerated Parents." *Corrections Compendium,* 16:11.

Corrections Compendium (1991b). "Electronic Monitoring Programs Grow Rapidly from 1986 to 1989." *NIJ Reports* No. 222. *Corrections Compendium* 16:14.

Corrections Compendium (1991c). "Survey: Sentencing Guidelines Determine Penalties in 17 Systems." *Corrections Compendium* 16:10–18.

Corrections Compendium (1991d). "Survey Shows High Public Support for Community Programs." *Corrections Compendium* 16:15.

Corrections Compendium (1992a). "Overcrowding Makes for

Dangerous Facilities in Illinois." *Corrections Compendium,* 17:16.

Corrections Compendium (1992b). "States Reports: The Courts and the Prisons." *Corrections Compendium,* 17:14.

Corrections Compendium (1993a). "Oregon Prison Riot May Be Due to Sentencing and Overcrowding." *Corrections Compendium,* 18:14.

Corrections Compendium (1993b) "Tough on Crime Law Increases Michigan Crime Rates." *Corrections Compendium,* 18:15.

Corrections Compendium (1994a). "Hiring of Correctional Officers Increasingly More Selective." *Corrections Compendium,* 19:8–16.

Corrections Compendium (1994b). "Prosecuting Criminal Enterprises." *Corrections Compendium,* 19:4–5.

Corrections Today (1995). "Supreme Court Limits Inmate Lawsuits." *Corrections Today,* 57:32.

Corsilles, Angela (1994). "No-Drop Policies in the Prosecution of Domestic Violence Cases: Guarantee to Action or Dangerous Solution?" *Fordham Law Review,* 63:853–881.

Cosgrove, Edward J. (1994). "ROBO-PO: The Life and Times of a Federal Probation Officer." *Federal Probation,* 58:29–30.

Costanzo, Mark and Lawrence T. White (eds.) (1994). "The Death Penalty in the United States." *Journal of Social Issues,* 50:1–197.

Cox, Barbara G. and Richter H. Moore, Jr. (1992). "Toward the Twenty-First Century: Law Enforcement Training Now and Then." *Journal of Contemporary Criminal Justice,* 8:235–256.

Courtless, Thomas F. (1989). "The Rehabilitative Ideal Meets an Aroused Public: The Patuxent Experiment Revisited." *Journal of Psychiatry and Law* 17:607–626.

Coyle, Kenneth R., John C. Schaaf, and James R. Coldren (1991). *Futures in Crime Analysis: Exploring Applications of Incident-Based Data.* Washington, DC: Criminal Justice Statistics Association, U.S. Bureau of Justice Statistics.

Craddock, Amy (1992). "Formal Social Control in Prisons: An Exploratory Examination of the Custody Classification Process." *American Journal of Criminal Justice,* 17:63–87.

Cragg, Wesley et al. (1992). "Reflections on Sentencing and Corrections." *Canadian Journal of Law and Jurisprudence,* 5:3–173.

Crank, John P. (1994). "Watchman and Community: Myth and Institutionalization in Policing." *Law and Society Review,* 28:325–351.

Crank, John P. (1996). "The Construction of Meaning During Training for Probation and Parole." *Justice Quarterly,* 13:265–290.

Crank, John P. and Robert Langworthy (1992). "An Institutional Perspective of Policing." *Journal of Criminal Law and Criminology,* 83:338–363.

Crank, John P. and Lee R. Rehm (1994). "Reciprocity Between Organizations and Institutional Environments: A Study of Operation Valkyrie." *Journal of Criminal Justice,* 22:393–406.

Crew, Robert E. Jr. (1993). "An Effective Strategy for Hot Pursuit: Some Evidence from Houston." *American Journal of Police,* 11:89–95.

Crew, Robert E. Jr., David Kessler, and Lorie A. Fridell (1994). "Changing Hot Pursuit Policy: An Empirical Assessment of the Impact on Pursuit Behavior." *Evaluation Review,* 18:678–688.

Criminal Justice Newsletter (1996). "Prison Litigation Reform Act Spawns Tests of Consent Decrees." *Criminal Justice Newsletter,* 27:1–2.

Crist, Charlie (1996). "Chain Gangs are Right for Florida." *Corrections Today,* 58:178–184.

Crocker, Lawrence (1992). "The Upper Limit of Justice Punishment." *Emory Law Journal,* 41:1059–1110.

Cromwell, Paul F. and George G. Killinger (1994). *Community-Based Corrections: Probation, Parole, and Intermediate Punishments.* 3d ed. St. Paul, MN: West Publishing Company.

Cromwell, Paul F., James N. Olson, and D'Aunn W. Avary (1991). "How Residential Burglars Choose Targets: An Ethnographic Analysis." *Security Journal,* 2:195–199.

Cronin, Roberta C. (1994). *Boot Camps for Adult and Juvenile Offenders: Overview and Update.* Washington, DC: U.S. National Institute of Justice.

Crosby, Catherine A., Preston A. Britner, and Kathleen M. Jodl (1995). "The Juvenile Death Penalty and the Eighth Amendment." *Law and Human Behavior,* 19:245–261.

Crouch, Ben M. and James W. Marquart (1990). "Resolving the Paradox of Reform Litigation, Prisoner Violence, and Perceptions of Risk." *Justice Quarterly,* 7:103–123.

Crutchfield, Robert D. et al. (1993). *Racial/Ethnic Disparities and Exceptional Sentences in Washington State.* Olympia, WA: Washington State Minority and Justice Commission.

Cullen, Francis T. and Lawrence F. Travis (1984). "Work as an Avenue of Prison Reform." *New England Journal on Criminal and Civil Confinement,* 10:45–64.

Cullen, Francis T. et al. (1985). "The Impact of Social Supports on Police Stress." *Criminology,* 23:503–522.

Culliver, Concetta C. (ed.) (1993). *Female Criminality: The State of the Art.* New York: Garland Publishing Company.

Cunningham, William C., John J. Strauchs, and Clifford W. VanMeter (1990). *Private Security Trends 1970 to 2000: The Hallcrest Report II.* Boston: Butterworth-Heinemann.

Curry, G. David and Irving A. Spergel (1992). "Gang Involvement and Delinquency among Hispanic and African-American Adolescent Males." *Journal of Research in Crime and Delinquency,* 29:273–291.

Cuvelier, Steven J. and Dennis W. Potts (1993). *Bail Classification Profile Project, Harris County, Texas: Final Report.* Alexandria, VA: State Justice Institute.

Czajkoski, Eugene H. (1992). "Criminalizing Hate: An Empirical Assessment." *Federal Probation,* 56:36–40.

Czajkoski, Eugene H. and Laurin A. Wollan Jr. (1986). "Opinion and Debate: Creative Sentencing—A Critical Analysis." *Justice Quarterly,* 3:215–239.

Dallao, Mary (1996). "Life Cut Short: Correctional Officer Killed in the Line of Duty." *Corrections Today,* 58:69–70.

D'Allessio, Stewart J. (1993). *Unemployment and the Incarceration of Pretrial Defendants.* Ann Arbor, MI: University Microfilms International.

D'Allessio, Stewart J. and Lisa Stolzenberg (1993). "Socioeconomic Status and the Sentencing of the Traditional Offender." *Journal of Criminal Justice,* 21:61–77.

D'Allessio, Stewart J. and Lisa Stolzenberg (1995). "The Impact of Sentencing Guidelines on Jail Incarceration in Minnesota." *Criminology,* 33:283–302.

Daly, Kathleen (1994). *Gender, Crime and Punishment.* New Haven, CT: Yale University Press.

Daly, Kathleen and Rebecca L. Bordt (1995). "Sex Effects and Sentencing: An Analysis of the Statistical Literature." *Justice Quarterly,* 12:141–175.

Daniels, Stephen (1984). "The Problem of Caseloads and Studying Court Activities Over Time." *American Bar Foundation Research Journal,* 4:751–795.

Dantzker, Gail, Arthur J. Lurigio, and Susan Hartnett (1995a). "Preparing Police Officers for Community Policing: An Evaluation of Training for Chicago's Alternative Policing Strategy." *Police Studies,* 18:745–770.

Dantzker, Gail, Arthur J. Lurigio, and Susan Hartnett (1995b). *Preparing Police Officers for Community Policing: An Evaluation of Training for Chicago's Alternative Policing Strategy.* Evanston, IL: Northwestern University, Center for Urban Affairs and Policy Research.

Dantzker, Mark Lewis (1989). "The Effect of Education on Police Performance: The Stress Perspective." Unpublished doctoral dissertation, University of Texas as Arlington. Ann Arbor, MI: University Microfilms International.

Das, Dilip K. (1983). "Conflict Views on Policing: An Evaluation." *Journal of Police,* 3:51–81.

Davey, Joseph D. (1994). "The Death of the Fourth Amendment Under the Rehnquist Court: Where Is Original Intent When We Need It?" *Journal of Crime and Justice,* 17:129–148.

Davidson, Bill (1968). "The Worst Jail I've Ever Seen." *Saturday Evening Post,* July 13, 1968:17–22.

Davies, Graham M. et al. (1995). "Seminar: A New Look at Eyewitness Testimony: Papers Presented at the BAFS Joint Seminar on 12 October 1994." *Medicine, Science and the Law,* 35:95–149.

Davis, Edward M. (1973). "Neighborhood Team Policing: Implementing the Territorial Imperative." *Crime Prevention Review,* 1:11–19.

Davis, Rob, Bruce Taylor, and Sarah Bench (1995). "Impact of Sexual and Nonsexual Assault on Secondary Victims." *Violence and Victims,* 10:73–84.

Davis, Robert (1994). "Washington Case Is a Test for '3 Strikes' Law." *USA Today,* June 21, 1994:A4.

Davis, Robert C. (1983). "Victim/Witness Noncooperation: A Second Look at a Persistent Phenomenon." *Journal of Criminal Justice,* 11:287–299.

Davis, Shirley (1990). "Participatory Management: A Technique for Reducing Probation/Parole Officer Burnout." Unpublished paper presented at the annual meeting of the Academy of Criminal Justice Sciences, Denver, CO (April).

Davis, Simon (1994). "Factors Associated with the Diversion of Mentally Ill Disordered Offenders." *Bulletin of the Academy of Psychiatry and the Law,* 22:389–397.

Davis, Su Perk (1990a). "Good Time." *Corrections Compendium,* 15:1–11.

Davis, Su Perk (1990b). "Survey: Parole Officers' Roles Changing in Some States." *Corrections Compendium,* 15:7–16.

Davis, Su Perk (1991). "Number of Furloughs Increasing—Success Rates High." *Corrections Compendium,* 16:10–22.

Dawson, John M. and Patrick A. Langan (1994). *Murder in Families.* Washington, DC: U.S. Department of Justice.

Dawson, Robert O. (1992). "An Empirical Study of *Kent*-Style Juvenile Transfers to Criminal Court." *St. Mary's Law Journal,* 23:975–1054.

Decker, Scott H. (1985). "Crime, Crime Rates, Arrests, and Arrest Ratios: Implications for Deterrence Theory." *Criminology,* 23:437–450.

Decker, Scott H. and C.W. Kohfeld (1984). "A Deterrence Study of the Death Penalty in Illinois, 1933–1980." *Journal of Criminal Justice,* 12:367–377.

Decker, Scott H. and C.W. Kohfeld (1985). "Crime, Crime Rates, Arrests, and Arrest Ratios: Implications for Deterrence Theory." *Criminology,* 23:437–450.

Decker, Scott H. and C.W. Kohfeld (1990). "The Deterrent Effect of Capital Punishment in the Five Most Active Execution States: A Time Series Analysis." *Criminal Justice Review,* 15:173–191.

DeJong, William (1994). *Preventing Interpersonal Violence among Youth: An Introduction to School, Community and Mass Media Strategies.* Washington, DC: U.S. National Institute of Justice.

del Carmen, Rolando V. (1995). *Criminal Procedure: Law and Practice.* 3d ed. Belmont, CA: Wadsworth.

del Carmen, Rolando V. et al. (1990). "Corrections and the Courts." *Corrections Today,* 52:34–70.

Delaware Executive Department (1984). *Recidivism in Delaware: A Study of Rearrest after Release from Incarceration.* Dover, DE: Delaware Executive Department, Statistical Analysis Center.

Denham, Robert N. (1996). "Correctional Education Put to the Test." *American Jails,* 10:66–68.

Denkowski, George C. and Kathryn M. Denkowski (1985). "The Mentally Retarded Offender in the State Prison System: Identification, Prevalence, Adjustment, and Rehabilitation." *Criminal Justice and Behavior,* 12:55–69.

Denno, Deborah W. (1994). "Gender, Crime and the Criminal Law Defenses." *Journal of Criminal Law and Criminology,* 85:80–180.

Dent, Helen and Rhona Flin (eds.) (1992). *Children as Witnesses.* Chichester, UK: Wiley.

DeSantis, John (1994). *The New Untouchables: How America Sanctions Police Violence.* Chicago: Noble Press.

Detroit Police Department (1983). *Mini-Station Personnel Training Manual.* Detroit, MI: Mini-Station Administration Unit.

DeWitt, Charles B. (1986). *Florida Sets Example with Use of Concrete Modules*. Washington, DC: National Institute of Justice.

DiCharia, Albert and John F. Galliher (1994). "Dissonance and Contradictions in the Origins of Marijuana Decriminalization." *Law and Society,* 28:41–77.

Dick, Andrew R. (1995). "When Does Organized Crime Pay? A Transaction Analysis." *International Review of Law and Economics,* 15:25–46.

Dickey, Walter J. (1995). *What Every Policymaker Should Know about Imprisonment and the Crime Rate*. Washington, DC: Campaign for an Effective Crime Policy.

Dickey, Walter J. and Dennis Wagner (1990). *From the Bottom Up: The High Risk Offender Intensive Supervision Program*. Madison, WI: Continuing Education and Outreach, University of Wisconsin Law School.

Dicks, Shirley (ed.) (1991). *Congregation of the Condemned: Voices Against the Death Penalty*. Buffalo, NY: Prometheus Books.

Dieter, Richard C. (1994). *The Future of the Death Penalty in the United States: A Texas-Sized Crisis*. Washington, DC: Death Penalty Information Center.

Diggs, David W. and Stephen L. Pieper (1994). "Using Day Reporting Centers as an Alternative to Jail." *Federal Probation,* 58:9–12.

DiIulio, John J. Jr. (ed.) (1990). *Courts, Corrections and the Constitution: The Impact of Judicial Intervention on Prisons and Jails*. New York: Oxford University Press.

Dillehay, Ronald C. and Michael T. Nietzel (1985). "Jury Experience and Jury Verdicts." *Law and Human Behavior,* 89:179–191.

DiPiano, John G. (1995). "Private Prisons: Can They Work? Panopticon in the Twenty-First Century." *New England Journal on Criminal and Civil Confinement,* 21:171–202.

Dixon, Jo (1995). "The Organizational Context of Criminal Sentencing." *American Journal of Sociology,* 100:1157–1198.

Dobash, Russel P. (1983). "Labour and Discipline in Scottish and English Prisons: Moral Correction, Punishment, and Useful Toil." *Sociology,* 17:1–27.

Doerner, William G. and Tai Ping Ho (1994). "Shoot—Don't Shoot: Police Use of Deadly Force Under Simulated Field Conditions." *Journal of Crime and Justice,* 17:49–68.

Donnelly, Patrick G. and Brian E. Forschner (1987). "Predictors of Success in a Co-Correctional Halfway House: A Discriminant Analysis." *Journal of Crime and Justice,* 10:1–22.

Dougherty, Joyce (1988). "Negotiating Justice in the Juvenile Justice System: A Comparison of Adult Plea Bargaining and Juvenile Intake." *Federal Probation,* 52:72–80.

Dressler, David (1969). *Practice and Theory of Probation and Parole*. New York: Columbia University Press.

Driscoll, Lois Regent (1984). "Illegality of Bribery: Its Roots, Essence, and Universality." *Capital University Law Review,* 14:1–42.

Drummond, Douglas S. (1976). *Police Culture*. Beverly Hills, CA: Sage.

Dubois, Philip L. (1990). "Voter Responses to Court Reform: Merit Judicial Selection on the Ballot." *Judicature,* 73:238–247.

Duffee, David E. and Edmund F. McGarrell (eds.) (1990). *Community Corrections: A Community Field Approach*. Washington, DC: Department of Justice, Bureau of Justice Statistics.

Duguid, Stephen (ed.) (1990). *Yearbook of Correctional Education, 1990*. Burnaby, CAN: Institute for the Humanities, Simon Fraser University.

Dumond, R.W. (1992). "The Sexual Assault of Male Inmates in Incarcerated Settings." *International Journal of the Sociology of Law,* 20:135–158.

Dunaway, David M. (1985). *A Legal Analysis of the Prevailing Law of Search and Seizure in Public Elementary and Secondary Schools*. Ann Arbor, MI: University Microfilms International.

Dundes, Lauren (1994). "Punishing Parents to Deter Delinquency: A Realistic Remedy?" *American Journal of Police,* 13:113–133.

Dunn, R.S. and M.M. Dunn (eds.) (1982). *The Papers of William Penn*, Vol. 2, *1680–1684*. Philadelphia: University of Pennsylvania Press.

Durham, Alexis M. III (1990). "Social Control and Imprisonment During the American Revolution: Newgate of Connecticut." *Justice Quarterly,* 7:293–323.

Durham, Alexis M. III (1994). *Crisis and Reform: Current Issues in American Punishment*. Boston: Little, Brown.

Dynia, Paul A. (1990). *Misdemeanor Trial Law: Is It Working?* New York: New York City Criminal Justice Agency.

Dynia, Paul A. et al. (1987). *Misdemeanor Trial Law Study: Final Report*. New York: New York City Criminal Justice Agency.

Eck, John E. (1995). *A General Model of the Geography of Illicit Retail Marketplaces*. Monsey, NY: Criminal Justice Press.

Edel, Wilbur (1995). *Gun Control: Threat to Liberty or Defense Against Anarchy?* Westport, CT: Praeger.

Eigenberg, Helen M. (1990). "The *National Crime Survey* and Rape: The Case of the Missing Question." *Justice Quarterly,* 7:655–672.

Eilers, Jennifer C. (1994). *Alternatives to Traditional Incarceration for Serious Traffic Offenders*. Charlottesville, VA: Virginia Transportation Research Council.

Einstadter, W.J. (1984). "Citizen Patrols: Prevention or Control." *Crime and Social Justice,* 21:200–212.

Eisenberg, Michael (1985a). *Release Outcome Series: Halfway House Research*. Austin, TX: Texas Board of Pardons and Paroles.

Eisenberg, Michael (1985b). *Factors Associated with Recidivism*. Austin, TX: Texas Board of Pardons and Paroles.

Eisenberg, Michael (1985c). *Selective Early Release: Research-Based Criteria*. Austin, TX: Texas Board of Pardons and Paroles.

Elliott, Delbert S. (1994). "1993 Presidential Address: Serious Violent Offenders: Onset, Developmental Course, and Termination." *Criminology,* 32:1–21.

Elliott, Delbert S. et al. (1983). *The Prevalence and Incidence of Delinquent Behavior, 1976–1980.* Boulder, CO: Behavioral Research Institute.

Elliott, Michelle (1995). "Child Sexual Abuse Prevention: What Offenders Tell Us." *Child Abuse and Neglect,* 19:579–594.

Elliston, Frederick A. and Michael Feldberg (eds.) (1985). *Moral Issues in Police Work.* Totowa, NJ: Rowman and Allanheld.

Ellsworth, Phoebe C. et al. (1984). "The Death-Qualified Jury and the Defense of Insanity." *Law and Human Behavior,* 8:81–93.

Ellsworth, Thomas (1990a). "The Actual and Preferred Goals of Adult Probation: A Study of Enforcement and Rehabilitation." Unpublished paper presented at the annual meetings of the Academy of Criminal Justice Sciences, Denver, CO (April).

Ellsworth, Thomas (1990b). "The Goal Orientation of Adult Probation Professionals: A Study of Probation Systems." *Journal of Crime and Justice,* 12:55–76.

Ellsworth, Thomas (1990c). "Identifying the Actual and Preferred Goals of Adult Probation." *Federal Probation,* 54:10–15.

El Nasser, Haya (1993). "Private Security Has Become Police Backup." *USA Today,* December 21, p. 9A.

Elson, John (1992). "Conduct Unbecoming." *Time,* December 14, p. 46.

Emerson, Deborah Day and Nancy L. Ames (1984). *The Role of the Grand Jury and the Preliminary Hearing in Pretrial Screening.* Washington, DC: U.S. Government Printing Office.

English, Kim, Susan M. Chadwick, and Suzanne K. Pullen (1994). *Colorado's Intensive Supervision Probation: Report of Findings.* Denver, CO: Colorado Division of Criminal Justice.

Epstein, Lee and Joseph F. Kobylka (1992). *The Supreme Court and Legal Change: Abortion and the Death Penalty.* Chapel Hill, NC: University of North Carolina Press.

Erez, Edna and Pamela Tontodonato (1990). "The Effect of Victim Participation in Sentencing on Sentence Outcome." *Criminology,* 28:451–474.

Erickson, Lori et al. (1992). "Architecture, Construction and Design." *Corrections Today,* 54:80–133.

Etheridge, Philip A. and James W. Marquart (1993). "Private Prisons in Texas: The New Penology for Profit." *Justice Quarterly,* 10:29–48.

Evans, Barry J., Greg J. Coman, and Robb O. Stanley (1992). "The Police Personality: Type A Behavior and Trait Anxiety." *Journal of Criminal Justice,* 20:429–441.

Evans, Robin (1982). *The Fabrication of Virtue: English Prison Architecture, 1750–1840.* New York: Cambridge University Press.

Evanson, Milton L. (1991). *Marijuana Use and Law Enforcement Personnel Policies by 1996.* Sacramento, CA: Peace Officer Standards and Training Commission.

Ewing, Charles Patrick (1991). "Preventive Detention and Execution: The Constitutionality of Punishing Future Crimes." *Law and Human Behavior,* 15:139–163.

Falk, James H. Sr. (1995). "Developing a Code of Ethics So COs Know How to Respond." *Corrections Today,* 55:110–120.

Farkas, Gerald M. and Robert H. Fosen (1983). "Responding to Accreditation." *Corrections Today,* 45:40–42.

Farkas, Mary Ann (1992). "The Impact of the Correctional Setting on the Research Experience: A Research Chronicle." *Journal of Crime and Justice,* 15:177–184.

Farnworth, Margaret and Raymond H. Teske, Jr. (1995). "Gender Differences in Felony Court Processing: Three Hypotheses of Disparity." *Women and Criminal Justice,* 6:23–44.

Farr, Kathryn Ann (1993). "Shaping Policy Through Litigation: Abortion Law in the United States." *Crime and Delinquency,* 39:167–183.

Farrington, David P. (1992). "Criminal Career Research: Lessons for Crime Prevention." *Studies on Crime and Crime Prevention,* 1:7–29.

Farrington, David P. and Roger Tarling (eds.) (1985). *Prediction in Criminology.* Albany, NY: State University of New York Press.

Faulkner, Rick (1994). "Networking in Community Corrections." *APPA Perspectives,* 18:23.

Faulkner, Samuel D. (1994). "A Ralph Nader Approach to Law Enforcement Training: Subject Control—Unsafe at Any Speed." *Police Studies,* 17:21–32.

Feeley, Malcolm M. (1983). *Court Reform on Trial: Why Simple Solutions Fail.* New York: Basic Books.

Feeley, Malcolm M. and Austin D. Sarat (1980). *The Policy Dilemma: Federal Crime Policy and the Law Enforcement Assistance Administration.* Minneapolis, MN: University of Minnesota Press.

Feld, Barry C. (1987). "The Juvenile Court Meets the Principle of the Offense: Legislative Changes in Juvenile Waiver Statutes." *Journal of Criminal Law and Criminology,* 78:471–533.

Feld, Barry C. (1988). "The Right to Counsel in Juvenile Court: An Empirical Study of When Lawyers Appear and the Differences They Make." Unpublished paper presented at the American Society of Criminology meeting, Chicago.

Feld, Barry C. (1991). "The Transformation of the Juvenile Court." *Minnesota Law Review,* 75:691–725.

Feld, Barry C. (1993a). "Criminalizing the American Juvenile Court." In *Crime and Justice: A Review of Research,* Vol. 17, Michael Tonry (ed.). Chicago: University of Chicago Press.

Feld, Barry C. (1993b). *Justice for Children: The Right to Counsel and the Juvenile Courts.* Boston: Northeastern University Press.

Feldberg, Michael (1985). "Police Discretion and Family Disturbances: Some Historical and Contemporary Reflections." In *Unhappy Families,* Eli H. Newberger and Richard Bourne (eds.). Littleton, MA: PSG Publishing Company.

Felkenes, George T., and Paul Peretz, and Jean Reith Schroedel (1993). "An Analysis of the Mandatory Hiring of Females: The Los Angeles Police Department Experience." *Women and Criminal Justice,* 4:31–63.

Felkenes, George T. and Jean Reith Schroedel (1993). "A Case Study of Minority Women in Policing." *Women and Criminal Justice,* 4:65–89.

Felkenes, George T. and Peter Charles Unsinger (1992). *Diversity, Affirmative Action and Law Enforcement.* Springfield, IL: Charles C. Thomas.

Felker, Charles J. (1990). "A Proposal for Considering Intoxication at Sentencing Hearings: Part II." *Federal Probation,* 54:3–14.

Field, Harlee (1987). "Commercial Juvenile Corrections: Anatomy of a Model." Unpublished paper presented at the annual meeting of the Academy of Criminal Justice Sciences, St. Louis, MO (March).

Fields, Charles B. (ed.) (1994). *Innovative Trends and Specialized Strategies in Community-Based Corrections.* New York: Garland.

Fields, Charles B., Harlee Field, and Frank P. Williams (1983). *Using and Improving Probation.* Huntsville, TX: Institute for Criminal Justice Policy Analysis.

Figueira-McDonough, Josefina (1992). "Community Structure and Female Delinquency Rates: A Heuristic Discussion" *Youth and Society,* 24:3–30.

Finch, Michael and Mark Ferraro (1986). "Empirical Challenge to Death-Qualified Juries: On Further Examination." *Nebraska Law Review,* 65:21–74.

Findlay, Mark (1992). "The Mafia Menace." *Criminal Organizations,* 7:3–17.

Findlay, Mark and Peter Duff (eds.) (1988). *The Jury Under Attack.* Sydney, AUS: Butterworths.

Finkel, Norman J. et al. (1994). "Killing Kids: The Juvenile Death Penalty and Community Sentiment." *Behavioral Sciences and the Law,* 12:5–20.

Finn, Peter and B. Lee (1985). "Collaboration with Victim-Witness Assistance Programs: Payoffs and Concerns for Prosecutors." *Prosecutor,* 18:27–36.

Fischer, Daryl R. and Andy Thaker (1992). *Mandatory Sentencing Study.* Phoenix, AZ: Arizona Department of Corrections.

Fisher, Robert, Kathryn Golden, and Bruce Heininger (1985). "Issues in Higher Education for Law Enforcement Officers: An Illinois Study." *Journal of Criminal Justice,* 13:329–338.

Fitzgerald, Robert and Phoebe C. Ellsworth (1984). "Due Process vs. Crime Control: Death Qualification and Jury Attitudes." *Law and Human Behavior,* 8:31–51.

Flango, Victor E. (1994a). "Court Unification and Quality of State Courts." *Justice System Journal,* 16:33–55.

Flango, Victor E. (1994b) "Federal Court Review of State Court Convictions in Noncapital Cases." *Justice System Journal,* 17:153–170.

Flango, Victor E. (1994c). *Habeas Corpus in State and Federal Courts.* Williamsburg, VA: National Center for State Courts.

Fletcher, George P. (1995). *With Justice for Some: Victims' Rights in Criminal Trials.* New York: Addison-Wesley.

Flood, Susan (ed.) (1991). *Illicit Drugs and Organized Crime: Issues for a Unified Europe.* Chicago: Office of International Criminal Justice, University of Illinois.

Florida Advisory Council on Intergovernmental Relations (1993). *Privatization as an Option for Constructing and Operating Jails.* Tallahassee, FL: Florida Advisory Council on Intergovernmental Relations.

Florida Advisory Council on Intergovernmental Relations (1994). *Intergovernmental Impacts of the 1994 Juvenile Justice Reform Bill.* Tallahassee, FL: Florida Advisory Council on Intergovernmental Relations.

Florida Department of Corrections (1990). *Boot Camp: A Twenty-Five Month Review.* Tallahassee, FL: Florida Department of Corrections, Bureau of Planning, Research and Statistics.

Florida Governor's Juvenile Justice and Delinquency Prevention Advisory Committee (1994). *Non-Delinquents Placed in Florida's Secure Juvenile Detention Facilities, 1993.* Tallahassee, FL: Florida Governor's Juvenile Justice and Delinquency Prevention Advisory Committee.

Florida Joint Legislative Management Committee (1992). *An Empirical Examination of the Application of Florida's Habitual Offender Statute.* Tallahassee, FL: Florida Joint Legislative Management Committee Economic and Demographic Research Division.

Florida Legislature Advisory Council (1993). *Intergovernmental Relations in Local Jail Finance.* Tallahassee, FL: Florida Legislature Advisory Council.

Florida Office of Program Policy Analysis (1995). *Status Report on Boot Camps in Florida Administered by the Department of Corrections and Department of Juvenile Justice.* Tallahassee, FL: Florida Office of Program Policy Analysis and Government Accountability.

Florida Probation and Parole Services (1984). *Preliminary Report on Community Control.* Tallahassee, FL: Florida Department of Corrections.

Florida Senate Committee on Corrections Probation and Parole (1993). *Sentencing Guidelines and the Management of the Prison Population: An Executive Summary of Events and Policy Choices.* Tallahassee, FL: Florida Senate Committee on Corrections Probation and Parole.

Florida Senate Committee on Executive Business Ethics and Elections (1991). *A Report on Alternative Methods of Jury Selection.* Tallahassee, FL: Florida Senate Committee on Executive Business Ethics and Elections.

Fogel, David (1978). *We Are the Living Proof.* Cincinnati, OH: Anderson Publishing Company.

Fogel, David (1979). *We Are the Living Proof.* Cincinnati, OH: Anderson Publishing Company.

Ford, David A. and Mary Jean Regoli (1993). *The Indianapolis Domestic Violence Prosecution Experiment: Final Report.* Indianapolis, IN: Indiana University, Department of Sociology.

Ford, Marilyn Chandler (1986). "The Role of Extralegal Factors in Jury Verdicts." *Justice System Journal,* 11:16–39.

Ford, Michelle E. and Jean Ann Linney (1995). "Comparative Analysis of Juvenile Sexual Offenders, Violent Nonsexual

Offenders, and Status Offenders." *Journal of Interpersonal Violence,* 10:56–70.

Forer, Lois G. (1994). *A Rage to Punish: The Unintended Consequences of Mandatory Sentencing.* New York: W.W. Norton.

Forst, Brian E. (1983). "Capital Punishment and Deterrence: Conflicting Evidence?" *Federal Probation,* 45:19–22.

Forst, Martin L. and Martha Elin Blomquist (1991). *Missing Children: Rhetoric and Reality.* Lexington, MA: Lexington Books.

Fort, Rodney (1991). *Benefit-Cost Analysis and the Community Protection Act.* Olympia, WA: Washington State Institute for Public Policy.

Fox, James G. (1984). "Women's Prison Policy: Prisoner Activism and the Impact of the Contemporary Feminist Movement: A Case Study." *Prison Journal,* 64:15–36.

Frank, James et al. (1996). "Reassessing the Impact of Race on Citizens' Attitudes Toward the Police: A Research Note." *Justice Quarterly,* 13:321–334.

Franke, Herman (1992). "The Rise and Decline of Solitary Confinement: Socio-Historical Explanations of Long-Term Penal Changes." *British Journal of Criminology,* 32:125–143.

Franz, Verl and David M. Jones (1985). "Politics and Police Leadership: The View from City Hall." In *Police Leadership in America: Crisis and Opportunity,* W.A. Geller (ed.). New York: Praeger.

Franz, Verl and David M. Jones (1987). "Perceptions of Organization Performance in Suburban Police Departments: A Critique of the Military Model." *Journal of Police Science and Administration,* 15:153–161.

Frazier, Mansfield B. (1995). *From Behind the Wall: Commentary on Crime, Punishment, Race and the Underclass by a Prison Inmate.* New York: Random House.

Freedman, Estelle B. (1981). *Their Sister's Keepers: Women's Prison Reform in America, 1830–1930.* Ann Arbor, MI: University of Michigan Press.

Friedman, Ruth (1988). "Municipal Liability for Police Misconduct: Must Victims Now Prove Intent?" *Yale Law Journal,* 97:448–465.

Friend, Roxanne et al. (1993). "Jails and Minorities." *American Jails,* 7:11–28.

Fukurai, Hiroshi, Edgar W. Butler, and Richard Krooth (1991). "Cross-Sectional Jury Representation or Systematic Jury Representation? Simple Random and Cluster Sampling Strategies in Jury Selection." *Journal of Criminal Justice,* 19:31–48.

Fulton, Betsy A., Susan B. Stone, and Paul Gendreau (1994). *Restructuring Intensive Supervision Programs: Applying "What Works."* Lexington, KY: American Probation and Parole Association.

Fyfe, James J. (ed.) (1985a). *Police Management Today: Issues and Case Studies.* Washington, DC: International City Management Association.

Fyfe, James J. (1985b). "Reviewing Citizens' Complaints Against the Police." In *Police Management Today,* James J.

Fyfe (ed.). Washington, DC: International City Management Association.

Fyfe, James J. (1988). "Police Use of Deadly Force: Research and Reform." *Justice Quarterly,* 5:165–205.

Fyfe, James J. and Mark Blumberg (1985). "Response to Griswald: A More Valid Test of the Justifiability of Police Actions." *American Journal of Police,* 4:110–132.

Gable, Ralph K. (1986). "Application of Personal Telemonitoring to Current Problems in Corrections." *Journal of Criminal Justice,* 14:167–176.

Galliher, John F., Gregory Ray, and Brent Cook (1992). "Abolition and Reinstatement of Capital Punishment During the Progressive Era and Early Twentieth Century." *Journal of Criminal Law and Criminology,* 83:538–576.

Gardner, Eugene J. (1992). "Regional Jails." *American Jails,* 6:45–47.

Garofalo, James and Richard D. Clark (1985). "The Inmate Subculture in Jails." *Criminal Justice and Behavior,* 12:415–434.

Garwood, M. (1985). "Two Issues on the Validity of Personnel Screening Polygraph Examinations." Unpublished paper presented at the 20th Annual Seminar of the American Polygraph Association, Reno, NV.

Gatz, Nick and Chris Murray (1981). "An Administrative Overview of Halfway Houses." *Corrections Today,* 43:52–54.

Geary, David Patrick (1975). *Community Relations and the Administration of Justice.* New York: Wiley.

Geary, David Patrick (1985). *Community Relations and the Administration of Justice.* New York: Wiley.

Geller, William A. and Hans Toch (1995). *And Justice for All: Understanding and Controlling Police Abuse of Force.* Washington, DC: Police Executive Research Forum.

George, B.J. Jr. (1990). "United States Supreme Court 1989–1990 Term: Criminal Law Decisions." *New York Law School Review,* 35:479–592.

Georgetown Law Journal (1971). "Police Perjury in Narcotics 'Dropsy' Cases: A New Credibility Gap." *Georgetown Law Journal,* 60:507–523.

Gerwitz, Marian (1987). *Court-Ordered Releases—November 1983.* New York: New York City Criminal Justice Agency.

Gettys, V.S. and J.D. Elam (1985). "Validation Demystified: Personnel Selection Techniques That Work." *Police Chief,* 52:41–43.

Gewerth, Kenneth E. and Clifford K. Dorne (1991). "Imposing the Death Penalty on Juvenile Murderers: A Constitutional Assessment." *Judicature,* 75:6–15.

Gibbs, John J. (1975). "Jailing and Stress." In *Men in Crisis: Human Breakdowns in Prison,* H. Toch (ed.). Chicago: Aldine.

Gibson, H. (1973). "Women's Prisons: Laboratories for Penal Reform." *Wisconsin Law Review,* 13:210–233.

Gilbert, James (1986). *A Cycle of Outrage: America's Reaction to the Juvenile Delinquent in the 1950s.* New York: Oxford University Press.

Gilliard, Darrell K. (1993). *Prisoners in 1992.* Washington, DC: U.S. Department of Justice.

Gilliard, Darrell K. and Allen J. Beck (1994). *Prisoners in 1993.* Washington, DC: Bureau of Justice Statistics.

Giordano, Peggy, Stephen A. Cernkovich, and M.D. Pugh (1986). "Friendships and Delinquency." *American Journal of Sociology,* 91:1170–1202.

Girdner, Linda K. and Patricia M. Hoff (1994). *Obstacles to the Recovery and Return of Parentally Abducted Children.* Washington, DC: U.S. Office of Juvenile Justice and Delinquency Prevention.

Gitchoff, G. Thomas and George E. Rush (1989). "The Criminological Case Evaluation and Sentencing Recommendation: An Idea Whose Time Has Come." *International Journal of Offender Therapy and Comparative Criminology,* 33:77–83.

Glaser, Daniel (1994). "What Works, and Why Is It Important? A Response to Logan and Gaes." *Justice Quarterly,* 11:711–723.

Glenn, Myra C. (1984). *Campaigns Against Corporal Punishment: Prisoners; Sailors, Women, and Children in Antebellum America.* Albany, NY: State University of New York Press.

Glick, Ruth (1978). *National Study of Women's Correctional Programs.* Washington, DC: National Institute of Law Enforcement and Criminal Justice.

Godfrey, Michael J. and Vincent Schiraldi (1995). *How Have Homicide Rates Been Affected by California's Death Penalty?* San Francisco: Center on Juvenile and Criminal Justice.

Godson, Roy, William J. Olson, and Louise Shelley (eds.) (1995). "Anticipating and Disrupting Organized Crime." *Trends in Organized Crime,* 1:1–125.

Goebel, Julius, Jr. (1971). *History of the Supreme Court, Antecedents and Beginnings to 1801,* Ray Roberts (ed.). New York: Macmillan.

Goetting, Ann (1985). "Racism, Sexism, and Ageism in the Prison Community." *Federal Probation,* 49:10–22.

Goetting, Ann (1992). "Patterns of Homicide among the Elderly." *Violence and Victims,* 7:203–215.

Golash, Deirdre (1992). "Race, Fairness and Jury Selection." *Behavioral Sciences and the Law,* 10:155–177.

Gold, Martin and D. Wayne Osgood (1992). *Personality and Peer Influence in Juvenile Corrections.* Westport, CT: Greenwood Press.

Goldkamp, John S. (1984). "Bail: Discrimination and Control." *Criminal Justice Abstracts,* 16:103–127.

Goldkamp, John S. and Michael R. Gottfredson (1984). *Judicial Guidelines for Bail: The Philadelphia Experiment.* Washington, DC: U.S. Government Printing Office.

Goldman, Sheldon (1985). "Reorganizing the Judiciary: The First Term Appointments." *Judicature,* 68:313–329.

Gomez, Marisa A. (1993). "The Writing on our Walls: Finding Solutions Through Distinguishing Graffiti Art from Graffiti Vandalism." *University of Michigan Journal of Law Reform,* 26:633–708.

Gonzales, Gil P. (1982). "*In re Myron:* Juvenile Confessions." *Criminal Justice Journal,* 5:349–358.

Goodman, Rebecca (1992). *Pretrial Release Study.* Minneapolis, MN: Hennepin County Bureau of Community Corrections, Planning and Evaluation.

Goodpaster, Gary (1983). "Judicial Review of Death Sentences." *Journal of Criminal Law and Criminology,* 74:786–826.

Goolkasian, Gail A., Ronald W. Geddes, and William DeJong (1985). *Coping with Police Stress.* Washington, DC: U.S. Department of Justice.

Gordon, Frank X. (1985). "The Judicial Image: Is a Facelift Necessary?" *Justice System Journal,* 10:315–324.

Gorer, Geoffrey (1955). "Modification of National Character: The Role of the Police in England." *Journal of Social Issues,* 11:25–32.

Gottfredson, Michael R. and Don M. Gottfredson (1988). *Decision Making in Criminal Justice: Toward the Rational Exercise of Discretion.* New York: Plenum.

Gottfredson, Stephen D. and Don M. Gottfredson (1985). "Screening for Risk among Parolees: Policy, Practice, and Method." in *Prediction in Criminology,* D. P. Farrington and R. Tarling (eds.). Albany, NY: SUNY Press.

Gottfredson, Stephen D. and Don M. Gottfredson (1990). *Classification, Prediction, and Criminal Justice Policy: Final Report to the National Institute of Justice.* Washington, DC: U.S. National Institute of Justice.

Gottfredson, Stephen D. and Don M. Gottfredson (1992). *Incapacitation Strategies and the Criminal Career.* Sacramento, CA: Law Enforcement Information Center, California Division of Law Enforcement.

Gottlieb, Barbara (1984). *Public Danger as a Factor in Pretrial Release: Summaries of State Danger Laws.* Washington, DC: Toborg.

Gottlieb, Barbara and Phillip Rosen (1984). *Public Danger as a Factor in Pretrial Release: Summaries of State Danger Laws.* Washington, DC: Toborg.

Gowen, Darren (1995). "Electronic Monitoring in the Southern District of Mississippi." *Federal Probation,* 59:10–13.

Graham, Michael H. (1985). *Witness Intimidation: The Law's Response.* Westport, CT: Quorum.

Grasmick, Harold G., Robert J. Bursik Jr., and Brenda Sims Blackwell (1993). "Religious Beliefs and Public Support for the Death Penalty for Juveniles and Adults." *Journal of Crime and Justice,* 16:59–86.

Graves, G. et al. (1985). *Developing a Street Patrol: A Guide for Neighborhood Crime Prevention Groups.* Boston: Neighborhood Crime Prevention Council, Justice Resource Institute.

Gray, Tara et al. (1991). "Using Cost-Benefit Analysis to Evaluate Correctional Sentences." *Evaluation Review,* 15:471–481.

Gray, Thomas A. and Eric D. Wish (1993). *Maryland Youth At Risk: A Study of Drug Use in Juvenile Detainees.* College Park, MD: Center for Substance Abuse Research.

Green, Bruce A. (1990). "The Good Faith Exception to the Fruit of the Poisonous Tree Doctrine." *Criminal Law Review,* 26:509–533.

Green, Helen Taylor (1993). "Community Oriented Policing in Florida." *American Journal of Police,* 12:141–155.

Green, Lorraine (1995). "Policing Places with Drug Problems: The Multi-Agency Reponse Team Approach." In *Crime and Place,* John E. Eck and David Weisburd (eds.). Monsey, NY: Criminal Justice Press.

Green, Maurice (1984). "Child Advocacy: Rites and Rights in Juvenile Justice." In *Advances in Forensic Psychiatry,* Robert W. Rieber (ed.). Norwood, NJ: Ablex.

Greenberg, David F., Ronald Kessler, and Colin Loftin (1983). "The Effect of Police Employment on Crime." *Criminology,* 21:375–394.

Greene, Edith (1986). "Is the Juvenile Justice System Lenient?" *Criminal Justice Abstracts* (March): 104–118.

Greenfeld, Lawrence A. (1996). *Child Victimizers: Violent Offenders and Their Victims.* Washington, DC: U.S. Department of Justice.

Greenstein, Steven C. (1994). *The Impact of Restrictions on Post-Indictment Plea Bargaining in Bronx County: The Processing of Indictments Already Pending."* Albany, NY: New York State Division of Criminal Justice Sources.

Greenwald, John (1990). "S & L Hot Seat." *Time,* October 1, pp. 34–40.

Greenwood, Peter W. (1982). *Selective Incapacitation.* Santa Monica, CA: Rand.

Greenwood, Peter W., J. Chaiken, and Joan M. Petersilia (1977). *The Criminal Investigation Process.* Lexington, MA: D.C. Heath.

Greenwood, Peter W. et al. (1994). *Three Strikes and You're Out: Estimated Benefits and Costs of California's New Mandatory Sentencing Law.* Santa Monica, CA: Rand.

Grieser, Robert C. (1989). "Do Correctional Industries Adversely Impact the Private Sector?" *Federal Probation,* 53:18–24.

Griffith, Winnie Ruth (1985). *Risk Prediction Models for Female Offenders.* Ann Arbor, MI: University Microfilms International.

Griffith, W.R. (1983). *Self-Report Instrument: A Description and Analysis of Results in the National Evaluation Sites.* Eugene, OR: Institute of Policy Analysis.

Grimes, Richard (1989). "The Regional Jail Concept." *American Jails,* 3:31–33.

Griset, Pamela L. (1994). "Determinate Sentencing and the High Cost of Overblown Rhetoric: The New York Experience." *Crime and Delinquency,* 40:532–548.

Griset, Pamela L. (1995). "Determinate Sentencing and Agenda Building: A Case Study of the Failure of Reform." *Journal of Crime and Justice,* 23:349–362.

Griswold, David B. (1985). "Controlling the Police Use of Deadly Force: Exploring the Alternatives." *American Journal of Police,* 4:93–109.

Grown, Mary C. and Roger D. Carlson (1993). "Do Male Policemen Accept Women on Patrol Yet? Androgyny, Public Complaints, and Dad." *Journal of Police and Criminal Psychology,* 9:10–14.

Guggenheim, Martin (1985). *The Rights of Young People.* New York: Bantam Books.

Guggenheim, Martin (1986). "Effective Assistance of Counsel for the Indigent Criminal Defendant: Has the Promise Been Fulfilled?" *New York University Review of Law and Social Change,* 14:1–276.

Gwinn, Casey G. (1995). "Can We Stop Domestic Violence?" *American Jails,* 9:11–19.

Haaga, John G., Richard Scott, and Jennifer Hawes-Dawson (1992). Santa Monica, CA: Drug Policy Research Center, Rand Corporation.

Haas, Kenneth C. (1994). "The Triumph of Vengeance over Retribution: The United States Supreme Court and the Death Penalty." *Crime Law and Social Change,* 21:127–154.

Hahn, Paul H. (1984). *The Juvenile Offender and the Law.* Cincinnati, OH: Anderson Publishing Company.

Hall, Jerome (1947). *Theft, Law and Society.* Indianapolis, IN: Bobbs-Merrill.

Hanewicz, Wayne B. (1985). "Discretion and Order." In *Moral Issues in Police Work,* Frederick A. Elliston and Michael Feldberg (eds.). Totowa, NJ: Rowman and Allanheld.

Haney, Craig (1984). "On the Selection of Capital Juries: The Biasing Effects of the Death-Qualification Process." *Law and Human Behavior,* 8:121–132.

Hanke, Penelope J. (1995). "Sentencing Disparities by Race of Offender and Victim: Women Homicide Offenders in Alabama, 1929–1985." *Sociological Spectrum,* 15:277–297.

Hans, Valerie P. and Neil Vidmar (1986). *Judging the Jury.* New York: Plenum.

Hanson, Kweku (1988). "Racial Disparities and the Law of Death: The Case for a New Hard Look at Race-Based Challenges to Capital Punishment." *National Black Law Journal,* 10:298–317.

Hanson, Roger A. and Henry W. K. Daley (1995). *Challenging the Conditions of Prisons and Jails: A Report on Section 1983 Litigation.* Washington, DC: U.S. Bureau of Justice Statistics.

Hanson, Roger A., Brian J. Ostrom, and William E. Hewitt (1992). *Indigent Defenders Get the Job Done and Done Well.* Williamsburg, VA: National Center for State Courts.

Harding, Christopher et al. (1985). *Imprisonment in England and Wales: A Concise History.* Dover, NH: Croom Helm.

Hardyman, Patricia L. (1993). *Design and Validation of an Objective Classification System for the Wyoming State Prison System: Final Report.* San Francisco: National Council on Crime and Delinquency.

Harer, Miles D. and Christopher Eichenlaub (1992). "Prison Furloughs and Recidivism." Unpublished paper presented at the annual meeting of the American Society of Criminology, Pittsburgh, PA (November).

Hargrave, G.E. (1985). "Using the MMPI and CPI to Screen Law Enforcement Applicants: A Study of Reliability and Validity of Clinician's Decisions." *Journal of Police Science and Administration,* 13:221–224.

Hargrave, G.E. and G. Berner (1986). "A 'Psychological Skills Analysis' for California Peace Officers." *Police Chief,* 53:34–36.

Harlow, Caroline Wolf (1994). *Comparing Federal and State Prison Inmates, 1991.* Washington, DC: U.S. Bureau of Justice Statistics.

Harris, M. Kay (1984). "Strategies, Values and the Emerging

Generation of Alternatives to Incarceration." *University Review of Law and Social Change,* 12:141–170.

Harris, M. Kay, Peter R. Jones, and Gail S. Funke (1990). *The Kansas Community Corrections Act: An Assessment of a Public Policy Initiative.* Philadelphia, PA: Prepared for the Edna McConnell Clark Foundation.

Harris, M. Kay et al. (1991). "Judicial Intervention in Local Jails." *Prison Journal,* 71:1–92.

Harris, Patricia M. (1986). "Is the Juvenile Justice System Lenient?" *Criminal Justice Abstracts* (March):104–118.

Harris, Patricia M. (1988). "Juvenile Sentence Reform and Its Evaluation: A Demonstration of the Need for More Precise Measures of Offense Seriousness in Juvenile Justice Research." *Evaluation Review,* 12:655–666.

Harrison, J. (1985). "Police Complaints: Pitfalls for the Unwary Litigant." *New Law Journal,* 135:1239–1240.

Harvard Law Review Association (1994). *A Uniform System of Citation.* Cambridge, MA: Harvard Law Review Association.

Hastie, Reid, Steven D. Penrod, and Nancy Pennington (1983). *Inside the Jury.* Cambridge, MA: Harvard University Press.

Hawaii Crime Commission (1984). *Mandatory Sentencing: A Preliminary Assessment.* Honolulu, HI: Hawaii Crime Commission.

Hawaii Office of the Auditor (1992). *Sunset Evaluation Report: Bail Bond Agents.* Honolulu, HI: Hawaii Office of the Auditor.

Haycock, Joel (1991). "Capital Crimes: Suicides in Jail." *Death Studies,* 15:417–433.

Heaney, Gerald W. (1991). "The Reality of Guidelines Sentencing: No End to Disparity." *American Criminal Law Review,* 28:161–232.

Heaney, Gerald W. et al. (1992). "Federal Sentencing Guidelines Symposium." *American Criminal Law Review,* 29:771–932.

Heard, Chinita A. (1993). "Forecasting Models for Managing a Changing Inmate Population: Implications for Public Policy." *Criminal Justice Review,* 18:1–11.

Heffernan, William C. (1985). "The Police and Their Rules of Office: An Ethical Analysis." In *Police Ethics: Hard Choices in Law Enforcement,* W. C. Heffernan and T. Stroupa (eds.). New York: John Jay.

Heller, Gerald W. (1990). "Effective Criminal Discovery: Rule 16's Hidden Potential." *Criminal Law Bulletin,* 26:99–122.

Henderson, Dwight F. (1971). *Courts for a New Nation.* Washington, DC: Public Affairs.

Henderson, Thomas A. and Cornelius M. Kerwin (1982). "The Changing Character of Court Organization." *Justice System Journal,* 7:449–473.

Hendricks, James E. and Jerome B. McKean (1995). *Crisis Intervention: Contemporary Issues for On-Site Interveners.* Springfield, IL: Charles C. Thomas.

Hengstler, Gary (1987). "Attorneys for the Damned." *American Bar Association Journal,* 73:56–60.

Henretta, John C., Charles E. Frazier, and Donna M. Bishop (1986). "The Effect of Prior Case Outcomes on Juvenile Justice Decision Making." *Social Forces,* 65:554–562.

Hepburn, John R. and Celesta A. Albonetti (1994). "Recidivism among Drug Offenders: A Survival Analysis of the Effects of Offender Characteristics, Type of Offense, and Two Types of Intervention." *Journal of Quantitative Criminology,* 10:159–179.

Hepburn, John R. et al. (1992). *The Maricopa County Demand Reduction Program: An Evaluation Report.* Phoenix, AZ: Maricopa County Evaluation Program.

Heper, Ian L., Richard L. Skok, and T.F. McLaughlin (1990). "Successful Correctional Officers." *Corrective and Social Psychiatry and Journal of Behavior Technology Methods and Therapy,* 36:46–53.

Heumann, Milton and Colin Loftin (1979). "Mandatory Sentencing and the Abolition of Plea Bargaining." *Law and Society Review,* 13:393–430.

Hewitt, John D., Eric D. Poole, and Robert M. Regoli (1984). "Self-Reported and Observed Rule-Breaking in Prison: A Look at Disciplinary Response." *Justice Quarterly,* 1:437–447.

Hickman, Kenneth G. (1990). "Urban Police Management." *Journal of Contemporary Criminal Justice,* 6:49–105.

Higgins, Scott (1996). "Making Sure Tomorrow's Correctional Facilities Stand the Test of Time." *Corrections Today,* 58:8.

Hirsch, Alan and Diane Sheely (1993). *The Bail Reform Act of 1984.* Washington, DC: Federal Judicial Center.

Hodge, John L. (1986). "Deadlocked Jury Mistrials, Lesser Included Offenses, and Double Jeopardy: A Proposal to Strengthen the Manifest Necessity Requirement." *Criminal Justice Journal,* 9:9–44.

Hoffman, Peter B. (1983). "Screening for Risk: A Revised Salient Factor Score." *Journal of Criminal Justice,* 11:539–547.

Hoffman, Peter B. (1994). "Twenty Years of Operational Use of a Risk Prediction Instrument: The United States Parole Commission's Salient Factor Score." *Journal of Criminal Justice,* 22:477–494.

Hoffman, Peter B. and James L. Beck (1985). "Recidivism among Released Federal Prisoners: Salient Factor Score and Five-Year Follow-Up." *Criminal Justice and Behavior,* 12:501–507.

Hogue, Mark C., Tommie Black, and Robert T. Sigler (1994). "The Differential Use of Screening Techniques in the Recruitment of Police Officers." *American Journal of Police,* 13:113–124.

Holeman, Herbert and B.J. Krepps-Hess (1983). *Women Correctional Officers in the California Department of Corrections.* Sacramento, CA: Research Unit, California Department of Corrections.

Holland, L.H. (1985). "Police and the Community: The Detroit Ministation Experience." *FBI Law Enforcement Bulletin,* 54:1–6.

Holmes, Malcolm D., Harmon M. Hosch, and Howard C. Daudistel (1993). "Judges' Ethnicity and Minority Sentencing: Evidence Concerning Hispanics." *Social Science Quarterly,* 74:496–506.

Holt, Ray and Richard L. Phillips (1991). "Marion: Separating Fact from Fiction." *Federal Prisons Journal,* 2:28–36.

Holten, N. Gary and Melvin E. Jones (1982). *The System of Criminal Justice.* 2d ed. Boston: Little, Brown.

Holton, C. Lewis (1995). "Once Upon a Time Served: Therapeutic Application of Fairy Tales with a Correctional Environment." *International Journal of Offender Therapy and Comparative Criminology,* 39:210–221.

Homans, George (1950). *The Human Group.* New York: Harcourt, Brace and World.

Homel, Ross (1994). *Flawed Order: The Administration of Justice in a 'Get Tough' Era.* Brisbane, AUS: Faculty of Education, Griffith University.

Hood, Jane C. and Stephen Rollins (1995). "Some Didn't Call It Hate: Multiple Accounts of the Zimmerman Library Incident." *Violence Against Women,* 1:228–240.

Hopper, Columbus B. (1985). "The Impact of Litigation on Mississippi's Prison System." *Prison Journal,* 65:54–63.

Horvath, Frank (1993). "Polygraph Screening of Candidates for Police Work in Large Police Agencies in the United States." *American Journal of Police,* 12:67–86.

Houk, Julie M. (1984). "Electronic Monitoring of Probationers: A Step Toward Big Brother?" *Golden Gate University Law Review,* 14:431–446.

Houston Police Department (1991). *Houston Police Department: Final Report Excerpts.* Washington, DC: Cresap.

Howells, Gary N., Kelly A. Flanagan, and Vivian Hagan (1995). "Does Viewing a Televised Execution Affect Attitudes toward Capital Punishment?" *Criminal Justice and Behavior,* 22:411–424.

Hudnut, William H. (1985). "The Police and the Polis: A Mayor's Perspective." In *Police Leadership in America: Crisis and Opportunity,* W.A. Geller (ed.). New York: Praeger.

Hudzik, John K. (1984). *Federal Aid to Criminal Justice: Rhetoric, Results, Lessons.* Washington, DC: National Criminal Justice Association.

Huff, C. Ronald (1990). "The Impact of a House Arrest Program on the Offenders, the Community, and the System." Unpublished paper presented at the annual meeting of the American Society of Criminology, Baltimore, MD (November).

Huff, C. Ronald, Arye Rattner, and Edward Sagarin (1996). *Convicted But Innocent: Wrongful Conviction and Public Policy.* Thousand Oaks, CA: Sage.

Hughes, Charles Evans (1966). *The Supreme Court of the United States.* New York: Columbia University Press.

Hughes, Robert (1987). *The Fatal Shore.* New York: Knopf.

Hull, Debra B. et al. (1991). "Sex Offenses and Offenders: Dynamics, Treatment." *Journal of Offender Rehabilitation,* 17:1–179.

Human Rights Watch (1995). *Children in Confinement in Louisiana.* New York: Human Rights Watch, Children's Rights Project.

Humphrey, Elaine S. (1992). *Day Reporting Program Profile.* Albany, NY: New York State Department of Correctional Services.

Humphrey, Elaine S. and Karl H. Gohlke (1993). *Profile of Participants: The Bedford Hills and Taconic Nursery Program in 1992.* Albany, NY: New York State Department of Correctional Services.

Humphries, Drew (1984). "Reconsidering the Justice Model." *Contemporary Crises,* 8:167–173.

Hunt, Geoffrey et al. (1993). "Changes in Prison Culture: Prison Gangs and the Case of the 'Pepsi Generation.'" *Social Problems,* 40:398–409.

Hunter, Susan M. (1985). "Issues and Challenges Facing Women's Prisons in the 1980s." *Criminal Justice Abstracts,* 17:129–135.

Hunter, Susan M. (1986). "On the Line: Working Hard with Dignity." *Corrections Today,* 48:12–13.

Hunzeker, Donna (1985). "Habitual Offender Statutes." *Corrections Compendium,* 10:1–5.

Hunzeker, Donna (1992). *Bringing Corrections Policy into the 1990s.* Denver, CO: National Conference of State Legislatures.

Hunzeker, Donna and Cindy Conger (eds.) (1985). *Inmate Lawsuits: A Report on Inmate Lawsuits Against State and Federal Correctional Systems Resulting in Monetary Damages and Settlements.* Lincoln, NE: Contact Center.

Immarigeon, Russ (1985). "Private Prisons, Private Programs, and Their Implications for Reducing Reliance on Imprisonment in the United States." *Prison Journal,* 65:60–74.

Inciardi, James A. (ed.) (1991). *Studies in Crime, Law and Justice,* Vol. 7, *The Drug Legalization Debate.* Newbury Park, CA: Sage.

Indermaur, David (1990). *Crime Seriousness and Sentencing: A Comparison of Court Practice and the Perceptions of a Sample of Public and Judges.* Washington, DC: Administrative Office of the U.S. Courts.

Ingley, Gwen Smith (1996a). "Inmate labor: Yesterday, Today and Tomorrow." *Corrections Today,* 58:28–32.

Ingley, Gwen Smith (1996b). "Position Statements Released." *Corrections Today,* 58:206–208.

Institute for Court Management (1983). *Evaluation of Telephone Conferencing in Civil and Criminal Court Cases.* Denver, CO: National Institute of Justice and the National Science Foundation; American Bar Association Action Commission to Reduce Court Costs and Delay.

Institute for Rational Public Policy, Inc. (1991). *Arizona Criminal Code and Corrections Study: Final Report to the Legislative Council.* Phoenix, AZ: Institute for Rational Public Policy.

Inwald, Robin (1985). "Administrative Legal and Ethical Practices in the Psychological Testing of Law Enforcement Officers." *Journal of Criminal Justice,* 13:367–372.

Iowa Equity in the Courts Task Force (1993). *Final Report of the Equality in the Courts Task Force.* Des Moines, IA: The Supreme Court of Iowa.

Irwin, John (1985). *The Jail: Managing the Underclass in American Society.* Berkeley: University of California Press.

Jackson, J.D. (1986). "The Insufficiency of Identification Evidence Based on Personal Impression." *Criminal Law Review,* 16:203–214.

Jackson, Mary S. (1994). "Drug Use Patterns among Black

Male Juvenile Delinquents." *Journal of Alcohol and Drug Education,* 37:64–70.

Jackson, Patrick G. (1987). "The Impact of Pretrial Preventive Detention." *Justice System Journal,* 12:305–334.

Jacobson, Jack M. (1977). "Procedural Due Process in Prison Disciplinary Hearings." *New England Journal on Prison Law,* 4:107–139.

Jamieson, Alison (1992). "Recent Narcotics and Mafia Research." *Studies in Conflict and Terrorism,* 15:39–51.

Jankowski, Louis (1991). *Probation and Parole 1990.* Washington, DC: Bureau of Justice Statistics.

Jeffries, Robert B. (1979). "Intent, Duress, and Necessity in Escape Cases." *Georgetown Law Journal,* 68:249–266.

Jenness, Valerie (1995). "Social Movement Growth, Domain Expansion, and Framing Processes: The Gay/Lesbian Movement and Violence Against Gays and Lesbians." *Social Problems,* 42:145–170.

Jensen, Magdeline et al. (1991). "The Sentencing Reform Act of 1984 and Sentencing Guidelines." *Federal Probation,* 55:4–57.

Johnson, Claire, Barbara Webster, and Edward Connors (1995). *Prosecuting Gangs: A National Assessment.* Washington, DC: U.S. National Institute of Justice.

Johnson, David R. (1981). *American Law Enforcement: A History.* St. Louis, MO: Forum.

Johnson, David R. (1995). *Illegal Tender: Counterfeiting and the Secret Service in Nineteenth-Century America.* Washington, DC: Smithsonian Institution Press.

Johnson, Edward E. (1983). "Psychological Tests Used in Assessing a Sample of Police and Firefighter Candidates." *Journal of Police Science and Administration,* 11:430–433.

Johnson, James B. and Philip E. Secret (1990). "Race and Juvenile Court Decision Making Revisited." *Criminal Justice Police Review,* 4:159–187.

Johnson, Kevin and Gary Fields (1995). "FBI Nabs 422 in Telemarketing Scams." *USA Today,* December 8, p. B1.

Johnson, Leonor-Boulin (1991). "Job Strain among Police Officers: Gender Comparison." *Police Studies,* 14:12–16.

Johnson, Leslie G. (1985). "Punishment in an Age of Scarcity: A Judicial Perspective." *Court Review,* 22:7–12.

Johnson, Sheri Lynn (1985). "Black Innocence and the White Jury." *Michigan Law Review,* 83:1611–1708.

Johnson, Tabatha R. (1993). *The Public and the Police in the City of Chicago.* Evanston, IL: Northwestern University, Center for Urban Affairs and Policy Research.

Johnson, Thomas A., Gordon E. Misner, and Lee P. Brown (1981). *The Police and Society: An Environment for Collaboration and Confrontation.* Englewood Cliffs, NJ: Prentice-Hall.

Johnson, Wesley W. and Mark Jones (1994). "The Increased Felonization of Probation and Its Impact on the Function of Probation: A Descriptive Look at County-Level Data from the 1980s and 1990s." *APPA Perspectives,* 18:42–46.

Johnson, Wesley W. et al. (1994). "Goals of Community-Based Corrections: An Analysis of State Legal Codes." *American Journal of Criminal Justice,* 18:79–93.

Johnston, Les (1992a). *The Rebirth of Private Policing.* New York: Routledge.

Johnston, Les (1992b). "Regulating Private Security." *International Journal of Sociology of Law,* 20:1–16.

Jones, Peter R. (1990). "Community Corrections in Kansas: Extending Community Based Corrections or Widening the Net?" *Journal of Research in Crime and Delinquency,* 27:79–101.

Jones, Susan Tilton (1992). "Evaluating Correctional Training: Is It Working?" *Corrections Compendium,* 17:1–6.

Joo, Hee John (1993). *Parole Release and Recidivism: Comparative Three-Year Survival Analysis of Four Successive Release Cohorts of Property Offenders in Texas.* Ann Arbor, MI: University Microfilms International.

Joo, Hee Jong, Sheldon Ekland-Olson, and William R. Kelly (1995). "Recidivism among Paroled Property Offenders Released During a Period of Prison Reform." *Criminology,* 33:389–410.

Josephson, Rose Lee and Martin Reiser (1990). "Officer Suicide in the Los Angeles Police Department: A Twelve-Year Follow-Up." *Journal of Police Science and Administration,* 17:227–229.

Jurik, Nancy C. (1985). "An Officer and a Lady: Organizational Barriers to Women Working as Correctional Officers in Men's Prisons." *Social Problems,* 32:375–388.

Jurow, George L. (1971). "New Data on the Effect of a 'Death-Qualified Jury' on the Guilt Determination Process." *Harvard Law Review,* 84:567–611.

Kadane, Joseph B. (1984). "After Hovey: A Note on Taking Account of the Automatic Death Penalty Jurors." *Law and Human Behavior* 8:115–120.

Kadane, Joseph B. and D. Kairys (1979). "Fair Numbers of Peremptory Challenges in Jury Trials." *Journal of the American Statistical Association,* 74:747–753.

Kadish, Sanford H. (1987). *Blame and Punishment: Essays in Criminal Law.* New York: Macmillan.

Kadish, Sanford H. (1994). "Supreme Court Review." *Journal of Criminal Law and Criminology,* 84:679–1175.

Kadish, Sanford H. (1995). *Blame and Punishment: Essays in the Criminal Law.* New York: Macmillan.

Kales, A.H. (1914). *Unpopular Government in the United States.* Chicago: University of Chicago Press.

Kalven, Jr. Harry and Hans Ziesel (1966). *The American Jury.* Boston: Little, Brown.

Kaplan, David A. and Bob Cohn (1991). "Palm Beach Lessons." *Newsweek,* December 23, pp. 30–31.

Kaplan, Howard B. (ed.) (1995). *Drugs, Crime and Other Deviant Adaptations: Longitudinal Studies.* New York: Plenum.

Kates, Don B. Jr. (1994). "Gun Control: Separating Reality from Symbolism." *Journal of Contemporary Law,* 20:352–379.

Katoh, Hisao (1994). "Prohibition of the Money Laundering as a Countermeasure against Organized Crime Groups (Yakuza or Boryokudan) in Japan." *Keio Law Review,* 7:21–41.

REFERENCES

Katz, Charles M. and Cassia C. Spohn (1995). "The Effect of Race and Gender on Bail Outcomes: A Test of an Interactive Model." *American Journal of Criminal Justice,* 19:161–184.

Kearney, William J. (1989). "Form Follows Function—And Function Follows Philosophy: An Architectural Response." *Juvenile and Family Court Journal,* 40:27–34.

Keating, J. Michael (1984). *Public Ends and Private Means: Accountability among Private Providers of Public Social Services.* Pawtucket, RI: Institute of Conflict Management.

Kelling, George L., Tony Pate, Duane Dieckman, and Charles E. Brown (1974). *The Kansas City Preventive Patrol Experiment: A Summary Report.* Washington, DC: Police Foundation.

Kelling, George L. and James Q. Wilson (1982). "Broken Windows: The Police and Neighborhood Safety." *Atlantic Monthly,* 249:29–38.

Kelly, Martin A. (1988). "Citizen Survival in Ancient Rome." *Police Studies,* 11:195–201.

Kennedy, Daniel B. (1984). "A Theory of Suicide While in Police Custody." *Journal of Police Science and Administration,* 12:191–200.

Kennedy, Daniel B. (1994). "Custodial Suicide." *American Jails,* 7:41–46.

Kennedy, Ludovic (1985). *The Airman and the Carpenter: The Lindbergh Kidnapping and the Framing of Richard Hauptmann.* New York: Viking Penguin.

Kenosha County Department of Social Services (1990). "Monitoring Juvenile Offenders: The Kenosha County, Wisconsin, Experience." *Journal of Offender Monitoring,* 3:1–7.

Kerce, Elyse W., Paul Magnusson, and Amy Rudolph (1994). *The Attitudes of Navy Corrections Staff Members: What They Think about Confinees and Their Jobs.* San Diego, CA: Navy Personnel Research and Development Center.

Kerle, Kenneth E. (1985). "The American Woman County Jail Officer." In *The Changing Roles of Women in the Criminal Justice System,* Imogene L. Moyer (ed.). Prospect Heights, IL: Waveland Press.

Kerle, Kenneth E. (1993). "Jails and Minorities." *American Jails,* 6:5.

Kerr, Norbert L. (1994). "The Effects of Pretrial Publicity on Jurors." *Judicature,* 78:120–127.

Kerr, Norbert L. and Robert J. MacCoun (1985). "The Effects of Jury Size and Polling Method on the Process and Product of Jury Deliberation." *Journal of Personality and Social Psychology,* 48:349–363.

Kerstetter, Wayne A. (1990). *Justice Pursued: The Legal and Moral Basis of Disposition in Sexual Assault Cases.* Chicago: American Bar Association.

Kerstetter, Wayne A. and Kenneth A. Rasinski (1994). "Opening a Window into Police Internal Affairs: Impact of Procedural Justice Reform on Third-Party Attitudes." *Social Justice Research,* 7:107–127.

Keve, Paul W. (1992). "The Costliest Punishment—A Corrections Administrator Contemplates the Death Penalty." *Federal Probation,* 56:11–15.

Key, Clarence Jr. (1991). *The Desirability and Feasibility of Changing Iowa's Sentencing Practices: Comparison Study of Five States and Their Sentencing Structures.* Des Moines, IA: Division of Criminal and Juvenile Justice Planning, Iowa Department of Human Rights.

Kindt, John Warren (1994). "Increased Crime and Legalized Gambling Operations: The Impact of the Socio-Economics of Business and Government." *Criminal Law Bulletin,* 30:538–555.

Kiser, George C. (1991). "Female Inmates and Their Families." *Federal Probation,* 55:56–63.

Klein-Saffran, Jody (1993). "Electronic Monitoring versus Halfway Houses: A Study of Federal Offenders." Ann Arbor, MI: University Microfilms International.

Klein-Saffran, Jody and Faith Lutze (1991). "The Effect of Shock Incarceration of Federal Offenders: Community Corrections and Post-Release Follow-Up." Unpublished paper presented at the annual meeting of the American Society of Criminology, San Francisco, CA (November).

Kleinig, John (ed.) (1989). "Ethics in Context: The Selling of Jury Deliberations." *Criminal Justice Ethics,* 8:26–34.

Klofas, John and Stan Stojkovic (eds.) (1995). *Crime and Justice in the Year 2010.* Belmont, CA: Wadsworth.

Knight, Barbara B. (1992). "Women in Prison as Litigants: Prospects for Post-Prison Futures." *Women and Criminal Justice,* 4:91–116.

Knight, Kevin, D. Dwayne Simpson, and Donald F. Dansereau (1994). "Knowledge Mapping: A Psychoeducational Tool in Drug Abuse Relapse Prevention Training." *Journal of Offender Rehabilitation,* 20:187–205.

Knowles, Lyle and Kenneth Hickman (1984). "Selecting a Jury of Peers: How Close Do We Get?" *Journal of Police Science and Administration,* 12:207–212.

Knox, George W., Brad Martin, and Edward D. Tromanhauser (1995). "Preliminary Results of the 1995 National Prosecutor's Survey." *Journal of Gang Research,* 2:59–71.

Koppel, Herbert (1984). *Sentencing Practices in 13 States.* Washington, DC: U.S. Department of Justice, Bureau of Justice Statistics.

Kornfeld, Alfred D. (1995). "Police Officer Candidate MMPI-2 Performance: Gender, Ethnic and Normative Factors." *Journal of Clinical Psychology,* 51:536–540.

Krakovec, Laura L. (1986). "Fourth Amendment: The Constitutionality of Warrantless Aerial Surveillance." *Journal of Criminal Law and Criminology,* 77:602–631.

Kratcoski, Peter C. (1994). *Correctional Counseling and Treatment.* 3d ed. Prospect Heights, IL: Waveland Press.

Kratcoski, Peter C. and Susan Babb (1990). "Adjustment of Older Inmates: An Analysis by Institutional Structure and Gender." *Journal of Contemporary Criminal Justice,* 6:264–281.

Krause, Melvyn B. and Edward P. Lazear (eds.) (1991). *Searching for Alternatives: Drug-Control Policy in the United States.* Stanford, CA: Hoover Institution Press.

Krause, Wesley and Marilyn D. McShane (1994). "A Deinstitutionalization Retrospective: Relabeling the Status Offender." *Journal of Crime and Justice,* 17:45–67.

Krisberg, Barry (1988). *The Juvenile Court: Reclaiming the Vi-*

sion. San Francisco: National Council on Crime and Delinquency.

Krisberg, Barry et al. (1985). *Planning Study for the Colorado Division of Youth Services.* San Francisco: National Council on Crime and Delinquency.

Krisberg, Barry et al. (1993). *Juveniles in State Custody: Prospects for Community-Based Care of Troubled Adolescents.* San Francisco: National Center for Crime and Delinquency.

Krueger, Robert F. et al. (1994). "Personality Traits Are Linked to Crime among Men and Women: Evidence from a Birth Cohort." *Journal of Abnormal Psychology,* 103:328–338.

Krug, Robert E. (1961). "An Analysis of the F Scale: Item Factor Analysis." *Journal of Social Psychology,* 53:288–291.

Kruttschnitt, Candace (1984). "Sex and Criminal Court Dispositions." *Journal of Research in Crime and Delinquency,* 21:213–232.

Kruttschnitt, Candace and Donald E. Green (1984). "The Sex-Sanctioning Issue: Is It History?" *American Sociological Review,* 49:541–551.

Kruttschnitt, Candace and Sharon Krmpotich (1990). "Aggressive Behavior among Female Inmates: An Exploratory Study." *Justice Quarterly,* 7:372–389.

Kunen, James S. (1983). *How Can You Defend Those People? The Making of a Criminal Lawyer.* New York: Random House.

Kunzman, E. Eugene (1995). "Preventing Suicide in Jails." *Corrections Today,* 57:90–94.

Kuykendall, Jack L. and David E. Burns (1983). "The Black Police Officer: An Historical Perspective." *Criminal Justice,* 19:41–45.

Kyle, Daniel G. (1995). *Corrections and Justice.* Baton Rouge, LA: Office of the Legislative Auditor.

Lacayo, Richard (1987). "Assault with a Deadly Virus." *Time,* July 20, p. 63.

LaFree, Gary D. (1985). "Official Reactions to Hispanic Defendants in the Southwest." *Journal of Research in Crime and Delinquency,* 22:213–237.

Lambuth, Lynn (1984). "An Employee Assistance Program That Works." *Police Chief,* 51:36–38.

Land, Kenneth C., Patricia L. McCall, and Karen F. Parker (1994). "Logistic Versus Hazards Regression Analyses in Evaluation Research: An Exposition and Application to the North Carolina Court Counselor's Intensive Protective Supervision Project." *Evaluation Review,* 18:411–437.

Lane, R. (1967). *Policing the City—Boston, 1822–1885.* Cambridge, MA: Harvard University Press.

Langan, Patrick A. (1994). "Between Prison and Probation: Intermediate Sanctions." *Science,* 262:791–793.

Langan, Patrick A. and Helen A. Graziadei (1995). *Felony Sentences in State Courts, 1992.* Washington, DC: U.S. Department of Justice.

Lanier, Charles S., Susan Philliber, and William W. Philliber (1994). "Prisoners with a Profession: Earning Graduate Degrees Behind Bars." *Journal of Criminal Justice Education,* 5:15–29.

Lanier, Mark M. and Cloud H. Miller III (1995). "Attitudes and Practices of Federal Probation Officers toward Pre-Plea/Trial Investigative Report Policy." *Crime and Delinquency,* 41:364–377.

Lanza-Kaduce, Lonn, Richard G. Greenleaf, and Michael Donahue (1995). "Trickle-Up Report Writing: The Impact of a Proarrest Policy for Domestic Disturbances." *Justice Quarterly,* 12:525–542.

LaPierre, Wayne R. (1994). *Guns, Crime and Freedom.* Washington, DC: Regency Publishing.

Larivee, John et al. (1990). "On the Outside: Corrections in the Community." *Corrections Today,* 52:84–106.

Latessa, Edward J., Lawrence F. Travis, and Harry E. Allen (1983). "Volunteers and Paraprofessionals in Parole: Current Practices." *Journal of Offender Counseling, Services, and Rehabilitation,* 8:91–106.

Latessa, Edward J. and Gennaro F. Vito (1988). "The Effects of Intensive Supervision on Shock Probationers." *Journal of Criminal Justice,* 16:319–330.

Laub, John H. and Bruce K. MacMurray (1987). "Increasing the Prosecutor's Role in Juvenile Court: Expectations and Realities." *Justice System Journal,* 12:196–209.

Lawrence, Richard A. (1984). "Professionals or Judicial Civil Servants? An Examination of the Probation Officer's Role." *Federal Probation,* 48:14–21.

Lawrence, Richard A. (1995). "Classrooms vs. Prison Cells: Funding Policies for Education and Corrections." *Journal of Crime and Justice,* 18:113–126.

LeBlanc, Marc, Gilles Cote, and Rolf Loeber (1991). "Temporal Paths in Delinquency: Stability, Regression, and Progression Analyzed with Panel Data from an Adolescent and a Delinquent Male Sample." *Canadian Journal of Criminology,* 33:23–44.

LeClair, Daniel P. (1990). *The Effect of Community Reintegration on Rates of Recidivism: A Statistical Overview of Data for the Years 1971 Through 1987.* Boston: Massachusetts Department of Corrections.

Lee, M. (1994). "Police Cautioning of Minors: In Whose Best Interests?" *Deviance et Societe,* 18:43–54.

Lee, W.L.M. (1901). *A History of Police in England.* London, UK: Methuen.

Leeke, William D. and Heidi Mohn (1986). "Violent Offenders: AIMS and Unit Management Maintain Control." *Corrections Today,* 48:22–24.

Leerhsen, Charles (1991). "'His Career Is Over.'" *Newsweek,* August 12, pp. 54–55.

Lefstein, Norman (1982). *Criminal Defense Services for the Poor: Methods and Programs for Providing Legal Representation and the Need for Adequate Financing.* Chicago: American Bar Association, Standing Committee on Legal Aid and Indigent Defendants.

Lehtinen, Marlene W. and Gerald W. Smith (1974). "The Relative Effectiveness of Public Defenders and Private Attorneys: A Comparison." *NLADA Briefcase,* 32:13–20.

Leidheiser, Stephen E. (1983). "Defense of Entrapment: The Confusion Continues." *Cumberland Law Review,* 13:374–395.

Lempert, R.O. (1975). "Uncovering Nondiscernible Differences: Empirical Research and the Jury-Size Cases." *Michigan Law Review,* 73:643–708.

Lester, David (1992). "Suicide in Police Officers: A Survey of Nations." *Police Studies,* 15:146–147.

Levinson, Marc R. (1983). "Should Licensing Commissions Put Police on Trial?" *Police,* 6:23–43.

Lewis, Dorothy Otnow et al. (1994). "A Clinical Follow-Up of Delinquent Males: Ignored Vulnerabilities, Unmet Needs, and the Perpetuation of Violence." *Journal of the American Academy of Child and Adolescent Psychiatry,* 34:518–528.

Libow, Julius (1993). "The Need for Standardization and Expansion of Nonadversary Proceedings in Juvenile Dependency Court with Special Emphasis on Mediation." *Juvenile and Family Court Journal,* 44:3–16.

Lieb, Roxanne, Lee Fish, and Todd Crosby (1994). *A Summary of State Trends in Juvenile Justice.* Olympia, WA: Washington State Institute for Public Policy, Evergreen State College.

Lieberg, Gregory J. (1996). "Computers Before and Now." *American Jails,* 9:23–26.

Lieberman, Jethro K. (ed.) (1984). *The Role of Courts in American Society.* St. Paul, MN: West Publishing Company.

Lieberman, Jethro K. and James F. Henry (1986). "Lessons from the Alternative Dispute Resolution Movement." *University of Chicago Law Review,* 53:424–439.

Lillis, Jamie (1994). "Prison Escapes and Violence Remain Down." *Corrections Compendium,* 19:1–8.

Lily, J. Robert (1985). "A Proposal for Evaluating Home Incarceration in Kenton County, Kentucky." Submitted to the Kentucky Department of Corrections.

Lilly, J. Robert (1992). "Review Essay: Selling Justice: Electronic Monitoring and the Security Industry." *Justice Quarterly,* 9:493–503.

Lilly, J. Robert, Richard A. Ball, and Jennifer Wright (1987). "Home Incarceration with Electronic Monitoring in Kenton County, Kentucky: An Evaluation." In *Intermediate Punishments: Intensive Supervision, Home Confinement, and Electronic Surveillance,* Belinda McCarthy (ed.). Monsey, NY: Criminal Justice Press.

Lindberg, Richard C. (1991). *To Serve and Collect: Chicago Politics and Police Corruption from the Lager Beer Riot to the Summergate Scandal.* Westport, CT: Greenwood Press.

Lindgren, Sue A. (1992). *Justice Expenditure and Employment, 1990.* Washington, DC: U.S. Department of Justice.

Lindner, Charles and Margaret R. Savarese (1984). "The Evolution of Probation: University Settlement and the Beginning of Statutory Probation in New York City." *Federal Probation,* 48:3–12.

Lindquist, Charles A. and John T. Whitehead (1986). "Correctional Officers as Parole Officers: An Examination of a Community Supervision Sanction." *Criminal Justice and Behavior,* 13:197–222.

Lippman, Matthew (1990). "The Necessity Defense and Political Protest." *Criminal Law Bulletin,* 26:317–356.

Lippold, Robert A. (1985). "Halfway Houses: Meeting Special Needs." *Corrections Today,* 47:46, 82, 112.

Little Hoover Commission (1990). *Runaway/Homeless Youths: California's Efforts to Recycle Society's Throwaways.* Washington, DC: Little Hoover Commission.

Litton, Gilbert and Linda Marye (1983). *An Evaluation of the Juvenile Diversion Program in the Orleans Parish District Attorney's Office.* New Orleans, LA: Mayor's Justice Coordinating Council, City of New Orleans.

Logan, Charles H. (1992). "Well-Kept: Comparing Quality of Confinement in Private and Public Prisons." *Journal of Criminal Law and Criminology,* 83:577–613.

Logan, Charles H. and Sharla P. Rausch (1985). "Why Deinstitutionalizing Status Offenders Is Pointless." *Crime and Delinquency,* 31:501–517.

Long, Lydia M. (1992). "A Study of Arrest of Older Offenders: Trends and Patterns." *Journal of Crime and Justice,* 15:157–175.

Long, Robert Emmet (ed.) (1993). *Banking Scandals: The S & L's and BCCI.* New York: H.W. Wilson.

Lopez, Antoinette Sedillo (ed.) (1995). *Latinos in the United States: History, Law and Perspective.* New York: Garland.

Lorr, Maurice and Stephen Strack (1994). "Personality Profiles of Police Candidates." *Journal of Clinical Psychology,* 50:200–207.

Lovell, David G. (1985). *Sentencing Reform and the Treatment of Offenders.* Olympia, WA: Washington Council on Crime and Delinquency.

Ludemann, Christian (1994). "Land Without Plea Bargaining? How the Germans Do It: Results of an Empirical Study." *EuroCriminology,* 7:119–140.

Lumb, Richard C. (1995). "Policing Culturally Diverse Groups: Continuing Professional Development Programs for Police." *Police Studies,* 18:23–44.

Lund, Dennis Wayne (1988). "Police Directed Preventive Patrol: Its Effect upon Personnel Motivation." Unpublished doctoral dissertation, Michigan State University. Ann Arbor, MI: University Microfilms International.

Lundman, Richard J. (1979). "Origins of Police Misconduct." In *Critical Issues in Criminal Justice,* R.G. Iacovetta and Dae H. Chang (eds.). Durham, NC: Carolina Academic Press.

Lurigio, Arthur J. and Dennis P. Rosenbaum (eds.) (1994). "Community Policing." *Crime and Delinquency,* 49:299–468.

Maahs, Jeffrey R. and Rolando V. del Carmen (1996). "Curtailing Frivolous Section 1983 Inmate Litigation: Laws, Practices and Proposals." *Federal Probation,* 59:53–61.

MacCornick, Austin (1931). *The Education of Adult Prisoners.* New York: Heath.

MacCoun, Robert J. and Tom R. Tyler (1988). "The Basis of Citizens' Perceptions of the Criminal Jury: Procedural Fairness, Accuracy, and Efficiency." *Law and Human Behavior,* 12:333–352.

MacCoun, Robert J., James P. Kahan, and James Gillespie (1993). "A Content Analysis of the Drug Legalization Debate." *Journal of Drug Issues,* 23:615–629.

Mack, Dennis E. (1992). "High Impact Incarceration Program: Rikers Boot Camp." *American Jails,* 6:63–65.

MacKenzie, Doris Layton (1990). "Boot Camp Prisons: Components, Evaluations, and Empirical Issues." *Federal Probation*, 54:44–52.

MacKenzie, Doris Layton and James W. Shaw (1993). "The Impact of Shock Incarceration on Technical Violations and New Criminal Activities." *Justice Quarterly*, 10:463–487.

MacKenzie, Doris Layton, James W. Shaw, and Voncile B. Gowdy (1993). *An Evaluation of Shock Incarceration in Louisiana*. Washington, DC: U.S. Department of Justice, Office of Justice Programs.

MacKenzie, Doris Layton and Claire C. Souryal (1991). "Boot Camps." *Corrections Today*, 53:90–115.

MacKenzie, Doris Layton and Claire Souryal (1994). *Multisite Evaluation of Shock Incarceration—A Final Summary*. Washington, DC: U.S. National Institute of Justice.

Macolini, Ruthann M. (1995). "Elder Abuse Policy: Considerations in Research and Legislation." *Behavioral Sciences and the Law*, 13:349–363.

Maguire, Kathleen and Ann L. Pastore (1995). *Bureau of Justice Statistics Sourcebook of Criminal Justice Statistics—1994*. Albany, NY: The Hindelang Criminal Justice Research Center, State University of New York at Albany.

Maguire, Kathleen and Ann Pastore (1996). *Sourcebook of Criminal Justice Statistics 1995*. Albany, NY: Hindelang Criminal Justice Research Center.

Maguire, Kathleen, Ann L. Pastore, and Timothy J. Flanagan (1993). *Bureau of Justice Statistics Sourcebook of Criminal Justice Statistics—1992*. Albany, NY: Hindelang Criminal Justice Research Center.

Mahan, Su (1989). "The Needs and Experiences of Women in Sexually Integrated Prisons." *American Journal of Criminal Justice*, 13:228–239.

Mahoney, Barry (1987). "Attacking Problems of Delay in Urban Trial Courts." *State Court Journal*, 11:4–10.

Malcolm, Joyce Lee (1994). *To Keep and Bear Arms: The Origins of an Anglo-American Right*. Cambridge, MA: Harvard University Press.

Manning, Peter K. (1977). *Police Work*. Cambridge, MA: MIT Press.

Ma-Omar, Jenhaw (1990). "Dimensions and Dynamics of Police Discretion: A Social Power Perspective and Discriminant Analysis." Unpublished doctoral dissertation, University of Minnesota. Ann Arbor, MI: University Microfilms International.

Marcus, Paul (1986). "The Entrapment Defense and the Procedural Issues: Burden of Proof, Questions of Law and Fact, Inconsistent Defenses." *Criminal Law Bulletin*, 22:197–243.

Marenin, Otwin (1989). "The Utility of Community Needs Surveys in Community Policing." *Police Studies*, 12:73–81.

Marenin, Otwin (1995). "The State of Plea Bargaining in Alaska." *Journal of Crime and Justice*, 18:167–197.

Marlette, Marjorie (1988). "Furloughs for Lifers Successful." *Corrections Compendium*, 13:11–20.

Marlette, Marjorie (1990). "Furloughs Tightened—Success Rates High." *Corrections Compendium*, 15:6–21.

Marley, C.W. (1973). "Furlough Programs and Conjugal Visiting in Adult Correctional Institutions." *Federal Probation*, 37:19–25.

Marquart, James W. (1986). "Doing Research in Prison: The Strengths and Weaknesses of Full Participation as a Guard." *Justice Quarterly*, 3:15–32.

Marquart, James W. and Julian B. Roebuck (1986). "Prison Guards and Snitches." In *Dilemmas of Punishment: Readings in Contemporary Corrections*, K.C. Haas and G.P. Alpert (eds.). Prospect Heights, IL: Waveland Press.

Marsh, Harry Lynn (1988). "Crime and the Press: Does Newspaper Crime Coverage Support Myths about Crime and Law Enforcement?" Unpublished doctoral dissertation, Sam Houston State University, Huntsville, TX.

Marshall, Chris E. and Vincent J. Webb (1994). "A Portrait of Crime Victims Who Fight Back." *Journal of Interpersonal Violence*, 9:45–74.

Marshall, Tony F. et al. (1985). *Alternatives to Criminal Courts: The Potential for Non-Judicial Dispute Settlement*. Brookfield, VT: Gower.

Martin, Dannie M. and Peter Y. Sussman (1993). *Committing Journalism: The Prison Writings of Red Hog*. New York: W.W. Norton.

Martin, Susan E. (1994). "'Outside Within' the Station House: The Impact of Race and Gender on Black Women Police." *Social Problems*, 41:383–400.

Martin, Susan E. (1995). "A Cross-Burning Is Not Just an Arson: Police Social Construction of Hate Crimes in Baltimore County." *Criminology*, 33:303–326.

Martinez, Pablo and Antonio Fabelo (1985). *Texas Correctional System: Growth and Policy Alternatives*. Austin, TX: Criminal Justice Policy Council.

Martinson, Robert (1974). "What Works? Questions and Answers about Prison Reform." *The Public Interest*, 35:22–54.

Marvell, Thomas B. (1994). "Is Further Prison Expansion Worth the Costs?" *Federal Probation*, 58:59–62.

Marvell, Thomas B. (1995). "Sentencing Guidelines and Prison Population Growth." *Journal of Criminal Law and Criminology*, 85:696–709.

Marvell, Thomas B. (1996). "Is Further Prison Expansion Worth the Costs?" *Corrections Compendium*, 21:1–5.

Marvell, Thomas B. and Carlisle E. Moody (1995). "The Impact of Enhanced Prison Terms for Felonies Committed with Guns." *Criminology*, 33:247–281.

Marx, Gary T. and Dane Archer (1971). "Citizen Involvement in the Law Enforcement Process." *American Behavioral Scientist*, 15:52–72.

Maryland Committee on Prison Overcrowding (1984). *Report*. Towson, MD: Maryland Criminal Justice Coordinating Council, Committee on Prison Overcrowding.

Maryland Criminal Justice Coordinating Council (1984). *Report*. Towson, MD: Maryland Criminal Justice Coordinating Council, Committee on Prison Overcrowding.

Maryland Department of Budget and Fiscal Planning (1986). *Review of the Maryland Parole Commission*. Annapolis, MD: Division of Management Analysis and Audits.

Mascolo, Edward G. (1983). "Emergency Arrest in the Home." *Prosecutor,* 17:30–35.

Maslach, Christina and Susan E. Jackson (1979). "Burned Out Cops and Their Families." *Psychology Today,* 12:59.

Mason, Mary Ann (1991). "A Judicial Dilemma: Expert Witness Testimony in Child Sex Abuse Cases." *Journal of Psychiatry and Law,* 19:185–219.

Massachusetts Halfway Houses, Inc. (1980). *MHHI (Massachusetts Halfway Houses Incorporated) Annual Report, 1980.* Boston: Massachusetts Halfway Houses, Inc.

Masters, Ruth E. (1994). *Counseling Criminal Justice Offenders.* Thousand Oaks, CA: Sage.

Mastrofski, Stephen Davis (1981a). "Policing the Beat: The Impact of Organizational Scale on Patrol Officer Behavior in Urban Residential Neighborhoods." *Journal of Criminal Justice,* 9:343–358.

Mastrofski, Stephen Davis (1981b). "Reforming Police: The Impact of Patrol Assignment Patterns on Officer Behavior in Urban residential Neighborhoods." Unpublished doctoral dissertation, University of North Carolina, Chapel Hill. Ann Arbor, MI: University Microfilms International.

Mastrofski, Stephen D. and R. Richard Ritti (1996). "Policing Training and the Effects of Organization on Drunk Driving Enforcement." *Justice Quarterly,* 13:291–320.

Mather, Lynn W. (1979). *Plea Bargaining or Trial? The Process of Criminal Case Disposition.* Lexington, MA: Lexington.

Matthews, Roger and Jock Young (eds.) (1992). *Issues in Realist Criminology.* Newbury Park, CA: Sage.

Matthews, Timothy, Harry N. Boone, Jr., and Vernon Fogg (1994). "Alternative Outcome Measures: The Concept." *APPA Perspectives,* 18:10–20.

Mauer, Marc (1985). *The Lessons of Marion: The Failure of a Maximum Security Prison: A History and Analysis, with Voices of Prisoners.* Philadelphia, PA: American Friends Services Committee.

Mauer, Marc and Tracy Huling (1995). *Young Black Americans and the Criminal Justice System: Five Years Later.* Washington, DC: Sentencing Project.

Mauer, Marc and Malcolm C. Young (1992). *Feasibility of the Expansion of Alternatives to Incarceration for Essex County, New Jersey.* Washington, DC: The Sentencing Project.

Mauro, Tony (1994). "For Senior Justice Blackmun, A Long and Agonizing Decision." *USA Today,* Feb. 23: 8A.

Maxwell, David A. (1993). *Private Security Law (Case Studies).* Stoneham, MA: Butterworth-Neinemann.

Maynard, D.W. (1982). "Defendant Attributes in Plea Bargaining: Notes on the Modeling of Sentencing Decisions." *Social Problems,* 29:347–360.

Mays, G. Larry (ed.) (1992). *Setting the Jail Research Agenda for the 1990s: Proceedings from a Special Meeting.* Washington, DC: National Institute of Corrections.

Mays, G. Larry and Tara Gray (eds.) (1996). *Privatization and Provision of Correctional Services: Context and Consequences.* Cincinnati, OH: Anderson Publishing Company.

Mays, G. Larry and Marilyn Houghtalin (1992). "Trying Juveniles as Adults: A Note on New Mexico's Recent Experience." *Justice System Journal,* 15:814–823.

Mays, G. Larry and William A. Taggert (1985). "The Impact of Litigation on Changing New Mexico Prison Conditions." *Prison Journal,* 65:38–53.

McAlary, Mike (1994). *Good Cop, Bad Cop: Detective Joe Trimboli's Heroic Pursuit of NYPD Officer Michael Dowd.* New York: Pocket Books.

McCaghy, Charles H. and Stephen A. Cernkovich (1991). "Polling the Public on Prostitution." *Justice Quarterly,* 8:107–120.

McCarthy, Belinda R. (1987a). *Intermediate Punishments: intensive Supervision, Home Confinement, and Electronic Surveillance.* Monsey, NY: Willow Tree Press.

McCarthy, Belinda R. (1987b). "Preventive Detention and Pretrial Custody in the Juvenile Court." *Journal of Criminal Justice,* 15:185–198.

McCarthy, Belinda and Robert Langworthy (eds.) (1988). *Older Offenders: Perspectives in Criminology and Criminal Justice.* New York: Praeger.

McCarthy, Belinda R. and Bernard J. McCarthy (1984). *Community-Based Corrections.* Monterey, CA: Brooks/Cole Publishing Company.

McCarthy, Belinda R. and Bernard J. McCarthy (1991). *Community-Based Corrections.* 2d ed. Monterey, CA: Brooks/Cole.

McConahay, J., C. Mullin, and J. Frederick (1977). "The Uses of Social Science in Trials with Political and Racial Overtones: The Trial of Joan Little." *Law and Contemporary Problems,* 41:205–229.

McConville, Mike and Chester Mirsky (1995). "Guilty Plea Courts: A Social Disciplinary Model of Criminal Justice." *Social Problems,* 42:216–234.

McCord, David M. (1995). "Toward a Typology of Wilderness-Based Residential Treatment Program Participants." *Residential Treatment for Children and Youth,* 12:51–60.

McCorkle, Richard C., Terance D. Miethe, and Kriss A. Drass (1995). "The Roots of Prison Violence: A Test of the Deprivation, Management, and 'Not-So-Total' Institution Models." *Crime and Delinquency,* 41:317–331.

McCormack, William U. (1994). "Supreme Court Cases, 1993–1994 Term." *FBI Law Enforcement Bulletin,* 63:27–32.

McCoy, Alfred W. and Alan A. Block (1992). *War on Drugs: Studies in the Failure of U.S. Narcotics Policy.* Boulder, CO: Westview Press.

McDonald, Douglas C. and Kenneth E. Carlson (1992). *Federal Sentencing in Transition: 1986–1990.* Washington, DC: Department of Justice, Bureau of Justice Statistics.

McDonald, Douglas C. and Kenneth E. Carlson (1993). *Sentencing in the Federal Courts: Does Race Matter? The Transition to Sentencing Guidelines, 1986–90.* Washington, DC: U.S. Bureau of Justice Statistics.

McDonald, William F. (1985). *Plea Bargaining: Critical Issues and Common Practices.* Washington, DC: U.S. National Institute of Justice by the Institute of Criminal Law and Procedure, Georgetown University.

McDowall, David and Colin Loftin (1992). "Comparing the UCR and NCS Over Time." *Criminology,* 30:125–132.

McGarrell, Edmund F. and Michael J. Sabath (1994). "Stakeholder Conflict in an Alternative Sentencing Program: Implications for Evaluation and Implementation." *Evaluation and Program Planning,* 17:179–186.

McGee, Richard A., George Warner, and Nora Harlow (1985). *The Special Management Inmate.* Washington, DC: U.S. National Institute of Justice.

McGough, Lucy S. (1994). *Fragile Voices in the American Legal System.* New Haven, CT: Yale University Press.

McGriff, M. David (1985). *A Test of the Incapacitation Theory on Burglars.* Ann Arbor, MI: University Microfilms International.

McGuire, James and Philip Priestley (1985). *Offending Behavior: Skills and Stratagems for Going Straight.* New York: St. Martin's.

McLeod, Donald K. (1979). "The Police Training Dilemma." In *Critical Issues in Criminal Justice,* R.G. Iacovetta and Dae H. Chang (eds.). Durham, NC: Carolina Academic Press.

McLeod, Maureen (1986). "Victim Participation at Sentencing." *Criminal Law Bulletin,* 22:501–517.

McMahon, Mickey (1995). "False Confessions and Police Deception: The Interrogation, Incarceration and Release of an Innocent Veteran." *American Journal of Forensic Psychology,* 13:5–43.

McManus, Patrick D. and Lynn Zeller Barclay (1994). *Community Corrections Act: Technical Assistance Manual.* College Park, MD: American Correctional Association.

McWhirter, Darien A. (1994). *Search, Seizure and Privacy.* Phoenix, AZ: Oryx Press.

Meachum, Larry R. (1986). "House Arrest: The Oklahoma Experience." *Corrections Today,* 48:102–110.

Meador, Daniel J. (1983). "An Appellate Court Dilemma and a Solution Through Subject Matter Organization." *University of Michigan Journal of Law Reform,* 16:471–492.

Mealia, Robert Michael (1990). "Background Factors and Police Performance." Unpublished doctoral dissertation, State University of New York at Albany. Ann Arbor, MI: Univerity Microfilms International.

Meeker, James W. "Criminal Appeals Over the Last 100 Years: Are the Odds of Winning Increasing?" *Criminology,* 22:551–571.

Meesig, Robert and Frank Horvath (1995). "A National Survey of Practices, Policies and Evaluative Comments on the Use of Pre-Employment Polygraph Screening in Police Agencies in the U.S." *Polygraph,* 24:57–136.

Megargee, Edwin I. and Joyce L. Carbonell (1985). "Predicting Prison Adjustment with MMPI Correctional Scales." *Journal of Consulting and Clinical Psychology,* 53:874–883.

Meisenhelder, Thomas (1985). "An Essay on Time and the Phenomenology of Imprisonment." *Deviant Behavior,* 6:39–56.

Melroy, J. Reid (1992). "Voluntary Intoxication and the Insanity Defense." *Journal of Psychiatry and Law,* 20:439–457.

Menard, Scott et al. (1992). "Residual Gains, Reliability and the *UCR-NCS* Relationship: A Comment on Blumstein, Cohen and Rosenfeld (1991)." *Criminology,* 30:105–132.

Menzies, Robert, Christopher Webster, and Diana Sepejak (1985). "Hitting the Forensic Sound Barrier: Predictions of Dangerousness in a Pre-Trial Psychiatric Clinic." In *Dangerousness Probability and Prediction,* Robert Menzies, Christopher Webster, and Diana Sepejak (eds.). Cambridge, UK: Cambridge University Press.

Meredith, Colin and Chantal Paquette (1992). "Crime Prevention in High-Rise Rental Apartments: Findings of a Demonstration Project." *Security Journal,* 3:161–188.

Merlo, Alida V. and Peter J. Benekos (1992). "Adapting Conservative Correctional Policies to the Economic Realities of the 1990s." *Criminal Justice Policy Review,* 6:1–16.

Mertens, William J. (1984). "The Fourth Amendment and the Control of Police Discretion." *Journal of Law Reform,* 17:551–625.

Metchik, Eric (1992). "Judicial Views of Parole Decision Processes: A Social Science Perspective." *Journal of Offender Rehabilitation,* 18:135–157.

Michigan Council on Crime and Delinquency (1993). *Trends in the Michigan Criminal Justice System: From Crisis to Chaos.* Lansing, MI: Michigan Council on Crime and Delinquency.

Middendorf, Kathi and James Luginbuhl (1995). "The Value of a Nondirective *Voir Dire* Style in Jury Selection." *Criminal Justice and Behavior,* 22:129–151.

Midwinter, Eric (1991). *The Old Order: Crime and Older People.* London, UK: Centre for Policy on Ageing.

Milin, Robert et al. (1991). "Psychopathology among Substance Abusing Juvenile Offenders." *Journal of the American Academy of Child and Adolescent Psychiatry,* 30:569–574.

Miller, D. (1985). "The Harassment of Forensic Psychiatrists Outside of Court." *Bulletin of the American Academy of Psychiatry and the Law,* 13:337–344.

Miller, E. Eugene (1977). "Halfway House: Correctional Decompression of the Offender." In *Corrections in the Community: Success Models in Correctional Reform,* E. Eugene Miller and M. Robert Montilla (eds.). Reston, VA: Reston Publishing Company.

Miller, E. Eugene and M. Robert Montilla (eds.) (1977). *Corrections in the Community: Success Models in Correctional Reform.* Reston, VA: Reston Publishing Company.

Miller, Edward (1990). "Executing Minors and the Mentally Retarded: The Retribution and Deterrence Rationales." *Rutgers Law Review,* 43:15–52.

Miller, Gilbert B. Jr. (1983). "Inmate Grievance Procedures Certified." *Corrections Today,* 45:76–77.

Miller, Herbert S., James A. Cramer, and William F. McDonald (1979). *Plea Bargaining in the United States: Phase I Report.* Washington, DC: U.S. Government Printing Office.

Miller, Jerome G. (1986). "Sentencing: What Lies Between Sentiment and Ignorance?" *Justice Quarterly,* 3:231–239.

Miller, Jerome G. (1991). *Last One over the Wall: The Massachusetts Experiment in Closing Reform Schools.* Columbus, OH: Ohio State University Press.

Miller, J. Mitchell and Lance H. Selva (1994). "Drug Enforcement's Double-Edged Sword: An Assessment of Asset Forfeiture Programs." *Justice Quarterly,* 11:313–325.

Miller, Larry S. (1985). "Jury Reform: An Analysis of Juror Perceptions of the Criminal Court System." *Criminal Justice Review,* 10:11–16.

Miller, Marc and Martin Guggenheim (1990). "Pretrial Detention and Punishment." *Minnesota Law Review,* 75:335–426.

Miller, Wilbur R. (1985). "Cops and Bobbies in the Mid-Nineteenth Century." In *Policing Society: An Occupational View,* W. Clinton Terry (ed.). New York: Wiley.

Milling, L. (1978). *Home Furlough Functions and Characteristics.* Hartford, CT: Connecticut Department of Corrections.

Milner, Joel S. (1992). "Sexual Child Abuse." *Criminal Justice and Behavior,* 19:1–792.

Milner, Joel S. and Kevin R. Robertson (1990). "Comparison of Physical Child Abusers, Intrafamilial Sexual Child Abusers, and Child Neglecters." *Journal of Interpersonal Violence,* 5:37–48.

Miner, Roger J. et al. (1987). "Symposium on Judicial Administration Research." *Justice System Journal,* 12:1–174.

Minnesota Corrections Crowding Task Force (1993). *Corrections Crowding in Minnesota.* St. Paul, MN: Minnesota Corrections Crowding Task Force.

Minnesota Probation Standards Task Force (1993). *Minnesota Probation: A System in Crisis.* St. Paul, MN: Minnesota Probation Standards Task Force.

Minnesota Program Evaluation Division (1994). *Sex Offender Treatment Programs.* St. Paul, MN: Minnesota Program Evaluation Division Office of the Legislative Audit.

Missouri Juvenile Justice Advisory Group (1993). *The Serious and Violent Juvenile Offender in Missouri 1993.* Jefferson City, MO: Missouri Department of Public Safety.

Mitchell, Chet (1990). "Intoxication and Criminal Responsibility." *International Journal of Law and Psychiatry,* 13:1–161.

Mitchell, John J. and Sharon A. Williams (1986). "SOS: Reducing Juvenile Recidivism." *Corrections Today,* 48:70–71.

Monahan, John (1984). "The Prediction of Violent Behavior: Toward a Second Generation of Theory and Policy." *American Journal of Psychiatry,* 141:10–15.

Moneymaker, James M. and W. Richard Janikowski (1990). "The Diminishing Scope of the Exclusionary Rule." *Criminal Justice Policy Review,* 4:105–114.

Montgomery, Imogene M. and Patricia McFall Torbet (1994). *What Works: Promising Interventions in Juvenile Justice— Program Report.* Washington, DC: U.S. Office of Juvenile Justice and Delinquency Prevention.

Montgomery, Reid H. Jr. (1984). *American Prison Riots, 1971–1983.* Columbia, SC: University of South Carolina Press.

Moore, Richter H. Jr. (1992). "Twenty-First Century Criminal Organizations and Their Members." Unpublished paper presented at the annual meeting of the American Society of Criminology. New Orleans, LA (November).

Morash, Merry and Robin N. Haarr (1995). "Gender, Workplace Problems, and Stress in Policing." *Justice Quarterly,* 12:113–140.

More, Harry W. (1992). *Special Topics in Policing.* Cincinnati, OH: Anderson Publishing Company.

Morley, Harvey N. and Robert S. Fong (1995). "Can We All Get Along? A Study of Why Strained Relations Continue to Exist Between Sworn Law Enforcement and Private Security." *Security Journal,* 6:85–92.

Morrill, S. (1984). "Tampa Likes Sector Patrolling." *Law and Order,* 32:37–40.

Morris, Stanley E. (1985). "Apprehending the Fugitive: U.S. Marshals Strike Back." *Police Chief,* 52:34–37.

Morton, Joann B. (ed.) (1991). *Change, Challenge and Choices: Women's Role in Modern Corrections.* Laurel, MD: American Correctional Association.

Motiuk, Laurence L., James Bonta, and Don A. Andrews (1986). "Classification in Correctional Halfway Houses: The Relative and Incremental Predictive Criterion Validities of the Megargee-MMPI and LSI Systems." *Criminal Justice and Behavior,* 13:33–46.

Mulcahy, Aogan (1994). "The Justification of 'Justice': Legal Practioners' Accounts of Negotiated Case Settlements in Magistrates' Courts." *British Journal of Criminology,* 34:411–430.

Mullen, Joan (1982). "Corrections and the Private Sector." *Privatization Review,* 1:10–19.

Mullen, Joan (1986). *Corrections and the Private Sector.* Washington, DC: U.S. Department of Justice, National Institute of Justice.

Munro, Fiona M. (1995). "Social Skills Differences in Aggressive and Non-Aggressive Male Young Offenders Within an Unfamiliar Social Situation." *Medicine Science and Law,* 35:245–248.

Muth, William R. and Thom Gehring (1986). "The Correctional Education/Prison Reform Link: 1913–1940 and Conclusion." *Journal of Correctional Education,* 37:14–17.

Myers, Laura B. and Sue Titus Reid (1995). "The Importance of County Context in the Measurement of Sentence Disparity: The Search for Routinization." *Journal of Criminal Justice,* 23:223–241.

Nagel, Ilene H. (1990). "Supreme Court Review." *Journal of Criminal Law and Criminology,* 80:883–1280.

Napper, G. (1986). "Partnerships Against Crime: Sharing Problems and Power." *Police Chief,* 53:45–46.

Natalini, Robert S. (1985). "Preventive Detention and Presuming Dangerousness under the Bail Reform Act of 1984." *University of Pennsylvania Law Review,* 134:225–250.

Nathan, Winifred (1984). "Whose Rights Are They Anyway? The Supreme Court and the Rights of Juveniles." *Children and Youth Services Review,* 6:329–344.

National Advisory Commission on Criminal Justice Standards and Goals (1973). *Report of the National Advisory Commission on Criminal Justice Standards and Goals.* Washington, DC: U.S. Government Printing Office.

National Association for the Care and Resettlement of Offenders (1993). *Opening the Doors: Women Leaving Prison.* London, UK: NACRO's National Policy Committee on Resettlement.

National Center for Missing and Exploited Children (1992). *Female Juvenile Prostitution: Problem and Response.* Washington, DC: National Center for Missing and Exploited Children.

National Center for Missing and Exploited Children (1994). *A Report Card to the Nation: Missing and Exploited Children, 1984–1994.* Arlington, VA: National Center for Missing and Exploited Children.

National Center for State Courts (1989). *Understanding Reversible Error in Criminal Appeals: Final Report.* Williamsburg, VA: National Center for State Courts.

National Center for State Courts (1990). *Bail Policy for Criminal Defendants Before, During and After Trial in Pennsylvania.* Andover, MA: National Center for State Courts, Northeastern Regional Office.

National Center for State Courts (1995). *State Court Caseload Statistics, 1993.* Williamsburg, VA: National Center for State Courts.

National Center for State Courts Information Service (1992). *Trends in State Courts.* Williamsburg, VA: National Center for State Courts Information Service.

National Employment Listing Service (1982). *The Police Employment Guide—1982 Edition.* Huntsville, TX: Criminal Justice Center, Sam Houston State University.

National Institute of Justice (1986). *Felony Court Case-Processing Time.* Washington, DC: U.S. Department of Justice.

National Institute of Justice (1991). *Private Security: Patterns and Trends.* Washington, DC: National Institute of Justice.

National Office for Social Responsibility (1987). *Reparative Work, Phase II: A Feasibility Study of an Alternative Punishment.* Alexandria, VA: National Office for Social Responsibility.

Nelson, E.K., Robert Cushman, and Nora Harlow (1980). *Program Models: Unification of Community Corrections.* Washington, DC: U.S. Government Printing Office.

Nelson, James F. (1994). *The Impact of Restrictions on Post-Indictment Plea Bargaining in Bronx County: A Comparative Analysis of Historical Practice and Initial Impact.* Albany, NY: New York State Division of Criminal Justice Services.

Nelson, W. Raymond and Russell M. Davis (1995). "Podular Direct Supervision: The First Twenty Years." *American Jails,* 9:11–22.

Nemeth, Charles P. (1992). *Private Security and the Investigative Process.* Cincinnati, OH: Anderson Publishing Company.

Nesbitt, Charlotte A. (1992). "The Female Offender: Overview of Facility Planning and Design Issues and Considerations." *Corrections Compendium,* 17:1–7.

Neubauer, David W. (1979). *America's Courts and Criminal Justice.* North Scituate, MA: Duxbury Press.

Neufeldt, David E. (1983). "Capturing Police Performance Policies." Unpublished doctoral dissertation, University of Arkansas. Ann Arbor, MI: University Microfilms International.

Nevares, Dora et al. (1990). *Delinquency in Puerto Rico: The 1970 Birth Cohort Study.* Westport, CT: Greenwood Press.

New Jersey Commission of Investigation (1994). *Money Laundering.* Trenton, NJ: New Jersey Commission of Investigation.

New York City Criminal Justice Agency (1992). *An Evaluation of the Impact of New York State's Felony Drug Statute.* New York: New York City Criminal Justice Agency.

New York Civil Liberties Union (1990). *Police Abuse: The Need for Civilian Investigation and Oversight.* New York: New York Civil Liberties Union.

New York Commission to Investigate Allegations of Police Corruption (1994). *Commission Report.* New York: New York Commission to Investigate Allegations of Police Corruption.

New York State (1984). *The Community Dispute Resolution Centers Program: A Progress Report.* New York: New York State Unified Court System.

New York State Department of Correctional Services (1989). *Follow-Up Study of First Six Platoons of Shock Graduates.* Albany, NY: New York State Department of Correctional Services, Division of Program Planning.

New York State Department of Correctional Services (1990). *The Second Annual Report to the Legislature: Shock Incarceration in New York.* Albany, NY: New York State Department of Correctional Services, Division of Parole.

New York State Department of Correctional Services (1991). *The Third Annual Report to the Legislature: Shock Incarceration in New York.* Albany, NY: New York State Department of Corrections, Division of Program Planning.

New York State Department of Correctional Services (1993). *Absconders and Parolees from Work Release: 1988–1992.* Albany, NY: New York State Department of Correctional Services.

New York State Division of Criminal Justice Services (1982). *Capital Punishment: A Review of the Issues.* Albany, NY: New York State Division of Criminal Justice Services.

Nicely, Michael C. (1994). "Good Neighbors: The U.S. Border Patrol's Community Resource Development Program." *FBI Law Enforcement Bulletin,* 64:8–11.

Nidorf, Barry J. (1995). "Recidivism: Let's Get Rid of It." *APPA Perspectives,* 19:6–10.

Nietzel, Michael T. (ed.) (1993). "Psychology and Law Enforcement." *Law and Human Behavior,* 17:151–200.

Nikitorov, Alexander S. (1993). "Organized Crime in the West and in the Former USSR: An Attempted Comparison." *International Journal of Offender Therapy and Comparative Criminology,* 37:5–15.

Niskanen, William A. (1994). *Crime, Police and Root Causes.* Washington, DC: Cato Institute.

Norland, Stephen and Priscilla J. Mann (1984). "Being Troublesome: Women on Probation." *Criminal Justice and Behavior,* 11:115–135.

Northern Kentucky Law Review (1982). "Selecting Judges in the States: A Brief History and Analysis." *Northern Kentucky Law Review,* 72:459–473.

"Noteworthy." (1991). *Corrections Compendium,* 16 (September): 14.

O'Brien, Barbara (1986). *Stress: Its Impact on the Recruitment and Retention of Policewomen.* Washington, DC: U.S. Government Printing Office.

Oettmeier, Timothy N. and W.H. Bieck (1989). *Integrating Investigative Operations Through Neighborhood Oriented Policing.* Houston, TX: Houston Police Department.

Oettmeier, Timothy N. and Mary Ann Wycoff (1994). "Police Performance in the Nineties: Practitioner Perspectives." *American Journal of Police,* 13:21–49.

Ogletree, Charles J. (1994). "Just Say No! A Proposal to Eliminate Racially Discriminatory Uses of Peremptory Challenges." *American Criminal Law Review,* 31:1099–1151.

Ohlin, Lloyd E. and Frank J. Remington (1993). *Discretion in Criminal Justice: The Tension Between Individualization and Uniformity.* Albany, NY: State University of New York Press.

O'Leary, Dennis (1994). "Reflection on Police Privatization." *FBI Law Enforcement Bulletin,* 63:21–26.

Olin, James W. (1995). "Local Inmate Work Programs." *American Jails,* 9:67–72.

Olivero, J. Michael and James B. Roberts (1990). "The United States Federal Penitentiary at Marion, Illinois: Alcatraz Revisited." *New England Journal on Criminal and Civil Confinement,* 16:21–51.

Orchowsky, Stan, Nancy Merritt, and Katharine Browning (1994). *Evaluation of the Virginia Department of Corrections' Intensive Supervision Program—Executive Summary.* Richmond, VA: Virginia Department of Criminal Justice Services.

Orsagh, Thomas and Mary Ellen Marsden (1985). "What Works When: Rational-Choice Theory and Offender Rehabilitation." *Journal of Criminal Justice,* 13:269–277.

Orsagh, Thomas and Mary Ellen Marsden (1987). "Inmates + Appropriate Programs = Effective Rehabilitation." *Corrections Today,* 49:174–180.

Osler, Mark W. (1991). "Shock Incarceration: Hard Realities and Real Possibilities." *Federal Probation,* 55:34–42.

Ostrom, Brian J. and Geoff Gallas (1990). "Case Space: Do Workload Considerations Support a Shift of Cases from Federal to State Court Systems?" *State Court Journal,* 14:15–22.

Padgett, John F. (1985). "The Emergent Organization of Plea Bargaining." *American Journal of Sociology,* 90:753–800.

Painton, Priscilla (1991). "The People vs. a Dynasty." *Time,* November 11, p. 47.

Palmer, John W. (1996). *Constitutional Rights of Prisoners.* 5th ed. Cincinnati, OH: Anderson Publishing Company.

Palmer, Ted (1992). *The Re-Emergence of Correctional Intervention.* Newbury Park, CA: Sage.

Parent, Dale G. (1988a). "Shock Incarceration Programs." *APPA Perspectives,* 12:9–15.

Parent, Dale G. (1988b). "Sentencing Purpose, Design and Operation of Shock Incarceration Programs." Unpublished paper presented at the annual meeting of the American Society of Criminology, Chicago, IL (November).

Parent, Dale G. (1989a). "Probation Supervision Fee Collection in Texas." *APPA Perspectives,* 13:9–12.

Parent, Dale G. (1989b). *Shock Incarceration: An Overview of Existing Programs.* Washington, DC: U.S. Department of Justice, Office of Justice Programs.

Parisi, Nicolette (1984). "The Female Correctional Officer: Her Progress Toward and Progress for Equality." *Prison Journal,* 64:92–109.

Parker, Edward A. (1990). "The Social Psychological Impact of a College Education on the Prison Inmate." *Journal of Correctional Education,* 41:140–146.

Paternoster, Raymond (1984). "Prosecutorial Discretion in Requesting the Death Penalty: A Case of Victim-Based Racial Discrimination." *Law and Society Review,* 18:437–478.

Patti, P. (1984). "New Concepts in Use of Force Reporting." *Law and Order,* 32:61–63.

Payne, D.M. and R.C. Trojanowicz (1985). *National Neighborhood Foot Patrol Center, Michigan State University.* East Lansing, MI: National Neighborhood for Patrol Center.

Peak, Kenneth J. and B. Grant Stitt (eds.) (1993). "Victimless Crime." *Journal of Contemporary Criminal Justice,* 9:1–69.

Pearson, Frank S. (1985). "New Jersey's Intensive Supervision Program: A Progress Report." *Crime and Delinquency,* 31:393–410.

Peat, Barbara J. and L. Thomas Winfree, Jr. (1992). "Reducing the Intra-Institutional Effects of 'Prisonization': A Study of Therapeutic Community for Drug-Using Inmates." *Criminal Justice and Behavior,* 19:206–225.

Penn and Schoen Associates, Inc. (1987). *Television and Police: Attitudes and Perceptions of the Police and the Public: A Study for the New York Police Foundation, Inc.* New York: Penn and Schoen Associates, Inc.

Pennsylvania Crime Commission (1992). *Racketeering and Organized Crime in the Bingo Industry.* Conshohocken, PA: Pennsylvania Crime Commission.

Pennsylvania Economic League, Inc. (1993). *Cost of Corrections in Pennsylvania.* Harrisburg, PA: Pennsylvania Economic League, Inc.

Penrod, Steven D., Solomon M. Fulero, and Brian L. Cutler (1995). "Expert Psychological Testimony on Eyewitness Reliability Before and After Daubert: The State of the Law and Science." *Behavioral Sciences and the Law,* 13:229–259.

Perkins, Craig A., James J. Stephan, and Allen J. Beck (1995). *Jails and Jail Inmates, 1993–1994.* Washington, DC: U.S. Bureau of Justice Statistics.

Perlin, Michael L. (1994). *The Jurisprudence of the Insanity Defense.* Durham, NC: Carolina Academic Press.

Perroncello, Peter (1995). "Toward a New Direct Supervision Paradigm." *American Jails,* 9:38–40.

Petersilia, Joan M. (1985a). "Community Supervision: Trends and Critical Issues." *Crime and Delinquency.*

Petersilia, Joan M. (1985b). *Probation and Felony Offenders.* Washington, DC: U.S. Department of Justice.

Petersilia, Joan M. (1986a). *Exploring the Option of House Arrest.* Santa Monica, CA: Rand.

Petersilia, Joan M. (1986b). "Exploring the Option of House Arrest." *Federal Probation,* 50:50–55.

Petersilia, Joan M. (1986c). *Taking Stock of Probation Reform.* Santa Monica, CA: Rand.

Petersilia, Joan M. (1987a). *Expanding Options for Criminal Sentencing.* Santa Monica, CA: Rand.

Petersilia, Joan M. (1987b). "Los Angeles Experiments with House Arrest." *Corrections Today,* 49:132–134.

Petersilia, Joan M. (1987c). "Prisoners Without Prisons." *State Legislatures* (August):22–25.

Petersilia, Joan M. (1988). *House Arrest.* Washington, DC: U.S. Department of Justice, National Institute of Justice.

Petersilia, Joan M. (1994). "Debating Crime and Imprisonment in California." *Evaluation and Program Planning,* 17:165–177.

Petersilia, Joan M., Allan Abrahamse, and James Q. Wilson (1990). "A Summary of RAND's Research on Police Performance, Community Characteristics, and Case Attrition." *Journal of Police Science and Administration,* 17:219–226.

Petersilia, Joan M., Susan Turner, and Joyce Peterson (1986). *Prison Versus Probation in California: Implications for Crime and Offender Recidivism.* Santa Monica, CA: Rand.

Petersilia, Joan M. et al. (1985). *Granting Felons Probation: Public Risks and Alternatives.* Santa Monica, CA: Rand.

Peterson, Ruth D. and John Hagan (1984). "Changing Conceptions of Race: Towards an Account of Anomalous Findings of Sentencing Research." *American Sociological Review,* 49:56–70.

Petrone, S. and M. Reiser (1985). "A Home Visit Program for Stressed Police Officers." *Police Chief,* 52:36–37.

Piehl, Anne Morrison (1992). *Probation in Wisconsin.* Milwaukee, WI: Wisconsin Policy Research Institute.

Piquero, Alex and Doris Layton MacKenzie (1993). "The Impact of an Alternative Program on Bedspace." Unpublished paper presented at the annual meeting of the American Society of Criminology, Phoenix, AZ (October).

Pisciotta, Alexander W. (1983). "Scientific Reform: The 'New Penology' at Elmira, 1876–1900." *Crime and Delinquency,* 29:613–630.

Plotkin, Marthal R. and Otwin A. Narr (1993). *The Police Response to the Homeless: A Status Report.* Washington, DC: Police Executive Research Forum.

Podkopacz, Marcy R. (1994). *Juvenile Reference Study.* Minneapolis, MN: Hennepin County Department of Community Corrections.

Pohlman, H.L. (1995). *Constitutional Debate in Action: Criminal Justice.* New York: HarperCollins.

Polk, Kenneth (1984). "Juvenile Diversion: A Look at the Record." *Crime and Delinquency,* 30:648–659.

Pollet, Susan L. (1993). "Parental Kidnapping: Can Laws Stem the Tide?" *Journal of Psychiatry and Law,* 31:417–445.

Pollock, Joycelyn M. and Ronald F. Becker (1995). "Law Enforcement Ethics: Using Officers as a Teaching Tool." *Journal of Criminal Justice Education,* 6:1–20.

Poole, Carol and Peggy Slavick (1995). *Boot Camps: A Washington State Update and Overview of National Findings.* Olympia, WA: Washington State Institute for Public Policy.

Popkin, Susan J., Lynn M. Olson, and Arthur J. Lurigio (1995). "Sweeping out Drugs and Crime: Residents' Views of the Chicago Housing Authority's Public Housing Drug Elimination Program." *Crime and Delinquency,* 41:73–99.

Porporino, Frank J. et al. (1992). "Prison Violence and Inmate Suicide and Self-Injury." *Forum on Corrections Research,* 4:2–39.

Potler, Cathy (1985). *A Neglected Population: Women Prisoners at Bayview.* New York: Correctional Association of New York.

Potter, Gary W. (1994). *Criminal Organizations: Vice, Racketeering, and Politics in an American City.* Prospect Heights, IL: Waveland Press.

Pound, R. (1940). "Principles and Outlines of a Modern Unified Court Organization." *Journal of the American Judicature Society,* 11:81–82.

Powis, Robert E. (1992). *The Money Launderers: Lessons from the Drug Wars—How Billions of Legal Dollars Are Washed Through Banks and Businesses.* Chicago, IL: Probus.

Pranis, Kay (1990). *Options in Criminal Corrections: A Study of Costs.* Minneapolis, MN: Minnesota Citizens Council on Crime and Justice.

Prentky, Robert A. (ed.) (1994). "The Assessment and Treatment of Sex Offenders." *Criminal Justice and Behavior,* 21:5–175.

President's Commission on Law Enforcement (1967). *President's Commission on Law Enforcement and the Administration of Justice.* Washington, DC: U.S. Government Printing Office.

Pretrial Resources Service Center (1994). *Commercial Surety Bail: Assessing Its Role in the Pretrial Release and Detention Decision.* Washington, DC: Pretrial Services Resource Center.

Price, Barbara R. and Natalie J. Sokoloff (eds.) (1995). *The Criminal Justice System and Women: Offenders, Victims and Workers.* 2d ed. New York: McGraw-Hill.

Pringle, P. (1955). *Hue and Cry.* London, UK: Museum Press.

Prior, L.E. (1985). "Polygraph Testing of Vermont State Police Officers." *Polygraph,* 14:256–257.

Prison Reform Trust (1984). *Beyond Restraint: The Use of Body Belts, Special Stripped and Padded Cells in Britain's Prisons.* London, UK: Prison Reform Trust.

Proctor, Jon L. (1994). "Evaluating a Modified Version of the Federal Prison System's Inmate Classification Model: An Assessment of Objectivity and Predictive Validity." *Criminal Justice and Behavior,* 21:256–272.

Provine, Doris Marie (1986). *Judging Credentials: Nonlawyer Judges and the Politics of Professionalism.* Chicago: University of Chicago Press.

Pugh, George (1985). "Situation Tests and Police Selection." *Journal of Police Science and Administration,* 13:172–177.

Quinlan, J. Michael et al. (1992). "Focus on the Female Offender." *Federal Prisons Journals,* 3:3–68.

Quinn, James F. and John E. Holman (1991). "The Efficacy of Electronically Monitored Home Confinement as a Case Management Device." *Journal of Contemporary Criminal Justice,* 7:128–134.

Racine, Trudy, Tom Vittitow, and Rick Riggs (1984). *Examining Potential Duplication Between Community Corrections Programs and District Court Probation Services.* Topeka, KS: Kansas Legislative Post Audit Committee.

Rackmill, Stephen J. (1994). "An Analysis of Home Confinement as a Sanction." *Federal Probation,* 58:45–52.

Radelet, Michael L., Hugo Adam Bedau, and Constance E. Putnam (1992). *In Spite of Innocence: The Ordeal of 400 Americans Wrongly Convicted of Crimes Punishable by Death.* Boston: Northeastern University Press.

Raeder, Myrna (1993). "Gender Issues in the Federal Sentencing Guidelines and Mandatory Minimum Sentences." *Criminal Justice,* 8:20–25, 56–63.

Raeder, Myrna (1995). "Determinate Sentencing and Agenda Building: A Case Study of the Failure of Reform." *Journal of Criminal Justice,* 23:349–362.

Rafter, Nicole H. (1983). "Prisons for Women." In *Crime and Justice: An Annual Review of Research,* Michael Tonry and Norval Morris (eds.). Chicago: University of Chicago Press.

Ragano, Frank and Nicholas Raab (1994). *Mob Lawyer.* New York: Scribner's.

Raine, Alinna P. and Frank J. Cilluffo (eds.) (1994). *Global Organized Crime: The New Empire of Evil.* Washington, DC: Center for Strategic and International Studies.

Rand, Michael R. (1991). *Crime and the Nation's Households, 1990.* Washington, DC: U.S. Department of Justice.

Rankin, Joseph H. and Edward L. Wells (1985). "From Status to Delinquent Offenses: Escalation?" *Journal of Criminal Justice,* 13:171–180.

Rasicot, James (1983). *Jury Selection, Body Language, and the Visual Trial.* Minneapolis, MN: AB.

Rasmussen, David W. and Bruce L. Benson (1994a). *The Economic Anatomy of a Drug War: Criminal Justice in the Commons.* Lanham, MD: Rowman and Littlefield.

Rasmussen, David W. and Bruce L. Benson (1994b). *Intermediate Sanctions: A Policy Analysis Based on Program Evaluations.* Washington, DC: Report Prepared for the Collins Center for Public Policy.

Rawlings, Philip (1992). *Drunks, Whores and Idle Apprentices: Criminal Biographies of the Eighteenth Century.* London, UK: Routledge.

Read, J. Don, John C. Yuille, and Patricia Tollestrup (1992). "Recollections of a Robbery: Effects of Arousal and Alcohol upon Recall and Person Identification." *Law and Human Behavior,* 16:425–446.

Ream, R.D. (ed.) (1985). "The Child and the Law: Special Bibliography Issue." *Children's Legal Rights Journal,* 6:1–70.

Reaves, Brian A. (1993). *Census of State and Local Law Enforcement Agencies, 1992.* Washington, DC: U.S. Department of Justice.

Reaves, Brian A. (1994). *Federal Law Enforcement Officers, 1993.* Washington, DC: U.S. Department of Justice.

Reaves, Brian A. (1996). *Local Police Departments, 1993.* Washington, DC: U.S. Department of Justice.

Reaves, Brian A. and Jacob Perez (1994). *Pretrial Release of Felony Defendants, 1992.* Washington, DC: U.S. Bureau of Justice Statistics.

Rebovich, Donald J. (1995). "Use and Avoidance of RICO at the Local Level: The Implementation of Organized Crime Laws." In *Contemporary Issues in Organized Crime,* Jay Albanese (ed.). Monsey, NY: Criminal Justice Press.

Reddington, Frances P. (1992). *In the Best Interests of the Child: The Impact of* Marales v. Turman *on the Texas Youth Commission.* Ann Arbor, MI: University Microfilms International.

Reed, Patricia A. (1983). "Pretrial Bail. A Deprivation of Liberty or Property with Due Process of Law." *Washington and Lee Law Review,* 40:1575–1599.

Reeves, R. (1992). "Approaching 2000: Finding Solutions to the Most Pressing Issues Facing the Corrections Community." *Corrections Today,* 54:74, 76–79.

Reger, Randall R. (1994). "The Consistently Inconsistent Application of Contempt Power in Juvenile Courts." *Journal of Crime and Justice,* 17:93–106.

Reiman, Jeffrey H. (1985). "Justice, Civilization, and the Death Penalty: Answering Van den Haag." *Philosophy and Public Affairs,* 14:115–148.

Reiss, Albert J. Jr. (1971). *The Police and the Public.* New Haven, CT: Yale University Press.

Reiss, Albert J. Jr. (1985). "Shaping and Serving the Community: The Role of the Police Chief Executive." In *Police Leadership in America,* William A. Geller (ed.). New York: Praeger.

Reiss, Albert J. Jr. and Michael Tonry (1993). "Organizational Crime." In *Beyond the Law: Crime in Complex Organizations,* Michael Tonry and Albert J. Reiss (eds.). Chicago: University of Chicago Press.

Reith, Charles (1938). *The Police Idea.* London, UK: Oxford University Press.

Reno, Janet (1996). "Juvenile Violence Arrest Rates Dropped Last Year, Reno Says." *Criminal Justice Newsletter,* 27:3.

Reulbach, Donna M. and Jane Tewksbury (1994). "Collaboration Between Protective Services and Law Enforcement: The Massachusetts Model." *Journal of Elder Abuse and Neglect,* 6:9–21.

Reuvid, Jonathan (ed.) (1995). *The Regulation and Prevention of Economic Crime Internationally.* London, UK: Kogan Page.

Reviere, Rebecca and Vernetta D. Young (1994). "Mortality of Police Officers: Comparisons by Length of Time on the Force." *American Journal of Police,* 13:51–64.

Reynolds, Morgan O. (1994). *Using the Private Sector to Deter Crime.* Dallas, TX: National Center for Policy Analysis.

Rhine, Edward E., William R. Smith, and Ronald W. Jackson (1991). *Paroling Authorities: Recent History and Current Practice.* Laurel, MD: American Correctional Association.

Rhode Island Governor's Commission to Avoid Future Prison Overcrowding (1993). *Report of the Governor's Commission to Avoid Future Prison Overcrowding and Terminate Federal Court Supervision Over the Adult Correctional Institution.* Providence, RI: Rhode Island Governor's Commission to Avoid Future Prison Overcrowding.

Rhodes, William (1991). "Federal Criminal Sentencing: Some Measurement Issues with Application to Pre-Guideline sentencing Disparity." *Journal of Criminal Law and Criminology,* 81:1002–1003.

Richardson, J. (1970). *The New York Police.* New York: Oxford University Press.

Richmond, C. (1970). "Expanding the Concepts of the Halfway House: A Satellite Housing Program." *International Journal of Social Psychiatry*, 16:986–1102.

Ridley, Ann and Louise Dunsford (1994). "Corporate Liability for Manslaughter: Reform and the Art of the Possible." *International Journal of the Sociology of Law*, 22:309–328.

Riley, Peter, Donald E. Stader, and James F. Lancaster (1995). "Curtailing Counterfeiting Operations . . . Fraudulent Documents." *Police Chief*, 62:31–57.

Ring, Charles R. (1989). "Probation Supervision Fees: Shifting Costs to the Offender." *Federal Probation*, 53:43–46.

Rison, Richard H. (1994). "Women as High-Security Officers." *Federal Prisons Journal*, 3:19–23.

Robbins, Ira P. (1990). "The Ostrich Instruction: Deliberate Ignorance as a Criminal *Mens Rea*." *Journal of Criminal Law and Criminology*, 81:191–234.

Roberts, Albert R. (ed.) (1994). *Critical Issues in Crime and Justice*. Thousand Oaks, CA: Sage.

Roberts, Dorothy E. (1994). "Foreword: The Meaning of Gender Equality in Criminal Law." *The Journal of Criminal Law and Criminology*, 85:1–78.

Roberts, Robert E. and Earl H. Cheek (1994). "Group Intervention and Reading Performance in a Medium-Security Prison Facility." *Journal of Offender Rehabilitation*, 20:97–116.

Robinson, David et al. (1992). "Focus on Staff." *Forum on Corrections Research*, 4:16–40.

Robinson, Dinah A. and Otis H. Stephens (1992). "Patterns of Mitigating Factors in Juvenile Death Penalty Cases." *Criminal Law Bulletin*, 28:246–275.

Robinson, Jeffrey (1994). *The Laundrymen: Inside the World's Third Largest Business*. London, UK: Simon and Schuster.

Rogers, Joseph W. and G. Larry Mays (1987). *Juvenile Delinquency and Juvenile Justice*. New York: Wiley.

Rogers, Robert (1993). "Solitary Confinement." *International Journal of Offender Therapy and Comparative Criminology*, 37:339–349.

Rohn, Warren and Trish Ostroski (1991). "Checking IDs: Advances in Technology Make It Easier to Monitor Inmates." *Corrections Today*, 53:142–145.

Rojek, Dean G. and Maynard L. Erickson (1982). "Delinquent Careers: A Test of the Career Escalation Model." *Criminology*, 20:5–28.

Rome, Dennis M., In Soo Son, and Mark S. Davis (1995). "Police Use of Excessive Force." *Social Justice Research*, 8:41–56.

Roper, Robert T. (1986). "A Typology of Jury Research an Discussion of the Structural Correlates of Jury Decision Making." *Justice System Journal*, 11:5–15.

Rosenberg, Irene Merker and Yale L. Rosenberg (1991). "*Miranda, Minnick*, and the Morality of Confessions." *American Journal of Criminal Law*, 19:1–34.

Rosenblum, Robert and Debra Whitcomb (1978). *Montgomery County Work Release/Pre-Release Program, Montgomery County, Maryland*. Washington, DC: U.S. Government Printing Office.

Rosenthal, Marguerite G. (1983). *Social Policy for Delinquent Children: Delinquency Activities of the U.S. Children's Bureau, 1912–1940*. Ann Arbor, MI: University Microfilms International.

Ross, David Frank, J. Don Read, and Michael P. Toglia (1994). *Adult Eyewitness Testimony: Current Trends and Developments*. Cambridge, UK: Cambridge University Press.

Ross, Jeffrey Ian (1995). "A Process Model of Police Violence." *Criminal Justice Policy Review*, 7:67–90.

Rothman, David J. (1983). "Sentencing Reforms in Historical Perspective." *Crime and Delinquency*, 29:631–647.

Rothwax, Harold J. (1996). *Guilty: The Collapse of Criminal Justice*. New York: Random House.

Rottman, David B., Carol R. Flango, and Sehdine R. Lockley (1995). *State Court Organization*. Washington, DC: Joint Effort Conference of State Court Administrators and National Center for State Courts.

Rowe, David C. and D. Wayne Osgood (1984). "Heredity and Sociological Theories of Delinquency: A Reconsideration." *American Sociological Review*, 49:526–540.

Rubin, H. Ted (1985a). *Behind the Black Robes: Juvenile Court Judges and the Court*. Beverly Hills, CA: Sage.

Rubin, H. Ted (1985b). *Juvenile Justice: Policy, Practice and Law*. New York: Random House.

Ruchelman, Leonard (1973). *Who Rules the Police?* New York: New York University Press.

Rudman, Cary J. and John Berthelsen (1991). *An Analysis of the California Department of Corrections' Planning Process: Strategies to Reduce the Cost of Incarcerating State Prisoners*. Sacramento, CA: California Assembly, Office of Research.

Runda, John C., Edward E. Rhine, and Robert E. Wetter (1994). *The Practice of Parole Boards*. Lexington, KY: Council of State Governments.

Rush, George E. (1994). *The Dictionary of Criminal Justice*. 4th ed. Guilford, CT: The Dushkin Publishing Group, Inc.

Rutherford, Andrew (1992). *Growing Out of Crime: The New Era*. 2d ed. Winchester, UK: Waterside Press.

Ryan, John P. and James Alfini (1978). "Trial Judges' Participation in Plea Bargaining: An Empirical Perspective." *Law and Society Review*, 13:486–495.

Ryan, T.A. (1984). *State of the Art Analysis of Adult Female Offenders and Institutional Programs*. Washington, DC: National Institute of Corrections.

Sachs, Andrea (1989). "Doing the Crime, Not the Time." *Time*, September 11, p. 81.

Sachs, Stephen H. et al. (1984). *Report on Security Conditions at Maryland Penitentiary's South Wing*. Annapolis, MD: Attorney General of Maryland.

Sagatun, Inger, Loretta L. McCollum, and Leonard P. Edwards (1985). "The Effect of Transfers from Juvenile to Criminal Court: A Loglinear Analysis." *Journal of Crime and Justice*, 8:65–92.

Saks, M.J. (1977). *Jury Verdicts*. Lexington, MA: Lexington Books.

Salzano, Julienne (1994). "It's a Dirty Business: Organized

Crime in Deep Sludge." *Criminal Organizations,* 8:17–20.

Saltzburg, Stephen A. and Kenneth R. Redden (1994). *Federal Rules of Evidence Manual.* Charlottesville, VA: Michie.

Sams, Julie P. (1986). "The Availability of the 'Cultural Defense' as an Excuse for Criminal Behavior." *Georgia Journal of International and Comparative Law,* 16:335–354.

Sanborn, Joseph (1993). "Philosophical, Legal, and Systematic Aspects of Juvenile Plea Bargaining." *Crime and Delinquency,* 39:509–527.

Sandhu, Harjit S., Salem Hmoud Al-Mousleh, and Bill Chown (1994). "Why Does Oklahoma Have the Highest Female Incarceration Rate in the U.S.? A Preliminary Investigation." *Journal of the Oklahoma Criminal Justice Research Consortium,* 1:35–43.

Sandys, Marla and Ronald C. Dillehay (1995). "First-Ballot Votes, Predeliberation Dispositions and Final Verdicts in Jury Trials." *Law and Human Behavior,* 19:175–195.

Sandys, Marla and Edmund F. McGarrell (1994). "Attitudes Toward Capital Punishment among Indiana Legislators: Diminished Support in Light of Alternative Sentencing Options." *Justice Quarterly,* 11:651–677.

Sandys, Marla and Edmund F. McGarrell (1995). "Attitudes Toward Capital Punishment: Preference for the Penalty or Mere Acceptance?" *Journal of Research in Crime and Delinquency,* 32:191–213.

Sarat, Austin (1985). "The Litigation Explosion, Access to Justice, and Court Reform: Examining the Critical Assumptions." *Rutgers Law Review,* 37:319–336.

Sarre, Rick (1993). *Police Use of Firearms: Issues in Safety.* Canberra, AUS: University of South Australia.

Satchell, Mitchell (1980). "The End of the line: Marion, Illinois." *Parade,* September 28, p. 6.

Saylor, William G. and Gerald G. Gaes (1991). *PREP Study Links UNICOR Work Experience with Successful Post-Release Outcome.* Washington, DC: U.S. Bureau of Prisons.

Scarfone, Anthony C. (1986). "The Mandatory Death Penalty for Murder by Lifers: Foregoing Procedural Safeguards on the Illusory Promise of Deterrence." *Syracuse Law Review,* 36:1303–1340.

Scharf, Peter and Arnold Binder (1983). *The Badge and the Bullet: Police Use of Deadly Force.* New York: Praeger.

Scheb, John M. II (1988). "State Appellate Judges' Attitudes Toward Judicial Merit Selection and Retention: Results of a National Survey." *Judicature,* 72:170–174.

Schiraldi, Vincent (1994). *Racial Disparities in the Charging of Los Angeles County's Third "Strike" Cases.* San Francisco: Center on Juvenile and Criminal Justice.

Schlatter, Gary (1989). "Electronic Monitoring: Hidden Costs of Home Arrest Programs." *Corrections Today,* 51:94–96.

Schmidt, Annesley K. (1985). "Deaths in the Line of Duty." *NIJ Reports,* 189:6–8.

Schmidt, Annesley K. (1986). "Electronic Monitors." *Federal Probation,* 50:56–59.

Schmidt, Annesley K. and Christine E. Curtis (1987). "Electronic Monitors." In *Intermediate Punishments: Intensive Supervision, Home Confinement, and Electronic Surveil-lance,* Belinda R. McCarthy (ed.). Monsey, NY: Criminal Justice Press.

Schneider, Anne L. (1984a). "Deinstitutionalization of Status Offenders: The Impact of Recidivism and Secure Confinement." *Criminal Justice Abstracts* (September): 410–432.

Schneider, Anne L. (1984b). "Divesting Status Offenses from Juvenile Court Jurisdiction." *Crime and Delinquency,* 30:347–370.

Schoenberg, Robert J. (1992). *Mr. Capone: The Real—and Complete—Story of Al Capone.* New York: William Morrow.

Schulhofer, Stephen J. (1985). "No Job Too Small: Justice Without Bargaining in the Lower Criminal Courts." *American Bar Foundation,* 13:221–229.

Schultz, Dorothy Moses (1993). "Policewomen in the 1950s: Paving the Way for Patrol." *Women and Criminal Justice,* 4:5–30.

Schumacher, Michael A. (1985). "Implementation of a Client Classification and Case Management System: A Practitioner's View." *Crime and Delinquency,* 31:445–455.

Schwartz, Ira M. and William H. Barton (eds.) (1994). *Reforming Juvenile Detention: No More Hidden Closets.* Columbus, OH: Ohio State University Press.

Schwartz, Ira M. and Chang Ming Hsieh (1994). *Juveniles Confined in the United States, 1979–1991.* Philadelphia: Center for the Study of Youth Policy, University of Pennsylvania.

Schweber, Claudine (1984). "Beauty Marks and Blemishes: The Coed Prison as a Microcosm of Integrated Society." *Prison Journal,* 64:3–14.

Scogin, Forrest, Joseph Schumacher, and Jennifer Gardner (1996). "Predictive Validity of Psychological Testing in Law Enforcement Settings." *Professional Psychology Research and Practice,* 26:68–71.

Scott, Robert Frank Jr., Robert Dean Hawkins, Jr., and Margaret Farnworth (1994). "Operation Kick-It: Texas Prisoners Rehabilitate Themselves by Dissuading Others." *Journal of Offender Rehabilitation,* 20:207–215.

Sechrest, Dale K. and Pamela Burns (1992). "Police Corruption: The Miami Case." *Criminal Justice and Behavior,* 19:294–313.

Sechrest, Dale K. and David Shichor (1993). "Corrections Goes Public (and Private) in California." *Federal Probation,* 57:3–8.

Segrave, Kerry (1995). *Policewomen: A History.* Jefferson, NC: McFarland and Company.

Seis, Mark C. and Kenneth L. Elbe (1991). "The Death Penalty for Juveniles: Bridging the Gap Between an Evolving Standard of Decency and Legislative Policy." *Justice Quarterly,* 8:465–487.

Seiter, R.P., J.R. Petersilia, and H.E. Allen (1974). *Evaluation of Halfway Houses in Ohio.* Columbus, OH: Ohio State University Program for the Study of Crime and Delinquency.

Serr, Brian J. and Mark Maney (1988). "Racism, Peremptory Challenges, and the Democratic Jury: The Jurisprudence of a Delicate Balance." *Journal of Criminal Law and Criminology,* 79:1–65.

Sevilla, Charles M. (1986). "Investigating and Preparing an In-effective Assistance of Counsel Claim." *Mercer Law Review,* 37:927–956.

Sexton, George E. (1995). *Work in American Prisons: Joint Ventures with the Private Sector.* Washington, DC: National Institute of Justice Program Focus.

Shaffner, Paula D. (1985). "Around and Around on Pennsylvania's Juvenile Justice Confession Carousel: This Time the Police Get the Brass Ring." *Villanova Law Review,* 30:1235–1266.

Shanahan, Michael G. (1985). "Private Enterprise and the Public Police: The Professionalizing Factors in Criminality." In *Police Leadership in America,* W.A. Geller (ed.). New York: Praeger.

Shane-DuBow, Sandra, Alice P. Brown, and Eric Olsen (1985). *Sentencing Reform in the United States: History, Content, and Effect.* Washington, DC: U.S. Department of Justice.

Sharbaro, Edward and Robert Keller (eds.) (1995). *Prison Crisis: Critical Readings.* Albany, NY: Harrow and Heston.

Shaw, Clifford and Henry D. McKay (1972). *Juvenile Delinquency in Urban Areas.* Chicago: University of Chicago Press.

Shaw, Clifford R. et al. (1929). *Delinquency Areas.* Chicago: University of Chicago Press.

Shaw, James W. and Doris Layton MacKenzie (1991). "Shock Incarceration and Its Impact on the Lives of Problem Drinkers." *American Journal of Criminal Justice,* 16:63–96.

Shaw, James W. and Doris Layton MacKenzie (1992). "The One-Year Community Supervision Performance of Drug Offenders and Louisiana DOC-Identified Substance Abusers Graduating from Shock Incarceration." *Journal of Criminal Justice,* 20:510–516.

Shawcross, Tim (1994). *The War Against the Mafia.* Edinburgh, SCOT: Mainstream Publishing.

Shawver, Lois (1987). "On the Question of Having Women Guards in Male Prisons." *Corrective and Social Psychiatry and Journal of Behavior Methods and Therapy,* 38:154–159.

Sheehan, Robert and Gary W. Cordner (1995). *Police Administration.* 3d ed. Cincinnati, OH: Anderson Publishing Company.

Shelden, Randall G. and William B. Brown (1991). "Correlates of Jail Overcrowding: A Case Study of a County Detention Center." *Crime and Delinquency,* 37:347–362.

Shelden, Randall G. John A. Horvath, and Sharon Tracy (1989). "Do Status Offenders Get Worse? Some Clarifications on the Question of Escalation." *Crime and Delinquency,* 35:202–216.

Sheley, Joseph F. (1994). "Drug Activity and Firearms Possession and Use by Juveniles." *Journal of Drug Issues,* 24:363–382.

Sheley, Joseph F. and James D. Wright (1995). *In the Line of Fire: Youths, Guns, and Violence in Urban America.* Hawthorne, NY: Aldine de Gruyter.

Sherman, Lawrence W. (1984). "Experiments in Police Discretion: Scientific Boom or Dangerous Knowledge?" *Law and Contemporary Problems,* 47:61–82.

Sherman, Lawrence W. (1985). "Becoming Bent: Moral Careers of Corrupt Policemen." In *Moral Issues in Police Work,* Frederick A. Elliston and Michael Feldberg (eds.). Totowa, NJ: Rowman and Allanheld.

Shichor, David (1993). "The Corporate Context of Private Prisons." *Crime Law and Social Change,* 20:113–138.

Shichor, David (1995). *Punishment for Profit: Private Prisons/Public Concerns.* Thousand Oaks, CA: Sage.

Shigley, Richard T. (1987). "The Emerging Professional Education Model for Police and the Minnesota Experience." Unpublished paper presented at the Academy of Criminal Justice Sciences meeting, St. Louis, MO (March).

Shilton, Mary K. et al. (1994). "Mandatory Minimum Sentencing." *IARCA Journal on Community Corrections,* 6:4–35.

Shinnar, Shlomo and Reuel Shinnar (1975). "The Effects of the Criminal Justice System on the Control of Crime: A Quantitative Approach." *Law and Society Review,* 9:581–611.

Shockman, Luke (1995). "White Collar Crime." *Minot (ND) Daily News,* December 16, p. B1.

Shute, Stephen, John Gardner, and Jeremy Horder (eds.) (1993). *Action and Value in Criminal Law.* Oxford, UK: Clarendon.

Sickmund, Melissa (1994). *How Juveniles Get to Juvenile Court.* Washington, DC: U.S. Office of Juvenile Justice and Delinquency Prevention.

Siedschlaw, Kurt (1990). "The Use of Performance Contracts in Community-Based Corrections." Unpublished paper presented at the annual meetings of the Academy of Criminal Justice Sciences, Denver, CO.

Sigler, Robert T. and Bridgett McGraw (1984). "Adult Probation and Parole Officers: Influence of Their Weapons, Role Perceptions and Role Conflict." *Criminal Justice Review,* 9:28–32.

Simmons, John A. et al. (1995). *Punishment: A Philosophy and Public Affairs Reader.* Princeton, NJ: Princeton University Press.

Simon, Jonathan (1993). *Poor Discipline: Parole and the Social Control of the Underclass.* Chicago, IL: University of Chicago Press.

Simon, Rita J. (1980). *The Jury: Its Role in American Society.* Lexington, MA: D.C. Heath.

Simone, Margaret V. (1984). "Group Homes: Succeeding by Really Trying." *Corrections Today,* 45:110–119.

Singer, Richard G. (1988). "Symposium: The 25th Anniversary of the Model Penal Code." *Rutgers Law Journal,* 19:519–954.

Skolnick, Jerome H. (1985). "Deception by Police." In *Moral Issues in Police Work,* Frederick A. Elliston and Michael Feldberg (eds.). Totowa, NJ: Rowman and Allanheld.

Skolnick, Jerome H. (1994). *Justice Without Trial: Law Enforcement in Democratic Society.* 3d ed. New York: Macmillan.

Skolnik, Howard L. et al. (1991). "Inmate Intervention Programs." *Corrections Today,* 53:92–203.

Skovron, Sandra Evans, Joseph E. Scott, and Francis T. Cullen (1989). "The Death Penalty for Juveniles: An Assessment of Public Support." *Crime and Delinquency,* 35:546–561.

REFERENCES

Slotnick, M. (1976). *Evaluating Demonstration Programs: Two Case Studies (Drug Treatment in a Parish Prison and a Community-Based Residential Facility).* New Orleans, LA: New Orleans Mayor's Criminal Justice Coordinating Council.

Slovenko, Ralph (1995). *Psychiatry and Criminal Culpability.* New York: Wiley.

Smith, Albert G. (1991). "Arming Officers Doesn't Have to Change an Agency's Mission" *Corrections Today,* 53:114–124.

Smith, Brent L. and Edward H. Stevens (1984). "Sentence Disparity and the Judge-Jury Sentencing Debate: An Analysis of Robbery Sentences in Six Southern States." *Criminal Justice Review,* 9:1–7.

Smith, David (1983). "The Demise of Transportation: Mid-Victorial Penal Policy." In *Criminal Justice History, An International Annual,* Vol. 3. Westport, CT: Meckler.

Smith, Michael Clay (1989). "Bad Checks, Debtor's Prisons, and Prosecuting Attorneys: *State v. Orth* and Criminal Justice Policy." *Criminal Law Bulletin,* 25:362–365.

Smith, Michael E. (1984). "Will the Real Alternatives Please Stand Up?" *New York University Review of Law and Social Change,* 12:171–197.

Smith, Michael R. (1994). "Integrating Community Policing and the Use of Force: Public Education, Involvement and Accountability." *American Journal of Police,* 13:1–21.

Smith, R.L. and R.W. Taylor (1985). "A Return to Neighborhood Policing: The Tampa, Florida Experience." *Police Chief,* 52:39–44.

Smith, Robert R. and M.A. Milan (1973). "Survey of the Home Furlough Policies of American Correctional Agencies." *Criminology,* 11:95–104.

Smith, Robert R. and D.A. Sabatino (1989). "American Prisoner Home Furloughs." Unpublished manuscript.

Smith, Robert R. and D.A. Sabatino (1990). "American Prisoner Home Furloughs." *Journal of Offender Counseling,* 10:18–25.

Smykla, John Oritz (1980). *Coed Prison.* New York: Human Sciences.

Smykla, John Ortiz (1981). *Community-Based Corrections: Principles and Practices.* New York: Macmillan.

Smykla, John Ortiz and William L. Selke (1995). *Intermediate Sanctions: Sentencing in the 1990s.* Cincinnati, OH: Anderson Publishing Company.

Snell, Tracy L. and Danielle G. Morton (1994). *Women in Prison.* Washington, DC: U.S. Bureau of Justice Statistics.

Snellenberg, Sidney C. (1986). "A Normative Alternative to the Death Penalty." Unpublished paper presented at the annual meeting of the Southern Association of Criminal Justice Educators. Atlanta, GA (September).

Snyder, Keith B. and Cecil Marshall (1990). "Pennsylvania's Juvenile Intensive Probation and Aftercare Programs." Unpublished paper presented at the American Society of Criminology meetings, Baltimore, MD (November).

Solomon, Rayman L. (1984). "The Politics of Appointment and the Federal Court's Role in Regulating America: U.S. Courts of Appeals Judgeships from T.R. to F.D.R." *American Bar Foundation Journal,* 2:285–343.

Sommers, Ira and Deborah R. Baskin (1994). "Factors Related to Female Adolescent Initiation into Violent Street Crime." *Youth and Society,* 25:468–489.

Song, Lin and Roxanne Lieb (1995). *Washington State Sex Offenders: Overview of Recidivism Studies.* Olympia, WA: Washington State Institute for Public Policy.

Sontheimer, Henry and Lynne Goodstein (1993). "An Evaluation of Juvenile Intensive Aftercare Probation: Aftercare Versus System Response Effects." *Justice Quarterly,* 10:197–227.

Sorensen, Jonathan R., James W. Marquart, and Deon E. Brock (1993). "Factors Related to Killings of Felons by Police Officers: A Test of the Community Violence and Conflict Hypotheses." *Justice Quarterly,* 10:417–440.

Sorensen, Jonathan R. and Donald H. Wallace (1995). "Arbitrariness and Discrimination in Missouri Capital Cases: An Assessment Using the Barnett Scale." *Journal of Crime and Justice,* 18:21–57.

Souryal, Sam S. (1995). *Police Organization and Administration.* 2d ed. Cincinnati, OH: Anderson Publishing Company.

South Carolina State Reorganization Commission (1990). *Evaluation of the Omnibus Criminal Justice Improvements Act of 1986: Section 3, 4, and 5, Second Year Report.* Columbia, SC: South Carolina State Reorganization Commission.

Spangenberg Group (1990). *Overview of the Fulton County, Georgia, Indigent Defense System.* West Newton, MA: Spangenberg Group.

Spelman, William (1988). *The Incapacitation Benefits of Selective Criminal Justice Policies.* Ann Arbor, MI: University Microfilms International.

Spelman, William (1994). *Criminal Incapacitation.* New York: Plenum.

Spelman, William (1995). "The Severity of Intermediate Sanctions." *Journal of Research in Crime and Delinquency,* 32:107–135.

Spergel, Irving A. (1995). *The Youth Gang Problem: A Community Approach.* New York: Oxford University Press.

Stack, Steven (1994). "Execution Publicity and Homicide in Georgia." *American Journal of Criminal Justice,* 18:25–39.

Stack, Steven and Ann Goetting (1995). "The Impact of Publicized Executions on Homicide." *Criminal Justice and Behavior,* 22:172–194.

Stack, Steven and Thomas Kelley (1994). "Police Suicide: An Analysis." *American Journal of Police,* 13:73–90.

St. Clair, James D. et al. (1992). *Report of the Boston Police Department Management Review Committee.* Boston: Management Review Committee.

Stanley, Alexander (1989). "Soul Brother No. 155413." *Time,* February 20, p. 40.

Steadman, Henry J., Margaret A. McGreevy, and Joseph P. Morrissey (1993). *Before and After Hinckley: Evaluating Insanity Defense Reform.* New York: Guilford.

Stearns, Gerry M. and Robert J. Moore (1993). "The Physical and Psychological Correlates of Job Burnout in the Royal

---

Canadian Mounted Police." *Canadian Journal of Criminology,* 35:127–147.

Steelman, Diane (1984). *Doing Idle Time: An Investigation of Inmate Idleness in New York's Prisons and Recommendations for Change.* New York: Correctional Association of New York.

Steen, Patricia (1991). *A Discussion of the Correctional System, Its Effects on Mother/Infant Relations and Recommendations for Reform.* Pacific Oaks, CA: Pacific Oaks College.

Steidel, Stephen E. (1994). *Missing and Abducted Children: A Law Enforcement Guide to Case Investigation and Program Management.* Arlington, VA: National Center for Missing and Exploited Children.

Steiger, John C. and Cary Dizon (1991). *Rehabilitation, Release and Reoffending: A Report on the Criminal Careers of the Division of Juvenile Rehabilitation "Class of 1982."* Olympia, WA: Juvenile Offender Research Unit, Department of Social and Health Services.

Steinberg, Marc I. (1975). "Right to Speedy Trial: The Constitutional Right and Its Applicability to the Speedy Trial Act of 1974." *Journal of Criminal Law and Criminology,* 66:229–239.

Steinberg, Marvin B. (1991). "The Case for Eliminating Peremptory Challenges." *Criminal Law Bulletin,* 27:216–229.

Steinke, Pamela (1991). "Using Situational Factors to Predict Types of Prison Violence." *Journal of Offender Rehabilitation,* 17:119–132.

Stephan, James J. and Tracy L. Snell (1996). *Capital Punishment 1994.* Washington, DC: Bureau of Justice Statistics.

Steppe, Cecil H. (1986). "Public Support: Probation's Backbone." *Corrections Today,* 48:12–16.

Stevens, Dennis J. (1994). "The Depth of Imprisonment and Prisonization: Levels of Security and Prisoners' Anticipation of Future Violence." *Howard Journal of Criminal Justice,* 33:137–157.

Stewart, Bob, Michael Lieberman, and William R. Celester (1994). "Hate Crimes: Understanding and Addressing the Problem." *Police Chief,* 61:14–18.

Stewart, Mary Janet, Edward L. Vockell, and Rose E. Ray (1986). "Decreasing Court Appearance of Juvenile Status Offenders." *Social Casework,* 67:74–79.

Stienstra, D. (1985). *Joint Trial Calendars in the Western District of Missouri.* Washington, DC: Federal Judicial Center.

Stitt, B. Grant (1988). "Victimless Crime: A Definitional Issue." *Journal of Crime and Justice,* 11:87–102.

Stitt, B. Grant and Robert H. Chaires (1993). "Plea Bargaining: Ethical Issues and Emerging Perspectives." *Justice Professional,* 7:69–91.

Stitt, B. Grant and Gene G. James (1985). "Entrapment: An Ethical Analysis." In *Moral Issues in Police Work,* Frederick A. Elliston and Michael Feldberg (eds.). Totowa, NJ: Rowman and Allanheld.

Stitt, B. Grant and Sheldon Siegel (1986). "The Ethics of Plea Bargaining." Unpublished paper presented at the annual meeting of the Academy of Criminal Justice Sciences. Orlando, FL.

Stohr, Mary K., Nicholas P. Lovrich, and Gregory L. Wilson (1994). "Staff Stress in Contemporary Jails: Assessing Problem Severity and the Payoff of Progressive Personnel Practices." *Journal of Criminal Justice,* 22:313–327.

Stohr, Mary K. et al. (1994). "Staff Management in Correctional Institutions: Comparing DiIulio's 'Control Model' and 'Employee Investment Model' Outcomes in Five Jails." *Justice Quarterly,* 11:471–497.

Stolzenberg, Lisa Ann (1993). "Unwarranted Disparity and Determinate Sentencing: A Longitudinal Study of Presumptive Sentencing Guidelines in Minnesota." Ann Arbor, MI: University Microfilms International.

Stone, William E. (1990). "Means of the Cause of Death in Texas Jail Suicides, 1986–1988." *American Jails,* 4:50–53.

Stotland, Ezra and Michael Pendleton (1989). "Police Stress, Time on the Job, and Strain." *Journal of Criminal Justice,* 17:55–60.

Strafer, G. Richard (1983). "Volunteering for Execution: Competency, Voluntariness, and Propriety of Third Party Intervention." *Journal of Criminal Law and Criminology,* 74:860–912.

Strawbridge, Peter and Deirdre Strawbridge (1990). *A Networking Guide to Recruitment, Selection and Probationary Training of Police Officers in Major Police Departments in the U.S.A.* New York: John Jay College.

Streib, Victor L. (1987). *Death Penalty for Juveniles.* Bloomington, IN: Indiana University Press.

Streib, Victor L. and Lynn Sametz (1989). "Executing Female Juveniles." *Connecticut Law Review,* 22:3–59.

Stroud, Carsten (1987). *Close Pursuit: A Week in the Life of an NYPD Homicide Cop.* New York: Bantam Books.

Stroup, Timothy (1985). "Affirmation Action and the Police." In *Police Ethics: Hard Choices in Law Enforcement,* W.C. Heffernan and T. Stroup (eds.). New York: John Jay.

Suchner, Robert W. and Jim Thomas (1989). "Judicial Decision Making in Prisoner Civil Rights Litigation." *Journal of Crime and Justice,* 12:109–145.

Suggs, D. and B.D. Sales (1978). "Using Communication Cues to Evaluate Prospective Jurors in the *Voir Dire.*" *Arizona Law Review,* 20:629–642.

Surrette, Raymond B. (1979). "Uncertainty and Organizational Reaction: The Special Case of Sheriff Elections and Arrests." Unpublished doctoral dissertation, Florida State University. Ann Arbor, MI: University Microfilms International.

Surrette, Raymond B. (1985). "Crimes, Arrests, and Elections: Predicting Winners and Losers." *Journal of Criminal Justice,* 13:321–327.

Sutherland, Edwin H. (1940> "White-Collar Criminality." *American Sociological Review,* 5:1–11.

Sutphen, Richard, David Kurtz, and Martha Giddings (1993). "The Influence of Juvenile's Race on Police Decision-Making: An Exploratory Study." *Juvenile and Family Court Journal,* 44:69–76.

Sykes, Gary W. (1985). "The Functional Nature of Police Reform: The 'Myth' of Controlling the Police." *Justice Quarterly,* 2:41–65.

Talley, Joseph E. and Lisa D. Hinz (1990). *Performance Prediction of Public Safety and Law Enforcement Personnel: A Study in Race and Gender Differences and MMPI Subscales.* Springfield, IL: Charles C. Thomas.

Tauro, Joseph L. (1983). "Sentencing: A View from the Bench." *New England Journal on Criminal and Civil Confinement,* 9:323–330.

Taylor, Jon Marc (1995). "A G.I. Bill for Correctional Officers." *Corrections Compendium,* 20:1–3.

Taylor, William Banks (1993). *Brokered Justice: Race, Politics, and Mississippi Prisons, 1798–1992.* Columbus, OH: Ohio State University Press.

Taylor, William J. (1985). "Training: ACA Priority." *Corrections Today,* 47:24–29.

Taylor, William J. (1992). "Tailoring Boot Camps to Juveniles." *Corrections Today,* 54:122–124.

Telecky, Judith (1996). "Increasing the Effectiveness of Parole Programs: The Texas Experience." *APPA Perspectives,* 20:26–28.

Tennenbaum, Abraham N. (1994). "The Influence of the *Garner* Decision on Police Use of Deadly Force." *Journal of Criminal Law and Criminology,* 81:241–260.

Terry, W. Clinton III (ed.) (1985). *Policing Society.* New York: Wiley.

Tewksbury, Richard A. (1994). "Improving the Educational Skills of Jail Inmates: Preliminary Program Findings." *Federal Probation,* 58:55–59.

Texas Bill Blackwood Law Enforcement Management Institute (1994). "Texas Bill Blackwood Law Enforcement Management Institute at Sam Houston State University." *TELEMASP Bulletin,* 1:1–11.

Texas Criminal Justice Policy Council (1992a). *Employment Services for Probationers: Evaluation.* Austin, TX: Texas Criminal Justice Policy Council.

Texas Criminal Justice Policy Council (1992b). *Interim Projections: Fiscal years 1992–1998.* Austin, TX: Texas Criminal Justice Policy Council.

Texas Criminal Justice Policy Council (1993a). *Impact Analysis of Proposed Changes in Good Time Policies.* Austin, TX: Texas Criminal Justice Policy Council.

Texas Criminal Justice Policy Council (1993b). *Review of Sentencing Reforms: Projected Impact and Recent Trends.* Austin, TX: Briefing to Senate Criminal Justice Committee.

Texas Office of the State Auditor (1993). *Tough Choices: Finding Ways to Balance Criminal Justice Policy and Criminal Justice Dollars.* Austin, TX: Texas Office of the State Auditor.

Thomann, Daniel A., Lois Pilant, and Sheldon Kay (1994). "Police Women in the 1990s." *Police Chief,* 61:31–55.

Thomas, Charles W. (1991a). "How Correctional Privatization Defines the Legal Rights of Prisoners." *The Privatization Review,* 6:38–58.

Thomas, Charles W. (1991b). "Prisoners' Rights and Correctional Privatization: A Legal and Ethical Analysis." *Business and Professional Ethics Journal,* 10:3–45.

Thomas, Charles W. (1994). "Growth in Privatization Continues to Accelerate." *Corrections Compendium,* 19:5–6.

Thomas, J.B. (1990). *Conspicuous Depredation: Automobile Theft in Los Angeles, 1904 to 1987.* Sacramento, CA: European University Study Series, California Attorney General.

Thomas, Wayne (1976). *Bail Reform in America.* Berkeley: University of California Press.

Thomas, Wayne (1977). *National Evaluation Program: Pretrial Release Programs.* Washington, DC: Law Enforcement Assistance Administration.

Thompson, Joel A. (1986). "The American Jail: Problems, Politics, and Prospects." *American Journal of Criminal Justice,* 10:205–221.

Thompson, Joel A. and G. Larry Mays (eds.) (1991). *American Jails: Public Policy Issues.* Chicago: Nelson-Hall.

Thompson, Linda S. (ed.) (1991). *The Forgotten Child in Health Care: Children in the Juvenile Justice System.* Washington, DC: National Center for Education in Maternal and Child Health.

Thornberry, Terence P., Rolf Loeber, and David Huizinga (1991). "Symposium on the Causes and Correlates of Juvenile Delinquency." *Journal of Criminal Law and Criminology,* 82:1–155.

Thornburgh, Dick (1991). "Symposium: Environmental Crime." *George Washington Law Review,* 59:775–999.

Thoumi, Francisco E. (1995). "Political Economy and Illegal Drugs in Columbia." In *Studies on the Impact of the Illegal Drug Trade, Vol. 2,* Francisco E. Thoumi (ed.). London, UK: Lynne Rienner.

Tiffany, Lawrence P. and Mary Tiffany (1990). *The Legal Defense of Pathological Intoxication—With Related Issues of Temporary and Self-Inflicted Insanity.* New York: Quorum Books.

Tilbor, Karen (1993). *Prisoners as Parents: Building Parenting Skills on the Inside.* Portland, ME: Muskie Institute of Public Affairs, University of Southern Maine.

Time (1988). "Inconceivable Sentence." June 6, p. 27.

Time (1993). "Rodney King, Live: The Central Figure in the L.A. Police Trial Testifies for the Prosecution." March 22, p. 21.

Timrots, Anita and Candice Byrne (1995). *Fact Sheet: Drug Use Trends.* Washington, DC: U.S. Office of National Drug Control Policy.

Tonry, Michael (1992). "Sentencing Commissions and Their Guidelines." In *Crime and Justice: A Review of Research,* Vol. 17, Michael Tonry and Norval Morris (eds.). Chicago: University of Chicago Press.

Tonry, Michael (1993). "Sentencing Commission and Their Guidelines." In *Crime and Justice: A Review of Research,* Vol 17, Michael Tonry (ed.). Chicago: University of Chicago Press.

Tonry, Michael (1994). "Racial Politics, Racial Disparities, and the War on Crime." *Crime and Delinquency,* 40:475–494.

Tonry, Michael (1995). *Malign Neglect: Race, Crime and Punishment in America.* New York: Oxford University Press.

Tonry, Michael and Kate Hamilton (eds.) (1995). *Intermediate Sanctions in Over-Crowded Times.* Boston: Northeastern University Press.

Tonry, Michael and Norval Morris (eds.) (1992). *Modern Policing.* Chicago: University of Chicago Press.

Tontondonato, Pamela (1986). "Criminal Career Behavior Patterns in a Cohort of Young Adult Males." Ann Arbor, MI: University Microfilms International.

Tooley, F. Jane (1972). "The Omaha Police-Community Relations Camp." *Police Chief,* 39:62–63, 288–289.

Torres, Donald A. (1985). *Handbook of Federal Police and Investigative Agencies.* Westport, CT: Greenwood Press.

Torres, Donald A. (1987). *Handbook of State Police, Highway Patrols, and Investigative Agencies.* Westport, CT: Greenwood Press.

Toure, Abati N. N. (1994). *The Impact of Criminal Justice on New York State's African and Latino Populations: A Focus on Corrections.* New York: New York State Association of Black and Puerto Rican Legislators.

Towberman, Donna B. (1992). "A National Survey of Juvenile Risk Assessment." *Juvenile and Family Court Journal,* 43:61–67.

Tracy, Paul E., Marvin E. Wolfgang, and Robert M. Figlio (1985). *Delinquency in Two Birth Cohorts: Executive Summary.* Washington, DC: U.S. National Institute for Juvenile Justice and Delinquency Prevention.

Travis, Jeremy (1995). *Solicitation for Research and Evaluation on Violence Against Women.* Washington, DC: U.S. Department of Justice.

Travisono, Anthony P. et al. (1986). "Special Needs Offenders: Handle with Care." *Corrections Today,* 48:4–80.

Trojanowicz, Robert C. (1990). "Community Policing Is Not Police-Community Relations." *FBI Law Enforcement Bulletin,* 59:6–11.

Trojanowicz, Robert C. and Dennis W. Banas (1985a). *Perceptions of Safety: A Comparison of Foot Patrol Versus Motor Patrol Officers.* East Lansing, MI: National Neighborhood Foot Patrol Center, Michigan State University.

Trojanowicz, Robert C. and Dennis W. Banas (1985b). *The Impact of Foot Patrol on Black and White Perceptions of Policing.* East Lansing, MI: National Neighborhood Foot Patrol Center, Michigan State University.

Trojanowicz, Robert C., M. Steele, and S. Trojanowicz (1986). *Community Policing: A Taxpayer's Perspective.* East Lansing, MI: National Neighborhood Foot Patrol Center, Michigan State University.

Trugman, Wendy Lynn (1986). "The Representative Jury Standard: An Alternative to *Batson v. Kentucky.*" *American Criminal Law Review,* 23:403–424.

Tunnell, Kenneth D. (1992). "Film at Eleven: Recent Developments in the Commodification of Crime." *Sociological Spectrum,* 12:293–313.

Tunnell, Kenneth D. and Larry K. Gaines (1992). "Political Pressures and Influences on Police Executives: A Descriptive Analysis." *American Journal of Police,* 11:1–16.

Turco, Ronald N. (1986). "Police Shootings: Psychoanalytic Viewpoints." *International Journal of Offender Therapy and Comparative Criminology,* 30:53–58.

Turner, Billy M. et al. (1986). "Race and Peremptory Challenge During *Voir Dire:* Do Prosecution and Defense Agree?" *Journal of Criminal Justice,* 14:61–69.

Turner, James Roger (1985). "Can Inmate Grievance Procedures Assist Management Decision Making? The Case of Florida's Prisons." Unpublished master's thesis. Florida State University, Department of Public Administration, Tallahassee, FL.

Turner, Jimmy (1994). "Preparing for Special Needs Offenders Takes Planning, Patience, and Flexibility." *Corrections Today,* 56:134–138.

Uniform Crime Reports (1996). *Uniform Crime Reports.* Washington, DC: U.S. Department of Justice.

U.S. Bureau of Justice Assistance (1992). *State Civil RICO Programs.* Washington, DC: U.S. Bureau of Justice Assistance.

U.S. Bureau of Justice Statistics (1993). *Use and Management of Criminal History Record Information: A Comprehensive Report.* Washington, DC: U.S. Bureau of Justice Statistics.

U.S. Bureau of Justice Statistics (1994a). *Elderly Crime Victims.* Washington, DC: U.S. Bureau of Justice Statistics.

U.S. Bureau of Justice Statistics (1994b). *Demonstrating the Operational Utility of Incident-Based Data for Local Crime Analysis: Reporting Systems in Tacoma, WA and New Bedford, MA.* Washington, DC: U.S. Bureau of Justice Statistics.

U.S. Code Annotated (1996). *U.S. Code Annotated.* St. Paul, MN: West Publishing Company.

U.S. Commission on Civil Rights (1993). *Police-Community Relations in Southern West Virginia.* Washington, DC: Commission on Civil Rights, West Virginia Advisory Committee.

U.S. Community Relations Service (1993). *Principles of Good Policing: Avoiding Violence Between Police and Citizens.* Washington, DC: U.S. Community Relations Service.

U.S. Congress Office of Technology Assessment (1987a). *The Electronic Supervisor: New Technology, New Tensions.* Washington, DC: U.S. Government Printing Office.

U.S. Congress Office of Technology Assessment (1987b). *Defending Secrets, Sharing Data: New Locks and Keys for Electronic Information.* Washington, DC: U.S. Government Printing Office.

U.S. Department of Justice (1976). *Two Hundred Years of American Criminal Justice: An LEAA Bicentennial Study.* Washington, DC: Law Enforcement Assistance Administration.

U.S. Department of Justice (1988). *Report to the Nation on Crime and Justice.* Washington, DC: U.S. Department of Justice, Bureau of Justice Statistics.

U.S. Department of Justice (1993). *Compendium of Federal Justice Statistics, 1990.* Washington, DC: U.S. Department of Justice.

U.S. Department of Justice (1995). *Survey of Criminal History Information Systems, 1993.* Washington, DC: U.S. Department of Justice.

U.S. Federal Bureau of Prisons (1993). *A Day in the Life of the Federal Bureau of Prisons.* Washington, DC: U.S. Department of Justice.

U.S. Federal Bureau of Prisons (1994). *State of the Bureau: Emergency Preparedness and Response.* Washington, DC: U.S. Department of Justice.

U.S. General Accounting Office (1985). *UNICOR Products: Federal Prison Industries Can Further Ensure Customer Satisfaction.* Washington, DC: U.S. General Accounting Office.

U.S. General Accounting Office (1992a). *Federal Jail Bedspace: Cost Savings, Greater Accuracy Possible in the Capacity Expansion Plan.* Washington, DC: U.S. General Accounting Office.

U.S. General Accounting Office (1992b). *Sentencing Guidelines: Central Questions Remain Unanswered.* Washington, DC: U.S. General Accounting Office.

U.S. General Accounting Office (1993a). *Federal Prison Expansion: Overcrowding Reduced But Inmate Population Growth May Raise Issue Again.* Washington, DC: U.S. General Accounting Office.

U.S. General Accounting Office (1993b). *Federal Prisons: Inmate and Staff Views on Education and Work Training Programs.* Washington, DC: U.S. General Accounting Office.

U.S. General Accounting Office (1995a). *Federal Fugitive Apprehension: Agencies Taking Action to Improve Coordination and Cooperation.* Washington, DC: U.S. General Accounting Office.

U.S. General Accounting Office (1995b). *Juvenile Justice: Minimal Gender Bias Occurred in Processing Noncriminal Juveniles.* Washington, DC: U.S. General Accounting Office.

U.S. General Accounting Office (1995c). *Law Enforcement Support Center: Name-Based Systems Limit Ability to Identify Arrested Aliens.* Washington, DC: U.S. General Accounting Office.

U.S. General Accounting Office (1995d). *Money Laundering: Stakeholders View Recordkeeping Requirements for Cashier's Checks as Sufficient.* Washington, DC: U.S. General Accounting Office.

U.S. House of Representatives Committee on the Judiciary (1994). *Prison Inmate Training and Rehabilitation Act of 1993.* Washington, DC: U.S. Government Printing Office.

U.S. Senate Committee on Governmental Affairs (1995). *Criminal Aliens in the United States.* Washington, DC: U.S. Senate Committee on Government Affairs.

U.S. Senate Committee on the Judiciary (1994). *Innocence and the Death Penalty.* Washington, DC: U.S. Government Printing Office.

U.S. Sentencing Commission (1987). *United States Sentencing Commission Guidelines Manual.* Washington, DC: U.S. Sentencing Commission.

U.S. Sentencing Commission (1991). *Special Report to the Congress: Mandatory Minimum Penalties in the Federal Criminal Justice System.* Washington, DC: U.S. Sentencing Commission.

U.S. Sentencing Commission (1995). *Cocaine and Federal Sentencing Policy.* Washington, DC: U.S. Sentencing Commission.

Uriell, Patricia (1984). *The Furlough Program: An Evaluation.* Manoa, HI: Youth Development and Research Center, School of Social Work, University of Hawaii.

Useem, Bert, Camille Graham Camp, and George M. Camp (1993). *Resolution of Prison Riots.* South Salem, NY: Criminal Justice Institute.

Utz, Pamela J. (1979). "Two Models of Prosecutorial Professionalism." In *The Prosecutor,* William F. McDonald (ed.). Beverly Hills, CA: Sage.

Vacho, Marla Marino et al. (1994). "Women in Prison." *Forum on Corrections Research,* 6:3–48.

Van den Haag, Ernest and John P. Conrad (1983). *The Death Penalty: A Debate.* New York: Plenum.

van Dijik, Jan J.M. (1994). "Understanding Crime Rates: On the Interactions Between Rational Choices of Victims and Offenders." *British Journal of Criminology,* 34:105–121.

Van Stelle, Kit R., Elizabeth Mauser, and D. Paul Moberg (1994). "Recidivism to the Criminal Justice System of Substance-Abusing Offenders Diverted into Treatment." *Crime and Delinquency,* 40:175–196.

Van Voorhis, Patricia (1993). "Psychological Determinants of the Prison Experience." *Prison Journal,* 73:72–102.

Van Voorhis, Patricia (1994). *Psychological Classification of the Adult Male Prison Inmate.* Albany, NY: State University of New York Press.

Van Voorhis, Patricia et al. (1991). "The Impact of Race and Gender on Correctional Officers' Orientation to the Integrated Environment." *Journal of Research in Crime and Delinquency,* 28:472–500.

Vaughn, Michael S. (1992). "The Parameters of Trickery as an Acceptable Police Practice." *American Journal of Police,* 11:71–95.

Vaughn, Michael S. (1993). "Listening to the Experts: A National Study of Correctional Administrator's Responses to Prison Overcrowding." *Criminal Justice Review,* 18:12–25.

Veneziano, Carol and Louis Veneziano (1995). "Reasons for Refraining from Criminal Activity." *American Journal of Criminal Justice,* 19:185–196.

Ventura, Louis A. and Charlene A. Cassel (1994). *The Effects of Forensic Mental Health Services in Reducing Criminal Recidivism of Mental Health Clients.* Columbus, OH: Department of Mental Health.

Verdeyen, Robert J. (1995). "Correctional Industries: Making Inmate Work Productive." *Corrections Today,* 57:106–110.

Vernick, Jon S. and Stephen P. Teret (1993). "Firearms and Health: The Right to Be Armed with Accurate Information about the Second Amendment." *American Journal of Public Health,* 84:1773–1777.

Vicary, Judith R. and Roland Good (1983). "The Effects of a Self-Esteem Counseling Group on male Prisoners' Self-Concept." *Journal of Offender Counseling, Services and Rehabilitation,* 7:107–117.

Violante, John M. and Fred Aron (1995). "Police Stressors: Variations in Perception among Police Personnel." *Journal of Criminal Justice,* 23:287–294.

Violante, John M., J.R. Marshall, and B. Howe (1985). "Stress, Coping, and Alcohol Use: The Police Connection." *Journal of Police Science and Administration,* 13:106–110.

Virdee, Satnam (1995). *Racial Violence and Harassment.* London, UK: Policy Studies Institute

Virginia Commission on Sentencing and Parole Reform (1995). *Report.* Richmond, VA: Commonwealth of Virginia.

Virginia Commission on Youth (1993). *Report of the Study of Serious Juvenile Offenders.* Richmond, VA: Commonwealth of Virginia.

Virginia Commission on Youth (1994). *Report of the Study of Barriers to the Development of Locally Designed Community-Based. Systems of Early Intervention Services.* Richmond, VA: Commonwealth of Virginia.

Virginia Department of Corrections (1995). *A Study of Prison Programs That Promote Maternal and Infant Bonding.* Richmond, VA: Commonwealth of Virginia.

Virginia Department of Criminal Justice Services (1993). *A Study of Domestic Violence Policies in Virginia's Law Enforcement Agencies.* Richmond, VA: Virginia Department of Criminal Justice Services.

Virginia State Crime Commission (1993). *Report on the Feasibility of Implementing Locally Operated Boot Camps for Juvenile Offenders.* Richmond, VA: Commonwealth of Virginia, Virginia State Crime Commission.

Virginia State Crime Commission (1994a). *Police Accountability.* Richmond, VA: Commonwealth of Virginia, Virginia State Crime Commission.

Virginia State Crime Commission (1994b). *Report of the Virginia State Crime Commission on Criminally Negligent Homicide.* Richmond, VA: Virginia State Crime Commission.

Vogel, Brenda (1996). "The Prison Law Library: From Print to CD-ROM." *Corrections Today,* 58:100–101.

Volenik, Adrienne E. (1986). *Sample Pleadings for Use in Juvenile Delinquency Proceedings.* Washington, DC: American Bar Association.

von Hirsch, Andrew (1984). "The Ethics of Selective Incapacitation: Observations on the Contemporary Debate." *Crime and Delinquency,* 30:175–194.

von Hirsch, Andrew (1985). *Past or Future Crimes: Deservedness and Dangerousness in the Sentencing of Criminals.* New Brunswick, NJ: Rutgers University Press.

von Hirsch, Andrew et al. (1994). "Sentencing Guidelines and Guidance." *Criminal Justice Ethics,* 13:3–66.

Vorenberg, James (1981). *Criminal Law and Procedure: Cases and Materials.* St. Paul, MN: West Publishing Company.

Wadlington, W. et al. (1983). *Children in the Legal System.* Mineola, NY: Foundation Press.

Waegel, William R. (1984a). "The Use of Lethal Force by Police: The Effect of Statutory Change." *Crime and Delinquency,* 30:121–140.

Waegel, William R. (1984b). "How Police Justify the Use of Deadly Force." *Social Problems,* 32:144–155.

Wagner, William F. (1978). "An Evaluation of a Police Patrol Experiment." Unpublished doctoral dissertation, Washington State University. Ann Arbor, MI: University Microfilms International.

Wahl, Otto F. and Arthur Lincoln Kaye (1991). "The Impact of John Hinckley's Insanity Plea on Public and Professional Publication." *American Journal of Forensic Psychology,* 9:31–39.

Wakefield, Holida and Ralph Underwager (1991). "Female Child Sexual Abusers: A Critical Review of the Literature." *American Journal of Forensic Psychology,* 9:43–69.

Waley-Cohen, Joanna (1991). *Exile in Mid-Qing China: Banishment to Xinjiang, 1758–1830.* New Haven, CT: Yale University Press.

Walker, Jeffrey T. and Louie C. Caudell (1993). "Community Policing and Patrol Cars: Oil and Water or Well-Oiled Machine?" *Police Forum,* 3:1–9.

Walker, Robert N. (1995). *Psychology of the Youthful Offender, 3/e.* Springfield, IL: Charles C. Thomas.

Walker, Samuel (1979). "Professionalism at the Crossroads: Police Administration in the 1980s." In *Critical Issues in Criminal Justice,* R.G. Iacovetta and D.H. Chang (eds.). Boston: Houghton Mifflin.

Walker, Samuel (1983). "Employment of Black and Hispanic Police Officers." *Academy of Criminal Justice Sciences Today,* 10:1–5.

Walker, Samuel (1984). "'Broken Windows' and Fractured History: The Use and Misuse of History in Recent Police Patrol Analysis." *Justice Quarterly,* 1:75–90.

Walker, Samuel (1989a). *Employment of Black and Hispanic Officers, 1983–1988: A Follow-Up Study.* Omaha, NE: Center for Applied Urban Research, University of Nebraska.

Walker, Samuel (1989b). *Sense and Nonsense about Crime: A Policy Guide.* 2d ed. Monterey, CA: Brooks/Cole.

Walker, Samuel (1993a). "Does Anyone Remember Team Policing? Lessons of the Team Policing Experience for Community Policing." *American Journal of Police,* 12:33–55.

Walker, Samuel (1993b). *Taming the System: The Control of Discretion in Criminal Justice.* New York: Oxford University Press.

Walker, Samuel and Lorie Fridell (1992). "Forces of Change in Police Policy: The Impact of *Tennessee v. Garner.*" *American Journal of Police,* 11:97–112.

Walla, Robert K. (1995). "Privatization of Jails: Is It a Good Move?" *American Jails,* 9:73–82.

Wallace, Harvey and Shanda Wedlock (1994). "Federal Sentencing Guidelines and Gender Issues: Parental Responsibilities, Pregnancy and Domestic Violence." *San Diego Justice Journal,* 2:395–427.

Wallace, LeAnn W. and Stevens H. Clarke (1986). "The Sentencing Alternatives Center in Greensboro, NC: An Evaluation of Its Effects on Prison Sentences." Unpublished paper presented at the annual meeting of the American Society of Criminology. Atlanta, GA (November).

Wallek, Lee (1991). *The Mafia Manager: A Guide to Success.* Highland Park, IL: December Press.

Wallerstedt, John F. (1984). *Returning to Prison.* Washington, DC: Bureau of Justice Statistics.

Walsh, Anthony (1990). "Twice Labeled: The Effect of Psychiatric Labeling on the Sentencing of Sex Offenders." *Social Problems,* 37:375–389.

Walsh, William F. (1989). "Private/Public Police Stereotypes: A Different Perspective." *Security Journal*, 1:21–27.

Walters, Stephen (1993a). "Changing the Guard: Male Correctional Officers' Attitudes Toward Women as Co-Workers." *Journal of Offender Rehabilitation*, 20:47–60.

Walters, Stephen (1993b). "Gender, Job Satisfaction and Correctional Officers: A Comparative Analysis." *Justice Professional*, 7:23–33.

Ward, David A. and Allen F. Breed (1985). *The United States Penitentiary, Marion, Illinois: Consultants Report Submitted to Committee on the Judiciary*. Washington, DC: U.S. Government Printing Office.

Warr, Mark and Mark Stafford (1984). "Public Goals of Punishment and Support for the Death Penalty." *Journal of Research in Crime and Delinquency*, 21:95–111.

Washington Indeterminate Sentencing Review Board (1992). *Report to the Legislature on the "Murder I Project."* Olympia, WA: Washington State Indeterminate Sentencing Review Board.

Washington State Department of Corrections (1993). *An Integrated Approach to Education, Work, and Offender Reintegration*. Olympia, WA: Washington State Department of Corrections.

Washington State Legislative Budget Committee (1983). *Prisoner Classification Issues: Performance Audit*. Olympia, WA: Washington State Department of Corrections.

Watson, Nelson A. and James W. Sterling (1969). *Police and Their Opinions*. Washington, DC: International Association of Chiefs of Police.

Watson, Patricia S. (1989). "The Homeowner's Right of Privacy in Garbage Left for Collection." *Criminal Law Bulletin*, 25:257–264.

Wayson, Billy L. et al., (1977). *Local Jails: The New Correctional Dilemma*. Lexington, MA: Lexington Books.

Webb, Gary L. (1984). *The Prison Ordeal*. Fayetteville, GA: Coker.

Websdale, Neil (1991). "Disciplining the Non-Disciplinary Spaces: The Rise of Policing as an Aspect of Governmentality in 19th Century Eugene, Oregon." *Policing and Society*, 2:89–115.

Wees, Greg (1996a). "Inmate Population Expected to Increase by 43% by 2002." *Corrections Compendium*, 21:1–4.

Wees, Greg (1996b). "Prison Construction Part One." *Corrections Compendium*, 21:9–19.

Weinreb, Lloyd L. (ed.) (1993). *Leading Constitutional Cases in Criminal Justice: 1993 Edition*. Westbury, NY: Foundation Press.

Weisburd, David, Elin Waring, and Ellen Chayet (1995). "Specific Deterrence in a Sample of Offenders Convicted of White-Collar Crimes." *Criminology*, 33:587–607.

Weisburd, David, Elin Waring, and Stanton Wheeler (1990). "Class, Status, and the Punishment of White-Collar Criminals." *Law and Social Inquiry*, 15:223–243.

Weisheit, Ralph A. and Kathrine Johnson (1992). "Exploring the Dimensions of Support for Decriminalizing Drugs." *Journal of Drug Issues*, 22:53–73.

Weisheit, Ralph A., Edward L. Wells, and David N. Falcone (1994). "Community Policing in Small Town and Rural America." *Crime and Delinquency*, 40:549–567.

Welsh, Wayne N. (1993). "Changes in Arrest Policies as a Result of Court Orders Against County Jails." *Justice Quarterly*, 10:89–120.

West, Paul (1988). "Investigation of Complaints Against the Police: Summary Report of a National Survey." *American Journal of Police*, 7:101–121.

Wettstein, Robert M. (ed.) (1992). "Cults and the Law." *Behavioral Sciences and the Law*, 10:1–140.

Whitaker, Catherine J. (1989). *The Redesigned National Crime Survey: Selected New Data*. Washington, DC: U.S. Department of Justice.

Whitaker, Gordon P. (ed.) (1984). *Understanding Police Agency Performance*. Washington, DC: U.S. Government Printing Office.

Whitcomb, Debra et al. (1994). *The Child Victim as a Witness*. Washington, DC: U.S. Office of Juvenile Justice and Delinquency Prevention.

White, Thomas W. (1989). "Corrections: Out of Balance." *Federal Probation*, 53:31–35.

White, Welsh S. (1980). "Death-Qualified Juries: The Prosecution Proneness Argument Reexamined." *University of Pittsburgh Law Review*, 41:353–406.

Whitehead, John T. and Charles A. Lindquist (1985). "Job Stress and Burnout Among Probation/Parole Officers Perceptions and Causal Factors." *International Journal of Offender Therapy and Comparative Criminology*, 29:109–119.

Whitehead, John T. and Charles A. Lindquist (1986). "Correctional Officer Job-Burnout: A Path Model." *Journal of Research on Crime and Delinquency*, 23:23–42.

Whitehead, John T. and Charles A. Lindquist (1987). "Determinants of Correctional Officer Professional Orientation." Paper presented at the American Society of Criminology meetings, Montreal, CAN.

Whitehead, John T. and Charles A. Lindquist (1992). "Determinants of Probation and Parole Officer Professional Orientation." *Journal of Criminal Justice*, 20:13–24.

Wicharaya, Tamsek (1995). *Simple Theory, Hard Reality: The Impact of Sentencing Reforms on Courts, Prisons and Crime*. Albany, NY: State University of New York Press.

Wiebush, Richard G. (1990). "The Ohio Experience: Programmatic Variations in Intensive Supervision for Juveniles." *Perspectives*, 14:26–35.

Wiebush, Richard G. (1991). *Evaluation of the Lucas County Intensive Supervision Unit: Diversionary Impact and Youth Outcomes*. Columbus, OH: Governor's Office of Criminal Justice Services.

Wiebush, Richard, Donna Hamparian, and Joe M. Davis (1985). *Juveniles in the Ohio Department of Youth Services Institutions, 1982–1984*, Part 1, *Juveniles*. Cleveland, OH: Ohio Serious Juvenile Offender Project.

Wilbanks, William (1985). "Predicting Failure on Parole." In *Prediction in Criminology*, David P. Farrington and R. Tarling (eds.). Albany, NY: State University of New York Press.

Wilkenson, T. and J. Chattin-McNichols (1985). "The Effectiveness of Computer-Assisted Instruction for Police Officers." *Journal of Police Science and Administration*, 13:230–235.

Williams, Frank P. III et al. (1982). *Assessing Diversionary Impact: An Evaluation of the Intensive Supervision Program of the Bexar County Adult Probation Department*. Huntsville, TX: Sam Houston State University.

Williams, Frank P. III and Marilyn D. McShane (1990). "Inclination of Perspective Jurors in Capital Cases." *Sociology and Social Research*, 74:85–94.

Williams, Gerald L. (1989). *"Making the Grade: The Benefits of Law Enforcement Accreditation*. Washington, DC: Police Executive Research Forum.

Williams, J. Sherwood et al. (1983). "Situational Use of Police Force: Public Reactions." *American Journal of Police*, 3:37–50.

Williams, Jimmy J. (1995a). "Race of Appellant, Sentencing Guidelines, and Decisionmaking in Criminal Appeals: A Research Note." *Journal of Criminal Justice*, 23:83–91.

Williams, Jimmy J. (1995b). "Type of Counsel and the Outcome of Criminal Appeals: A Research Note." *American Journal of Criminal Justice*, 19:275–285.

Williams, Levi (1984). "A Police Diversion Alternative for Juvenile Offenders." *Police Chief*, 51:54–57.

Williford, Lori (1996). "Teaching Self-Management Skills to Young Offenders." *Corrections Today*, 58:85–86.

Willison, David (1984). "The Effects of Counsel on the Severity of Criminal Sentences: A Statistical Assessment." *Justice System Journal*, 9:87–101.

Willman, Jr., Herb C. and Ron Y. Chun (1974). "Homeward Bound: An Alternative to the Institutionalization of Adjudicated Juvenile Offenders." In *Alternatives to Imprisonment: Corrections and the Community*, George C. Killinger and Paul F. Cromwell, Jr. (eds.). St. Paul, MN: West Publishing Company.

Willoughby, K.R. and W.R. Blount (1985). "The Relationship Between Law Enforcement Officer Height, Aggression, and Job Performance." *Journal of Police Science and Administration*, 13:225–229.

Wilson, George P. (1985). "Halfway House Programs for Offenders." In *Probation, Parole, and Community Corrections*, Lawrence Travis III (ed.). Prospect Heights, IL: Waveland Press.

Wilson, James Q. (1968). *Varieties of Police Behavior: The Management of Law and Order in Eight Communities*. Cambridge, MA: Harvard University Press.

Wilson, James Q. (1974). *Varieties of Police Behavior*. New York: Atheneum.

Wilson, James Q. (1983). *Thinking About Crime*. New York: Basic Books.

Wilson, James Q. and Joan M. Petersilia (eds.) (1996). *Crime*. San Francisco: ICS Press.

Winer, Anthony S. (1994). "Hate Crimes, Homosexuals, and the Constitution." *Harvard Civil Rights Civil Liberties Law Review*, 29:387–437.

Winfree, L. Thomas Jr. et al. (1994). "Drug History and Pris-

onization: Toward Understanding Variations in Inmate Institutional Adaptations." *International Journal of Offender Therapy and Comparative Criminology*, 38:281–296.

Winsberg, Morton D. (1993). "Are Crime Waves in the United States Regional or National?" *Journal of Criminal Justice*, 21:517–520.

Winters, Clyde Ahmad (1992). "Socio-Economic Status, Test Bias and the Selection of Police." *Police Journal*, 65:125–135.

Witham, Donald C. (1985). *The American Law Enforcement Chief Executive: A Management Profile*. Washington, DC: Police Executive Research Forum.

Wolfgang, Marvin E. (1983). "Delinquency in Two Birth Cohorts." In *Prospective Studies of Crime and Delinquency*, Katherine Tilmann Van Dusen and Sarnoff A. Mednick (eds.). Boston: Kluwer-Nijhoff.

Wolfgang, Marvin E., Robert M. Figlio and Thorsten Sellin (1972). *Delinquency in a Birth Cohort*. Chicago: University of Chicago Press.

Wood, Dorothy, Jean Verber, and Mary Reddin (1985). *A Study of the Inmate Population of the Milwaukee County Jail*. Milwaukee: Wisconsin Correctional Service and Benedict Center for Criminal Justice.

Wood, Jeff and Diane Sheehey (1994). *Guideline Sentencing: An Outline of Appellate Case Law on Selected Issues—September 1994*. Washington, DC: Federal Judicial Center.

Woods, Gerald (1993). *The Police in Los Angeles: Reform and Professionalism*. New York: Garland.

Wooldredge, John D. and Kimberly Masters (1993). "Confronting Problems Faced by Pregnant Inmates in State Prisons." *Crime and Delinquency*, 39:195–203.

Wooldredge, John D. and L. Thomas Winfree Jr. (1992). "An Aggregate-Level Study of Inmate Suicides and Deaths Due to Natural Causes in U.S. Jails." *Journal of Research on Crime and Delinquency*, 29:466–479.

Woolner, Ann (1994). *Washed in Gold: The Story Behind the Biggest Money-Laundering Investigation in U.S. History*. New York: Simon and Schuster.

Wooten, Harold B. and Mary K. Shilton (1993). "Reconstructing Probation: What Prosecutors, Defense Attorneys and Judges Can Do." *Criminal Justice*, 7:12–15, 48–50.

Worden, Alissa Pollitz (1991). "Privatizing Due Process: Issues in the Comparison of Assigned Counsel, Public Defender, and Contracted Indigent Defense Systems." *Justice System Journal*, 16:390–418.

Worden, Alissa Pollitz (1993). "Counsel for the Poor: An Evaluation of Contracting for Indigent Criminal Defense." *Justice Quarterly*, 10:613–637.

Wren, Thomas E. (1985). "Whistle-Blowing and Loyalty to One's Friends." In *Police Ethics: Hard Choices in Law Enforcement*, William C. Heffernan and Timothy Stroup (eds.). New York: John Jay Press.

Wright, Kevin N. (1985). "Developing the Prison Environment Inventory." *Journal of Research in Crime and Delinquency*, 22:257–277.

Wright, Kevin N. (1993). "Prison Environment and Behavioral Outcomes." *Journal of Offender Rehabilitation*, 20:93–113.

Wright, Kevin N., Todd R. Clear, and Paul Dickson (1984).

"Universal Applicability of Probation Risk-Assessment Instruments: A Critique." *Criminology,* 22:113–134.

Wright, Richard A. (1995). "Rehabilitation Affirmed, Rejected and Reaffirmed: Assessments of the Effectiveness of Offender Treatment Programs in Criminology Textbooks." *Journal of Criminal Justice Education,* 6:21–39.

Wunder, Amanda (1994). "Working for the Weekend: Prison Industries & Inmate-Employees." *Corrections Compendium,* 20:9–22.

Wunder, Amanda (1995a). "Corrections Budgets, 1994–1995." *Corrections Compendium,* 20:5–16.

Wunder, Amanda (1995b). "Teaching Life Skills to Mississippi Prisoners." *Corrections Compendium,* 20:1–3.

Wynkoop, Timothy F., Steven C. Capps, and Bobby J. Priest (1995). "Incidence and Prevalence of Child Sexual Abuse: A Critical Review of Data Collection Procedures." *Journal of Child Sexual Abuse,* 4:49–66.

Yanich, Danilo (1990). *The Pace of Justice: Processing Criminal Cases in Delaware.* Newark, DE: Delaware Public Administration Institute, University of Delaware.

Yarborough, Tinsley E. (1984). "The Alabama Prison Litigation." *Justice System Journal,* 9:276–290.

Zamble, Edward and Frank J. Porporino (1988). *Coping, Behavior, and Adaptation in Prison Inmates.* Secaucus, NJ: Springer-Verlag.

Zaragoza, Maria S. et al. (1995). *Memory and Testimony in the Child Witness.* Thousand Oaks, CA: Sage.

Zaslaw, Jay G. (1989). "Stop Assaultive Children—Project SAC Offers Hope for Violent Juveniles." *Corrections Today,* 51:48–50.

Zatz, Marjorie S. (1994). "Race, Ethnicity and Determinate Sentencing: A New Dimension to an Old Controversy." *Criminology,* 22:147–171.

Zawitz, Marianne W. (1995) *Guns Used in Crime.* Washington, DC: U.S. Department of Justice.

Zeisel, Hans (1971). " . . . And Then There Were None: The Diminution of the Federal Jury." *University of Chicago Law Review,* 38:710–795.

Zimbardo, Philip G. (1994). *Transforming California's Prisons into Expensive Old Age Homes for Felons: Enormous Hidden Costs and Consequences for California's Taxpayers.* San Francisco: Center on Juvenile and Criminal Justice.

Zimmerman, Joseph F. (1981). *The Government and Politics of New York State.* New York: New York University Press.

Zimring, Franklin E. and Gordon Hawkins (1995). *Incapacitation: Penal Confinement and the Restraint of Crime.* New York: Oxford University Press.

Zingraff, Matthew and Randall Thomson (1984). "Differential Sentencing of Men and Women in the USA." *International Journal of the Sociology of Law,* 12:401–413.

Zorza, Joan and Laurie Woods (1994). *Analysis and Policy Implications of the New Domestic Violence Police Studies.* New York: National Battered Women's Law Project.

Zupan, Linda L. (1986). "Gender-Related Differences in Correctional Officers' Perceptions and Attitudes." *Journal of Criminal Justice,* 14:349–361.

Zupan, Linda L. (1991). *Jails: Reform and the New Generation Philosophy.* Cincinnati, OH: Anderson Publishing Company.

Cases Cited

Alabama v. White, 496 U.S. 325 (1990), 133–134
Apodaca v. Oregon, 406 U.S. 404 (1972), 252
Argersinger v. Hamlin, 407 U.S. 25 (1972), 209–210
Arizona v. Evans, 115 S.Ct. 1185 (1995), 133
Arizona v. Hicks, 480 U.S. 321, 107 S.Ct. 1149 (1987), 60
Augustus v. Roemer, 771 F.Supp. 1458 (1991), 66
Baldasar v. Illinois, 100 S.Ct. 1585 (1980), 209–210
Baldwin v. New York, 399 U.S. 66 (1970), 231–232
Ballard v. Walker, 772 F.Supp. 1336 (1991), 66
Ballew v. Georgia, 435 U.S. 223 (1978), 233
Barker v. Wingo, 407 U.S. 514 (1972), 64, 198
Batson v. Kentucky, 476 U.S. 79 (1986), 153, 238–239
Beatham v. Manson, 369 F.Supp. 783 (1973), 352
Beech v. Melancon, 465 F.2d 425 (1972), 135
Bell v. Wolfish, 441 U.S. 520 (1979), 347
Bennis v. Michigan, _U.S._, 116 S.Ct. 994 (1996), 9
Berkemer v. McCarty, 468 U.S. 420 (1984), 54
Blanton v. City of North Las Vegas, Nev., 489 U.S. 538 (1989), 231–232
Bordenkircher v. Hayes, 437 U.S. 357 (1978), 215
Borning v. Cain, 754 F.2d 1151 (1985), 353
Bouiles v. Ricketts, 518 F.Supp. 687 (1981), 353
Bourjaily v. United States, 482 U.S. 171 (1987), 43
Brady v. Maryland, 373 U.S. 83 (1963), 206
Brady v. United States, 397 U.S. 742 (1970), 214–215
Brandenburg v. Ohio, 395 U.S. 444 (1969), 58
Breed v. Jones, 421 U.S. 519 (1975), 414
Breeden v. State, 622 A.2d 160 (1993), 65
Brinegar v. United States, 338 U.S. 160, 69 S.Ct. 1302 (1949), 60
Brown v. Doe, S.D.N.Y. 803 F.Supp. 932 (1992), 342
Burch v. Louisiana, 99 S.Ct. 1623 (1979), 252
California v. Ciraolo, 476 U.S. 207, 106 S.Ct. 1809 (1986), 60
California v. Greenwood, 486 U.S. 35 (1988), 129
California v. Lovercamp, 118 Cal.Rptr. 110 (1974), 72
Campbell v. Grammer, C.A.8 (Neb.) 889 F.2d 797 (1989), 342
Carroll v. United States, 267 U.S. 132 (1925), 130

Chambers v. Maroney, 399 U.S. 42 (1970), 130
Chimel v. California, 395 U.S. 752 (1969), 130
Clark v. Heard, 538 F.Supp. 800 (1982), 184
Clemmons v. United States, 721 F.2d 235 (1983), 218
Cohen v. California, 403 U.S. 15 (1971), 59
Colorado v. Connelly, 479 U.S. 157 (1986), 62
Commonwealth v. Hillhaven Corp., 687 S.W.2d 545 (1984), 195
Commonwealth v. Shaffer, 326 N.E.2d 880 (1975), 71
Cook v. City of New York, 578 F.Supp. 179 (1984), 344–345
Cooper v. California, 386 U.S. 58 (1967), 130
COPPAR v. Rizzo, 357 F.Supp. 1289 (1973), 145
County of Riverside v. McLaughlin, 500 U.S. 441 (1991), 181–182
Cunningham v. Ellington, 323 F.Supp. 1072 (1971), 135
Davis v. United States, 397 U.S. 969 (1969), 181
Dickey v. Florida, 398 U.S. 30 (1970), 198
Dillingham v. United States, 423 U.S. 64 (1975), 198
Division of Corrections v. Neakok, 721 P. 2d 1121 (1986), 385
Doggett v. United States, 505 U.S. 647 (1992), 198
Dow Chemical Co. v. United States, 476 U.S. 227, 106 S.Ct. 1819 (1986), 60
Duncan v. Louisiana, 391 U.S. 145 (1968), 188–189, 231–233
Eddings v. Oklahoma, 455 U.S. 104 (1982), 432–433
Eissa v. United States, 485 A.2d 610 (1984), 58
Ex parte Crouse, 4 Whart. 9 (1839), 399, 401
Fare v. Michael C., 442 U.S. 97 (1979), 414–415
Fletcher v. Peck, 6 Cr. 87 (1810), 153
Fowler v. Graham, 478 F.Supp. 90 (1979), 352
Frazier v. Stone, 515 S.W.2d 766 (1974), 282
Furman v. Georgia, 408 U.S. 238 (1972), 4–6, 285–287
Ganey v. Edwards, 759 F.2d 337 (1985), 352
Garner v. Memphis Police Department, 36 CrL 3233 (1979), 136
Garner v. Memphis Police Department, 710 F.2d 240 (1983), 136
Gates v. Collier, 390 F.Supp. 482 (1975), 352, 354
Georgia v. McCollum, 505 U.S. 42 (1992), 240
Ghen v. Rich, 8 F. 159 (1881), 5

Author Index

Subject Index

Photo Credits